Bible Commentary

by
E. M. Zerr

Volume V
Matthew—Romans

ISBN 1-58427-185-X

Guardian of Truth Foundation
P.O. Box 9670
Bowling Green, Kentucky 42102
www.truthbooks.net
1-800-428-0121

Foreword: The E.M. Zerr Bible Commentaries

Cecil Willis
Reprinted From *Truth Magazine* XX:26 (June 24, 1976), pp. 3-5

The Cogdill Foundation, which publishes *Truth Magazine*, has obtained exclusive publication rights to the six volume *Bible Commentary* written by Brother E.M. Zerr. . . .

Information About E.M. Zerr

Brother Zerr was quite well-known among a group of very conservative brethren, but he may not have been known among brethren in general. Hence, a little information concerning him is here given. Edward Michael Zerr was born October 15, 1877 in Strassburg, Illinois, but his family soon thereafter moved to Missouri. He was the second of six children born to Lawrence and Mary (Manning) Zerr. Brother Zerr's father was reared as a Catholic, but after he married Mary Manning, he obeyed the gospel. At the age of seventeen, young Edward was immersed into Christ in Grand River, near Bosworth, Missouri.

In June, 1897 young Brother E.M. Zerr received a letter from A. L. Gepford asking him to go to Green Valley, Illinois, and to preach in his stead. His first sermon was entitled, "My Responsibility as a Preacher of the Gospel, and Your Responsibility as Hearers." In the years between delivery of this first sermon on July 3, 1897, and the delivery of his last sermon on October 25, 1959, Brother Zerr preached about 8,000 sermons, from California to Connecticut, and from Washington to Arizona. It is noteworthy that his last sermon was built around Matt. 13:44, and was entitled "Full Surrender." Brother Zerr preached the gospel for a little over 60 years.

Among the brethren with whom Brother Zerr was most frequently associated, it was then common to have protracted periods of concentrated Bible studies, commonly referred to as "Bible Readings." Young Brother Zerr attended a three month "Bible Reading" conducted by the well-known teacher, A.M. Morris, in 1899. During this study which was conducted at

Hillsboro, Henry County, Indiana, Brother Zerr stayed in the home of a farmer named John Hill. After leaving the John and Matilda Hill farm, "E.M." began correspondence with their daughter, Carrie. The following year, while attending a "Bible Reading" conducted by Daniel Sommer in Indianapolis, "E.M." and Carrie were married, on September 27, 1900. The newlyweds took up residence in New Castle, Indiana, where their four children were born, one of whom died in infancy.

In 1911, Brother A.W. Harvey arranged for Brother Zerr to conduct a "Bible Reading" which continued for several months at Palmyra, Indiana. These "Bible Readings" usually consisted of two two-hour sessions daily. Young Brother Zerr's special ability as a teacher was soon recognized, and he continued to conduct such studies among churches of Christ for 48 years. Edward M. Zerr died February 22, 1960, having been in a coma for four months following an automobile accident at Martinsville, Indiana. His body was laid to rest in the little country cemetery at Hillsboro, Indiana, near the church building in which he had attended his first "Bible Reading."

Brother Zerr's Writings

In addition to his oral teaching and preaching, Brother Zerr was a prolific writer. He was a regular contributor to several religious periodicals. Brother Zerr also composed the music and lyrics of several religious songs. Two of these, "The True Riches," and "I Come to Thee," may be found in the widely used song book, *Sacred Selections.*

One of the books written by Brother Zerr is entitled *Historical Quotations,* and consists of the gleanings from 40,000 pages of ancient history and other critical sources which he read over a period of twenty years. These quotations are intended to explain and to confirm the prophetic and other technical statements of the Bible. Another book, a 434 page hard-cover binding, consists of a study course containing 16,000 Bible questions. This book, *New Testament Questions,* has at least 50 questions on each chapter of the New Testament. A smaller book, *Bible Reading Notes,* consists of some of the copious notes which Brother Zerr made in connection with the "Bible Readings" which he conducted. But the crowning success of his efforts was the writing of his six volume commentary on the whole Bible.

These six volumes were published between 1947 and 1955. Brother Zerr has the unique distinction, so far as is known to this writer, of being the only member of the church to write a commentary on the entire Bible. Many other brethren have written excellent and valuable commentaries on various books of the Bible, but no other brother has written on the entire Bible.

The writing of this commentary consumed more than seven years of full-time labor. In order that he might devote himself without interruption to this herculean effort, Brother Zerr was supported by the Newcastle church during this seven year period. It is unfortunate, in this writer's judgment, that other competent men have not been entirely freed of other duties that they might give themselves to such mammoth writing assignments. Through *Bible Commentary*, Brother E.M. Zerr, though dead since 1960, will continue to do what he liked best to do—conduct "Bible Readings" for many years to come. The current printing is the fifth printing of the Old Testament section (four volumes) of the commentary, and the sixth printing of the New Testament section (two volumes).

Many Christians spend but little money on available helps in Bible study. Some own perhaps only a *Cruden's Concordance*, a Bible dictionary of some kind, and then *Johnson's Notes*. It would be interesting to know how many copies of B.W. Johnson's *The People's New Testament Commentary With Notes* have been sold. If I were to hazard a guess, it would be that at least 1,000,000 copies of this superficial commentary have been sold. *Johnson's Notes* contains the printing of the entire New Testament text in both King James Version and the English Revised Version (the predecessor to the American Standard Version), and his comments, all contained in two volumes. In fact, a single volume edition also is available. Thus one is buying two copies of the New Testament, and B. W. Johnson's *Notes*, in one or two volumes. So necessarily, *Johnson's Notes* are very brief.

If brethren somehow could be made acquainted with Brother Zerr's *Bible Commentary*, it is possible that it could be as widely used as has been *Johnson's Notes*, first published in 1889. Brother Zerr printed very little of the Bible text in his commentary. He assumed you would have your own Bible nearby. To have printed in the commentary the entire Bible would have required at least three other volumes. While it would have been helpful to have the Bible text printed by the comments, this unnecessary luxury would have been very expensive, since we all have copies of the Scriptures already. Furthermore, Brother Zerr intended that one be compelled to use his Bible, in order that his commentary never supplant the Sacred text.

A Word of Caution
I am sure that Brother Zerr, were he yet living, would advise me to remind you that his *Bible Commentary* is only that of a man, though a studious man he was. In fact, in the "Preface" to this set of books, just such a word of warning is sounded by Brother Zerr. The only book which we recommend without reservation is the Bible! But Bible commentaries, when viewed merely as the results of many years of study by scholarly men, can be very helpful to one.

Brother Zerr spent his life-time working among those brethren who have stood opposed to "located preachers" and to "Bible Colleges." However, he has not "featured" these distinctive views in his *Bible Commentary*. If one did not know of these positions held by Brother Zerr, he might not even detect the references to them in the commentary. However, I want to call such references to your attention. Along with the opposition to "located preachers," Brother Zerr also held a position commonly referred to as "Evangelistic Oversight." This position declares that until a congregation has qualified elders appointed, each congregation should be under the oversight of some evangelist. With these positions, this writer cannot agree. References to these positions will be found in his comments on Acts 20:28; Eph. 3:10; 3:21; 4:11; 1 Tim. 5:21; 2 Tim. 4:5, and perhaps in a few other places that do not now come to memory. Brother Zerr also took the position that a woman should never cut or even trim her hair. His comments on this position will be found at 1 Cor. 11:1-16.

But aside from a very few such positions with which many of us would disagree, Brother Zerr's *Bible Commentary* can be very helpful. Some restoration period writers of widely used commentaries held some rather bizarre positions regarding the millennium. Brethren scruple not to use *Barnes' Notes*, in spite of his repeated injection of Calvinism, and *Clark's Commentary*, in spite of his Methodist teaching.

Brother Zerr's *Bible Commentary* is far superior to *Johnson's Notes*. Though there are some extraordinarily good volumes in the well-known Gospel Advocate commentaries, there also are some notoriously weak volumes in this widely used set. Viewed from the point of consistent quality, Brother Zerr's *Bible Commentary* is superior to the Gospel Advocate set. Some brethren whom I consider to be superior exegetes of the Word have highly recommended Zerr's *Bible Commentary* and have praised the splendid and incisive way in which he has handled even those "hard to be understood" sections of God's Word.

Our recommendation regarding E.M. Zerr's six volume commentary can be paraphrased from the words of a well-known television commercial: "Try it; you'll like it!"

PREFACE to the NEW TESTAMENT COMMENTARY

When I began to write a commentary on the New Testament I realized that I would not be able to answer all the questions in advance that might arise in the mind of the reader. · I learned this truth in my experience of teaching a class orally. After going into much detail explaining a chapter and then calling for questions, I have been surprised at the points that were suggested which I had overlooked. And in a work where no opportunity can be had for a hearing from the student it would be impossible to avoid all such omissions. But it was my purpose to deal with every question occurring to me, no matter how unimportant it might seem to the advanced student, using such words and phrases as are understood by the average reader. I could not hope to meet the demands of the overcritical or those who might feel themselves qualified from the standpoint of the scholarship of the world. My intention has been to write a "commentary for the common man."

A word of caution will be given as to the proper use of a commentary. It should not be considered as an authority but only as a means of suggestion for the various fields of thought. Very often an explanation will be self-evident when it is stated and will need no further proof of its correctness. Yet the thought might not have occurred to the reader had he not seen the suggestion. This truth gives one of the main purposes of a commentary. If the comment is not thus evident, the reader should carefully investigate for himself before accepting the explanation. And if the author has cited the grounds for his statement, the reader should examine all such proof with all the care possible, in justice to himself as well as to the author. Regardless of any preconceived opinions, the reader should approach the commentary with a mind that is like a clean sheet of paper, ready to receive and record any truth that he may find that is sustained by satisfactory evidence. In conclusion of this paragraph, a commentary should be given the same kind of treatment that its author would receive were he doing his teaching orally. He should be heard respectfully and full consideration be allowed for all of his statements. They should be compared with all the proofs or evidences available, then be accepted or rejected according to whether they are in harmony therewith or not.

The reader should see the preface to Volume 1 of the Old Testament Commentary, since many statements therein as to the general plan of this work apply to it as a whole. Also the list of works given in that preface have been consulted in the writing of the New Testament Commentary. All of those works named are classed as "authorities" in their respective fields. While on this subject I will add a few lines in explanation of the definitions in the lexicon. Thayer sometimes defines a Greek word as it applies in specific passages, and at other times he gives its meaning in general. This distinction has usually been called to the attention of the reader. And also, what he offers as the direct meaning of the word is printed in italics, and if he has any personal comments or explanation of his own definition, that is printed in common type. I sometimes quote both kinds because a learned writer of a lexicon certainly knows why he has offered his definition of the word being considered. In addition to the "authorities" mentioned I have consulted commentaries and writings of religious teachers. No man knows it all, and frequently one can obtain valuable suggestions and references to sources of information that he otherwise would have missed. In the use of these works I have observed the same rules of caution toward them that I have asked the reader to maintain in his use of this Commentary.

The Author

Bible Commentary

MATTHEW 1

Verse 1. The word *book* is from the Greek word BIBLOS and is defined by Thayer, "A written book, a roll or scroll." *Generation* is from GENESIS which Thayer defines, "used of birth, nativity." *Book of the generation.* This phrase is commented on by the same author as follows: "A book of one's lineage, i. e. in which his ancestry or his progeny [ancestors from whom he is a descendant] are enumerated." *David; Abraham.* Matthew wrote his book for the special benefit of the Jews is the reason he did not go any farther back than to Abraham. He was the first patriarch to whom the promise of the Messiah was made and their interest in Him would hence not include any earlier ancestors. After Abraham the most important man in the ancestry of Christ was David, so the record makes mention of him. The word for *book* means generally any written document, but in this place it applies only as a title for the family history of the ancestors of Christ which will include verses through 17.

Verse 2. Abraham had more than one son but the promised seed was to come through his son Isaac (Genesis 21: 12; Romans 9: 7), hence Matthew goes from Abraham to Isaac in the record. Isaac also had more than one son and it was stipulated that Jacob was the one through whom the line was to go (Genesis 25: 23; Romans 9: 12, 13) thus the author goes from Isaac to Jacob in his tracing of the blood line. Jacob also had many sons who figure in an important manner in the history, but only one of them (Judah, here called Judas) could be used in the blood line, so the significant wording is *Judas and his brethren.* This idea of singling out the particular one in each family was observed all down the line. I have gone into detail in this verse to set forth the subject, and such details will not need to be repeated in all of the following verses.

Verse 3. *Thamar* is called Tamar in Genesis and she was the daughter-in-law of Judah. The account of how she became the mother of his sons is in Genesis 38.

Verse 4. *Aram* is in the form of Ram in the Old Testament account.

Verse 5. *Booz* is Boaz in the account found in the Old Testament. His mother *Rachab* is called Rahab in Joshua 6: 25; she was the woman in Jericho. This verse names two women who were connected with the blood line of Christ (Rachab and Ruth) who were not direct descendants of Abraham. However, this should not confuse us because it was customary in ancient times to ignore the daughters in the family registers. But these women were so outstanding in their parts of the great drama that the inspired writer gives them special mention.

Verse 6. Here the record takes on an additional phase of importance. In the days of Samuel the prophet the people of Israel clamored for a king in order to be like the nations around them. The Lord was displeased with their request but suffered them to have a king. The first one was Saul of the tribe of Benjamin, but he was so unrighteous that God took the throne from him and his family and even shut out that tribe from the royal line. The throne was then given to the tribe of Judah which had possession of the kingdom in Jerusalem until the Babylonian captivity. David was the first man to occupy the throne from that tribe, hence the words *David the king.* All of the rest to be named in the blood line were kings also but the fact will not be mentioned. This special notice was given to David because he was the first man to be in both the royal and blood lines. And in having such a place in the history of Israel he became the most important type of Christ as king, hence the various references to Him as sitting on the throne of his father David. The term "father" refers to the blood line and the term "throne" refers to the royal line. The mother of Solomon is referred to but not named as were Rachab and Ruth. No reason is given in the Scriptures for this variation in the mention of persons. It is worth considering, however, that of the many wives that David had, this one was the mother of both Solomon and Nathan (1 Chronicles 3: 5). The significance of this is in the fact that both of these sons of David were direct ancestors of Christ; Solomon's line coming down to Joseph the (foster) father, and

Nathan's coming down to Heli the father of Mary. Hence, the two blood streams from David coming through the two sons who were full brothers, were brought together by the marriage of Joseph and Mary.

Verse 7. *Roboam* is Rehoboam in the Old Testament and *Abia is Abijam*.

Verse 8. *Joshaphat* is Jehoshaphat, *Joram* is Jehoram, and *Ozias* is Uzziah in the O. T.

Verse 9. *Joatham* is Jotham, Achaz is Ahaz and *Ezekias* is Hezekiah formerly.

Verse 10. *Manasses* is spelled Manasseh and *Josias* is the same as Josiah.

Verse 11. *Jechonias* has three different forms in the Old Testament but the one generally used is Jehoiachin. He was not the last temporal king that the people of Israel ever had; there was one more (Zedekiah). But while he was a son of Josiah, he had been placed on the throne in Jerusalem by the king of Babylon (1 Kings 24: 17), having deposed Jehoiachin and taken him to Babylon as a captive. But the blood line remained with him, hence the present verse words it *Jechonias and his brethren.* Also, the words *about the time they were carried away to Babylon* are explained by the facts just mentioned in this paragraph.

Verse 12. *After they were brought to Babylon.* Family life was not discontinued even though the Jews were in captivity. The inspired writer is able to give us the names of lineal descendants that he wished to use in connecting the blood line from Abraham to Christ. Not all of the succeeding names are given nor was that necessary. The present verse virtually covers the 70 years of the captivity, for it was in the days of *Zorobabel* (Zerubbabel) that they came out of it (Ezra 3: 2).

Verses 13-15. This paragraph covers the space of over four centuries, from the return after the captivity to the time of Jacob, father of Joseph. It is evident that not all of the men in the blood line are named, but only enough of them to show the connection of the list as that would affect the ancestry of Jesus.

Verse 16. The use of the term "begat" is not used here because Joseph was only the foster father of Jesus. But the verse states that he was the husband of Mary in order to show how the two blood streams from David

were joined. *Husband* is from ANER which is the only word for "husband" in the New Testament. It is so rendered 50 times and by "man" 156 times. The word cannot hence be known to designate a married man except by the connection in which it is found. *Jesus who is called Christ.* The specific meaning of the first word is "saviour" and the last is defined "anointed." The force of the combined title is "Saviour and King."

Verse 17. *Generations* is from GENEA and Thayer's definition at this place is, "The several ranks in the natural descent, the successive members of a genealogy." The three sets of 14 generations are so arranged for the sake of uniformity as an aid to the memory. There are several names omitted and a man may be said to have begotten a person when it really means a generation or more later. This manner of speaking was done before this; for instance, in Daniel 5: 18 Belshazzar is spoken of as the son of Nebuchadnezzar whereas he was his grandson. The count of the generations is based on the ones named in the chapter. By strict count there are 40 instead of 42 as the three sets of 14 would require; this is because David and Jechonias are each counted twice.

Verse 18. The meaning of espousal as compared with marriage will be considered at verse 20. *Before they came together* means before they began living together as husband and wife. *Found with child* should be considered separately from the words *of the Holy Ghost.* Joseph did not know that her condition was produced by a miracle but thought she had been impure. The inspired writer adds the italicized words for the information of the reader. The meaning of the clause is as if it said "she was found with child (which later proved to be by the Holy Ghost)."

Verse 19. *Being a just man* denotes that Joseph was kind and considerate, yet was conscientious and unwilling to ignore the moral law. Because of this he planned to *put her away* which means to break the engagement. He had such a personal regard for her that he did not want to expose her to public disgrace, yet he did not think it would be right to live with her.

Verse 20. While Joseph was pondering the subject the angel of the Lord appeared and explained the situation. He further advised him to proceed with their plans because Mary was pure from all wrong. She is here called his *wife* and in Luke 2: 5 she is called his "espoused wife." All this is because in Biblical times an espousal was regarded as binding, as to the obligation, as the actual marriage.

Verse 21. The angel not only told Joseph the cause of Mary's condition, but even told him what to call the child when born. Proper names in ancient times usually had some specific meaning, hence the name Jesus, meaning "Saviour," was to be given to this son to be born of Mary, because he was designed to save his people from sin.

Verse 22. The information was also given Joseph that what was happening was in fulfillment of prophecy, all of which would meet his approval because he was a believer of the inspired word.

Verse 23. The angel then quoted the prophecy to which he had referred which is in Isaiah 7: 14. The thing of special importance is that the child was to be born of a *virgin*, an event that could not occur by the laws of natural reproduction alone. *God with us.* This signifies that since the body of this child was both divine and human, it meant that it would be virtually the presence of God with man, hence he was to be called by the name of Emmanuel which has that meaning.

Verse 24. *Did as the angel of the Lord had bidden him* denotes that what follows in this verse and the next will be in obedience to the command of the angel. *Raised from sleep* is explained by the fact that in ancient times God used various means in communicating His will to the people (Hebrews 1: 1) and one of them was by dreams. After the dream had delivered the desired information to Joseph, it was time for him to arise out of sleep and proceed with the program pointed out by the angel.

Verse 25. Joseph took Mary into his home in fulfillment of his espousal and on the instructions of the angel. *Knew her not* is a Biblical expression for the intimate relation of the sexes. The reason Joseph did not have this relation with Mary now was because the angel had told him that her son was to be born of a virgin, which required that at the time of the birth his mother must never have had intimate relations with a man. *Till she had brought forth* has to mean that after the birth of Jesus, Joseph lived with Mary in the intimate relation of

husband and wife, else the language is meaningless and deceptive. It therefore proves that Mary did not continue to be a virgin, but lived with her husband in the relationship of a wife, and her children by that marriage will be met with in later chapters of this book.

MATTHEW 2

Verse 1. *Bethlehem* was a small town not far from Jerusalem, and *Judea* was one of the three divisions or territories into which Palestine was divided in the time of Christ. Judea was the most important part of the country in that it contained the important city of Jerusalem, which was the capital and place of the temple of the Jews. *Herod the king.* I shall quote from history regarding this man who occupied so prominent a place in the affairs of God's people: "This year was born Herod the Great, who was afterwards king of Judea (for he was twenty-five years old when he was first made governor of Galilee in the year before Christ 47). His father was Antipas, a noble Idumaean, and his mother Cyprus of an illustrous family among the Arabians . . . By country therefore he was an Idumaean, but by religion a Jew, as all other Idumaeans were from the time that Hyrcanus brought them all to embrace the Jewish religion, of which I have above given an account." Prideaux's Connexion, year 72. "But Antigonus, by way of reply to what Herod had caused to be proclaimed, and this before the Romans, and before Silas also, said, that they would not do justly if they gave the kingdom to Herod, who was not more than a private man, and an Idumean, i. e., a half Jew." Josephus, Antiquities, Book 14. Chapter 15, Section 2. The Herodian family figures prominently in the New Testament history, and the various members of it will be identified by their individual names as they appear in the passages. *Wise men* is from MAGOS which Thayer defines at this place as follows: "Oriental wise men (astrologers) who, having discovered by the rising of a remarkable star that the Messiah had just been born, came to Jerusalem to worship him." The original word is used with reference to both good and evil men, but the whole context indicates that it was used in the former sense in the present instance. We are sure that the case of the shepherds as recorded in Luke 2 was not an accident, likewise the fact that the star led the wise men correctly would show their standing with the Lord. Furthermore, God spoke to them in a dream (verse 12) on the matter which again proves that the visit of the wise men to Jerusalem was under the direction of God. Since the New Testament was not yet written, this event would be another to come under Hebrews 1: 1. *East* is defined by Thayer, "eastern region, the east." The term therefore refers not merely to the direction from which the wise men came, but the country in general lying in that direction from Palestine. The guidance of the star was general only and directed them to Jerusalem. This was doubtless by the hand of God, to bring them in contact with those who were concerned in this grand occasion, particularly Herod who was destined to play such an important part in the drama.

Verse 2. When the wise men reached Jerusalem they made inquiry, seeking the exact location of the newborn *king of the Jews*. This specific statement is another proof that the whole movement of these men was under the instruction of the Lord. *Seen his star in the east* denotes where they were when they first saw the star, not that it was merely in the east when they saw it. It was over Jerusalem when they reached the city, for verse 9 describes it as moving immediately before them even to the extent of detailed guidance in the local territory. They gave as their mission only the desire to *worship* the newborn king. It might be wondered as to how an infant could be worshiped by wise men, seeing that the general idea seems to restrict that word to some specified schedule of religious performance. The word in its several English forms is used in various connections in the New Testament, and also comes from many different Greek originals. These Greek words are also rendered by other words in the Authorized Version. I shall give a complete list of these words, showing where they occur as the original for *worship*, followed by other words (if any) by which they have been translated in the New Testament. The figure after the word denotes the number of times the word is so rendered. DOXA, Luke 14: 10. Worship 1, dignity 2, glory 144, honor 6, praise 4, glorious 6. EUSEBEO, Acts 17: 23. Shew piety 1, worship 1. THERAPEUO, Acts 17: 25. Cure 5, heal 38, worship 1. THRESKEIA, Colossians 2: 18. Religion 3, worshiping 1. LATREUO, Acts 7: 42; 24: 14, Philip-

pians 3: 3; Hebrews 10: 2. Do service 1, serve 16, worship 3, worshiper 1. NEOKOROS, Acts 19: 35. Worshiper 1. PROSKUNTES, John 4: 23. Worshiper 1. SEBAZO, Romans 1: 25. Worship 1. SEBOMAI, Matthew 15: 9; Mark 7: 7; Acts 16: 14; 18: 7, 13; 19: 27. Worship 6, devout 2, devout person 1, religious 1. SEBASMA, 2 Thessalonians, 2: 4. Devotion 1, that is worshiped 1. THEOSEBES, John 9: 31. Worshiper of God 1. PROSKUNEO is rendered "worship" 58 times in the New Testament and is never rendered by any other word. Not one of the Greek words in this group is used of the public services of the church when translated by the word "worship." This list will not be copied again, so the reader is advised to mark it for ready reference.

Verse 3. Herod was only half Jew and was appointed to the office of ruler by the Romans, who had acquired control of the country. He was fearful of losing the throne when he heard that a child of Jewish blood had been born and was spoken of as king of the Jews. He was therefore troubled or disturbed in mind. All Jerusalem with him was troubled also, because there were a great many men in the city who depended upon him for the place of dignity that they were permitted to enjoy.

Verse 4. Herod was an Idumaean by nation but a Jew in religion. He thus had learned something of the Old Testament Scriptures, and knew that it had been prophesied that a king was some day to be born to the Jewish nation. However, he was not sufficiently informed to locate the town where it was to take place. He called upon the priests and scribes for the information because they were supposed to be able to give it. (See Leviticus 10: 11; Deuteronomy 17: 9; Malachi 2: 7.)

Verse 5. Concordances and other works of reference were not in use at the time of this history, but the scribes were familiar with the scriptures from having to copy them so often. It is not much wonder then that they could give Herod the information.

Verse 6. As proof of their statement they quoted from Micah 5: 2 which designates where the birth was to occur and also what the child predicted was to do. *Rule* is from POIMAINO and sometimes it means to feed or nourish. Thayer defines it in this place by, "To rule, govern," and he explains the word elsewhere as meaning, "of the overseers (pastors) of the church." It should be observed that the new-born king was to rule the people of Israel, not the political world.

Verse 7. Herod evidently believed that the star appeared at the same time as the birth and that would give him a point from which to reckn the age of the child. He called the wise men privately because his entire behaviour was prompted by craftiness.

Verse 8. The wicked king doubtless believed the prophecy, for he sent the wise men to Bethlehem in search of the child. *Diligently* is from AKRIBOS which Thayer defines, "exactly, accurately, diligently." Hence they were not only to be diligent or earnest in their investigation, but were to be careful that the information that they obtained was reliable. It will be understood that Herod's claim of wanting to worship the child was made in hypocrisy.

Verse 9. The wise men were obedient to Herod for the present in that they started on their journey to Bethlehem. That was a small town not far from Jerusalem and could have been easily found without any special aid. But it was necessary that they not only go to the right town but also that they find the particular house where the child was at that hour. The community was full of people who had come in response to the decree of Caesar (Luke 2: 1-3). It might not have been known that a child had been recently born among the throng, and an inquiry would not likely bring any accurate information. Hence the star, which evidently had temporarily disappeared, came into view again and went as an escort for the wise men, going even to the very house where the infant was then being nursed.

Verse 10. Having been led from their home country by the star, the confidence of the wise men had already been pretty well established. Now that it reappeared just at the time they were starting on the final lap of their journey, their confidence was made stronger and hence they had great rejoicing.

Verse 11. They worshiped him, not the mother. For the meaning of *worshiped* see the note at verse 2. *Gifts* is from DORON and Thayer says in this place that it means "gifts offered as an expression of honor." An infant this young could not have personal appreciation for material articles,

hence the performance was in token of their recognition of his dignified importance. It was customary in old times to show recognition of either social or official rank by making presents. (See Genesis 32: 13; 1 Samuel 10: 27 and the comments on those passages.)

Verse 12. To be *warned* ordinarily conveys the idea of danger, but it might not concern the person receiving the warning but someone else to whom he was to deliver the message. The word is from CHREMATIZO and Thayer defines it, "To be divinely commanded, admonished, instructed." The meaning is that God instructed the wise men not to return by way of Jerusalem. The word would include the idea of danger, but it would be concerning the child Jesus and not the wise men directly. Had they gone back through Jerusalem they would have been forced to meet up with Herod, and that would have given them no way to keep the information from him that would have meant harm to Jesus.

Verse 13. *When they were departed* indicates that the angel gave these instructions to Joseph at the same time that he started the wise men on their journey homeward.

Verse 14. This verse indicates that Joseph arose while it was yet night, for it was under the darkness that he started for Egypt. This is another instance showing promptness in obeying the command of the Lord. Abraham manifested a similar attitude about the offering up of his son as recorded in Genesis 22: 3.

Verse 15. The writer completes the part of his story that pertained to Egypt in order not to break into the line of thought, and he will resume it a little later on. In giving instructions for Joseph to come with his son out of Egypt, the prophecy in Hosea 11: 1 was fulfilled the second time; first time was in the days of Moses.

Verse 16. The original word for *mocked* has a somewhat varied meaning, but in the present instance it denotes that Herod regarded the actions of the wise men as intended for a trifling with him. Whether they had such a motive or not, he was much enraged at the slight upon his dignity. But he was not to be frustrated (as he thought) in his wicked plot to make away with the child whom he regarded as his rival. He therefore formed the plan to draw a

dragnet around the territory of Bethlehem in the hopes of entrapping the
child Jesus, and he placed the maxi-
mum· age at two years. It had been
that long since he made his inquiry
of the wise men which he supposed
was the time of the royal birth. This
plot might have accomplished his satanic purpose had it not been for the
intervention of the Lord as recorded
in verse 13. Many people have been
confused between the slaughter of
these infants and the one in Egypt in
the time of Moses. In that case the
male children only were to be slain,
while no distinction was made in the
present instance. Pharaoh was concerned only about children who might
become soldiers to make war against
him and hence he ordered just the
males to be killed. Herod would not
risk the excuse that could have been
offered by some in sparing their infants had the girls been exempted,
hence the passage says that *all the
children* were ordered slain. That
word is from PAIS which Thayer defines is this place by the following:
"1. a child, boy or girl; . . . plural infants, children."

Verse 17. When one inspired writer
makes an application of another inspired statement, it leaves us with no
uncertainty as to its meaning. Thus
we know that Jeremiah had the
"slaughter of the innocents" in mind
when he wrote Jeremiah 31: 15.

Verse 18. The context of the statement in Jeremiah had to do with the
sorrows of ancient Israel at the hands
of the heathen nations. Many of them
had been slain or otherwise mistreated
by these foreign people. Rama (or
Ramah) was near Jerusalem and
Rachel was buried in that district.
She was an important "mother in
Israel" and her name is used to represent the mothers in Israel generally.
Following a practice of the Old Testament prophets in going from their
time to that of the New Testament for
a like occurrence, Jeremiah looked forward to another when the near kin of
Rachel would be cruelly mistreated.
This was done when Herod caused so
many of the Jewish children to be
slain, hence the reference of Matthew
to that prophecy of Jeremiah.

Verse 19. Sometimes angels were
sent in visible form to communicate
with man on behalf of God, and at
others they came only in an inspired
dream which was the way it was done

to Joseph in Egypt when it was necessary to give him information.

Verse 20. He was instructed to leave
Egypt and return because the ones
who sought to slay the child were
dead. The first instructions were general and designated only that he
should return to the *land of Israel*
which would include Galilee as well
as Judea.

Verse 21. This verse is still in the
general form and merely states that
Joseph brought the child and his
mother into the *land of Israel*, and in
so doing he carried out the first instructions of the angel delivered to
him in the land of Egypt.

Verse 22. It was after the Lord informed him of the reign of Archelaus
that Joseph was afraid to enter Judea
which was only one part of the *land
of Israel*. The word *notwithstanding*
is not in the original and serves no
good purpose by being injected into
the text and should be ignored. The
verse simply means that God warned
(same word as in verse 12) Joseph
about the son of Herod, and that
caused him to change his course and
enter another part of the land of
Israel called Galilee.

Verse 23. The city to which Joseph
went with his family was Nazareth,
which was the former home of Mary
(Luke 1: 26, 27). This seems to have
been a mere coincidence for them to
settle at this place, but we may be
sure that God had a hand in all of
the affair. The writer says it was in
fulfillment of a prophecy that *He was
to be called a Nazarene*. The last word
is not in any prophecy of the Old
Testament. The term is derived from
the formation of the name Nazareth
which seems to signify "a sprout or
branch," and under such like terms
Jesus is referred to in Isaiah 11: 1;
53: 2; Jeremiah 23: 5; 33: 15; Zechariah 3: 8; 6: 12.

MATTHEW 3

Verse 1. *In those days* is indefinite
and it is at least a quarter of a century after the close of the preceding
chapter. In that chapter (verse 21)
Jesus was but a "young child" while
now he is about 30 years old (Luke
3: 23). *Baptist* is from the Greek
word BAPTISTES which Thayer defines,
"a baptizer; one who administers the
rite of baptism," hence the name John
the Baptist. It is sometimes asked
why a man would come to baptize in
a wilderness where there are no people

to baptize nor any water available for such a purpose. Both assumptions are wrong, for while the territory was not settled or inhabited, there was nothing to prevent the people of the settlements going out to him, which they did (verse 5). Also the word does not mean a place where there would be no water. *Wilderness* is from EREMOS which Thayer defines, "an uncultivated region fit for pasturage." There would not likely be much pasturage where there was no water. Besides, Judea was not so large a region but that the river of Jordan could be reached for the purpose of baptizing.

Verse 2. *Repent* is from METANOEO and Thayer defines it here as follows: "To change one's mind for the better, heartily to amend with abhorrence for one's past sins." To amend means more than a mere state of the mind; it requires that one do something about it. BASILEIA is the only word in the Greek New Testament for "kingdom." It has several phases of meaning and hence I consider it well to give a pretty extensive quotation from the lexicons as to their definitions: "1. royal power, kingship, dominion, rule. 2. a kingdom i. e. the territory subject to the rule of a king. 3. properly the kingdom over which God rules . . . the kingdom of the Messiah . . . the rule of God, the theocricy . . . God's rule, the divine administration."—Thayer. I have quoted only such words in Thayer's lexicon as are in italics, which denotes the direct definition, omitting for the sake of space his many remarks on the word. The same rule will be followed in quoting from the other lexicons: "1. dominion, reign, rule. 2. a kingdom, dominion, realm."—Robinson. "A kingdom; royalty, dignity, power, reign, rule, sovereignty, dominion."—Groves. "A kingdom, realm, i. e. the region or country governed by a king; kingly power, authority, dominion, reign."— Greenfield. This paragraph may not be quoted again in full, hence the reader is urged to study it carefully to discover its shades of meaning, also to make a note of its location for ready reference. *At hand* is from EGGIZO and means "is near," which denotes that it was not yet in actual existence in the days of John the Baptist.

Verse 3. The prophecy cited is in Isaiah 40: 3 where the prophet passes from a favorable turn in the affairs of ancient Israel to the time when prepa-rations were to be made for Christ's entry upon the new dispensation. *Make his paths straight* has the idea of preparing a path for another to use afterward. By taking down the high and rough places and taking out the sharp curves, the other party could make better progress in his travels. Of course this is all figurative and refers to the work of John in bringing about a reformation among the Jews. Such a work would get a group of people in better frame of mind and character to receive the more advanced work of Christ.

Verse 4. In Zechariah 13: 4 a false prophet is described as wearing a rough garment to deceive the public, indicating that such a garment was an article of clothing peculiar to a prophet. It was appropriate that John the Baptist, who was a true prophet, wear such a piece made from the hair of camels. The girdle served as a belt to hold the loose garment close to the body. Leviticus 11: 22 included the locust among clean foods that the Jews were permitted to eat. *Wild honey* is so called because it was made by wild bees and deposited in hollow trees or crevices of rocks. Honey is one of the purest of foods in the vegetable class, and locusts could be classed with the animal kind. John the Baptist, therefore, had a somewhat balanced though simple diet.

Verse 5. The text does not say that every individual in these districts was baptized, but that great throngs from all of them came out to be baptized.

Verse 6. *Baptized* is from BAPTIZO which Thayer defines first, "Properly to dip repeatedly, to immerse, submerge. 2. to cleanse by dipping or submerging, to wash, to make clean with water." Strong defines it, "To make whelmed (i. e. fully wet)." From this meaning of the word we can understand why John was baptizing in *Jordan*, not at or nearby. *Confessing their sins* is the simple phrase used here, but in Mark 1: 4 and Luke 3: 3 it is worded "baptism of repentance." The meaning of the passage is that the people professed to have repented of their sins and were baptized on that declaration.

Verse 7. The *Pharisees* and *Sadducees* were two leading sects of the Jews in the time of Christ. They had some radical differences which will be described in another place. There were some principles, however, which they both had in common and one of them was hypocrisy, and both made great claims of excellence which they did not possess. This, too, will be described elsewhere. *Generation of vipers* is a figure of speech meaning a class of vile and poisonous characters. They came to the baptismal services of John for the outward appearance it made. In his preaching John exhorted the people to repent and be baptized for the remission of sins, in order to escape the wrath of God. He had not specified any classes, so the response of these sects was an outward admission of their being sinners though their attitude was one of self-righteousness.

Verse 8. *Meet for repentance* means for them to prove by their works that they have really repented. A mere sorrow or regret for sin does not constitute repentance in the sight of the Lord, but the guilty one is expected to reform his life by ceasing to do the things that were wrong.

Verse 9. John was an inspired man and could read the thoughts of these boastful pretenders. But aside from this truth, the language of these Jews indicated their pride of ancestry. (See John 8: 33.) John did not intend to belittle the importance of Abraham, but he meant that having descended through the line of that great patriach did not entitle them to any special favors in their wrong doing. It was God's will that Abraham's lineal descendants become the special race for His purposes, but that was not because no other plan would have been possible. As far as power or ability was concerned, He could have caused the stones to become impregnated with the divine germ of life so that they could give birth to children to be enrolled in the register of Abraham's seed. Such a possibility as described above existed though the Lord never intended to do such a thing. There was another feat, however, that was as wonderful as that, which was to convert Gentile heathen into descendants of Abraham by faith. (See Romans 4: 11.)

Verse 10. This verse is figurative and general and denotes the judgments of God against sin. An ax lying at the root of a tree suggests a probable attack upon it. The instrument is near but inactive, yet ready to be used if and when a decision is made against the tree. The fact on which the decision will be made is that the tree does not produce good fruit. I do not believe this verse applies to the Jewish nation as a whole for there was only one "tree" of the Lord that could be considered. The words *every tree* indicate that John was speaking of individuals all of whom were exhorted to repent and thus escape the wrath of God. The condemnation to such wrath was starting through the preaching of John, but the final result of rejecting that preaching would not come until the great judgment day. Being an inspired man John the Baptist was able to predict the future lot of all classes of men who were in his hearing, even to the punishment of fire awaiting the unsaved at the time of the final judgment. This prepares us to understand the following two verses.

Verse 11. There are three baptisms referred to in this verse, one administered by John and two by the Lord; the two were in the future when John spoke. The three baptisms were in different elements, namely, water, Holy Ghost and fire, and the three were for that many different kinds of subjects. The water baptism administered by John was performed upon penitent Jews and it was for the remission of their sins. The Holy Ghost baptism administered by the Lord was performed upon the apostles and it was to "guide them into all truth" (John 16: 13). The baptism with fire to be administered by the Lord (at the judgment day) upon the unsaved and it is for the purpose of punishment. The simple pronoun *you* is used by John because he knew that in his audience were men who would become apostles and hence would receive the baptism of the Holy Ghost. He knew also that some of his hearers would live and die in their sins because they would be too stubborn to repent, and these would receive the baptism of fire. But he spoke to the multitude as a whole and intended the two baptisms to be applied to the ones deserving them. This explains Acts 1: 5 and 11: 16 where the baptism of the Holy Ghost only is mentioned because the apostles were the only ones being considered. *Shoes not worthy to bear* is an allusion to the customs of that time. Loose sandals were worn in foot travel and upon entering a home they were removed and taken charge of by a servant. By way of illustration John regarded himself as unworthy even to bear the shoes of the one who was soon to come after him in the work of further reformation.

Verse 12. The figures now change and are drawn from a different source. In verse 10 they were based upon the work of horticulture, while in this they are upon that of agriculture. *Fan* is from PTUON and is defined "a winnowing-shovel" in Thayer's lexicon. Grain was piled down on a smooth place called the threshing floor and trampled out by oxen or beaten with a large club called a flail. Then an instrument like a broad shovel was used to scoop up the shattered grain and toss it up into the wind so the chaff could be blown to one side. The grain was stored in the garner (granary) and the chaff was burned. The process is used to illustrate the separation of the wicked from the good at the day of judgment. The good will be taken to the garner which is heaven, and the wicked will be cast into the lake of fire. The terms ordinarily used to describe the threshing process do not cover all of the phases of the work as it pertains to humanity, hence John qualified the fire by the word *unquenchable* which comes from the Greek word ASBESTOS and Thayer's definition is, "unquenchable." There will be only one judgment day and hence no continual gathering of chaff to cast into the fire. There is but one explanation, therefore, for using unquenchable fire, and that is that the wicked will not be put out of existence as literal chaff is, but will continue to exist and burn endlessly, and that will require a fire that cannot be put out.

Verse 13. Jesus had spent his life through childhood and early manhood with his parents at Nazareth which was in Galilee. The time came when he was to enter upon his life's work and he had reason for starting it with being baptized. There was only one man baptizing people then and that was John the Baptist, hence Jesus left his home and came into Judea where John was baptizing in the Jordan.

Verse 14. John did not know the divine identity of Jesus until the baptism had taken place (John 1: 33), therefore his remarks were not prompted by that subject. They were cousins according to the flesh and about the same age. It is reasonable to conclude that John knew Jesus as a near relative and humbly placed himself in a lower rank of excellence. All that John knew as to the purpose of water baptism was that it was for the remission of sins. Someone had to start the great work of reform without being baptized himself, and of the two John considered Jesus to be the more worthy of the honor.

Verse 15. Had the remission of sins been the only result to be accomplished by baptism, Jesus would not have come to John at all for it because he had no sins to be remitted. Hence it was necessary for John to be informed of the reason why Jesus made the request. *Fulfill* is from PLEROO and Thayer's definition at this passage is, "to perform, execute." *Righteousness* is from DIKAIOSUNE and Thayer defines it as follows: "b. integrity, virtue, purity of life, uprightness, correctness in thinking, feeling, and acting. Matthew 3: 15; 5: 6, 10, 20; 6: 33." Note that nothing in the definition requires any act in the nature of repentance or confession, hence Jesus who had no sins to confess could adopt the definition in his reason for requiring baptism. But while he had no sins to confess he did have a duty to "perform," and by so doing he could maintain his "integrity." When this explanation was made to John he promptly performed the baptism and thus cooperated in the act that Jesus said would be fitting or becoming.

Verse 16. If Jesus went up *out of* the water it was necessary that he go down into it, and that would agree with the definition of "baptize" as given at verse 6. The heavens were opened *unto him* and *he saw* the Spirit in the form of a dove. This together with John 1: 32-34 indicates that Jesus and John were the only witnesses of this remarkable event. It was fitting that John be permitted to see it since that was the sign the Lord had given him by which he was to recognize the One for whom all this preparatory work was being done.

Verse 17. If only the eyes of John and Jesus saw the heavens open and the bodily shape of the dove, it would be reasonable to. conclude that their ears only heard these words. It also indicates one reason why the words "hear ye him" were not added as they were at chapter 17: 5. The Father here acknowledged Jesus as his Son after he had *fulfilled* his righteous duty of being baptized. But his life's work was only beginning and hence it was not time to give the command to hear him.

MATTHEW 4

Verse 1. *Led up of the spirit* denotes that Jesus was divinely instructed to go into the *wilderness* (same place as chapter 3: 1) and submit to the test. *Tempted* is from PEIRAZO and has various shades of meaning in the New Testament. I shall copy most of the italicized words in Thayer's definition which constitutes his direct description of the word: "To try, i. e. 1. to try whether a thing can be done; to attempt, endeavor. 2. to try, make trial of, test. To solicit to sin, to tempt. To inflict evils [afflictions] upon one in order to prove his character and steadfastness of his faith." The context must be considered in each case to determine which part of the definition applies. The word *devil* is from two originals in the Greek New Testament which are DAIMONION and DIABOLOS. Thayer defines the first, "1. the divine Power, deity, divinity. 2. a spirit, a being inferior to God, superior to men . . . evil spirits as the messengers and ministers of the Devil." (It is the word frequently thought of for demons.) The second word is defined, "prone to slander, slanderous, accusing falsely . . . false accuser, slanderer . . . In the Bible and in ecclesiastical writings THE DIABOLOS is applied to Satan." The rule is that when the plural word "devils" is used it comes from the first word above, and if singular, "the devil," it is from the second word and means Satan.

Verse 2. A man would not have to go forty days without food to become hungry in the ordinary sense or degree. The meaning is that by the end of that period the pangs of hunger became severe.

Verse 3. *Tempter* is from the same word as "tempted" in verse 1, and the person doing the tempting is the devil also defined in that verse. The devil knew that the great issue at stake was the divinity of Christ, hence the suggestion he made was a challenge for Him to prove his claim. There is no doubt with us (and neither was there with the devil) as to Christ's ability to do the thing suggested. But Christ never used his miraculous power or divine character in his own behalf. He was here to set an example for his followers who were to be taught the lesson of self-denial. It would have been inconsistent to ask his disciples to resist temptation when they had only their natural powers for support, while He overcame his trials by falling back on his divine power. Another thing that would have made it wrong for Christ to turn the stones into bread

is that it would have been an act proposed by the devil. It is wrong to have any fellowship with Satan in any act, even though it might be right in itself.

Verse 4. In quoting the statement that is in Deuteronomy 8: 3, Jesus showed his respect for the inspired word of God and set a worthy example for others. He ignored the challenging phase of the preceding verse and based his reply on the principle that physical satisfaction is not the only thing that should interest a person in this life. One might be abundantly supplied and contented physically and yet lack the more important food which is for the inner man and is found in the words of God.

Verse 5. Thayer's definition for the original of *taketh* is, "1. to take to, to take with one's self, to join to one's self." The word does not mean that Jesus was carried against his will to the place, but that He accompanied the devil as a further step in the procedure of the test to which he was being put. The word *pinnacle* is a subject of some uncertainty in the several works of reference that I have consulted as to what part of the temple is meant. It is evident that a specific place is meant for the Greek definite article is used in the original text, making it read "the pinnacle" instead of "a pinnacle." But regardless of all these considerations the point is that it was a place high enough to have caused death to one who would fall from it.

Verse 6. Much importance has been attached by commentators to the devil's omission of the words "in all thy ways" from his citation to Psalms 91: 11, 12. The word *ways* is from DEREK which Strong defines, "a course of life or mode of action," regardless of whether that course is right or wrong. The context must determine in each case whether it is the one or the other. To say that casting himself down would have been wrong is to assume the very point in question. Had it been right for him to perform such a stunt as the devil suggested, then the passage which he cited would have given the assurance of divine protection according to the passage in Psalms.

Verse 7. The word for *tempt* is similar to the one in verse 1 but is a stronger word and is defined by Thayer, "To prove , test, thoroughly tempt." Jesus quoted Deuteronomy 6: 16 and thus it will be well to look at that passage and consider the connection. It says not to tempt God as they tempted him in Massah. That refers to Exodus 17: 2, 7 where the people complained because of their thirst and questioned if the Lord was among them. It was trying (one meaning of tempt) on the patience of God to hear such attacks upon His power and goodness. That justifies the comment of Thayer in his definition of the word when he says, "by irreligion and immorality to test the patience or avenging power of Christ." God's longsuffering is infinite for people who sincerely rely on Him for help, even to the last degree of indulgence for their unusual requests. But He will not suffer being approached in the spirit of challenge just to see if He can and is willing to gratify their disrespectful curiosity.

Verse 8. If the reader will examine the various definitions of *kingdom* given in chapter 3: 2, he will learn that the word sometimes means the territory ruled by a king; in other words, it is something that can be seen with the fleshly eye. However, the rulership of such realms would necessarily involve much *glory*, so the devil called the attention of Jesus to that feature. A miracle or supernatural performance had to be done in order to make such a display before the eyes of Jesus, but that does not present any difficulty for the Bible has numerous instances that show he has been suffered to use such power when it suited the Lord's plan to have it so.

Verse 9. In the corresponding passage in Luke 4: 6 the devil makes a stronger claim than is recorded here. He says that he possesses the "glory" of all these realms of the world and Jesus does not deny it; the following passages will also bear out his claim. (John 14: 30; 16: 11; Ephesians 2: 2.) In this verse the devil promises to give up his control of the glory existing in the kingdoms of the world and turn it over to Jesus. The only condition he requires is that Jesus fall down and *worship* him. See the note in comments on chapter 2: 2 for the meaning of *worship*. Regardless of what phase of that word the devil had in mind, to have complied with the proposition would have been sin and that would have for ever disqualified Him from being a perfect sacrifice.

Verse 10. The word *satan* is spelled the same in both Greek and English and the definition in Thayer's lexicon (the part written in italics) is the single word "adversary" when used as a proper name, and "a Satan-like man" when used figuratively. Jesus used it as a proper name in this verse and thus identified him with "the devil" in this account of the temptation. *Get thee hence* means for him to leave which he will do in the next verse. *Worship* is from PROSKUNEO and *serve* is from LATREUO, and both of them are found in the long note on the word "worship" at chapter 2: 2.

Verse 11. Luke 4: 13 adds the words "for a season" to the statement here that "the devil leaveth him." This is significant and adds force to the statements in Hebrews 2: 17, 18; 4: 15 which indicate that Jesus was subject to temptation all through his life on earth. These temptations came whenever the devil or his servants had an occasion to try their hand. For the present the devil has gone the limit of his resources, for 1 John 2: 16 says that "all that is in the world" is the "lust of the flesh, lust of the eyes and pride of life." He used these three with Eve and won over her. He used them in the temptation of Christ in the wilderness and was defeated. The item of bread was an appeal to the lust of the flesh; the display of the kingdoms of the world appealed to the lust of the eyes, and the idea of casting himself from the pinnacle appealed to the pride of life in that it would only be pride that would prompt a person to perform some sensational exploit. Having been defeated in this encounter with Jesus, the devil quit the scene to await another opportunity.

Verse 12. The account of John's imprisonment is in the 14th chapter, being inserted there to explain a remark that was made by the Herod who was reigning then. We are not told in this place why Jesus departed from Galilee, but the purpose is indicated in John 4: 43-45. *When Jesus had heard.* Jesus did not have to obtain information about the activities of men by the ordinary means of hearing (John 2: 23-25), so the phrase is used merely to state the occasion on which he left Judea. It means as if it said "upon the report," etc., Jesus left Judea and went to Galilee. The word *hear* is from AKOUO and has various shades of meaning which must be understood in each passage according to the connection. The word is so important that I believe it will be well to give a quotation from Thayer's lexicon on the definitions of the word. I shall quote the parts in italics since that is his direct definition, while the words in regular type are his own comments and explanation of the definitions. I urge the reader to make note of it and be prepared to consult it as occasion suggests. "To be endowed with the faculty of hearing. To attend to; consider. To understand, perceive the sense of what is said. To get by hearing, learn. A thing comes to one's ears, to find out (by hearing), learn (hear of); to learn. To comprehend, understand. To perceive any one's voice. To give ear to one, listen, hearken. To yield to, hear to one; to listen to, have regard to. To perceive the distinct words of a voice. To yield obedience to a voice."

Verse 13. *Nazareth* was a town in Galilee where the parents of Jesus lived after coming back from Egypt. Now he moves his residence to another town in the same province called Capernaum. From now on when mention is made of "his own city" it will mean this place, while the term "his own country" will still mean the vicinity of Nazareth.

Verse 14. *That it might be fulfilled* does not always mean that a certain thing was done just so a particular prophecy might be fulfilled, although it will sometimes mean that. In every such passage it will be well to consider it in the light of saying, "and in so doing the prophecy was fulfilled which," etc.

Verse 15. The prophecy of Isaiah 9: 1, 2 is quoted which was fulfilled when Jesus took up his residence in the city of Capernaum. Sometimes more than one place would have the same name, hence the inspired writers gave several marks of identity by which the correct one would be known.

Verse 16. Heathen darkness had brooded over the communities around Capernaum, but the presence and teaching of Jesus penetrated that gloom and gave the people the benefit of spiritual light which fulfilled an important prophecy of the scriptures.

Verse 17. *From that time* denotes that Jesus began his public teaching after his baptism and not before. Likewise, men are not regarded as the Lord's workers today until they have been baptized. It indicates also that they are expected to begin working for Him as soon as they are baptized. In most respects the preaching of Jesus was like that of John in that its main subject was to require men to repent in view of the nearness of the king-

dom of heaven. Each of them taught that the kingdom was *at hand* which would mean that it did not exist in fact in their lifetime. Moreover, it also shows that it was soon to appear which disproves the teaching of the present day by some that the kingdom is still in the future.

Verse 18. According to John 1: 35-42 these two brothers were disciples of John. They had not ceased their regular occupation since there was nothing wrong about it and the command of John that his disciples repent would not interfere with their business. They were fishermen by occupation and were in the act of casting a net into the water when Jesus came by. That was the principal means of fishing in those days; the other was with a hook (Matthew 17: 27).

Verse 19. We note that the Lord did not say anything to these men as to their personal conduct. They had already been converted by John and hence nothing was wanting along that line. John's work was to "prepare the way of the Lord" by persuading men and women to repent and be baptized. That made it entirely proper for Jesus to call upon them to enter the work for which they had been prepared. *Make you fishers of men.* That was a psychological appeal to these men in view of their usual occupation. Jesus did not belittle or even criticize their business, but only promised to give them an improved opportunity to work at the trade of fishing. He intended for them to have better bait (spiritual meat) and take more valuable fish, the souls of men.

Verse 20. In leaving their nets they gave up their secular occupation for the sake of following Christ. A similar but fuller statement will soon be made of two others whom Jesus will call.

Verse 21. *Zebedee* is referred to in the reference works simply as a Jew who was a fisherman by trade. The information that he was the father of the two apostles, James and John, will be useful in other places for distinguishing them from other men with the same names. These brothers were called by Jesus and no particulars are given as to why they were called.

Verse 22. This contains the fuller statement referred to in verse 20; the brothers left the ship *and* their *father*. This would not have been necessary if nothing but information were the object. It would be taken for granted that they could not follow Jesus without leaving their father as well as all other objects at home. The lesson is that love for earthly relatives should not be regarded above service for Christ.

Verse 23. The word *synagogue* occurs many times in the New Testament and I will give Thayer's definition of the original Greek: "In the N. T. 1. an assembly of men. 2. a synagogue, i. e. a. an assembly of Jews formally gathered together to offer prayer and listen to the reading and exposition of the Holy Scriptures. b. the building where those solemn assemblies are held." The first meaning of the word is virtually the same as a congregation and then it came to be applied to the building in which the people met. Thayer says the following historically on the subject: "Synagogues seem to date their origin from the Babylonian exile. In the time of Jesus and the apostles every town, not only in Palestine but also among the Gentiles, if it contained a considerable number of Jewish inhabitants, had at least one synagogue, the larger towns several or even many."

The law of Moses made no provision for these buildings, yet there was nothing in its teaching that would prohibit them. The national worship was conducted at Jerusalem where the tabernacle and later the temple were located. Such services, which consisted in the animal sacrifices and burning of incense, also the service of the showbread and burning of oil on the golden candlestick, must all be conducted at Jerusalem only. But other items of Jewish worship might be performed in any place available and hence these many synagogues that are mentioned throughout the New Testament.

The word *gospel* is from EUAGGELION, and its universal definition in the lexicons is "glad tidings" or "good news." Any specific additional meaning to be attached to it must be obtained through the connection in which it is used. Hence in the present verse the words *gospel of the kingdom* simply means the good news that the kingdom is at hand. There is not much difference between *sickness* and *disease*. The first especially refers to the symptoms of nausea and the second to some bodily weakness. In taking care of *all manner* of ailments Jesus proved his superhuman power.

Verse 24. Syria embraced most of the country including Palestine and the region north and northeast of it. Such beneficial work as Jesus was doing would naturally be reported so that would cause him to become famous. The personal interest that people would have in such subjects as sickness and other afflictions would bring them forth to have Jesus relieve them. *Possessed with devils* will be explained in another place.

Verse 25. The preceding verse makes a general statement of the territory from which the afflicted people came; this specifies some parts of that vast area.

MATTHEW 5

Verse 1. This and the next two chapters constitute what is commonly called the "sermon on the mount," so called because the verse says that the Lord *went up into a mountain.* The text does not specifically state why Jesus went up to this place further than to say he did it *seeing the multitudes.* However, since the distinction is made between the multitudes and the disciples, we may reasonably conclude that the purpose was to be less hindered in the teaching of the ones who were really interested in it, and not moved only by curiosity or desire for temporal favors. *Disciples* is from MATHETES which Thayer defines, "A learner, pupil, disciple . . . the twelve apostles." The word has a broader or narrower application according to the way it is used, and the connection must always be considered in determining its meaning in a given case. Thayer's remarks included with the definition also show the word sometimes means those who favored Jesus and "became his adherents." That is its most prevalent meaning and the one it has in the present verse.

Verse 2. *Opened his mouth and taught them* is very significant. In all of God's dealings with man He has never influenced him in his moral and spiritual conduct except by the use of words, either written or spoken, and hence Jesus followed that plan in talking to his disciples about things pertaining to the kingdom of God. In this great sermon Jesus lays down many principles of life that pertained to the time before the kingdom was set up, and others were to be applied afterward. Where a distinction is necessary to the understanding of any passage I shall so state it.

Verse 3. *Blessed* is an adjective coming from the Greek word MAKARIOS, and Thayer defines it simply by the words "blessed, happy." In the Authorized Version it is rendered by the first

43 times and by the second 6 times. These verses are usually called "beatitudes," and Webster's definition of that word is, "Consumate [complete] bliss; blessedness." It will be well for us to think of the word in the sense of being happy as that is the more familiar word. To be *poor in spirit* means to recognize one's need of spiritual help. Such characters are the ones who will accept the kingdom of heaven.

Verse 4. There could be no happiness in the fact of mourning but it is by way of contrast. The new system that Jesus was about to set up would provide the only genuine relief from the sorrows of this world.

Verse 5. The word for *meek* is PRAOS which Thayer defines, "gentle, mild, meek." It is a contrast with the fierce and domineering spirit so often shown by the members of earthly kingdoms, especially the rulers. To *inherit* is generally defined in the lexicons "to receive by lot." Thayer's definition of this verse is, "to partake of eternal salvation in the Messiah's kingdom." *The earth* is the same that is referred to in 2 Peter 3: 13 which the apostle says was promised to the righteous.

Verse 6. To hunger and thirst after righteousness means to be eager to learn what constitutes a righteous life. It does not stop there, for when a man is hungry he not only seeks to find some food, but also is ready to partake of it. This means that the ones whom Jesus was blessing would be eager to do that which is right.

Verse 7. The single English word "mercy" is Thayer's definition of the word here. It is defined in the English dictionary to mean to be sparing in inflicting even punishment that is due another. It does not call for endorsement of wrong or for overlooking it, but to be considerate of the other person.

Verse 8. When disconnected from all qualifying terms the word *pure* simply means "unmixed"; something that is not combined with any other substance, and hence it could mean either good or bad. An object that has no good in it would be pure evil. When the connection shows it is used in a good sense (as in our verse) it means a heart not mixed up with the evils of a sinful world. The definition of the Biblical heart will be given in another place.

Verse 9. Every statement of scripture must be understood in harmony with others on the same subject for the words of inspiration do not contradict each other. James 3: 17 says the wisdom from above is *first* pure *then* peaceable, and Paul in Romans 12: 18 commands us to live at peace with all men "if possible." The verse here means that disciples are to make every scriptural effort to be at peace with each other, and also to bring about a peaceable settlement between others who are at variance. Such will be *called the children of God* because He deals with mankind on that principle.

Verse 10. Thayer defines the original at this place, "to harass, trouble, molest," and he says that it may be done "in any way whatsoever," hence the persecution may be against one's body or his mind. But this must be done because the victim is righteous, and has no reference to accidental affliction, or punishment for wrong doing. These persons have the qualities of the citizens in the *kingdom of heaven*.

Verse 11. This verse is similar in thought to the preceding one except that it is considering only the persecution of the mind. The evil things said against a disciple must be done in falsehood to bring him under the application of this blessing.

Verse 12. This verse continues the thought of the preceding one. It will be nothing new for the Lord's disciples to be treated unjustly, for the righteous prophets were thus treated in former years. The *rejoicing* is to be for having been classed with the righteous prophets. The reward will come after this life is over and the victims have been admitted into heaven.

Verse 13. The teaching of Jesus contains many illustrations drawn from nature and the customs of mankind. *Salt* has two outstanding qualities; preservation of articles with which it comes in contact, and rendering food more agreeable to the taste. The lives of true disciples will shed the truth among men by example and teaching, and thus contribute to the salvation of their souls. And next, the trials or hardships of this life will be easier to bear, will "taste better" for having the salt of divine truth mixed with them. But if the salt *losses its savour* ("to make flat and tasteless") it will not be of any use either as a preservative or palliative. The first *it* is a pronoun for *the earth* which cannot be salted if *it* (the salt) has lost strength. Such salt is fit for nothing but to be trodden upon as the soil of the ground. Likewise, if the disciples of Christ cease to be an influence for good—cease to practice the principles taught by their Master, they will finally be rejected and trodden upon by the Judge.

Verse 14. Disciples of Christ are the light of the world in much the same sense that they are the salt of the earth. The righteous lives they exhibit and the truth they spread among their fellowmen will reflect the light that comes from the Lord. The *hill* is the mountain or government of Christ and the light of divine truth shines forth from that exalted position like the glow of light from a city upon a hill.

Verse 15. It is possible for a strong light to be rendered useless, which would be done if a man lighted a lamp and then put some vessel over it. But men do not do such things in temporal matters; only in spiritual things do they act thus foolishly.

Verse 16. Jesus does not wish his disciples to act so unreasonably as the description in the preceding verse implies. *Let your light shine* does not call for any special effort to bring attention to the good light that has been made. If a host just makes a good light and leaves it uncovered, the guests will see it and give proper credit for the favor. *Your light* and *good works* are mentioned in direct connection which shows they mean the same. It is not necessary for one to boast of his good works in order to have men see them; all that is necessary is to perform the works. However, the doer of these good deeds for the benefit of others, must also live a good life otherwise or in addition to his benevolence, or his good deeds will be rendered ineffective in the mind of men. ("Let not then your good be evil spoken of.") *Glorify* is from DOXAZO and Thayer's definition at this place is, "to praise, extol, magnify, celebrate." It is the Greek word for "glorify" in every place in the Authorized Version. The reason men will glorify God for these lives of the disciples is because they know that such conduct is not the natural result of the fleshly motives.

Verse 17. Jesus lived and completed his work on earth while the law of Moses was in force. He taught that men should respect and obey that law, yet he gave many instructions that were not specifically set forth in that system. That was because he was getting ready to bring into the world another system of laws that were to be different from the old. This opened the way for the critics to charge him with being opposed to the law of Moses. In answer to such erroneous notions he used the difference between *destroying* and *fulfilling.* He was not in the world for the first but for the second. The Old Testament writings had predicted that a son of David was to come into the world and give it a new religious law. Because of such predictions, the very things Jesus taught of a different character constituted a fulfilling of the law.

Verse 18. *Verily* is from the Greek word AMEN which occurs 150 times in the New Testament. In the Authorized Version it is rendered "amen" 50 times and "verily" 100 times. Thayer defines the word as follows: "surely, of a truth, truly; most assuredly; so it is, so be it, may it be fulfilled." These various phrases define the word according to the connection in which it is used, whether at the beginning or ending of a passage, etc. *Till heaven and earth pass* is a phrase denoting the certainty of the fulfillment of the law of God. The material universe will pass away, but not until it has served the purpose of the Creator. Likewise, the law will not pass away until it has all been fulfilled. *Jot* is from IOTA which is the smallest letter of the Greek alphabet and was originally written as a subscript under the regular line. *Tittle* is one of the diacritical marks used by the Greeks in their writings. The two terms are used to illustrate the importance that Jesus attached to the law. Even such apparently small points of the law as these will not be dropped until they have been fulfilled.

Verse 19. The commandments of the law will not be in force in the kingdom of heaven. The thought is that a man who would break the least of these commandments while they are in force shows the wrong attitude toward divine law. Such a person would not rank very high in the kingdom of heaven after it has been set up.

Verse 20. *Exceed* is from the same Greek word that is used in 2 Corinthians 3: 9, and we know that it is there used in the sense of quality and not quantity. Jesus means that his disciples must have a better kind of righteousness than the Pharisees practiced, for theirs was done for appearance and came from the lips only. A full description of the Pharisees will be found in connection with the comments at chapter 16: 12. The kingdom of heaven was to be entered into only by men who were converted in heart and whose actions were induced by a genuine acceptance of the Lord's commandments.

Verse 21. In half a dozen places in this chapter Jesus quotes some things that were said in *old time* which means the time that was regulated by the law of Moses. He does not discredit the authority of the Sinaite lawgiver, but shows how some changes or additions will be made in the teaching for the kingdom of heaven. He being the Son of God and the one who will be the king on the throne of David when the church is set up, it was appropriate that he begin showing some of the contrasts between the two. Those contrasts will generally consist in making a more spiritual application of the ancient laws, and/or in tightening their requirements so as to make them more rigid.

One of such items was the law of trial for murder, that such a crime would lay a man under charges to be heard by the *judgment.* This is from the Greek word KRISIS and I shall give the definition of two lexicons: "The college of judges (a tribunal of seven men in the several cities of Palestine; as distinguished from the Sanhedrin, which had its seat at Jerusalem . . . Matthew 5: 21, 22)." — Thayer. "A judgment seat, tribunal, put for a court of justice, judges, i. e. the smaller tribunals established in the cities of Palestine, subordinate to the Sanhedrin; see Deuteronomy 16: 18; 2 Chronicles 19: 5. According to the Rabbins they consisted of 23 judges; but Josephus expressly says the number was seven."—Robinson. Even as serious a crime as murder was considered as only being in danger of facing this secondary court of justice.

Verse 22. Jesus is teaching that under the standards of right and wrong that he will establish, being angry with a brother *without a cause* will endanger one before the same *judgment* seat as murder did in old time. As a further indication of increased strictness, to give way to one's temper to the extent of calling his brother *Raca* (a term of reproach meaning empty-headed or senseless), would endanger him before the greater

court; the *council* which was the Sanhedrin. Still increasing the picture of responsibility, to accuse a brother of being a *fool* will put a man in danger of hell fire. According to Thayer, Robinson and Greenfield, the word for *fool* means "a wicked rebel against the Lord." And it should be noted that all of the evil actions are on condition that they are *without a cause.* The word *hell* is from GEHENNA which refers to the lake of unquenchable fire into which the wicked will be cast after the judgment. A fuller definition of the English word "hell" as it is used in the New Testament will be given in another part of the COMMENTARY.

Verse 23. *Therefore* is said because the last subject treated was the sin of showing the wrong attitude toward a brother. Under the law of Moses the Jews were encouraged to bring voluntary gifts to be consecrated to the Lord on the altar of sacrifices. These were in addition to the sacrifices specifically required on stated occasions or for specific purposes. Such an act was supposed to indicate that the giver was very much devoted to the Lord, and yet at the very time he might recall that his brother had a complaint against him. Such a complaint, for instance, could consist of calling him "a fool" according to the preceding verse.

Verse 24. One command is no more important than another, neither may one duty be made to take the place of another. But the gifts presented at the altar were expected to proceed from the heart, which would not be the case if a man would refuse to make a matter right with his brother. In other words, a ritualistic service should not be treated as a substitute for one of humility and brotherliness. Hence the man was directed to postpone his altar service until he had made it right with his brother.

Verse 25. This verse is in the nature of good advice concerning disputes with a fellow citizen on the subject of a debt. A conscientious attorney will advise his client to "settle the case out of court" if possible, which is the gist of this admonition from Jesus. *Whiles thou art in the way with him* means while they are still out of the jurisdiction of the judge. A man would better suffer some loss and remain a free man, rather than risk having the case decided against him and then have to spend a term in prison because of being unable to pay the sum assessed. All of this is to be understood in the light of an old law where a man could be put into prison for a debt.

Verse 26. Had the man offered to settle privately he might have been let off upon the payment of a part of the debt. If he lets it go on through court he may have to lie in prison until the entire debt is paid to which will be added the "court costs."

Verse 27. This verse introduces another place where Jesus shows that his laws will be stricter than the old ones. The law against adultery pertained to the physical act only as it was pronounced "by them of old time."

Verse 28. This passage has been strained out of its true meaning. To say it means a man sins if he thinks of the subject of sex at all in connection with a woman would be to fly in the face of much scripture. In 1 Corinthians 7: 2 Paul instructs a man to marry in order to "avoid fornication," and yet he could not have been in any danger of that sin unless he had been mindful of the subject in connection with some woman. The apostle does not condemn him for the mere fact of that state of mind and hence we should not construe the teaching of Jesus to make it condemn him. The thought is of a man who has no intention of honorable marriage, but who indulges his mind with the subject and who cultivates an imagination on the subject in a case where he knows he could not carry out his inclinations without violating the moral law, either because he or the woman would not be free to consummate the union.

Verse 29. A physical operation will not cure a moral evil of the mind. If a man were deprived of his natural eyes it would not prevent him from thinking of the woman towards whom he had been looking with evil intent. But the loss of so valuable an organ as the eye is used to illustrate the extent of sacrifice that one should make in order to rid himself of an evil action of body or mind. A friend or an occupation may seem to be as valuable as the eye, yet one should better go on through life without it rather than enjoy it a few years and then he be lost entirely.

Verse 30. The lesson in this verse is exactly the same as that in the preceding one, using the hand instead of the eye for the illustration. A full definition of the word *hell* will be given here and may not be repeated in full again. The reader should mark the place for convenient reference when needed. The word comes from three different Greek words in the New Testament. I shall give Thayer's definition, based upon his knowledge of history and of the language: "GEHENNA, the name of a valley on the S. and E. of Jerusalem . . . which was so called from the cries of the little children who were thrown into the fiery arms of Moloch, i. e. of an idol having the form of a bull. The Jews so abhorred the place after these horrible sacrifices had been abolished by King Josiah (2 Kings 23: 10), that they cast into it not only all manner of refuse, but even the dead bodies of animals and of unburied criminals who had been executed. And since fires were always needed to consume the dead bodies, that the air might not become tainted by their putrefaction, it came to pass that the place was called GEHENNA PUROS [Gehenna fire]." The following are all the places in the New Testament where the word *hell* comes from GEHENNA. Matthew 5: 22, 29, 30; 10: 28; 18: 9; 23: 15, 33; Mark 9: 43, 45, 47; Luke 12: 5; James 3: 6.

HADES is defined by Thayer as follows: "1, a proper name, Hades, Pluto, the god of the lower regions, the nether world, the realm of the dead . . . it denotes, therefore, in Biblical Greek, Orcus, the infernal regions, a dark and dismal place . . . the common receptacle of disembodied spirits." Following are all the places in the New Testament where the word *hell* comes from HADES: Matthew 11: 23; 16: 18, Luke 10: 15; 16: 23; Acts 2: 27, 31; Revelation 1: 18, 6: 8; 20; 13, 14. The word *hell* comes from TARTAROO in one place only which is 2 Peter 2: 4, and the definition is not very different from that of hades. To sum up, HADES is the place where all disembodied spirits go at death regardless of whether they are good or bad. TARTAROO is that part of HADES where the spirits of the wicked go at death. GEHENNA is the lake of unquenchable fire into which the whole being of the wicked (body soul and spirit) will be cast after the judgment.

Verse 31. The law referred to is in Deuteronomy 24: 1 which required a man to give his wife a writing that showed she had not deserted him, but that he had compelled her to go away. We know that was the purpose of that law, for the next verse says she may become another man's wife. If she did not have the writing no man would risk marrying her for fear she was a deserter. If the writing had been done the husband was considered as having done full justice to his wife. But Jesus is going to show this to be another instance where his law will be stricter than the old.

Verse 32. Jesus never taught anything at one time that disagreed with what he taught at another. This verse should be considered in connection with chapter 19:9 which is a fuller statement. The mere putting away of a wife does not constitute adultery, for there may be cases where a man would have to put his wife from him in order that he might live a Christian life. A woman might be guiltless as far as the intimate subject is concerned, and yet develop such a character and conduct herself in such a manner as to prevent a man from doing his full duty as a disciple of Christ; this idea is taught in chapter 10: 34-39. But unless his wife also is guilty of immorality the husband is not permitted to marry another. Neither would the wife who is put away for some cause other than immorality have the right to marry another under the regulations of the kingdom of heaven that Jesus was soon to set up.

Verse 33. *Forswear* means to make a false oath, or to testify under oath that which one does not intend to fulfill. The reference is to Leviticus 19: 12 where false oaths were expressly forbidden. Jesus cites the saying in contrast between his ruling and the old.

Verse 34. As to whether an oath is true or false is not the question with Jesus, for he forbids his disciples to make any oath at all. When a man makes an oath he backs it up by the authority of some power supposed to be great enough to make the oath good. That is why Jesus mentions various things by which men might pronounce an oath. The Jewish people had come to think they should not swear by the name of God, but Jesus shows it is as bad to swear by heaven since that is God's throne.

Verse 35. On the same basis as the above, they should not swear by the earth since it, too, is a part of the seating place of God, being his footstool. Jerusalem was the city of the great King who was God in the old system and will be the city of the new

king when the kingdom of heaven is set up.

Verse 36. If a man cannot even cause one hair of his head to change its color at his will, it would be foolish to rely upon it for making his oath good.

Verse 37. *Yea, yea; Nay, nay* means to let the statements be simply that of affirming what is in the positive class and denying the negative. The laws of the state do not require any man to make an oath if he declines to do so, but will accept his affirmation at the same value as an oath. Since that is true, there could be no good reason for wanting to add the oath, which is the reason Jesus said it *cometh of evil.*

Verse 38. In a number of places the old law did require the kind of penalty that is described in this verse. That was to be done as a legal act and not a personal one. Jesus teaches that no personal retaliation was to be permitted under the pretense of that law. If a man is actually harmed he has the right to appeal to the law of the land as it is in authority for that purpose (1 Timothy 1: 9, 10), but he should not take the law into his own hands.

Verse 39. The sermon on the mount is largely a document of principles and not specific rules, and the spirit of the teaching is to be followed instead of the letter. This very verse is an indication of the correctness of the aforesaid conclusion, for no one would be expected literally to turn a cheek toward a would-be smiter.

Verse 40. Men wore inner and outer garments in old time. Using the circumstance as an illustration only, as was done with the cheek, Jesus teaches that if a man insists on having one's outer garment, just let him have the other also.

Verse 41. Under some peculiar customs of the old times there seems to have been one of providing an escort for a man making a journey. However, the lesson is the same as that contained in the preceding verses which is that the disciples of Christ should show a willingness to be imposed on rather than wanting to impose on others.

Verse 42. In all of the teaching of the scripture regarding the granting of favors, we should consider what Jesus says in Matthew 7: 6. We should always try to learn whether the person asking a favor is worthy before granting it. If we find that he is, then we may give him what he asks and lend him what he wishes to borrow.

Verse 43. The passages that were cited for the saying in this verse are Leviticus 19: 18 and Deuteronomy 23: 6. Jesus is still on the line of contrasts between his teaching and the old, and that introduces the subject of *love* which has caused some difficulty with students of the Bible. They think that Christians are required to have love in cases where it seems impossible. The difficulty lies in not understanding that the English word *love* comes from two words in the Greek New Testament which have different meanings. I shall give the information gleaned from the lexicons and the reader should make note of it for reference.

One of the Greek words in verb form is AGAPAO, and it is defined in part as follows: "To love, to be full of goodwill and exhibit the same: Luke 7: 47; 1 John 4: 7; with accusative [objective] of a person, to have a preference for, wish well to, regard the welfare of: Matthew 5: 43; 19: 19; Luke 7: 5; John 11: 5; Romans 13: 8; 2 Corinthians 11: 11; 12: 15; Galatians 5: 14; Ephesians 5: 25, 28; 1 Peter 1: 22, and elsewhere; often in the epistle of John of the love of Christians towards one another; of the benevolence which God, in providing salvation for men, has exhibited by sending his Son to them and giving him up to death, John 3: 16; Romans 8: 37; 2 Thessalonians 2: 16; 1 John 4: 11 . . . of the love which led Christ, in procuring human salvation to undergo sufferings and death, Galatians 2: 20; Ephesians 5: 2; of the love which God has for Christ, John 3: 35; 10: 17; 15: 9; Ephesians 1: 6. When used of love to a master, God or Christ, the word involves the idea of affectionate obedience, grateful recognition of benefits received: Matthew 6: 24; 22: 37; Romans 8: 28; 1 Corinthians 2: 9; 8: 3; James 1: 12; 1 Peter 1: 8; 1 John 4: 10, 20, and elsewhere. With an accusative [objective] of a thing AGAPAO denotes to take pleasure in the thing, prize it above other things, be unwilling to abandon it or do without it; . . . to welcome with desire, long for; 2 Timothy 4: 8."—Thayer. "To love (in a social or moral sense)."—Strong. In the noun form it is from AGAPE and defined in part as follows: "a purely biblical word. . . . In signification it follows the verb AGAPAO; consequently it denotes 1. affection, good-will, love, be-

nevolence: John 15: 13; Romans 13: 10; 1 John 4: 18. Of the love of men to men; especially of that love of Christians toward Christians which is enjoined and prompted by their religion, whether the love be viewed as in the soul or as expressed; Matthew 24: 12, 1 Corinthians 13: 4-8; 2 Corinthians 2: 4; Galatians 5: 6; Philemon 5, 7; 1 Timothy 1: 5; Hebrews 6: 10; 10: 24; John 13: 35; 1 John 4: 7; Revelation 2: 4, 19, etc. Of the love of men towards God; . . . of the love of God towards Christ; John 15: 10; 17: 26. Of the love of Christ towards men: John 15: 9; 2 Corinthians 5: 14; Romans 8: 35; Ephesians 3: 19: . . . 2. Plural AGAPAI, agapae, love-feasts, feasts expressing and fostering mutual love which used to be held by the Christians before the celebration of the Lord's Supper, at which the poorer Christians mingled with the wealthier and partook in common with the rest of food provided at the expense of the wealthy: Jude 12."—Thayer. "From AGAPAO; love, i. e. affection or benevolence; specifically (plural) a love-feast."—Strong. The other word for love is PHILEO, a verb, and is defined in part as follows: "1. To love; be friendly to one, Matthew 10: 37; John 5: 20; 11: 3, 36; 15: 19; 16: 27; 20: 2; 21: 15-17; 1 Corinthians 16: 22; Revelation 3: 19; . . . to love, i. e. delight in, long for, a thing . . . to love to do with pleasure: 3. As to the distinction between AGAPAN and PHILEIN: the former by virtue of its connection with AGAMAI, properly denotes a love founded in admiration, veneration, esteem, like the Latin diligere, to be kindly disposed to one, wish one well: but PHILEIN denotes an inclination prompted by sense and emotion, . . . Hence men are said AGAPAN God, not PHILEIN; and God is said AGAPESAI TON KOSMON (John 3: 16), and PHILEIN the disciples of Christ (John 16: 27); Christ bids us AGAPAN (not PHILEIN) TOUS ECHTHROUS (Matthew 5: 44), because love as an emotion cannot be commanded, but only love as a choice . . . As a further aid in judging of the difference between the two words compare the following passages: John 11: 5, 36; 21: 15-17 . . . From what has been said, it is evident that AGAPAN is not, and cannot be, used of sexual love."—Thayer. "To be a friend to (denoting personal attachment, as a matter of sentiment or feeling: while AGAPAO is wider, embracing especially the judgment and the deliberate assent of the will as a matter of principle, duty and propriety).".—Strong.

These definitions are somewhat detailed, and for the convenience of the reader, I shall condense the two and the information of the lexicons will be the authority for the statements. One word means that sentiment of feeling such as a man will have for his wife or other close friend. The other is that feeling of interest that a man can have in another's welfare that would prompt him to try to save him if possible, regardless of his unpleasant disposition that might naturally provoke a feeling of dislike.

Verse 44. *Love your enemies* is explained with the note on the preceding verse. *Bless* is from EULOGEO which Thayer defines, "2. to invoke blessings, Matthew 5: 44," or to wish something good of another. *Curse* is from KATA-RAOMAI and Thayer defines it in this place as follows: "To curse, doom, imprecate [ask or wish for] evil on." The clause means that while an enemy is wishing for some evil to come on us, we should be wishing something good for him. *Do good to them that hate* us does not mean to do him a favor that he could use in the furtherance of his evil intentions, but do something that will actually benefit his soul. To pray for our persecutors denotes that we ask the Lord to help us overcome the evil one with righteous deeds in the hope of leading him into a reforming of his life.

Verse 45. Children are supposed to be like their parents in disposition and actions. The disciples of Christ should be like their Father in heaven in that they are not selfish or partial in the bestowal of favors. God gives the blessings of nature on all classes alike, because these favors are not supposed to be rewards for righteous living, and hence their bestowal could not be regarded as an endorsement of their lives.

Verse 46. *Love* here is from AGAPAO, and the word is defined in the long note at verse 43. From that it can be seen that Jesus disapproves of the selfishness that would lead us to benefit only those who are willing to benefit us. Even the publicans were willing to do that, although that class of citizens was not thought of very highly.

Verse 47. To salute means to "pay one's respects to" in the way of polite greeting. We should show that much courtesy even to those who are not in our class; not be "clannish."

Verse 48. *Perfect* is from TELEIOS and the simple meaning of the word is "completeness." When anything or person is all that is expected of it, it can be said to be complete and hence perfect. It is taken for granted that human beings are not expected to possess all of the traits that God has, but the spirit of impartiality is one characteristic that man can possess in common with God. If he does then he is complete on that score and hence is like the Father in heaven.

MATTHEW 6

Verse 1. *To be seen* is the key to this verse. To say it means we should do all of our good deeds unknown to others would make it contradict chapter 5: 16 where others were to *see our good works.* But our motive in doing good deeds should not be to be seen of men. If we do so, we will get only the reward that men can give us in the form of praise, for the Father will not give us any reward for it.

Verse 2. The three words *sound a trumpet* are from SALPIZO which Thayer defines "to sound a trumpet." The same author comments on the word as follows: "To take care that what we do comes to everybody's ears, to make a noise about it." In the preceding verse the alms were done in order to be seen of men. This verse goes further and sounds the trumpet in order to be sure the deeds will be seen. *Hypocrite* is from HUPOKRITES which Thayer defines as follows: "1. one who answers, an interpreter. 2. an actor, stageplayer. 3. in Biblical Greek a dissembler, pretender, hypocrite." The word originally had no moral significance, meaning only a man who went upon the stage to play a certain role in a drama. It then got into the moral and religious language to mean a man who acts a part on the stage of human experiences. The word means one who pretends to be something he knows he is not. *Have their reward.* The first word is defined, "To have received all that one can expect." The praise of men is what these hypocrites sought and that is what they will have; nothing else.

Verse 3. *Hands* cannot literally know anything hence we have to conclude this verse means we should not make a great ado over our good deeds.

Verse 4. *Alms in secret.* We have seen in verse 1 and chapter 5: 16 that our good deeds are not required to be done literally in secret. The meaning of this verse, therefore, must be that we should do good even in cases where men may not realize the good we have done. But God knows all things and will give full credit where it is due.

Verse 5. The place of the praying is not what is condemned, but the motive, *to be seen*, is the thing that is wrong. At any proper time it would be right to pray even on the streets, but it must not be done for show. *Have their reward* virtually means they may not expect any further reward. (See verse 2.)

Verse 6. The servants of the Lord may offer either private or public prayers in lawful service to Him. Both kinds should be considered in connection with this chapter. But it is improper to pretend to be offering a private prayer and yet do it in a way to attract attention. This verse means that if a disciple actually means his prayer to be private he should seek a private place to offer it.

Verse 7. *Vain repetitions* is explained in the lexicon to mean saying the same things over and over again for the sake of taking up time, or for the purpose of making a favorable impression. *Heathen* is from ETHNIKOS which Thayer defines, "3. in the New Testament savoring of the nature of pagans, alien to the worship of the true God, heathenish." *Much speaking* means the same as vain repetitions as to its motive. Many prayers of disciples of Christ today have unnecessary phrases that would come under the disapproval of Jesus. Our prayers should be brief and simple and made to pertain to the occasion that caused the prayer to be called for.

Verse 8. Prayer is not for the purpose of informing God about our needs for He already knows that. It is an occasion of showing our faith in the Heavenly Father.

Verse 9. After *this manner* denotes that Jesus only intended this to be an example of the kind of prayers he wished his disciples to offer. It therefore is not "the prayer he taught his disciples to pray." There are no set forms of service in the kingdom of heaven as to the wording of them. *Hallowed* is from HAGIAZO and is defined, "to render or acknowledge to be venerable, to hallow." It is equivalent to saying that the name of our Father is holy.

Verse 10. Both John and Jesus had taught that the kingdom of heaven was at hand. That would mean that it was near but not yet set up. The prayer for the kingdom to come would therefore be a scriptural one for the disciples to offer at that time. However, it would be unscriptural to make that prayer today since the kingdom is *in earth* now. *As in heaven*. God's rule had been going on for centuries in heaven, hence the prayer was to recognize that fact while praying for it to take place on the earth. Such a prayer indicated two things; that the disciples wished the kingdom to come, and also that they believed in the promise of Christ that it was to come soon.

Verse 11. There are two outstanding thoughts in this verse. *Daily* is from a Greek word that means "necessary," showing they were to pray for what they needed and not what they merely desired. And *this day* indicates that prayer should be offered daily.

Verse 12. God does not have to be given an example of righteous performances before He will do it. But if a disciple is unwilling to forgive those indebted to him, the Lord will not regard him as worthy of such a favor. (See chapter 18: 23-35.)

Verse 13. *Temptation* is from a word that sometimes means "adversity, affliction, trouble," and *evil* is from one meaning "hardships." God never leads men into sin and the words are not used in that sense in this place. The clause is simply a prayer for God to help the disciples in the trials of life. *For thine is the kingdom*, etc., is given as a reason for believing that God could control the elements of creation according to His will, and hence he would be able to give the disciples this assistance. For the meaning of the word *amen* see the comments at chapter 5: 18.

Verses 14, 15. See the comments on verse 12 for the explanation of these.

Verse 16. Fasting was never commanded as a regular practice, but it was voluntarily done on particular occasions as an outward symbol of grief or penitence or great anxiety. The act was approved by the Lord when prompted by a sincere motive. But the hypocrites wished to obtain the praise of men for fasting when they had not actually abstained from food long enough to produce any visible effects on their countenance. To accomplish their purpose they would *disfigure* their faces and then put on a sad look. Thayer defines the word *disfigure*, "to deprive of lustre, render unsightly; to disfigure." This was done in order to appear unto men *to fast* or appear as men fasting.

Verse 17. When David was ready to cease fasting (2 Samuel 12: 20) at the death of his child he arose and washed himself. Jesus instructed his disciples to proceed with the usual customs of daily life in spite of their season of fasting. That would tend to the opposite effect of the disfigurement that the hypocrites practiced for attention.

Verse 18. *Appear not unto men to fast.* By following the usual routine as described in the preceding verse the disciples would not appear to be men on a fast. That would take them out of the class of hypocrites who made a show of their performance in order to receive the praise of men. God who knows the hearts of men would see and reward the devotions of His servants as would be fitting.

Verse 19. *For yourselves* is the key to this verse and is in line with 1 Timothy 6: 18. To say the passage forbids the accumulation of property beyond the present day needs would be to set some scriptures against others. We may lay up something for the future but not simply *for ourselves;* it is that "we may have to give to him that needeth" (Ephesians 4: 28). When we have thus accumulated a surplus we must be careful not to trust in it or become attached to it lest we make it an idol.

Verse 20. In addition to the reasons against hoarding described in the preceding verse, it is also foolish from the standpoint of an investment. Our idle wealth may be attacked and taken by thieves and all be lost for any good use. But the treasures in heaven, which consist of the credits from God for our righteous lives, will be safe because no thief will ever be admitted to that place, neither will any form of decay be possible there. That is why Paul used the impressive words, "Laying up in store for themselves a good foundation against the time to come, that they may lay hold on eternal life" (1 Timothy 6: 19).

Verse 21. This is another reason for not hoarding material wealth *for ourselves,* because that will become the object of our greatest interest which will lead to a form of idolatry. Doubtless that is the reason for Paul's statements in Ephesians 5: 5 and Colossians 3: 5. The heart is the inner man and the seat of emotions and the cause of activities. If that is centered in worldly wealth it will induce man to devote his attentions upon it to the neglect of God.

Verse 22. The human body is again used for illustration, the eye being the particular part for the comparison. This organ is the only one that admits light into the body and hence complete dependence upon it is necessary. *Single* is from HAPLOUS which Thayer defines by, "good, sound." The literal fact is that if a man's eyes are sound or normal he will be able to receive all the light that is offered him.

Verse 23. *Evil* is defined in the lexicon to be "in a bad condition." *If the light that is in thee be darkness.* If the only means one has for receiving light be darkness (which it would be if it became in bad condition), then the darkness would be great because one has no other means of seeing. The lesson in this illustration is that a man has only one means of receiving spiritual light which is his intellect or mind. It is that part of his being by which he either accepts or rejects spiritual light. (See John 3: 19-21.) Therefore if that mind is rendered "unsound" by the love of darkness or evil deeds, "how great is that darkness."

Verse 24. In the time of Christ and the apostles the country had many slaves and the relation of master and slave was referred to frequently in the speech and literature. If a man belonged to a certain master he would not be able nor even should desire to serve another or to divide his services. If he so much as attempted to do so he would be brought to punishment by his rightful master. Jesus made his own application of the illustration by comparing it to God and *mammon.* That word is derived from a Chaldean one that is defined, "what is trusted; treasure; riches." We have seen in verses 19-21 above that our wealth can become an idol in our hearts, and that would make it another god that would be a rival of the true God. The lesson is that we must not try to divide our devotion between God and anything or anyone else.

Verse 25. *Therefore.* If you are going to serve God and not riches, you will not be so concerned about temporal things which do not constitute the object of your chief devotions. *Take no thought* is from MERIMNAO, which Thayer defines, "to be anxious; to be troubled with cares." It is the word for *be careful* in Philippians 4: 6 where the connection shows it means not to be too much concerned but to look to the Lord for help. Hence Jesus does not mean that his disciples were to be indifferent about the needful things of life, but they should not be overanxious about it. The reasoning the Saviour offers is both simple and forceful. The body and the life within it are certainly more valuable than the clothing for the body or the food for the life. But they already possessed the major blessings, then why have any doubts about God's ability and willingness to give them the minor ones?

Verse 26. This verse is not intended to encourage indolence on the part of man, for the fowls cannot perform the scientific works of production while man is able to do so. The idea is that since these helpless creatures are abundantly supplied without their own help, it shows the power and willingness of the Creator to accomplish all that is necessary. Therefore the servants of God should have full confidence in His ability and willingness to supply all the needs of man that he cannot obtain for himself.

Verse 27. Undue anxiety will not add the slightest amount to one's size, hence it is useless to be concerned about the necessities of life to the extent of foolish worry.

Verse 28. This verse has the same lesson as verse 26 except it has to do with clothing only. The lilies are as helpless as the fowls and do nothing to produce their outward appearance and growth.

Verse 29. The glory of Solomon's royal robes was artificial, made by the art of man, and doubtless was unexcelled by any other king of his time. His general surroundings also were the greatest of his time. (See 1 Kings 10.) The glory and beauty of the flower is natural and hence is made directly by the hand of the Creator without the instrumentality of man, which shows the ability of God to accomplish the utmost in the field of adornment and clothing.

Verse 30. Grass is from CHORTOS and is defined in the lexicon, "grass, herbage, hay, provender." The lily is of the vegetable kingdom and hence is in the general class of the herbs. Which is comes from ONTOS which is defined, "truly, in reality, in point of fact . . . that which is indeed."—Thayer. The thought is that this beautiful lily is actually in existence but only for a brief time. Notwithstanding its uncertain and short existence, God thinks enough of it to give it a beauty that far excels that of Solomon. Certainly, then, He will not forget man who is made in His image. Cast into the oven refers to the use of light fuel such as leaves and grass that was burned in the portable baking stoves of many homes in that day. Smith's Bible Dictionary says the following of these ovens: "The eastern oven is of two kinds—fixed and portable. The latter is adapted to the nomad [traveling] state. It consists of a large jar made of clay, about three feet high and widening toward the bottom, with a hole for the extraction of the ashes. Each household possessed such an article, Exodus 8: 3, and it was only in times of extreme dearth that the same oven sufficed for several families; Leviticus 26: 26. It was heated with dry twigs and grass, Matthew 6: 30, and the loaves were placed both inside and outside of it."

Verse 31. This verse is a summing up of the thoughts in the verses starting with 25 and the repetition is for the purpose of emphasis.

Verse 32. Gentiles is from ETHNOS and refers to the nations in general out over the world. God knows all about our needs for He has created the very bodies that have them, hence he certainly will not refuse to provide what is necessary to support them.

Verse 33. There is nothing that we really have to do in making a living that will need to interfere with our work in the kingdom of God. The point is that we must be concerned first about the righteousness belonging to the kingdom. While doing that we can also do what is necessary for our temporal needs, and it is in that way that "all these things shall be added unto us."

Verse 34. Again the exhortation comes not to be overanxious about the morrow which means the future in general. Evil is from KAKIA and Thayer defines it at this place, "evil, trouble." The thought may well be expressed with a familiar one "don't borrow trouble" from the future. Also by another household saying not to try to "cross a bridge before we get to it." Sufficient unto the day, etc., means that each day has enough trouble for itself without looking ahead and worrying about some evil that may never come anyway. When the morrow comes, if it brings trouble to us it will then be time enough to think about it. We will be able then to care for it in the way just set forth in this chapter.

MATTHEW 7

Verse 1. *Judge not.* These words are often quoted by people who resent being corrected for their wrong doing. Such persons fail to consider that the word has a very wide range of meaning and that they should learn the bearing of it in any particular place before applying it to themselves. Were they asked if they believe the Bible contradicts itself in any way they would say no, yet the same Greek word is used in John 7: 24 where Jesus says for us to judge. But it may be replied that Jesus says to judge "righteous judgment." That is the very point, and hence our present verse simply means not to judge unrighteously. But if a judgment is according to the truth and facts in a case then it would be righteous judgment and not forbidden by this verse.

Verse 2. With the first verse explained this one should not be difficult. If a man passes unrighteous judgment upon another he lays himself open to condemnation. In other words, if a man condemns another without evidence, it will indicate that he is himself the guilty one and is trying to divert attention from himself to another.

Verse 3. The terms *mote* and *beam* are used figuratively to illustrate the inconsistency of a hypocrite. Two wrongs do not make one right, neither must a man profess to be "as pure as an angel" before he has the right to condemn sin in others. It should be noted that both these men were afflicted in the same manner (in the eye), only one was less than the other. The illustration pictures a man with a serious obstruction in his eye and wanting to operate on the eye of another who is much less affected. In practice it would be like a man condemning another for getting drunk every Saturday night when he was himself drinking every day.

Verse 4. This continues the thought of inconsistency just described.

Verse 5. A hypocrite is one who pretends to be what he knows he is not. This man pretends to have unaffected eyes, yet he knows better if he is able to recognize what is an affection in the other's eye. That is, he knows his own eye is not right if he can understand that a mote renders the other man's eye defective.

Verse 6. *Dog* sometimes means a sodomite (Deuteronomy 23: 18; Revelation 22: 15) or other impure man, but it is here associated with literal swine and hence should be understood as meaning the brute creatures. Both animals were classed as impure and unclean under the law and hence are used to illustrate unworthy human beings. The lesson in the verse is that we should not bestow favors upon those who are not worthy. If a man spends money in unrighteous indulgencies, we should turn a deaf ear to him when he makes a cry of poverty and destitution.

Verse 7. The favors of God are offered to us on conditions. Thus the invitation to *ask* is restricted to the things that are "according to his will" (1 John 5: 14). The promise of obtaining what we seek for is to be in harmony with chapter 6: 33, and the same principle would apply to knocking, which is merely a sign that we wish to be admitted into the favor of God.

Verse 8. This is an assurance of fulfillment of the preceding verse, the key to it being in the words *every one*. Since God is no respecter of *persons* (Acts 10: 34), it follows that all who meet the conditions set forth in the preceding verse will be favored of God without partiality as to who the individual is.

Verse 9. A humane father would not answer a son's request for bread with a stone.

Verse 10. Or will he substitute a fish with a serpent in his son's request.

Verse 11. *Being evil* is used as a contrast with God. The disciples would admit that they were sinful men and yet were humane in their treatment of their children. Certainly, then, a divine Father will be kind to his children. It is significant that He will give *good things* to them who ask him, not just anything they might think they needed. Even an earthly humane father might deny a request of his son if the thing asked for should not be the best thing for his welfare.

Verse 12. *Therefore* is from oun and Thayer's over-all definition of it is as follows: "Then, therefore, accordingly, consequently, these things being so," and Robinson and Greenfield define it in virtually the same way. The conclusion is drawn from the facts and truths set forth in verse 7-11. God will not refuse to grant necessary favors to His children, and even sinful man will not refrain from granting like requests to a relative. Using this as an example. we should even not wait to be asked for a needed favor since we would not refuse the thing if requested, but should voluntarily advance the favor, such as we would expect from others under the same circumstances. *This is the law and the prophets* is equivalent to "on these hang all the law and the prophets" (chapter 22: 40). If we love our neighbor as ourselves we will do to him as we would expect him to do to us. We will not steal his property, or invade his home, or falsify on him, or seek to kill him, etc., because we would not want him to do so unto us.

Verse 13. A companion passage to this is Luke 13: 23-30 where the connection shows the subject is eternal salvation after the judgment day. *Enter ye in,* therefore, means to enter into eternal life. Jesus first describes the way that leads to destruction. *Gate* and *way* are used figuratively, because there is no specific route established for the purpose of taking people to eternal death. It means that the opportunities for entering or starting on this evil way are many and the kind of life that will lead to death of the soul is so easy that it is compared to a wide or roomy one; that is the reason that many go that way. It is the universal practice of man to follow the course of least resistance in this life. Such is the way of sin because there are only a few people who will oppose a man who wishes to follow a life of sin.

Verse 14. Both Thayer and Robinson give "narrow" as one definition of the original for *strait*. *Narrow* is from THLIBO and is defined by Thayer, "A compressed way, i. e. narrow, straitened, Matthew 7: 14; figuratively to trouble, afflict, distress." From the definition we understand the road to eternal life is one in which the traveler will be pressed with hardships and persecutions. It is also narrow in the ordinary sense of that word because the travelers go as individuals as far as responsibility is concerned, and just one man does not need a wide path; the going is "single file." *Find* is from HEURISKO and Thayer's first definition is. "To come upon, hit upon, to meet with; to find a thing sought." Not many people are looking for a way of life that will bring them hardships and tribulation, hence Jesus says *few there be that find it.*

Verse 15. *False prophets* comes from PSEUDOPROPHETES which Thayer defines, "One who, acting the part of a divinely

inspired prophet, utters falsehoods under the name of divine prophecies, a false prophet." The same author explains *sheep's clothing* to mean "the skins of sheep." A wolf having the skin of a sheep around him would be like these evil men who are posing as the prophets of God.

Verse 16. *Know them by their fruits.* The wolf would soon show his true character by his ravenous attack upon the unsuspecting sheep. A thorn bush or thistle will finally prove itself to be such by bearing thorns instead of fruit.

Verses 17, 18. These verses are a direct statement of facts upon which the foregoing comparison was based. The statements are absolute and describe conditions that are normal, not those that may only seem to be. However, an evil tree without exception will be unable to bear good fruit. If a tree that is or was naturally good appears to bear evil fruit it is because something has been done to it to interfere with its regular function and virtually turned it into an evil tree. We know that such a change is possible in the life of a man, for a good one may fall from his righteous course of life and become evil and henceforth bear evil fruit in his life.

Verse 19. In the literal field, a farmer will remove an evil tree to make room in his orchard for a good one, and will do away with the bad tree by burning it. The lesson is that if men do not bear good fruit, which means to practice good deeds while in this life, the great Owner of the garden will cast them into fire.

Verse 20. This verse is the conclusion of the important comparison of good and bad trees which applies to the lives of men in this world.

Verse 21. *Lord* is from KURIOS and means, "One who has control of a person, the master." The mere addressing one as a master without doing what he expects of his servant is inconsistent. Such empty professors will not be admitted into the kingdom of heaven, because there will be things that need to be done by its citizens.

Verse 22. Neither may a servant select his own type of activities according to what suits his preferences and expect to be rewarded for it. If that should be permitted there would be much necessary though less apparently glorious work neglected. The works described in this verse were possible in the days of miracles and Jesus does not deny the claims of these one-sided servants.

Verse 23. In spite of the ritualistic performahces or works of display which these men did, there was something of the practical that was lacking. They did only what suited them and were content to construct a character that did not respect all the sayings of Christ. For this reason Jesus says he *never knew you*, which means he never recognized or endorsed them as being true servants.

Verse 24. No doubt the people described in the preceding verse lived a life that made a fair appearance to others because their deeds seemed out of the ordinary. Yet they were not well founded because they were not backed up by a program of practical obedience to the whole law of useful service. A house must not only be pleasing to the eye of an admirer in order to stand, but it must be founded on something solid. Hence Jesus compares the all-around and serviceable man to one who not only put some desirable things into the construction of his building, but who was careful to underlay it with a rock foundation.

Verse 25. The elements of the weather are used to illustrate the final test that will be put upon every man's life. The trials of this world will have their part to play in the great drama, but the final test will come when the Lord tries all mankind at the bar of the last judgment when Christ sits upon the throne of judgment.

Verse 26. The man who builds a house on the sand is like one who estimates his needs by present conditions only. In the absence of water and wind, sandy ground would seem about as firm as a rock, or at least enough so that it would appear firm and hard and suitable to hold up a house. Likewise, if no tests were made of a man's work in this life, either now or at the judgment, then one kind of spiritual structure might be as acceptable as another and hence he might as well do as he sees fit about it.

Verse 27. But the test is sure to come and the house on the sand will fall. *Great will be the fall* because it will be the loss of a soul.

Verse 28. The word for *astonished* is defined by "amazed" in the lexicon, which was caused by the *doctrine* or teaching of Jesus. *People* is from oCHLOS and that Greek word has been rendered by company 7 times, multi-

tude 79, number 1, people 82, press 5. It has a wide range of definitions in the lexicon such as, "a crowd; multitude of men who have flocked together in some place, a throng; the common people; a multitude." From chapter 5: 1 and 8: 1 we cannot conclude that it means all the people of the territory heard him in the mount, yet a considerable number did follow the Lord to that place as those desiring to learn of him.

Verse 29. *Having authority, not as the scribes.* The scribes were not inspired men neither were they in any official position. Their business was to copy the law and then quote it to the people for their information; they could only say "it is written." Jesus was the Son of God and could speak independent of all written documents, although he always respected what had been written by Moses and the prophets.

MATTHEW 8

Verse 1. The *multitudes* evidently were the ones Jesus left behind in chapter 5: 1 when he went up into the mount. Their interest did not seem to be strong enough to take them up the place where they would have to climb. Now that he is again on the lower level they are ready to go along after him. *Followed him* refers to their bodily movement in walking with him and not to any particular attitude of mind toward his teaching.

Verse 2. The leper *worshiped* Jesus which would mean only that he assumed a position of respect. See the long definition of the word at chapter 2: 2. The law of Moses required a leper to maintain a safe distance from others (Leviticus 13: 45, 46), hence the conduct of this man could be only one of courtesy. Leprosy was incurable except by miraculous power, and Jesus had previously proved his ability to cure bodily ailments by his miraculous power (chapter 4: 23, 24).

Verse 3. Jesus was willing to heal the leper and did so both by physical contact and word of mouth. The healing was *immediate* and not like the pretended working of miracles today where the patient is exhorted to "hold out with faith and finally be cured."

Verse 4. There was no medical cure for leprosy known to the ancients but sometimes a leper was cured miraculously. And after the physical cure had been accomplished, a ceremonial cleansing was required under the law which included certain sacrifices. (See

Leviticus 14.) The Mosaic law was in force in the time of Christ, hence he commanded this man to comply with that ordinance pertaining to leprosy. *For a testimony unto them.* When the former leper presented himself before the priest to perform this service, it was proof that a miraculous cure had been done and hence another bit of evidence would be furnished of the power of Jesus.

Verse 5. The Funk and Wagnalls New Standard Bible Dictionary defines a *centurion* as follows: "The commander of a 'century,' i. e., a hundred men, the sixtieth part of a legion, in the Roman army." This man was a Gentile, being an official in the Roman military forces. But the fame of Jesus had reached the ears of all classes, and they believed that the benefit of his mercy was to be enjoyed by any who were afflicted.

Verse 6. The word *Lord* in the original has several shades of meaning, one of which is "sovereign, prince, chief." This centurion had not become a disciple of Jesus and hence he did not address him as *Lord* from that standpoint. But he had learned enough about his great work to believe him to be be a superior person in wisdom and power. He therefore appealed to him on behalf of his servant who was sick of the palsy which was a form of paralysis that retained a considerable amount of feeling in the parts.

Verse 7. Jesus was able to give "absent treatment" as effectively as otherwise. However, the proposal to come to the home of the centurion drew from him an expression of complete faith. He had not even requested that Jesus come, but only appealed to him in the attitude of a simple trust in his power and willingness to do something for him.

Verse 8. This verse gives us one reason why the centurion had not askel Jesus to come to his home; he did not feel worthy of such a guest. He therefore was to be satisfied with the favor to his servant though absent, and expressed his belief thus.

Verse 9. This verse indicates that the good things the centurion said in the preceding verse did not come out of a desire to use empty flattery, because he gave a logical reason for his statement. *Under authority . . . under me* is a very significant line of argument. The centurion had the power to give commands to servants who were *under* him, even though he was himself *under* another. Jesus, on the other hand, was under no one (as the centurion thought) and hence should be able to exercise unrestricted authority. This was in line with one definition for *Lord* which is: "One who has control of a person, the master."

Verse 10. A ·meaning of *marvel* is "to admire." Jesus could not be surprised or impressed as if by some unexpected occurrence for his wisdom was divine. Therefore we are to understand this to mean he was filled with admiration for this unusual exhibition of faith. *So great faith, no, not in Israel.* The centurion was not a member of the nation of Israel but belonged to the idolatrous Gentiles. Yet he showed more faith than the people who were supposed to possess great confidence in the seed of Abraham.

Verse 11. *East and west* is used figuartively to mean the earth or world in general, not merely the land of the Jews that was virtually restricted to the land of Palestine. *Kingdom of heaven* means the "everlasting kingdom" that is promised in 2 Peter 1: 11 to the faithful. To *sit down* means to become a guest and admitted to the hospitality of a home. It is used in this place to refer to the favors that will be given to the faithful in the Eternal Home after this life on earth is over.

Verse 12. *Children* is from HUIOS and Thayer's definition at this place is, "those for whom a thing is destined." It does not necessarily mean those who had actually become members of the kingdom, but those who would logically have been expected to be foremost in entering it as were the Jews. The fathers of that nation, Abraham and Isaac and Jacob, had lived faithfully under the system that was in force over them (the Patriarchal Dispensation), but their descendants of the later centuries in the time of Christ rejected the teaching of their great *seed* and will be rejected in the day of judgment. Paul set forth this same thought in his speech at Antioch (Acts 13: 46).

Verse 13. Having concluded his speech to the hardened Jews, Jesus gave his final attention to the centurion by promising him the favor he requested. *As thou hast believed* means that the centurion would receive the favor he believed he would, namely, the healing of his servant at once by the simple word of Christ. Hence the statement that the servant *was healed in the selfsame hour* is given in direct connection.

Verse 14. One observation we should make here is that Peter had a wife, contrary to the dogma of the church of Rome. - *Laid* means she was prostrated with the fever as if thrown down by the force of the disease.

Verse 15. In this case Jesus saw fit to make bodily contact. We are not told here whether he said anything, but in Luke 4: 39 it says he "rebuked the fever." This healing also was immediate and complete for the woman was able to perform the work of administering to them.

Verse 16. Thayer defines *even* in this passage to mean, "from our three to six o'clock P. M." That accounts for the many things that seem to have been done yet on that same day. *Possessed with devils* will be explained at verse 28, but it should be noted here that healing the sick was distinguished from casting out devils. It is also stated that Jesus did both *with his word*.

Verse 17. *That it might be fulfilled* does not always mean that a certain thing was done just so a particular prophecy might be fulfilled, although it will sometimes mean that. Whichever the case may be, it will be well to consider it in the light of saying, "and in so doing the prophecy was fulfilled which," etc. The prophecy cited here is in Isaiah 53: 4.

Verse 18. Sometimes the multitudes were so great that it interfered with the work of Jesus (Mark 2: 4; 3: 9; Luke 8: 19). That was the case here and hence Jesus gave orders for them to depart unto the *other side* (of the Sea of Galilee).

Verse 19. A full description of the work and character of the *scribes* will be given at chapter 13: 52, but I will state now that they were a very important group of men among the Jews. They made great pretentions of learning and wished to be recognized as an indispensable class. This scribe came to Jesus with an air of one who was deeply concerned in the work of the new teacher who was gaining so much fame among the people. But Jesus knew his heart as he always did all other men, and knew that he had mixed motives in his apparent devotional attitude.

Verse 20. To *follow* Jesus at that time meant to go bodily over the country with him and with no certain arrangement for personal comfort. The foxes and birds had fixed places of abode and always knew where they would lodge. However, we should not take the saying of Jesus to mean that he would be like a friendless wayfarer with no chance of accommodations at night. We are sure that he had friends (such as the family of Lazarus) who gladly opened their homes for him. But he did not hold possession of any such a place so that he could provide the comforts of temporal life for his followers, hence there was no object in following him with such luxuries in view. There is no ground for saying this verse is a statement to show how "poor" Jesus became as a popular notion claims for it.

Verse 21. It is unreasonable to suppose that this man's father was actually dead at this time, for had that been the case he would not have been away from home. The necessary conclusion is, then, that the father was aged and likely to pass away almost any time, and the son presented this family duty as an excuse for not going abroad over the country with Jesus.

Verse 22. As the father was not yet dead, and this man professed to be a disciple of Jesus and hence *alive* spiritually, he should leave the temporal work of a burial to those who were *dead* spiritually. The general lesson in the case is that even as important a circumstance as a funeral should not be allowed to interfere with the spiritual services we owe to Christ.

Verse 23. The *disciples* were that part of the crowd that professed to be the followers of Jesus in belief as well as wanting to go along with him in the traveling. We would naturally conclude that the multitude could not enter the ship.

Verse 24. In the Scriptures as in any other literature, we should deal with figurative language according to reason. We know that had the ship been literally *covered* with the water, the disciples would have already perished and would not have been able to speak. The meaning of the passage is, therefore, that the ship was filling and that unless it was stopped they would perish.

Verses 25, 26. The disciples had been with Jesus and had seen his power over great obstacles. They should have had such confidence in him that as long as he was with them no harm could come. Their failure to take that view of it was the reason for charging them with "little faith." Jesus then did what they should have confidently expected him to do; he stilled the tempest.

Verse 27. Each new miracle seemed to fill the disciples with astonishment. The distinguishing feature of this event would lie in the fact that it was inanimate things that Jesus controlled. That is indicated by their word *obey*, which ordinarily would require intelligent response which the storm could not do.

Verse 28. Gergesenes (also called Gadarenes) was situated near the eastern shore of the Sea of Galilee. The *tombs* were caves in the rocks that were used for the burial of the dead. They were generally open so that persons could enter and leave them as occasion suggested. It was in this kind of a place that the Lord met the two afflicted men. *Possessed with devils* all comes from the Greek word DAIMONIZOMAI. Another Greek word that is always (with one exception) rendered by "devil in the Authorized Version is DAIMONION. These two Greek words are so frequently related that I shall consider them both in the comments at this verse. I shall quote from both Thayer and Robinson as they discuss the words in their lexicons. Because of the important history that they give in connection with their specific definitions, I think it will be well to give the reader the benefit of this authentic information. It will be so necessary in various places in our study of the New Testament, that I urge the reader to make it convenient to consult it carefully any time it is referred to. First will be Thayer on DAIMONIZOMAI:

"In the N. T. DAIMONIZOMENOI are persons afflicted with especially severe diseases, either bodily or mental (such as paralysis, blindness, deafness, loss of speech, epilepsy, melancholy, etc.), whose bodies in the opinion of the Jews (see DAIMONION) demons had entered, and so held possession of them as not only to afflict them with ills, but also to dethrone the reason and take its place themselves; accordingly the possessed were wont to express the mind and consciousness of the demons dwelling in them; and their cure was thought to require the expulsion of the demon." Next is Thayer on DAIMONION "1. the divine Power, deity, divinity . . . 2. a spirit, a being inferior to God, superior to men . . . evil spirits or the messengers and ministers of the devil . . . to have a demon, be possessed by a demon, is said of those who either suffer from some exceptionally severe disease, Luke 4: 33; 8: 27; or act and speak as though they were mad, Matthew 11: 18; Luke 7: 33; John 7: 20; 8: 48. . . . According to a Jewish opinion which passed over to Christians, the demons are the gods of the Gentiles and the authors of idolatry. . . . The apostle Paul, though teaching that the gods of the Gentiles are a fiction (1 Corinthians 8: 4; 10: 19), thinks that the conception of them has been put into the minds of men by demons, who appropriate to their own use and honor the sacrifices offered to idols." Next will be Robinson on DAIMONIZOMAI:

"In New Testament, to have a demon or devil, to be a demoniac, to be possessed, afflicted, with an evil spirit; found only in the Gospels." Next is Robinson on the Greek word daimonion: "1. generally a deity, a god, spoken of heathen gods, Acts 17: 18. 2. specifically a demon. In the New Testament, a demon, devil, an evil spirit, an unclean spirit. These spirits are represented as fallen angels, 2 Peter 2: 4; Jude 6; and are now subject to Satan as their prince, Matthew 9: 34; 25: 41; 2 Corinthians 12: 7; Revelation 12: 9. They were held to have the power of working miracles, but not for good, Revelation 16: 14; to be hostile to mankind, John 8: 44; to utter the heathen responses and oracles, Acts 16: 17; and to lurk in the idols of the heathen, which are hence called daimonia, devils, 1 Corinthians 10: 20. . . . They are likewise represented as the authors of evil to mankind, both moral and physical."

Verse 29. These devils were fallen angels (see note on preceding verse), and had been in the place of torment in Hades (2 Peter 2: 4; Jude 6) where they would have remained until *the time* of judgment for which they were being reserved. They had been enjoying a short relief from that torment by being in these human creatures. They knew they would be doomed eternally at the last judgment, but if they could remain on earth until that day they would escape that much torment. But now if Jesus sends them back to their place in Hades, they will again be tormented *before the time* of the great judgment day that is awaiting all intelligent beings.

Verses 30, 31. Rather than go back to their previous place in Hades, these devils preferred to inhabit the swine because then (as they thought) they would get to remain on the earth until the judgment of the last day.

Verse 32. Their request was granted but it did not benefit them very long. The possession of devils sometimes caused great physical derangement in men, and here it produced a madness in the swine that caused them to plunge into the water and perish.

Verse 33. Such an event was so unusual that the keepers fled into the city and reported the whole thing to the people.

Verse 34. The people came out to where Jesus was and requested him to leave the community. That could not have been on account of the one afflicted with the devils for in Mark's account (Mark 5: 19, 20) he was benefited and became a preacher of Jesus. The only conclusion possible is they feared others might lose some of their stock.

MATTHEW 9

Verse 1. Having been requested to leave the country of the Gergesenes, Jesus took passage in a ship and recrossed the Sea of Galilee. *His own city* means Capernaum as may be learned in chapter 4: 13 where he changed his residence.

Verse 2. The *palsy* was a form of paralysis and rendered a man helpless. Jesus knew the hearts of all men and hence the words *seeing their faith* does not mean that what he saw was what gave him the information. The conclusion must be that what Jesus saw was an outward indication of faith. But the palsied man was not doing anything, hence as far as the direct evidence shows, the men carrying the bed were the only ones who had faith. Thus we have no positive authority for saying that the patient had any faith, notwithstanding which, the Lord gave him forgiveness for his sins. We also have no evidence that such a favor was being sought when they brought him to Jesus, but rather that they merely wished to have the afflicted man cured. *Son* is from TEKNON and Thayer renders it in this place, "affectionate address, such as patrons, helpers, teachers, and the like, employ."

Verse 3. *Blaspheme* is from a Greek word of virtually the same form, BLASPHEMEO, and Thayer defines it, "To speak reproachfully, rail at, revile, calumniate [accuse falsely]." In his own comments on the word he says it means, "Specifically of those who by contemptuous speech *intentionally* [emphasis mine, E. M. Z.] come short of the reverence due to God or to sacred

things." Thus we see they accused Jesus of showing disrespect for God in claiming authority to forgive. In Mark's account of the same event they make that item the basis of their accusation (Mark 2: 7).

Verse 4. The scribes were afraid to make their accusation so that others could hear it, but Jesus knew their thoughts and exposed them.

Verse 5. The thing Jesus declared to be done was invisible and thus open to question. He then proposed to make another declaration that would be visible if accomplished. *Whether it is easier* means that if he has the authority to do the one he also has it to do the other, for one would be no harder to do than the other for one endowed with divine power as he claimed to be.

Verse 6. Jesus then proposed to prove his *power* (from EXOUSIA meaning authority) to perform the invisible by doing the visible. Addressing the palsied man, Jesus told him not only to arise, but to take up his bed and go home. This evidently was the bed on which he was lying when the men came to carry him to Jesus.

Verse 7. It would require something more than imaginative "mind over matter" to enable a helpless paralytic to walk and carry a piece of furniture.

Verse 8. The aforesaid logic was suggested to the minds of the multitude and they expressed themselves to that effect. Nothing is said about the attitude of the accusers, and they doubtless hung their heads in shame. *Glorify* is from DOXAZO and Thayer defines it in this place, "to praise, extol, magnify, celebrate." *Given such power unto men.* The last word is from ANTHROPOS, and its universal meaning as given by Thayer is, "A human being, whether male or female," and hence the distinction is made between the brute creation and human beings. We are not told how much this multitude knew about the dual character of the person of Christ, but the outstanding appearance was that he was a man. That is why they marveled at his authority and might which could be accounted for only by giving the credit to God.

Verse 9. *Receipt of custom* is from one Greek word that means "tax office." The man who had charge of the taxes was called a publican, and that subject will be explained in detail in the next verse. Matthew was connected with that work when Jesus came along, and he was called to follow which he did. He was baptized by John since Jesus "came unto his own" who were the ones whom John baptized and prepared for him. It was in keeping with his instruction from John, therefore, for him to quit his secular employment and follow at the call of him for whom he had been made ready.

Verse 10. All men are sinners to some extent, but they are named as a class in this passage which means they were unrighteous in their life as a whole and hence regarded as an unworthy group. They are also classed with the *publicans* which shows they also were regarded as an unworthy group. They are referred to frequently in the New Testament, and I shall quote from the works of reference for the information of the reader.

"The class designated by this word [publican] in the New Testament were employed as collectors of the Roman revenue. The Roman senate farmed the direct taxes and the customs to capitalists who undertook to pay a given sum into the treasury, and so received the name of *publicani*. Contracts of this kind fell naturally into the hands of the *equites* [*military orders*], as the richest class of Romans. They appointed managers, under whom were the *portitores*, the actual custom-house officers, who examined each bale of goods, exported or imported, assessed its value more or less arbitrarily, wrote out the ticket, and enforced payment. The latter were commonly natives of the province in which they were stationed, as being brought daily into contact with all classes of the population. The name *publicani* was used popularly, and in the New Testament exclusively, of the *portitores*. The system was essentially a vicious one. The *portitores* were encouraged in the most vexatious or fraudulent exactions, and a remedy was all but impossible. They overcharged whenever they had an opportunity, Luke 3: 13; they brought false charges of smuggling in the hope of extorting hush-money, Luke 19: 8; they detained and opened letters on mere suspicion. It was the basest of all livelihoods. All this was enough to bring the class into ill favor everywhere. In Judea and Galilee there were special circumstances of aggravation. The employment brought out all the besetting vices of the Jewish character. The strong feeling of many Jews as to the absolute unlawfulness of paying tribute at all made matters worse. The scribes who discussed the question, Matthew 22: 15, for the most part answered it in the negative. In addition to their other faults, accordingly, the publicans of the New Testament were regarded as traitors and apostates, defiled by their frequent intercourse with the heathen, willing tools of the oppressor. The class thus practically excommunicated furnished some of the earliest disciples both of the Baptist and of our Lord. The position of Zacchaeus as a "chief among the publicans," Luke 19: 2, implies a gradation of some kind among the persons employed." — Smith's Bible Dictionary, article, Publican.

"TELONES, 1. a renter or farmer of taxes; among the Romans usually a man of equestrian [one who rides on horseback] rank. 2. a tax-gatherer, collector of taxes or tolls, one employed by a publican or farmer-general in collecting the taxes. The tax-collectors were, as a class, detested not only by the Jews but by other nations also, both on account of their employment and of the harshness, greed, and deception, with which they prosecuted it."—Thayer. "TELONES, a farmer of the taxes or customs, one who pays to the government a certain sum for the privilege of collecting the taxes and customs of a district. . . . Whence in the English Version, a publican. The public revenues of the Greeks and Romans were usually thus farmed out; and among the latter the purchasers were persons of wealth and rank, and in the later periods chiefly of the equestrian order. . . . The farmers-general had also sub-contractors, or employed agents, who collected the taxes and customs at the gates of cities, in seaports, on public ways, bridges, and the like. . . . In the New Testament in the later sense, a toll-gatherer, collector of customs, publican, the object of bitter hatred and scorn to the Jews, and often coupled with the most depraved classes of society."—Robinson's Greek Lexicon. This long note will not be copied again, hence it will be important that the reader make careful note of its location for reference as occasion requires.

Verse 11. The information given with the comments on the preceding verse shows the moral and social standing of the *publicans and sinners*. The significance of *eating* with others was different in ancient times from what it is now. I shall quote from Funk and Wagnalls Standard Bible Dictionary on this subject: "The moral aspects of eating are taken account of in a series of prescriptions and prohibitions on the manner, time, and articles to be eaten. 'Eating together' was a sign of community of life, and symbolized either adoption into the household, or entrance into irrevocable [unbreakable] covenant (Jeremiah 41: 1). This conception underlies the sacrificial meal in which God is taken as a participant. It was the worst form of treason, therefore, to break a covenant entered into through the ceremony of eating together." The Pharisees who pretended to be very righteous, wanted to appear shocked that a righteous teacher like Jesus would defile himself by associating with these low characters, especially on such an intimate occasion as eating a meal together.

Verse 12. Jesus does not admit that the Pharisees are as righteous as they claim, but if they are, they are inconsistent in criticizing Jesus for associating with sinners. These sinners are spiritually sick and are the very ones who need treatment. Incidently, the Lord made a declaration that condemns those who deny the good work of physicians. It is claimed that medicine is unnecessary, that it is not a good thing, and that sick people can be healed without a physician. And this in spite of the statement in Proverbs 17: 22 that medicine "doeth good," and that Jesus said that the sick *need a physician.*

Verse 13. *Learn what that meaneth.* Learn the meaning of the statement, *I will have mercy and not sacrifice.* I request the reader to "learn" its meaning by consulting Isaiah 58: 3; Ezekiel 34: 1-4; Hosea 6: 6; Joel 2: 13; Micah 6: 6-8. By these passages it will be learned that the self-righteous Jewish leaders in former times imposed on the poor and common people, then tried to get things even before the Lord by offering big material sacrifices. Under those circumstances the Lord would want these leaders to leave off their sacrifices until they had showed mercy to the unfortunate populace. Jesus wanted these same pretentious Jewish leaders before him to get this lesson so they would cease their selfish attitude toward the "sinners." A physician does not make calls at homes where all are in good health, and on that principle Jesus came to call on the sinners of the earth because they are the ones who are spiritually sick. If the Pharisees were as righteous as they professed to be, they

should not expect Jesus to pay much attention to them.

Verse 14. Fasting was never commanded as a regular practice but was voluntarily done in times of grief or anxiety. At the time of this conversation John the Baptist had been slain, which is recorded later in this book, and his disciples were fasting in honor of his memory. Not that they were doing so just at the time they came to Jesus, but had been doing so *oft* or at intervals since his death.

Verse 15. Jesus represents himself as a bridegroom who is still present with the *children* which is used in the sense of friends. These friends would have no occasion to fast or mourn for their bridegroom because he was still with them. Fasting under these circumstances would be inappropriate. *Days will come* refers to the time when he would be taken from them and when that time happens they will mourn (Mark 16: 10).

Verses 16, 17. I have made one paragraph of the two verses because they are on the same subject, and whatever comments I wish to make will have a common application to both verses. But I shall first explain the literal meaning of the terms used, after which I shall offer my comments on the application. When fabric is old it is shrunk, and also weakened with age and easily torn. If a hole in it is repaired with new and unshrunk cloth, it will pull loose in shrinking and tear the old cloth. Bottles were made of the skins of animals, being closed tightly around the mouth somewhat like a leathern pouch. While these pouches are new they are moist and capable of expanding without bursting. New wine has to expand as it ferments, and if it is put into old pouches that have become dry, the expansion of the liquid will burst these vessels. The usual explanation of these illustrations is that it represents the folly of trying to mix the *new* religion that Jesus was introducing with the *old* one that Moses gave to the people of God. I do not believe that is the purpose of the illustrations and will give the reasons for my statement.

It would be an abrupt change of subject from anything that had been said for several chapters. Nothing in the conversation between Jesus and the audience would call for the injection of a highly figurative argument concerning the comparative merits of the Old and New Testaments. On the other hand, the importance of the work of

John and Christ, and of the truth that the first was to be replaced by the second, would justify some further teaching from Jesus on it. If the old garment and old bottles represent the old law, on which and into which the new law should not be put, then what constitutes the old cloth and old wine that is to be attached to it? I believe the whole point is simply a lesson on the subject of appropriateness. The disciples of John could fittingly mourn because he had been taken from them. Jesus was still with his disciples and they could not appropriately mourn. It will be well to recall the words of Solomon in Ecclesiastes 3: 4, "A time to weep, and a time to laugh; a time to mourn, and a time to dance."

Verse 18. The word for *ruler* is defined by Thayer, "A ruler, commander, chief, leader." The word could hence be applied to various persons, but in this verse it means, "of the officers presiding over the synagogues." For a description of these synagogues and their uses see the comments at Matthey 4: 23. This man was a Jew and had learned enough about the work of Jesus to have the faith that he expressed. He was consistent in his attitude, for if a person has the power to perform other miracles he also can raise the dead. Modern professed miracle workers betray their fradulent practices by refusing even to try raising the dead, because they know they have no miraculous power.

Verse 19. Jesus had previously showed his ability to work miracles by "absent treatment" (chapter 8: 13). He therefore had some special reason for going to the ruler's house.

Verse 20. On the way to the ruler's house an afflicted woman sought relief from a chronic case of hemorrhage of blood of twelve years' standing. Her only contact with Jesus was that of touching the hem of his garment. There was no literal curative properties in the clothing of the Lord, but the woman thought there was and her faith was manifested by touching it which induced him to favor her.

Verse 21. The woman expressed her faith in words only to herself.

Verse 22. Jesus could read the thoughts of mankind and knew the woman *said within herself*. Turning, he made no mention of her touching his garment, but granted her the cure because of her faith. As usual, the recovery from her disease was immediate.

Verse 23. By this time Jesus had reached the ruler's house. As he entered he saw the *minstrels* (musicians) and the people *making a noise*. These words are from THORUBEO which Thayer defines at this place, "to wail tumultuously." The instruments that such minstrels used were flutes and they could be made to produce a turbulent "noise."

Verse 24. *Not dead but sleepeth.* The Bible as well as secular compositions uses both figurative and literal language, and the distinction should always be remembered or confusion may result. I shall quote Webster on the two words: "figurative, 2. Expressing one thing in terms normally denoting another with which it may be regarded as analogous [similar]; as figurative language, sense. Literal, 4. Of senses of words, conveying the primary meaning, — opposed to figurative." With this authentic information we may form a convenient and correct formula as follows: "Figurative language is that based on appearances regardless of the facts; literal language is that based on the facts regardless of appearances." Jesus used the figurative because when a person is dead he "appears" to be asleep. The people did not recognize the figure but thought he was speaking literally and hence they *laughed him to scorn*. The last word is not in the original and the statment should merely say that they laughed at him. The same kind of circumstance as to language occurred in the case of Lazarus in John 11: 11 and 14, except that Jesus used both figurative and literal language for his disciples.

Verse 25. This is another instance where Jesus saw fit to make bodily contact in performing the miracle. However, that would not account for it as far as any physical cause was concerned, for the same procedure would not raise the dead if performed by another without the possession of supernatural power.

Verse 26. *Fame* is from the Greek word PHEME and one word in Thayer's definition is, "report." The idea means to express the fact of the extent of the news about the deed, not so much the thought of Jesus from the standpoint of notoriety.

Verse 27. These blind men must have heard this report referred to in the preceding verse. *Son of David* means he was descended from David in the blood line. Many people in Palestine were familiar with the prediction in the law that the Messiah was to come through that line. Their addressing him with this title not only acknowledged him to be possessed with miraculous power (others had possessed that), but that he was the fulfiller of the law and the prophets.

Verse 28. The blind men did not lose heart but followed Jesus until he had entered another house, and there they came to him for relief. Jesus knew all hearts and was aware of the faith in the minds of these men, but a public profession of faith is one of the acts that puts a man in favorable light before the Lord.

Verse 29. *According to your faith* is said on the same principle as that said to the centurion in chapter 8: 13, "as thou hast believed."

Verse 30. *Eyes were opened.* Thayer explains the last word to mean, "to restore one's sight," hence the passage does not mean their eyelids had been closed.

Verse 31. Did not Jesus know these men would immediately begin to spread the report of their wonderful recovery? They would have been the most unnatural and ungrateful persons in the country to have received such an unspeakably gracious blessing and then not tell anyone about it. But Jesus did not want the public to think he was doing miracles just for the sake of fame. Should anyone accuse him of it, there would be plenty of witnesses to deny the accusation because they had heard him ask the favored ones not to make an ado about it.

Verse 32. *Dumb, possessed with a devil.* The reader should consult the long quotation from the lexicons that is given at chapter 8: 28. It will there be seen that being possessed with a devil did not always produce the same effect on the people. In the case of our present verse it produced dumbness in the man.

Verse 33. The relief sought was granted although the fact is not stated except to take it for granted. It was the man that was dumb, not the devil, for when it was cast out the man spake. *It was never so seen in Israel.* This was the remark of the uninspired multitudes but it was true, for it was not contradicted by even the Pharisees.

Verse 34. The Pharisees could not deny the fact of the casting out of the devil, but tried to rob Jesus of due credit by attributing his power to Satan. This subject will be dealt with in chapter 12: 22-32.

Verse 35. Jesus taught in the syna-gogues because he could meet the Jews assembled there to hear the reading of the Scriptures. *Gospel of the kingdom* means the good news that the kingdom of heaven was near. Healing *every* sickness and disease is significant. Modern professed miracle workers will select such ailments that are not apparent so that their failure to effect a cure cannot be known.

Verse 36. The multitudes were worn out by foot travel in their quest for the favors they hoped to get from Jesus. Their condition caused him to be moved with pity, which fulfilled the many predictions that he was to be a man who could "be touched with the feeling of our infirmities" (Hebrews 4: 15).

Verse 37. There were so many people who needed help that neither Jesus nor any other man could be bodily present with all of them. That is what he meant by *harvest plenteous, laborers few.*

Verse 38. The prayer intimated in this verse will call for something definite to be done. Jesus will himself bring about a fulfillment in the next chapter.

MATTHEW 10

Verse 1. *His twelve disciples.* Jesus had many disciples, but he selected twelve out of the group to be his apostles. In Mark 3: 14 it is stated that these men were designated as the ones who should "be with him." This was to be one of the qualifications required of the original apostles. (See Acts 1: 21, 22.) These men were to be "laborers" sent forth into the harvest as was asked by the Lord in the preceding chapter. Since they were to be separated at least at short intervals from him, they would need to be qualified to back up their work by miracles of various kinds. *Power* is from EXOUSIA which also means "authority." With the appointment that Jesus made they were given the right and ability to execute the mission.

Verses 2-4. There are three accounts or lists of the twelve apostles; here, in Mark and in Luke. The men are the same ones but the names of some of them are not the same, and the three accounts do not give them in the same order. For the purpose of identification I shall number the list as given by Matthew from 1 to 12 consecutively, using it as a schedule for the other two. The list given by Mark 3: 16-19 should be numbered as follows to correspond with these in

Matthew: 1, 3, 4, 2, 5, 6, 8, 7, 9, 10, 11, 12. Number the list in Luke 6: 14-16 as follows: 1, 2, 3, 4, 5, 6, 8, 7, 9, 11, 10, 12. All of the men with the same number are the same regardless of the name. *Who also betrayed him* is said to distinguish the traitor from the brother of James who has the same name in one list, although the betrayal had not taken place when this was written.

Verse 5. This and the following verses through 5 constitute what is familiarly known as the first commission. It was limited as to the territory or people to whom they were to go. All people who were not full blooded Jews were regarded as Gentiles. Samaritans were distinguished from the Gentiles because they were a mixed race, part Jew and part Gentile, both in their blood and in their religion. This history of their origin is recorded in 2 Kings 17, and explained in volume 2 of this Commentary.

Verse 6. *Lost sheep.* The Jewish nation had been imposed upon and neglected by the leaders for generations, hence they were compared to sheep who were lost in the wilderness, deserted by their shepherd. That is why Jesus had compassion on them and thought of them as being "scattered abroad, as sheep having no shepherd" (chapter 9: 36).

Verse 7. At this time the kingdom of heaven was *at hand,* which shows it was near but not yet in existence as a fact. Hence we know that John the Baptist (who was then dead) did not set up the kingdom as some people teach today.

Verse 8. These apostles were able to perform the same kind of miracles that Jesus did, and that included the power to *raise the dead.* Pretended miracle workers today refuse even trying to raise the dead on the ground that the early disciples were restricted to miracles on the living. The present passage disproves their doctrine and exposes their hypocrisy. *Freely received, freely give.* The apostles received all their power from Jesus—it was not a natural trait—hence they should pass its benefits to others.

Verse 9. These metals refer to the coins used in those days. The reason they were not to provide themselves with them will be explained in the next verse.

Verse 10. A *scrip* was a provision bag, used in the same manner as the modern lunch basket. They were also told not to take any extra clothing besides what they wore as they started. The reason given is that *the workman is worthy of his meat.* They were to be supported by the people among whom they labored. Since those people were Jews, and hence already disposed somewhat in their favor, it would be reasonable to expect some returns for their work. Later, when they were to go among the heathen, and especially as they would be without the immediate support of Jesus, they were to "look out" somewhat for themselves. (See Luke 22: 35-38.)

Verse 11. *Enquire* is from EXETAZO which Thayer defines, "To search out; to examine strictly, inquire." This would require the apostles not merely to ask some person whom they might meet as to what house it would be well to enter, but they were to take whatever means would be necessary to obtain reliable information. After finding a house worthy of their visit they were to confine their work in that town to that house. The reason for this restriction is shown in verse 23.

Verse 12. The enquiry mentioned above would include the added information they would receive through the attitude manifested by the residents of a house upon entering it. A house might be selected temporarily because of some apparently favorable indications, and the test would be concluded after meeting the people on the inside. This would be introduced by an act of courtesy in the form of *salutation.* That word is from ASPAZOMAI and Thayer defines it at this place, "To salute, greet, wish well to."

Verse 13. After the investigation has been completed, if the house is found to be worthy, their *peace* or good wishes was to be bestowed upon it. That would be accompanied with their delivering of a message of good news of the kingdom. If the house was found to be unworthy, their peace was to return to them, and that means their good wishes would be recalled.

Verse 14. A group of citizens that were such as to be regarded as unworthy, would be the kind that would reject the offered blessings of the apostles. *Shake off the dust of your feet.* People traveled on foot and thus picked up the particles of soil on the way. This act was purely a symbolic one, for there would be no contamination in the dust due to the character of the people. It meant that all responsibility for their fate was to be left at their own door, seeing they would not receive the favors offered them by their good visitors.

Verse 15. *Be more tolerable* in popular language would mean to "stand a better chance." Sodom and Gomorrha were very wicked cities, yet their opportunities for knowing better were far less than those of the cities to be visited by the apostles. These conditions made them less responsible and hence less to answer for. It should be noted that the difference was to be made *in the day of judgment*. That is, in making up the verdict as to the eternal fate of people, the Judge will consider these facts as to their opportunities. After the day of judgment nothing is said about any difference.

Verse 16. If a sheep had to be put into the midst of wolves he would not escape being attacked but by the best kind of behavior. He should not make any unnecessary movement toward one of these beasts for that would attract his attention. Instead, he should go about his search for food or whatever he was seeking, using his good judgment and not doing any harm to the interests of the beasts. The simple lesson was that the apostles were to be discreet in their dealings with the people they met.

Verse 17. The *councils* were the sanhedrins, the highest courts the Jews were permitted to have at that time, and the synagogues were the buildings where they met for religious purposes. (See the description of them at Matthew 4: 23.) The object in forcing the apostles into these places was to persecute them from both the secular and religious standpoints as far as their authority permitted.

Verse 18. Not being satisfied with what they could accomplish in their own assemblies, the Jews would drag the apostles before the rulers of the Roman Empire where they would hope to obtain some decrees against them. *For a testimony* does not mean the persecutors would hail the apostles into those courts for the purpose of hearing the testimony against themselves. Jesus meant that such a circumstance would give them an opportunity thus to speak against them and all the sinful men of the nations.

Verse 19. This verse is in line with the comments on the preceding one, that the calling of the apostles before the various courts was to be turned into an opportunity for speaking the truth. They were not to be worried as to what kind of speeches they were to ᵐake, for they would be furnished

with the necessary material for the speech. *In that same hour* indicates that the subject matter would be adapted to the circumstances of the occasion when it arrived.

Verse 20. This verse states the means by which the apostles were to speak, that they would be guided by the Spirit of their Father.

Verse 21. The same oposition to truth that would bring the apostles into the courts, will also divide between the members of families. This prediction is made specifically in Luke 12: 53 where Jesus is speaking of the results of his teaching.

Verse 22. *Hated . . . name's sake.* Because of their loyalty to the name of Jesus, men would hate the apostles wherever they labored. *Endureth to the end* means those who hold out faithful to the end of the persecutions will be saved or divinely blessed.

Verse 23. To endure persecution does not mean that one must needlessly expose himself to possible death. If he can escape without compromising any truth or evading any duty, he should do so and thus be able to do good elsewhere. The apostles would have plenty of places in which to preach, therefore when their work was rejected and their lives endangered in one city, they were to flee into another. Even then they would not have time to visit all the cities in Israel until their period for working would be ended. That was the reason for the restrictions mentioned in verse 11.

Verse 24. The word *above* means the disciple and servant are not any better than their master and lord, or any more entitled to escape persecution than they.

Verse 25. *Enough to be as.* It should be regarded as a favor not to be any more liable to persecution than they. Since the master of the house has already been virtually called Beelzebub (chapter 9: 34), the servants may expect the like treatment.

Verse 26. The persecutors perform their evil deeds often in an underhanded and cowardly manner. But their works will finally be exposed and all false charges disproved.

Verse 27. *Darkness* and *light* are used figuratively, and have the same meaning as the next clause. Jesus taught his apostles many things while they were alone with him, and they were then expected to tell them to others publicly. The *housetops* were flat in those times and used very much in the same manner as our verandas or sidewalks. (See Deuteronomy 22: 8; Matthew 24: 17; Acts 10: 9.) That would give the apostles an opportunity to preach to the people in a public manner.

Verse 28. Mere human beings can cause us to die physically, but Jesus teaches that they cannot go any further in their work of destruction while someone else can. All this proves that death as we use that term does not end it all, hence the materialists are shown to be teachers of false doctrine. God is the One who can *destroy* (cast) our whole being in *hell*, therefore we should *fear* or respect Him. See the note at chapter 5: 30 for the lexicon explanation of *hell*.

Verse 29. God's care for his creatures is the point in this verse. A sparrow was of such little commercial value that two of them could be bought for a farthing, one of the smallest of coins; yet every time one of them is brought down God sees it.

Verse 30. Before finishing the subject of the sparrow, Jesus makes direct reference to the value of the human being. *Numbered* is from the Greek word ARITHMEO, and Thayer defines it with the one word only that we have in our Authorized Version. Robinson defines it, "To number, to count." The meaning is that each hair is counted or considered.

Verse 31. If God takes such notice of the sparrow which has such small value, He certainly will not overlook man who is destined never to cease his existence.

Verse 32. The fear of persecution might cause some to deny Christ, so this verse is properly placed in the midst of that subject. *Confess* is from HOMOLOGEO, and I shall give Robinson's definition of the word because it is more condensed: "To speak or say together, in common, i. e., the same things; hence to hold the same language, to assent, to accord, to agree with." To confess one, then, means to admit being in agreement with him and endorsing his teaching. Of course Jesus will not need to agree with the teaching of his disciples except to acknowledge that the disciples had accepted the teaching given them by the Lord.

Verse 33. This verse is simply the opposite of the preceding one.

Verse 34. *Peace* is from EIRENE and the primary definition in Thayer's lexicon is, "A state of national tranquility; exemption from the rage and

havoc of war." His definition in our verse is, "Peace between individuals, i. e., harmony, concord." Jesus uses the word *peace* in a restricted or figurative sense, and hence the word *sword* is also thus used, and the meaning will be explained in the verses following.

Verse 35. The conditions described in this verse are the opposite of the specific definition of "peace" in the preceding one. These relatives will be set at variance with each other because some of them will accept the teaching of Christ and some will not.

Verse 36. Not only will distant relatives be opposed to each other, but right in a man's household there will be members who will become his personal enemies because he is determined to accept Christ's teaching.

Verse 37. The only way to prevent the above difficulty is to reject the doctrine of Christ. If one does that it proves that he loves his earthly relatives more than he does Christ, in which case he becomes unworthy of his Lord. That will put him in the class mentioned in verse 33 and he will be rejected at the last day.

Verse 38. The *cross* is used figuratively in this place. The original word is defined by Thayer simply, "A cross." However, the same author cites us to some history that explains the language of Jesus as follows: "The judicial usage which compelled those condemned to crucifixion themselves to carry the cross to the place of punishment, gave rise to the proverbial expression [about bearing the cross], which was wont to be used of those who on behalf of God's cause do not hesitate cheerfully and manfully to bear persecutions, troubles, distress,—thus recalling the fate of Christ and the spirit in which he encounters it."

Verse 39. The key word in this verse is *life* which comes from PSUCHE in both cases. The word has been rendered in the Authorized Version by heart 1 time, life 40, mind 3, soul 58. Among the phrases in Thayer's long definition are the following: "Breath; the vital force; life; that in which there is life; the soul; the seat of the feelings, desires, affections; the soul as an essence which differs from the body and is not dissolved by death." From the above information we may learn that man has an outer and an inner life. Expressed in another way, he has a physical life and an inner life that can be saved spiritually. Both kinds of life must be considered in this verse which will make it read as follows: "He that findeth [or is working for] his earthly life shall lose his spiritual life." Of course the last half of the verse means just the opposite, but we may extend the language and say that if a man actually loses his earthly or outer life (verse 28) for the sake of Christ, he will gain eternal life.

Verse 40. Jesus and his Father are one in purpose, and both were upholding the apostles who had been chosen. Of necessity, then, the attitude of the people towards any one of the three would count for all of them.

Verse 41. The apostles were classed as prophets under the new order of things under Christ. To receive one of these *in the name of a prophet* means to receive him because he is a prophet of the Lord. *Prophet's reward* means the reward such as a prophet can bestow. The same principle applies to receiving a righteous man for his reward.

Verse 42. These "little ones" are the same disciples referred to in earlier verses of the chapter. Kindness of ever so little a character shown to them is the same as doing so to Jesus and will be rewarded in due time. This is the same lesson that is taught in Matthew 25: 40.

MATTHEW 11

Verse 1. All the words *it came to pass* are from GINOMAI and that word is used over 400 times in the Greek New Testament. It has a wide range of meanings and has been rendered in the Authorized Version by, be done 82 times, be 249, be made 69, become 42, come 53, come to pass 82, and others. In places where it is rendered 'came to pass" it has the simple meaning, "it happened." *Made an end* means for the time being, for Jesus gave them commandments many times afterward. When the twelve disciples are mentioned it always means the apostles. Having given his apostles their "first commission," Jesus resumed his own work of *teaching* and *preaching*. There is not much difference between these two words when applied to the words of Jesus. The specific meaning of the first is "to instruct," and the other is, "to proclaim or announce."

Verse 2. This is the third time that the imprisonment of John has been referred to without relating its events.

(See chapter 4: 12; 9: 14, 15.) The account of it will be found in chapter 14: 1-12. John sent two of his disciples on an inquiry to Jesus. Let it be noted that it was his own disciples he sent, not those of Jesus who were daily near him and seeing his miracles on the sick and infirm.

Verse 3. I do not believe that John made this inquiry through any weakness of his own faith. That would have been a serious fault after the kind of preaching he had done. His own languishing in prison even should not have put any strain on his faith for he had preached to the people and told them concerning Christ and himself that "He must increase, but I must decrease," so that his persecution would harmonize with his own preaching. And had it been the case that his faith was weakening, Jesus would certainly have said something of a reproving character either to or about him. But he not only did not do that, but the entire speech that he made afterwards at verses 7-14 about John was highly complimentary. I am persuaded that it was for the reassurance of his own disciples who had not been seeing the miracles that Christ's disciples had seen. No doubt John believed that by getting his disciples in the immediate presence of Jesus on the occasion of the inquiry, they might get to see some of those evidences for themselves. This idea is borne out by the account in Luke 7: 21 which says "in that same hour he cured many of their infirmities," etc.

Verse 4. Having "performed" doubtless for the benefit of John's disciples, he sent them back to John with the instruction to show him "again" about these miracles that they had just seen. The language shows that John had previously known about them, hence the report would not bring him any additional news. It might be asked why they should go tell John if the circumstance was just for their benefit. Well, the mission in the mind of John would have been accomplished, but their duty would not have been performed until they reported, and of course Jesus would not interfere with that.

Verse 5. This verse is the same account of the deeds which Luke says Jesus did "in that same hour." They all were things that required miraculous power unless we except the preaching of the gospel to the poor. That would require the miracle of inspiration but not the physical kind that is usually meant.

Verse 6. *Not be offended* is from SKANDALIZO and Thayer defines it at this place, "To be offended in one," and he explains his definition to mean, "i. e., to see in another what I disapprove of and what hinders me from acknowledging his authority." Jesus was giving so many evidences of the authority in his possession that no doubt should be had as to whether he was the one "that should come," and they need not "look for another."

Verse 7. The importance of John and his work will be the subject of some verses, all of which will show that Jesus had a high regard for him. A *reed* is a tall and slender stem that would be swayed easily by the wind. Such would illustrate a man with little stability and one who could be easily influenced. The question of Jesus implied that John was not that kind of a man.

Verse 8. A man who was accustomed to the soft and luxurious life of royal palaces would be unsuited for work out in the wilderness. But the prophecy had foretold that the forerunner of Jesus was to operate in the wilderness, hence no surprise should be felt over the rough outdoor raiment of John the Baptist.

Verse 9. Coming more specifically to the office of John, the subject of a prophet was mentioned. The ordinary prophet was a man who wrote and/or spoke general predictions that would have widespread fulfillment. John had himself been the fulfiller of other prophecies and hence he was *more than a prophet*.

Verse 10. Jesus makes references to the predictions that had been made of John, which are recorded in Isaiah 40: 3, 4; Malachi 3: 1. The pronouns *I* and *my* stand for God, *thy* and *thee* refer to Christ, and the *messenger* means John the Baptist.

Verse 11. Up to the time of John's birth there had never been a greater prophet than he, for he not only fulfilled other prophecies, but uttered some himself that were of the greatest importance. Notwithstanding, he never was permitted even to see the kingdom of heaven, much less to set up and be "in it." For that reason the least person in that kingdom would be greater than John in the sense of having superior advantages over him, the privileges only possible to those who are members of the final masterpiece of Heaven in the salvation of mankind.

Verse 12. This verse is used by some to prove that the kingdom of heaven was in existence in the days of John. There have been several passages under observation that would forbid such a conclusion, hence we should seek for an explanation of the apparent contradiction. An organization is like a house in that it exists in preparation before it does in fact. Passing a site and seeing some digging of soil and unloading of material, a man may say to his friend: "This is our new school house." He would mean it was the school house in preparation. John began to "prepare" a people for Christ and thus it was the kingdom of heaven in preparation. But John's work was opposed even by force and hence it is said that the kingdom suffered violence.

Verse 13. After Malachi completed his book, there was not one word of inspiration from heaven recorded until the voice of John was heard in the wilderness. That is, there was silence until his teaching about the kingdom introduced the new subject.

Verse 14. *Elias* in the New Testament is the form for Elijah in the old. Malachi 4: 5 prophesied that "Elijah the prophet" was to come, which Luke 1: 17 words" in the spirit and power of Elias." John the Baptist was not Elias in person (for he had gone to heaven, 2 Kings 2: 11), but had the same kind of *spirit* (PNEUMA) and *power* (DUNAMIS) as he, and hence he is called by his name.

Verse 15. This is an emphatic call to attention, meaning that all who are blessed with the faculty of perceiving the sense of the divine teaching should use that faculty by attending to what is said.

Verse 16. *Markets* is from AGORA which Thayer defines, "1. any collection of men, congregation, assembly. 2. place where assemblies are held." The same author further explains: "In the New Testament the forum or public place,—where trials are held, Acts 16: 19; and citizens resort, Acts 17: 17; and commodities are exposed for sale." At such a place persons of all ages and classes would gather sometimes only for pastime. *Children* here is from PAIDARION which Thayer defines, "A little boy, a lad." These children were gathered to amuse each other. One set was to "furnish the music" and the other set was to respond.

Verse 17. But the set that was to respond was hard to please which was used by the Lord to illustrate the people of that generation in their attitude toward John the Baptist and himself. The one set of children first played on their pipes or flutes, but the others would not respond by dancing. Thinking they were not in the mood for jollity, they next set up a wailing sound and the others refused to respond to that, too, showing that they were determined not to be satisfied with anything that was done.

Verse 18. *Neither eating nor drinking.* No man can live without eating and drinking, but John did not eat among the people or from their supplies. He dwelt in the wilderness and lived on locusts and wild honey. *He hath a devil.* This charge is not recorded in any place except in the words of Jesus, but that makes it an established fact. They meant by such an accusation that John was a maniac or "out of his mind" to live as he did. That was the meaning that was attached to such a charge as may be seen in the following passages. John 7: 20; 8: 48, 49, 52.

Verse 19. Jesus did the very opposite as to his social activities and did eat "with publicans and sinners" (chapter 9: 11), yet that did not suit the people so they represented him as a man especially interested in his appetites. *Wisdom is justified of her children.* The last word is from a Greek word that means something that is produced by another. The wisdom that John and Christ showed in their different manner of life will be justified by the good results (the product or children) of their work, which was adapted to the peculiar circumstances in which they moved.

Verse 20. The key to this verse is that *they repented not.* God does not condemn unrighteous persons rashly on the mere fact of their sinfulness, but it is when they have been admonished and refuse to repent. (See Revelation 2: 5, 16; 3: 3.)

Verse 21. These cities first named were not literally as wicked as Tyre and Sidon, but they had received more opportunities for learning better. Those ancient cities would have shown a better spirit in that they would have *repented*, which is the idea of importance in the passage.

Verse 22. Notice the toleration was to be *at the day of judgment,* not afterward. See the comments on this thought at chapter 10: 15.

Verse 23. The same comparison is to be made between the cities of this verse as was made in verse 21. *Exalted unto heaven* is a figure of speech, based on the fact that Jesus was an inhabitant of Capernaum by choice (chapter 4: 13), and hence it had the advantage of his presence. *Hell* is from HADES, and the literal meaning of it is the abode of disembodied spirits after death. However, it is used figuratively in this passage, since its fate is contrasted with what would have been that of Sodom under as favorable opportunity, namely, that *it would have remained until this day.* The prediction of Jesus is that the city will sink into a state of forgetfulness. The prophecy has been fulfilled because the works of reference can only tell of various places that claim to have been its location. Funk and Wagnalls Standard Bible Dictionary says, "Its present site is a matter of dispute," and Smith's Bible Dictionary declares, "It is impossible to locate it with certainty."

Verse 24. For *more tolerable* see the comments on verse 22.

Verse 25. The Pharisees professed to have superior wisdom, yet their hearts had become so hardened with selfishness that the important principles of responsibility had been *hid* from their perception. *Babes* is a figurative term for the honest and humble people who were ready to hear the lessons of truth offered to them.

Verse 26. The endearing term of Father is used here, to which Jesus had joined that of Lord in the preceding verse. Jesus endorsed the work of God with NAI which is translated *even so.* Thayer defines it, "Yea, verily, truly, assuredly, even so." The beautiful reason for his endorsement was that it "seemed good in thy sight." The best of reasons for any action of God is that He considers it to be good.

Verse 27. The complete intimacy between Jesus and God is the main point, and he indicates it by using the terms Father and Son. In anticipation of the full delivering of authority to him (chapter 28: 18), he says *all things are delivered.* No person will be permitted to benefit from this great intimacy but the one to whom the Son reveals it, and that will be only the man who accepts the Son.

Verse 28. The willingness of Jesus to share the forementioned blessing with others is indicated by the rest of this chapter. This whole passage is often called Christ's world-wide invitation. To *labor* means to be distressed with the hardships of life, especially those brought about by sin. The kind of rest to be given will be shown next.

Verse 29. *Yoke* is from ZUGOS, which has been rendered in the Authorized Version by yoke 5 times and pair of balances 1. The word is used as an illustration of the obligation that one must accept as a co-worker with Jesus in the service of righteousness. *Learn of me* is consistent with the whole situation, for if a man expects to serve his yokefellow he should desire to know something about him. That learning will reveal that the owner of the yoke is meek and lowly which means he is humble and interested in the welfare of the unfortunate ones of earth. The *rest* is to be for the *soul*, not that a disciple of Jesus will be an idler in the vineyard. But while his body may be bent down with the toils of the service and from its persecutions imposed by the enemy, the inner man will be at peace and rest in the Lord. (See 2 Corinthians 4: 16.)

Verse 30. *Easy* is from a word that means it is not harsh nor galling because it is made correctly. If a yoke for a beast is made to fit his body, he can pull a heavy load without any injury to his shoulders, and that would make a big burden comparatively light. On that principle the service that Christ places upon the shoulders of his disciples is adapted to their needs and abilities, which makes it easy to bear.

MATTHEW 12

Verse 1. *At that time* is a phrase that does not have any specific meaning as to date. On the same event Mark 2: 23 and Luke 6: 1 word the thought "it came to pass." It is the writer's way of introducing another subject, and if the particular date is important in determining the meaning it must be learned by the context. Corn in the Bible means small grain such as wheat or barley, and *ears of corn* means the heads. Deuteronomy 23: 25 gives the public the right to make a personal use of this grain while in the field, but it was not permitted to cut any of the straw with a sickle.

Verse 2. The Pharisees knew about this law and hence could not accuse them of trespass. They were so eager to find fault, however, that they charged them with breaking the law of the sabbath.

Verse 3. Two wrongs never make one right, but these Pharisees pretended to have so much respect for David and other of the fathers or ancestors, that it was fair to refer to him in this manner to expose their hypocrisy.

Verse 4. The incident is recorded in 1 Samuel 21 when David was fleeing from Saul. He did not eat of the bread that was then on the table, but that which had been put back for the use of the priests after the table had been supplied with new loaves. While it was intended *only for the priests*, yet an emergency existed which allowed David and his men to eat. Likewise, the disciples were out from home with Jesus and were in need of food, and that justified them in eating in this way because the necessities of life do not constitute a violation of the sabbath law.

Verse 5. To *profane* means to make a secular use of a thing. Numbers 28: 9, 10 shows the priests performing the manual labor of handling an animal in the sacrifice. John 7: 22, 23 tells of a child being circumcised even on the sabbath day. The surgical act of performing circumcision was a manual one and hence technically violated the sabbath law. But it was understood that if an emergency or positive commandment called for some physical act even on the sabbath day, then the regular law as to its observance did not apply or bind the parties to its usual observance.

Verse 6. The temple was holy and it was the place where these manual performances were done. *In this place* means the case of Jesus and his disciples, and that it was of more importance at that time than the sanctity of the sabbath day.

Verse 7. This subject is explained at chapter 9: 13.

Verse 8. The title *Son of man* is used only by Jesus himself, and it applies especially to him because he was born of a member of mankind, as well as having been begotten of God. *Lord of the sabbath* does not imply that he would belittle the law of the holy days. He was with his Father in all of the works of creation, also in the issuing of laws and dispensations for the conduct of human beings. Any lawmaking power has the right to alter its own edicts if and when it sees fit to meet an emergency, hence Jesus was within his rights in the above conduct.

Verse 9. The use of the synagogues is explained at· Chapter 4:23. Jesus entered into such a place and there met another opportunity of performing a good work, also of exposing the hypocrisy of the Jews who were present.

Verse 10. Jesus was not long in meeting such an opportunity as referred to in the preceding verse. A hand *withered* means one that had been cut off from obtaining its normal share of moisture and nourishment from the circulation. The condition would be caused by some permanent obstruction that could not be cured by natural means. The account here says *they asked him*, while the accounts of the same event in both Mark 3:2 and Luke 6:7 say they *watched him*. There is no contradiction for the last two passages explains the first to mean that they were asking that question in their minds. This conclusion is borne out by the 8th verse of Luke 6 which says, "But he knew their thoughts." The idea is that they had an accusing suspicion of him in their minds that Jesus would probably heal the man, then they could charge him with breaking the sabbath.

Verse 11. But, knowing their thoughts Jesus anticipated their verbal question and asked one himself. The manual labor necessary to lift a sheep out of a pit would be far greater than what is required to heal an afflicted man. Yet these critics would not hesitate performing that kind of deed even on the sabbath day.

Verse 12. The contrast between the value of a man and a sheep is so evident that they could not give Jesus any answer to his question. *Lawful to do well* was putting the case in an unexpected form. It ignored the technical fact of a physical action on the sabbath day and expressed the more important and unanswerable idea of doing well. They could not deny that it would be doing well to relieve a man of an affliction, neither would they presume to say that any time existed when it would be wrong to do well.

Verse 13. The hand only was afflicted, hence the man could use his arm to extend the hand toward Jesus. We have no doubt that Jesus could have healed the man without any ac-

tion on his part, but it has always been a feature of the Lord's dealings to require man to cooperate with Him. This was exhibited as an act of faith on the part of the afflicted man when he reached out his hand and so he received the favor of a cure.

Verse 14. The Pharisees displayed the very depths of wickedness in wanting to destroy Jesus. They could not deny the good done to the afflicted man, neither could they answer the reasoning that Jesus put to them, so the next resort was to destroy him. *Council* is from SUMBOULION and does not mean the sanhedrin, but a meeting especially called in the form of a consultation.

Verse 15. Jesus always knew what was going on and prevented the wicked designs of the Pharisees by leaving the scene. He was not intimidated from continuing his good works, for when the multitudes followed him he healed all that were afflicted.

Verse 16. *Not make him known.* See the comments at chapter 9:30.

Verse 17. *That it might be fulfilled* is explained at chapter 4:14.

Verse 18. The quotation is from Isaiah 42:1-3 which is the Old Testament form of Esaias. The pronouns of the first person refer to God. Gentiles means the nations in general. The favor of Christ's work was finally to be given the people of the world.

Verse 19. *Strive* is from ERIZO which Thayer defines, "To wrangle, engage in strife." *Cry* is from KRAUGAZO and defined, "To cry out, cry aloud." It means that Jesus was not to be a noisy, loud-mouthed person. His voice was not to be heard in *the streets;* he was not to be an ordinary "street preacher."

Verse 20. The figures in this verse are used for the same purpose as the preceding verse, to illustrate the gentleness and quietness with which Jesus was to go about his work. A reed in normal condition is not very resistant, much less if it has been bruised. Jesus would not use enough violence even to break such an article. *Smoking flax* denotes the wick in a candlestick that is being used as a light. Jesus would not use enough violence even to snuff out that imperfect light. He was to maintain that spirit until he had completed his work and was ready to sit upon his throne.

Verse 21. The word *Gentile* comes from different Greek words and they also are rendered by different words in the Authorized Version. The general meaning of the word is that it refers to the people of the world who are not Jews. The Mosaic system was for the Jews only while that given by Christ was for universal benefit.

Verse 22. Being *possessed with a devil* is explained at chapter 8: 28. It was the man who was rendered blind and dumb, for when the devil was cast out the man spoke.

Verse 23. It was known by many that David was to have a descendant who would be a wonderful man in many respects. When they saw these mighty works being performed by Jesus, they concluded that he was that one predicted by the prophets.

Verse 24. The Pharisees could not deny the fact of the casting out of the devil, for the people were there and saw the evidence of it. They thought of robbing Jesus of his proper credit by reflecting against the power by which he did it. It was known that Beelzebub (Satan) had displayed supernatural power, hence it seemed convenient to reason that he could be working through Jesus, little realizing how their inconsistency would soon be exposed and turned against them.

Verse 25. *Jesus knew their thoughts.* The Pharisees did not always express themselves directly to Jesus because they were too cowardly to do so, but they would make their remarks to the multitude. But they could not escape exposure in that way because the Lord always knows what people are thinking. He therefore made this argument based on the unreasonableness of their statement. For Beelzebub to assist Jesus in casting out the devils, beings in the same wicked moral class as Satan himself, would be like a kingdom engaging in conflict with itself which would certainly bring it to ruin.

Verse 26. Satan is one of the names of Beelzebub and he would be interested in the same conditions that would be favorable to the other devils, and surely would not cooperate with Jesus or any other person in opposing their interests.

Verse 27. Jesus did not admit that these persons really did cast out devils, they just made that claim such as the case in Acts 19: 13. But their position on the subject gave Christ another basis for exposing their inconsistency. They would not admit that their children did their work by the help of Beelzebub, for that would be classing

them as unworthy of respect as they were trying to place Jesus.

Verse 28. Taking for granted, then, that Christ was doing his work by the Spirit of God, it would prove his claim that he was the one to bring the kingdom of God to them.

Verse 29. This verse is another argument against the accusation of the Pharisees. Whoever can enter forcefully into a man's house and plunder him must be stronger than he. Likewise, to overcome Satan and cast him out of his lodgings, one would have to be stronger than he. Therefore, it could not be Satan doing this for that would be making him stronger than himself.

Verse 30. This verse is a conclusive statement of principle on which Jesus regards all intelligent creatures. There is no neutrality between the kingdom of Christ and that of Satan. A man may refuse to be outwardly an advocate of the kingdom of Christ but still wish to profess being in favor of it. But in that case he will be regarded as an active worker in the kingdom of Satan and against that of Christ.

Verse 31. *All manner of sin.* This phrase is so direct and complete that it will not admit a single exception but the one that Jesus makes. (More on this thought in the next verse.) The original word for *blasphemy* is defined by Thayer as follows: "Universally, slander, detraction, speech injurious to another's good name."

Verse 32. Sometimes persons will attempt to formulate a description of some very wicked actions. They may think they have an unanswerable argument when they tell of the vicious things that have been said about Christ, and state that such conduct as that must be the "unpardonable sin" if there ever was any. Yet our present verse is directly against that because it specifically says that speaking against the Son of man "shall be forgiven." It should be noted that the Scriptures in no place calls this the "unpardonable" sin. We do not know that it would be impossible for God to pardon this sin, but we are told plainly in these two verses that *it shall not be forgiven. Neither in this world, neither in the world to come.* The original word for *world* is AION and one meaning of it is "age." When Jesus spoke this passage the Jewish age was in force, and the Christian age was to come. The blasphemy against the Holy Spirit would not be forgiven under either dispensation. This sin will be described in detail at Mark 3: 30. To say that the world to come means the life in heaven would imply that some sins will be forgiven at that time which we know is not true. All sin, whether "pardonable" or not will have to have been forgiven before the judgment day for any person to enter into that life. At that time the status of every intelligent being will be as described in Revelation 22: 11.

Verse 33. *Make* is said in the sense of describe or consider or classify. The clause means that as a bad tree cannot produce good fruit, so the good work of casting out a devil could not be done by a wicked character like Satan.

Verse 34. *Generation of vipers* is defined by Thayer, "Offspring of vipers," and the same author explains his definition thus: "Addressed to cunning, malignant, wicked men." On the principle that a corrupt tree cannot produce good fruit, these wicked Pharisees are unable to bring forth good fruit in the way of righteous words or deeds. It is under that rule of reasoning that Jesus accuses them of having an evil heart, because the words of their mouth were evil against the Holy Spirit.

Verse 35. See the preceding verse for the explanation of this.

Verse 36. The original for *idle* is AEGOS, and its proper or literal meaning is to be worthless or meaningless. Such a word not only cannot convey any good impression to the hearer, but it might be mistaken for something the speaker never intended. To make that use of language would therefore be wrong and will have to be accounted for.

Verse 37. See the comments at chapter 11: 19 on the word *justified*, to learn in what sense a man may be justified by his words. It should be noted that the text does not say a man will be justified by his words *only*.

Verse 38. The word *sign* is from SEMEION which has been rendered in the Authorized Version by miracle 22 times, sign 51, token 1, wonder 3. Jesus worked miracles for a testimony to those who were honestly disposed toward information, but there is no case on record where he did it to gratify mere curiosity. These Jews had just witnessed the casting out of the devil, and that should have convinced them that Jesus was a good man to say the least. This present request was in the nature of a challenge, and it also was in line with the leading characteristic of their race (1 Corinthians 1: 22).

Verse 39. For the reasons expressed in the preceding paragraph, Jesus called them an evil generation and refused to perform any miracle at that time. However, he was willing to stake his reputation as a prophet on an event yet to come.

Verse 40. Just as certainly as Jonas spent three days and three nights within the whale, so the Son of man will spend that much time in the heart or inner part of the earth. The subject has two significant parts as it pertains to the test that Jesus proposed. If he spends a stipulated time only in the earth, then he must come forth unharmed as Jonas did from the whale, which would prove him to be a man under the care of God. Likewise, if and when that occurs it will prove Jesus to have been a true prophet at the time he spoke this to the Jews.

Verse 41. We know that Christ will be the only one to sit on the throne of judgment at the last day, hence all apparent statements to the contrary are to be understood in some accommodative sense. The word *condemn* is from KATAKRINO which Thayer defines, "b. by one's good example to render another's wickedness the more evident and censurable." If the men of Nineveh were willing to repent at the preaching of a man like Jonas, there will be no excuse for people who have had that of the Son of man given them.

Verse 42. The lesson of responsibility based upon opportunity is that in the preceding verse and is the same in this. If as notable a person as a queen would come so far to hear the wisdom of a man, surely the people should show greater interest in the wisdom of such a person as Jesus. This woman is called the *queen of the south* because the country of Sheba was a great distance from Judea and was south as to direction and in such a trip signified that a great territory was represented.

Verse 43. Jesus made some arguments based on the practices and beliefs of the people without necessarily endorsing those beliefs. (See comments at verse 27.) The Jews believed that the devils haunted the deserts, but made raids into the places of civilization to torment human beings. One of those devils was cast out of a man and it went back to its regular dwelling place (according to the Jewish notion) but could not find a satisfactory spot to rest.

Verses 44, 45. A man's body is likened to a house and hence the clearing out of the demon is called the sweeping and cleaning of a house. The demon saw the place he had just been occupying in such an inviting condition that he wanted to share it with his special friends and took them with him. Logically, then, that man was in worse condition than he was the first time. Let the reader remember that Jesus is only using this notion of the Jews for an illustration, not that he endorses it, and it serves as a likening of what was to come to their race. The things used for the story existed only in the belief of the Jews, but the thing it was used to illustrate was to come as an actual experience upon the nation. The Jews at first accepted the Gospel and furnished many recruits, but the nation as a whole turned against it and became unbelievers. Their city was finally destroyed and they became the object of scorn in the eyes of the peoples of the world.

Verse 46. *Brethren* is from ADELPHOS which Thayer defines as follows: "1. A brother (whether born of the same two parents, or only of the same father or the same mother): Matthew 1: 2; 4: 18 and often. That 'the brethren of Jesus,' Matthew 12: 46, 47; 13: 55; Mark 6: 3 (in the last two passages also sisters; Luke 8: 19; John 2: 12; 7: 3; Acts 1: 14; Galatians 1: 19; 1 Corinthians 9: 5, are neither sons of Joseph by a wife before Mary (which is the account in the Apocryphal Gospels), nor cousins, the children of Alphaeus or Cleophas (i. e., Clopas) and Mary, a sister of the mother of Jesus (the current opinion among the doctors of the church since Jerome and Augustine), according to that use of language by which ADELPHOS like the Hebrew . . . denotes any blood-relation or kinsman, but own brothers, born after Jesus, is clear principally from Matthew 1: 25; Luke 2: 7 . . . where, had Mary borne no other children after Jesus, instead of HUION PROTOTOKON, the expression HUION MONOGENE would have been used, as well as from Acts 1: 14; John 7: 5, where the Lord's brethren are distinguished from the apostles." For the convenience of the reader and to save him from confusion, I will state that this quotation from the lexicon shows that Jesus had fleshly brothers who were the children of Joseph and Mary, and that Mary did not remain a virgin after the birth of Jesus as the Romanists teach.

Verse 47. Jesus never disrespected his mother but treated her as any man should the woman who had given him birth, but the people needed the lesson that is set down here, and it was for their benefit that he spoke.

Verse 48. The question does not indicate that Jesus intended to ignore his family relations, or that he did not recognize them; it was not asked for that purpose.

Verse 49. After the aforesaid remark, Jesus pointed toward his disciples as an answer to his own question. Since the persons included in the gesture were men and women, while he named three relationships regarding family ties, we know he had some figurative sense in mind for the terms.

Verse 50. The only proper relationship that can be produced by obedience to the will of God is that of brethren. Thus the conclusion is necessary that no earthly relative should be regarded as near to one as our fellowship with Christ.

MATTHEW 13

Verse 1. The conversation reported at the close of the preceding chapter took place in a house. It was on that same day that Jesus went out and sat down on the shore.

Verse 2. A person as interesting as Jesus would not be left to himself very long if the people know where he is, so we are told that *great multitudes* came unto him. The second word is from a Greek original that means the populace or people in general, and that alone would indicate a goodly number of men and women. Then the other word emphasizes the expression so that we understand that a very large audience came together. Jesus wished to be heard by the multitude and that suggested also that he be seen. For this twofold purpose he entered a ship where he could be in the position of a public speaker with his audience on the shore that doubtless was elevated rearward on the order of an inclined floor of an auditorium.

Verse 3. The literal meaning of the original for *parable* is, "A placing of one thing by the side of another."— Thayer. As to the results of such a placing, or the reason or reasons why it is done, that has to be determined by the context in eac.. ...e. (See the comments at verse 11.) Caution should be observed in the study of the parables not to make them mean more than was intended. Jesus spoke about thirty parables all pertaining to the plan of salvation that he intended to set up among men. Surely that many would not have been necessary just for the sake of emphasis. The conclusion is that different parts of that plan were considered in the various parables. No one illustration could be large enough to cover all the phases of the one plan of salvation that was to be given to the world. As a result of the above truths, there may be some features of one parable that do not fit in with the Gospel plan at all. That is because the whole story had to be told in order to make it understood at the point where it does apply. Then another parable will be given that will cover the points in its application where the other one seemed not to be fitting. The parables of our Lord were drawn both from nature and art, and from the customs of man in the conduct of his public and private affairs in all of life's relations.

Verse 4. In the days before machinery, seed was sown by the system known as broadcasting, even as such seeding is done sometimes today. In such a work a man could not have full control of the direction of the seed and hence did not always deposit it where it might have been desired. *Way side* is from HODOS which Thayer defines, "A traveled way." In such a place the surface would be packed down and hard so that the seeds could not find any opening to bury themselves in the soil. Being thus exposed, they would soon catch the eyes of the birds and be devoured.

Verse 5. Stony ground is that where small rocks are mixed with the surface of the soil, thereby limiting the amount of earth at any given spot. *Forthwith* means *"immediately,"* and the seed sprang up in that way because it ran out of material for growth in the ground, hence it had to come up into the open where it could feed on air and sunlight. But having been thus impelled upward prematurely, the root part of the plant was incomplete and therefore was weak.

Verse 6. Sunlight is necessary for plant life and growth, but other elements must accompany it; it must have a "balanced diet." This plant was deprived of the moisture and

mineral food that should have been supplied in the ground. Not having such necessities, the one article in the menu (that of the sun) was too much and the result was fatal.

Verse 7. *Thorn* is from AKANTHA which Thayer defines, "A thorn, bramble-bush, brier." It is a plant that grows near the ground in the nature of coarse grass. That is why the soldiers could plat it into a wreath or crown to place on the head of Jesus (Matthew 27: 29). The seeds of this plant were not visible at the time of the sower's work, but when the growing season came they sprang up with all other vegetation. Being more rugged and wild than the good seed deposited by the farmer, they soon choked out all the other plants just as weeds will often smother out the good grass today.

Verse 8. The *good ground* would be that where the three forementioned obstacles were not present. Yet with all that advantage it should be noted that the crop was not the same in every place as to the amount, which will be explained at verse 23.

Verse 9. See comments for this statement at chapter 11: 15.

Verse 10. Attention is called to the fact that the question the disciples asked pertained to *them*, the multitude.

Verse 11. A familiar statement that may be heard on the parables is as follows: "Jesus spoke in parables in order to make his teaching easier to be understood by the people." Such a statement is exactly opposite of the truth, for this very verse says, in answer to the question of the disciples, that it was *not given* to the multitudes to know the mysteries of the kingdom of heaven. It may be replied that it was because this knowledge of the mysteries was not possessed by the multitudes that the parables were given to explain them. But that is not correct, for even the disciples did not understand the meaning of the parables until Jesus had them to himself and explained them. A natural question now is in regard to the present day. May we speak of the parables as a means of making the subject plainer in our teaching of the subjects of the New Testament? The answer is that we may, and the reason is that we have both the illustration (the parable) and the thing illustrated with us which is the church and the Gospel, and we can show the comparison. The kingdom had not yet been started when Jesus spoke to the multitudes and hence it was not time to introduce them to all of its mysteries or unrevealed truths.

Verse 12. Jesus had told the disciples that it was not given to the multitudes to know the mysteries of the kingdom, and in this verse he begins to tell them why. We would think it impossible to take from a man something that he hath not, hence we must look for some figurative or accommodative use of this language. A useful illustration of the subject is in John 15: 2. Every branch had been given an opportunity to bear increase but it did not do so. Hence the branch itself was to be removed from the vine. The multitudes had been given the words of Moses and the prophets, yet they refused to see in them the beauties of the kingdom of heaven in predicted form. Now it was certainly just to keep them still in the dark as to those beauties (mysteries) until such time as the whole world would have a full description of the system in detail.

Verse 13. The first clause of this verse is similar in meaning to verse 11. *Seeing see not*, etc., means that they were given the ability and opportunity to see and hear but they would not use them.

Verse 14. Failing to use the means of information within their reach is the subject of this verse. The prophecy referred to is in Isaiah 6: 9, 10.

Verse 15. The condition described is with reference to their moral or spiritual situation, but the natural organs are named by way of illustration. Gross means "To make fat; to make stupid (to render the soul dull or callous)." And this was not an accident that came to them, for the verse states the motive they had for bringing on the condition. It was done deliberately for fear they might hear some truth that would expose their evil deeds and later lead them into the service of Christ.

Verse 16. The disciples were willing to use their opportunities for obtaining information and hence were pronounced as blessed of the Lord. That was why they were admitted into the explanation of the mysteries of the kingdom of heaven, while the multitudes were not permitted to receive anything but the unexplained parables.

Verse 17. This verse sounds as if some others who were righteous were in the same class as these multitudes in that they had not seen or heard either. The apparent difficulty is explained by going back to the time when the Lord did not expect the people to have a full knowledge of the divine plan. But even the things they could have discerned by proper attention to what was revealed, the Pharisees had failed to grasp because of their hardness of heart. *Which ye see* and *which ye hear* is spoken in prospect as if Jesus said, "which ye are going to hear," meaning the explanation of the parables which comes in the next and following verses.

Verse 18. This verse invites the disciples to listen and they will hear the inner meaning of some of the "mysteries" that had not been told even to the prophets.

Verse 19. Failure to understand might not always be a fault, yet we know it is used as one in this case. The original word is SUNIEMI, and its general meaning is, "to set or bring together," and the definition is explained to mean, "to put the perception and the thing perceived together; to set or join together in the mind." It denotes that the hearer will give careful attention to what is said so as to arrive at the thought intended by the speaker. Of course a person will not understand what is said to him if he refuses to give it due consideration. As a further result, that person will soon forget all that was said to him and the thought will be lost as was the seed that fell on the hard or beaten ground.

Verses 20, 21. *Anon* is from a word that is defined "immediately" in Thayer's lexicon. It does not indicate that one can be too ready to accept the word, but he may be influenced more by enthusiasm than serious consideration. Such a person may be sincere in his motives, but he has failed to consider that the same word that he received with so much joy for the present, will need to be retained as firmly in the future. He will have to endure opposition from the enemies because of his devotion to the truth, and when that comes if he yields to the foe he becomes *offended* which means to stumble and reject the word he had heard so joyfully.

Verse 22. See the comments at verse 7 for a description of these thorns. *Care* is from MERIMNA and Thayer's simple definition is, "Care, anxiety," and he explains his definition to mean, "anxiety about things pertaining to this earthly life." Robinson defines it, "Care, anxiety, anxious thought," and his comment on it is, "as dividing up and distracting the mind." It means to be so concerned about the things of worldly interest that one neglects to give proper attention to spiritual matters. *Deceitfulness of riches* means the false pleasures that one may have by means of his wealth. He should not be thus deceived because "the fashion of this world passeth away" (1 Corinthians 7: 31).

Verse 23. The good ground is the heart or mind that *understands*, and this word is explained at verse 8. The hundred, sixty and thirty fold is different in amount only. It is all good wheat, but not all men even in the good class have the same ability or capacity for producing results. The Lord is not concerned about the amount of work a man accomplishes in the vineyard just so he does what he can.

Verse 24. The reader should first see the comments at verse 3 about the right use of parables. The one now before us is for a different purpose from the one just concluded. The main point in this is to show what is going to take place at the judgment day. But in order to explain why that will be done it is necessary to tell what was going on in the world before that. In relating those details the Lord mentions some things that do not represent the activities within the church. The items of the parable will first be given and the explanation will follow a little later in the chapter. It starts with the simple fact that a man sowed *good seed* in his field as no man would sow any other kind in his own territory.

Verse 25. *While men slept* means the time when mankind was usually asleep, and that would be the most likely time for an enemy to get in his evil work. *Tares* is from zizanion, and Thayer's description of it is, "A kind of darnel, bastard wheat, resembling wheat except that the grains are black," and Robinson says of it, "At first having a close resemblance to them" [good grain]. A common idea is that the tares were growing in such a way that the roots of them and the wheat were entwined so that a man could not pull up the one without uprooting the other. This is a mistake, and instead, it is the resemblance that is considered and which will be considered also below.

Verse 26. There was enough difference as the growing proceeded that some informed servants recognized the presence of the tares and were puzzled about it.

Verse 27. The servants asked their master for an explanation.

Verse 28. He explained that an enemy had done it. The natural conclusion with the servants was that he would want them to gather the tares out of the field.

Verse 29. The close resemblance between the tares and the wheat might cause some of the servants to mistake the one for the other while the plants were not fully matured.

Verse 30. By harvest time the growth will be completed and hence no harm can be done to the wheat even if it is pulled up. Also by that time the distinction will be clearer so that the reapers whose experience guides them in the harvesting work will be able to make the separation between the things that should not remain together.

Verse 31. The parable of the tares was dropped for the present because the multitudes were still present and the explanation was not to be for them. Before dismissing them Jesus spoke two shorter parables, one of which was about the mustard seed.

Verse 32. The point in this parable is the extent to which the kingdom of heaven was to grow from a very small beginning. The variety of mustard that is considered is the garden kind or that which is cultivated. The word is from sinapi and Thayer describes the plant as follows: "The name of a plant which in oriental countries grows from a very small seed and attains to the height of 'a tree'—ten feet or more." The birds of the air need not be thought as being the largest kind for the text does not require such a conclusion. There are many varieties of small birds that could easily perch in the branches of a plant ten feet high. The kingdom of heaven started in one city and with only a few hundred members at most, but it spread until it became universal and people of all nations sought spiritual shelter in it.

Verse 33. The next parable is contained in this one verse. The meaning is somewhat the same as the preceding one but from a different standpoint. The nature of leaven is to work its way through the mixture in which it has been deposited. If nothing interferes with its operation it will continue until it converts all of the material into a nature like itself. The leaven of the Gospel was deposited at Jerusalem and it spread its influence until it reached to the extremities of "the whole" world or was carried out according to the great commission (Romans 10: 18; Colossians 1: 23).

Verse 34. *Without a parable* applies to the multitudes at such times as Jesus was using to talk about the kingdom of heaven (verse 11).

Verse 35. In speaking the parables Jesus fulfilled a prophecy spoken by David in Psalms 78: 2. *World* is from KOSMOS and means the people of the earth.

Verse 36. The first verse of this chapter states that Jesus went out of the house where he spoke to the multitudes. He now dismissed them and went back into the house, and when the disciples came to him they asked for an explanation of the tares and wheat.

Verse 37. The sower is the Son of man or Jesus the Christ.

Verse 38. The field is the *world* (mankind in general) and not the church as some people teach. *Good seed are the children* means the good seed (which is the divine truth) produces children for the kingdom of heaven. The tares are the children or product of evil teaching. These evil men are people of the world who would not accept the kingdom of heaven and the Lord's teaching.

Verse 39. *Devil* is from DIABOLOS which means Satan or Beelzebub. He has always been an enemy of righteousness and has used his influence to keep men out of the kingdom of the Lord. *World* in this and the following verse is from AION and means age; specifically the age of the earth. Angels have been instruments of God since the human family has existed. They are said to be the reapers, and the same prediction is made of their part in the last harvest as recorded in Revelation 14: 14-20.

Verse 40. All refuse material that accumulates in the course of a growing season generally is disposed of at the time of harvest. Thus it will be done with the tares at the harvest time which will be at the end of the world.

Verse 41. One meaning of the word for *kingdom* is, "The territory subject to the rule of a king," and Jesus said (chapter 28: 18) that "all power is given unto me in heaven and in earth." This shows that the whole inhabited earth is the kingdom of Christ in this broad sense. Hence the wicked characters in the world will be taken out of it at the last day and cast into the fire.

Verse 42. *Wailing and gnashing of teeth.* The subject of endless punishment will be fully considered at chapter 25: 46. It will be stated here however, that the phrase in italics indicates a condition of conscious torment.

Verse 43. *Then* is an adverb of time and refers to the condition just after the harvest which is at the end of the world. In 1 Corinthians 15: 24 Paul says that Jesus will give up his kingdom when he comes and deliver it to his Father. That is why this verse says that the righteous will then shine as the sun in the kingdom of their Father.

Verse 44. The lesson in this parable is the value of salvation, and hence the sacrifice that one should make willingly in order to obtain it. The treasure represents the salvation which Jesus brought and deposited in the same field that is a part of the parable of the tares. When a man "finds" that salvation through hearing the Gospel and desires to obtain it, he will devote all his time and talents for that purpose.

Verse 45. This parable teaches the same lesson as the preceding one on the value of salvation. One word in the definition for *goodly* is, "genuine." There are many things that appear as pearls but are only imitation. This merchant was not wishing anything but the real and hence he was *seeking* for it.

Verse 46. Salvation also is something for which a man should seek (chapter 6: 33), and he should be just as careful to find the genuine and not some imitation. Like the parable, there are systems made by man that have the appearance of being good, like "simulated pearls," but upon examination will be found to be false. And there is no reason for anyone to be deceived for the Scriptures will make it very clear as to what the salvation from God is like. When a man finds it he must devote his entire attention to it in order to retain this *pearl of great price*.

Verse 47. When a man casts a net

into the water he does not know what may be taken because he cannot see the fish until the net is drawn out. Likewise, no man can read the mind of another, and when he offers the Gospel to the world he cannot see the hearts of those who profess to accept it.

Verse 48. After the fishing time is over the net will be drawn out and taken to the shore where the good fish can be separated from the others. In like manner the Gospel fish net will be spread out on the shore of the judgment. Then all those persons who have deceived their fellow men will be exposed before the eye of the great Judge.

Verse 49. As in the parable of the tares, the angels are represented as the servants of the Lord in separating the good from the bad at the end of the world.

Verse 50. This verse takes the same comments as verse 42.

Verse 51. Jesus was still talking to his disciples, the multitudes having been dismissed (verse 36), hence it was appropriate for him to ask them if they understood what had been said. We recall that the disciples who were following Jesus had shown enough sincere attention to the things that had been recorded to have formed a commendable idea of the matters, which entitled them to the explanation of the "mysteries" of the kingdom. But some of the teaching of Jesus was more literal or direct so that honest minds like these would be able to grasp it without special explanation. Hence we are not surprised that they answered his question with *yea Lord*.

Verse 52. One important key word in this verse is *scribe*, and I shall give some information from the writings of learned authors upon the work of this special class of men. The word is from GRAMMATEUS and Thayer's general definition of it is, "1. A clerk, scribe, especially a public scribe, secretary, recorder . . . 2. In the Bible, a man learned in the sacred writings, an interpreter, teacher." This definition of the word is based on the special work of these men. On this subject Robinson in his lexicon says the following: "The scribes had the charge of transcribing the sacred books; whence naturally arose their office of interpreting difficult passages, and deciding in cases which grew out of the ceremonial law. Their influence was of course great, and many of them were members of

the Sanhedrin." As further consideration of this subject, we observe that mechanical means of recording literature were not in existence in Biblical times, hence the copies of the law had to be made by hand. Such frequent contact with the sacred writings naturally made these men familiar with the text, and they could be relied on to quote from it when occasion called for it. With this knowledge of the Old Testament to begin with, after a scribe received the instruction belonging to the kingdom of heaven he would be qualified to offer the treasures of sacred knowledge from both the *New* and *Old* Testaments.

Verse 53. *Finished these parables* refers to the ones in this chapter.

Verse 54. Jesus was in Galilee all the time he was teaching these parables and hence he was already in his *own country* with reference to the province. Thus the term has specific reference to the vicinity of Nazareth ,where he had been brought up. Having lived there in his boyhood and early manhood, the people were acquainted with his humble life and hence they were astonished when they heard his teaching and saw his works.

Verse 55. The people were acquainted with much of the family history of Jesus and never knew of any training he had gone through to give him the talents he was now displaying. There could be no question about his general standing as a citizen for they knew all of these nearest relatives and could mention them by name. For comments on the term *brethren* see those at chapter 12: 46.

Verse 56. The Romanists insist that Mary always remained a virgin, and that when his "brethren" are mentioned it means his disciples since they are known by the name of brethren also. That is true, but when so used it includes all of the disciples regardless of sex. If that had been the meaning intended in verse 55 there would have been no reason to mention *sisters* in this verse for they would have been included in the other.

Verse 57. *Offended* is from SKANDA-LIZO and Thayer's definition at this place is, "To find occasion of stumbling," and he explains his definition to mean, "To see in another what hinders me from acknowledging his authority." Jesus uttered the familiar proverb about a prophet's honor in his own country. People are inclined to have more respect for a teacher who is unknown to them than for their acquaintances. Jesus did not state any reason for this and hence I am unable to explain it.

Verse 58. Pretended miracle workers try to explain their failure at performing certain miracles on the ground of the unbelief of the multitude. They will refer to such passages as the present verse and try to hide behind it. They ignore the point that Jesus did do some of his works in spite of the unbelief of the multitude. The reason their unbelief restricted his mighty works so that he did not *many* of them was their unbelief which rendered them unworthy. (See chapter 7: 6 and Mark 6: 5.)

MATTHEW 14

Verse 1. The Herodian family was a prominent one in the days of Christ and the early years of the church. Its head was Herod the Great who had several sons by a number of wives. The name "Herod" became a family title and the various members had personal names that made distinctions between them. The different members of the Herodian family held offices of greater or lesser importance in Palestine and figured largely in the affairs of the church as well as the nation. The one in this verse was Herod Antipas, son of Herod the Great. *Tetrarch* originally meant "ruler of a fourth part of some territory," but finally came to mean one who had the rulership over a small part of any district to which he might be assigned.

Verse 2. Hearing of the fame of Jesus, Herod thought he would have to make some kind of an explanation of it since he could not deny the facts. He doubtless had a sort of guilty feeling over the way he had treated John the Baptist and it gave him this weird-like impression. He explained the matter to his servants by saying that John had come back to life and was doing these mighty works in the person of Jesus. However, this return to life on earth to which Herod referred was not a part of the general resurrection that is taught in the Scriptures, but to a belief that many people had that is described in the histories and other works of reference as "transmigration."

I shall quote Webster's definition of the word: "Act or instance of transmigrating; specifically, the passing of the soul at death into another body or successive bodily forms, either human or animal; also *(often transmigration of souls)*, the doctrine that souls so pass." We know that such a doctrine did not originate with any true teacher from God, although many of His professed people took up with it. The idea of repeated transmigrations was based on the theory of Brahma, the Hindu name of the Supreme Being. I shall quote from Myers Ancient History (pages 99, 100) on this matter: "A chief doctrine of Brahmanism is that all life, apart from Brahma, is evil, is travail and sorrow. . . . The only way to redemption from evil lies in communion with and final absorption with Brahma. But this return to Brahma is dependent upon the soul's purification, for no impure soul can be reabsorbed into Brahma. . . . As only a few in each generation reach the goal, it follows that the great majority of men must be born again, and yet again, until all evil has been purged away from the soul and eternal repose is found in Brahma. He who lives a virtuous life is at death born into some higher caste, and thus he advances towards the longed-for end. The evil man, however, is born into a lower caste, or perhaps his soul enters some unclean animal. This doctrine of rebirth is known as the transmigration of souls." While this doctrine originated with the heathen teachers, it had become widely known in the time of Christ and the apostles and was reflected even in the opinions of some of the Jews. That made it necessary for our Saviour and his apostles to deal with it (Matthew 16: 14; Mark 8: 28; Hebrews 6: 2), hence the reader should make himself familiar with this paragraph for future reference when the subject may be mentioned.

Verse 3. The imprisonment and slaying of John the Baptist had taken place several months before this but nothing was stated on the subject at the time. Now the remark of Herod being recorded by Matthew brought up the subject which might leave the reader in confusion, hence he interrupts his story and goes back to tell that incident, beginning with this verse and running through verse 12. The cause of the trouble was the marriage of Herod with the wife of his brother Philip I.

Verse 4. John the Baptist told Herod that it was unlawful for him to have her. That would have been a true accusation for more than one reason, but the most outstanding one was the fact that his brother Philip was still living.

Verse 5. Herod would have slain John in spite work, but was kept from it by the force of public opinion which held John in high esteem as a prophet of God. Besides, Herod might not personally have been inclined so harshly towards him if he had not been influenced by his wicked wife. Mark 6: 19 tells us that she quarreled with John and would have put him to death had she been able to do so.

Verse 6. But an unexpected event gave her the opportunity she wanted to accomplish her wicked purpose that was prompted by an adulterous heart. Herod celebrated his birthday by a banquet to which he invited the high men of rank in his estate. The text does not state that his program included the following performance, but for some reason the daughter of his wife by a previous marriage danced before him and his guests. The word for *dance* is ORCHEOMAI which Thayer defines simply, "to dance." Robinson defines it, "to lift up, to raise aloft; to leap, to dance." Young's definition is, "to lift up (the feet), dance." There is no intimation of any display of musical rhythm, but on the other hand from the definitions of the word in the lexicons, and also from the effects her dancing had on the adulterous mind of Herod, the conclusion is clear that the girl exposed herself before the eyes of that lustful king. It says it *pleased Herod*, and that pleasure overcame his better judgment.

Verse 7. Herod was so overcome by the effect of the girl's appearance before his eyes that he seems to have lost his reason. He told her with an oath and without any stipulation that she could have whatever she asked, and Mark's account says that Herod extended his offer to include half of his kingdom.

Verse 8. *Before instructed of her mother.* Herodias knew the nature of Herod, in that he was willing to marry her while her husband was living. Doubtless it was her suggestion that caused the girl to dance before the group and display her charms in the way she did. She further prompted her daughter what to do in case her dancing produced the effect she anticipated. Consequently she asked for the head of John the Bapist in a *charger* which means a large dish. The wicked woman would not risk merely requesting the death of John for she would never be sure that it was carried out. But if his head is severed from his body and brought to her she would know the deed was done.

Verse 9. The king was not expecting such a request as this and he was doubtless genuinely sorry because of it. But he had bound his promise with an oath in the knowledge of his royal guests, and pride as well as a false notion of the sacredness of an oath, though a sinful one, prevailed over his personal sentiments so that he commanded the wish to be granted and gave orders to the executioner to behead the righteous man.

Verse 10. John was in prison and the beheading was done there.

Verse 11. The head of John the Baptist was placed in a dish and brought to the damsel. The head of that forerunner of Christ, the one who had been foretold by the prophets, the man whose preaching aroused the multitudes of all Judea, was severed from his body because he dared to rebuke a lustful man and woman for their wickedness. Of course the damsel was true to the orders of her mother and delivered this reward of her own immoral actions to the vicious woman waiting for it.

Verse 12. *His disciples* means the disciples of John. They got possession of his body and buried it, then went and told Jesus because they knew that he would be concerned.

Verse 13. *When Jesus heard it* means what the disciples of John had just reported. Hence the whole narrative including the works of Jesus goes back to the time of the death of John and proceeds again from there. Jesus wished some privacy or at least some relief from the presence of the crowds after receiving the sad news, and hence he went into a ship and journeyed to a place not much inhabited. Notwithstanding, the people came in throngs on foot to follow him.

Verse 14. The patience and love of Jesus knew no bounds. He went out to this place for a little relaxation from the press of the multitudes, but when they came on after him his compassion asserted itself and he healed their sick.

Verse 15. It was getting on towards the close of day and the crowds were lingering in the presence of Jesus. Thinking they might not realize the hour and thus would let darkness find them without provisions, the disciples suggested that Jesus send them into the villages for food.

Verse 16. This situation provided the occasion of one of the most noted of the miracles of Jesus. The faith of the disciples was to be tested, also they were to receive a lesson on the subject of cooperation; Jesus told them to feed the people.

Verse 17. The reply of the disciples indicates they had no miraculous power, and that they thought they were expected to feed the multitudes from their own private stores. Hence they explained how scant was their supply of food.

Verse 18. The amount of supplies the disciples had would not have been even a taste for the crowds, but the lesson was that whatever man has, whether little or much, must be contributed to the cause if he expects the Lord to make the project effective.

Verse 19. *Grass* is mentioned which indicates that the place was not without moisture even though it was called a desert. The word means a territory that was not occupied generally by people. It would be more orderly to serve a large crowd if sitting than while standing. Looking up to heaven was a gesture of recognition of the source of the good things at hand. *Blessed* is from EULOGEO and Thayer's first definition is, "to praise, celebrate with praises." The clause means that Jesus took the bread in his hands before serving, then looked up toward heaven and "Praised God from whom all blessings flow." It was orderly to pass the bread out through the hands of the disciples, besides it made them partakers with Jesus in the service of the hour.

Verse 20. Even had the whole multitude been able each person to have tasted of the amount of bread the disciples had, it would not have been a miracle although a remarkable thing. They not only tasted but ate—not only ate but were filled; which could not have been accomplished naturally with five loaves. And to show that *filled* was not figurative there were twelve baskets full of fragments taken up. Why bother with these scraps when it was so easy to obtain bread with Jesus with them? John 6: 12 reports the same event and adds the reason given by Jesus was "that nothing be lost."

Verse 21. It may have been only a coincidence that there was one loaf to each thousand men, but by leaving out the enumeration of the women and children that figure of pro rata was obtained.

Verse 22. Jesus *constrained* or commanded his disciples to enter a ship and go across the sea before him. He wished to dismiss the multitudes which would require some considerable time because of the large number of them.

Verse 23. Before joining the disciples Jesus retired to a mountain to pray, so that by the time evening had come he was alone. That would be a very suitable situation for prayer with his Father.

Verse 24. In the meantime a storm had come up and the disciples were having difficulty with their ship. *Wind was contrary* means the wind was blowing against them or in the opposite direction to that in which they wished to row. Evidently Jesus was expecting such a condition and selected the occasion for one of his great miracles.

Verse 25. The *fourth watch* was the same as our three o'clock in the morning, as the twelve hours of the night were divided into four divisions of three hours each, beginning at six in the evening. Thus the hour that Jesus went toward the disciples was still in darkness although not very far from the time of daylight.

Verse 26. Peering out over the sea in the darkness the disciples saw an object on the surface of the water coming toward them. While it was still in the darkness of night, yet it was not total darkness, so that an object could be discerned but not very distinctly. The sight startled them and they cried out with fear because they thought it was a spirit. Ordinarily a spirit is not supposed to be something that can be seen, but the original for this spirit is PHANTASMA which means a phantom or something that appears to exist but which belongs to the unseen world. There is enough of the superstitious in most people to make them have a weird or uneasy feeling in the presence of such an appearance, hence the disciples cried out in their fright.

Verse 27. They did not recognize Jesus from his appearance but did know his voice, hence the Lord spoke to let them realize who was coming to them.

Verse 28. We are not told the motive that Peter had in wanting to walk on the water. If it was from a desire to make a show, the Lord certainly knew how to humble him.

Verse 29. Peter actually got started walking on the surface of the sea and hence had evidence that it was Jesus who was dealing with him miraculously. This should have reassured him that no harm need come to him.

Verse 30. The power of the Lord is not affected by any apparent difficulties. Peter had started on his journey over the sea and had evidence that Jesus was there. He also should have remembered the previous event (chapter 8: 23-27) in which the sea was calmed by the Lord's voice. But his human nature got the better of him and he began to sink. Of course Jesus would not let his disciple perish, but he used the occasion to rebuke him by allowing him to think he was going to sink and perish.

Verse 31. The Lord chastised him at the same time he was rescuing him by accusing him with having little faith. A good lesson may be obtained for all of us from this event. It does not require as much faith to appear firm when everything is favorable. The test comes when it appears that things are against us, and it is then that we should think of the words of Paul in Romans 8: 31, "If God be for us, who can be against us?"

Verse 32. Whether it was the mere presence of Jesus in the ship that quieted the storm we are not told, or that he commanded it to be so as he did in the case referred to above. What we know is that when he entered the vessel the wind ceased.

Verse 33. The circumstance had a deep effect on the men in the ship and caused them to *worship* Jesus. See the comments on chaper 2: 2 for the meaning of that word. The worship in this case took the form of a confession that Jesus is the Son of God. That was one purpose of the miracles that Jesus performed according to John 20: 30, 31, and not merely to gratify the curiosity of idle or disinterested people.

Verse 34. The storm being over, the ship resumed its journey and landed on the western shore of Galilee at the country of Gennesaret.

Verse 35. The fame of Jesus had become known in this territory. After his arrival the sick were sent for and brought into the presence of the man who was known as the healer of all kinds of diseases.

Verse 36. Touching the garment of Jesus had no curative effect in itself, but the act showed their faith and they were healed as a reward for it, on the same principle as that of the woman in chapter 9: 20-22.

MATTHEW 15

Verse 1. See the comments on chapter 13: 52 for a description of the scribes. The Pharisees were a leading sect of the Jews who made great pretentions of righteousness. They, with the scribes, were enemies of Jesus and frequently tried to get him into trouble with either the Sanhedrin or the Romans.

Verse 2. The Pharisees and others who stood with them doctrinally placed great stress on the traditions of those who were the elders or forefathers in the Mosaic system. In most cases they held these traditions to be of more importance than the written law of Moses, and where there was a disagreement between them they perverted the written law in favor of the tradition. One of such rules had to do with washing the hands at certain specified times. This was not done as a necessary act of sanitation but was one of the self-imposed rituals of the elders among the Jews. The disciples were busy with the important affairs of their work with Jesus and did not observe such ceremonies. But the critics thought they had a cause for accusation against them and came to Jesus with their complaint.

Verse 3. It was a much worse fault to set the traditions of the elders against the positive requirements of the Mosaic law than it was to ignore the customs of the fathers, and that was the accusation that Jesus made against these critics.

Verse 4. The law of Moses plainly required a man to honor his parents (Exodus 20: 12). The word *honor* in the commandment to which Jesus referred comes from the Hebrew word KABED which Strong defines, "In a good sense (numerous, rich, honorable): causatively [as a cause], to make wealthy." The definition of the word which Moses wrote, as well as the reasoning of Jesus on the subject, shows that honoring one's parents included the financial support of them also.

Verse 5. A man's parents are in need of the good things of life and look to their son for help. But he puts them off with the excuse that the money that he would otherwise have spent on them so that they would have *profited* by it, had been "earmarked" for the Lord's treasury. This was hypocrisy on their part for they never carried out their claim of devoting the money to the cause of the Lord. Besides, the law never intended that money should be put into the public treasury that was needed for dependents.

Verse 6. The Pharisees taught that if a man withheld his support of his parents on the pretense of giving it to the Lord, he would be exempt from the commandment in Exodus 20: 12, thus putting their tradition above the law.

Verse 7. A hypocrite is one who professes to be what he knows he is not. See the comments at chapter 6: 2 for the lexicon definition and other accounts of the word. *Well did Esaias prophecy* means the prophet did well in predicting these characters.

Verse 8. Generally speaking, the lips and mouth pertain to the fleshly or outer man, and the heart refers to the inner man. The Biblical heart is the occasion of so much confusion among religious teachers that I shall give the reader a description of it as will be taken from the lexicon definition of original Greek. With one exception (PSUCHE in Ephesians 6: 6) the word in the New Testament is from KARDIA and I shall quote Thayers definitions (the part in italics) for it in its various applications: "1. a. the vigor and sense of physical life. b. the soul or mind, as it is the fountain and seat of the thoughts, passions, desires, appetites, affections, purposes, endeavors. Specifically of the understanding, the faculty and seat of intelligence. Of the soul so far forth as it is affected and stirred in a bad way or good, or of the soul as the seat of the sensibilities, affections, emotions, desires, appetites, passions. 3. used of the middle or central or inmost part of any thing, even though inanimate." This Greek word occurs 158 times in the New Testament and is not rendered by any term but "heart" in the Authorized Version. From the extended definition as well as by the various connections in which it is used, it is plain that when "heart" is not used figuratively it means the mind or intelligence of man. This ex-

plains how a person's mouth or lips can say one thing while the heart does not really mean it, and thus he is acting hypocritically.

Verse 9. *Worship* is from SEBOMAI which Thayer defines, "to revere, to worship." The people of whom Jesus was speaking professed to have great respect for him and that is the sense in which he said they worshiped him. *In vain* is defined "fruitlessly" and means that the pretended reverence they had for Jesus would not bring them any favor from him as long as they taught the doctrine of human authority instead of that of the man they claimed to honor but whose teaching they were rejecting.

Verse 10. *He called the multitude.* This was not for the purpose of explaining a parable of the church, but to show them why he had accused them of inconsistency in their undue emphasis on washing the hands.

Verse 11. Jesus was not ignoring the need for cleanliness, but was teaching the lesson of putting moral and spiritual matters above the physical. If a man permits a particle of dirt to enter his mouth and into the stomach it cannot do him any harm for the system will take care of it. Jesus will explain this subject to his disciples a few verses farther on in the chapter.

Verse 12. *Were offended* denotes that they stumbled at the saying of Jesus, and because of it they were unwilling to recognize him as having the wisdom or authority to make a declaration upon the conduct of others.

Verse 13. Jesus was willing to stake his right to speak and the correctness of what he said on the outcome. Every plant not planted by his Father was to be rooted up. If the work of Jesus was not authorized of God, then it would not stand and he would be exposed as an impostor. On the other hand, if his work holds fast it will prove him to have been a true teacher and one over whom the Pharisees had no reason to stumble. This statement had special reference to the church or kingdom that he was about to set up, for in Ezekiel 34: 29 a "plant" is predicted and the context there (verses 20-31) plainly shows that it has reference to the church.

Verse 14. *Let them alone* is defined by Thayer, "c. to let go, let alone, let be; to disregard." It means for the disciples not to lose any time or spend any efforts on them as it would be useless. A further reason for ignoring them was the danger involved in following or associating with them. They were blind leaders and those who would follow them are as blind as they. That would mean that all of them would share the same fate and fall into the ditch or go astray.

Verse 15. Peter called the teaching of Jesus about washing and eating a parable. However, it was not a parable of the kingdom (chapter 13: 11), hence Jesus had called the multitudes to him to give that lesson. But it was somewhat indirect or figurative and the apostles did not understand it.

Verse 16. The expression of Jesus sounds as if he were surprised at the lack of understanding shown by his disciples, when he was supposed to know all about man and not to be surprised at anything. That is not the point, but he said this to them as a mild rebuke for their slowness in thinking out the matter.

Verse 17. Mere filth that is not in the nature of disease germs goes through the stomach and other digestive organs and is separated from food particles the same as the other waste matter, and it is then discharged from the body without having done it any harm. A draught corresponds with our modern sanitary stool.

Verse 18. The things that come *out of* the mouth orginate in the heart, and if they are evil it indicates an impure and a defiled heart. (See chapter 12: 34.)

Verse 19. See again the definition of the heart at verse 8 and it will be observed why the things mentioned in this verse are said to come from it.

Verse 20. Certainly no man can entertain an interest in murder and the other things named in verse 19 and not be defiled. They affect his character while the soil passing from the hands into the mouth has no relation to that.

Verse 21. *Coasts* means region and Jesus went to that surrounding these cities.

Verse 22. *Woman of Canaan* is indefinite because all the land west of the Jordan was generally known as Canaan, and there were both Jews and Gentiles living there. However, the term was used to designate this. woman as outside the class recognized as Jews. This woman not only recognized Jesus as Lord but also as a son of David. The latter term was specific and meánt that she believed him to be the descendant of David according to the prophets, for many of the Gentiles were acquainted with the Old Testament. This woman's daughter was possessed with a devil which is explained at chapter 8: 28.

Verse 23. Jesus had his own way of trying out the faith of those who sought favors of him, and he used it here by appearing to ignore the woman. But she was not to be discouraged by this seeming indifference, for she continued crying after him until the disciples became impatient and asked Jesus to send her away.

Verse 24. Instead of directly doing as the disciples requested, Jesus merely gave the woman to understand that she was not in the class to which he was sent. See the comments at chapter 10: 6 for the meaning of *lost sheep*.

Verse 25. This did not entirely discourage the woman for she repeated her plea accompanied with an attitude of worship towards Jesus.

Verse 26. Jesus made his answer much more in the nature of an argument in figurative form. *Dog* is from KUNARION which Thayer defines, "a little dog." No special disrespect was intended to her personally by this term, for it was commonly known that the Jews were regarded as God's children, and the Gentiles would logically be in a lower class. Besides, Jesus knew the heart of the woman whose faith he was drawing out, and purposely furnished her the illustration by which she could make one of the most touching appeals I have ever known. With all this in view, he compared the Jews to God's children, the favors he was bestowing on them to the bread provided by the Father, and the Gentiles to the little dogs that might be playing at the feet of their master.

Verse 27. The woman was not discouraged nor even hurt at the Lord's comparison. Instead, she accepted the classification as a good basis for her persistence. After the children have been abundantly fed, the scraps are generally gathered up and given to the dogs. She would be satisfied with a temporal favor from Jesus in the healing of her daughter ,even though it would be like the crumbs compared with the loaves of spiritual blessings that he was daily bestowing on his disciples.

Verse 28. *Great is thy faith*. This was indicated by her patience or endurance. She had full confidence at the start in the ability of Jesus to perform her request, but her persistence showed her faith in his willingness to do so if she did not give up too soon. In this she has set an example for those of us who profess to believe in the goodness and power of God. We are often too apt to "lose heart" and cease looking to the Lord for his grace. This is the subject of one of the parables of Jesus recorded in Luke 18: 1-8. The faith of the Canaanite woman was rewarded with the immediate recovery of her daughter.

Verse 29. The region of Tyre and Sidon where Jesus was teaching and working bordered on the Sea of Galilee but was an area a mile wide and several miles long. He now came nearer to the sea and went up into a mountain where he received the multitudes.

Verse 30. As usual Jesus had a great following because his fame had gone all over the country. Afflicted people who were unable to travel alone were brought to Jesus and *cast* down at his feet. This word might give us an unfavorable impression as it seems to indicate an act of impatience if not indifference. It is from the Greek word RHIPTO and Thayer's definition at this place is the simple phrase, "to set down." He then explains his definition to mean, "(with the suggestion of haste and want of care), of those who laid their sick at the feet of Jesus, leaving them at his disposal without a doubt that he could heal them." They were not disappointed for the text says *and he healed them*.

Verse 31. Again Jesus proved his ability to work all kinds of miracles and did not have to select his cases as do the pretenders of miracle-working today. A remarkable thing about the event is that *they glorified the God of Israel*. Everyone knew that an ordinary man could not accomplish such wonderful works, hence they attributed it to the *God of Israel* (not any of the gods of the Gentiles). That was the main purpose Jesus had in performing his great deeds according to John 20: 30, 31.

Verse 32. Once more the compassion of Jesus asserted itself in behalf of the multitude whose interest had kept them in his presence for three days. Of course there would be no opportunity for procuring food out there in that mountainous area. *Fasting* is from NESTIS and Thayer's definition is, "fasting, not having eaten." The mere fact of being without food during the time necessary to reach a market would not cause them to *faint in the way*, but they would already be weak, having not eaten for three days.

Verse 33. It is strange the disciples seem to have forgotten the event of chapter 14: 15-21; probably they had not forgotten it but took that way of asking Jesus to take care of the case in hand as he did the other time.

Verse 34. The supply of food in the possession of the disciples was nothing compared with the needs of the multitude, but Jesus was still inclined to require his disciples to have a part in the good work.

Verse 35. For the sake of orderliness the multitudes were told to sit down.

Verse 36. In this case Jesus *gave thanks*, in the instance of chapter 14: 19 he "blessed" which was virtually the same meaning as was explained at that place.

Verse 37. *And were filled*. See the comments on this phrase at chapter 14: 20, also John 6: 12 as to why the scraps were taken up.

Verse 38. No disrespect was intended by the writer in giving the number of men and only an indefinite reference to the women and children. In old times it was the custom to list families and other groups of human beings according to the men only.

Verse 39. The multitudes were given sufficient nourishment to overcome the effects of their three-day fast and were dismissed. Magdala was a city on the western shore of the Sea of Galilee and it is sometimes mentioned by other names.

MATTHEW 16

Verse 1. A full description of these two sects will be given at verse 12. They were opposed to each other in various respects, but often forgot their differences and united in opposing Christ or his apostles. Their motive in coming to Jesus here was to tempt or test him. Had they been honestly seeking for evidence of the might and wisdom of the Lord he would have granted the request, but he never performed a miracle to gratify mere curiosity or to meet a challenge.

Verse 2. Jesus referred them to

their own study of the heaven in which they professed to know how to figure out the future by the present indications.

Verse 3. *The signs of the times* were as clearly portrayed in the Scriptures as were the weather signs, yet they pretended there was nothing on record to indicate the work and purpose of Jesus. Since this was only a pretended necessity for additional evidence Jesus called them hypocrites.

Verse 4. This subject of the sign of Jonas is explained at chapter 12: 40.

Verse 5. The preceding verse says that Jesus departed from the multitude. He and his disciples had been in the vicinity of Magdala which is on the western shore of the Sea of Galilee. They then crossed over the sea, and verses later in the chapter show that they were to spend some time in an uninhabited territory where there would be no opportunity to purchase provisions. Jesus knew the disciples had forgotten to attend to that matter (Mark 8: 14 says they had one loaf), and decided to use the fact as a basis for a test of their faith in him as one who could and would care for them.

Verse 6. Without mentioning bread directly, Jesus warned them against the *leaven* of the Pharisees and Sadducees whom they knew to be two evil groups of Jews.

Verse 7. There is no logical connection between literal leaven and these sects as far as the disciples were considering it. But a guilty conscience sometimes interprets an unrelated statement as a rebuke and that is what they did about Christ's remark.

Verse 8. Jesus accused his disciples of small faith because they were disturbed over as trival a matter as a shortage of bread. Had there been no visible prospects for food at all for the present, their general knowledge of past experiences should have given them confidence that nothing serious would be allowed to happen to them.

Verses 9, 10. It seems that man needs to have his faith renewed from time to time on account of his unreliable memory. Moses had seen all the mighty works of God in Egypt and the Red Sea, yet when he was told that nation was to be given an abundance of flesh to eat he wondered where the Lord would get it. (See Numbers 11: 18-23.)

Verse 11. Jesus needed only to state

that he was not considering bread when he used the term *leaven*, for the disciples then concluded rightly that he had used if figuratively.

Verse 12. The disciples made the correct interpretation of the comparison and applied it to the *doctrine* or teaching of those two sects. I shall give the description of these prominent groups of the Jews as may be learned from reliable works of reference. "What I would now explain is this, that the Pharisees have delivered to the people a great many observances by succession from their fathers which are not written in the law of Moses; and for that reason it is that the Sadducees reject them, and say that we are to esteem those observances to be obligatory [binding] which are in the written word, but are not to observe what are derived from the tradition of our forefathers." Josephus, Antiquities, Book 13, Chapter 10, Section 6.

"In addition to the books of the Old Testament, the Pharisees recognized in oral traditions a standard of belief and life. They sought for distinction and praise by the observance of external rites and by the outward forms of piety, such as ablutions, fastings, prayers, and alms-giving; and, comparatively negligent of genuine piety, they prided themselves on their fancied good works. . . . A Sadducee, a member of the party of the Sadducees, who, distinguished for birth, wealth, and official position, and not averse to the favor of the Herod family and of the Romans, hated the common people, were the opponents of the Pharisees, and rejecting tradition acknowledged the authority of the Old Testament alone in matters pertaining to faith and morals; they denied not only the resurrection of the body, but also the immortality of the soul and future retribution, as well as the existence of angels and spirits." These last two quotations about the Pharisees and Sadducees are the historical remarks of Thayer in his Greek lexicon, the original words being PHARISAIOS and SADDOUKAIOS. Having given an extended account of these two sects for the information of the reader, I shall summarize it by saying that the false doctrine of the Pharisees was that the tradition of the fathers was of equal authority with the written Scriptures. That of the Sadducees was that there would be no resurrection of the body and consequently no future life.

Verse 13. Jesus and his disciples having landed on the eastern shore of the Sea of Galilee they journeyed northward until they came into the *coasts* or vicinity of Caesarea Philippi. This is to be distinguished from the Caesarea that was on the eastern shore of the Mediterranean Sea. The place got its name by the desire of Herod Philip who wished to honor Caesar and himself both by a twofold name. That was accomplished by the name which we have just read as the double name includes both Caesar and Philip. Jesus concluded it was time to introduce the most serious phase of his own authority and purposes. He opened the subject by inquiring about the current opinions concerning himself; not of his doings but of his identity. He had been out among the people long enough for them to have formed some kind of ideas as to his real standing as a public teacher. He could not have asked this question for information for he already knew what was in man (John 2: 24, 25). Hence it was asked to bring out the contrast that should be existing between the opinions of the common people and that of the men who had been chosen to be the apostles after Jesus was ready to leave this world.

Verse 14. All of the persons named had died, hence the reference to them in connection with Jesus was on the theory of the transmigration of souls. See the explanation of that subject with the comments on chapter 14: 2.

Verse 15. Jesus then came out with the climax of the conversation. The answer to the question he was going to ask would be read by future generations. The apostles had been with him and seen his work and heard his teaching. It remained to be shown by the answer whether that association had made any better impression on them than was expressed by the common people. Jesus asked *them* (all of the apostles) for their estimate of him regarding his identity.

Verse 16. Jesus had addressed his question to all of the apostles, but it would not be expected that all of them would speak at once in answering the question. Peter was generally the spokesman for the others, and if what he said did not agree with them they would have made it known. The reply that Peter gave to the question embraced all that Jesus claimed to be. The word *Christ* means "anointed" and as it applied in this case it meant that Jesus was *the* one that God would recognize as a ruler in the kingdom. *The Son* is equivalent to the phrase "only begotten Son" in John 3: 16. God has numerous sons from a spiritual standpoint, but Jesus is the only one who is the offspring of the person of God. The *living* God signifies that he is not the offspring of the idol gods for they are lifeless objects.

Verse 17. Bar-jona means son of Jona, and the full name is given to distinguish him from others who were named Simon. *Flesh and blood hath not revealed it.* Peter could not have received this information from any human source, hence it had to come from the Father in the way of divine inspiration.

Verse 18. I do not believe it is necessary to trouble ourselves about a grammatical basis for arguments that are frequently made over the original Greek words for *Peter* and *rock*. It is true that they are different from each other to some extent. But if we should consider them only in their literal meaning they are similar. But we know that Jesus did not mean to tell Peter that he was to be "the rock" on which the church would be built. It is also clear from other passages that Peter is in the foundation of the church but so are all the apostles (Ephesians 2: 20). Then we cannot single out this one apostle and say that he is the foundation rock as the Romanists teach. The rock on which Christ intended to build his church was his own divinity that was embodied in the confession that Peter had just made. Much questioning also is done as to the antecedent of *it;* but that, too, is needless for we know that Jesus meant everything that would be necessary to accomplish his purpose of building his church. *Gate* is from PULE and Thayer defines it, "access of entrance into any state." *Hell* is from HADES and means the state or place of the soul after death. Jesus knew he must die and that his soul would go through this entrance to Hades, but that those gates would not be able to retain him, for he would come out from within them into life again so that he could perfect his work of setting up his church.

Verse 19. *Keys* is from KLEIS which Thayer defines, "a key. Since the keeper of the keys has the power to open and to shut, the word is figuratively used in the New Testament to denote power and authority of various kinds." There is nothing significant about the plural form of the word, but it is a part of the same figure that Thayer uses in his definition. The man who has charge of a building carries a group of keys, hence the word is used in the plural form; literally there is but one key to the kingdom of heaven and that is obedience to the requirements of the Gospel. Jesus was speaking directly to Peter because he was the spokesmen for all the rest. We know it was not meant that Peter alone was to have the keys, for Jesus said virtually the same thing in John 20: 21-23 and he was talking to all of the apostles. *Whatsoever thou shalt bind on earth shall be bound in heaven,* etc. This is Christ's own comment on the *keys of the kingdom.* He intended to send the Spirit upon the apostles to "guide them into all truth" (John 16: 13), so that they would make no mistake in telling men what they must do to be saved. Being thus inspired, their teaching to men would be according to the will of heaven and hence it would be ratified there. *Whatsoever thou shalt loose,* etc., means the like thought on the negative side of the subject. No one has the right to bind any doctrine on men that was not required by the apostles. While on this verse it should be observed that in this conversation with the apostles, Jesus speaks of the church and the kingdom of heaven in the same sense, showing that no distinction is to be made today, for the kingdom is afterwards spoken of as being in existence (Matthew 26: 29; Romans 14: 17; Colossians 1: 13; 4: 11; 1 Thessalonians 2: 12; Hebrews 12: 28; Revelation 1: 9).

Verse 20. A command similar to this one is in chapter 17: 9, except that a certain time was set before which the disciples were not to make the specific announcement of the divinity of Christ. The crowning fact that was to prove that great claim of Jesus was to be his resurrection after three days. The public ministry for the general teaching about the kingdom that was at hand was drawing nearer to its close, and Jesus did not wish to release this fundamental truth unto the world prematurely.

Verse 21. See the remarks of the preceding paragraph about the progress of the ministry of Jesus. Since it was in that stage, it was time to begin preparing the minds of the apostles for the tragic events not far

ahead, including the death and resurrection of their Lord with whom they had been so closely associated in the work.

Verse 22. The idea that Peter had in this impulsive speech was that something certainly would be done to prevent the thing Jesus had predicted. His own action recorded in John 18: 10 indicated that he was willing to help prevent the tragedy.

Verse 23. The primary meaning of Satan is "adversary," and when Peter intimated that he would try to prevent the thing that Jesus declared would be done he became an adversary to him. *Savourest* means to be thinking about some subject of personal interest, and in this case it was the idea of an earthly kingdom that occupied the mind of Peter. He wanted such a kingdom to be set up because of what it would mean to him, and certainly such an event would require the living presence of the king. A part of Thayer's definition of the original for *offence* is, "an impediment placed in the way." Were Peter to have his wishes carried out in this matter it would have been an impediment to the great plan that Jesus had in view.

Verse 24. *After* is from OPISO and Thayer explains the word at this place to mean, "to follow any one as a guide, to be his disciple or follower." *Deny* is from APARNEOMAI which Thayer defines, "to deny," and explains the definition to mean in this passage, "to forget one's self, lose sight of one's self and one's own interests." Figures of speech are based upon some literal fact. *Take up his cross* is a reference to the rule of compelling a condemned man to carry his own cross to the place of execution. If the victim became unable to bear it alone, someone would be made to take up the rear part and help carry it, walking after the other to the place of execution. (See Luke 23: 26.) The present verse means that a professed follower of Jesus must be willing to help bear the trials and self-denials that were practiced by him.

Verse 25. This verse is explained at chapter 10: 39.

Verse 26. *World* and *soul* are used in the same sense as the two kinds of life in the preceding verse. The thought is that the things of this world are altogether not as valuable as the soul of man, and that if one were to exchange his soul to gain this world it would be a transaction without profit.

Verse 27. It has been nineteen centuries since Jesus uttered the words of this verse, but he wished his disciples to have something to look for as a reward for their sacrificing everything necessary to save their soul and gain that which is worth more than all this world. They were expected to rely on the promise of Christ because of their faith in him, because the reward would not come in their lifetime.

Verse 28. The preceding verse gives the promise of reward for faithful work at the second coming of Christ. As a guarantee of the surety of that promise, Jesus told them that some of them in his presence would live to see the great event that was to prepare men for that last day of accounts. They were promised the honor of seeing the Son of man in another manner; he was to be seen spiritually in his kingdom. We incidentally may obtain an important truth by this statement. The kingdom was set up in the time of those apostles, and that disproves the heresy taught by some today that the kingdom is still in the future.

MATTHEW 17

Verse 1. *After six days* means after the last conversation Jesus had with his disciples. There seems to have been a peculiar nearness between Jesus and these three apostles, for they are mentioned as a sort of trio a number of times (Mark 5: 37; 14: 33). Jesus selected them to be witnesses of the unusual scene that he knew was coming, and took them with him into a high mountain.

Verse 2. *Transfigured* is from META-MORPHOO which Thayer defines, "To change into another form, to transfigure, transform," and he comments on the word as follows: "To be resplendent with divine brightness; used of the change of moral character for the better." It is the word for "transformed" in Romans 12: 2, and for "changed" in 2 Corinthians 3: 18. It is the source of our English word "metamorphosis" which Webster defines, "2. A striking alteration in appearance, character, or circumstances." With all this authoritative information before us, we understand the meaning of our verse is that Jesus underwent a change in his appearance so that his face shone, and even his raiment was glistening white. However, his body was not replaced literally, and the change in his appearance did not

prevent the apostles from recognizing him.

Verse 3. We have a very interesting assemblage here. The apostles had not died and hence represented the fleshly state. Elias (Elijah) had been transferred to heaven without death and represented the eternal state. Moses had died and represented the intermediate state. There were good men from each of the three states of intelligent creatures, thus representing the whole universe of beings responsible to God for their past or present conduct. A person in the flesh cannot see spiritual beings ordinarily, but God can adapt all circumstances to whatever purpose the case demands. He wished the apostles to see these men from the intermediate and eternal states and performed such miraculous changes as were necessary. That was done either upon the eyes of the apostles or the form of the other men.

Verse 4. In Mark's account of this event he states that Peter "wist not [knew not] what to say." He was overcome by the scene, yet had a feeling of reverence towards the three great persons in the group; Jesus, Moses and Elias, and proposed providing a suitable housing place that they might be retained longer.

Verse 5. This announcement was like the one that God made at the baptism of Jesus with the additional word *hear ye him.* (See chapter 3: 17.) At the time of his baptism Jesus had not performed any of his great works nor done any of his teaching. He now was nearing the close of his earthly work and the apostles were supposed to be ready for an authoritative declaration concerning the rank and position of him with whom they had been so closely associated. The setting of the conversation was significant due to the importance of the main characters in the scene. Moses was the lawgiver of the Old Testament system and Elias (Elijah) was one of the great prophets who lived under that system. Those men were not to be regarded as the authorities under whom the apostles will be expected to work, but instead they were to take their instructions from the Son in whom the Father was well pleased; they were to *hear him.*

Verse 6. *Afraid* is from PHOBEO and Thayer says the word in this place means, "to be startled by strange sights or occurrences." The appearance of the two men from the other states did not overcome them, but this mighty voice and its announcement struck them with a feeling of awe so that they prostrated themselves on the ground.

Verse 7. Jesus assured his apostles that nothing would harm them.

Verse 8. The purpose of the great scene was accomplished and Moses and Elias returned to their proper places. *They saw no man.* The last two words are from OUDEN which Strong defines, "Not even one, i. e., none, nobody, nothing." This indefinite form of speech was appropriate in view of the unusual manner in which Moses and Elias had appeared, for they were evidently not just like other men except to such a degree that they could be recognized by the apostles.

Verse 9. For the explanation of this verse see the comments at chapter 16: 20.

Verse 10. The disciples mistook the Elias spoken of by the scribes to be that prophet literally, who was to announce the mission and divinity of Jesus. Now they were forbidden to make a like statement until after that divinity has been proved by the resurrection. If they were not allowed to make statements on that subject, why should Elias be permitted to do so.

Verse 11. *Shall come* is future tense in form but Jesus was only quoting the prophecy of Malachi. To *restore* means to bring about a reformation in the lives of the people of Israel (Malachi 4: 6; Luke 1: 16, 17).

Verse 12. Jesus then explained that it was not in person that Elias was to come. In other words, by describing the treatment that "Elias" received from the people who did not recognize his place in God's plan, the disciples perceived the point of the Lord.

Verse 13. The disciples did the proper kind of reasoning and it gave them the correct conclusion, and was a demonstration of the thoughts offered at chapter 13: 16, 17.

Verse 14. The act of the man kneeling down to Jesus was one form of worship. The reader should see the various meanings of the word in the comments at chapter 2: 2.

Verse 15. Being possessed with a devil did not affect all people alike. That could be caused by either of two things; the peculiar condition of the victim at the time or the kind of devil that had entered into him. In the present case it caused the son to become a *lunatick* according to the Authorized Version. This word is from SELENIAZOMAI which Thayer defines, "To be moon-struck; to be epileptic," and in commenting on the word he says, "epilepsy being supposed to return and increase with the increase of the moon." Of course the people named the condition according to their theories as to the causes of disease, not knowing that it was the presence of the devil.

Verse 16. *Could not cure him* denotes the belief that the son had some serious disease as was explained in the preceding verse. It is true that the being possessed with a devil would sometimes result in a disease, in which case the casting out of the devil would be equivalent to performing a cure.

Verse 17. This criticism concerning the lack of faith was meant for the disciples as we shall see at verse 20. *How long*, etc., was an expression of displeasure at the amount of long-suffering he was called upon to show towards them. Then addressing the father of the child he told him to bring the afflicted one to him.

Verse 18. When anyone is being dealt with because of some condition brought on by his own sin, he is the person who is rebuked. Being possessed with a devil was not a sin but an affliction, hence the Lord rebuked the devil. The child was cured *from that very hour* which was unlike the performances of professed miracle workers today who insist on having "plenty of time."

Verse 19. When Jesus chose his twelve apostles and sent them out to preach, he told them also to perform certain miracles. Among them was that of casting out devils (chapter 10: 8), hence it was natural for them to be concerned about their failure.

Verse 20. The charge of their *unbelief* means their faith did not go far enough; it did not grow as it should. Jesus then used the mustard grain for an illustration of that subject. It will help us to grasp the meaning of the comparison if we consider the same event as recorded in Luke 17: 6. The apostles asked the Lord to "increase" their faith, and in answer to the request he made the comparison to the grain of mustard seed. We also should remember the comparison between this grain and the kingdom of heaven in Matthew 13: 31, 32. It is clear, therefore, that the reference to the mustard seed was on the principle of growth. Their faith should have grown instead of their expecting Jesus to "increase" it by some special means independent of their own part in the matter. Of course a grain of mustard seed or any other seed could not grow had not the Creator furnished it with the materials necessary for that growth in the earth and air. And likewise, Jesus had given abundance of evidence by his miracles and teaching to have caused them to have increase in their faith to the point where they could not only cast out this devil, but also remove a mountain if such needed to be done.

Verse 21. *Howbeit* is an obsolete word meaning "nevertheless," indicating that some special point is about to be made. *This kind* is from GENOS which Thayer defines, "The aggregate of many individuals, of the same nature, sort, species." *Goeth out* is from EKPOREUOMAI which Thayer defines, "To go forth, go out, depart." He explains the definition to mean, "demons, when expelled, are said to go out (to wit from the human body): Matthew 17: 21." Robinson defines the word, "To go out of, to go or come forth," and he explains it to mean, "Spoken of demons, absolutely Matthew 17: 21." We do not know why this class of devils required the special performance of prayer and fasting before yielding and coming out of human beings. We are certain, however, that at some time Jesus had given his apostles the instructions that should have induced them to show the faith necessary to be patient and use the weapons of prayer and fasting against the devil. Their faith had not led them that far and hence they failed to overcome the devil.

Verse 22. Before leaving Galilee Jesus predicted his betrayal.

Verse 23. Not only was Jesus to be turned over to wicked men of the world, but he was to be killed and raised the third day. The apostles were *exceeding sorry* because of the prediction of his death, and that sorrow seemed to blind their minds to the other prediction of his resurrection. When the sad affair had taken place the disciples showed such forgetfulness as we may learn in Luke 24: 13-27.

Verse 24. Capernaum was a city of Galilee and the chosen residence of Jesus (chapter 4: 13). When he and

his apostles entered this city Peter was approached by those who collected the tax that was for the upkeep of the temple. Robinson says this was "the yearly tribute to the temple paid by every Jew," hence Peter was asked if his master did not pay that tax.

Verse 25. Peter answered in the affirmative and intended to speak to Jesus about it. But when he came into the house where Jesus was he *prevented him* which means he could read his mind and hence anticipated what he was going to say. But the Lord changed the subject somewhat and the *tribute* he mentioned is from a word that means custom or taxes that should be levied upon foreigners.

Verse 26. Jesus and his apostles were citizens of that nation and would not rightly be under obligation to pay such a tax.

Verse 27. While not strictly bound to pay this tax, Jesus decided to pay it rather than offend the collectors, and enabled Peter to get the money by a miracle.

MATTHEW 18

Verse 1. The apostles believed that the kingdom of heaven that Jesus had been announcing was to be a restoration of the old Jewish government with perhaps some additional features suited to the times. They maintained this idea even after the resurrection (Acts 1: 6). With such a system in mind it was natural for them to ask the question of this verse, for in earthly governments there are men of superiority in rank.

Verse 2. *Little child* is from PAIDION and according to Thayer it means a young child somewhat advanced in age beyond infancy; and old enough to have developed some traits of character. Jesus used this child for an illustration of the kind of temperament that would be of the greatest esteem in the kingdom of heaven.

Verse 3. *Be converted* has reference to the general rule that was to apply after the kingdom of heaven was set up, and not especially to these apostles. They had been baptized by John upon repentance and had been converted from their past course of life. But even then they were in need of a change of mind on the subject of true greatness, otherwise they would not be fit to become members of the kingdom when the time came. But the verses on this matter state the subject as it was to apply to all people in their attitude towards Jesus and his followers. *Become as little children* refers to the humility that must accompany any professed belief in Christ and desire for his kingdom.

Verse 4. The comparison is made directly in this verse. Literal children were not to become members of the kingdom, for they do not need it, but men and women must become *as* these children on the matter of humbleness.

Verse 5. *Such little child* means the same as the *little children* of verse 3. To *receive* such a person means to be friendly with him or show hospitality because of his humble character. This is to be done in the name of Christ or because he is a humble disciple of his and is trying to mold his life after his teaching.

Verse 6. To *offend* means to cause to stumble or go wrong, which indicates it has reference to those old enough to be responsible for their conduct and also liable to temptation. Such a person is called a *little one* figuratively because he has complied with verse 3. Physical death by drowning would be a mild fate in comparison with that awaiting one who has caused a humble disciple of Christ to stumble and fall.

Verse 7. *Offences* means causes of stumbling or occasions in which a person meets with temptation. *Needs be* is from ANAGKE and the simple definition of Thayer is, "necessity," and he explains his definition to mean, "imposed either by the external condition of things, or by the law of duty, regard to one's advantage, custom, argument." In a world as large as this with its multiplied hundreds of activities and other circumstances, it would be unreasonable to expect it ever to be free from these temptations. However, that does not justify any man who is responsible for some specific case of offence.

Verses 8, 9. Since each man is responsible for his own conduct, he should overcome the cause of stumbling whatever it may be in his particular case. The lesson taught by the discarding of the hand and eye is explained at chapter 5: 29, 30. *Everlasting* is from AIONIOS which Thayer defines, "without end, never to cease, everlasting." *Hell* is from GEHENNA and is explained at chapter 5: 30.

Verse 10. To despise means to belittle or treat with disrespect, especially to do so because of the humble position in life that the person has. *These little ones* are the same as are described in verse 3. *Their angels* means the guardian angels that God employs in His care for his children. In Acts 12: 15 mention is made of "his angel" when the disciples at a prayer meeting were told that Peter was at the gate. Thayer defines the original word, "angel, messenger of God," and he comments on the word as follows: "Guardian angels of individuals are mentioned in Matthew 18: 10; Acts 12: 15." We have other evidence that God uses his angels in the care and watchfulness necessary for the welfare of righteous people (Psalms 91: 11; Hebrews 1: 13; Acts 27: 23). We do not know how or when these angels work, for that is entirely in God's part of the divine providence. It is enough for us to have the assurance that such holy creatures are serving God in our behalf.

Verse 11. The American Standard Version and some other translations omit this verse on the ground that it is not in the early Greek manuscripts. But the same thought is contained in chapter 9: 13, so we lose nothing either way we consider the passage.

Verse 12. I believe this verse indicates the preceding one is genuine, for it is directly in the same line of thought. If Jesus came to save that which is lost it would be like a shepherd who would leave the sheep that were safely in the fold and go in search of the one that had gone astray.

Verse 13. We should observe that it is *rejoicing* and not merely love that the shepherd manifests over the sheep when it is found. He still esteems the 99 as highly as ever, but there is not the occasion for joyous demonstrations over them that there is for the one just recovered.

Verse 14. This verse goes back to all of the others that speak of the *little ones*. We are sure they mean the humble disciples and not literally the small boys and girls for they are not in any danger, not being responsible for their conduct.

Verse 15. When Jesus was on earth he taught many things that could apply only while he lived, and others that were to become a part of the permanent law of his kingdom. The passage starting with this verse is one of the latter, for it includes mention of the church (verse 17) and that would have to be after he had gone back to his Father. Furthermore, there is nothing in the teaching of the apostles that disagrees with this passage, hence we are bound to conclude it is a law of the Lord today. The first thing a brother should do if another does him wrong, is to tell him to his face in the absence of any other person, and without having said a word to anyone else. It may be that the brother does not realize what he has done and will gladly adjust the difficulty. In such an event the trouble will be settled and it should never be made known to another one.

Verse 16. If the conversation fails to bring a reconciliation it will be evident that a more public knowledge of the affair will have to come. As a protection against any misunderstanding, the next meeting should have one or two witnesses that all things that are said may be proved in case further dealing becomes necessary.

Verse 17. These witnesses are to be intercessors also, for this verse speaks of the possibility that the offender will not *hear* them. This denotes that it will be proper for them to have something to say in this second meeting as well as being witnesses in case further controversy is necessary. If this meeting is a failure, the matter will have to become a public affair and the offended party should take his case to the church. The church has the right to hear the complaint and the report of the witnesses, and if it concludes the accused is guilty he should be required to make proper amends. If he refuses to do so he should be excluded which is equivalent to placing him in the same class as the heathen (people of the world) in that he will be put into the realm of Satan (1 Corinthians 5: 5).

Verse 18. This verse is explained at chapter 16: 19.

Verse 19. One important function of the church is shown in verse 17 and that was still in the mind of Jesus when he spoke the words of this verse. The apostles are given special attention because they were in the church first (1 Corinthians 12: 28). But some things can be done without the presence of an apostle; the assurance of this verse comes under that class. We know that an apostle could perform his special function without the presence of another (Acts 19: 6), yet this verse requires at least that two shall

be present, hence this passage applies to disciples generally. The reason that *two* of the disciples is mentioned is that is the minimum of them that can compose a unit of the church referred to in verse 17. *Agree* is from SUM-PHONEO which Thayer defines, "To be in accord, to harmonize, i. e., to agree together." It should be understood that they must agree in the things that are right, which were to be taught in other portions of the law of Christ. In other words, the Lord wishes his church to be united in its activities and perform as a whole while in the doing of things pertaining to the spiritual welfare of all. (See 1 Corinthians 5: 4 and 2 Corinthians 2: 6.)

Verse 20. *For* is from GAR which Thayer defines, "Truly therefore, verily as the case stands," which indicates that the conclusion of this verse is based upon the truth stated in the preceding one. *In* is from EIS and the passage means for them to gather into the name of Christ. But the name of Christ is confined to his church since all authority and glory must be given him through that body (Ephesians 3: 21). Jesus will always be present in spirit when any group of two or more disciples is assembled according to verse 19 and 2 Corinthians 2: 10.

Verse 21. *Seven* is a prime number and in figurative language means completeness. The question of Peter was equivalent to asking if he should go to the limit in forgiving.

Verse 22. If seven means completeness then it would not be possible to go any further in the extension of mercy. We therefore understand the statement of Jesus here to have been spoken figuratively for the sake of emphasis.

Verse 23. See the comments at chapter 13: 3 on the scope and subject matter of the parables. No one of them was intended to cover everything pertaining to the scheme of human redemption. Some of them were suggested by a special circumstance, and then Jesus spoke a parable to compare the incident or conversation that called for it. The subject of selfishness toward those who have done us wrong, while forgetting our own sins, was suggested by the question that Peter asked of Jesus. The sins of one brother against another are illustrated by a commercial relationship, evidently because that would make the point easier to see. Yes, this parable was spoken to make the subject easier to understand, but Jesus was talking to his disciples and not to the multitude.

Verse 24. With the material subject as an illustration we would realize that ten thousand talents ($2,000,000) would constitute a great obligation.

Verse 25. According to ancient laws a debtor and his family could be sold into slavery by his creditor to recover the debt; this master threatened to use that law.

Verse 26. The servant *worshiped* his lord by falling down and humbly asking for mercy. See the long note at chapter 2: 2 for the various meanings of that word.

Verse 27. It was compassion and not financial justice that caused this lord to forgive the debt. He did not deny the existence and justice of the debt his servant owed him, but was willing to forget about it because it was so great.

Verse 28. Gratitude should have prompted this man to show kindness to all others with whom he would have any dealings. Instead, he found a man who owed him a hundred pence ($1,600) and demanded payment, at the same time handling him brutally.

Verse 29. This servant prostrated himself and made the same plea that the creditor had made to his lord, assuring him of making payment as soon as possible.

Verse 30. Another ancient law permitted a debtor to be put into prison if he failed to make payment. While there he would be induced in some way to make arrangements to pay his debt.

Verse 31. The ungrateful servant may have thought he would not be exposed to his kind master, but fellow-servants were aware of his conduct and reported it to him. Likewise man often thinks he can elude the eyes of the Lord but all things are known to Him.

Verse 32. The only reason the lord of this servant forgave his debt was that he *desired* it, not that it was a favor he had earned. In like manner we are taught that our Master is pleased for us to ask Him for the favor we seek (chapter 7: 7-11).

Verse 33. A simple request brought the remission of a vast obligation in favor of this servant. That fact should have induced him to grant this comparatively small favor that was so earnestly requested by his fellow-servant.

Verse 34. *Tormentors* is from BASANISTES and this is the only place where the word is used in the Greek New Testament. Thayer defines it, "One who elicits [obtains] the truth by the use of the rack, an inquisitor, torturor." It is used here to mean an officer who uses strong pressure to force the debtor into the acknowledgment of his debt and to take some action necessary to meet it.

Verse 35. If unworthy man will not forgive his fellow being, he need not expect the Father to forgive him, but instead to deliver him into a place of endless punishment where he will be "tormented" (Matthew 25: 46).

MATTHEW 19

Verse 1. Jesus had been in Galilee for some time and then moved into the region on the east side of Jordan. Just across the river was the territory of Judea which is the meaning of the words *coasts of Judea beyond Jordan.*

Verse 2. As usual, great crowds followed him and he healed them *there.* That was different from the way it is done or professed to be done by the false workers of miracles today, who require that the patient have faith and come back for more help.

Verse 3. Jesus answered all questions that were put to him that were of importance, and that of divorce was certainly in that class. The Pharisees were not sincerely seeking information when they asked this question, for the writer says they asked it *tempting him.* But for the benefit of others who could hear him and for those who would read it in the record, the Lord gave his explanation of the delicate subject.

Verse 4. Jesus went back to the beginning of man, and all discussions of this subject should go there for the proper basis of whatever is said. It should be observed that both words *male* and *female* are singular, showing that the Lord intended that one partner only should be engaged with another in this union.

Verse 5. *For this cause* means because God made one man for one woman to reproduce the race. That being true, they must be free from all other human beings in this relationship. That will make it necessary for the man (he being the aggressor and head in all of the social affairs of life as is evident all through the Bible) to *leave* his parental home in order to form a union with a female and thus establish another family. *Leave* is from KATALEIPO which Thayer defines, "To leave behind; to depart from, leave; to forsake, leave to one's self," etc. Certainly it does not mean that he must desert his parents in other respects, but in the matter of forming a union for the perpetuation of the race, a man must act independently with regard to this physical relationship. Most human laws regarding the "age of consent" have ignored this Biblical law of God. When a male is old enough to perform the marriage act he is instructed that he may leave his parents and contract marriage with a female. *Cleave* is from KOLLAO which Thayer defines, "To glue, glue to, glue together, cement, fasten together; join one's self to, cleave to." This "joining" is accomplished by the act that makes them one flesh according to the closing statement that *they twain shall be one flesh.*

Verse 6. *Are no more twain* is a positive proof that the fleshly union that is formed by the first intimate relationship is permanent, and not that the fact of being *one flesh* applies only at the time the act is being performed as some people teach. It is stated that God has joined this man and woman into one flesh, and the only "ceremony" that was used was the fleshly act. Were there no human laws on the subject, the fleshly act would be the only thing that would constitute marriage in heaven's sight. But as man began to multiply on the earth and social conditions became more complex, the need for laws of regulation to keep the relation between the sexes pure was recognized by human leaders and such laws were enacted. The only thing God has to do in such laws is to recognize them and to require His creatures to obey them. *What God joined . . . no man put asunder.* The Lord would not make a ruling against a sin that could not be committed. The fact that He did forbid *man* to sever this union which He alone had formed by the intimate relation proves that such a putting asunder can be committed. The only conclusion that is possible, then, is that the union will be put asunder when either party to it has relation with another; that act will form another union which will sever the preceding one.

Verse 7. It was natural for them to ask this question, for they knew that the law which Moses gave did not hold strictly to the foregoing requirements.

Verse 8. Jesus did not say that the original law of marriage had been repealed. Neither did he say that Moses ignored it and "permitted" them to divorce their wives as it is so frequently stated. There is a vast difference between permitting a thing and suffering it. The first is equivalent to an endorsement but the second means only to tolerate something under protest. The people had become so hardened in worldliness that the original law was held off for the time being. But that period of indulgence was over when Jesus spoke and man was to be held to the law of marriage as it existed from the beginning and as Jesus stated it in verses 4 and 5.

Verse 9. This verse names the only ground on which a married man or woman may be divorced and remarry lawfully in the sight of God. Fornication forms another fleshly union and automatically breaks the previous one. By that same token the innocent one is free and may remarry without committing adultery. To say that there is no exception to the law of marriage and divorce is to contradict Jesus, for he plainly says that fornication is an exception. Let it be noted that it is the remarriage where no guilt of fornication exists that constitutes the sin of adultery. There are cases where a person may need a divorce other than because of fornication on the part of the companion. In such instances the legal separation may be obtained but the said person would not have the scriptural right to remarry as long as the other one remained clear morally.

Verse 10. The disciples had heard the conversation between Jesus and the Pharisees and doubtless were given information that was very new to them. See the comments at verse 3 about answering questions for the benefit of the hearers besides those who asked them. This explanation about the strictness of the marriage relation gave the disciples a feeling of hesitancy about contracting marriage. They expressed that feeling with the saying *it is not good to marry.* They meant that the best thing for a man to do is to abstain from marriage altogether.

Verse 11. That was too strong a saying for more than one reason, and Jesus replied that not all men could receive or adopt *this saying*, meaning the words in italics in the preceding verse. Jesus meant that it would not be a good thing for men generally to adopt that rule of life, and that only certain men could safely refrain from entering the marriage relation and he proceeded to describe them.

Verse 12. The only means God created for the perpetuation of the human race was the fleshly union of the sexes. As an inducement for man to cooperate with Him in this he established the mutual attraction of the male and female for each other. Like most blessings from God, this one was subject to misuse and unlawful enjoyment. For this reason the institution of family relationship was given so that human beings could have a lawful means of gratification and at the same time accomplish the divine edict to "multiply and replenish the earth." From the foregoing truths we may understand that it is a moral risk for a man to decide against entering marriage, for he will be tempted to yield to his sexual inclinations unlawfully. But a eunuch may safely refrain from it and thus adopt the saying of the disciples "not to marry," because such a person is free from this fleshly tendency.

The Lord then named three classes of these eunuchs. The one is a person who was born without this normal function and hence would not have any inclination toward the opposite sex. Another is a man who has been mutilated by others for whatever reason, and by such action has been robbed of his manly powers. The third one is a man who has been able so to subdue this fleshly tendency that the opposite sex makes no appeal to him. The apostle Paul was one of such characters (1 Corinthians 7: 7). Outside of these three classes of eunuchs the only divine safeguard against unchastity is the institution of marriage, and the proper exercise of the function in that relationship of husband and wife. (See 1 Corinthians 7: 5.)

Verse 13. *Little children* is not figurative but means literally a small child. The parents recognized Jesus as an individual who could bestow a blessing according to his own wisdom on these helpless creatures. The disciples were still somewhat confused as to the nature of the work that Jesus intended to accomplish. With this erroneous view of it, they considered this act on the part of the people as an interruption and rebuked them in the hearing of Jesus.

Verse 14. The key word in this passage is *such*, and if the disciples had recalled the lessons of chapter 18: 1-5 they would not have uttered their rebuke. Jesus did not say that the kingdom of heaven would contain little children, but it was to have men and women who had become *such* persons by repentance and humility.

Verse 15. The Son of God would not have to make a physical contact with a person in order to bestow a blessing. The act of putting his hands on the little children was a form of caress or endearment.

Verse 16. The man who came to Jesus was evidently a Jew in good standing and understood what the law required of its followers. But he also must have learned something about Jesus and his teaching *(Master* is from a word that also means teacher), and had the idea that something very different would have to be done to obtain what he was offering to the world, hence the question stated in this verse.

Verse 17. *None good but God.* Jesus did not deny being a good person, for in John 10: 11 he even affirmed that he was the good shepherd. Since he was a member of the Godhead, he wished this man to know that in calling him good it was equivalent to calling him God, since all goodness comes from Him. He then gave the young man an answer to his question which was doubtless different from what he expected. When he told him to *keep the commandments* he did not understand to what he could have reference since the regular commandments of the law had already been his rule of life.

Verses 18, 19. He asked Jesus to specify the commands that were meant and he repeated the six of the decalogue that pertained to dealings between man and man.

Verse 20. Jesus did not question the statement of the young man that he had kept all of those laws, hence we may conclude that this claim was true. But Jesus was here to set up another kingdom with other laws, and perhaps something would need to be added to the life of this young man who had lived up to the letter of the law. He doubtless asked confidently *what lack I yet?*

Verse 21. We need not think this man was merely pretending to be interested, for there is nothing in the conversation of Jesus that indicated that he had an unfavorable feeling toward him; instead; as Mark's account gives it (chapter 10: 21) he loved the young man. But he could read the minds of men and he knew this man was a rich Jew and that he was devoted to his wealth. It is not necessarily wrong to be wealthy, but it is so when one is attached to his riches as this man was. That would constitute an "emergency" that required special legislation, hence Jesus told him the thing he lacked was the separation of his wealth from personal use and devotion of it to others.

Verse 22. This shaft "hit its mark" for the young man went away sorrowing because of his great possessions. What he ever did about it we are not told.

Verse 23. *Hardly* is from DUSKOLOS which Thayer defines, "with difficulty." The sacrifices that a rich man is called upon to make enter so deeply into his devotion to the business of getting more money, that it is difficult for him to bring about that change in his manner of life.

Verse 24. *Needle* is from RHAPHIS which Thayer defines, "a needle," and he shows that the word comes from RHAPTO which means, "to sew." Donnegan defines rhaphis, "a needle, awl, or other instrument for sewing." The Authorized version renders this verse correctly, for the words are so defined in the lexicon of the Greek language.

Verse 25. The disciples knew that a camel could not naturally go through the eye of a needle, and they took the comparison to mean that few if any persons could be saved.

Verse 26. Jesus supplied the point the disciples overlooked, namely, that a thing impossible with men does not have to be so with God. He could actually take a camel through the eye of a needle, but in doing so there would be some kind of change made in the camel's body that its earthly master could not cause it to make. A rich man can be saved, but it cannot be if he continues in his devotion and trust in his riches.

Verse 27. The apostles then saw the point and understood that the illustration of the camel and needle meant that one must go to the utmost in sacrificing his personal interests in order to secure the favors that the kingdom of heaven offers to the world.

Peter spoke to Jesus on behalf of the other apostles as he was generally the spokesman for them. He stated that they had *forsaken all* to follow Jesus and asked what it would bring to them. We should bear in mind that following Jesus as he meant it was to leave their homes bodily so as to travel over the country *with him.* (See Mark 3: 14 on being "with him.")

Verse 28. *Regeneration* is from PALIG-GENESIA which has a very extensive meaning in Greek literature, but its proper definition is, "new birth, reproduction, r e n e w a l, recreation."— Thayer. It occurs only twice in the New Testament and the other place is Titus 3: 5 where it is used in connection with "washing." Hebrews 10: 22 says that it is our bodies that are washed and the connection there also shows that it applies to persons who have been regenerated by obedience to the Gospel. Hence it is clear that Jesus was speaking of the Christian Dispensation, after the kingdom of heaven was set up and he would be its king, sitting in glory at his Father's right hand. But he arranged his rule of government by delegating the writing of the law to his twelve apostles. That law was to be in force unto the end of the world (chapter 28: 20), and in that figurative way they would be occupying the twelve thrones. *Twelve tribes of Israel* is a figure of speech based on the fact that under the Jewish system God's people were grouped into that many tribes. Under the Gospel system there is only one tribe but the law is administered by the twelve apostles, hence Christians are referred to as twelve tribes. (See Acts 26: 7; James 1: 1.)

Verse 29. These apostles had forsaken all of their earthly interests for the time being that they might be with Jesus literally in his journeys among the people. But it was not to be permanent, for, when the personal ministry of Christ was completed, they could resume their former manner of life, at least to some extent. But even that temporary self-denial was to be rewarded with such good things (Mark 10: 30 adds "now in this time"), and after the judgment it was to bring eternal life.

Verse 30. This verse is a statement of general principles. The words *first* and *last* do not always mean chronologically but sometimes are used with reference to importance. If any specific sense is to be attached to them in any case, the connection will have to be considered in determining the meaning. But the words usually mean that persons who are expected to be foremost in accepting the truth are often the least concerned, and vice versa.

MATTHEW 20

Verse 1. Jesus was still talking to his disciples when he spoke the following parable. It was to illustrate the principle mentioned and commented upon in the last verse of the preceding chapter. The application of the parable will come in verse 16, but the whole story had to be told to bring out the point. A vineyard means usually a place where grapes are grown, but the word could be understood to denote any place where plants are cultivated. *Early in the morning* means the beginning of the day, for the next time he went out it was still only the third hour of the day.

Verse 2. The penny was equivalent to about 17 cents in our money. The value of the wages is not important in the parable as it was spoken for another purpose.

Verse 3. The householder found he needed more workers and went out about the third hour (9 A. M. our time) and found *others* unemployed which indicates he had secured the first laborers in this place. *Marketplace* is from AGORA and it is defined in the lexicon of Thayer as follows: "In the New Testament the forum or public place,—where trials are held, and citizens resort, and commodities are exposed for sale." It is easy to see why a man would go to such a place to hire workmen.

Verse 4. No stipulated amount was stated but the laborers were promised whatever was right. They evidently agreed with the terms for it states *they went their way.*

Verse 5. The householder went back for more men at noon and 3 P. M. and made the same bargain for it says *and did likewise.*

Verse 6. The last time he went was about the *eleventh hour* which would correspond with our 5 P. M., an hour before quitting time at least, depending on what part of the eleventh hour it was when he hired them.

Verse 7. He asked them why they were idle and they said that no man had offered them any work. That being a valid explanation, the house-

holder engaged them to work with the same promise he made the ones hired from the third hour and on through the day. The use that is made of the "eleventh hour" item is entirely off of the purpose of the parable, but because of the widespread idea existing concerning it, I think it will be well to give some notice to it. The error to which I refer is the doctrine that a person professing repentance on his deathbed should be compared to these men in the *eleventh hour.* There is no comparison for these men went to work as soon as they had an opportunity while the deathbed man had been offered work by the Gospel ever since he was of responsible age. Also, these men had whatever was left of the eleventh hour and all of the twelfth to work, while the deathbed man has let the whole day of life go by and he has no opportunity to work at all.

Verse 8. There is no special rule in business that caused the paymaster to begin with the ones hired last. However, by telling the parable in that order Jesus brought out the idea of the lesson which is in verse 16. These men were last as to time and the chronology of events but they were first or foremost in receiving the Lord's estimation.

Verse 9. These "eleventh-hour" men did not know how much they were to receive, only that it was to be "whatever is right." They made no complaint and hence showed a willingness to be fair and agreeable.

Verse 10. *They supposed* expresses the basis on which most of the erroneous doctrines of men are formed. There is no scripture for the theories hence they rely on their own judgment and it is usually along the line of what they were wanting to begin with. These "early" laborers did not complain when the wage rate was stated, and neither was the paymaster cutting it short at the end of the day. But they were measuring themselves by others in the laboring group which is an unwise principle to act upon according to Paul in 2 Corinthians 10: 12.

Verse 11. They complained to the very man who made the bargain with them in the morning and with whom they found no fault when they hired to him.

Verse 12. *Made them equal with us* was a false accusation. The householder was only carrying out his contract as he had done with them. The "eleventh-hour" men had gone to work at the first opportunity and the others had done no better than that. When they accepted the offer of employment they knew they would have to do a full day's work which would extend through the hottest part of the work period.

Verse 13. *I do thee no wrong* was a truthful statement for the householder was living up to his contract made at the time of employment.

Verse 14. *That thine is* denotes that these men wanted more than was coming to them. When the paymaster put the penny into their hands he gave them all that was rightfully theirs. That means that had they obtained more than the penny they would have gone home with property that did not belong to them.

Verse 15. This householder could have given his money to anyone he chose regardless of all others and been within his rights since it was his own. *Eye evil because* means they had an envious eye when they saw the good favor bestowed upon the others.

Verse 16. This verse shows the point intended to be made by the parable. The ones who were first in point of time were the last (or least inclined) in showing an attitude of appreciation towards the householder, and Jesus made that application of the circumstances. While on the subject he added a statement that is not always made when the first clause is used. Many called, few chosen. The governments of the world call many men to appear for possible induction into the armed services, but when they are examined only a few pass the test and are chosen. All men are called by the Gospel and many accept the call. But only a few out of that group will qualify themselves for the final test at the judgment by a righteous life. That is why 2 Peter 1: 10 exhorts Christians to "give diligence to make their calling and election [choosing] sure."

Verse 17. *The twelve disciples* always means the twelve apostles.

Verse 18. This is the second time that Jesus made this sad prediction (chapter 16: 21). No reply was made by the apostles this time, the rebuke from Jesus to Peter on the other occasion evidently not being forgotten.

Verse 19. The Jews could condemn a man to death but they did not have the authority to execute it (John 18: 31). That is why they had to take their cases to the Roman or secular courts (here called *the Gentiles*) to get such a sentence carried out.

Verse 20. In Mark 10: 35 these brethren are identified simply as the sons of Zebedee as they would also be recognized to be in our verse. The reason for the seemingly unnecessary phrase *mother of Zebedee's children* is that she spoke for her sons, whereas the account in Mark tells us only of their desire. The woman first worshiped Jesus before asking her favor. (See the long definition of "worship" at chapter 2: 2.)

Verse 21. Since Jesus knew what was in man's mind it was not necessary for him to ask this question for information. However, it is the will of the Lord for his creatures to show their confidence in Him by asking, although he knows what they need before they ask (see chapter 6: 8). The woman's request was based on the same erroneous idea of the kingdom of heaven that people generally had while Jesus was on earth. She thought it was to be in the nature of an earthly kingdom, and that the persons who were permitted to occupy seats nearest the king would have some special advantages.

Verse 22. There was more than one reason for saying they did not know what they were asking for, one of them being their ignorance of what was in store for Jesus. But they thought they were prepared in mind to take whatever might come in their association with the king and doubtless they were sincere in their answer. While they had not asked for that experience, Jesus asked them the question and got an affirmative reply.

Verse 23. The *cup* and *baptism* are used figuratively and refer to the persecutions that were destined to come upon Christ and his followers. They indeed were to have that experience as Jesus informed them. Since Jesus was to be the king it would naturally fall to someone else to do the seating of him on the throne. That is why he said of it that it *is not mine to give.* However, he did say that the Father would give the honor to them for whom it is prepared.

Verse 24. This conversation between Christ and the two brethren was heard by the ten other apostles. We are not told why they were indignant, but evidently it was because of the ambition of the two in wanting to be seated above the others in places of authority. Jesus had already told them (chapter 19: 28) that all of them would have important positions in the kingdom which should have made them grateful and satisfied.

Verse 25. It was necessary so often for the apostles to be corrected in their erroneous notion of the kingdom of heaven, because they thought of it in the same light as the governments of the world. Jesus reminded them that in such kingdoms a person who is great is the one who has the most authority, and such a man often uses that greatness to impose upon his fellow citizens.

Verse 26. In the kingdom that Christ was going to set up, phases that would involve greatness and popularity were to be opposite those in worldly kingdoms; in the institution of Christ true greatness was to consist in service to others. *Minister* is from DIAKONOS and one meaning of the word in the lexicon is "servant."

Verse 27. *Servant* is from a different word than *minister* in the preceding verse. It is a stronger term and is compared to a slave. Such a word was used because the apostles were so much in the dark as to the character of the coming kingdom that it took unusual language to get them to see the point.

Verse 28. As a proof that the kingdom of Heaven was to be different from others, Jesus cited his own example of condescension. Although he was to be its king, he came among men as the greatest of servants, and crowned that service by giving his life.

Verse 29. As a rule there were many people following Jesus as he went from place to place but they were not all going with the same motive. Some were sincerely seeking for more teaching, some were interested in his miraculous cure of their diseases, and others were following with selfish interests in the temporal favors (John 6: 26).

Verse 30. For the significance of *son of David* see comments at chapter 15: 22.

Verse 31. The multitude did not want the journey interrupted. *Because*, etc., expresses the motive of the multitude and not the opinion of the inspired writer. The persistence of the blind men was like that of the woman of Canaan in chapter 15: 22-28 and it showed their great faith as Jesus said about the woman.

Verse 32. Jesus halted and asked the blind men what they wanted. He did not ask them to come in to him since they were blind and that would have been a hardship on them.

Verse 33. A man's eyesight is one of the most precious faculties he possesses, and it was the one thing that was uppermost in the minds of these unfortunates.

Verse 34. When Jesus so willed it he made bodily contact with persons he wished to favor. These men showed their appreciation by joining the group following Jesus.

MATTHEW 21

Verse 1. Jesus usually traveled on foot, but he was now to make a change in his mode of going and sent two of his disciples to secure the means of doing so.

Verse 2. Jesus knew all things that pertained to his activities and hence could tell the disciples what they would find in the nearby village.

Verse 3. "The earth is the Lord's and the fulness thereof" (1 Corinthians 10: 26), therefore it was right for Jesus to "commandeer" these beasts. It was not an act of taking them just because he had the authority to do so, but it was because they were needed. Take note that he needed *them* and not the mother or colt only.

Verse 4. Matthew explains that what is about to take place had been prophesied in the Old Testament and it is recorded in Zechariah 9: 9.

Verse 5. Any statement of an event may include more than is specifically mentioned but it will never take in less than is named. Verses 3 and 4 clearly stated that the mother and the colt were to be loosed and brought to Jesus. Also in verse 7 both colt and mother were brought and the people put their clothes on *them*. And now our present verse cites a prophecy which definitely predicts that Jesus was to ride on an ass *and* its colt. Most commentators believe that Jesus rode the colt only, and that the mother was taken along because of a humane feeling for the mother and her young offspring. It is true that neither of the other three accounts says a thing about the mother, but that could be accounted for by the fact that the use of an unbroken colt was the unusual feature of this event and hence it only is given notice by them. If it should be questioned how one man could ride two beasts, the explanation is that he would sit on the back of the mother and place his feet on the colt in the place of stirrups. This would identify the rider as the one foretold by the prophet, while the fact of riding only one would not be so rare as to attract attention. Even the riding of an unbroken colt would not be so unusual because somebody had to ride it for the first time, and besides this, the public crowd would not know it was an unbroken animal since it would be under control of this supernatural rider.

Verses 6, 7. This paragraph merely records the doing of the things commanded.

Verse 8. It was an ancient custom to honor an approaching dignitary by making a carpet of garments and the foliage of trees on which he might proceed. It says *a very great multitude* made this display of honor. It was at the season when the Passover was soon to be observed by the Jews, and great numbers were at Jerusalem from all over the world to attend that feast in obedience to the law of Moses.

Verse 9. *Hosanna* is a Greek word and Robinson defines it, "Save now, succor now, be now propitious." He says further that it is from a Hebrew word that means a joyful acclamation." Thayer's definition agrees with this but is more condensed. The passage means an expression of good will to him who is able to save others because he is a descendant of David. *Blessed is he*, etc., is an acknowledgment that Jesus was coming to their city in the name of the Lord.

Verse 10. The foregoing conversation was taking place as Jesus was entering the city. When he reached the inside the people were *moved*. That word is from SEIO which Thayer defines, "to shake, agitate, cause to tremble; to quake with fear." This means the citizens of the city in general who were not informed upon the state of affairs nor upon the prophecies that were being fulfilled; they were the ones *moved*. In their agitation and fright they asked *who is this?*

Verse 11. *The multitude* means the group that had been witnessing the entrance of Jesus into the city. They were aware of what was going on and what connection it had with the iden-

tity of Jesus, and they gave the information to the citizens.

Verse 12. The reader should see my comments on Deuteronomy 14: 24-26 in Volume 1 of the Old Testament Commentary. It was right to sell doves and other creatures to be used in the services at the altar, and it was necessary to have an exchange table to trade local money for the foreign, because the money brought in by foreigners was not good in the markets of Judea. But it was wrong to transact that business in the temple because it was intended for the religious services only. They having committed an outrage against the sacred temple, it was proper for Jesus to treat them as outlaws and force them' out of the place they were desecrating.

Verse 13. It is *written* is cited from Isaiah 56: 7 where the prophet was writing about the restoration of the Jews after the captivity, but where he also included some words that referred to the age of the church. Jesus called the temple as it was used then a *den of thieves* because they were taking advantage of the situation to charge undue fees for their transactions; they were profiteering.

Verse 14. This work that Jesus did was far different from that of the "thieves." They were in it for unrighteous gain while Jesus was doing good to the unfortunate people by healing their infirmities.

Verse 15. The original word for *crying* is defined in the lexicon, "to speak with a loud voice," and means the children let themselves be heard in shouting their good wishes for Jesus. The chief priests and scribes were *sore displeased* evidently because they were envious of the attention that he was receiving.

Verse 16. These envious men called the attention of Jesus to the cries of the children as if to suggest that he stop the disturbance, but in reality as an expression of their displeasure caused by their envy. The quotation Jesus made is in Psalms 8: 2, and in both places the words *babes* and *sucklings* have about the same meaning. Both mean small children but the first denotes those who are somewhat the older of the two. The simple, childlike trust that a little one shows in the existence and goodness of God is one of the sweetest things that can be seen in this world. Even those still young enough to be feeding at the breast will manifest characteristics that can be explained only by the fact that they are the handiwork of a gracious Creator.

Verse 17. Bethany was a small village about two miles from Jerusalem. Although it was an unimportant town from the standpoint of size, it was very noted by the things that took place there. It was the home of Lazarus and his two sisters where Jesus was always a welcome guest. On the present occasion we are merely told that Jesus left the presence of this envious crowd and spent a night in the quiet little village.

Verse 18. The body of Jesus was both human and divine and subject to the needs of bodily maintainance the same as other men. At this time he sought to satisfy his hunger by the use of the fig which is indeed a wholesome food.

Verse 19. In the account given at Mark 11: 13 the statement is added: "For the time of figs was not yet." Our verse says that Jesus found only leaves on the tree when he expected to find fruit also. If it was not the time for figs why would Jesus curse the tree for not having the fruit as well as the leaves? This matter is explained by the editor's note on Josephus, Wars, Book 3, Chapter 10, Section 8, as follows: "It may be worth our while to observe here, that near this lake of Gennesareth grapes and figs hang on the trees ten months of the year. We may observe also, that in Cyril of Jerusalem, Cateches, 18, section 3, which was delivered not long before Easter, there were no fresh leaves of fig trees, nor bunches of fresh grapes in Judea, so that when Mark says (11: 13), that our Saviour, soon after the same time of the year, came and 'found leaves' on a fig tree near Jerusalem, but 'no figs,' because the time of 'new figs' ripening 'was not yet,' he says very true; nor were they therefore other than old leaves which our Saviour saw, and old figs which he expected, and which even with us commonly hang on the trees all winter long."

Jesus cursed the fig tree for having leaves but no fruit, since its opportunity for bearing the one was as good as the other, regardless of whether it was the old or new crop that was expected. Many people have moralized on this circumstance and compared the leaves to the empty profession of righteousness that men make and the absence of fruit to the failure of doing one's duty to the Lord. We may make our own comparison to it for the purpose of an illustration, but nothing in the text indicates that to have been in the mind of Christ. Rather, it was just another opportunity to perform a miracle for the instruction of the disciples, for that was the only subject they discussed about it afterward. *Presently* is from PARACHREMA which Thayer defines, "Immediately, forthwith, instantly," and Robinson says, "On the spot, forthwith, straightway."

Verse 20. This verse indicates that the disciples made their remark at the time when Jesus pronounced the curse upon the tree, but according to Mark 11: 20, 21 it was the next day. However, our verse does not disagree with that for it only says "when the disciples saw it," meaning the complete withering away of the tree, and that could have been the next day. Hence we should understand the word *presently* in the preceding verse to have been used in a figurative or comparative sense.

Verse 21. For comments on the extent of faith here see chapter 17: 20..

Verse 22. In *prayer, believing* corresponds in thought with chapter 17: 21. In that passage the faith was to be connected with a season of "prayer and fasting." The part that was performed by the disciples in each instance was an evidence of their faith.

Verse 23. *When he was come into the temple* was the day after Jesus had driven the moneychangers out. It was that act the chief priests and elders meant when they called upon him for his authority to perform it.

Verse 24. Jesus never evaded any proper question that was asked of him. However, rather than directly accuse them of insincerity he chose to expose them by a counter inquiry. He promised to answer their question if they would do likewise to his.

Verse 25. The fact of John's baptism was not denied by anyone, the only question being his authority for teaching and practicing it. John either was doing so by the authority of the Lord of heaven or merely as a work of man, and they were asked to say which they thought it was. But the question, although a perfectly fair one, put them in an embarrassing position because of the inconsistency of their general conduct. If they were to admit that John's baptism was from heaven they could not explain why they did not endorse it.

Verse 26. They were afraid to accuse John of acting on man's authority because of the pressure of public opinion that was favorable to his work. These hypocritical leaders of the Jews did not have much love for the common people, yet they wanted to hold on to their esteem for the sake of popularity.

Verse 27. They refused to answer and falsely stated that they *could not* tell, for they had an abundance of evidence that John was a man of God. Jesus also refused to answer their question but did not misrepresent his position as did the Pharisees; he simply said *neither tell I you.*

Verse 28. This is a parable of two brothers and hence refers to people of the same family group. The contrast, then, is not between Jews and Gentiles as some of the parables apply. The first son was the publicans and harlots of the 31st verse, and the second was the chief priests and elders of verse 23. Both sons were asked to work for their father, likewise all ranks of Jews were invited to accept the work of preparation for the kingdom of heaven soon to be set up.

Verse 29. The publicans and harlots did not actually refuse the favors offered them, but that action of the son was supposed in order to show the better disposition in that they thought better of the offered favors than did the others.

Verse 30. This verse was virtually carried out as stated, for the chief priests and elders made great pretensions of being interested in the work of John and Jesus, but in the final test they refused to work at it.

Verse 31. The kingdom of heaven was not set up in fact in the earth lifetime of John, but his work was that kingdom in preparation, and whatever attitude anyone showed toward his work was counted for or against the kingdom.

Verse 32. *In the way of righteousness* means the way of life that John taught was righteous. But the self-righteous Jews only pretended to accept his teaching and did not actually do so (chapter 3: 7, 8; 21: 25). But the publicans accepted the teaching of John and came to his baptism and so fulfilled the parable.

Verse 33. Unlike the preceding parable, this one has to do with the Jews and the Gentiles. The Jews were God's exclusive people for 15 centuries but did not appreciate their good fortune and even mistreated the righteous prophets and other teachers who were sent among them. Finally the Gentiles were admitted into the family of God on an equal basis with the Jews. The story of the householder was told in detail to bring out these truths, some of which were still future when Jesus spoke. God was the householder and the services and benefits of the Mosaic system were "hedged" about with the Lord's oversight (Isaiah 5: 1-7).

Verse 34. It takes time to produce fruit, hence the householder did not expect any products until the proper time and then he sent special servants to get them.

Verses 35, 36. This refers to the mistreatment that the Jews showed to the prophets and other righteous teachers who were sent among them by the Lord.

Verse 37. Jesus was a Jew and was sent to that nation as the rightful heir of all that his Father possessed, and he should have been reecived with great respect.

Verse 38. Being the heir, if he could be removed there would seem to be no one to claim the property, hence the workers planned to make away with him.

Verse 39. The wicked workers carried out their plot and slew the son of the householder. It refers to the treatment that Jesus was soon to receive at the hands of the wicked Jews in thrusting him into the hands of the Gentiles to be killed.

Verses 40, 41. Jesus asked the hearers for their opinion of the case. Still thinking of some literal case of earthly relationship, they answered correctly as to what would happen to such husbandmen.

Verse 42. Jesus began opening their understanding of the parable by referring to a prediction in the Old Testament. They doubtless were aware of this statement and must have begun to see the light that was exposing them.

Verse 43. The Lord made a literal application of the parable to the Jewish nation of which his hearers were members. The nation that was to be given the kingdom was the Gentiles. This does not mean that the Jews would be barred from the kingdom of heaven, but they no longer would be the sole workers in the Master's vineyard.

Verse 44. *This stone* means Christ who is the stone of verse 42 that had been rejected by the builders, meaning the leaders in the Jewish nation. There are two applications of the illustrations about the *falling* upon the stone and its *falling upon* the victim. It would be bad enough to fall down on a stone for one would be hurt thereby, but it would be far worse for that stone to be elevated and then fall upon that same one. So the Jewish nation had stumbled over this stone and it was complaining about it. The leaders had even tossed it aside as unfit even to be used at all in the building. But it was to be elevated to be the head stone in the building and from that position was to fall (figuratively speaking) upon the nation and demolish it. That event took place in A. D. 70 when the Romans overthrew Jerusalem and disorganized the Jewish commonwealth. The illustration applies also to individuals in general. Those who "stumble at the word" (1 Peter 2: 8) will be offended in this world, and at the judgment they will be crushed by the weight of Christ's authority and sent into eternal ruin in the lake of fire prepared for the devil and his angels (chapter 25: 46).

Verse 45. The Jewish nation as a whole was to suffer in the fate predicted by the parable, but the *chief priests* and *Pharisees* were especially responsible which truth they realized when they heard the parable.

Verse 46. *Sought to lay hands* means they tried to think of some way they could use to overpower Jesus. *Feared the multitude* is to be understood in the same light as was their fear over John the Baptist in the 26th verse.

MATTHEW 22

Verse 1. Mark reports the parable of the wicked husbandmen which we have just studied in the preceding chapter. He also tells us (chapter 12: 12) that after the parable the chief priests and Pharisees left the hearing of Jesus, hence the present parable was spoken to the multitudes in general.

Verses 2, 3. This parable was to show the attitude of the Jews toward the kingdom of heaven as it contrasted with that of the Gentiles. The Lord chose a very familiar subject for the illustration, that of a marriage and the feast that was given to the guests. *Call them that were bidden.* Invitations were sent out some time before the date of the wedding, and as that time approached the invited guests were notified that the date of the wedding had arrived and for them to be present. The Jews were told in the Old Testament that the kingdom of heaven was going to be set up but no definite date was stated to them. *They would not come.* The Jews were not very responsive to the invitation offered to them to partake of the good things provided by Jesus.

Verse 4. Perhaps the invited guests did not take these servants seriously, or they thought there was no need to hurry as the time was not so near. So the king sent out more servants who told the guests that even the animals intended for the wedding feast were killed and prepared for the occasion and that they should come on. Many of these details have no direct bearing on the application but needed to be told to make the story complete. The point is that the Jews were pleaded with to accept the kingdom of Christ but they did not show the interest they should.

Verse 5. Some were more interested in their worldly possessions than in the things that pertained to their spiritual welfare.

Verse 6. Others were more active in their opposition to the work of the King and persecuted the servants. They went so far as to put to death the most prominent ones which included John the Baptist, the apostles and even the son (Jesus).

Verse 7. This verse was literally fulfilled by the wars between the Jews and the Romans. That conflict ended with the destruction of Jerusalem in 70 A. D. I shall quote from Myers Ancient History, page 499, which shows the fulfillment of this prediction: "The accession of Flavius Vespasian marks the beginning of a period, embracing three reigns, known as the Flavian Age (A. D. 69-96). Vespasian's reign was signalized both by important military achievements and by stupendous public works undertaken at Rome. After one of the most harassing sieges recorded in history, Jerusalem was taken by Titus, son of Vespasian. The temple was destroyed, and more than a million Jews that were crowded in the city are believed to have perished. The miserable remnants of the nation were scattered everywhere over the world. Josephus the historian accompanied the conqueror to Rome. In imitation of Nebuchadnezzar, Titus robbed the temple of its sacred utensils and bore them away as trophies. Upon the triumphal arch at Rome that bears his name may be seen at the present day the sculptured representation of the seven-branched golden candlestick, which was one memorial of the war."

Verse 8. *They which were bidden* means the Jews who were first called to the honors of the kingdom of heaven. Were not *worthy* or deserving on account of the way they treated the notice that it was time to come to the wedding feast.

Verse 9. When the Jews had been given the first opportunity of accepting the Gospel and they rejected it, the servants of Christ turned to the Gentiles. This is clearly taught in Acts 3: 26; 13: 46; 28: 27, 28.

Verse 10. *Highways* means the world in general whereas the first invitation was restricted to the Jews. (chapter 10: 5, 6.) *Bad and good.* Even in the world there is a difference between men both socially and morally. But no man is so bad but the Gospel can purify and redeem him, and no one is so good that he does not need its saving qualities in order to be worthy of attending the wedding feast.

Verse 11. The date setting of the parable has been changed and the time is at the end of the world when Jesus will come to claim his bride. (See Revelation 19: 7.) In the Bible an espousal or engagement for marriage is spoken of in the same sense as the actual marriage in many respects (Genesis 19: 14; Matthew 1: 20). The reason is that when two persons have pledged themselves to become husband and wife they are as bound morally as if they had entered into the relationship. In other words, an "engagement ring" would be as much of a bond morally as the "wedding ring," so that if while the first only has been offered and accepted, either party should be intimate or even familiar with a third, it would be considered as an act of unfaithfulness. That is why Paul wrote what he did about the "espousal" of the Corinthians to Christ, in the second epistle, chapter 11: 1, 2. Hence the portions of the parable we have considered thus far pertain to the courtship and engagement only, but

this verse transfers the story to the time of the actual marriage. *Had not on a wedding garment.* For the sake of unity in appearance all the guests were expected to have on a uniform especially appropriate for the occasion.

Verse 12. *And he was speechless.* It was customary for a man arranging a wedding to provide garments for the occasion so that all would be in orderly appearance. It would therefore not be on account of poverty or lack of opportunity to procure the garment that this man was not wearing one, hence he was *speechless* because he had no excuse. The garment to be worn by the guests at the marriage of the Lamb is "the righteousness of saints" (Revelation 19: 8). This robe has been provided by the Lord and offered to the espoused bride without money and without price (Isaiah 55: 1; Romans 13: 14), hence there will be no excuse for any professed Christian to appear at the day of judgment not properly adorned.

Verse 13. The figurative or illustrative part of the parable is now dropped and the direct application is made. Those who are found wanting at the day of judgment will be cast into the place of punishment spoken of in chapter 25: 46.

Verse 14. See the comments at chapter 20: 16 for the explanation of this.

Verse 15. *Took counsel* means the Pharisees consulted together to decide upon some plan to *entangle* Jesus in his talk. The word is from PAGIDEUO which occurs in no other place in the New Testament. Thayer defines it, "to ensnare, entrap," and he explains the definition to mean, "of the attempt to elicit [draw out] from one some remark which can be turned into an accusation against him."

Verse 16. *Herodians* is from the Greek word HERODIANOI. Thayer and Robinson define it the same, but the latter gives more information in his historical comments and I shall quote his definition and the comments as follows: "Herodians, partisans [those who take sides] of Herod Antipas, and therefore supporters of the Roman dominions in Palestine; which the Pharisees were not. It was consequently a political rather than a religious party; though it would seem to have embraced many Sadducees." This information explains why the Pharisees sent the Herodians to Jesus. They had no particular love for those people, but as they (the Herodians) were in sympathy with the political interests of the Romans of whom Caesar was king, they would try harder to get Jesus to say something that would get him into trouble with the government. They made their approach with a series of compliments that were pure flattery as verse 18 shows.

Verse 17. In their ignorance of the nature of the kingdom of heaven they thought that Jesus would be opposed to all other governments. Were that the case he naturally would oppose giving them financial support. Had he answered them to that effect it would have been ground for accusing him of disloyalty to the "powers that be."

Verse 18. Jesus called these men *hypocrites* because they pretended they wanted information, when they knew that was not the case as verse 15 plainly indicates.

Verse 19. Jesus met the situation in a manner that was doubtless unexpected. Instead of answering their question with a direct yes or no, he asked for a piece of the very kind of money that was being used in paying for the government's finances.

Verse 20. *Image and superscription* means the human likeness on a coin, and the words that are stamped on it in connection with the image. The coins of all nations are made with the likeness either of their rulers or other important persons in the government. The key to the difficulty which confronted these hypocrites is in the words of Christ after they handed him the coin, *whose . . . is this?*

Verse 21. In their answer they committed themselves beyond recall, for they directly said the whole thing belonged to Caesar, the very article that he was asking people to give to him as tribute. No one would say it is not "lawful" to give to a man what belongs to him. They had said this money belonged to Caesar, hence it would be lawful to give it back to him. And by the same token it would be right to give to God what belongs to him, namely, their religious devotion.

Verse 22. Robinson defines the original for *marveled*, "to wonder, to be astonished, to be amazed." Hence we are not to get the idea these hypocrites had any great respect for Jesus, but they were so defeated in their attempt to entrap him that they were capable only of silent astonishment.

That is why they *left him and went their way* with nothing more to say.

Verse 23. See at chapter 16: 12 for more complete details on the doctrine of the Sadducees. *The same day* was the day the Herodians failed in their attempt to entrap Jesus, and the Sadducees thought they would try it. It is a proper argument to confront a man with an actual inconsistency that comes from his teaching, for whenever a man is inconsistent he is bound to be wrong, but the Sadducees either misunderstood or wilfully misrepresented the Lord's position concerning the resurrection. He did not teach that men would resume their earth life after they came from the grave. Neither did he teach that the resurrected righteous (and they are the only ones being considered here) could engage in such a manner of life even if they desired.

Verse 24. They correctly repeated the law of Moses on this subject which is recorded in Deuteronomy 25: 5, which also was a ruling of Judah in Genesis 38: 8, 9 in the Patriarchal Dispensation.

Verses 25-28. The Sadducees described a case (whether supposed or actual does not matter) in which they thought the position of Jesus would find great difficulty. It is evident that if a woman should meet seven men alive, each of whom had legally been her husband, she would be embarrassed to say the least as also would the men. But their supposed problem was based on the theory that human beings were to recognize each other after the resurrection in the same way they did when they lived on the earth. There are some Sadducees now with reference to this matter of future recognition. Such a theory is fathered by the wish which is based on a fleshly desire, and which has to deny the teaching of 1 Corinthians 15: 42-54; Philippians 3: 21; 1 John 3: 2.

Verse 29. *Err, not knowing the scriptures.* At the time Jesus was speaking the New Testament had not been written, hence he had reference to the Old Testament. That book does not say much about the future state, yet had the Sadducees been as familiar with it as they pretended to be they would have understood that in the next world the marriage relation will not be continued because it will not be needed. The beginning paragraphs of Genesis reveal the command given to the first man and woman to multiply and replenish the *earth*. After the earth ceases to be there will be no need for the marriage relation. *Nor the power of God.* The Sadducees supposed they could disprove the truth of a resurrection by describing a situation that would make it impossible without causing great domestic trouble. They should have understood that nothing is "too hard for the Lord" (Genesis 18: 14).

Verse 30. Note it 'does not say the saved of earth will become angels, but they will be *as* angels, and that only as regards the marriage relation for they are without sex. It is true that whenever the Bible makes any reference to the gender of angels it is always the masculine. That is due to a rule of language that when reference is made to intelligent creatures by a pronoun, if the gender is not specifically known the masculine is always used.

Verse 31. Jesus was going to make a reference to the Scriptures (which he said they did not know) to prove that another life is taught in them. The Sadducees professed to believe that writing, so they should be impressed with what will be shown to them.

Verse 32. The passage referred to is in Exodus 3: 6. The argument Jesus made was based on two great truths. God is not the God of the dead as the Sadducees would admit; yet Abraham, Isaac and Jacob had been in their graves for centuries. The conclusion is, then, that although the bodies of these patriarchs were dead, something else about their beings was still living. And if their spirits can live outside of their fleshly bodies, there should be no difficulty in believing that they could be reunited with those bodies and thus be resurrected.

Verse 33. No wonder the multitudes were astonished at the doctrine (teaching) of Jesus, for it put the Sadducees to silence.

Verse 34. The Pharisees *were gathered together* for the purpose of consultation as in verse 15. Their object was to plot some way of entrapping Jesus in his talk.

Verse 35. Thayer defines the original for *lawyer* as follows: "One learned in the law, in the New Testament an interpreter and teacher of the Mosaic law." Because of his profession this man could pretend to be interested in the law, and hence his approach to Jesus would have an outward appearance of being an honest one. However, the inspired writer says his purpose in asking the question was to tempt Jesus.

Verse 36. The question would seem to be prompted by a good motive since it pertained to the law. But it was unfair because the Lord never put any more of His authority behind one commandment than another. (See James 2: 10, 11.) Had Jesus specified one command as being greater than another, the lawyer would have accused him of showing discrimination between things that were equal as to their divine origin.

Verse 37. Jesus stated to him the commandment that requires wholehearted love for God, against which even this lawyer could not have any objection.

Verse 38. The Lord did not say that even this was the greatest, only that it was great. And it was great because it was the *first* one, which was proper since it pertained to God, and everyone would agree that God comes before all other beings.

Verse 39. If the lawyer thought he had caught something by the word *great* on which to make an ado, he was soon deprived of that motive because Jesus said the next one was *like* it. He then stated the commandment to love one's neighbor as one's self.

Verse 40. The first four commandments pertain especially to man's attitude toward God, and the other six have to do with man to man. (See Exodus 20: 1-17.) If a man loves God with all his heart he will observe the four commandments that pertain to Him; and if he loves his neighbor as himself, he will observe all of the six that pertain to that neighbor. That is why Jesus said that the whole law and prophets *hang* on these two. That word is from KREMANNUO which Thayer defines, "To be suspended, to hang," and he explains it as follows: "The meaning is, all the law and the Prophets (i. e., the teaching of the Old Testament on morality) is summed up in these two precepts."

Verse 41. The Pharisees had been trying to entrap Jesus with questions they thought could not be truly answered. That is, could not without contradicting something in his teaching, but they failed as we have seen. Now the Lord turned and put a question to them that was fair, and yet which would be impossible to explain without exposing some of their opposition to him.

Verse 42. The Pharisees did not profess to dislike Jesus (they dared not because of public opinion, chapter 21: 46), but pretended to regard him only as a good man and not divine. When they answered the question of Jesus by saying he was the son of David they only recognized his blood relation to the great ancestor, not that he was anyone higher than a human being.

Verse 43. If Christ was no more to David than an earthly descendant why did he call him Lord. This question was based on a statement in Psalms 110: 1 which the Pharisees would have to accept unless they denied the Scriptures which they would not do.

Verse 44. The first *Lord* is God and the second is Christ. The pronoun *my* in the first instance refers to David and the second to God. Using names instead of pronouns, the verse means that God invited Christ to sit on His right hand until He had made Christ's enemies his (Christ's) footstool. The point at issue is that in this statement David acknowledged Christ to be his Lord.

Verse 45. The argument of Jesus was, how could David recognize Christ as his Lord if he was only his son as the Pharisees claimed.

Verse 46. The verse says that no man could answer the question. The reason is that they either did not know or were unwilling to acknowledge the divine-human character of Christ's being. This put an end to the tempting questions of the multitude, for they were completely defeated in their hypocritical attacks on the great Teacher.

MATTHEW 23

Verse 1. The audience that heard this remarkable chapter was composed of the *multitude* and the *disciples*. The first 12 verses were addressed to that part of the multitude designated *scribes and Pharisees*, and what should be the attitude of the disciples toward that group.

Verse 2. Moses wrote the law that was to regulate the Jews during that dispensation. After he died it was the duty of others to teach and enforce it upon the nation, and that was a work done by the scribes and Phari-

sees which is the meaning of their *sitting in Moses' seat.*

Verse 3. The scribes and Pharisees had no authority on their own account, but the law which they enforced was just as binding as was the personal teaching of Moses while he was living. The inconsistency of a teacher does not lessen the force of what he teaches if it is according to the law. These scribes and Pharisees were hypocrites and failed to "practice what they preached," yet the disciples were told to obey the law regardless of the unfaithfulness of these teachers; that was because the law of Moses was still in force at the time Jesus was speaking. Note the two words *observe* and *do* that were to be recognized by the disciples. A truth or declaration should be *observed* or respected although it may not contain any direct command for action. But a practical commandment must be not only observed but also must be *done.*

Verse 4. The scribes and Pharisees would apply the duties taught in the law in a severe measure when concerned with others. *With one of their fingers* is a figure of speech, for a burden that could be moved with one finger would not be very heavy. It means they were not willing to exert themselves in the least toward practicing the commandments of the law. One reason they took such an attitude was the fact that they exaggerated the duties actually required by the law in order to oppress the common people.

Verse 5. *Their works* refers to the things these hypocrites did, which were done with a vain motive and that they might be seen of men. "Make broad their phylacteries" may be explained by a quotation from Smith's Bible Dictionary as follows: "Phylacteries were strips of parchment, on which were written four passages of Scripture, Exodus 13: 2-10, 11-17; Deuteronomy 6: 4-9, 13-23, in an ink prepared for the purpose. They were then rolled up in a case of black calfskin, which was attached to a stiffer piece of leather, having a thong one finger broad and one and a half cubits long. They were placed at the bend of the left arm. Those worn on the forehead were written on four strips of parchment, and put into four little cells within a square case on which the letter . . . was written. The square had two thongs, on which Hebrew letters were inscribed. That phylacteries were used as amulets [charms] is certain and was very natural. The expression 'they make broad their phylacteries,' Matthew 23: 5, refers not so much to the phylactery itself, which seems to have been a prescribed breadth, as to the case in which the parchment was kept, which the Pharisees, among their other pretentious customs, Mark 7: 3, 4; Luke 5: 33, etc., made as conspicuous as they could. It is said that the Pharisees wore them always, whereas the common people only used them at prayers." *Borders* is from KRASPEDON which Thayer defines, "A little appendage hanging down from the edge of the mantle or cloak." He explains his definition, "The Jews had such appendages attached to their mantles to remind them of the law, according to Numbers 15: 37." For more detailed comments on this curious subject, see those at Numbers 15: 37-41 in volume 1 of the Old Testament Commentary.

Verse 6. *Rooms* means places at the table while eating, some of them being regarded as more honorable than others. *Chief seats* means the first or front seats in the synagogues that gave the occupants a prominent view of the audience.

Verse 7. *Markets* were places of general interest where men gathered either to buy or to sell their wares, or to converse on various topics. It was usual to see large crowds in such places and they were so public that no one was of any special importance; but these scribes and Pharisees wished to receive special notice by the crowd. The Mosaic system had no officials with the title of *Rabbi;* the term was created by the Jews to mean one of dignity and respect. It carried with it the idea of some great one deserving special attention. Thayer defines the original, "My great one, my honorable sir." The Pharisees wanted it repeated to give it more emphasis.

Verse 8. The titles of distinction could be used with various intent, hence that of Rabbi could denote a great leader which was not to be ascribed to private disciples.

Verse 9. By the process of elimination we know this verse does not mean our fleshly father for that is a respect all men are commanded to show. Nor can it mean in the sense of one who leads us to be born into the kingdom, for Paul claimed that relationship to Timothy (1 Timothy 1: 1). The conclusion is clear, then, that this verse

means not to call any man *father* as a religious title or one of authority.

Verse 10. The original for *master* not only means a leader, but also denotes a great and authoritative teacher. Christ is the only one in the kingdom of heaven that is deserving of that distinction (chapter 28: 18).

Verse 11. This is explained in comments on chapter 18: 1-4.

Verse 12. We have learned that true greatness consists of sincere humility and a desire to be of service to others. But if a man strives for worldly greatness he will be brought down by the Lord under a state of enforced humiliation.

Verse 13. Up to now Jesus has been talking to his disciples in this chapter, and a part of that conversation has been about the scribes and Pharisees. From here to the close of the chapter he will be speaking directly to them. A hypocrite is one who pretends to be something he knows he is not. (See at chapter 6: 2.) These Jews knew that their pretensions were false as their evasive conversations showed. *Shut up the kingdom.* They not only refused to receive the teaching of John and Jesus and thus get ready for the kingdom that was at hand, but did all they could to keep others from doing so. Eight times in this chapter Jesus pronounces *woe* upon the scribes and Pharisees. The word is an interjection and means a term of grief or dismay, and when spoken by an inspired man means that great calamity is in store for those referred to.

Verse 14. *Devour* is from KATESTHIO which Thayer defines at this place, "To devour i. e., forcibly appropriate." *Houses* is from OIKIA and the same lexicon defines it in this passage, "Property, wealth, goods." They took advantage of the unfortunate widows who were helpless because of the power of the scribes and Pharisees. After enlarging their own estates at the unjust expense of the widows, they came to the places of devotion and uttered prayers that were unusually long. *Greater damnation.* The Bible speaks of only one Gehenna or lake of fire into which the unsaved will be cast after the judgment, therefore the actual punishment will be the same for all who are put into that place. The second word in italics also means condemnation and applies to the estimate that the Lord will place on the wrong deeds of these men. A judge may sentence two men to prison for life, yet he may utter a severer condemnation upon one while in his speech of pronouncing sentence than upon the other.

Verse 15. The English word "proselyte" means one converted or brought over from one faith to another. The word has virtually the same meaning in the Bible, for the Gentiles were permitted to embrace Judaism, and when they did so they were called proselytes. The Jews recognized a distinction between the extent to which some Gentiles made the change which resulted in such classifications as "proselytes of the gate" and "proselytes of righteousness." The latter went farther than the former and conformed to all of the requirements of the law of Moses. But this distinction need not concern us as far as the present verse is concerned. The point is that the scribes and Pharisees professed great zeal in making proselytes, but through their deceptive methods of pressing their own traditions upon the converts ahead of the written law, they confused them and made them worse characters than themselves. *Twofold more the child of hell.* This is plainly a figurative statement, for no one can be any more than once a child of another. The word *child* is used in the sense of one who is worthy of or entitled to a thing. This should be understood in the light of comments on "greater damnation" in the preceding verse.

Verse 16. The point in this verse is their inconsistency of making a technical distinction between things where there was no difference in principle. It was a usual practice of these pretenders to make a show of importance by performing oaths, yet they evaded their self-assumed obligation by naming the temple in their oaths and claiming it was not binding. But they insisted that if others made their vows in the name of the gold attached to the temple they would not dare break it since the gold was holy.

Verse 17. Jesus showed their inconsistency in that if the gold was sacred it was the temple that made it so, being attached to and forming a part of the structure.

Verses 18-22. The same argument is made in these verses as that in verse 17. The attachment between the altar and the gift upon it, or between the temple and Him who dwells therein (who is God), or between heaven and the throne therein with its Occupant—that attachment makes the obligation equal all around. The word *guilty* in verse 18 means the same as *debtor* in the 16th verse; the person is under obligation to perform the oath.

Verse 23. The Jews were required by the law to give a tenth of the products of their land to the Lord's service. The plants named were small ones of the mint family and of small value commercially, yet these Pharisees were very scrupulous to turn over the *tithe* (tenth) as required. At the same time they were so attentive to those comparatively small matters, they were indifferent about such weighty matters as judgment, mercy, and faith. Notice Jesus did not say for them to replace the one by the other, but to observe both the small and great things.

Verse 24. The point in this verse is the same as in the preceding one but expressed with different terms. Both the gnat and camel were among the creatures classed as unclean by the law of Moses. When the Jews made wine they strained it through a fine cloth to get out all the objectionable objects. Strain *at* should be translated strain *out*, and means they were so particular about having the wine pure they would strain out a gnat, but would swallow a camel (figuratively speaking). The meaning is, they would make a big ado about minor matters but overlook the duties of great importance.

Verse 25. This verse is intended to teach the same lesson as the preceding one by using the figure of a cup kept for drinking purposes. The inside is where the material is placed that is to be consumed, not the outside. By cleansing the outside instead of the inner part, they showed that their pretended care in the cleansing performance was for the appearance only.

Verse 26. The activities necessary for cleansing the inside would also affect the outside if the process should be carried out completely and sincerely.

Verses 27, 28. The inconsistency and hypocrisy of the scribes and Pharisees is the principal subject of many of these verses, and Jesus uses various figures and comparisons for his purpose. *Whited sepulchres* is the object used in this paragraph for the comparison, and the occasion of their being whited is explained in Smith's Bible Dictionary as follows: "A natural cave enlarged and adapted by excavation, or an artificial imitation of one, was the standard type of sepulchre. Sepulchres, when the owner's means permitted it, were commonly prepared beforehand, and stood often in gardens, by roadsides, or even adjoining houses. Kings and prophets alone were probably buried within towns. 1 Kings 2: 10; 16: 6, 28. Cities soon became populous and demanded cemeteries, Ezekiel 39: 15, which were placed without the walls. Sepulchres were marked sometimes by pillars or by pyramids. Such as were not otherwise noticeable were scrupulously 'whited,' Matthew 23: 27, once a year, after the rains before the passover, to warn passers-by of defilement."— Article, *burial.* The beautiful appearance of these whitewashed places contrasted with the decayed and unclean bones within, and the fact was used by Jesus to illustrate the outward fair pretentions of the hypocrites that were opposite to the corruptions of their hearts.

Verse 29. The prophets had been dead for centuries and were placed in tombs at the time of their death. The word for *build* is defined at this place by Thayer, "To restore by building, to rebuild, repair." To *garnish* is defined, "To ornament, adorn." There was nothing wrong in the work of these scribes and Pharisees respecting the treatment of the burial places of the prophets.

Verse 30. Neither would there have been anything objectionable about what they said regarding the history connected with those prophets, had the remarks been in harmony with their own conduct in the same matters which were the subject of the history.

Verse 31. The point Jesus made was upon the admission of these pretenders that it was their fathers who had slain the prophets. That fleshly relation would not have placed any blame on them had it not been a prominent practice of them to justify their lives by boasting of their great ancestry.

Verse 32. This verse is partly in a sense of irony. It is as if Jesus had said: "Since you are the fleshly descendants of those murderers, you may be expected to show their traits in their moral and spiritual character. In so doing you will fully measure up to the wickedness of your ancestors."

Verse 33. *Serpents* and *vipers* are virtually the same creatures as to general classification, being slightly different in variety. The outstanding characteristics of both are deception, poison and filthiness. John the Baptist called those people by the term "vip-

ers" in chapter 3: 7. *How can ye escape, etc.* The fire of *hell* (Gehenna) will have been prepared for the devil and his angels (chapter 25: 41), hence it will logically be the final destiny of the offspring of such wicked characters.

Verse 34. Jesus concluded his direct denunciation of the scribes and Pharisees, and the rest of this speech is made up of predictions against them soon to be fulfilled. He began it by foretelling how they would abuse the righteous men and prophets that would yet be sent to them in that generation.

Verse 35. See the comments on verse 32. By *filling up the measure* of their wicked ancestors, the scribes and Pharisees brought to a climax the long career of murder beginning with the slaying of Abel and including Zacharias in 2 Chronicles 24: 20, 21.

Verse 36. *All these things* means the predictions and charges of the two preceding verses, together with the judgments that were soon to come upon that generation.

Verse 37. The storm that Jesus just predicted was to have its climax upon the capital city of Jerusalem. Seeing that calamity so near, he uttered the lamentable words of this verse. The many attempts to awaken the city to a sense of its evils and the results to follow are compared to the care that a hen manifests in offering her wings for the protection of her brood. And the refusal of the citizens to accept that warning is compared to a flock of chickens that would not come under the wings spread out for them.

Verse 38. *Desolate* is from EREMOS which Thayer defines, "Solitary, lonely, desolate, uninhabited." The word is used figuratively and represents Jerusalem as a house that has resisted all attempts to save it. The city had continued in its attitude of wickedness, unmindful of all the offers of mercy that Jesus extended towards her, and he then sadly left her to her fate that was to come in 70 A. D. by the hand of the Romans.

Verse 39. *Blessed is he that cometh,* etc., was said before (chapter 21: 9), so that we may think of the present statement as if it said "till ye shall AGAIN say." However, the other time it was said to him in person, while the next time it will be said to him spiritually. And that cannot be when he *cometh in his kingdom* on Pentecost, for it was to be after the "house" was left desolate which did not come till 70 A. D. at the destruction of Jerusalem. Hence all conclusions are eliminated except that it means when the Jews accept Christ (Romans 11: 26; 2 Corinthians 3: 14-16). When that time comes the name Jerusalem will be extended to mean the spiritual starting point of the church and hence its citizens (including the Jews), will recognize Jesus as the Messiah of the Old Testament and will thus say "blessed is he that cometh in the name of the Lord."

MATTHEW 24

Verse 1. The speech of Jesus recorded in the preceding chapter took place in the temple that was the pride of the Jews. After going out, the disciples called his attention to the *buildings* (architecture) of the structure, evidently admiring its wonderful appearance which the Jews boasted of requiring "forty and six years" to construct as we may read in John 2: 20.

Verse 2. The remarks of the disciples gave an opportunity that was appropriate for Jesus to make an important prediction. He made the simple statment that not one stone would be left resting upon another. In Luke 19: 43, 44 a more detailed account of the disaster is given, in which it is shown how it was to be accomplished.

Verse 3. The disciples had learned from the teaching of Jesus that the world was someday to come to an end. (See chapter 11: 22, 24; 12: 41, 42; 13: 39.) Because of that teaching they erroneously concluded that the predictions about the destruction of the temple were to be fulfilled at the same time as the end of the world. They also understood that the destruction of the world was to occur when Jesus comes again. With these ideas in mind they asked him to tell them *when shall these things be.* That was the one and only question they intended to ask, and the rest of the verse is only a specification of the things they thought were to happen at the time of the end of the world. However, their intended single question involved two great events, namely, the destruction of Jerusalem and the end of the world which we now know to have been at least nineteen centuries apart.

Because of the radical conditions and various human transactions to occur in connection with the destruction of Jerusalem, Jesus knew that ambitious men would take advantage of the disturbed state of affairs to make statements about the coming of Christ the second time and thus de-

ceive the people. In order to prepare the disciples against being so deceived, he gave them the teaching that is in this memorable chapter. He gave a description of things to occur at the destruction of Jerusalem, then went ahead to his second coming and depicted some of the things to happen then. He alternated these two subjects throughout the chapter, going back and forth from one to the other in more or less detail, so that his disciples could see the difference between the two events and thus not be deceived. There are a few intervening verses not directly connected with either of the main subjects which will be explained as we come to them. With those exceptions, the chapter should be marked off as follows. Verses 4-26, destruction of Jerusalem; verse 27, 2nd coming of Christ; verse 28, destruction of Jerusalem; verses 30, 31, 2nd coming of Christ; verses 34, 35, destruction of Jerusalem; verses 36-51, 2nd coming of Christ. Trusting the reader will constantly observe which group of verses we are in, I shall now comment upon the verses in their order.

Verse 4. The warning to *take heed* indicates a condition that might be misunderstood or even unnoticed if it were treated with an attitude of indifference. By heeding the signs Jesus gave, the disciples would be able to detect the false prophets.

Verse 5. *Come in my name* means they will take upon themselves the name of Christ as they come among the people. Just because they will be wearing that name they will deceive many who will not look any farther into the subject than the sound of the name.

Verse 6. The destruction of Jerusalem was brought about by the war between the Jews and the Romans. That conflict did not begin in Judea but was going on farther up in Palestine for some time before. The report of the battles in the distance reached the ears of the people in Judea, and that is why Jesus said they would *hear of wars and rumors of wars. Be not troubled . . . end is not yet.* The first rumors of war will not mean that *the end* of Jerusalem is right upon them.

Verse 7. The Roman Empire was composed of many nations, and when the war against the Jews broke out it threw the whole empire into commotions. These various smaller units of governments in the empire were thrown into confusion and many of them began fighting each other. A state of war often produces shortages in the necessities of life which brings famine and pestilence. A literal earthquake is never caused by warfare, but God has brought them about at numerous times to mark His concern for the conditions. In the present case it was one of the signs the disciples were given by which they could see the approaching storm.

Verse 8. The word *sorrows* is from ODIN which Thayer defines, "the pain of childbirth, travail-pain, birth-pang." The suffering destined to come upon the nation and city of the Jews is compared to the pangs of childbirth. And as the full development of those pains are preceded by brief and comparatively light ones, warning the expectant mother that her time is near, so these rumors of wars reaching the ears of the people of Jerusalem are compared with the preliminary labor pains.

Verse 9. The preceding verse deals with the conditions a short time prior to the actual suffering in Judea, and the present one brings their history down upon the area itself. *Deliver you up* means the persecutions that were to be imposed upon the Jewish citizens by the Romans, especially those who had become Christians.

Verse 10. There will be several references in this chapter to Josephus' history of the wars of the Jews and Romans. That history is divided into books, chapters and paragraphs or sections. For the sake of brevity and also clearness, the reader should understand that the numbers used in the references will mean those three divisions respectively. The confusion caused by the war resulted in much violence even between the Jews. I shall quote from Josephus, 5-6-1. "Now while the factions fought *one against another*, the people were their prey, on both sides, as we have said already; and that part of the people who would not join with them in their wicked practices, were plundered by both factions. . . . And when the parts that were interposed between their possessions were burnt by them, they left a space wherein they might *fight with each other;* for this internal sedition did not cease even when the Romans were encamped near their very walls . . . for they never suffered anything that was worse from the Romans than they *made each other suffer.*"

Verse 11. This is the same prediction that is made in verse 5.

Verse 12. Many people are affected by their surroundings whether good or bad. *Iniquity* means a state of lawlessness, and because that condition was coming upon the country a great number of disciples were going to become cold in their love for God.

Verse 13. *Endure unto the end* first means to remain faithful to the Lord until the end of that war. It would also be true of those who might be slain in the general turmoil provided they were faithful till death.

Verse 14. *World* is from a Greek word that Thayer defines, "The inhabited earth." *The end* means the end of Jerusalem as the climax of the war. That event occurred in 70 A. D., and the Gospel was to have been offered to all the nations of the (civilized) world by that time. Hence the great commission of the apostles (chapter 28: 19 and Mark 16: 15) was fulfilled in the first century, which agrees with Romans 10: 18 and Colossians 1: 23. The Lord was not willing for Jerusalem to be destroyed until the Gospel had been offered to the entire extent of human inhabitants on earth, hence He supervised the whole revolution as far as the dates were concerned.

Verse 15. The prediction referred to is in Daniel 9: 27; 11: 31. *Abomination of desolation* means the Roman army and it is so called because its presence and effects will bring a state of desolation to the city of Jerusalem. *Stand in the holy place* is referred to by the words *standing where it ought not* in Mark 13: 14. It is so described because the area around Jerusalem was regarded as holy ground, and the presence of a hostile heathen army was considered as a desecration of the place.

Verse 16. However offensive the presence of a Roman army would seem, the Lord used it as a signal for his disciples to flee for safety while it was possible. In the church history of Eusebius, chapter 5, in a foot note is the following. "But the people of the church in Jerusalem had been commanded by a revelation, vouchsafed [guaranteed as safe] to approved men there before the war, to leave the city and to dwell in a certain town of Perea called Pella."

Verse 17. Houses had flat roofs and the buildings were joined one against another even unto the end of the street at the wall. If a man had gone up there for some reason and saw the army of the Romans near he did not need to come down, but could go from one roof to another until he reached the wall.

Verse 18. The man in a field should not regard his personal belongings at home of more importance than his safety, and hence it would be better to flee immediately for safety.

Verse 19. Women in the condition described could not well travel.

Verse 20. Wintry weather would not be convenient time to travel. *Neither on the sabbath day.* The law of Moses has nothing to say about a "Sabbath-Day's Journey," but that was a tradition of the Jews based on a strained interpretation of Exodus 16: 29 and Joshua 3: 4. On that ground the pious Jews in the time of Christ thought it was wrong to travel more than two thousand cubits on the sabbath day. A person attempting to go further on that day would be hindered by these Jews who would seek to punish him for what they thought was a violation of the law. Jesus was not endorsing the tradition, but he knew it would be an obstacle against speedy traveling and hence expressed the prayerful wish on behalf of his disciples.

Verse 21. That the predictions of this verse were fulfilled can be proved by a number of historians. However, I shall quote from Josephus only on this point because he was a Jew and hence had a genuine interest in that nation. Moreover, not being a Christian, his testimony as a historian that so completely verifies the predictions of Jesus will be of special value. I will first quote direct from his own estimate of the sufferings of the Jews in Jerusalem in his preface to the history of the war. "Because it had so come to pass, that our city Jerusalem had arrived at a higher degree of felicity [happiness] than any other city under the Roman government, and yet at last fell into the sorest calamities again. Accordingly it appears to me, that the misfortune of all men, from the beginning of the world, if they be compared to those of the Jews, are not so considerable as they were; while the authors of them were not foreigners neither." If Josephus had intended to point out the exact fulfillment of Christ's predictions, he could not have used stronger language. That was not his purpose, for he was not a disciple of Jesus and hence had no personal interest in him. But he was an able and truthful historian and gave us the facts of history. In giving the readers some details of the sufferings endured by the people in the city I shall not quote verbatim as it would require too much space. Instead, I shall make the statements and give the references to his history of the Jewish war, that the reader may find them and see the full account by consulting the volume, The Wars of the Jews.

The troubles of the people of Jerusalem during the war were many and great for they were divided into three seditious factions (5-1-1), provisions were wantonly destroyed (5-1-4), they ate corn unground and uncooked (5-10-2), children would snatch the last morsel from the parent, and the mother from the infant. Children were lifted from the ground by the food they held in their mouths. People were beaten who ate their food before the robbers arrived. Those who were suspected of having hidden some food were tortured by having sharp stakes driven up into their lower bowels (5-10-3), and the famine consumed whole families. Many died as they were burying others. There was no lamentation as the famine confounded all natural passions. A stupefying silence and awe overcame them (5-12-3). Some had swallowed their money, and then had their bodies ripped open by robbers (5-14-4). Some searched the sewers and manure piles for food (5-13-7) and ate hay, old shoes and leather (6-3-3). A mother roasted and ate her son (6-3-4); bloodshed was so great as to quench fire in the houses (6-8-5).

Verse 22. If the conditions in Jerusalem that have been predicted should continue indefinitely, no one would be able to survive the ordeal. *Elect* is from EKLEKTOS which Thayer defines in this and many other passages, "1. chosen by God, to obtain salvation through Christ," and other passages teach us that what one gets through Christ is to be accomplished through obedience to his commandments. When the siege and turmoil in Jerusalem came upon the city and surrounding territory, there were many men and women of both Jews and Gentiles who had become Christians and they are the ones meant by *the elect.* For the sake of these persons the Lord decreed to bring the conflict to a close as soon as the general purpose of it had been accomplished.

Verse 23. *Then* means while these times of tribulation were going on. The false prophets would use the disturbed condition as a pretext for pointing to some outstanding men and calling some one of them by the name of Christ and that the 2nd coming was upon the world. The warning was that such agitators were not to be believed.

Verse 24. These false prophets were to be able to make such an application of the unusual happenings that even the *elect* (the Christians) would almost be misled by it. The faith of these elect of God in the teaching of Christ was so great that it made them easy victims of the shrewd false prophets. *If it were possible* means that the *elect* would really be deceived had not Christ forewarned them.

Verse 25. This short verse is for the purpose of defeating the plots of the false prophets to mislead the elect, by impressing the seriousness of it on them beforehand.

Verse 26. On the basis of the general warning that was given by Christ, the disciples were not to pay any attention to the false prophets. They would think to mislead the multitudes by claiming that Christ had come for a certainty, but that it would be necessary to make a special search for him. They will even announce that Christ is hiding in some secret place or was strolling out in the desert. Jesus warned them not to believe any such statements because that was not to be the manner of his second coming.

Verse 27. Having warned against letting false prophets take advantage of the disturbed conditions at the time of the Jewish wars to announce the second coming, Jesus then goes over to that event to explain how it will be then. That is why this verse was listed in the comments at verse 3 as the "second coming of Christ." The universal and simultaneous appearance of Jesus at his second coming is compared to that of a flash of lightning. It does not appear in spots only and require that one's attention be called to it before it is observed. When Jesus comes he will be seen by all classes at the same time (Revelation 1: 7). There are false prophets in the world today who have been predicting the second coming of Christ, even setting the very date when it was to occur. But the dates all proved to be wrong, so in order to "save face" they

have changed their story and now declare that he did actually come but was seen only by his "witnesses." The prophecy of Jesus and John contradicts the theory and shows that all of these so-called "witnesses" are frauds.

Verse 28. This verse comes back to the destruction of Jerusalem, in which Jesus uses a habit of birds hovering about a dead creature preparatory to devouring it. Were a bird seen flying around over a certain place we would understand that he scented something which he intended soon to attack for food. This very practice of an eagle is referred to in Job 39: 30. The same is used figuratively in the case of our subject, because the eagle was inscribed on the banners of the Roman army. (Josephus, Wars, 3-6-2.) The fact was mentioned as another sign that would indicate the attack of the Romans upon Jerusalem, seeing the ensigns gathering round the city as a flock of eagles would hover over a carcase.

Verse 29. The most of this chapter is in answer to the inquiry of the apostles which pertains to the two great events, the destruction of Jerusalem and the second coming of Christ. This verse is not on either of those subjects, but is a prediction of events that would concern the church and the world, beginning *immediately after* the events of the destruction of Jerusalem. Of course it is figurative for the literal sun and other heavenly bodies were not involved in the things predicted. The sun refers to Christ, the moon to the church, and the stars to teachers and other leading men in the church. Soon after the destruction of Jerusalem the influence of evil in the Roman government and the schemes of ambitious men in the kingdom of heaven combined and brought on the period known in religious literature as The Dark Ages, which lasted until the Reformation. During all that time there were faithful disciples in the world, but since the Bible was taken from the common people, it greatly interfered with the light of divine truth that comes from Christ through the church, and taught by faithful men in the church. All this is what is meant by the statements about the sun, moon and stars ceasing to shine. The same thing is meant by the words, *the powers of heaven shall be shaken,* for all of these sources of light were powers that originated in heaven, but they were *shaken* (agitated) by the revolution of the Dark Ages.

Verse 30. *Then* means after the period predicted in the preceding verse. The Dark Ages lasted until the work of Luther and the other Reformers. That was another revolution in the religious and political world that broke up the union of church and state. After that event the Lord took up the second one of the great subjects that he had been describing since the disciples made their inquiry in verse 3. The length of time that was to elapse before the second coming is not important, but what is of much concern is that the second coming of Christ was not to be until after the Dark Ages. But it is also important that it is to be the next major event in the list of those in the present schedule. The mourning of humanity at that time is the same as John predicted in Revelation 1: 7, and the coming in the clouds is the same as was predicted in Acts 1: 11 and Jude 14.

Verse 31. The prediction that a trumpet will be heard when Jesus comes again is also made in 1 Corinthians 15: 52 and 1 Thessalonians 4: 16. We observe also that the second coming of Christ will occur at the same time the world is to come to an end. In this verse the coming of Christ is accompanied with the work of the angels in gathering the *elect* (saved ones) of Christ, and in Matthew 13: 39 we are told that the angels will do this at the end of the world.

Verse 32. This and the following verse are some of the "exceptions" mentioned at verse 3. They are thrown in to suggest to the disciples the use that should be made of the "signs of the times." He referred to the common fig tree that was so prevalent in Palestine. The preliminary appearance of leaves was observed and from the fact a conclusion was formed that a change of seasons was near.

Verse 33. By using the same kind of logic with the signs that Jesus had predicted, the disciples could know when the first of the two great events was about due. We know this verse has the application to that event, for the disciples were to be living so that they could *see all these things*, and of course we are sure that they were not to live to see, bodily, the signs of the near approach of the second coming of Christ.

Verse 34. In keeping with the preceding verse we may conclude that the present one is in the bracket of the destruction of Jerusalem. *Generation* is from GENEA, which Thayer defines at this place, "The whole multitude of men living at the same time." Jesus spoke these words in about 30 A. D., and the destruction of Jerusalem was in 70 A. D. We know that the entire population would not have died in 40 years, so the prediction was fulfilled according to the words of our Lord.

Verse 35. *Heaven and earth* means the objects composing the material universe such as the earth, sun, moon and stars. They are destined to pass away at the day of judgment, but the truths spoken by Jesus will not fail; they will always be the truth.

Verse 36. From this verse through the end of the chapter the subject is the second coming of Christ and things that will take place in connection with it. At the time Jesus spoke these words no angel even, much less any man, knew when the end of the world was to come. *My Father only* might mean that not even Christ knew it, but I would not be too positive about that. The intimacy between the everlasting Father and Son would suggest the possibility of their having this knowledge in common. However, we are sure that no man knows of it, so that men who presume to predict the date must be regarded as false prophets of whom Jesus warned the disciples to beware.

Verse 37. The comparison intimated is shown in the next verse.

Verse 38. None of the things mentioned in this verse were wrong. The great mistake was in being wholly absorbed in their temporal interests and not paying any attention to the admonitions of Noah "a preacher of righteousness" (2 Peter 2: 5).

Verse 39. *Knew not* means they were so concerned with the affairs of this life they did not realize their danger until the flood was upon them, and then it was too late to avoid the disaster. So the coming of Christ will be upon the world in a surprise event even as the flood was in the days of Noah. He and his family were not overtaken by the flood because that patriarch believed the warning of the Lord. Likewise when Jesus comes again there will be some righteous people looking for him and will not be overtaken and found unprepared (1 Thessalonians 5: 4).

Verse 40. *Taken* is from PARALAMBANO which Thayer defines at this and several other places. "To take to, to take with one's self, to join to one's self." So it does not mean that one man will be taken out of the field and the other left there. That will be impossible since the field will be destroyed with the earth. It means one of the men will be taken to Christ as part of the good harvest, while the other will be rejected and gathered with the tares to be burned.

Verse 41. Grain was ground by rolling one millstone round over another by means of a lever fastened to the stone. The separation of these women will be done on the same basis as that of the two men in the preceding verse. Both cases show that the Lord's people and those of the world may engage together in any honorable occupation while performing work necessary to a livelihood. That is why Jesus said "Let both grow together until the harvest" [end of the world] (chapter 13: 30).

Verse 42. To *watch* means to be alert and thoughtful concerning one's duty to the Lord, and then regardless of when he comes the servant will be ready.

Verse 43. *Broken up* is from DIORUSSO and the definition in Thayer's lexicon, is, "To dig through," referring to the attempt to force an entrance into a house. One difference between the coming of a thief and that of the Lord is that the householder did not have any warning that any such attempt would be made upon his house. But we do have warning that Christ is coming again to judge the world and we are not told when, hence the necessity of being always awake and watching. An incidental bit of information may be obtained from this illustration of Jesus. The householder would have been compelled to use force in protecting his home and the Lord made a reference to the subject in an approving attitude. That shows that it is right for one to protect his home and family, even though he has to use force against force.

Verse 44. *In such an hour as ye think not.* Unlike the time of the destruction of Jerusalem, the second coming of Christ will not be heralded by specific signs. Instead, the world in general will be going on in the pursuit of earthly interests, feeling a sense of security and satisfaction, and hence will be taken by surprise as it is awakened to a sense of the awful doom just upon it (1 Thessalonians 5: 1-3).

Verse 45. Jesus finished his speech in parable form, likening himself to a householder who took his leave of the members of his house for a season, instructing them that he would return at some date not announced then. This householder appointed one of his servants to have charge of affairs during his absence, in seeing that the members were served their food at proper times. The practical application is to be made to the service that the disciples of the Lord are expected to render in the house of God.

Verse 46. The servant does not know when his lord will return, but if he is always faithful to his duty it will not matter when it occurs, for his faithfulness is what will bring him the blessing of the master of the house.

Verse 47. In the literal procedure of the parable the promotion of the faithful servant would be the thing usually expected. In its application it means that the faithful servants of Christ will be promoted to the higher enjoyment of heaven.

Verse 48. A servant might be attentive to his duties for a while, but if more time went by than was expected, he may conclude that his lord has postponed his coming for an indefinite period. (See 2 Peter 3: 3, 4.)

Verse 49. Under the impression that "there is plenty of time yet" this servant will relax his vigilance and turn the good treatment of his fellow servants into mistreatment of them; he will even join in the unrighteous practices of some of them. Likewise, some professed disciples of Christ often get tired of faithful service in the kingdom and give way to a life of sin.

Verse 50. Such a worldly life has the tendency of blunting the mind with regard to spiritual matters. It even may blot from his mind the memory of all the warnings of the Lord. In such a case his coming will be unexpected to him hence it will take him by surprise and find him not ready for a favorable meeting.

Verse 51. *Cut him asunder* means to sever him from the Lord's household. An unthinking and self-gratifying servant is not as bad in the abstract as a hypocrite, for such a character that professes to be what he knows he is not is among the worst of sinners. But since both of these individuals are to have their portion together, it teaches us that there is only one lot awaiting the unsaved at the day of judgment. We ordinarily think of a gnashing of the teeth as a much stronger demonstration than weeping. The use of the two is very significant as applied to those condemned in the lake of fire. Gnashing the teeth will be caused by the bodily pain, while weeping (also defined "lamentation") will be the expression of the mind, caused by the realization of what the person has missed of joy, and what he has brought upon himself by his life of sin while in the world.

MATTHEW 25

Verse 1. *Then* is an adverb of time and applies to the second coming of Christ predicted in the preceding chapter. The word specifies the exact part of the parable that is to be applied, namely, the sudden announcement of the approach of the bridegroom. The whole story had to be told in order to explain the particular point at which the application was to be made.

Verse 2. Wisdom and foolishness are opposite terms which could have numberless applications depending on the connection in which they are used.

Verses 3, 4. The present application is to the ones who took their lamps only (the foolish), and the wise were those who took extra oil in the vessel besides that already absorbed and retained by the wick. The lamps were shallow bowls with a projection resembling the spout of a water pitcher. A wick of twisted flax was placed in this spout extending down into the vessel which was supposed to be supplied with olive oil. The foolish virgins neglected to see that their lamps had oil in them.

Verse 5. *Slumbered and slept.* The first word properly means to be drowsy so as to nod, the last one means to go on into more complete sleep. This happened because the bridegroom was longer than expected in making his appearance. As to the usual hour for the wedding, Smith's Bible Dictionary says, "When the fixed hour arrived, which was generally late in the evening," etc. While it was late it evidently was not often as late as midnight, which explains why *all* of the virgins fell asleep, the wise as well as the foolish.

Verse 6. This *cry* was a strong sound for the original is defined in the lexicon, "a crying, outcry, clamor." That was made necessary by the lateness of the hour and the sleeping state of the virgins.

Verse 7. *Trimmed* is from KOSMEO

which Thayer defines, "To put in order, arrange, make ready, prepare."

Verse 8. Putting the lamps in order would include lighting them as well as pinching off the charred end of the wick. Not until after lighting them did the foolish virgins realize they had neglected to "fill their lamps." There would be enough of the oil still retained in the wicks to start the light, but in a short while they would begin to grow dim. *Gone out* is rendered "going out" in the margin which is correct. When the flame began to go down they realized what was the trouble and appealed to the wise virgins for oil from their vessels.

Verse 9. The capacity of the old style lamp was limited and it would have been foolish for the wise to reduce their supply at the last moment.

Verse 10. Ordinary judgment should have told these virgins that it was too late to go on a shopping errand, especially at that time of night. The approach of the bridegroom had been announced with an urgent clamor which indicated that the preparatory period was over and that the event of the hour was about to start.

Verse 11. The word *Lord* is erroneously capitalized which indicates that it means Christ. The person referred to was the one having charge of the wedding activities, and the term as used by the virgins was one of respect only.

Verse 12. *I know you not* denotes he did not recognize them as being entitled to be present at the wedding. The approach of the bridegroom had been announced in no uncertain terms, and these people should have been already there if they were among the invited guests. Coming after the door was closed indicated to this master of ceremonies that they were would-be intruders who were coming out of a wrong motive.

Verse 13. *Watch therefore* are the words that express the lesson intended by the parable. It is the same that was set forth by the parable of the unfaithful servant in the closing verses of the preceding chapter.

Verse 14. Jesus spoke another parable that teaches the duties of the Lord's servants from another angle. Note that the man delivered unto his servants *his* (the man's) goods. In 1 Timothy 6: 7 Paul says "we brought nothing into this world, and it is certain we can carry nothing out." On that basis we should realize that what is in our hands does not belong to us, but it is delivered to us as a trust which the parable shows.

Verse 15. *Talent* is from TALANTON and Thayer defines it, "The scale of a balance, a balance, a pair of scales; a talent." He also explains it to mean, "a weight, varying in different places and times; a sum of money weighing a talent and varying in different states and according to the changes in the laws regulating the currency." The specific value of the talent is of no importance for the purpose of the parable. It is used merely as a means of expressing the different degrees of responsibility of the servants. Note the different amounts delivered to the servants was based on *his several ability*. The lord knew the abilities of his servants and assigned to them the tasks that corresponded with their ability.

Verses 16, 17. Each of these men did exactly the same thing with the money entrusted to him. By *trading* or making the proper use of the money they doubled it.

Verse 18. The only comment I will make here on the third man, is that he at least did not misuse or lose it; further comments will be made at verse 25.

Verse 19. *Reckoneth with them* means he called upon them for a report.

Verse 20. The only report this man could or needed to make was that he had doubled his lord's money, and had the extra talents to show for it.

Verse 21. *Good and faithful* are the words that signify the lesson in the parable. Jesus combines the application with the telling of the parable by stating the reward awaiting the faithful servant. That reward will be to enter into the joy of his Lord, which means the joy provided by the Lord to be shared together in heaven.

Verse 22. This servant's report was exactly the same kind as that of the first one, namely, that he had doubled his lord's money by trading.

Verse 23. It is significant that each of these two men received the same sentence from their lord, notwithstanding there was a great material difference in the amounts they had to return to him. But each servant was *faithful* to the trust bestowed upon him, which is the basis on which man will be judged at the last day. Some men have more ability than others and hence they will be required

to accomplish more. But if everyone is faithful to the extent of his power and opportunity he will receive the one and only reward in store, which is the entrance into the joy of the Lord.

Verse 24. Every one of the charges this servant made against his lord was false. He made them as a basis for his failure to do anything with the money that was put into his hands. But while they were false accusations, they will be turned against him as we shall see at verse 27.

Verse 25. This verse illustrates what may be called negative goodness in the light of some theories. There are multitudes who think they can expect to be saved by merely abstaining from active wrong doing. That if they avoid doing anything at all they certainly could not be accused of doing any wrong act. The man with one talent seems to have taken that view of the case. But there are many passages that condemn the sin of omission, such as Hebrews 2: 3. This man thought that by burying the money it would be preserved for its owner. Even if that could have been accomplished with literal money, the rule will not hold good in the application. A man's talent will not remain fixed as to quality while in this world. If it is not put to good use, it will be corrupted by contact with the evil elements around it.

Verse 26. This servant was both *wicked* and *slothful;* wicked in making false accusations against his lord, and slothful in being indolent to do something with the money. *Thou knewest,* etc., does not mean that his lord admitted the accusations, but used them as a basis for the condemnation in the following verse.

Verse 27. *Oughtest therefore.* If this lord was as exacting as the servant pretended to think he was, that was one great reason he should have been eager to do something that would satisfy him and hence avoid receiving his severe rebuke and sentence. *Exchanger* is from TRAPEZITES which Thayer defines, "A money-changer, broker, banker, one who exchanges money for a fee, and pays interest on deposits." Such a business in Palestine was occasioned by the coming of people from various countries. Their money was not good in the local markets, which made it necessary to exchange it for current money of Palestine. *Usury* is the interest these exchangers would pay local citizens who were willing to lay their money on the banker's table to be used in the exchange business. In the spiritual application it means that if we make the proper use of the opportunities the Lord has furnished us, we will become better and improve as the years go by. The third man was not condemned for not having as much to give his lord, but for not having any interest at all. In other words, he was condemned on the principle of being unfaithful to the trust that was given over to him.

Verse 28. The lord wished his money to be put to some use so as to bring him proper returns. The man with the ten talents at hand when the accounting was made had proved his good business judgment and hence was entrusted with this other one.

Verse 29. *Hath not, he hath* might seem to be contradictory terms, but in the language of monetary dealings they are not. The second term is the principal and the first is the interest. Since the man had no interest to show, he was not allowed to retain the principal. In the spiritual application if a man does not make good use of his opportunity while in this life, he will not have another privilege. (Revelation 22: 11.)

Verse 30. No earthly lord ever treated his servants as this verse indicates. It is the conclusion that Jesus makes to the lesson of the parable. For *weeping* and *gnashing of teeth* see the comments on chapter 24: 51.

Verse 31. Many of the passages of a descriptive character in the Bible are worded like the transactions of men. We know from all the direct teaching of the New Testament that Christ will be the sole judge of the human family (Acts 17: 31) at the day of final accounts. No conversation or other participation will be allowed upon the part of human beings. Therefore all the parables and other passages that speak of such actions are used figuratively. They truly represent what would be the result were the mentioned conversations to be permitted. But aside from such parts of the various descriptions, the direct predictions will take place. For instance, the Son of man will actually come with the angels (2 Thessalonians 1: 7), and will sit upon the *throne of his glory* which means the throne of judgment.

Verse 32. *All nations* denotes that no human beings will escape the judgment bar of God, in which He will have seated his Son as the sole judge.

The people will be divided into only two groups, for all human creatures will belong to one or the other, no third group. The reference to sheep and goats is for an illustration only. It is based on the practice of a shepherd who is getting ready to lead his flock into a fold for permanent shelter. While out over the fields some goats may have straggled in among the sheep, and the shepherd would not want them in his fold.

Verse 33. There is no moral value of a man's right hand over his left, but the separation had to be made and the assignment to these respective hands is so worded for its psychological effect.

Verse 34. While Jesus will be the judge, he will pronounce sentence in harmony with the wishes of his Father who has created and prepared all good things. *Foundation* is from KATABOLE, defined in Thayer's lexicon, "a founding," and that means the starting of something. World means the universe in general, but has special reference to the orderly arrangement of things that were intended for the occupancy of man. God intended from the start to have a place of joy and happiness into which the creature man would be admitted after qualifying himself for it. It will be the inheritance of this place (here called a kingdom) that the royal judge will invite the righteous to have.

Verse 35. See the comments at chapter 13: 3 on the scope of the parables. In the present one Jesus had only one point to impress which will be brought out as the comments proceed. But as it is in most of them, the whole story must be told to make the point of application clear. Administering food to the hungry and drink to the thirsty would be classed among "good works" as that term is commonly used. Hospitality is likewise so considered according to Hebrews 13: 2.

Verse 36. Clothing the naked and visiting ("looking after") the sick are both among good works pertaining to our relation with each other. *In prison* does not mean in the sense of a penal institution; at least it was not being used as such in this case, because it was the disciple of Jesus who was there. It means a guard house in which the enemy was confining a captive for the purpose of persecution. If the disciple was in a regular penal structure he was placed there on a false accusation. The case of Paul in

Rome (2 Timothy 1: 16-18) is not exactly in point, for he was in his own hired house. Yet he was a virtual prisoner because he was chained to an officer, and while in that situation the disciple Onesiphorus "came unto him."

Verses 37-39. The righteous will think that Jesus meant all these things were done for him personally. They did not remember having any such experiences and made inquiry as to when it was to which he referred.

Verse 40. This verse tells us the main object of the parable. Jesus is not on earth in person and hence we cannot show him such personal favors as these good sheep are said to have done. But his disciples who are his and our brethren are here, and we always have opportunities for doing them good. (See Galatians 6: 10.)

Verse 41. The extent of this *everlasting fire* will be explained at verse 46. But for the present it should be noted that it was not originally designed for man, but for the devil and his angels. These angels evidently mean the fallen angels who had sinned and were cast down from heaven (2 Peter 2: 4; Jude 6).

Verses 42, 43. The same list of good works is named in the sentence against the folks on the left hand as was said to the others. It might be well to note that these people were not condemned because of any wicked thing they had done. See the comments on verse 25 about the negative principle in the conduct of life.

Verses 44, 45. The ones on the left will have the same misunderstanding about the personal treatment that the others had, and they will be given the same explanation. They might have sometimes professed an interest in the needs of their brethren, but their expressions of sympathy were not accompanied with anything practical and hence no good was accomplished. In James 2: 14-16 is a statement on this angle of the subject.

Verse 46. *These* means the ones on the left hand of the king and the *righteous* are the ones on the right. *Punishment* is from KOLASIS which Thayer defines, "correction, punishment, penalty." Such words do not indicate a condition where the victim is unconscious or has been annihilated as certain persons teach. *Everlasting* and *eternal* are both from AIONIOS which Thayer defines, "Without end,

never to cease, everlasting." This definition applies to the word that is used to describe the future state of both the saved and the unsaved. Whatever can be said as to the duration of the eternal life of the saved, applies with equal force to the duration of the punishment of the unsaved. No man who professes to believe the Bible will say that eternal life will ever end, so neither can he consistently say that the punishment of the unsaved will ever end. Both classes will exist consciously in their respective circumstances without end.

MATTHEW 26

Verse 1. *All these sayings* refers to the speeches Jesus made to his disciples following his last visit to the temple. His work on earth was about to come to an end and he turned his attention to the events that were soon to come.

Verse 2. The passover was a feast of the Jews that was instituted in Egypt on the night of the slaying of the firstborn of the Egyptians (Exodus 12). It became one of the annual feasts of the nation at which time all the males were required to go to the city of Jerusalem where it was celebrated in commemoration of the Egyptian event. *After two days* would come the regular date which was Friday, the 14th day of the 1st month. Jesus and his apostles ate the feast two days before the regular time. As proof of this, the italicized words above indicates it, and John 18: 28 records a statement that shows the Jews had not yet eaten of the passover, although it was the day after Jesus and his apostles had eaten theirs. There was a reason for his observing it at this time for he knew that he was to die the next day and hence would not get to partake of it if he waited for the established time. This should not confuse us any in view of the emergency, and also the authority of Jesus. Chapter 12: 8 states that the Son of man is Lord of the sabbath, and he certainly is Lord of other days also.

Verse 3. *Then assembled* means a gathering of the members of the Sanhedrin, the highest court of the Jews in the time of Christ. The word is usually rendered "council" in the New Testament, but it is sometimes referred to as an assembly as it is in this verse. The word is from the Greek, SUNEDRION which Thayer defines,

"Any assembly (especially of magistrates, judges, ambassadors), whether convened to deliberate or to pass judgment; in the Scriptures 1. any session of persons deliberating or adjudicating [judging]. 2. specifically, the Sanhedrin, the great council at Jerusalem." He follows his definition with the following information. "Consisting of seventy-one members, viz., scribes and elders, prominent members of the high-priestly families (hence called . . .), and the high-priest, the president of the body. The fullest periphrasis [wordy description] for Sanhedrin is found in Matthew 26: 3; Mark 14: 43, 53. The more important causes were brought before this tribunal, inasmuch as the Roman rulers of Judea had left to it the power of trying such cases, and also of pronouncing sentence of death, with the limitation that a capital sentence pronounced by the Sanhedrin was not valid unless it were confirmed by the Roman procurator [an agent]. The Jews trace the origin of the Sanhedrin to Numbers 11: 16." All of this information from Thayer is important, and the reader should make a note of it for ready reference, for the subject will be mentioned several times in the New Testament study.

Verse 4. We have learned in the preceding paragraph that the Sanhedrin could not lawfully put anyone to death. That is the reason the Jews had this consultation to devise some plot to kill Jesus by a trick of subtilty.

Verse 5. The Jews were not concerned about disturbing the holy feast, but wished to avoid any conflict with the people. In other words, they were acting on policy more than on principle and wished to retain their popularity.

Verse 6. The writer now goes back a few days to relate some incidents that happened while Jesus was in Bethany. In chapter 21: 17 is the account of his going out to that village nearby where he lodged over night. In John's account (John 12: 1, 2) we are told that when he was there a supper was made in his honor, which our present verse says was in the house of Simon the leper. The law of Moses required a leper to dwell apart from society (Leviticus 13: 46), hence we should conclude that Simon had been miraculously cured by the Lord, and he was designated "the leper" to distinguish him from several other men with the same name.

Verse 7. According to John 12: 3 this woman was Mary a sister of Lazarus. Funk and Wagnalls Standard Bible Dictionary says the following of this box. "Alabaster (origin of the word unknown): Mineral carbonate of lime. A white stone much used in antiquity to ornament buildings and for vases and small bottles for holding precious ointment." Mark 14: 3 says the woman broke the box and poured the ointment on his head. No reason is given for breaking the box, but at least it shows she intended to use all the ointment.

Verse 8. According to John 12:4-6 it was Judas who made the complaint. And the same passage explains his motive to have been a selfish one. John calls him a thief and Jesus calls him a devil in John 6: 70, all of which accounts for his conduct.

Verse 9. It was true that such a product was costly (about fifty dollars' worth) to be used in what might have been considered an unprofitable way. But it was not really his thoughts of economy that caused Judas to make his remark. He was a covetous man and it hurt him to see that much value bestowed upon another.

Verse 10. *Good work* is used in the sense of a good act or deed, not so much as a manual effort which we know it was not. What constituted this a good deed will be explained in the comments on verse 12.

Verse 11. Jesus did not criticize the idea of giving something to the poor. He instructed the rich young man (chapter 19: 21) to give his possessions to the poor. Neither did he question the motive of Judas in making his complaint. He left that subject for some other to do as John did in the passage cited at verse 8. But he made a statement that pertained to the subject of using present opportunities that are soon to pass. He was to leave the world in a short time and that would stop all chances of doing him a bodily favor, while they would never cease to have the opportunity of helping the poor.

Verse 12. *For my burial.* It was an old custom to anoint the dead and use spices at the time of burial. (See 2 Chronicles 16: 14; John 19: 40; Luke 23: 56). Mark 14: 8 quotes Jesus as saying, "She is come aforehand to anoint my body to the burying." Since it was customary to bestow such treatment on the human body it would be regarded as a good deed to perform it. Mary evidently believed that she would not have as good an opportunity for this service if she waited until after the death of Jesus. However, whether this tells the motive for her coming aforehand or not, the mere desire to do honor to the body of her Lord was regarded favorably. This subject furnishes us with some suggestions concerning an inquiry often heard as to whether the use of flowers and other items on funeral occasions is right. Of course all good things are liable to abuse, and the extravagant spending of money for flowers is wrong. But we have convincing proof that it is proper to give respectful attention to the body because it is made in the image of the Creator. Any unnecessary mutilation of the body, therefore, would be wrong, which would condemn the desecrating act of cremation.

Verse 13. This means that the deed of the woman would become a part of the Gospel record and hence would be mentioned wherever the sacred book went.

Verse 14. The covetous heart of Judas was evidently stirred by the "waste" of something that would have brought in a goodly sum of money, and since it was bestowed upon Jesus, the thought occurred to him that he could recover some of it by betraying him to the Jews for money.

Verse 15. He asked the priests to make him an offer for which he would carry out the wicked deed. They *covenanted* (contracted) to give him thirty pieces of silver. According to the Oxford Cyclopedic Concordance it would be about twenty dollars today.

Verse 16. Immediately after the bargain was made, Judas watched for an opportunity to fulfill it by pointing Jesus out in the way stated in verse 48.

Verse 17. Matthew resumes his history at the place where he left it at verse 5. *Feast of unleavened bread.* The 14th day of the first month was the time of the passover (Exodus 12: 6), and it was to be eaten with unleavened bread (verse 8). And the seven days following were also days in which they were to eat unleavened bread (Leviticus 23: 5, 6). For more details about these days of unleavened bread, see the comments at Exodus 12: 15 and Leviticus 23: 6, 7 in volume 1 of the Old Testament Commentary. Jesus and his apostles ate their passover two days before the regular time

(verse 2), and hence all the other items as to dates were set back correspondingly. The entire eight days beginning with the 14th came to be referred to as the feast of unleavened bread, so that the day of the passover (14th) would be called *the first day of unleavened bread* as we see it here; hence these italicized words apply to Christ and his apostles only in this place and the like statements in the other Gospels accounts. This being a special date for them, the disciples wished some instructions where to arrange for the passover, knowing Jesus would not eat it in any public place with the Jews.

Verse 18. Jesus directed them to go to a certain man in the city and deliver the request of their Master to him. Notice Jesus called it *my time;* that is, his time of crucifixion was at hand and he needed to eat the passover that evening. Also, since it was a special date, he wanted to eat it in a private house and hence made the request for the use of this man's house to be occupied by him and his apostles.

Verse 19. *Made ready the passover.* Jesus and his disciples were under the law of Moses and of course they made this preparation according to the directions recorded. Exodus 12: 5-9 has its first application in Egypt which was before the law was given from Sinai, but the same regulations were followed afterward. That means the disciples prepared the animal as directed, and also procured a supply of unleavened bread.

Verse 20. One of the great advantages of having more than one account of the life of Christ is the fact that the same details are not given in all of them. The things that happened on this last night of Christ before his death are not given in strict chronological order. For the convenience of the reader I shall write a list of references, and if he will read them in exactly the order as given he will have a connected record of what took place on that night. Luke 22: 14-18; 21-23; John 13: 23-30; Luke 22: 19, 20. It is important that the passages be read just as the references show, not taking in a single verse not indicated nor leaving out one. I shall now comment on the verses of this chapter in their order. *Even* is from opsios and has a somewhat indefinite meaning as to any exact hour, but all lexicons agree that it means toward the end of the day.

Verse 21. Jesus had divine knowledge and hence was aware of the intentions of Judas.

Verse 22. *They were exceeding sorrowful.* This was a sincere sorrow on the part of all except the guilty one, for he could not have any sorrow (at this time) for something that he was wanting to do.

Verse 23. The apostles had asked Jesus who was going to betray him but he did not answer them all. According to John 13: 22-26 John was leaning on Jesus' bosom and hence was near him. Peter beckoned to him to ask Jesus who it was, and when Jesus told him, Judas did not hear the answer. The answer was accompanied with the act of dipping a piece of bread in the dish containing the flesh and its broth. Jesus reached into the dish at the same time that Judas did, which was the sign to the other apostles that answered their question of who was to be the betrayer.

Verse 24. *Son of man goeth.* The last word is from HUPAGO which Thayer defines at this place, "To withdraw one's self, to go away, depart." Jesus knew that it was destined for him to leave the world through the treachery of one of his professed friends (Psalms 41: 9). However, this decree against him was not to relieve the perpetrator of the deed from the guilt of wrong doing. We have learned that Judas was called a thief and a devil before he had ever performed this evil deed (John 6: 70; 12: 6), hence it did not change his character in the least for God to use him as the agent in the necessary act. *Woe to that man.* Why pronounce a woe upon Judas if he was selected as this agent, is a natural inquiry. It was because of his motive in doing it, which was to obtain some money to gratify his covetous heart. Another thing, even this deed would not need to have caused him to be lost. The Jews on the day of Pentecost were accused of murdering Jesus, yet they were given the opportunity of obeying the Gospel for the remission of their sins. If Judas who was guilty only of betraying Christ, had repented from a godly sorrow and obeyed the Gospel he could have been saved also. But Jesus knew he would not do this, hence he made the prediction of this verse.

Verse 25. Judas could not have asked the question for information, for he had already contracted with the chief priests to betray his Lord. All of the others had asked the same question and if he kept silent it would be so conspicuous that his guilt would be manifest to all in the group.

Verse 26. *Blessed* is from EULOGEO and Thayer defines it in this passage, "To praise, celebrate with praises." We should understand, therefore, that it does not mean to bestow some miraculous quality upon the bread. The conclusion is strengthened by the giving of thanks for the cup, and we know that the cup is as important as the bread. If the bread required some miraculous quality to be given to it to produce the desired effect on the communicants, then surely the cup would have also required something more than the simple act of thanksgiving. *Brake* is from KLAO which is defined by Thayer, "To break," and he then adds the comment, "used in the New Testament of the breaking of bread." He also cites Matthew 14: 19; 15: 36, and other places where we know it refers to the act of dividing a loaf so that more than one person could properly partake of it. Thus we see the word has no religious significance, but states what is a physical necessity in order that the communicants could *eat* of it which is the only religious phase about the handling of the bread. *This is my body.* The Romanists insist that this statement must be taken literally and not to be understood in the sense of the bread as only a representation of his body. That reasoning would make nonsense of the other passages where the language is just as direct. For instance, in 1 Corinthians 10: 4 where Paul is speaking of the Israelites in the wilderness and of their drinking of a rock, he says "that rock was Christ." The record of that event is in Exodus 17: 6 where Moses literally smote a literal rock and thus provided drinking water for the congregation. We know that rock was only a piece of material, so that the statement of Paul means it was a type or representation of Christ who furnishes water of spiritual life. On the same principle, the bread represents the body of Christ because his body had to be given to provide spiritual food for mankind.

Verse 27. It might be asked why the cup was not "blessed" if it is as important as the bread; it was. The definition of "blessed" is, "to praise, celebrate with praises," as may be seen in comments on the preceding verse. In thanking God for the cup one would thereby be praising it. Matthew uses the two terms, blessed and thanks, as being the same in principle. *Drink ye all of it* means for all of them to drink of it. The priests of Rome insist on doing the drinking for the others, which is a contradiction of the instructions that Jesus gave to his disciples.

Verse 28. *Blood of the New Testament.* Under the Old Testament the blood that was shed was that of beasts, but the blood of the New was that of the Lamb of God. *Shed for many.* None but the Jews received the benefit of the blood shed in the animal sacrifices, while the blood of Christ offers benefits to the whole world (Romans 3: 25; 1 John 2: 2), which includes Jews and Gentiles without distinction.

Verse 29. The passages cited at verse 20 show that when Jesus spoke the words of this verse they were still in the passover feast, and hence he said them before verses 26-28 of the present chapter. Therefore, when the fruit of the vine was served in the institution of the Lord's supper he did not partake. That would be appropriate, for that supper was to celebrate the death of Christ (1 Corinthians 11: 26), and a man would not be expected to memorialize his own death. *Until I drink it new in my Father's kingdom.* Yes, Jesus does partake of the cup, but it is in a spiritual sense only. When disciples are eating and drinking of the Lord's supper he is present in spirit even as he promised that he would be (chapter 18: 20).

Verse 30. According to Thayer and Robinson this hymn was one of the Psalms of David. The mount of Olives was the site of Gethsemane which will be explained at verse 36.

Verse 31. While on their way to the mount of Olives Jesus said many things to his apostles. Chapters 14, 15, 16 and 17 of John were spoken as they were going, but Matthew records only what is in verses 31-35. *Shall be offended* or be caused to stumble. It means that something was going to happen that would cause them to falter in their devotion to Christ. This lack of devotion was to be manifested by the fact of their deserting him and fleeing. Jesus said it was written and we may read the prediction in Zechariah 13: 7.

Verse 32. *After I am risen* explains what Jesus meant in the preceding verse by being smitten. The stroke was to be so severe that it would cause his death, but he predicted that he was to rise from the dead.

Verse 33. Peter was a man of an impulsive temperament and inclined to make rash statements and to perform rash acts, such as that recorded in John 18: 10. The emphatic statement recorded here, therefore, is not surprising or should not be.

Verse 34. Jesus made a specific prediction of what Peter would do; not only specific as to the act but also as to the time of the night in which it would occur.

Verse 35. Even the pointed predictions of Jesus did not calm the rash spirit of Peter, but he repeated his declaration with an added item, that he would die before he would betray Jesus. His enthusiastic vows seemed to affect the other disciples for they all repeated his declaration.

Verse 36. The journey from the upper room and the passover to the garden of Gethsemane was ended. When they reached the border of the garden Jesus instructed the group to be seated while he went on farther to pray. I shall quote from Smith's Bible Dictionary on the item of Gethsemane. "A small 'garden,' Matthew 26: 36; Mark 14: 32, situated across the brook Kedron, John 18: 1, probably at the foot of Mount Olivet, Luke 22: 39, to the northwest and about one-half or three-quarters of a mile English from the walls of Jerusalem, and 100 yards east of the bridge over the Kedron. There was a 'garden' or rather an orchard, attached to it, to which the olive, fig and pomegranate doubtless invited resort by their hospitable shade."

Verse 37. Leaving the most of the group at the place where they first paused, Jesus took with him Peter and the sons of Zebedee (James and John), and went on into the garden with them. The humanity in his nature now began to manifest itself which caused him to be sorrowful and heavy hearted.

Verse 38. Jesus expressed his feelings to the three disciples and told them to tarry there while he stepped aside to pray. *Sorrowful, even unto death.* This is a highly colored figure of speech, meaning that he felt sad enough to die.

Verse 39. Having asked the three disciples to tarry and watch, Jesus wished to be alone with his Father and hence went a little farther away from them before beginning his prayer. He prayed that *this cup* might pass from him if it was the will of his Father. A common error in the comments heard today is to apply this cup to the suffering and death on the cross. Jesus rebuked Peter for thinking he could rescue him from that cup (John 18: 11), saying that the cup of death was necessary to fulfill the scripture. He certainly would not ask the Father, then, to save him from it. No, the *cup* to which he referred was *this cup*, meaning the present agony through which he was going. That cup of agony is forcefully described in Luke 22: 40-44. Jesus only asked that he be spared the terrible nervous agitation which he was at that time enduring. But it was not God's will to spare his Son even that much, so he was compelled to go through with it, until his agony brought out the great drops of sweat that was likened to thickened blood.

Verse 40. After his first prayer Jesus came back to the three disciples and found them asleep. We might wonder why he did not rebuke them more severely, but Luke 22: 45 says they were "sleeping for sorrow." Even that should have been overcome by the spirit of watchfulness, but at least we are pleased that it was not from indifference.

Verse 41. *Watch and pray* denotes the two sides of the scheme of salvation, the human and the divine. Watching is a duty of man in order that he may not be overtaken or surprised by temptation. (See Galatians 6: 1.) While doing what is humanly possible, it is proper to look for help from God if man goes to Him in prayer. *Spirit* and *flesh* are the two parts of a human being; the first is the inner man and the other is the outer. The first is inclined to the better way of life and the other is more inclined to evil. A good picture of these two is presented in Romans 7: 15-25.

Verse 42. Notice Jesus says *this* cup which denotes something present with him then. See the comments on the subject at verse 39.

Verse 43. The eyes of the disciples were heavy with the fatigue of sorrow.

Verse 44. Jesus prayed three times and each time his prayer was on the same subject. His persistence was on the principle that faith should be enduring and not inclined to give up easily. See the teaching on this subject in Luke 18: 1-8. It should be noted that each of the prayers was made on condition that they were as God willed.

Verse 45. Jesus perceived the depressed condition of his disciples and decided to let them sleep undisturbed for a little while since the critical hour was about on hands. *Is betrayed* is in the present tense as to grammatical form but really means "is to be betrayed." Yet it is put in this form to indicate the event was very near.

Verse 46. We do not know how much time passed between this and the preceding verse. It could not have been long, yet there was enough time for the disciples to get a short but undisturbed nap. Jesus saw Judas and the crowd with him approaching, and roused the disciples from their sleep.

Verse 47. Jesus was concluding his speech to the disciples when Judas arrived in his immediate presence. To avoid confusion as to why he was not with the group of disciples that Jesus left at the border of the garden, the reader should see the passages cited at verse 20. He should particularly note from John 13: 30 that Judas left them while the passover was still taking place, hence he was never near them again until the present verse. *Staves* is from a Greek word that means "clubs," and the possession of such weapons indicated an attitude of cruelty and disrespect. Even an ordinary policeman usually refrains from using his club (billy) unless there is resistance, but Jesus had never even indicated that he would "resist arrest" as a guilty lawbreaker might do. No wonder he asked them (Luke 22: 52) if they thought they had to deal with him as they would a thief.

Verse 48. *Hold him fast.* Judas had no doubt of the ability of Jesus to escape from the hand of the mob and really expected him to do so. Then if the priests complained of their loss and demanded the recovery of the money on a pretense of fraud, he could remind them of his warning and thus reject their complaint. Had things turned out as he expected, Judas would have procured the money which his covetous heart craved, and at the same time Jesus would not have been any worse off.

Verse 49. *Hail* means a salutation that comes from a Greek word denoting a friendly greeting that includes good wishes. It is as if Judas had said, "Master, I give you my good wishes for your happiness," and then pretended to verify his wishes by a kiss.

Verse 50. *Friend* is from ETAIROS which Thayer defines, "a comrade, mate, partner." *Wherefore* is from some Greek terms that virtually mean "for what purpose." The verse denotes as if Jesus said, "Judas, we have been comrades for over three years, then why is it that you come to me in this manner?" Just then the mob took charge of Jesus.

Verse 51. John 18: 10 tells us it was Peter who made this attack on the servant.

Verse 52. Some people use this verse to condemn capital punishment, but instead of condemning it the opposite is true. To *take the sword* under the circumstances where Peter did is the act of a private, unofficial man. Had he gone to the limit in his act it would have caused the death of the servant and that would have made him a murderer since he did not represent the law. And if that had occurred, Jesus said that he should himself have perished with the sword, that being one of the means of lawfully executing a murderer under the criminal law of the land.

Verse 53. Had it been right to defend Jesus with force, he could have prayed his Father who would have sent him twelve legions (about 72,000) of angels.

Verse 54. But if that had been done it would have prevented the scripture prophecies of his death from being fulfilled. Jesus knew all through his life that he was to die as a sacrifice for the sins of the world, to replace the animal sacrifices of the Mosaic system and make one offering for all time (Hebrews 10: 1-5).

Verse 55. Jesus rebuked the mob for coming out against him armed as if he were a thief. He reminded them of former opportunities of taking him and they did not do so nor even try to. All this showed their evil motive in the present movement.

Verse 56. Matthew is making the statements in this and the following verses. He is telling us that the deeds of this crowd were done in fulfillment of the predictions in the scriptures. The rebuke that Jesus gave Peter, also his submission to the attacks of the mob, seemed to dishearten all the disciples so that they *forsook him and fled.* By that act they fulfilled the predictions in Isaiah 53: 3 and Zechariah 13: 7.

Verse 57. *Led him away to Caiaphas.* John 18: 13 says they led him to Annas first who was the father-in-law of the high priest. Just what official position (if any) this Annas had at this time is a disputed point. But he was a former high priest and perhaps as a preliminary hearing Jesus was taken before him through respect for his former position, and in view of his relation to Caiaphas.

Verse 58. Peter's curiosity prompted him to follow Jesus as they led him away to the officers. But he also began to show the cowardice which he afterward displayed in the court by following Jesus *afar off.* He wanted to be near enough to see what was going on but not so near as to be suspected of being connected with him in any way that might be embarrassing or endanger his own life and liberty.

Verse 59. The persons referred to here were leading men of the Jews who composed the *council* (Sanhedrin). The description of this court and the extent of its powers may be seen at verse 3. Before they could obtain any action from the Roman court, the Sanhedrin must first try and condemn the prisoner. *Sought false witness* is very significant. They knew that nothing could be said truthfully against Jesus, hence they would have to rely on witnesses who were willing to give false testimony.

Verse 60. *But found none.* That is, no man was willing to testify to any act on the part of Jesus that would have made him guilty of a capital offence under the law of Moses. However, at last two witnesses came forward who said they had something to offer the court about the prisoner.

Verse 61. The testimony of these had nothing to do with any capital offence. Had Jesus said what they claimed, it still would not have made him guilty of anything serious, but only a claim as to what he said he could do if he chose. But even this was false, for he never said anything like what they affirmed. Another thing, according to Mark 14: 59, even these two witnesses disagreed with each other, and that would have thrown their testimony out of court had it been even on the subject of capital offences. According to Deuteronomy 17: 6; 19: 15 there must be at least two witnesses who testify to the same thing before a man could be condemned to death.

Verse 62. The high priest was surprised that Jesus did not make any reply to the testimony of these witnesses. He tried to get him to say something or other but failed.

Verse 63. *But Jesus held his peace.* There is a familiar rule that "silence gives consent" which would mean that if a man refused to deny a charge made against him it was taken as an admission of guilt. Under most circumstances that would be true, but Jesus knew he was bound to be condemned to die regardless of whether he replied or not. Besides, the pretended testimony was so ridiculous and contradictory that he considered it as beneath his dignity, hence he treated their statments with silent contempt. For an officer to *adjure* another person means to place him under oath. The high priest did this to Jesus and placed him under oath *by the living God.* Having bound Jesus with such an oath he asked him *whether thou be the Christ, the Son of God.* This introduced another subject, different from the one for which he was supposed to be brought into the council. The question pertained to his divinity and hence was a vital one, being the central fact of the entire system that Jesus was introducing into the world. Of course he would not be silent on that and his answer will be given in the next verse.

Verse 64. *Thou hast said* is an affirmative answer to the question of the high priest. *Nevertheless* is used in the sense of "moreover, furthermore," etc. It thus is not a restriction on or modification of what was just said, but i n t r o d u c e d additional thoughts. Jesus did not stop with merely answering the question about his divinity, but announced some things that were to happen because of his divine Sonship with God. *Ye shall see* agrees with Revelation 1: 7 which says that *every eye* shall see him when he comes to the earth again. The prediction was a blow to the pride of the high priest, not because he was told that he would see Jesus when he comes, but because it predicted that he (Jesus) was to occupy a throne of glory. The high priest was at that very hour presiding in a meeting that was prejudiced against the prisoner, and he as president had manifested his sympathy with the accusers.

. **Verse 65.** Decisions of the Sanhedrin were to be made by the vote of the members who should be uninfluenced by any interested person. The high priest violated the rules of justice

by announcing a conclusion ("he hath spoken blasphemy") before they had voted.

Verse 66. With such a breach of justice to influence them, it is no wonder that the assembly answered the question of the high priest as they did. It was all the more to be expected when their own personal sentiments were previously set against the prisoner because of his frequent rebukes of their wicked lives. *He is guilty of death* means that he is guilty of a crime that calls for the death penalty. Under the law of Moses a man who was guilty of blasphemy against God was to be put to death (Leviticus 24: 16). Jesus was not guilty, but the high priest had pronounced him so, hence the way was opened for the assembly, which was overwhelmingly moved by the spirit of a mob, to agree with the decision of the president and condemn the prisoner.

Verse 67. The Sanhedrin could pronounce a sentence of death but it could not execute it, hence they gratified their wicked hearts by this contemptible treatment of Jesus. According to Numbers 12: 14 and Deuteronomy 25: 9 it was regarded as a disgrace to have another spit in one's face. Thayer says to buffet means "to strike with the fist, give one a blow with the fist," which would be intended to cause pain. To smite with the open hand was not so much to cause pain as it was to treat with contempt.

Verse 68. *Prophesy* is from PRO-PHETEUO which Thayer defines at this place, "To utter forth, declare, a thing which can only be known by divine revelation." In a crowded condition no one person would be distinctly visible so that the belittling act of slapping with the hand could be done without its being seen as to who really did it. (See Mark 5: 27-31.) This act was an unmanly challenging of Christ's knowledge.

Verse 69. *Sat without in the palace.* We should remember that the present session of the Sanhedrin was held in the headquarters of the high priest (verse 57). *Palace* is a somewhat indefinite word in the Bible, but a common view of it is a building surrounded with an uncovered court. Sometimes the word is used to designate the building only, and at others it means the courtyard around it; the session of the Sanhedrin was held in the building. *Peter sat without in the palace* means he was out in the courtyard of the palace. The text does not tell us why the damsel asked Peter the question, but the same thing was asked him by another damsel, and still one of the crowd asked this question. All of them received the same negative answer, hence it is reasonable to conclude it was a part of the Lord's plan to bring about the threefold denial that was predicted in verse 34. This question about Peter's being *with* Jesus and the cowardly denial is significant, and shows that the fact of association with another makes him a partaker of whatever he is doing. (See Romans 1: 32.) Of course Jesus was not doing anything wrong, and if Peter had been true to his profession so strongly expressed in verses 33-35, he would gladly have admitted his friendly association with the Lord and rejoiced in sharing in his persecutions. (See Acts 5: 41.)

Verse 70. Peter not only denied being an associate of Jesus, but uttered a falsehood by saying he did not know him. The fear of sharing in the persecutions of Jesus caused him to say this and thus added another sin to the ones previously committed.

Verse 71. This *porch* was a place a little further away from the main building. The statement of the first damsel alarmed him and he was induced to move farther away. But even at this place his presence was noticed and a maid connected him with Jesus.

Verse 72. Peter emphasized his denial this time with an oath.

Verse 73. We are not told which person did the speaking this time, only that it was someone of the group standing near. The statement was made in an argumentative mood which shows they had heard his former denials (verse 70). *Bewrayeth* is the same as saying his speech "gave him away" or proved him to be what they were saying. Different communities and groups had their own dialects or brogues in their conversation. These people knew the dialect of Jesus and recognized that of Peter as being the same.

Verse 74. This time Peter thought he should make his denial still more emphatic than he had the first two instances. *Curse* is from KATANATHE-MATIZO which Thayer defines, "to call down direct evils on, to curse vehemently." *Swear* is from OMNURUI and the same lexicon defines it, "to swear; to affirm, promise, threaten, with an oath." The sentence means that Peter expressed the wish that some great misfortune would come to him if what he said was not true. And to give force to his declaration he made an oath in connection with it. As soon as he had concluded his statement the cock crew. Mark 14: 30 says the cock would crow twice, but that Peter would make his third denial before the second crowing. Verse 72 of that chapter says the cock crew the second time after this third denial.

Verse 75. *And Peter remembered the word of Jesus.* Luke 22: 61 says that *the Lord turned and looked upon Peter.* The place where Jesus was being tried was so arranged that he could be seen from the space outside where Peter was. Jesus hence could be seen by the apostle, and when the cock crew the third time he turned and gave him an accusing look that reminded him of what was said in verse 34. This brought him to his better thinking and filled him with genuine sorrow (Godly sorrow, 2 Corinthians 7: 10); his immediate reaction was to go out from the crowd to himself and weep bitterly.

MATTHEW 27

Verse 1. The Sanhedrin pronounced the death sentence against Jesus and that was as far as it could go under the power that the Roman government granted to it. The members of the court then consulted or planned the next move they would have to make to get this sentence affirmed by the officer who had the necessary power.

Verse 2. They *bound him* which was unnecessary as far as security of the prisoner was concerned, for Jesus had not given any indication of even wishing to escape. But it was customary to put some kind of shackle on a man who was a prisoner, and the feeling of this mob was such that it would certainly not make any exception of Jesus. *Pilate the governor* was an officer appointed by the Romans to represent the empire in parts of Palestine. His presence in Jerusalem at this time, and also some other useful information will be explained by a quotation from Smith's Bible Dictionary. "He was appointed A. D. 25-6, in the twelfth year of Tiberius. His arbitrary administration nearly drove the Jews to insurrection on two or three occasions. One of the first acts was to remove the headquarters of the army from Caesarea to Jerusalem.... It was the custom for the procurator [governor or agent] to reside at Jerusalem during the great feasts, to preserve order, and accordingly, at the time of our Lord's last Passover, Pilate was occupying his official residence in Herod's palace. Caesarea was the official headquarters for the Roman government in Palestine, which accounts for the mention of Pilate's temporary presence in Jerusalem at this time.

Verse 3. *Condemn* is a legal and judicial term as used in this place. Thayer defines the original, "To give judgment against one, to judge worthy of punishment, to condemn." The word is stronger than a mere accusation and means that the case had been decided officially against Jesus and that no way could be used for him to escape death. Judas had not expected this to happen; see the comments on this subject at chapter 26: 48. The pronouns are to be understood as follows: "When he [Judas] saw that he [Jesus] was condemned." *Repented himself* does not mean that Judas had repented in the sense of "repentance unto salvation" (2 Corinthians 7: 10), for in that case his conduct afterward would have been righteous. Instead, it means he reversed the money part of the transaction by returning the pieces of silver.

Verse 4. Judas knew from the start that Jesus was innocent, but expected him to resort to his miraculous power to escape from the hands of the mob. He had a guilty conscience but it was overruled by the effect of his disappointment so that he did not have the moral courage to do the right thing. *What is that to us* means they were not concerned about the affairs of his conscience.

Verse 5. Casting the pieces of silver down in the temple indicated that Judas was offering the money to the sacred service as "conscience money."

Verse 6. The priests understood the purpose of Judas to be that the money was to be put into the treasury. They pretended to have great respect for the sacredness of the temple, notwithstanding they had treated the one who was "greater than the temple" (chapter 12: 6) with the deepest disrespect.

Verse 7. *Potter's field.* After all the clay suitable for the making of pottery has been taken from a field, the land is of little use and hence very cheap commercially. A plot of such land was bought with this money and devoted to the burying of strangers or persons unknown to the community. From this circumstance comes the name "potter's field" today, a portion of cemetery grounds where poor people may bury their dead free of charge for the ground.

Verse 8. The *field of blood* was so called because it was purchased with the money that had been paid to Judas for his betrayal of Jesus. The priests had called it *the price of blood* (verse 6), and thought it was not fitting to put such "tainted money" into the treasury of the temple.

Verse 9. *Was spoken by Jeremy* [Jeremiah] *the prophet.* This prophecy is actually in the book of Zechariah, chapter 11: 13. Various explanations have been offered for this apparent contradiction, but I consider the most reasonable one to be that which is based on the outstanding prominence of Jeremiah. He was so highly respected that he was looked upon as a sort of "dean of prophets," and hence the prophecy was accredited to him in a complimentary or honorary sense.

Verse 10. *Lord appointed me.* The first person of the pronoun is used because the passage represents Christ as the speaker, and *the Lord* would be the Father who had *appointed* him to suffer this shame.

Verse 11. *Thou sayest* is equivalent to giving an affirmative answer. This conversation is referred to by Paul in 1 Timothy 6: 13 in which it is called "a good confession." This indicates that the confession required of men may be made in any form of speech that amounts to such a profession of faith.

Verse 12. *He answereth nothing.* This fulfilled Isaiah 53: 7, "As a sheep before her shearers is dumb, so he openeth not his mouth."

Verses 13, 14. Pilate was surprised at the silence of Juses in the face of accusations made by the chief priests. This was the same thing that happened in the presence of the high priest (chapter 26: 62).

Verse 15. *Governor was wont to release* means it was customary for him to do so. The feast of the passover was celebrated on the part of the civil powers by releasing a prisoner. There is little or no information available today as to when or how the custom started. Selection of the one to be favored was left to the voice of the people or unofficial crowd, not to the chief priests or other officers.

Verse 16. *They* means the people who had this prisoner in confinement for the security of the public. He is said to have been a *notable* prisoner. Thayer says this word means "notorious, infamous" [of bad report]. This bad name is explained in Mark 15: 7 which says he had committed murder and insurrection in connection with others.

Verse 17. All of the pronouns in this verse refer to the *people*, described in verse 15. Since they were the ones who must name the prisoner to be released, it was necessary for Pilate to ask them this question. *Barabbas* or *Jesus.* Pilate believed that Jesus was innocent of the accusations being made against him, but he ···as powerless to make any decision in the matter. However, as a suggestion which he thought would influence the crowd in their decision, he named Barabbas and Jesus. This prisoner was such a wicked character that surely they would not want him turned loose upon society. He thought they would reason that "of two evils it is better to choose the lesser." If they would do this it would result in the discharge of Jesus without any responsibility on his (Pilate's) part. It is possible they would have done as Pilate expected had it not been for the fact that will be explained at verse 20.

Verse 18. *They* in this verse means the chief priests (Mark 15: 10) who had been responsible for the arrest of Jesus. Since that was the case Pilate thought the *people* would not be so prejudiced against him and would certainly vote in favor of his release rather than such a dangerous character as Barabbas.

Verse 19. There is nothing to indicate this to have been a miraculous dream. It is natural for the exciting events occurring in one's presence to make an impression on the mind, and that in turn would cause dreams to come in sleep. The innocence of Jesus was so evident that even this pagan wife of the governor was concerned about what might come to her husband if he should have any part in persecuting such a *just man.*

Verse 20. While Pilate was waiting for the decision of the crowd, the *chief priests and elders* were busy among them, using their persuasive powers to influence the decision. They were not permitted to have any public voice in the selection, hence they accomplished their wicked purpose by working on the people who did have such a voice.

Verse 21. Pilate repeated his question to the people. Acting upon the influence of the chief priests and elders, the crowd named Barabbas as the one to be released.

Verse 22. If such a notorious criminal as Barabbas was to be given his freedom, surely as just a man as Jesus would not be dealt with very severely, hence the somewhat challenging question was asked as to what should be done with the man who was called Christ. Their answer that he was to be crucified, was to carry out the sentence imposed by the Sanhedrin but which it did not have the authority to execute.

Verse 23. There is nothing in the text that indicates any knowledge on the part of Pilate as to the charge upon which Jesus had been brought into his court. It is true the crowd accused him of perverting the nation (Luke 23: 2), but that was not any authoritative testimony for it was made by this mob at the moment. According to Matthew 26: 64-66 the point at which the Sanhedrin voted Jesus guilty was when he claimed to be the Son of God. Pilate, however, did not know anything about that (as far as we know), hence it was logical for him to ask the crowd the question stated. They refused to answer Pilate's question although they knew the pretense the Sanhedrin used in rendering its verdict. But they also knew that such a decision would not have much weight in a secular court, hence they ignored the question of the governor and repeated their wicked demand instead.

Verse 24. Although Pilate was a Roman official, he was somewhat acquainted with the Jewish history because of the frequent appearances of the leading men of that nation in Roman affairs. In Deuteronomy 21 is a provision in the law to dispose formally of a case of death for which it was not known who was responsible. The elders of the city nearest the body that was found were technically held to be guilty, or at least to have guilty knowledge thereof. The Lord knew that in some cases this would be unjust toward innocent persons, so a ceremony was ordained that included the washing of the hands which settled the case and cleared them of all responsibility. Pilate thought he could use that ceremony and thus avoid all responsibility for the death of Jesus. He failed to consider, however, that the Mosaic ceremony was in force only in cases where the elders actually were innocent or did not know anything about the case, while Pilate did have knowledge of the merits of the case and even had pronounced Jesus not guilty (Luke 23: 4). He therefore could not escape responsibility by this misuse of the law intended only for the protection of the innocent.

Verse 25. The people understood from this performance of Pilate that he was hesitating because of a conscientious regard for the possible results of turning Jesus over to crucifixion. In order to remove that obstacle and secure the desired decree, they uttered the awful statement, *His blood be on us, and on our children.* This rash sentence proved to be a prediction that was fulfilled forty years later. In the year 70 A. D. the city of Jerusalem was destroyed by the Romans and the Jewish people suffered untold miseries in the siege. That event was a part of the Roman military strategy, but God caused it to come upon the Jews because they had slain His own Son.

Verse 26. It was a custom with the Romans to scourge a prisoner who was to be executed. There were various methods of administering this punishment. Luke 23: 22 reveals that Pilate proposed to chastice Jesus and let him go. That would have been a compromise with the hopes of pacifying the Jews and yet not being so harsh upon Jesus. But the mob would not accept it, so Pilate followed the cruel practice and scourged Jesus, after which he turned him over to the mob to have him crucified.

Verse 27. Of course the people of the Jews could not personally perform this execution since they were not officers of the Roman government. That action was to be done by the soldiers, who took the victim into the *common hall* which the margin correctly renders "governor's house"; here they brought the entire band of soldiers. There was no need for such a military display for Jesus was not showing any disposition to resist. It was done through pomp and to humiliate the doomed man by their show of power.

Verse 28. *They stripped him.* This was after Jesus had been scourged, for that operation required that his clothing be removed first according to Smith's Bible Dictionary. This denotes that after the scourging was performed his clothing was replaced upon his wounded body. Scarlet was one of the royal colors of Rome, and the placing of this robe on the body of Jesus after it had been stripped the second time, was in mockery because he had said he was a king.

Verse 29. The actions of this verse also were done in mockery of the claim of Jesus that he was a king of the Jews. For a crown they used *thorns*, which comes from the same Greek word as that used in chapter 13: 7. Thayer defines the word, "A thorn, bramble-bush, brier." It means something that was not visible at the time the sowing was done, for it was afterward that the thorns "sprang up." The plant used as a mocking as well as a painful article was the kind that could be *platted* or woven into a crown and then pressed down upon the head of Jesus. Kings usually hold a baton or rod in their hand which was called a scepter when so used, indicating the authority of the throne. For that purpose a *reed* was placed in his hand in mockery of his claim as king. Smith's Bible Dictionary gives the following information on the reed that grew in Palestine. "A stronger reed, Arundo donax, the true reed of Egypt and Palestine, which grows 8 or 10 feet high, and is thicker than a man's thumb. It has a jointed stalk like a bamboo, and is very abundant on the Nile." There is something very pathetic about this item of the mocking ceremony. The placing of a crown on the head would require only that Jesus would not resist, but to put a reed *in his right hand* would be possible only by his cooperation, for an object like that would have to be grasped in order for the act to be a success. All of this was in keeping with the prediction of nonresistance that was made in Isaiah 53: 7 and Acts 8: 32, 33. It is fitting that a king would be saluted respectfully in the manner described in this verse, but these wicked men did it in mockery.

Verse 30. Isaiah 53: 3 predicts that Jesus was to be "despised" which means to be treated with contempt or belittled. That was fulfilled when they *spit upon him*, which was done also when he was in the high priest's house (chapter 26: 67). They next took the reed out of his hand and struck him on the head. That indicated that he was to be dispossessed of the authority he claimed to have, and then be punished by the very authority he claimed to represent as king.

Verse 31. After completing their shameful mockery, they replaced the robe with his own clothing and started the "last mile" of his life toward the place of crucifixion.

Verse 32. Simon did not "bear the cross alone," but helped Jesus with the burden. See the comments on this subject with the reference cited at chapter 16: 24.

Verse 33. No genuine believer in Christ would wish to lessen the respect that is so universally held for "the scenes of Calvary," yet it should be understood that most of the sentimental expressions on the subject are prompted by the general facts connected with the crucifixion. Even the poetic term "Mount Calvary" is not justified except figuratively as may be seen by the information now to be offered to the reader. *Golgotha*, rendered "Calvary" in Luke 23: 33," is from the Greek word KRANION which Thayer and Robinson define by the simple term "a skull." Smith's Bible Dictionary says the following in an article entitled Golgotha. "The Hebrew name of the spot at which our Lord was crucified. Matthew 27: 33; Mark 15: 22; John 19: 17. By these three evangelists it is interpreted to mean the 'place of a skull.' Two explanations of the name are given: (1) that it was a spot where executions ordinarily took place, and therefore abounded in skulls; or (2) it may come from the look or form of the spot itself, bald, round and skull-like, and therefore a mound or hillock in accordance with the common phrase— for which there is no direct authority —'Mount Calvary.' Whichever of these is correct, Golgotha seems to have been a known spot."

In his comments on the word "Calvary," Robert Young, author of the Analytical Concordance to the Bible, says the following: "This name occurs only in Luke 23: 33, and is not a proper name, but arises from the translators having literally adopted the word Calvaria (i. e., "a bare skull"), the Latin word by which the Greek word is rendered in the Vulgate [a Latin version of the Scriptures]. This *Kranion* is simply the Greek translation of the Chaldee *Golgotha*. The place of crucifixion is by each of the four evangelists called Kranion, and is in every case translated *Calvaria* in the Vulgate, and in every place but that in Luke the English version translates the word by 'scull.' There is no sanction for the expression 'Mount Calvary,' for it is only 18 feet high."

Verse 34. According to both Smith's Bible Dictionary, and Funk and Wagnalls Standard Bible Dictionary, this gall was made from the poppy plant which grew in abundance in Palestine. That, combined with the vinegar which would be somewhat alcoholic, composed a stupifying product that would act as an easement from pain. Jesus would not drink it because he was not willing to do anything to make his sufferings any less severe. Incidentally, we have an important bit of information as to what the verb "drink" means. The passage says that Jesus "tasted" of the mixture but would not "drink," which shows there is a difference between the two. Christians are commanded to "drink" of the fruit of the vine, not just taste of it. There is no need to consume a regular serving of it as one would to quench thirst, but we are expected to partake of it enough that it can be said we drink and not merely taste as is commonly done. Most churches do not provide enough of the fruit of the vine in the Lord's supper to meet the requirement of the ordinance.

Verse 35. The crucifixion of Jesus forms so important a part of the plan of human salvation, that I believe the reader should have some information on the manner of performing the act itself. I shall quote a description of it as may be found in Smith's Bible Dictionary. "The one to be crucified was stripped naked of all his clothes, and then followed the most awful moment of all. He was laid down upon the implement of torture. His arms were stretched along the cross-beams, and at the center of the open palms the point of a huge nail was placed, which, by the blow of a mallet, was driven home into the wood. Then through either foot separately, or possibly through both together, as they were placed one over the other, another huge nail tore its way through the quivering flesh. Whether the sufferer was also bound to the cross we do not know; but, to prevent the hands and feet being torn away by the weight of the body, which could 'rest upon nothing but four great wounds,' there was, about the centre of the cross, a wooden projection strong enough to support, at least in part, a human body, which soon became a weight of agony. Then the 'accursed tree' with its living human burden was slowly heaved up and the end fixed firmly in a hole in the ground. The feet were but a little raised above the earth. The victim was in full reach of every hand that might choose to strike. A death by crucifixion seems to include all that pain and death can have of the horrible and ghastly,—dizziness, cramp, thirst, starvation, sleeplessness, traumatic [shock from a wound] fever, tetanus, publicity of shame, long continuance of torment, horror of anticipation, mortification of unattended wounds, all intensified just up to the point at which they can be endured at all, but all stopping just short of the point which would give to the sufferer the relief of unconsciousness. The unnatural position made every movement painful; the lacerated veins and crushed tendons throbbed with incessant anguish; the wounds, inflamed by exposure, gradually gangrened; the arteries, especially of the head and stomach, became swollen and oppressed with surcharged blood; and, while each variety of misery went on gradually increasing, there was added to them the intolerable pang of burning and raging thirst. Such was the death to which Christ was doomed. The crucified was watched, according to custom, by a party of four soldiers, John 19: 23, with their centurion, Matthew 27: 54, whose express office was to prevent the stealing of the body. This was necessary from the lingering character of the death, which sometimes did not supervene even for three days, and was at last the result of gradual benumbing and starvation. But for this guard, the persons might have been taken down and recovered as was actually done in the case of a friend of Josephus. Fracture of the legs was especially adopted by the Jews to hasten death, John 19: 31. In most cases the body was suffered to rot on the cross by the action of sun and rain, or to be devoured by birds and beasts. Sepulture [burial] was generally therefore forbidden; but in consequence of Deuteronomy 21: 22, 23, an express national exception was made in favor of the Jews. Matthew 27: 58. This accursed and awful mode of punishment was happily abolished by Constantine."

Parted his garments. We learn from the aforesaid quotation that the victim to be crucified was stripped of his clothing before the crucifixion. It was a custom that the soldiers performing the execution should have this raiment as extra pay in addition to their wages

as soldiers. According to John 19: 23 there were four of them, corresponding to the four parts to be nailed, the two hands and two feet, and hence there would be four parts to be shared by them. *Casting lots.* Most of the garments were so made that they could be divided into parts without any damage to them. But John 19: 23, 24 says the coat was made by weaving into one piece without any seams, and therefore it could not be divided without ruining it. Accordingly, the soldiers agreed to decide the question by casting lots for the garment. This action fulfilled the prediction in Psalms 22: 18. *That it might be fulfilled.* The bearing on this kind of phrase is explained in the comments on chapter 4: 14.

Verse 36. Consult the preceding verse for the reason why they watched him.

Verse 37. *Accusation written.* It was a custom of the Romans to place a tablet on the cross over the head of the victim on which was written the accusation for which he was crucified. In the present case the "crime" was that he was *Jesus the king of the Jews.* According to John's account (John 19: 21) the chief priests objected to the wording of this inscription, which will be commented upon at that place.

Verse 38. The scripture does not tell us the motive of the Romans for crucifying these thieves at this particular time and in the position with Jesus as stated. But we can understand the part the Lord had in it, for it fulfilled a prediction in Isaiah 53: 12 that "he was numbered with the transgressors."

Verse 39. Thayer says this wagging of the head was "expressive of derision." A similar movement is recorded in Job 16: 4 and Psalms 109: 25. *Reviled* is a stronger term and comes from the same Greek word as "blaspheme." Thus by the movement of their body and their word of mouth, these cruel people showed their contempt for the Lamb of God who was at that very hour making the supreme sacrifice that creatures like them might have an opportunity of being saved.

Verse 40. To blaspheme means to speak evil, whether in direct falsehood or otherwise. The preceding verse says they reviled him which means to blaspheme, and the present verse tells us some of the false things they said. Jesus never said he would destroy the temple (John 2: 19), hence this was one of the blasphemous falsehoods they uttered against him. IF *thou be the Son of God* denotes they understood what was the real issue between Jesus and his enemies. It was not about his personal life nor his knowledge, but it was his identity. That is why the devil dwelt on that question in the temptations (chapter 4: 3, 6), and why Jesus asked the question stated in chapter 16: 13, 15 and 22: 42. All the other questions and facts in the life of Christ are important only in so far as they pertain to the fundamental claim that he is God's Son.

Verse 41. The reproachful sayings in the preceding verse were from the crowd in general. This verse specifies the chief priests and scribes as the ones who were mocking Jesus. They had been against him all through his public work, so it is not surprising that they would join in the mob clamor at this time.

Verse 42. *Saved others* refers to the miraculous cures that Jesus did for people. *Himself he cannot save* means he cannot deliver himself from the cross. This was another falsehood, and it ignored the incident in the garden when Peter thought to defend him against bodily attack (chapter 26: 51-54). They professed that they would believe in him if he would come down from the cross. This was a hypocritical claim for Jesus had done many works in their presence that were as great as this would have been, yet they refused to acknowledge him as the Lord.

Verse 43. *Let him deliver him* means for God to deliver his Son from the cross. This was as insincere as the statement of the preceding verse. They must have known that God would have the same reason for not interfering with the crucifixion as Jesus had for not resisting it.

Verse 44. This reproach from the thieves was as much out of place as any such a thing could be. There was no honorable reason why they were in the difficulty of the hour, for they could have avoided it by the right conduct. But Jesus was so situated from the fact that his conduct was righteous. We are glad that one of them did see the situation in the proper light and so expressed himself. (Luke 23: 39-43.)

Verse 45. The sixth and ninth hours corresponds with our noon and three in the afternoon. This darkness is predicted in Joel 2: 30, 31 and is referred to by Peter in Acts 2: 19, 20. It seems that nature was draped in mourning during the last hours of this human-divine sacrifice. And to add to the gloom, the Father withdrew his comforting grace so that Jesus made a strong outcry, "My God, my God, why hast thou forsaken me?" In order that the Son of God might make a complete sacrifice, that he might "pour out his soul unto death" (Isaiah 53: 12), he was left unattended in his painful solitude, no soothing hand to calm the nervous agitation with a caressing touch, but, deserted by all his friends and mocked by his enemies, compelled to die for the unjust.

Verse 46. *Eli, Eli, lama sabachthani* is from Hebrew words as Jesus uttered them. Then Matthew translates them into Greek, which the translators of King James render in English for us, *My God, my God, why hast thou forsaken me?* This bewailing sentence is recorded as a prophecy in Psalms 22: 1.

Verse 47. The Hebrew word that Jesus used is similar in sound to the Greek for Elias, and that misled the bystanders to think he was calling for Elias who had been predicted to come into the world as his forerunner (Malachi 4: 5).

Verse 48. In John 19: 28, 29 where this part of the event is recorded, Jesus is reported to have said he was thirsty. Thus in our present verse we are told that a person standing near offered him a drink of vinegar (sour wine), serving it with a sponge on a reed. That was the most convenient way either of serving or receiving it under the circumstances. This was done merely to quench his dying thirst and not as an opiate since it did not have the gall mixed with it which he had refused (verse 34).

Verse 49. Others, with less sympathy with Jesus in his distress, were willing to let him linger on in pain to see if his friend Elias (as they supposed) would come to his rescue and take him down from the cross.

Verse 50. When a human being is at the point of death from exhaustion, he is generally unconscious, or if not, he is very weak and would not be expected to make a strong cry. An exception to this would be when the patient is in delirium and hence acting with abnormal energy and without intelligent expression. No part of this description can apply to Jesus at this point. He not only was conscious, but his mind had not entered that stage where it would be acting mechanically, for according to Luke 23: 46 this "loud voice" was immediately followed by the all impressive words, "Father, into thy hands I commend my spirit." Our present verse says he yielded up the *ghost*, which comes from the same Greek word as spirit. So this outcry was evidently the final expression of one who, though ready to die, being "crucified through weakness" (2 Corinthians 13: 4), was able by the force of the will to make a triumphant shout as he was ready to leave the scenes of death and go to his Father.

Verse 51. This veil separated between the holy and most holy rooms in the temple. Through it the high priest went on the day of atonement to offer a service of blood for the sins of the people (Leviticus 16: 29, 30). Jesus died at the hour that the animal was slain for the sacrifices, and hence it was fitting that this veil be rent at the same time, signifying that the great High Priest was ready to offer himself as a ransom for all. The quaking of the earth and rending of the rocks was God's method of opening the graves, the significance of which will be explained in the next two verses.

Verse 52. *Graves were opened.* The tombs are meant which were in the form of caves that either were natural or were hewn out of a rock (verse 60), and another stone placed at the entrance to close the burial place. The earthquake loosened these stones and made them roll away thus *opening* the *graves* or tombs. A saint is anyone who is devoted to the service of God. These could not have been Christians because the church had not been set up. They were persons from one or all of the following groups of servants of God; those who had lived and died under the Patriarchal or Jewish dispensations, or disciples who had been called by the preaching of John or Christ, and who had died within the three years of their personal ministry. The rising of these saints forms a link in a very important chain of thought, which will be dealt with at Romans 8: 29, 30. For the present, however, I will state that these saints never died again.

Verse 53. One thing that is often overlooked in referring to this event, and that is that it was *after his resur-*

rection that the saints arose. That was in order to make Christ the first one to come from the dead to die no more (Acts 13: 34; 26: 23). Also, it was necessary for it to occur this close to the resurrection of Jesus in order that he could be the first "among many brethren" (Romans 8: 29). The *holy* city means Jerusalem because it was the capital of the Jewish nation in its religious system.

Verse 54. The centurion and the other watchers were filled with awe by the demonstration. It was not at the resurrection of anyone for that had not taken place yet. But they saw and felt the shaking of the earth at the same time that Jesus died, and knew that some supernatural power was the cause of it. They were pagans and did not know God as Christians know him, but they did know that Christ claimed to be His son, and the demonstration convinced them that he was what he claimed to be.

Verse 55. These women were faithful to the last, but with feminine timidity they stood some distance away watching. They had come from the same district where Jesus was brought up, Galilee, and had served him on various occasions.

Verse 56. Mary Magdalene was the woman whom Jesus cured of demons (Mark 16: 9); Mary the mother of James and Joses was the mother of Jesus (Mark 6: 3); the mother of Zebedee's children was the mother of James and John (Mark 10: 35).

Verse 57. Luke 23: 50, 51 says that Joseph was a counsellor which means that he was a member of the Sanhedrin. That passage states also that he "had not consented to the counsel and deed of them," meaning the Sanhedrin. Decisions of that body were made by the voice of the members (Matthew 26: 65, 66), and when the case of Jesus was presented, Joseph did not vote with those who condemned him. It should be noted that Joseph was a *rich man*, also that he was "a good man and a just," and that he was a disciple of Jesus. All of this disproves the teaching of some that a man cannot be a true disciple of Jesus and still be a rich man. It is the trusting in riches that will condemn a man (Mark 10: 24; 1 Timothy 6: 17, 18). But if he will "do good" with his riches he will thereby lay up for himself a good foundation against the time to come, and lay hold upon eternal life. Had Joseph not been a rich man he might not have been able to purchase the burial place that was used to give the body of Jesus the respect that even any human body deserves, much more that of the Son of God. Another thing, by the fact of this man's being rich it fulfilled the prediction that Christ "made his grave with the rich" (Isaiah 53: 9). That same prophecy includes a grave with the wicked which means the people of the world from whom Joseph purchased the place.

Verse 58. Joseph knew he would have to make special provisions and obtain a legal permit in order to take charge of the Lord's body. As an explanation of that subject I shall quote again a part of the statement from Smith's Bible Dictionary. "In most cases the body was suffered to rot on the cross by the action of sun and rain, or be devoured by birds and beasts. Sepulture [burial] was generally therefore forbidden." The statement that *Pilate commanded the body to be delivered* shows that a considerable amount of "red tape" was necessary in procuring the body of one who had been crucified.

Verse 59. Joseph wrapped the body in a winding sheet of clean linen. In the comments at verse 35 it is shown that a person to be crucified was stripped of all his clothing, hence the immediate need for using this linen cloth, for under the circumstances there was no opportunity for getting a burial shroud.

Verse 60. John 19: 38-40 says that Joseph had a helper in this loving service, the man who came to Jesus by night (John 3: 1, 2). This gives us the information that Nicodemus became friendly with Jesus at least, and was willing not only to assist in the work of burying the Lord, but contributed a substantial amount of valuable products to be used in the burying according to the Jewish manner of such a ceremony. The tomb was hewn out of the rock and might well be compared to the burial chambers that are made in the walls of modern mausolems in the public cemeteries. The body was borne by these two men and laid in this cavity as it would be deposited on a couch. To close it a great stone was rolled up against the opening.

Verse 61. The *other Mary* was the mother of Jesus (verse 56). These women found a seat opposite where Jesus was buried and "beheld where he was laid" (Mark 15: 47), which explains their concern about the stone when they were coming the day after the sabbath with spices, intending to anoint his body (Mark 16: 1-3).

Verse 62. The day before any holy or sabbath day was called a preparation (Mark 15: 42), and this would apply to every holy day, not only the regular weekly sabbath. The day of the passover was a holy day (Leviticus 23: 4, 5), hence the day before it would be a preparation. The passover came on Friday the 14th, thus it would naturally be a day that *followed the day of preparation*, and also the day following the crucifixion. On that day the leading Jews came to Pilate with their request.

Verse 63. The Jews reminded the governor of the claim of Jesus that he would rise from the dead after three days. Yes, Jesus did declare such a thing, and the Jews had no misunderstanding of the words. But when they had a wicked motive prompting them, they perverted them to serve their hypocrisy (chapter 26: 61).

Verse 64. I do not believe these Jews actually feared the disciples would steal the dead body of their Lord; what could they do with it? Besides, they were discouraged and in no mood for trying any rash means of what at best could only have been propaganda that would soon have been exposed. But these Jews were foolish enough to think that a seal over the tomb would prevent Jesus from breaking it, just as there are people today foolish enough to think that by having their bodies cremated they can escape the lake of fire. *Error* and *deceiver* are from Greek words with virtually the same meaning. The *last error* means the last deception, and the thought was that if they let the disciples succeed in their plan, then they (the Jews) would be worse beaten at the game than they were the first time.

Verse 65. Pilate reminded them of the watch in existence already, which consisted of various regulations as to the number of men to be on the watch at a time and the number of hours each group was required to be on duty. In addition to this, Pilate authorized them to make the tomb as secure as possible.

Verse 66. Acting upon the authority of Pilate, they put a Roman seal on the tomb and appointed the watchmen to be on duty at the grave.

MATTHEW 28

Verse 1. The particular time at which the 24-hour period was supposed to start has been a disputed point, and that is because no absolute and universal rule was observed by all people. According to this verse the period began in the morning. Thayer defines *began to dawn* to mean, "To grow light, to dawn." And Mark 16: 2 refers to the same event as being "at the rising of the sun," all of which indicates that at least in some cases the 24-hour day was from sunrise to sunrise. However, we should not overlook that it was after the sabbath was past for the text says *end of the sabbath* which Thayer defines, "the sabbath having just past." The two Marys were the same as those mentioned in 27: 61; Mary Magdalene and Mary the mother of Jesus.

Verse 2. There *was* a great earthquake. The marginal renders it "had been," which is correct, for Mark 16: 4 says that when the women arrived at the tomb they found the stone rolled away from the sepulchre. The angel was not afraid to break the seal that the Jews had caused to be placed upon the tomb, for he did not flee but rather remained and sat upon the stone.

Verse 3. Lightning is very bright and penetrating and a fitting comparison for the counterance of an angel. Snow-whiteness is an emblem of purity and well represents the kind of being who would come down from heaven.

Verse 4. The keepers were the members of the watch who were stationed there to see that no person would disturb the tomb. When this angel ignored the entire setup and removed the stone it was a great surprise to the watchers who were soldiers. No wonder it filled them with fear and trembling and rendered them helpless.

Verse 5. As far as the text shows, the angel paid no attention to the members of the watch, but he addressed encouraging words to the women. Being on a mission from heaven he was endowed with the information that would be useful in his work. By this he was aware of the purpose of the women who appeared at this time.

Verse 6. Not only had Jesus risen, but he had left the scenes of the tomb. As a visual evidence of the Lord's resurrection, the women were invited to come and see the place where he had lain.

Verse 7. After a look at the empty tomb they were bidden to go qiuckly and tell the good news to the disciples. They were later to see Jesus in Galilee, the district where he had lived until he was ready for his public ministry.

Verse 8. The *fear* of these women was the same as profound respect, and the great joy was caused by the wonderful fact that their Lord was alive again. Their joy would not let them be selfish, but they went running to bring the word to the disciples.

Verse 9. Jesus had left the tomb before the women arrived, and as they were leaving he met them and gave them a joyous greeting. The reader should see the note on the subject of "worship" at chapter 2: 2 and note the various shades of meaning of the word. In our present verse the only outward demonstration indicated was their grasping the feet of the Lord. This act of respectful condescension could very properly be called one of worship and is included in the definition of the word.

Verse 10. This is the same message the angel gave the women at the tomb. Christ's *brethren* means his disciples (John 20: 17, 18), and they were promised to be met by him in his home country of Galilee.

Verse 11. *Some of the watch* means the men who had been on duty at the tomb. They doubtless did their duty in seeing that no man disturbed the tomb, but they were powerless to prevent what the angel did. As faithful watchmen they made a true report of what had transpired. However, this was before they had been approached on the bribery proposition and agreed to make the foolish statement mentioned above.

Verse 12. Gave the money unto the *soldiers* means the men who had been appointed to guard the grave from disturbance by the disciples.

Verse 13. The absence of the body of Jesus from the tomb could not be denied, hence the story of stealing it was made up to account for the empty tomb. There are at least two weak points in this story. If they were asleep they could not know what was going on; also, such a lack of faithfulness as watchers was punishable by death and they would not likely have risked it. But money will do wonders and it seems to have had its effect on these soldiers.

Verse 14. Thayer says to persuade means "to win one's good will." Pilate was a wavering sort of governor as had been shown in this case, and they felt sure they could influence him to let the soldiers off without punishment. Another thing, they said *if this come to the governor's ears; there is* no proof that he ever heard the report.

Verse 15. This foolish report was circulated *among the Jews* which is very significant. They were the ones who wanted to believe it and pretended to do so. There is no account of any knowledge of it among the people in general.

Verse 16. The women were told by the angel (verse 7) to give the disciples the word, and in verse 10 Jesus gave them the same message. Hence this verse reports the journey to Galilee, the very mountain spot for the meeting having been designated. *Eleven* disciples were in the group because Judas had taken his own life before the crucifixion of his Lord (chapter 27: 5).

Verse 17. All we can say of this *worship* is that what they did comes within the definition of the word as given at chapter 2: 2. Thayer defines the original of *doubt*, "to doubt, to waver." It indicates a frame of mind that might be expressed by a familiar saying, "it is too good to be true."

Verse 18. In the Authorized Version the word "power" comes from two Greek words, with only a few exceptions, which are DUNAMIS and EXOUSIA. There is a partial blending of these words in their meaning so that they are used somewhat interchangeably, but each has its main or proper meaning. According to Thayer the first word means, "strength, ability, power; inherent power, power residing in a thing by virtue of its nature." He defines the second word, "power of choice, liberty of doing as one pleases; leave or permission." For convenience the first may be defined as "personal strength or ability," the second as, "the right or privilege bestowed on one." The word in this verse is EXOUSIA, which means that God bestowed upon Christ full right to rule over his kingdom.

Verse 19. *Teach* is from MATHETEUO and is defined by Thayer, "to make a disciple; to teach, instruct." Its main application is to bring persons into a relationship with Christ that they never had before. *All nations* is equiva-

lent to "every creature" in Mark 16: 15. The Mosiac system was given to the Jews only, while the Gospel was given to both Jew and Gentile. To do this teaching among all nations would require ability to speak in every language, and none but the apostles had that ability. It is a perversion of scripture, therefore, to apply this commission to preachers of today. *In* is from EIS which means "into" as used here. The Father, Son and Holy Ghost are a unit in the Godhead and hence "name" is singular. Whoever is baptized into one is baptized into all three, therefore one baptism is all that is necessary and right. The scripture in no place presents this as a formula to be spoken by the administrator of baptism, and when he says these words he is merely announcing to the hearers what he is doing.

Verse 20. *Teaching* is from DIDASKO and means to instruct in general. The ones to be instructed were those that Christ had commanded. In order that no mistake would be made, the Comforter (Holy Spirit) was to be sent to "bring all things to their remembrance" (John 14: 26). *I am with you always, even unto the end of the world.* The authority of the apostles was to be in force to the end of the world. Christ is not with them in person any more than he is with all Christians in person. But the words of the apostles are written in the New Testament and they are as binding on us now as if they were here in person and as if Jesus also had remained on earth in person. So there can be no successors to the apostles in this world because they are still in their own proper place of authority under Christ and will be until the end.

MARK 1

Verse 1. Mark was not one of the apostles, but was inspired to write an account of the life of Christ. He is mentioned a few times in the New Testament which will be noticed as we come to them. *Beginning of the gospel* is his introduction to the story of Christ, indicating the point in the history at which he was to begin his book.

Verse 2. This verse states the beginning point that was referred to in the preceding verse, that it was the time when Jesus was ready to start in his public work. But since that was to be preceded immediately by the work of the forerunner, John the Baptist, the author opens his story with several verses about that great man. This verse cites a prophecy in Malachi 3: 1, referring to John the Baptist as a messenger to go before the face of Christ to prepare the way for him.

Verse 3. See comments on Matthew 3: 1 for the explanation of *wilderness*.

Verse 4. *Baptism of repentance* denotes that baptism was caused by sincere repentance. (See Matthew 3: 7, 8.) *For* is from EIS and means in order to remission of sins.

Verse 5. *All the land of Judea* means that people came to John from all that country, not that every person was baptized. *Confessing their sins* was the verbal evidence that they had repented, and submission to baptism was the active evidence.

Verse 6. See the comments at Matthew 3: 4 for explanation of this verse.

Verse 7. This is John's first mention of the one who was to follow him. The reference to shoes is an allusion to the customs of that time. Loose sandals were worn in foot travel and upon entering a home they were removed and taken charge of by a servant. By way of illustration John regarded himself as unworthy even to unfasten the shoes of the one *mightier* than he.

Verse 8. *With* is from EN and means "in," referring to the element in which the persons were baptized. The baptism of the Holy Ghost was to be performed by the one coming after John and that was Christ. He was to give the Holy Ghost (Spirit) in overwhelming measure to his apostles to "guide them into all truth" (John 16: 13).

Verse 9. The preceding eight verses concludes the introduction referred to in verse 1. This and the next verse includes both John and Jesus, which will be all that Mark will record directly of the work of John, and any reference that may be made to him will be as a matter of history. *In those days* denotes that while John was to come before Jesus, yet their introduction to the world was to be virtually at the same time. Jesus came from Nazareth where he had lived since the return of his parents with him from Egypt (Matthew 2: 23). The reason for his baptism is explained in Matthew 3: 13-15.

Verse 10. If Jesus came *up out of* the water, then he had gone *down into* it. That was made necessary for the body to be baptized which was done by immersion. He (John) saw the

Spirit descending upon him (Jesus). John had been previously told that he would see such a thing take place (John 1: 33).

Verse 11. The voice from heaven was that of God, who openly recognized Jesus as his Son after he had been baptized, and he also added the important truth that he was *well pleased* in his Son.

Verse 12. Having been recognized formally as the Son of God, Jesus would not enter into his work until he had been tested. The word *spirit* always comes from the same Greek word, whether good or evil spirits, human or divine spirits, are meant; the connection here shows it means the *Holy Spirit*. Driveth is from EKBALLO which Thayer defines at this place, "to command or cause one to depart in haste." This is virtually the same in meaning as Matthew's statement that Jesus was "led up of the Spirit" (4: 1).

Verse 13. This verse gives a general summing up of the different things that took place with Jesus in those forty days: for the details see Matthew 4: 1-11. *Gospel of the kingdom* means good news that the kingdom of heaven was about to be set up.

Verses 14, 15. *Time is fulfilled* means the predictions of the start of the kingdom of God as to time had been fulfilled. On that ground Jesus commanded them to *repent and believe the gospel*. Why did he put repentance before belief? A fuller statement on the same subject is in Acts 20: 21. The work of John and Jesus was among the Jews only. They were still under the Mosaic system in which God was the only personality they were supposed to serve. But they had become slack toward God and were obligated to repent on behalf of Him, then come with clean hands to the new system and believe the Gospel. It was like telling a debtor to pay up his old debts before asking a new creditor to accept him.

Verse 16. This Simon was Simon Peter according to Matthew 4: 18, who, with his brother Andrew, was the first man called from his secular occupation to travel with Jesus bodily over the country and to be with him constantly.

Verse 17. Using their own occupation as a basis for his figures of speech, Jesus compared the proposed work of these men with what they had been doing. They were still to be fishers, but were to fish after men with the bait of the Gospel.

Verse 18. They could not use their temporal nets in the new business and hence had to forsake them. Their interest was indicated by their *straightway* forsaking the nets.

Verse 19. James and John were the ones elsewhere called "Zebedee's children."

Verse 20. All of these men were only required to come along with Jesus. No initiation act was required of them because John had already baptized them. We know that he was to prepare a people for Christ, and Jesus accepted these men as they were which shows that they had been made ready for his service. John had but one method of preparing men for Christ which ended with baptism. So we must conclude these men had been baptized by John the Baptist to await service under Christ.

Verse 21. Capernaum was a city on the shore of Galilee, and Matthew 4: 13 tells us that Jesus made it his dwelling place. He entered the synagogue on the sabbath because there would be people there whom he could teach. For more information about synagogues see the information offered in connection with Matthew 4: 23.

Verse 22. This verse is explained at Matthew 7: 28, 29.

Verse 23. The man with an *unclean spirit* was possessed with a devil. This subject is considered at length at Matthew 8: 28.

Verse 24. Of course we must understand that the devil did his talking with the mouth of the victim which is signified by the expression "possessed with the devil." Note that references to this devil are in both the singular and plural numbers. That is because though there might be a legion of them within a man (chapter 5: 5-13), there would be one as spokesman. The devil knew Jesus because he had once been with him in heaven but was cast out because of sin (2 Peter 2: 4; Jude 6; Luke 10: 18). It was not surprising, then, that they did not want anything to do with Jesus.

Verse 25. *Jesus rebuked him* and not the man, for the being possessed with a devil was an affliction and not a fault. The devil not only was commanded to come out of the man, but to make no remarks about the situation.

Verse 26. *Cried with a loud voice* may seem to contradict the statements in the preceding paragraph. No, this cry was forced from the victim by the injury which the devil inflicted on him as he was coming out.

Verse 27. People had been known to be possessed with devils for some years, but until the time of Christ no one was able to expel them. And notice that it was not done by any bodily contact, but solely by the authority of Jesus which was so great that when he commanded the devils they obeyed. No wonder the people were amazed and started to talk about it among themselves.

Verse 28. An event like the casting out of devils without any apparent means would be reported by everyone who heard about it. As a result the fame of Jesus spread at once throughout Galilee which was the district in which Capernaum was located.

Verse 29. Jesus and the first four disciples whom he called entered into the home of Simon and his brother.

Verse 30. Simon Peter was a married man for mention is made of his wife's mother. This does not harmonize with the doctrine of Rome which denies the right of marriage to all of the clergy. It is replied that Peter left his wife so that he could be qualified to serve in the capacity of head of the church. That also contradicts the scripture, for 1 Corinthians 9: 5 tells us that he was leading his wife about with him, and that was in Paul's day. *Anon they tell him of her* means they told him of the case of sickness as soon as he entered into the house.

Verse 31. The only physical thing that Jesus did was to lift up the woman with his hand. But that act alone would not have recovered her, for any man could have done that. And the encouraging act of lifting her from the bed did not merely give her an imaginary impulse as a "shot in the arm" might cause, but she was able to minister to the group which would require something more than nervous will power.

Verse 32. This verse includes regular diseases and also the being possessed with devils which shows there was a difference between the two kinds of afflictions. The presence of devils sometimes caused diseases similar to those to which mankind was always subject, but such cases could be cured only by casting out the devils.

Verse 33. Jesus was still in the home of Peter and his brother where he had healed the mother of Peter's wife, also had recovered others of their afflictions. This caused such a stir throughout the city that great crowds gathered at the door.

Verse 34. *Divers diseases* means many kinds of diseases. *Suffered not the devils to speak, because they knew him.* These devils would not have deserved any credit for proclaiming the divinity of Christ; that is, it would not have been an act of faith but of knowledge. They made such a declaration once and were rebuked for it (verses 24, 25), and Jesus still was not willing to be upheld by such characters.

Verse 35. Jesus was human as well as divine, and therefore he preferred to be alone with his Father at certain times. There is a foolish theory that Jesus and God are one in person. If that were true, to whom did he pray in that solitary place? The theory breaks down under the weight of its own absurdity.

Verse 36. Jesus was not allowed to be alone very long. Since he went out there *a great while before day* it is reasonable to say that as soon as it came the usual hour to arise, Peter discovered his absence and he took his group and went in search of him.

Verse 37. They did not know exactly where he was for it says *when they had found him.* They told Jesus that all men were seeking for him, but the motive for their search is not revealed by the text.

Verse 38. The main purpose of Jesus in his personal ministry was to preach the good news of the kingdom. The working of miracles was one of the "side lines" of his mission, performed to give testimony to the genuineness of his teaching. Because of that he stated that they should go into other towns to preach, and that he had come out into the world for that purpose.

Verse 39. The Jews would be gathered in their synagogues to read the Scriptures and perform other acts of worship. That gave Jesus an opportunity to preach the good news, then back up his authority by casting out devils or other miraculous works.

Verse 40. Leprosy was an incurable disease and a man afflicted with it was required to live apart from society (Leviticus 13: 45, 46). This leper had been convinced by the other miracles of Jesus that he could also heal him of leprosy if he was willing.

Verse 41. Leprosy was contagious only by physical contact, therefore when Jesus touched the leper he proved his faith in the power that the Father had given him. In connection with the physical contact he also uttered the word of cleansing.

Verse 42. *As soon as he had spoken* the man was cleansed from his leprosy. This denotes that his physical contact would not have been necessary as far as the healing was concerned. We should note that Jesus did not require a period of time for his accomplishment but did it *immediately.* Modern so-called faith healers must have an indefinite period, telling their patients that "it takes time," and that if their faith "holds out" they will be healed. This proves that all such "faith-cure" persons are frauds.

Verse 43. The next verse will show what this charge was and why it was given.

Verse 44. Leprosy was incurable by any natural means, but it could be cured by miracle, such as the case of Naaman in 2 Kings 5. And when a Jew had been cured of the disease physically, he was still required to perform certain services for his ceremonial cleansing which included the offering of sacrifices and other materials. That is what Jesus meant that this man should *offer for his cleansing.* (See Leviticus 14: 1.)

Verse 45. This verse indicates why the man was told not to report his case to any man. The people were so worked up over it that they interferred with the work of Jesus and caused him to go into desert places which were those not populated.

MARK 2

Verse 1. Jesus did not remain in the desert indefinitely, but returned to Capernaum which was his last residence. Of course he would not escape the knowledge of the crowd for the word passed around that he was in a certain house.

Verse 2. The crowd filled the house to capacity and then kept coming until they could not all get in hearing distance of the door. But to all who were within that limit Jesus did his preaching.

Verse 3. The palsied man was *brought* to the place, which shows he was helpless and had nothing to do with the affair as far as the text states.

Verse 4. The *press* means the crowd that had gathered about the door. Matthew records this event but says nothing about their going down through the roof. In Luke 5: 19 they are said to have made an opening through the roof by taking up the tiling. Houses were made with flat roofs which were covered over with roofing tile. These could be taken up without any damage to the building just as many styles of roof tiles can be handled today. After making this opening through the roof, they let the couch bearing the sick man down right into the immediate presence of Jesus.

Verse 5. Jesus saw *their* faith; nothing said about the faith of the patient.

Verses 6, 7. These scribes were *reasoning in their hearts* but Jesus knew what they were thinking, for he always knew what was in man.

Verse 8. Jesus let them know that he knew what they were thinking about.

Verse 9. *Whether is easier* means to ask them which would be easier for him to do, for if he had authority from God he could do the one as readily as the other.

Verses 10, 11. Jesus demonstrated his power to perform miracles of the invisible kind by doing the visible. He told the palsied man to arise and carry his bed.

Verse 12. Again the result of Christ's word was *immediate.* When the man arose and carried his bed in their presence the people were amazed and declared they had never seen such a deed before. A more detailed discussion of this case is at Matthew 9: 2.

Verse 13. The *sea side* was that of Galilee where Jesus spent a great part of his time. The crowds were generally interested in his teaching and followed after him for that and also for the physical benefits obtained by his hands.

Verse 14. This man was Matthew Levi, one of the apostles and writer of the book with that name. *Receipt of custom* means the place where taxes were received, and this identifies him as a publican. Jesus told Levi to follow him which he did without any preparation further than what John

the Baptist had done. (See chapter 1: 20.)

Verse 15. These *publicans and sinners* were not some special sects as were the Pharisees and Sadducees, but were people who were regarded as being in the lower ranks of society. They were thus classed especially by the Pharisees who made such a claim of righteousness. (See comments at Matthew 9: 10 about the publicans.)

Verse 16. These self-righteous people were not fair enough to speak to Jesus directly, but satisfied their envy by attacking his disciples. Eating with another in old times was regarded as a strong recognition of social rank, hence this particular criticism was hurled at Jesus over the shoulders of his disciples.

Verse 17. If these critics were as righteous as they claimed, then they did not need the presence of Jesus any more than a man in health would need a physician. It is the sinner who needs the services of a Saviour and that would call for the attention that Jesus was giving to these "sinners." This does not mean that Jesus regarded the Pharisees as righteous men, but he was merely using their own claims against them.

Verse 18. Fasting was never commanded as a general practice, but it was customary to do so in times of distress or anxiety. John the Baptist was dead and his disciples were fasting in his memory. *They* (the Pharisees) came and criticized the disciples of Jesus for not fasting.

Verse 19. This verse has reference to some customs in connection with marriages. *Children* is used figuratively and refers to some invited guests who took pleasure in the presence of the bridegroom. After the wedding he would leave and these special friends would lament his absence which would be appropriate.

Verse 20. This verse applies the illustration to the disciples who were destined finally to mourn the absence of their Lord. (See chapter 16: 20).

Verses 21, 22. The lesson here is one of doing things in an appropriate manner and at the proper time. A full treatment of the whole parable is given at Matthew 9: 14-17.

Verse 23. Deuteronomy 23: 24, 25 gave the Jews the right to make personal use of the grain in the field but not to take any away. Thus no complaint could be made for their eating this corn which was a small grain such as wheat or rye.

Verse 24. The Pharisees pretended to object because they were doing this on the sabbath day. But Jesus will show them that one law is no more sacred than another.

Verse 25. *Have ye never read* implies that they had read that account, but were ignoring the event for the time being because it would condemn them for inconsistency.

Verse 26. The bread that David ate was that which had been on the table in the tabernacle for seven days, then was set back for the use of the priests. But it had served its religious purpose and therefore it was no desecration of it for David to eat it, especially as it was an emergency.

Verse 27. *The sabbath was made for man* means the day was set aside for man's benefit in providing him a time for relaxation from labor. But since the use of food is as important as rest, it is right to provide that food even if it must be done on this day in an emergency.

Verse 28. No law is any greater than the authority behind it. Christ and his Father worked together in giving to man the law of the sabbath, therefore this Son would have the right to adjust that law to any condition suggested in his wisdom.

MARK 3

Verse 1. *Withered hand* means that something had shut off the circulation from that member and it had pined away for lack of moisture, rendering it useless.

Verse 2. The Pharisees were always pretending to be zealous about the law, though they did not keep it themselves. Jesus was performing his good deeds on every day of the week, but they knew they could not object to what he was doing, hence they pretended to be offended because he did some things on the sabbath day. So they had their eyes set upon him with a wicked interest, hoping he would heal this man on that day and thus give them a pretext for accusing him.

Verse 3. Jesus knew their thoughts but proceeded to heal the man.

Verse 4. Before going further with the case, Jesus anticipated their accusation with a question they were not expecting. He put the matter on the basis of doing good or evil, saving life

or destroying it, and asked them which should be done on the sabbath day. They would not answer because either way they answered would have condemned them.

Verse 5. Another word in Thayer's definition of the Greek for *anger* is "indignation," and it means that Jesus was greatly agitated over the hardness of their hearts. However, it did not keep him from performing the good deed for the man. He was told to *stretch forth his hand* which shows that his arm was not affected. As soon as he stretched forth his hand it was cured without any bodily contact from Jesus that we know of.

Verse 6. Having been defeated in their attempts to convict Jesus under the law, the Pharisees decided to try some other plan, which was to get him to say something that would set himself against the government. For the account of how they did this and my comments on it, see at Matthew 22: 16-21. The *Herodians* were some Jews who were favorable to Herod's family relations and the Romans.

Verse 7. Jesus went to the Sea of Galilee and that drew the crowds after him again, both from the immediate vicinity and Judea.

Verse 8. Jerusalem was in Judea, but the writer thought it good to specify some of the important centers of population in that district as well as others. *Idumaea* was the same as Edom, a country east of the Jordan. *Tyre* and *Sidon* were important cities of Phoenicia, a country bordering on the Mediterranean Sea. The fame of Jesus reached into all these places and people came from them to see him.

Verse 9. *Small ship* means a small boat that could take Jesus from the pressure of the crowd, and yet permit him to be seen and heard by the people.

Verse 10. This verse explains why the people thronged about Jesus.

Verse 11. *Unclean spirits* is another name for devils that afflicted the people.

Verse 12. See chapter 1: 34 on why the unclean spirit was forbidden to preach Jesus.

Verse 13. Jesus called these men out of the group of disciples following him.

Verse 14. This is the appointment of the twelve apostles. They were expected to *be with him continuously* except as he would send them out on missions.

Verse 15. The word *power* is from EXOUSIA which means authority primarily, and Jesus bestowed it upon his apostles. In so doing he enabled them to heal sicknesses and cast out devils which would make their authority effective.

Verse 16-19. There are three of the Gospel accounts that give the list of the twelve apostles. The persons are the same but the names not always, since some of them had more than one name. For the sake of space the reader is asked to see the complete treatment of this subject at Matthew 10: 4. *Which also betrayed him* was said prospectively as the betrayal of Jesus had not yet taken place.

Verse 20. Jesus was kept so busy teaching the people and administering to their afflictions that there was no opportunity for him and his apostles to have their meals.

Verse 21. *His friends* is rendered "those belonging to him" by the "Englishman's Greek New Testament," and that agrees with the marginal reading that says "kinsmen." When they said *He is beside himself* they meant they thought he was carried away with the intensity of the situation. But Jesus continued his teaching and good work in spite of the apparent protest of his relations.

Verse 22. The scribes are explained at Matthew 13: 52. They would not deny the fact of his casting out devils, but pretended to believe that he got his power for the work from Beelzebub (Satan).

Verse 23. The foolishness of their theory was shown by this question. Even a wicked being like Satan would not be working against himself.

Verses 24, 25. The same point is made by supporting a kingdom that divided itself into opposing groups, for such a kingdom would soon be overthrown by the internal strife.

Verse 26. This is the same as verse 23.

Verse 27. The illustration is this. A man must overthrow another in order to plunder his house, and to do that he would have to be stronger than the man of the house. If Satan casts out Satan, then we have the foolish conclusion that Satan is stronger than Satan which is so absurd that no reply was possible.

Verse 28. This verse takes in every manner of sin that could be named except the one that will be designated in the next verse.

Verse 29. To blaspheme means to speak violent and evil things against another; it implies things said with the intention of insulting or injuring another. To be guilty of such a sin against the Holy Ghost (Spirit) meant to be without a chance of pardon.

Verse 30. The sin against the Holy Ghost was charged against these Jews because *they said he hath an unclean spirit*. This narrows the subject down to one item, thus ruling out all human efforts to imagine something that "surely is the 'unpardonable' sin if ever there was one." For a complete discussion of this subject see Matthew 12: 24-28, and the comments that are made upon those verses.

Verse 31. *There came then.* Verse 21 tells of the "friends" of Jesus who wanted to take charge of him but were not able to do so. Whether these family relatives were the ones meant in the former verse I cannot say, or perhaps they were anxious to attempt what the other relatives failed to accomplish. At any rate, they came as near as they could and tried to get the attention of Jesus.

Verse 32. The multitude tried to help them get his attention by telling him that it was his mother and brethren who wanted to talk to him.

Verse 33. The reply of Jesus was not intended as a slight upon his family but a mild rebuke for the crowd. It is as if he had said, "why should my mother and brethren be allowed to alter my work of salvation?"

Verse 34. Jesus prepared to point out the persons deserving more attention just then than his family relatives, and called attention to the crowd that had gathered closely about him, to whom he had been preaching the truth.

Verse 35. The same person (notice it is in singular number) could not be both sister and brother at the same time. The idea is, then, that doing the will of God is more important than being the fleshly relations of Christ.

MARK 4

Verse 1. This chapter corresponds with Matthew 13.

Verse 2. A parable is the placing of one thing beside another for the purpose of an illustration. The reader should see the precautionary comments offered at Matthew 13: 3 as to the right use to make of the parables.

Verse 3. *Hearken* means a special call to attention.

Verse 4. Seed was sown by hand only, in Bible times, and that would make it natural for it to fall into various places as the parable shows. *Wayside* was a beaten path where the ground was hard so that the seed could not find any opening to bury itself.

Verse 5. The soil over the *stones* would be scarce and the seed would soon use up all the strength in the ground, and that would force it to spring up at once toward the sun and atmosphere for sustenance.

Verse 6. However, the full strength of the sun would be too much for the tender plant because it did not have a completed root, as a result it would be scorched and die.

Verse 7. These *thorns* were a plant defined in the lexicon as "a bramble-bush, brier." The plant was not in sight when the sowing was done, but at the growing time it sprang up and choked out the good seed, it being a hardier plant.

Verses 8, 9. The good ground brought forth various amounts of the good seed which was the only difference; the quality was the same in all.

Verse 10. *Asked of him the parable* signifies they did not understand the meaning of it. See the comments on Matthew 13: 11 as to why the apostles needed to have the parables explained to them aside from the crowd.

Verse 11. *Them that are without* refers to the people who were not disciples. This also is explained in the comments referred to in the preceding verse.

Verse 12. This unusual language means that the people did not use the opportunities they had been given to grasp the truths of Heaven. That refusal to open their eyes and ears to the things offered them is likened to a man who has eyes and ears, but refuses to use them for fear he will see and hear things that will condemn his manner of life.

Verse 13. The parable of the sower is so natural that the apostles should have seen the lesson in it. The question of Jesus is a mild rebuke and implies that they should bestir themselves a little more and not lean so heavily on him for instruction.

Verses 14, 15. Jesus loved his disciples, and notwithstanding their apparent dullness he wished to give them the information they desired. *The sower soweth the word* is very brief, but it indicates that the things that happened afterward were no fault of the sower. As seed remaining on the surface of the ground would soon be picked up by the birds, so if men do not take the good seed into their hearts, Satan will have a chance at it and will soon take it away with his many subjects of worldly interests.

Verse 16. These people were more enthusiastic over the newly-found subject than they were serious. Hence what they did was done somewhat in the spirit of excitement.

Verse 17. Excitement is momentary and such an interest is not very deep-seated. When the real test comes of facing the attacks of worldly enemies, such people become offended which means they stumble over the word.

Verse 18. As far as the text shows, these people gave attention to what was said and understood it. If they failed to produce any fruit from it the reason was something else besides not knowing about the value of the word which they had heard.

Verse 19. This verse explains why the word did not produce a crop with these people even though they understood it. *Cares of this world* denotes that concern and anxiety that some people have over the things of this life. They give so much attention to those things that it crowds out their consideration for the word. *Deceitfulness of riches.* Many people think that if they can accumulate a large amount of wealth that it will bring them happiness. But they are being deceived, for the so-called pleasures that can come only through money are temporal and at best are uncertain. Solomon says of this, "For riches certainly make themselves wings; they fly away as an eagle toward heaven" (Proverbs 23: 5).

Verse 20. The good ground illustrates those who not only *hear* the word but also receive it; not only that but go to work with it to make it reproduce. The different amounts that were produced merely denotes that some good people have more ability to produce than others, but the Lord asks us only to be faithful and do what we can.

Verse 21. In purely temporal or material things, men will act with better judgment than they do in things moral and spiritual. A man would not make a light for the accommodation of his guests, then put something over it that would prevent them from benefiting by it. Neither should we allow some careless conduct keep our possible influence for good from being seen by those about us. (See Matthew 5: 15, 16.)

Verse 22. All evil deeds will some day be exposed by the Lord. Our good deeds, therefore, should be permitted to be a benefit to others, and not be lost upon them by some unwise conduct on our part.

Verse 23. This verse means for men to make use of their opportunities to hear the truth as the Lord provides it for them through his servants.

Verse 24. The admonition as to what we hear is connected with the statement about the measure. The thought is that the more and better attention we give to what is said to us, the more benefit we will receive from what is said.

Verse 25. To take from one which he does not have is explained at Matthew 25: 29.

Verse 26. This short parable has an important lesson. What we do becomes an influence that lives and acts even when we are not aware of it. How necessary it is, then, that we guard our every act.

Verse 27. *Knoweth not how.* We do not understand how God makes things grow in the material kingdom, yet it makes its development notwithstanding our lack of that knowledge. Likewise, our work in the kingdom of God will have its reward in its proper time and in the Lord's own way even though we cannot always understand how it is.

Verse 28. This shows that everything in God's creation is accomplished by growth.

Verse 29. The lesson should be grasped that it takes faith and patience to accomplish the desired results in the service of the Lord. (See Galatians 6: 9.)

Verse 30. These questions were asked to get the attention of the hearers.

Verse 31. According to historical information the mustard seed that was produced in Palestine was the smallest of all those that grew in that country.

Verse 32. The physical growth of the little seed is like that which is expected to be made in the things pertaining to the kingdom of God. From small beginnings the work of the Lord may grow on until it is of service to many around us.

Verse 33. *As they were able to hear it.* Jesus did not wish to deliver his teaching in greater amounts or depths than they would be able to grasp. (See John 16: 12.)

Verse 34. This verse is explained at Matthew 13: 11.

Verse 35. The multitudes sometimes were so great that it made a hindrance to the work of Jesus. He never actually refused to serve them when in their midst, but would move to other parts of the country. Thus he told his disciples they would pass over to the other side which meant the other shore of the Sea of Galilee.

Verse 36. Jesus dismissed the multitudes which is the meaning of the phrase *sent them away,* for they would not all depart. *They took him* denotes they would not leave him entirely alone, but some of them found the *other little ships* nearby. Just how far they tried to accompany him is not stated. Doubtless most of them remained on the same side of the sea until he returned, for verse 21 states that when he came back "much people gathered unto him."

Verse 37. After starting across the sea a violent storm arose. *It was now full* is a figure of speech meaning that the boat was filling, and unless something could be done it would soon be literally filled and sink.

Verse 38. Jesus was asleep which shows that the water had not yet reached to him as he lay *on a pillow.* In their fright they awoke him and cried for him to rescue them.

Verse 39. Jesus was more severe in his language to the storm and sea than he was to the disciples. He rebuked both storm and waves and commanded them to *be still.* Both of them were dumb objects and could not render intelligent obedience, hence their response proved the authority of the Master to rule as his wisdom directed.

Verse 40. The disciples were intelligent beings and hence Jesus gave them a mild rebuke, charging them with having little faith.

Verse 41. One meaning of the original word for *feared* is, "To be filled with awe and amazement." They wondered what manner of man it would be who could regulate dumb objects of creation with his mere word.

MARK 5

Verse 1. Gadarenes (also called Gergesenes) was situated near the eastern shore of the Sea of Galilee, and it was there that Jesus went ashore.

Verse 2. The *tombs* were caves in the rocks that were used for the burial of the dead. They were generally open so that persons could enter and leave them as occasion suggested. It was at this kind of place that the Lord met the man with an *unclean spirit*.

Verse 3. *No man could bind him.* The effect of being possessed with an unclean spirit (devil) was not always the same. Sometimes it produced great prostration, at others it caused insanity, and in the present case it brought abnormal strength together with manifestations of insanity at times.

Verse 4. Attempts were made to bind this man but the chains would not hold. No man could *tame* him means he could not be subdued because of his strength.

Verse 5. This shows that he was not only unnaturally strong, but he was vicious and wild and showing the traits of an insane man.

Verse 6. However, it was the outward or human part of this creature that was performing the things described and that was because he was possessed of this devil and had to do as the evil spirit directed him. The devil himself was perfectly intelligent, for he caused the man to run and meet Jesus and perform some act of respect that is called *worship*. (See the note on that subject at Matthew 2: 2.)

Verse 7. *What have I to do with thee* is the same as asking Jesus what he is about to do. To *adjure* means to put a person under oath, which would be an unauthorized act on the part of the devil. The demand was that Jesus would not torment him.

Verse 8. This verse explains the demand of the preceding verse. If the devil is required to leave the man he may have to return to his former place in Hades which would mean the torment that he adjured Jesus not to inflict upon him.

Verse 9. The pronouns *he* and *we* are not the same in grammatical number. That is because one devil was the spokesman for the others. It is orderly for one or more beings interested in

the same thing to let one do the talking. The apostles observed that practice according to Matthew 17: 4; Acts 2: 14.

Verse 10. Speaking on behalf of the other devils, he requested Jesus not to send them *out of the country.* That was the main point of interest, not so much the idea of remaining in the man. (See the comments on verse 8.)

Verse 11. The swine was one of the unclean beasts under the law of the Jews, but we do not know whether they were interested in them commercially or not.

Verse 12. *All the devils besought* denotes the same thought set forth in verse 9 concerning a spokesman who represented the others.

Verse 13. The devils did not gain any advantage by entering the swine, but Jesus granted their request without volunteering any information. Whether they were suffered to enter other human beings or had to return to their former place in Hades we are not told.

Verse 14. The feeders saw what the swine did, but the text does not state if they knew what caused it. What happened when the people came out afterward, however, shows that they understood that Jesus had something to do with it.

Verse 15. The mentioning of seeing Jesus and the man at the same time indicates the people connected Jesus with the whole event. *They were afraid.* This man had defied all attempts to subdue him even with a chain, now he was seen sitting quietly and in his right mind. The situation was so overwhelming that it filled the ·people with terror and confusion.

Verse 16. The feeders explained what was done and what happened to the swine.

Verse 17. No harm had been done to the unfortunate man, hence the only conclusion possible is they were afraid some more of them would lose their swine.

Verse 18. It was natural for the man to make such a request as this verse states.

Verse 19. Jesus had more important things for the man to do, and that was to tell the good news to his friends. He was to relate it in connection with the thought that the Lord *had compassion* on him.

Verse 20. Decapolis was a district east of the Jordan, and it was in that region that the grateful man spread the news of his recovery which caused the crowd to gather.

Verse 21. Jesus returned to the western shore of Galilee, and, as usual, the crowds began to gather about him, doubtless with various motives.

Verse 22. *Ruler* is from ARCHI-SUNAGOGUE, and Thayer's explanation is, "It was his duty to select the readers or teachers in the synagogue, to examine the discourses of the public speakers, and to see that all things were done with decency and in accordance with ancestral usage." *Fell at his feet* manifested great respect and much anxiety.

Verse 23. The simple ceremony of laying his hands on the daughter would not have been necessary had Jesus seen fit to accomplish the cure without it, but the request was the ruler's way of indicating his faith in the great Healer.

Verse 24. It was nothing unusual for the crowds to follow Jesus, but the statement is added that they thronged him. That is an introduction to the event that is to follow soon, especially as to certain parts of it.

Verse 25. This woman was afflicted with a chronic hemorrhage of 12 years' standing.

Verse 26. This verse is one of the passages that are perverted into meaning just the opposite of their real teaching. The woman had grown worse in spite of her being treated by physicians. The fact is used by many "drug-less healers" to prove that physicians are useless, even though Jesus said in Matthew 9: 12 that the sick need a physician. But the very statement that this woman had not been benefited by the physicians is proof that others had been helped by them.

Verse 27. This woman touched the garment of Jesus on the same principle that the ruler wanted him to touch the body of his daughter.

Verse 28. *For she said* means that she said it to herself.

Verse 29. The woman obtained the relief she sought and it was *straight-way*. That was the manner of miraculous cures and not a requirement that much time be given as in the case of the fraudulent "faith-cure" workers of today.

Verse 30. *Virtue* is from DUNAMIS and is one of the words for "power." It says that Jesus knew of the virtue going out of him, not that he felt the loss of the power. He knew it because he had divine knowledge of what was being done. His question was for a test of the woman, but the disciples thought it was for information.

Verse 31. *Thou seest the multitude* means that the whole crowd was touching him (see the comment on verse 24), and it seemed strange to them to ask such a question.

Verse 32. Jesus was continuing his test of the woman's trust in him.

Verse 33. The woman thought she had unintentionally committed some wrong. She came trembling and prostrate before Jesus and told him the truth.

Verse 34. The statement Jesus made to the woman denotes that it was not the contact with the garment that cured her, but the faith that was manifested by the act. *Go in peace* was said to assure her that she had not done anything wrong.

Verse 35. One miracle is no harder to perform than another but these people thought there was a difference. There are some things the Lord cannot do because they are not right, but no miracle is impossible merely because it is too hard.

Verse 36. Jesus overheard the word that was brought to the ruler, and he gave him an assurance of favor if he continued to have faith.

Verse 37. The group had neared the ruler's house when the message of death was brought. Jesus stopped the crowd at that place and permitted the trio of apostles to accompany him, the same ones specified on other occasions (Matthew 17: 1; 26: 37).

Verse 38. When Jesus arrived at the house a tumultuous crowd had gathered and the people were weeping and wailing as was the custom upon a death in a home.

Verse 39. *Not dead, but sleepeth.* This is figurative language, and the reader is cited to the comments on this subject at Matthew 9: 24.

Verse 40. They laughed at Jesus because they did not understand the two kinds of language. No reason is stated for putting the group out of the house, but it was appropriate to treat the people so in view of the hasty and undignified attitude they showed toward Jesus. He then took the parents of the girl, together with the three apostles, and entered the room where the body lay.

Verse 41. Jesus took the damsel by

the hand because it was his plan in this case. However, that fact alone was not the power that was to bring the dead to life, otherwise any man could bring a dead person to life again.

Verse 42. The girl was twelve years old and hence was able naturally to walk after her illness was gone. The astonishment was caused by the fact that a dead person had been brought back to life.

Verse 43. The Lord permitted Mark to record this case in his Gospel, hence there was nothing wrong in the case being known. But it was the practice of Jesus to be humble and not glory over his miraculous deeds, so he gave instructions frequently that people should not spread the report of what they had received.

MARK 6

Verse 1. *Open country* means that where Nazareth was located (Matthew 4: 13). The reference cited tells that Jesus adopted Capernaum as his residence and many of his mighty works were done there, but he occasionally paid a visit to his boyhood home. Let it be noted that his disciples (apostles) followed him to Nazareth.

Verse 2. *From whence hath this man these things.* Jesus had lived in this town until he was thirty years old and they were intimately acquainted with him. It had been but a little while since he went away, and when he came back and they saw his deeds and heard his teaching it was somewhat puzzling to them.

Verse 3. The remarks in this verse were said by way of assuring themselves of the identity of Jesus. A peculiar trait of the human mind has produced a well-known saying, "Familiarity breeds contempt." The citizens seemed to think that one with whom they were so intimately acquainted would be unable to accomplish such a great work. (For comments on *brethren* see Matthew 12: 46.)

Verse 4. In this verse Jesus merely states the fact commented upon in the preceding verse, without expressing any opinion on it either for or against.

Verse 5. *Could* is from DUNAMAI which Thayer defines, "to be able, have power," and he explains his definition, "whether by virtue of one's own ability and resources, or of a state of mind, *or through favorable circumstances* (emphasis mine, E. M. Z.),or by permission of law or custom." The words emphasized explain in what sense

Jesus could not do much in this place; the circumstances were unfavorable. The fact that he did heal "a few sick folks" shows it was no lack of ability in Jesus.

Verse 6. Jesus was divinely inspired and knew all that was in man, hence nothing could surprise him that was done by human beings. The word *marvel* means that Jesus took special note of the gross unbelief of the people of Nazareth and decided to go elsewhere to do his work.

Verse 7. This is sometimes referred to as "the first commission," in contrast with "the great commission" of chapter 16: 15, 16. The wisdom of working in pairs is shown by the plan Jesus used in this case. Paul frequently had one or more brethren with him as he went out into the field. *Power* is from EXOUSIA which means authority or right. It was fitting to use such a word because the unclean spirits were intelligent beings and could logically be addressed by commands.

Verse 8. The staff was a walking stick and would be needed from the start, hence they were permitted to provide that. A *scrip* was the same as a modern lunch basket. They were supposed to be given their necessities by the people among whom they worked on the ground that "the workman is worthy of his meat" (Matthew 10: 10).

Verse 9. Sandals were needed immediately, like the walking stick, therefore they were permitted to provide that before starting, and one coat was placed on the same basis.

Verse 10. They were to make only one house stop in each city.

Verse 11. Shaking off the dust was an old custom practiced to indicate a feeling of disgust against a person or place; I have no information as to its origin. *More tolerable . . . in the day of judgment*, not afterwards. To use some everyday language, some people will have a harder time in getting past the judgment than others. The reason is that some have more and better opportunities than others.

Verse 12. *They* means the twelve apostles who went out under the commission as stated in verse 7. Matthew 10: 7 tells us also that they preached the news that the kingdom of heaven was at hand and that repentance therefore was necessary.

Verse 13. They cast out devils by the power or authority that Jesus gave them (verse 7), and performed the other miracles by the same means. Anointing with oil is connected with healing the sick. The significance of that is expressed by one writer by saying, "Its use implied that God was the healer." That is correct, but it does not explain how it does so. The idea is that oil of olives is no active medicine and could not effect a cure of sickness alone. The conclusion would be, then, that a greater power was working in connection with the oil. (See James 5: 14.)

Verse 14. This was Herod Antipas, son of Herod the Great. His remarks about Jesus are explained in the note at Matthew 14: 2 on "transmigration."

Verse 15. The writer interrupts his story of Herod to report what some others were saying about Jesus. The same is given in the conversation Jesus had with the apostles when they came into the coasts of Caesarea Philippi (Matthew 16: 13, 14).

Verse 16. This verse repeats verse 14 with the added statement that Herod beheaded John.

Verse 17. The persecution began with the imprisonment of John which was spite work, caused by Herodias whom he had unlawfully married, she being the wife of his brother.

Verse 18. John told Herod it was not lawful for him to have this woman. The law that he violated by that marriage is in Leviticus 18: 16; 20: 21.

Verse 19. John's rebuke especially angered Herodias who would have killed John if she could have done as she felt about it.

Verse 20. The original word for *feared* has a twofold meaning, depending on the way it is used. This entire verse shows a friendly attitude toward John hence it means that Herod respected him. It was this kind of fear that was in the way of the wicked designs of his wife. But as vicious a person as she can plot and accomplish her wickedness by indirect methods as we shall see.

Verse 21. *Convenient* is defined, "seasonable, timely, opportune." The verse means that Herod's birthday fu :. hed a convenient time for the wo .an to carry out her plot.

V erse 22. Herodias knew the lustful character of Herod, a character that explains his willingness to take his own brother's wife unlawfully, and she therefore conceived a plan to capture him. She instructed her daughter

to go into the party and dance before the eyes of the men. It is not reasonable to suppose that Herod was a judge of "art" so that the performance of the girl impressed him from that standpoint. Besides, if that were his motive, just an expensive personal gift would have been all that she would have expected. The eastern dances were of a licentious character, displaying the figure in a way to appeal to the lustful eyes of the witnesses. Herod's baser nature was so inflamed that he exceeded all the customs and promised to give the girl anything she might ask.

Verse 23. The man was so overcome in his passion that he did not stop with a mere promise, but backed it up with an oath, and also specified the maximum limit to which she could go in her wish which was the half of his kingdom.

Verse 24. The damsel had accomplished the satanic effect that her mother planned, and she then went to her for further instructions, and was told to ask for the head of John the Baptist. This verse states the wish in general terms and the next will be more specific to suit the horrible designs of the revengeful woman.

Verse 25. Following her mother's instructions the girl came back into the presence of Herod and requested the head of John *in a charger* or large dish. By having the head in this way the wicked woman would know that she had been successful in her plot.

Verse 26. The king was sorry because he knew that John was a righteous man. But his pride of position under the eyes of the guests, together with a false notion of the sacredness of oaths, prevailed over his better judgment and feelings.

Verse 27. The executioner went to the prison and beheaded John, which was done with a sword, that being before the days of other mechanical means.

Verse 28. The head was brought in a large dish and given to the girl. That would seem to make the deal regular since she was the one who had earned the gift by her immoral performance. Of course she could do as she pleased with the award, hence she gave it to her mother who had plotted the affair.

Verse 29. *His disciples* means the disciples of John. All that was left for them to do was to give respectful and loving attention to the headless body.

I have been unable to find any information on what became of the head of this righteous man.

Verse 30. The apostles made this report under the commission of verses 7-13.

Verse 31. The crowds were so dense that it interfered with their meals. The people kept coming and going until Jesus instructed his disciples to get away for a while.

Verse 32. They slipped away from the crowd and took a boat for a desert place.

Verse 33. But they did not escape from the eyes of all the people. They saw and recognized Jesus and were determined not to let him get entirely from them. They could not follow him in boats, but went on foot with such speed that they were at the place ahead of him and met him as he landed.

Verse 34. *When he came out* denotes when he left the boat and came ashore. The compassion of the Lord was always one of his ruling principles. His opinion of this mixed throng that had come *out of all cities* is compared to a flock that has been deserted by the shepherd. Such a group of people would furnish the kind that was hungering and thirsting after righteousness (Matthew 5: 6), hence it says *he began to teach.*

Verse 35. The disciples finally became concerned about the comfort of the multitude. It was a desert place, which merely means it was not inhabited and hence contained no markets of any kind where food could be purchased.

Verse 36. They suggested that Jesus dismiss the people that they might go into the villages *round about* to buy some food, for they had not brought any such supplies when they came out there.

Verse 37. The disciples did not understand how Jesus meant for them to feed them.

Verse 38. These few loaves and fishes would not supply even a taste for all the multitude, but the lesson should be gathered that the Lord expects man to do what he can in accomplishing desired results.

Verse 39. *Sit down by companies* means to form groups for the orderly passing of food. *Green grass* does not grow where there never is any moisture, so the desert does not mean an infertile spot.

Verse 40. *By hundred and fifties.* This was according to the uneven condition of the land, making it more convenient to have smaller groups in some places and larger groups in others, adapting the size of the groups to the surface conditions.

Verse 41. Jesus blessed the bread by giving thanks to God for it. The reason for breaking the bread was the same for breaking it in the Lord's Supper, and that was only because more than one person was to partake of it. Jesus handed the pieces of bread to the disciples so they could serve the multitude.

Verse 42. Jesus did not satisfy their hunger by performing a miracle on their appetite, for it says they were all *filled.* The miracle was in multiplying the bread as it was being passed through the crowd.

Verse 43. Another proof that no miraculous effect was given to the bread so as to satisfy the hunger, is the fact that they found all these scraps left after the meal.

Verse 44. *Five thousand men,* and Matthew 14: 21 adds "besides women and children."

Verse 45. Bethsaida was a town of Galilee, and Jesus gave his disciples instructions that they were to return by boat to that region, while he remained to dismiss the people so they could return to their homes.

Verse 46. Having sent the multitudes away, Jesus retired to a mountain to pray.

Verse 47. The boat had been making its way for several hours until evening overtook it. Still later in the night a severe wind came down upon the sea, blowing against the boat so that the rowers were having difficulty with the vessel. Jesus saw the situation and went to their rescue the *fourth watch* which was 3 A. M.

Verse 48. While it was night, it was possible to discern a form coming towards them and they were frightened. They thought it was a *spirit* which is from PHANTASMA which means some kind of disembodied being with a visible form.

Verses 49, 50. The familiar words, "It is I; be not afraid," assured them of their safety.

Verse 51. The presence of Jesus in the boat had a quieting effect on the storm. The disciples were baffled by the event and overwhelmed by amazement.

Verse 52. *Heart was hardened* means it was stunned to the extent of inaction, forgetting for the time being that Jesus had only a few hours before fed the thousands.

Verse 53. Gennesaret was a narrow strip of country on the east shore of Galilee.

Verse 54. *They* means the people of Gennesaret who had seen Jesus before and knew about his great works of compassion on behalf of the unfortunate.

Verse 55. The people began at once to gather up the sick folks and carry them in beds to wherever they knew that Jesus was pausing.

Verse 56. *Streets* is from a word that means marketplaces, not an ordinary thoroughfare as one might think. They were centers where people in all the walks of life gathered, and they expected Jesus to be there a part of the time. When he did come he was requested to let the sick people touch his clothing. Such a request was a sign of their faith and Jesus rewarded it by healing them of their diseases.

MARK 7

Verse 1. The Pharisees were a religious sect of the Jews, and the scribes were those whose business it was to copy the law of Moses and expound it unto the people. Both of these groups were constant foes of Jesus because he rebuked their hypocrisies.

Verse 2. These people were always watching to find a cause of complaint. They thought they had found something when they saw the disciples eating without washing.

Verse 3. This did not refer to ordinary cleansing but to a tradition of the elders.

Verse 4. The tradition required that they wash their hands as a ceremony under certain conditions, regardless of whether the act was necessary or not.

Verse 5. They based their criticism on the fact that the disciples had disregarded the tradition of the elders, not that they had gone contrary to the rules of sanitation.

Verse 6. Jesus directly called those people hypocrites and said that Esaias (Isaiah) had prophesied about them. They spoke one way and their heart was interested in another.

Verse 7. Regardless of the apparent goodness of the worship that is offered to God, if it is based on the command-ments of men the worship is vain or useless.

Verse 8. A person would have the privilege of maintaining his own notions about such things as ceremonial washing of hands and service vessels, provided that was as far as it went. But these people exalted those practices above the commands of God, even to the extent of substituting them for the divine law.

Verse 9. *Full well* applies to the truthfulness of the statement and not to what the Pharisees were doing; truly, ye reject, etc. *That ye may keep* denotes they could not keep such traditions as theirs in the way they desired without disregarding the commandments of the Lord.

Verse 10. The kind of traditions Jesus was condemning is specified in this and a few following verses. First, he cited one of the positive commandments God gave through Moses, that a man should honor his parents. And this honor included the obligation of administering to their needs.

Verse 11. *Corban* is defined in the lexicon, "a gift offered to God." These Pharisees pretended to have put their money into the Lord's treasury instead of using it to provide some benefit for their parents.

Verse 12. On the pretense that they had put their money into the treasury, they claimed exemption from considering their parents as dependents.

Verse 13. In the aforesaid practice they made their traditions more important than the inspired law that had been delivered to them by the hand of Moses.

Verse 14. Jesus next turned his attention to the people in general. He wished them not to misunderstand what he had said about washing the hands.

Verse 15. He did not mean to belittle the importance of cleanliness. The Pharisees were dealing with the subject in a ceremonial way only, as if the soil on one's hands would cause some moral or spiritual bad effect. Jesus was denying that and then stating what would in reality defile one. This is as far as he went in his explanation to "the people." (See the reason why at Matthew 13: 11.)

Verse 16. This means for every man to use his opportunities for hearing the truth.

Verse 17. After getting to themselves, the disciples asked Jesus to explain the parable to them. He did so as explained by the note cited at **verse 15.**

Verse 18. Jesus repeated the statement about the outward filth entering a man.

Verse 19. The reason it does not defile a man is because it is not retained, but is eliminated from the body along with other waste matter. A *draught* was similar to our modern sanitary stool.

Verse 20. The mere fact of its coming out is not what defiles a man. The idea is that such things as will soon be named are what makes a man defiled, and the issuing forth of them reveals what the defilements are.

Verse 21. The things named in this and the following verse are not done "on the spur of the moment," but are the deliberate intentions of the heart, and that is why they are said to defile a man. *Adulteries* can be committed first in the heart (Matthew 5: 28). Fornication is virtually the same in the eyes of the Lord, but human laws make a difference and the scripture condemns both so there will be no doubt. *Murder* is taking human life unlawfully after it has been premeditated which is done in the heart.

Verse 22. A man does not *steal* accidentally but plans to do it. *Lasciviousness* is filthy desire and they are begun in the heart. *An evil eye.* Thayer says, "Since the eye is the index of the mind, the following phrases have arisen," then he includes the one italicized. *Blasphemy* is wicked speech that is prompted by the heart.

Verse 23. These things defile a man because they corrupt his heart and then his life through the manner of conduct they induce him to practice.

Verse 24. Jesus left the vicinity of the Sea of Galilee and went on across the country to that lying near the Mediterranean Sea in which were the cities of Tyre and Sidon. He wished to have some privacy and entered into a house for that purpose. *Could not be hid.* Jesus did not wish to be always performing miracles to accomplish his purposes, but often took the same course that other men would take under the same circumstances. In the present case the shelter of a house was not enough to hide him.

Verse 25. This woman's daughter had an *unclean spirit* which means was possessed with a devil. This daughter was *young* and ordinarily would not be unrighteous in her man-

er of life, but the possession of a devil was an affliction and not a fault.

Verse 26. In the time of Christ all persons who were not Jews were regarded as Gentiles whatever their nationality might be, hence this woman being Greek is rendered Gentile in the margin. By nation she was a Syrophenician which is a compound word meaning a mixture of the Phoenician and Syrian territories. The writer mentions this as an explication of the attitude that Jesus at first maintained in testing her faith.

Verse 27. The Greek word for *dog* is not the one ordinarily used for that animal, but one that Thayer defines as "a little dog." It refers to a creature that would be like a child's pet and allowed to play about the table while its master was eating. The crumbs that fell would not be denied the dog and the circumstance was used for an illustration. Jesus purposely used that story to suggest the humble speech the woman made.

Verse 28. The woman did not resent the comparison, but was willing to accept the temporal healing of her daughter as crumbs, and leave the bread of the Lord's teaching to the children of his Father's family, namely, the Jews.

Verse 29. The woman said just what Jesus wished her to say, and as a reward he assured her that the devil had been driven out of her daughter.

Verse 30. She found it as Jesus stated upon her return home. After such an experience as the girl had suffered (Matthew 15: 22 says she was "grievously vexed"), she would be somewhat prostrated, so the mother found her daughter lying on a bed.

Verse 31. Decapolis was a region on the east side of the Jordan. So Jesus left the western part of Palestine, crossed the country and over Jordan and on to the coast of the Sea of Galilee.

Verse 32. This man was suffering with a bodily ailment of his hearing, and that had caused him to be defective in his speech. People learn to talk from childhood by hearing others, and if they cannot hear they may not learn to talk.

Verse 33. This physical contact was the plan that Jesus saw fit to use in this case, not that he could not have healed the man otherwise.

Verse 34. EPHPHATHA is a Greek word and the King James translators retained it in the text, then gave the definition of it which is the same that is in Thayer's lexicon, namely, "be thou opened." *Looking up to heaven* indicated that he was looking to God for cooperation as he always worked as a partner with his Father.

Verse 35. As usual, the cure was *straightway* and not a prolonged affair.

Verse 36. *Charged them tell no man.* Jesus did not want the people to think that he was working miracles just with the motive of becoming famous.

Verse 37. The proof these people had that Jesus did all things well was the fact that visible changes came to the man with whom they were so well acquainted.

MARK 8

Verse 1. Jesus did many of his works through cooperation with his disciples.

Verse 2. The compassion of Jesus was caused by the lack of food among the multitudes. That would be emphasized by the motive that had kept them there for three days, which was that they might hear the teaching He was giving.

Verse 3. For comments on this verse see those on Matthew 15: 32.

Verse 4. It is strange the disciples forgot the occasion of chapter 6: 35-44.

Verse 5. Jesus never had to ask questions for information (John 2: 24, 25), but he often asked them as a means of drawing the disciples into the matter at hand, to let them feel a sense of responsibility concerning the welfare of others.

Verse 6. They were to sit down for the sake of orderliness. The bread was first handed to the disciples who then *did set* ("place near"—Thayer) the bread before them.

Verse 7. *He blessed* is equivalent to "gave thanks" in the preceding verse.

Verse 8. Having the baskets of scraps left denoted that their being filled was not just an imagination. This is especially significant in view of the fact that they had been fasting for three days and must have been very hungry.

Verse 9. Matthew 15: 38 says this many men besides women and children.

Verse 10. After dismissing the people Jesus got into a boat and came to the region of Dalmanutha, a town on the west side of the Sea of Galilee.

Verse 11. It is honorable to ask questions for information, but the Pharisees asked them as a temptation of Jesus, thus acting in their usual hypocritical manner.

Verse 12. *Sighed deeply* means Jesus made a deep groan over the perversity of those people. He did not consider them worthy of much attention. In Matthew 16: 4 he did tell them about Jonah, but that was not what they really wanted.

Verse 13. Leaving the crowd, Jesus again recrossed the sea.

Verse 14. They were about to enter a region where public markets were scarce at best, which ought to have prompted the disciples to make special provision for it. Jesus knew they had forgotten about it and used the circumstance to test them.

Verse 15. The disciples knew that the Pharisees and Herod were in an unfavorable light with Jesus, but they did not grasp the comparison that was made to leaven.

Verse 16. "A guilty conscience needs no reproof" is an old saying, and it about describes the state of mind the disciples were in. There was scarcely any connection between what Jesus said and the fact of their having forgotten to take bread.

Verse 17. They had done their reasoning to themselves but Jesus knew about it and rebuked them for their dullness of heart which almost amounted to unbelief.

Verse 18. This verse means they did not use their faculties to arrive at just conclusions, even when they had visible facts on which to base their reasoning.

Verses 19, 20. To show that it was not a lapse in their memory, Jesus specified that part of the previous feedings that especially demonstrated the greatness of the miracle (the amount of scraps left) and they remembered both instances.

Verse 21. Jesus rebuked them with a question as to their understanding. Matthew 16: 12 states that the disciples then did understand what Jesus meant by leaven.

Verse 22. The request for Jesus to touch the man showed their faith in his power.

Verse 23. Jesus anointed the man with saliva and touched his eyes.

Verse 24. Men looked like trees walking to this man; that is, he saw that much but the vision was indistinct.

Verse 25. Jesus next touched the man's eyes and he saw clearly. This circumstance has been referred to by some as an answer to our claim that miraculous cures were instantaneous. But it is no valid argument, for Jesus just saw fit to perform two miracles, and each was instantaneous. To be like the modern so-called miracles, the man should have been receiving repeated treatments and the sight returning gradually, little by little, until he could see clearly. Instead, as soon as Jesus touched the man's eyes the first time he could see objects. Had nothing more been done he would always have seen that well. So that each of the miracles was complete and instantaneous.

Verse 26. See the comments on Mark 7: 36 for the present verse.

Verse 27. The origin of the name Caesarea Philippi is explained at Matthew 16: 13. The question Jesus asked his disciples was for the introduction to the more important subject of the faith they had in him.

Verse 28. These opinions were based on the doctrine called "transmigration," which is explained by a note at Matthew 14: 2.

Verse 29. *Whom say ye* was addressed to all the apostles, but Peter usually was the spokesman and he made the confession of faith on behalf of the others.

Verse 30. This charge was not like the one in verse 26 and others as it had nothing directly to do with his miracles. It meant that it was not time to "release" the fundamental claim of his divinity to the whole world.

Verse 31. It was near enough to the end to introduce the sad information of how Jesus was to be treated by the Jewish leaders. This one verse covers the persecution, death and resurrection of Jesus. But it seems that Peter noticed only the bad part of it and overlooked the glorious assurance of the resurrection. Doubtless that was because he was still under the delusion that Jesus was to set up an earthly kingdom, which he could not do if he died a violent death.

Verse 32. With that error in mind Peter spoke against the prediction of Jesus.

Verse 33. Satan accomplished his purpose in the garden by contradicting the saying of God. Peter contradicted the statement of Jesus and hence he called him by that name. *Savourest* means to be interested in a thing, and Jesus meant that Peter was

interested in a temporal kingdom instead of the spiritual kingdom of God.

Verse 34. *Cross* is used figuratively and means that following Christ requires one to make sacrifices. Many things must be denied to a man who tries to serve Jesus.

Verse 35. Two kinds of life are considered in this verse. The passage would read that whoever seeks to save his temporal life at the expense of righteousness will lose his spiritual life. And of course the opposite is true of the man who puts spiritual things above everything else.

Verse 36. *Profit* means to obtain from an investment more than was put into it. If a man buys the whole world with the price of his soul he will be a loser, for the price paid is many times more valuable than the thing purchased.

Verse 37. This verse has the same thought as the preceding but with a different figure. It is compared to a man pawning his soul for the pleasures of this world. When he would wish to redeem his soul from the "pawn shop" of the world he will not be able because the things of the world will then be gone out of existence.

Verse 38. Whosoever *therefore*. Since a wasted life will have nothing with which to redeem the soul, it is folly to disregard Jesus (be ashamed of him) in this world. Such a man will be disregarded by Jesus when he is in his presence and that of his angels.

MARK 9

Verse 1. This statement of Jesus denotes that the kingdom of heaven was not yet set up, and also it was to come in the lifetime of some men then living. Since all of the people living then are dead, we know that the kingdom of heaven has been in existence for centuries and that much teaching on that subject today is false.

Verse 2. *Six days after* the conversation of the preceding verse is what is meant. These are the three apostles whom Jesus frequently took with him on special missions. To be transfigured means to take on another appearance.

Verse 3. White raiment indicates purity and heavenly splendor. A *fuller* is a cleanser of cloth and no man in that occupation could put a garment into the condition of whiteness that appeared upon the body of Jesus.

Verse 4. Elias is the same as Elijah of the Old Testament who went to heaven in a whirlwind (2 Kings 2: 11) and hence never died. Moses was the lawgiver of the Old Testament and died (Deuteronomy 34: 5). Peter, James and John had not died and were therefore still in the flesh. So at this event the three states of man were represented, the fleshly, the intermediate and the eternal.

Verse 5. Peter had a feeling of hospitality and wished to provide for the guests, which indicates they had the appearance of men who could be cared for in earthly housing.

Verse 6. *Wist* is an obsolete word meaning he knew not what to say, or, he did not realize what he was saying. *Sore afraid* means they were exceedingly amazed.

Verse 7. The announcement from the cloud was like the one heard at the baptism of Jesus except it had the words, *hear him.* The earthly work of Jesus was virtually completed and the authority of the Son of God over Moses and the prophets was thus announced in this important assembly.

Verse 8. The purpose of the visit of the special guests was accomplished, and when the apostles rallied from their amazement they noted the absence of Moses and Elias.

Verse 9. This vision was so special that the public in general was not yet ready for its announcement. (See the comments on chapter 8: 30.)

Verse 10. The restriction Jesus placed on them which was connected with the resurrection confused the apostles. They discussed the subject among themselves and then decided to ask Jesus a question.

Verse 11. The apostles did not realize that *Elias* was used figuratively only.

Verse 12. Jesus affirmed the prediction that Elias was to come *first* and *restore all things*, which means to get things in readiness for Christ.

Verse 13. Jesus then explained that the prediction had been fulfilled. This matter is explained in more detail at Matthew 17: 10-12.

Verse 14. *Came to his disciples* means the ones Jesus left waiting while he was in the mount. The scribes were generally at hand with their critical questions, and when they could not approach Jesus they contacted his disciples.

Verse 15. *The people* means the crowd in general who were usually in a favorable frame of mind toward Jesus. Their attention was called to him and they were *greatly amazed* or surprised. But they were favorably impressed by his sudden appearance for they came and saluted him.

Verse 16. Jesus asked the scribes why they were questioning the disciples. As far as the text goes they never answered the question put to them by Jesus.

Verse 17. One of the multitude (not one of the scribes) announced to Jesus that he had brought his son unto him. That denotes that he came with his son expecting to meet Jesus. But as he was not with the disciples the father had turned the case over to them. A *dumb spirit* is stated because it had that effect on the boy. We know it does not literally mean the devil that was dumb for when Jesus commanded it to come out (verse 26) it *cried* which shows the spirit itself was not dumb.

Verse 18. These symptoms were the effects this particular spirit had on the boy. The possession of evil spirits did not always work the same, the reason for which is not made known in the text. The father then stated that the disciples could not cast the evil spirit out of his son.

Verse 19. This charge of faithfulness was meant for the disciples (Matthew 17: 20).

Verse 20. These terrible symptoms were the results of being possessed with a devil. The devils knew Jesus and feared him, but as a desperate piece of vengeance when this one saw Jesus he overcame the boy and inflicted the injuries mentioned.

Verse 21. This son had been possessed with the devil most of his life.

Verse 22. The child evidently would have lost his life had it not been for friends.

Verse 23. *All things are possible* as far as the Lord's power is concerned, but he does not bestow that power unless the case is regarded worthy, and that point is frequently (not always) determined by the degree of faith manifested.

Verse 24. *Believe* and *unbelief* seem like opposite terms. The man said he did believe, so the request meant that his faith should be made stronger.

Verse 25. Jesus did not want the commotion to become too great so he did his work promptly. The devils are intelligent beings is the reason the Lord could command them.

Verse 26. The spirit *cried* which shows it was not dumb, but it had produced dumbness at times in the boy. Having suffered these attacks from early childhood the boy was exhausted when the devil was cast out so that he appeared to be dead.

Verse 27. Jesus then cured the boy of his weakness so that he arose.

Verse 28. The disciples were baffled over their failure to cast out the devil, and when they had a chance alone they asked Jesus to explain this failure.

Verse 29. The account that Mark gives is very brief. For a fuller treatment of the subject see the text and my comments at Matthew 17: 20, 21.

Verse 30. This verse means that Jesus wished to have as much privacy as possible. His public work was about over and it was unnecessary to meet the public as he had.

Verse 31. Jesus warned his disciples of what was coming, and the same things had been prophesied in the Old Testament.

Verse 32. The language of Jesus was plain and he used words that were in common use. The reason the disciples did not understand them was their delusion of an earthly kingdom they thought he was going to set up.

Verse 33. Jesus did not need to ask questions for information (John 2: 25), but this was his way of bringing the subject before the disciples, for he knew they had been disputing about it as they were going to Capernaum.

Verse 34. *They held their peace* because they felt ashamed as well as surprised that he could read what had not been intended for him even to hear. They had an earthly form of kingdom in mind that Jesus was to set up, and were contending among themselves about who should be in the highest position as a member of it.

Verse 35. True greatness is the subject of this speech of Jesus. In earthly kingdoms it is usual for men to seek prominence and try to become great from the standpoint of authority over others. In the kingdom of heaven it is just the opposite of that. One reason is that this kingdom is an absolute monarchy, and in such a government any attempt of the citizens to attain to greatness in the nature of authority must be interpreted as an infringement upon the king.

Verse 36. This child was small for Jesus took him in his arms, after he had placed him in full view of the apostles.

Verse 37. Receiving a little child in the name of Christ means to do so because of the comparison between them. A man who will do that is bound to have a humble attitude, and humility is what constitutes true greatness in the kingdom of Christ. *Receiveth not me, but him, etc.* This denotes the close association between Christ and his Father. No person can obtain any favor from one of them if he ignores the other.

Verse 38. We notice that no denial was made as to whether the man actually was casting out devils. The complaint was that he was not walking along bodily in the same crowd with Jesus and the twelve. John did not understand that only the apostles were required to "be with him" in that sense. (See chapter 3: 14.)

Verse 39. The fact the man was actually casting out devils proved that he was a true disciple. Had he been a mere pretender he would have failed as did the men reported in Acts 19: 13-16 who were brought to such shameful defeat.

Verse 40. There is no actual neutrality with regard to matters pertaining to Christ. A man may not be very active in an unrighteous life, but unless he is active in the service for Christ he is counted as being "on the other side" (Obadiah 11).

Verse 41. This is to be understood in the same light as verse 37.

Verse 42. When a man becomes like a little child he is then classed as a *little one* in the sense of the word here. This is evident from the truth that he can be *offended* which means to stumble or do wrong, and that is possible only with a person of responsible age and mentality.

Verse 43. *Offend* means to cause to stumble or do wrong. The hand is a valuable member of the body and is used to illustrate anything one might be cherishing but that causes him to do wrong. One would give up the hand if it became diseased and endangered the whole life of the man. Likewise, we should sacrifice any practice or associate however dear, if our spiritual welfare should be endangered by it. A description of *hell* as it is defined in the lexicon may be seen with comments on Matthew 5: 30.

Verse 44. All of the illustrations that are ever used here or elsewhere as to the duration of punishment, must be interpreted to mean that the unsaved will be in punishment that will be conscious and endless. *Their worm dieth not* is commented upon by another writer in better language than I can produce as follows: "The awfully vivid idea of an undying worm, everlastingly consuming an unconsumable body." The reason the worm will not die is that the body will not be consumed, even though in the midst of an unquenchable fire, and hence there will always be something to keep the worm alive.

Verse 45. The foot is used instead of the hand, otherwise the lesson in this verse is the same as that in verse 48 on the subject of making self-denials.

Verse 46. *Worm dieth not* is explained at verse 44.

Verse 47. This is the same lesson as in verses 43 and 45.

Verse 48. See verse 44 for the explanation of this.

Verse 49. *Salted with fire.* Here we see fire used figuratively for salt. Salt, through its preserving qualities, tends to perpetuate an object brought into contact with it. It is thus connected with the fire of perdition because of the perpetual duration of that fire. Salt is used with the idea of perpetuation in Numbers 18: 19.

Verse 50. Just as salt is used to illustrate the perpetuation of the punishment of the wicked, so it also can preserve and perpetuate the good qualities of man. Jesus exhorted the disciples not to let the salt of their good lives lose its strength. They could *have peace one with another* by using the salt of brotherly love.

MARK 10

Verse 1. *Arose from thence* refers to Capernaum where Jesus had been teaching, and started on the journey toward Jerusalem. *By the farther side* is the same as saying *by way of* that region; the route traveled was along the eastern side of the Jordan. As usual, the crowds gathered about Jesus and he taught them.

Verse 2. In Matthew's account of this conversation (chapter 19: 3) the Pharisees add the words "for every cause." Mark says they asked the question for the purpose of tempting Jesus. They hoped he would say something that would disagree with the law and thus give them an occasion for accusing him.

Verse 3. Instead of answering direct, Jesus asked them to repeat the law of Moses on the subject of the question they professed to have in mind.

Verse 4. They stated the law correctly as far as they went, and that law may be seen in Deuteronomy 24: 1.

Verse 5. Jesus did not deny their citation but explained the reason for the law; the people were not in the favorable attitude for the strictness of enforcement, and as an emergency some tolerance was extended to them.

Verse 6. Jesus also informed them that it was not always that way, and his teaching soon indicated that a return to the original ruling would be required after the kingdom of heaven was set up. The original order was that God made them *male* and *female;* singular on both sides, not male and females.

Verse 7. *For this cause* means for the cause soon to be stated, a man should leave his father and mother and cleave to his wife. The word *cleave* means that he should join his body with hers in the fleshly relationship.

Verse 8. The result of that cleaving was to be that the two bodies would become one in the flesh. Not only would they be one flesh at the time of the union, but it was to be permanent, for it says they would be *no more twain, but one flesh.*

Verse 9. It says that God joined these two, and that was because the ordinance was authorized of God. The fleshly union made them one and the unfaithfulness of either would be the way that the union could be *put asunder.*

Verse 10. The disciples wished to have further information.

Verse 11. The wish was granted by the statement of this verse. The simple fact of divorcing a wife does not constitute adultery, but the remarriage to another (except when the wife has been unfaithful, Matthew 19: 9) does.

Verse 12. The same rule applies to a wife that does to a husband.

Verse 13. It is natural for people to want their children admired and even to be fondled. These children were brought to Jesus for that purpose, and it is not any surprise that such a desire would exist, especially in view of the importance of this great "friend of man." The disciples evidently thought that Jesus had more important things to do than to notice children.

Verse 14. Jesus overheard the objections of his disciples and concluded it was an appropriate time to give them a lesson touching the principles of his kingdom soon to be set up. *Of such* should be noted, for it is very significant. Little children were not to become members of the kingdom, for they do not need it. The point is that the spirit of those who are acceptable members of the kingdom of heaven must become like that of a little child.

Verse 15. *Receive the kingdom of God as a little child* means they must become *as* the child in spirit, otherwise they will not be welcomed into the kingdom.

Verse 16. Jesus then gave an example of his own teaching by taking the children in his arms and bestowing upon them a caressing touch. *Blessed them* means he pronounced his good wishes upon them.

Verse 17. The teaching of Jesus had given the impression that something special would be required in order to have eternal life. No doubt this man (who Matthew says was young, chapter 19: 20) sincerely desired eternal life, but he had no idea what he would be required to do in obtaining it.

Verse 18. *None good but one* is explained at Matthew 19: 17.

Verse 19. These six commandments of the Decalogue are the ones that pertain to man's dealing with man. Jesus knew that in this man's case the extra law he would give would also be in that class.

Verse 20. The man claimed to have kept all of these and Jesus did not deny it.

Verse 21. A part of Thayer's definition of the original for *love* is "to regard the welfare of." Knowing the situation with the young man, Jesus considered that his spiritual welfare was at stake. He decided to show him what would be necessary to assure him of that welfare, which was to dispose of his riches.

Verse 22. The man's attachment to his riches was the occasion of this *grief*.

Verse 23. *How hardly shall they . . . enter the kingdom of God.* The reader should see the comments covering this whole event at Matthew 19: 20-27.

Verse 24. The words *trust in riches* gives the key to this subject, which is expressed also by Paul in 1 Timothy 6: 17, and is virtually the same as "the love of money" in the same chapter and verse 10.

Verse 25. This needle is explained in the comments cited in verse 23.

Verse 26. The disciples were taking a purely physical view of the subject.

Verse 27. With God all things are possible as far as power is concerned.

Verse 28. *Have left all* meant they had literally left their homes in order to travel with Jesus in his journeys through the country.

Verse 29. Many things had to be left behind if they went with Jesus in this kind of a journey, for they would have been encumbrances to the work.

Verse 30. *Now in this time* refers to the life on earth with these apostles, but after their bodily association with Jesus had been fulfilled. They were to have their homes and families for their personal use again (such as Peter rejoining his wife, 1 Corinthians 9: 5), but would be required to endure persecutions for the sake of their religion. *World to come* means the age after the judgment in which the righteous will enjoy eternal life.

Verse 31. This important language is commented upon at Matthew 19: 30.

Verse 32. Jesus had told his disciples that he was to be mistreated (chapter 8: 31), and they seemed to think he should not voluntarily go to Jerusalem. When they saw that he was even foremost in the journey they were amazed. Although they followed along after him they were under a feeling of terror.

Verse 33. Instead of trying to lessen their fears by painting the picture in some favorable colors, Jesus repeated what he had said to them before. *Deliver him to the Gentiles* was to be because the Jews could not execute the death sentence.

Verse 34. Jesus usually included the resurrection in his predictions of his death.

Verse 35. This request was for the sake of James and John, but Matthew 20: 20, 21 states that their mother made the plea to Jesus.

Verse 36. The Lord knows what we need or want before we ask him, but he desires that we ask him (Matthew 6: 8).

Verse 37. This request was based on their idea of an earthly kingdom.

Verse 38. The disciples did not realize what was involved in their request. They thought only of the glory that was supposed to come upon those in positions of authority in the kingdoms of the world. The cup and baptism that Jesus mentioned were figurative, referring to the trials that were in store for those who were associated with Christ in the kingdom of heaven.

Verse 39. Without realizing what it meant, the disciples indicated they were ready to accept the cup and baptism. Even in a spiritual kingdom, such a cup and baptism as Jesus meant were to be expected, hence he told them they would have that experience.

Verse 40. *Is not mine to give* is explained at Matthew 20: 23.

Verse 41. The other apostles were displeased with James and John. It evidently was because of their desire to be seated above the others in places of authority.

Verse 42. Jesus found it necessary so many times to explain the fundamental difference as to true greatness between his kingdom and those of the world. In them the strongest are the ones who exercise the rule of authority and domination.

Verses 43, 44. It was to be the opposite of that in the kingdom of heaven. In it the truly greatest citizens will be the ones who render the most service to others.

Verse 45. The principle of service as a sign of true greatness was practiced by the Son of man notwithstanding he was to be the king. He devoted his life on earth to service unto others, then crowned that service by giving his life for the benefit of the whole world that all might be saved who would serve him.

Verse 46. Jesus came to Jericho after crossing the Jordan on the way to Jerusalem. As he and his disciples with a great number of other people were leaving that city, they passed a blind beggar sitting by the wayside.

Verse 47. This man had been asking for the necessities of life only, for he did not expect any of the people to be able to do anything for his blindness. But the fame of Jesus had reached his ears, and learning that he was passing by it prompted him to ask for a more important favor.

Verse 48. The crowd thought the blind man was interrupting the work of Jesus, but he was made more persistent by the attempt to quiet him.

Verses 49, 50. Whoever was given the command to call the blind man gave him a kindly greeting. Upon information that Jesus had heard his plea he arose and went to him. He cast away his outer garment that he might move more easily.

Verse 51. Jesus knew the nature of the man's affliction, but wished him to express his request as an indication of his faith. (See comments at verse 36).

Verse 52. For the sake of his faith the Lord granted the unfortunate man his sight. Notice that it was *immediately* as all truly miraculous cures were done.

MARK 11

Verse 1. The mount of Olives was near Jerusalem (Acts 1: 12) and the towns named were on or near the mount. They are mentioned to indicate *how* "nigh" they were.

Verse 2. Jesus usually traveled on foot, and being so near the city he would not change his mode of travel just from being tired. But he wished to prepare for the fulfilling of a certain prophecy by procuring this animal. He instructed his disciples to bring him a colt tied in a nearby village, one that had never been "broke to ride."

Verse 3. They were given the authority to take the colt, equipped with the all-sufficient explanation to its owners that *the Lord hath need of him.*

Verse 4. They found the colt tied at an intersection of two streets, or rather, where they came together as "a fork in the road."

Verse 5. The inquiry was made of them that Jesus had anticipated. It was quite natural to ask for an explanation when others besides the owners were taking possession of this untrained colt.

Verse 6. Their explanation was accepted as Jesus said it would be.

Verse 7. *Brought the colt . . . he sat upon him.* Jesus rode the mother of the colt also although Mark does not say so. For an explanation of this subject see the comments on Matthew 21: 5.

Verse 8. When a dignitary was approaching, it was customary to make a carpet on which he might proceed. These people did so with the materials at hand, namely, their outer garments. Some found the *branches* or leaves of palm trees to use for a carpet.

Verse 9. *Hosanna* is defined in the comments on Matthew 21: 9.

Verse 10. *Our father David.* These people were Jews who had come to Jerusalem to attend the feast of the Passover. They were acquainted with the prophecies that David was to have a descendant who was to sit on his throne and here recognized Jesus as that person. (See Psalms 132: 11).

Verse 11. This verse mentions only in general terms the visit of Jesus to the temple. In Matthew 21: 12, 13, is the account of his casting out the moneychangers, and it is also mentioned in verse 15 of this chapter. Having purged the temple, Jesus went out to the nearby village of Bethany to stay over night.

Verse 12. In the morning they returned from Bethany and Jesus became hungry.

Verse 13. See the comments at Matthew 21: 19 for the explanation of the fig tree.

Verse 14. *No man eat fruit of thee* is the *curse* pronounced upon the fig tree.

Verse 15. This verse describes what is referred to at verse 11 and in the passage in Matthew. The chronological order of the events is not quite the same in Mark as it is in Matthew, but the facts are the same so that no contradiction exists.

Verse 16. This verse means Jesus stopped all commercial activities in the temple.

Verse 17. The place where this saying is written is Isaiah 56: 7. Jesus called it a *den of thieves* because they were taking advantage of the situation to charge undue fees for their transactions; they were profiteering.

Verse 18. The scribes and chief priests *feared him* in the bad sense of that word. They were afraid of an uprising among the people if they did any harm to Jesus.

Verses 19, 20. On the return to Jerusalem they observed the fig tree that Jesus had cursed. So completely did this "curse" affect the fig tree that it had withered from its top to its roots.

Verse 21. Peter called the attention of Jesus to the fig tree, evidently in a manner that indicated his astonishment.

Verse 22. The first reply of Jesus was that it requires faith in God.

Verse 23. No miracles were performed by Jesus or his apostles for the mere gratification of curiosity, or just to make a show of power. If any good reason appeared for removing a mountain in this way it could be done, for one miracle is as easy as another as far as power is concerned.

Verse 24. Even miracles that are right and needed cannot be performed without the proper degree of faith. (See Matthew 17: 19-21.)

Verse 25. The word *stand* does not refer to the posture of the body, but is a term that applies to the established practice of praying. Besides, the things Jesus instructs to be done in connection with praying to God are just as necessary in any other position of the body as they are in that of standing.

Verse 26. The duty of forgiving others in connection with our plea for pardon, mentioned in this and the preceding verse, is taught in Matthew 6: 12-15.

Verse 27. The old foes of Jesus were these men who met him in the temple.

Verse 28. *These things* means the driving of the moneychangers out of the temple.

Verses 29-33. For an explanation of this passage see Matthew 21: 24-27.

MARK 12

Verse 1. See the comments at Matthew 13: 3 as to the right use of Parables. For other comments as to the householder see Matthew 21: 33.

Verse 2. *At the season.* It takes time to produce fruit, hence the householder did not expect any products until the proper time when he sent a special servant for them.

Verses 3-5. This refers to the mistreatment that the Jews showed to the prophets and other righteous teachers who were sent among them by the Lord.

Verse 6. Jesus was a Jew who was sent to that nation as the rightful heir of all his Father's possessions, and he should have been received with great respect.

Verse 7. Being the heir, if he could be removed there would seem to be no one to claim the property, hence the workers planned to make away with him.

Verse 8. The wicked workers carried out their plot and slew the son of the householder, which refers to the treatment that Jesus was soon to receive at the hands of the wicked Jews.

Verse 9. According to Matthew's account (chapter 21: 40, 41), this answer to the question of Jesus was made by the Jews. Having in mind some literal case of an earthly vineyard, they answered correctly, not realizing that their own answer would condemn them for their wicked attitude towards the servants of God.

Verses 10, 11. Jesus began opening their understanding of the parable by referring to a prediction in the Old Testament.

Verse 12. They doubtless were aware of this statement and must have begun to see the light that was exposing them. But they were restrained from doing anything to Jesus because of their fear of public sentiment that was favorable to him.

Verse 13. *Herodians* were a family party among the Jews who favored the Romans. This is described more extensively in the comments on Matthew 22: 16.

Verse 14. After some expressions of pure flattery these hypocrites came out with their question. They had the delusion that the kingdom which Jesus was soon to set up would be a temporal one, and hence a rival of the Roman Empire. In that case he would logically disapprove of any financial support of Caesar. If they could get him to say so, they would have a basis for accusing him of being an enemy of the lawful government.

Verse 15. Knowing their hypocrisy, Jesus did not answer directly by "yes" or "no," but asked to see a piece of money.

Verse 16. The coins of about all countries have the image of some important person on them, and also some saying or motto is inscribed thereon. Jesus took the critics by surprise by asking to whom the coin belonged. They answered correctly that it was the property of Caesar. Incidentally, this very coin was the kind that was used in paying the tribute to Caesar's government.

Verse 17. Anyone would have to say it is right to give back to a man that which is rightfully his. They just had said the coin belonged to Caesar, so it was natural that Jesus would tell them to give it back to him. In so doing they would be performing the very thing they asked Jesus if it was lawful to do. *They marveled* means they were amazed and so stunned that they had nothing more to say.

Verses 18-23. To save space let the reader see comments on Matthew 22: 23-28.

Verses 24, 25. For the explanation of this paragraph see Matthew 22: 29, 30.

Verse 26. *Book of Moses* is so called because God inspired him to write it. God declared himself to be the God of these patriarchs whom the Sadducees professed to love.

Verse 27. God is not a God of the dead (which these Sadducees as well as everyone else admitted), yet these patriarchs had been in their graves for centuries. That proves there is something in man that lives after the body is placed in the grave.

Verse 28. In Matthew's account of this conversation (chapter 22: 34-40) it is stated that the purpose of this question was to tempt Jesus, while the present passage says nothing about that. Instead, the latter part of the conversation indicates a favorable attitude toward Jesus. Both phases of it are true and explanable on a reasonable basis. After the scribe put the tempting question to Jesus, the reply was so unanswerable that he was drawn over to the better view of it and brought forth the good remarks reported of him. The question asked of Jesus was unfair because no one of God's commands is any more important or greater than another.

Verse 29. The one great difference would be the contrast between God and man. Logically, then, a command to love God would come first in the sense of priority.

Verse 30. This command requires that God shall be loved with all the powers of man.

Verse 31. The preceding command is first in priority, but the second one is like it in the sense of authority that is back of it.

Verse 32. The scribe was affected by the answer of Jesus and verified it. He went farther and stated the reason why we should love the Lord wholeheartedly, and that was because there is only one God.

Verse 33. The scribe summed up in this verse what constitutes the entire Decalogue, in that he cites the two commandments on which all the law and prophets hung (Matthew 22: 40). The reason he assigned for his conclusion was that it was better than burnt offerings. A man might offer whole droves of animals for the outward show, but not actually be moved by genuine love for God or man.

Verse 34. The kingdom of God had not been set up when this conversation took place, hence no actual distance could exist between it and any person as to specific items required for entrance into it. But the scribe expressed a principle of life that was so different from that of the Pharisees, that Jesus meant he was advocating ideas that were much like what would be required of persons in the kingdom when it did become a fact on earth. This conversation silenced the critics so that none of them asked Jesus any more questions.

Verse 35. Many of the Jews admitted that Christ was an actual descendant of David according to the flesh, but denied that he was divine or related to him spiritually.

Verse 36. Jesus then quoted Psalms 110: 1 where David referred to him as "my Lord."

Verse 37. The question put to them was how Christ could be both a son of David and also his Lord. *Common people* has been referred to from a sentimental motive as if it was a contrast between the humble folks and the self-righteous scribes and Pharisees. We may say these people were of that type if we offer our remarks as a comment, but the word does not mean that. It is from POLUS which means "the masses."

Verse 38. *Long clothing* was worn to attract attention and obtain special salutations in public such as the market places where many people resorted.

Verse 39. *Chief seats* means the front pews that faced the audience, and uppermost *rooms* at feasts means the highest seats, those that gave an advantage of display.

Verse 40. *Devour widows' houses* means they took advantage of them to obtain their property. For more detailed comments on this verse see the comments on Matthew 23: 14.

Verse 41. This money was a voluntary offering made for the upkeep of the temple. The rich cast in *much* in actual count of the money.

Verse 42. This widow cast in *two* mites instead of "one" as generally stated.

Verse 43. Jesus stated in literal language what he meant comparatively.

Verse 44. Jesus explained his statement to mean that the widow made the sacrifice in that she gave all that she had. The rich gave much and yet had much left and hence did not make any sacrifice.

MARK 13

Verse 1. The Jews admired the temple because of its apparent firmness, being remodeled and reinforced through forty and six years of work (John 2: 20).

Verse 2. Notwithstanding the seemingly indestructible form of the building, Jesus predicted that the time was coming when it not only would be wrecked, but the destruction would be so great that all the stones would be scattered out over the ground.

Verse 3. The mount of Olives was near Jerusalem (Acts 1: 12), and Jesus went from the temple to that place and sat down. The usual trio of disciples, Peter, James and John, was joined by Andrew, and they asked Jesus privately for information.

Verse 4. The subject matter of this and the remaining verses of the chapter is the same as that in Matthew 24. It has been dealt with in much detail at that place and the reader is urged to consult those comments. In view of saving space, the comments in the present chapter will be brief and the reader may supplement the information obtained in this chapter with the more exhaustive remarks in Matthew.

Verse 5. The false prophets would purposely confuse the destruction of Jerusalem with the second coming of Christ, and he warned his disciples to beware.

Verse 6. It was known that a great person to be hailed as the Christ was predicted by the prophets, and these impostors would take advantage of the disturbed conditions to make a claim to the prophecy before the readers of the Old Testament.

Verse 7. These *wars* were the conflicts going on in the northern parts of Palestine and Syria between the Romans and Jews and other people.

Verse 8. The Roman Empire was made up of various small nations, and they were set in motion of war activities against each other by the general disturbance between the Romans and Jews. *Beginnings of sorrows* is commented upon in Matthew 24: 8.

Verse 9. *They shall deliver you up* refers to the false teachers who were to come among the people. When the disciples resisted they were persecuted and put to death.

Verse 10. By the time the wars ended in the destruction of Jerusalem, the Gospel was preached in all the countries of the world. (Romans 10: 18.)

Verse 11. The apostles were assured of moral and spiritual victory even though they were brought before the courts. The things necessary to be said would be given them by inspiration from the Father.

Verse 12. These family troubles would be caused by the fact that some of the members would be true followers of Christ and others would not. (Matthew 10: 34-37.)

Verse 13. *All men* would hate the true disciples for the same reason that their own family relations would turn against them. *Endure unto the end* means to the end of the turmoil caused by the Jewish wars.

Verse 14. *Abomination of desolation* means the Roman army that was a heathen group. *Standing where it ought not* refers to the territory of Jerusalem which was considered as holy ground. *Flee to the mountains.* (See Matthew 24: 16.)

Verse 15. Houses had flat roofs and the buildings joined one against the other. The roofs were used in much the same way that a veranda is today. If a man was on the roof of his house when he saw the Roman army, he should go from one roof to another until he reached the wall of the city and then get down and flee.

Verse 16. The man in the field should not wait to recover anything.

Verse 17. A woman in the condition described here could not travel very well.

Verse 18. Winter would be a difficult time to travel, hence the prayer suggested.

Verse 19. See particularly the long historical quotation at Matthew 24: 21.

Verse 20. The elect means the people who had elected or chosen to serve the Lord. For their sake the Lord was going to bring an end to the Jewish wars.

Verse 21. The scene is changed here and Jesus is talking about his second coming. The disturbances of the Jewish war about Jerusalem would give a pretext for the false prophets to say it was the end of the world, and would announce some certain person to be the Christ who was predicted by the prophets.

Verse 22. *Signs and wonders* would be- in the form of some kind of trickery, and even the elect (verse 20) would be deceived were they not warned beforehand.

Verse 23. This verse is to emphasize the warning already given.

Verses 24, 25. This paragraph is explained in detail at Matthew 24: 29.

Verse 26. *Then* means that after the long period of the Dark Ages which is the subject of the preceding paragraph, the next great event which the Lord was considering in this broad space of centuries was the second coming of the Son of man.

Verse 27. This verse denotes the day of judgment, when the heavenly reapers, the angels, would gather up the people of God from all over the world.

Verse 28. Jesus interrupts his main subject to make an illustration. People judge the nearness of summer by the appearance of the fig tree.

Verse 29. The presence of the Roman army and other conditions would indicate that the things predicted of Jerusalem were about to be fulfilled.

Verse 30. The original word for *generation* is defined, "all of the people living at one time." The persons living when Jesus was speaking would not all be dead before *these things* (the destruction of Jerusalem) would be fulfilled.

Verse 31. It was intended that the universe was to pass away, but the sayings of Christ were to hold firm until they had been fulfilled.

Verse 32. The verse corresponding with this in Matthew 24: 36 says nothing about the Son directly. Our present verse specifically mentions him and hence the comments here are to be more decisive than the ones at the former passage. But whether the Father has seen fit to tell him about it since then is another question.

Verse 33. If we are always watchful and living right, it will not matter when he comes, for we will be prepared to meet him with joy.

Verse 34. This short parable has the important lesson of the necessity of being faithful to the trust bestowed upon the servants of Christ.

Verse 35. The periods named are parts of the 24-hour day when people are usually the least active. That would be the special reason for being watchful.

Verse 36. *Coming suddenly* shows that the second coming of Christ will not be a drawn-out affair. That is taught also in 1 Corinthians 15: 52; 1 Thessalonians 4: 16.

Verse 37. The duty of being watchful is on the shoulders of everyone.

MARK 14

Verse 1. *After two days.* See the comments on Matthew 26: 2 on this unusual circumstance. *Passover and of unleavened bread.* The Passover was a day on which all leaven was put out of the houses, and the seven days following had the same restrictions.

Verse 2. The Jews were more concerned about the condition of society than they were about the killing of Christ, even though it might have been on a holy day.

Verse 3. See the comments on Matthew 26: 7 for the explanation of this verse.

Verse 4. The word *some* has specific reference to Judas (John 12: 4).

Verse 5. Judas pretended to be concerned about the poor, but his real motive was covetousness (John 12: 6).

Verse 6. *Good work* is explained at length at Matthew 26: 12.

Verse 7. *Poor with you always* denotes we will always have poor people with us.

Verse 8. *She hath done what she could* is a significant statement. No special amount of service is required of us but we are expected to do what we can for Christ.

Verse 9. This means that the deed of this woman would become a part of the Gospel record and hence would be mentioned wherever the sacred book went.

Verse 10. Judas was peeved because the ointment was "wasted" on Jesus and he conceived the idea of counteracting the deed through the cowardly betrayal.

Verse 11. By the transaction for money at the expense of the freedom of Jesus, the traitor hoped to "recover" what he thought was lost by the act of the woman.

Verse 12. It was the *first day of unleavened bread* for Jesus and his apostles. See again the comments on Matthew 26: 2.

Verse 13. The pitcher of water was merely an item by which the disciples were to contact the right man, who would be going to a certain house.

Verse 14. The man with the pitcher seems to have been used as a guide for the apostles. When they followed him into the house they were to speak next to the householder and ask to be shown the guestchamber to be used for the Passover.

Verse 15. The Lord had caused the householder to have a room reserved for their use.

Verse 16. The preparation for the feast was done by the apostles.

Verse 17. Let it be noted that the twelve (apostles) were still with Jesus.

Verse 18. The prediction as to the one to betray Jesus was not made yet.

Verse 19. *They began ... to say ... Is it I,* which includes Judas, for had he not joined in the inquiry, his silence would have been significant.

Verse 20. The *dish* means the vessel containing the flesh of the lamb used in the Passover. It was customary to dip a piece of bread in the broth and then eat it. Jesus did this at the same time with Judas so as to answer the question they all had asked.

Verse 21. Judas refused to repent after his dark deed and therefore he went to perdition (John 17: 12). This is why Jesus said it would have been good for him not to have been born.

Verse 22. The events of this last night are not all given in any one place, and the ones that are given are not in chronological order. See the note and references on this point with the comments at Matthew 26: 20. I shall now comment on the verses as they appear in the present chapter. Jesus *blessed* the bread by giving thanks for it. He broke it as an act of decency because more than one person was to eat of it. Otherwise the breaking of it has no religious significance to us.

Verse 23. Instead of "blessing" the cup he *gave thanks,* which shows that the two terms mean the same and that nothing supernatural was done to the "emblems."

Verse 24. The Old Testament used the blood of beasts, while the blood of the New Testament is that of Christ. *Shed for many* which means the whole world, although many will reject its benefits through unbelief.

Verse 25. The passage cited at verse 22 shows that our present verse was spoken while they were still engaged in the Passover feast.

Verse 26. According to Thayer and Robinson this *hymn* was a Psalm of David.

Verse 27. To *be offended* denotes that one falters or stumbles in his devotions. The prediction quoted is in Zechariah 13: 7.

Verse 28. Jesus always included his resurrection in the predictions of his death. He not only was to arise but would come into the presence of his apostles again.

Verse 29. Peter was always sincere in his general principles of life, but he was rash and did things from impulse as he did in this declaration.

Verse 30. Jesus was specific and predicted Peter's third denial would be before the second cock crowing.

Verse 31. This pointed prediction only caused Peter to be more positive in his assurance of faithfulness, even to the point of dying with Christ. The emphatic attitude of Peter seemed to stir up the others so that they agreed to the same promise of loyalty.

Verse 32. On this verse see the comments at Matthew 26: 36.

Verse 33. Leaving most of the apostles where they first paused, Jesus took with him Peter, James and John and went on into the garden. The humanity of his nature now beagn to manifest itself which caused him *to be sore amazed, and to be very heavy.*

Verse 34. *Exceeding sorrowful unto death* is a highly-colored figure of speech, meaning he felt sad enough to die. Wishing for still more privacy he left them here.

Verse 35. Jesus went still farther from the three so as to be alone with his Father. He prayed that if possible *the hour* might pass from him. This is the same prayer that is termed "cup" in Matthew 26: 39. The crucifixion was not to take place until the next day, so we know that the prayer about this "cup" and "the hour" could not refer to the cross. (See also the comments at Matthew 26: 39.)

Verse 36. This prayer had *to do* with *the hour* just commented upon.

Verse 37. Their sleeping was not from mere indifference. (See Luke 22: 45).

Verse 38. The flesh is what gave way and caused the apostles to fall asleep. Jesus admonished them to let their spirit or better part of their being have more influence over them and lead them into a more watchful attitude.

Verse 39. The prayer in this instance was the same as that in verses 35, 36.

Verse 40. *Eyes were heavy* because of their grief and worry over the situation.

Verse 41. Jesus had gone away the third time and now when he came back he found them sleepy as before. In his great compassion he bade them go on and take a nap. But it was not for long because the mob was seen coming toward the garden.

Verse 42. Jesus then roused the apostles with the announcement that the one who was to betray him was at hand.

Verse 43. Jesus had no sooner said the words of the preceding verse than the mob approached with Judas in the lead. *Staves* is from a word that means "clubs," as if they were hunting for some hardened criminal who was a foe of society.

Verse 44. The sign agreed upon was a kiss and they were to watch for that demonstration. *Lead him away safely.* (See the comments at Matthew 26: 48.)

Verse 45. The mere act of kissing Jesus would have seemed too cold, hence Judas added warmth to the salutation by recognizing him as *Master.*

Verse 46. *They* means the mob composed of the chief priests and scribes.

Verse 47. The one who used the sword was Peter (John 18: 10). See the remarks that Jesus made to Peter and my comments on the same at Matthew 26: 52.

Verse 48. Jesus charged the mob with coming out against him as if he had been a thief who deserved to be taken with the unrefined weapons like clubs.

Verse 49. It was rather late for them to be showing such concern on behalf of public safety. Jesus was in the temple and other public places daily before this. When a dangerous person is at large (such as these clubs would imply), it is the custom not to "stand on ceremony" but to take such a person at once. Jesus then explained the seeming contradiction in their conduct by saying that it fulfilled the scriptures.

Verse 50. *They all* means the apostles. Seeing Jesus was being taken without any resistance, they concluded that all was lost and in their fright they fled.

Verses 51, 52. Mark is the only one of the writers who records this event. There is no information as to the identity of the young man. *Linen* is from the Greek word SINDON which Thayer defines, "thing made of fine cloth." He then explains it by saying, "so of a light and loose garment worn at night over the naked body." Robinson gives virtually the same definition and explanation as that of Thayer. That accounts for the fact that the young man had nothing else on. It was night, and the commotion had attracted his attention so that without taking time to dress he went to the scene of excitement. The apostles had just fled while the young man still followed along after Jesus. The men of the mob thought he was sympathizing with Jesus and decided to arrest him. This frightened him so that he escaped by giving up his nightrobe.

Verse 53. The chief priests assembled to discuss what to do about the case.

Verse 54. Peter was afraid to be known as a friend of Jesus so he followed *afar off.*

Verse 55. *And found none* means they could not find anyone who was prepared to testify as they desired. They wanted to get some person to affirm some word or act of Jesus on which they could secure the death sentence.

Verse 56. There were plenty of men who would have been disposed to give such testimony, but since they were falsifying their statements did not agree and hence their pretended testimony was rejected.

Verse 57. Other pretended witnesses told what they had heard Jesus say.

Verse 58. A look at John 2: 19 will show how grossly these men falsified.

Verse 59. No wonder these so-called witnesses did not agree. When men conspire to bear false testimony they are sure to overlook something that will expose them.

Verse 60. The high priest was surprised that Jesus did not reply.

Verse 61. Jesus said nothing in reply to the falsehoods of these men; in that way he fulfilled the prophecy in Isaiah 53: 7. The high priest then asked Jesus a question touching his personality which was the same as his divinity. That was important and we will see that he answered it.

Verse 62. Jesus not only answered the question of the high priest, but added a prediction that was in line with his divinity and authority as a king.

Verse 63. Decisions of the Sanhedrin were made by vote, supposed to be based on the testimony of valid witnesses. The statement of Jesus agitated the high priest so that he declared there was no need for witnesses.

Verse 64. The high priest called for the vote of the assembly and *they all* condemned Jesus to death. This means that all who voted at all did so. There were some who did not take part in the voting (Luke 23: 50, 51).

Verse 65. The Jews could pass a sentence of death but could not execute it. But they gratified their wicked feeling against Jesus by gross personal mistreatment. The things they said and did to him would not be permitted today in any responsible court, regardless of what sentence might have been pronounced.

Verses 66, 67. The point to be noted is that being *with Jesus* was regarded as significant. Association indicates fellowship or participation.

Verse 68. Peter understood it that way, for he denied it very emphatically, then moved out farther in his fearfulness and stopped at the porch. At that instant the cock crowed the first time.

Verse 69. This maid spoke to the people standing by and not to Peter. She made the declaration on her own information (indicating Peter), "this is one of them."

Verse 70. Peter denied her statement which made his second denial. The next time it was the people standing near who made the statement, and they supported their claim by referring to the similarity of speech used by Peter and Jesus and his disciples.

Verse 71. *Curse* and *swear* are explained at Matthew 26: 74. This made the third time that Peter denied even knowing Jesus or having been with him.

Verse 72. Matthew says this second crowing was immediately after the third denial (chapter 26: 74). This fact, (together with the look that Jesus gave him, Luke 22: 61), recalled the specific prediction of Jesus about his denials. *When he thought thereon, he wept,* or, upon considering the whole event, he was overwhelmed with remorse. Matthew 26: 75 says "he went out and wept bitterly." The conduct of Peter was different from that of Judas. Both men were disappointed over the way matters were going with Jesus, and the things they had said or done. But Judas destroyed his own life while Peter repented through godly sorrow.

MARK 15

Verse 1. *In the morning* was the day after the scenes in the garden, and the meeting in the palace of the high priest. The Jews had gone as far as they could under the law, so the next step was to take Jesus before Pilate who was the Roman governor.

Verse 2. To be a king under the Romans might imply some rivalry, but Pilate restricted his question to the Jews, which would not mean any necessary opposition to the law of the land. To the question of Pilate Jesus merely said *thou sayest it.*

Verse 3. To the accusation of the chief priest Jesus made no reply, not even to the extént of denying them, although they pertained to his alleged conduct.

Verse 4. Pilate called the attention of Jesus to the accusations, doubtless thinking that he had not noticed them, or at any rate had not observed the nature of them.

Verse 5. It is usual for a prisoner to deny the charges made against him, whether he cares to defend himself or not. Jesus did neither which caused Pilate to wonder.

Verse 6. It was customary to celebrate that feast with the release of a prisoner to be selected by the people, not the officers or priests.

Verse 7. Pilate knew about the situation, and he therefore was aware that Barabbas was a noted criminal whom no good society could tolerate.

Verse 8. While the governor was delaying his action the *multitude* began clamoring for him to follow up with the usual practice.

Verse 9. Pilate thought this would give him an opportunity of releasing Jesus without clearing him of the sentence the Sanhedrin had pronounced against him.

Verse 10. The chief priests had no voice in selecting the prisoner to be released. They had caused Jesus to be delivered into the hands of this court with an envious motive. In view of that, Pilate thought the people would take a better view of the case and call for the release of Jesus.

Verse 11. It is possible that they would have done so, had the chief priests not *moved* or influenced them to call for the release of Barabbas.

Verse 12. Pilate was evidently surprised at the selection of the people. If they were willing to have so wicked a prisoner as Barabbas turned loose upon the community, they certainly could not wish for anything severe to be done to as harmless a person as Jesus, hence he asked them directly for their verdict concerning him.

Verse 13. They cried out *again.* Mark does not tell of their having made this demand before, but Matthew 27: 21 gives that instance.

Verse 14. According to Mark's account the Jews would not state any *evil* against Jesus, but John 18: 30 reports that they accused him of being a "malefactor," which merely means an evildoer, so that they evaded the governor's question.

Verse 15. It was a practice of some of the courts to scourge a condemned prisoner before delivering him to the executioners. It was a harsh ordeal imposed on his bare body.

Verse 16. *The whole band* means a part of the army to be used as executioners.

Verse 17. Purple and scarlet were the royal colors, and this kind of robe was put on Jesus in mockery. The crown of thorns was for the same purpose because he had claimed to be a king, and also in order to torture him in his humiliation.

Verse 18. This was a salutation of mockery and contempt.

Verse 19. These men did not *worship* Jesus in any proper manner as we may well conclude. (See the note on "worship" at Matthew 2: 2.)

Verse 20. After these acts of mockery were concluded, the soldiers replaced the robe with his own clothing. Matthew, Mark and John mention the crown of thorns and also the robe of royal colors. They tell of the removal of the robe but neither of them says a word about removing the crown of thorns. We can reasonably conclude that our Lord was compelled to wear the instrument of mockery and torture throughout the six long hours of the scenes of the cross.

Verse 21. *Compel Simon . . . to bear his cross.* (See notes at Matthew 16: 24.)

Verse 22. See a full explanation of *Golgotha* at Matthew 27: 33.

Verse 33. This mixture is explained in the comments at Matthew 27: 34.

Verse 24. The act of crucifixion is so cruel that a detailed description of it, as given by the works of reference, is given in the comments at Matthew 27: 35.

Verse 25. The *third hour* corresponds with our nine o'clock A. M.

Verse 26. *Accusation is defined,* "The crime of which one is accused." Hence those who passed by would see that

Christ was crucified for being The King of the Jews!

Verses 27, 28. The scripture referred to is in Isaiah 53: 12.

Verse 29. Again the mob misquoted Jesus, for he never said he would destroy the temple. What he did say is recorded in John 2: 19.

Verse 30. There can be no question that Jesus had the power to come down from the cross. Had he done so, however, the scriptures could not have been fulfilled (Matthew 26: 24; Isaiah 53: 7-10).

Verse 31. This remark of the chief priests fulfilled Luke 4: 23.

Verse 32. *That we may see and believe* was a hypocritical statement. They had known of miracles that Jesus performed that called for as much power as this would have required, yet they were still in unbelief. *They that were crucified with him* means the thieves. According to Luke 23: 40-42, one of them repented of his saying and appealed to Jesus for mercy and asked to be remembered.

Verse 33. Jesus had been on the cross three hours when the darkness started (verse 25). It lasted until the ninth hour which was three o'clock P. M.

Verse 34. See the comments at Matthew 27: 46 for use on this verse.

Verse 35. This is explained at Matthew 27: 47.

Verse 36. In John 19: 28, 29 is the record of why this vinegar (sour wine) was served to Jesus. He had expressed his condition which was one of thirst, the kind that so often comes upon one at the approach of death.

Verse 37. *Cried with a loud voice.* This is commented upon at some length at Matthew 27:50. *Gave up the ghost* (or spirit), which proves that man possesses something besides his flesh which leaves the body at death.

Verse 38. A description of the importance of this veil is at Matthew 27: 51.

Verse 39. According to Matthew 27: 54, the earthquake and other demonstrations in the natural creation, helped to convince the centurion that it was no ordinary person who had just died and was thus accorded such distinction.

Verses 40, 41. These women were faithful to the last, but with feminine timidity they had stood some distance away watching. They had come from the same district where Jesus was brought up, Galilee, and had served him on various occasions.

Verse 42. *The day before the sabbath* is a general explanation, meaning that every sabbath or holy day is preceded by a preparation day. Whatever manual exercise would be needed in preparing food and other necessary articles for life must be done on these preparation days. The regular Passover came on Friday the fourteenth. Jesus was crucified on the day before, which was the reason for saying this was *the preparation*.

Verse 43. Being a *counsellor* means he was a member of the Sanhedrin. For extended comments on this man see those at Matthew 27: 57.

Verse 44. Pilate was surprised that Jesus was dead. Crucifixion causes a slow death and the victim usually has to suffer on and on for hours until late in the night, and this was the cause of Pilate's surprise. To make sure that Joseph was not planning to recover Jesus alive, the governor sent the centurion to see if Jesus had died.

Verse 45. The centurion reported that Jesus was dead, and Pilate then gave the body to Joseph. This good man had made special provision for the care of the body. For further comments on this phase of the subject see at Matthew 27: 58.

Verse 46. John 19: 38-40 tells us that Nicodemus assisted Joseph in this service of Love. He was the man who had come to Jesus by night (John 3: 1, 2).

Verse 47. The women witnessed the burial of Jesus and the rolling of the stone against the door of the sepulchre, which explains their concern in chapter 16: 3.

MARK 16

Verse 1. The word *sabbath* is singular in number and Thayer defines it, "The seventh day of each week." It corresponds with our Saturday which also is the seventh and last day of each week.

Verse 2. *Early in the morning* and *rising of the sun* are phrases used in the same sense. This agrees with Matthew 28: 1, and shows that the 24-hour period of time began and ended in the morning; not at sundown or midnight.

Verse 3. This verse is referred to at chapter 15: 47.

Verse 4. Matthew 28: 2 says the

angel rolled the stone away from the sepulchre.

Verse 5. *Entering.* It will be well again to quote the description of a sepulchre as given by Smith's Bible Dictionary. "A natural cave enlarged and adapted by excavation, or an artificial imitation of one, was the standard type of sepulchre." Hence we understand the sepulchre as a whole was a spacious cavity, in the far side of which would be a sepcific spot arranged for a body; the outside entrance would be closed with a stone. This *young man* is called an angel by Matthew which is not strange. Angels often appeared on earth in the form of men, and the long white garment of this person agrees with that idea.

Verse 6. The angel spoke encouragingly to the women, and let them know he was aware of their purpose in coming to the tomb. As an evidence for their eyes that Jesus was gone he led them to the spot where he had been laid.

Verse 7. *Tell his disciples, and Peter.* This does not mean that Peter was not a disciple; but he had denied Jesus three times, and it was fitting that his attention be especially called to the evidence that his Lord was alive again as he had predicted.

Verse 8. The whole scene was so unusual and solemn that the women were virtually overcome, and were speechless for the time being.

Verse 9. The first few verses of this chapter pertains to the scenes at the sepulchre. This verse begins to tell of things that took place elsewhere after the resurrection. The *seven devils* had nothing to do with the character of Mary Magdalene (it being an affliction), for she was a good woman and was interested in the work and fate of Jesus (Matthew 27: 61; 28: 1; Mark 16: 1; John 19: 25; 20: 14, 15).

Verse 10. *They mourned and wept* fulfills chapter 2: 20.

Verse 11. It was somewhat on the principle of a phrase "too good to be true" that the disciples *believed not.* But according to Luke 24: 25 Jesus rebuked the disciples for such unbelief.

Verse 12. *Appeared in another form.* Luke 24: 16 explains that the disciples' eyes were *holden* (restrained) so that they did not know him. Doubtless the unusual character of the report so overcame them that they were confused. Under such conditions a person whom they well knew would not look natural.

Verse 13. These disciples reported what they had seen and heard, and the ones to whom they told the story were as doubtful as themselves.

Verse 14. *The eleven* means the apostles except Judas who had hanged himself. We should note that these apostles at this time *believed not.* Jesus rebuked them for their unbelief in the face of testimony of those who had seen him after his resurrection.

Verse 15. This and the following verse corresponds with Matthew 28: 19, 20. It is commonly referred to as The Great Commission, although the New Testament does not so name it. *World* is from KOSMOS which has a wide range of meaning, but its usual sense is, "the inhabitants of the earth." *Preach* is from KERUSSO which Thayer defines, "to be a herald; to officiate as a herald; to proclaim after the manner of a herald." He then explains his definition, "always with a suggestion of formality, gravity, and an authority which must be listened to and obeyed." The word may be used occasionally in a general sense, but its primary meaning is to tell something that is new. That is why an apostle had to be inspired because he would be expected to publish the Gospel for the first time, and to the people of various languages. *Creature* is from the same original word that is used in Colossians 1: 23 where Paul says that the Gospel had then been preached to every creature which is under heaven. Whatever Jesus meant by *every creature,* Paul says it had been done, and hence the "great commission" was carried out by the apostles. That means that when a preacher says he is preaching under the "great commission" he is perverting the scripture.

Verse 16. *He that believeth* necessarily means to believe what is preached which is the Gospel; the good news of the death and resurrection of Christ for the sins of mankind. The believing must be followed by being *baptized.* That word is from the Greek word BAPTIZO which Thayer defines, "To cleanse by dipping or submerging, to wash, to make clean with water; to overwhelm." Robinson defines it, "to dip in, to sink, to immerse." *Saved* is from SOZO which Thayer defines, "To rescue from danger or destruction," hence it does not cover all that may follow in a person's life. A man might be rescued from drowning, and afterwards he could carelessly fall into the water again and perish. If a man does not believe the Gospel he will be condemned regardless of whether he is baptized or not, hence it was not necessary to mention baptism on the negative side.

Verses 17, 18. *Them that believe* are the believers of the preceding verse. It cannot be restricted to the apostles on the ground that "believe" is in the present tense, for verse 14 says that even the apostles did not believe at the time Jesus was speaking. *Follow* means to attend or accompany one, and refers to the spiritual gifts that were bestowed upon Christians in the first years of the Gospel age (Acts 6: 8; 19: 6; 1 Corinthians chapters 12, 13, 14; Ephesians 4: 8-14; James 5: 14, 15). Matthew then names some of the miracles that Christians were enabled to perform in that period.

Verse 19. The ascension is reported also in Luke 24: 51 and Acts 1: 9.

LUKE 1

Verse 1. I have consulted a great number of works of reference, such as histories, Bible Dictionaries, encyclopedias, lexicons and critical concordances; also a number of commentaries, and all agree that Luke is the author of the book we are now studying. For the sake of saving space, I do not think it necessary to list all of these works, in view of the unity in their statements making the conclusion well founded. Many of them state also that Luke was not a born Jew, and that he was a doctor of medicine. He was not an apostle but was inspired to write a record of the Gospel.

Verse 2. Luke was not an eyewitness of the things on which he writes, but they were told him by those who were. In copying down the things told him he would be qualified by inspiration, even as the Spirit guaranteed the accuracy of the memory of the apostles which was promised by Jesus before he left them (John 14: 26).

Verse 3. So thorough was the report these witnesses gave Luke that he says it caused him to have *perfect* ("exact" —Thayer) understanding of the whole story. The book of Luke was addressed to Theophilus who was an outstanding, educated Christian, according to the Bible Dictionaries. Being addressed to one individual does not affect its importance for others, any more than does the fact that Paul wrote four of his epistles to individuals do so.

Verse 4. The special purpose Luke had in writing to this man was that he might be assured of the instructions he had already received.

Verse 5. Luke, like Matthew, begins his record at the time just prior to the birth of Jesus. However, unlike Matthew, he first gives us the history concerning the parentage of John the Baptist. It was in the days of Herod (The Great) who was king of Judea. *Course of Abia* is explained at 1 Chronicles 24 in volume 2 of the Old Testament Commentary. All priests had to be descendants of Aaron but that was not required of their wives, hence Luke gives us the added information that Elizabeth was also from Aaron.

Verse 6. This couple lived up to all requirements of the law, which proves that it was not physically impossible to do so as some teach. Paul was another who did this according to Philippians 3: 6.

Verse 7. *They had no child, because* that *Elizabeth was barren.* This is a significant statement that contrasts with the practice of some professed Christians who are childless from choice. Such people treat with contempt the first object of marriage by practicing birth control. Not only was Elizabeth barren, but she and her husband were in advanced age as were Abraham and Sarah (Genesis 11: 30; 17: 17), yet they did not give up hope (verse 13).

Verse 8. *Order of his course.* (See the comments at verse 5).

Verse 9. This *custom of the priest's office* is described in Exodus 30: 7-10.

Verse 10. The *whole multitude* were obeying Leviticus 16: 17.

Verse 11. The altar of incense was in the first holy room of the temple, and incense was burned on it daily. *Right side;* on Zacharias's right hand as he stood facing the altar in the service.

Verse 12. The people were not permitted to accompany the priest in this place (verse 10), hence the appearance of an angel there caused Zacharias to be disturbed.

Verse 13. *Prayer is heard* and *bear thee a son* are phrases that are related; he had been praying for a son. This was one thing that caused Luke to say this couple was righteous. Had they been opposed to children and tried to avoid having them, they would not have been righteous. The promise of a son included instructions for his name.

Verse 14. Not only was Zacharias to rejoice over this son, but many others would have reason to be glad for his birth because of the great work he was to do in preparing a people for the king of heaven.

Verse 15. *Great in the sight of the Lord* whether the world admired him or not. *Drink neither wine nor strong drink* was a qualification of a Nazarite under the law (Numbers 6: 1-4). During his entire life he was to be under the guidance of the Spirit.

Verse 16. This verse shows the fulfillment of Malachi 4: 6.

Verse 17. Elias (Elijah) was a powerful prophet in the Old Testament, and John was to be given a spirit of power like his. *Turn the hearts of the fathers*, etc., refers to the same as at verse 16. *A people prepared for the Lord* means the people whom John baptized in preparing a people for Christ.

Verse 18. The promise of a child under the conditions seemed so nearly impossible that Zacharias overlooked the evidence of the miracle already before him, that of the presence of an angel in that exclusive spot.

Verse 19. This was not merely an angel, but was one of the two who only are named in the Bible. This one was from the immediate presence of God where he usually stood, ready to do the bidding of the occasions as they came up.

Verse 20. Zacharias was to receive a sign that would be both an evidence and a mild punishment, *because he believed not the words*. This dumbness that was to come at once would start the evidence, and when it was completed it would strengthen the meaning.

Verse 21. The people waited according to the law, but Zacharias was detained longer than the regular service usually required which caused them to wonder.

Verse 22. *A vision* is defined as something that appears to one either while awake or asleep. As Zacharias had become speechless since he entered the temple, the people realized that something supernatural had occurred.

Verse 23. *Days of his ministration were accomplished.* The priests took turns in the service which is explained in the comments at 1 Chronicles 24: 6, volume 2 of the Old Testament Commentary.

Verse 24. *Hid* is from PERIKRUPTO which Thayer defines, "to conceal on all sides or entirely, to hide," and he explains his definition, "to keep one's self at home." It is the usual custom for expectant mothers to keep in retirement the last months of the period, but Elizabeth did the reverse. Nothing is said about her continuing the retirement after the five months, hence we would not think the other was done out of false modesty. A reasonable conclusion is that she was still under the feeling that it was "too good to be true," and before telling the good news to her friends, she decided to await the five months which would be the time for life to be evident.

Verse 25. After the five months had shown that she was to become a mother, she then commented by *saying* (last word of the preceding verse) that it was the Lord who had dealt thus with her. In bestowing this upon Elizabeth she commented that it would take away her *reproach.* To be unable to bear children in those days was considered a *reproach*, and it is still so considered with those who respect the first commandment regarding the divine object of marriage.

Verse 26. *Sixth month* means the sixth since the conception by Elizabeth. The same angel who appeared to her at the first was sent on a similar mission to Nazareth.

Verse 27. A virgin is a person who has not had any relations with the opposite sex. The connection must show in each case whether the virgin is a male or female. Since this one was *espoused* (engaged) to a man we know it means a female. *House* is from OIKOS and Thayer defines it at this place, "stock, race, descendants of one," which denotes that Joseph was a descendant of David.

Verse 28. *Hail* is a friendly greeting, indicating that some good news is about to be given to the person addressed. This was to be given to Mary as a special favor peculiar to women, and it was to be from the Lord.

Verse 29. *Troubled* means "agitated," and it was caused by the unexpectedness of the situation, and she was wondering what it all meant.

Verse 30. Seeing the disturbed condition of Mary, the angel assured her there was nothing to fear, but that God had selected her as an object of His favor.

Verse 31. *Womb* is from GASTER, and this is the only place where it comes from that Greek word. Also, this is the only place in the Bible where a statement of conceiving is joined with the word womb; this is significant. Matthew 3: 9 says that God could raise up children even from the stones. To promise Mary (a single girl) a son might have been taken to mean that God would give her a son in some miraculous way independent of her own body. Hence it was necessary to tell this virgin that she was to conceive *in her womb*. The name of the son also was selected for her at this time.

Verse 32. Verses 28 and 30 contain all that the angel said by way of praise for Mary. After that he spoke of the greatness to be bestowed upon her son. *Son of the Highest* is the same as calling him the Son of God. *Throne of David* means the throne which David (his great ancestor) had prophesied should be given him (Psalms 132: 11).

Verse 33. *House of Jacob* is a phrase often used to mean the Jewish nation in general, and later referring to the people of God spiritually whether Jew or Gentile. The kingdom of this "son of David" and of Mary was to stand for ever. (See Daniel 2: 44.)

Verse 34. *I know not a man.* This cannot mean that Mary had no male acquaintance, for she was even engaged to one. The word *know* is from GINOSKO, and Thayer says at this place the word means, "the carnal [sexual] connection of male and female." Robinson says virtually the same thing, except that he gives it as his definition of the word at this place. Mary meant that she was not being intimate with any man, which she thought would be necessary to conceive in her womb. We are taught an important lesson in morals here. The fact of being engaged was as binding in Biblical times as the actual marriage as far as obligations towards each other were concerned, but it did not authorize any intimacies until the time of marriage.

Verse 35. The Holy Ghost (Spirit) is an invisible, though personal being, and that is why he could enter into and take charge of the womb of Mary without any conscious participation on her part. The germ of life necessary to fertilize that of the female was thus deposited in the proper place by this holy Being, sent directly from God and authorized to represent Him in this union. Therefore, the angel concluded, the person to be brought

forth from this union was to be called the Son of God. This is the only instance in which God ever did a thing like this, and that is the reason Jesus is called the *ONLY* begotten Son of God. From the conception and ever afterward through the period of expectancy, the experience of Mary was like that of all mothers.

Verse 36. The Greek word for *cousin* has an indefinite meaning, and may apply to any relative not as near as brother or sister. Mary had not expressed any doubt of the miracle that the angel just promised. However, he supported the promise by reporting another one along the same line, that her cousin was already six months along in her expectancy, notwithstanding she was *called barren*.

Verse 37. This verse is the angel's explanation of the two miracles of conception. God cannot do anything wrong, but nothing is impossible with Him because it is too hard.

Verse 38. This speech of resignation of Mary is one of the sweetest passages ever made. There is no sign of exultation over her special favor, but a meek submission as a handmaid, unto the word of the Lord. The angel delivered his message and departed.

Verses 39, 40. It was a sweet and confidential meeting these happy women had with each other. This joy was mutual, but Mary's evidence was only the word of the angel for as yet there was no physical evidence of her conception, while Elizabeth had that of the living child within her own body.

Verse 41. It is usual for an unborn babe at that period to manifest a movement of life, but this was a miraculous instance since it not merely moved but *leaped*. Besides, it occurred as an immediate result of the voice of Mary acting through the ears of Elizabeth. The explanation is in the closing sentence, *Elizabeth was filled with the Holy Ghost*.

Verse 42. The entrance of the Spirit into Elizabeth inspired her so that the words she spoke from here through verse 45 are those of inspiration. The blessing pronounced on Mary was emphasized by the one upon *the fruit of thy womb*.

Verse 43. *Mother of my Lord.* Elizabeth could have known this only by having been filled with the Holy Ghost, for the angel said nothing about it as far as we are told.

Verse 44. An unborn babe is unconscious, so the physical movement of this one was a reaction to the effect produced in the mind of Elizabeth; it was *for joy* of hers that caused the stirring of the babe in her womb.

Verse 45. *She that believed* refers to Mary who had no physical evidence as yet. (See the comments at verses 39, 40.) Elizabeth then gave Mary an assurance of the fulfillment of the promises, and that was an expression of her inspired mind.

Verses 46. To *magnify* the Lord denotes a desire to "esteem highly," not that any human being can contribute anything to the greatness of the Lord.

Verse 47. Mary is not making any technical distinction between her soul and her spirit. Her entire inner being was filled with praise for the greatness of the Lord.

Verse 48. *Low estate* refers to the humble station in life she had occupied; now she will receive the good esteem of all generations, but not that she would be worshiped.

Verse 49. Mary attributes her *great* favor to the One with a holy name.

Verse 50. The mercy will endure continuously to all who fear Him.

Verse 51. Since we know that Elizabeth was enabled by the Spirit to speak with supernatural wisdom, we may properly conclude Mary to have been doing the same thing.

Verse 52. *He hath* is general as to tense, and means that God always recognizes humility and rewards it with His favor, but deposes those who exalt themselves.

Verse 53. These statements are figurative in form, but teach the same principles as those in the preceding verses.

Verse 54. *Holpen* means helped Israel *in remembrance* or in view of his wonted mercy.

Verse 55. Abraham was the father of the Jewish race, and God had promised him an heir who should bless the world, which Mary was recalling to mind.

Verse 56. Mary visited with Elizabeth until the time for the birth of her son, then she returned to her own home in Nazareth in Galilee.

Verse 57. Elizabeth gave birth to a son at the usual time after conception.

Verse 58. *Shewd great mercy* refers to the former condition of barrenness that had been overcome. Rejoiced with her is an example of Romans 12: 15.

Verse 59. The covenant with Abraham as well as the law of Moses required this rite (Genesis 17: 12; Leviticus 12: 2, 3). The law did not specify the age when the child should be named, but custom had established the time of circumcision for it. It happens frequently even today that people outside the family will presume to name the new baby. It was understandable why they would suggest the name of his father as that had long been another custom.

Verse 60. Elizabeth did not resent their wanting to pick a name for her baby, only they did not have the right one.

Verse 61. These people even argued the question which reminds us of 1 Peter 4: 15.

Verse 62. It is strange that the father had not been consulted in the first place, instead of waiting until they wanted him to decide a dispute. *Made signs* means they beckoned by a nod or something similar what they wanted him to do.

Verse 63. Zacharias had been dumb since the appearance of Gabriel (verse 20), hence his calling for a *writing table* which means a tablet. *They marveled* because Zacharias said the babe's name *is* John, indicating that the matter had been previously decided, which it had been by the angel (verse 13).

Verse 64. *Mouth was opened immediately* fulfills verse 20. He had two reasons for praising God; the birth of a son and the recovery of his speech.

Verse 65. *Fear* means a general feeling of respectful consideration for the wonderful things that had occurred. *These sayings* or happenings were reported extensively all through the country of Judea.

Verse 66. *Laid them up in their hearts* denotes that they kept them in mind. *What manner of child shall this be!* This remark was caused by the unusual circumstances connected with his conception and birth.

Verse 67. Being filled with the Holy Ghost made Zacharias' prophecies inspired.

Verse 68. This was said in view of the work of John in reforming the Jewish people, preparing them for the work of Christ (See Malachi 4: 6).

Verse 69. This whole speech of Zacharias was on a theme that combined the work of John and Christ, with the weight of it in favor of the latter. This priest was happy to be the father of the forerunner of the Saviour of his people. *Horn of salvation* refers to the power that Christ would · have to be able to save the people.

Verse 70. Christ had been foretold by the prophets through Old Testament times, in places too numerous to mention at this place.

Verse 71. *Saved from our enemies* has reference to the suffering the Jews were undergoing from the heathen powers, as well as from the influences of sin.

Verse 72. *This holy covenant* pertains to the promise of Christ.

Verse 73. This oath to Abraham is recorded in Genesis 12: 3; 18: 18; 22: 18.

Verse 74. This is the same in meaning as verse 71.

Verse 75. Zacharias places salvation on condition of lifelong righteousness.

Verse 76. *Thou, child,* has specific reference to his own son who had just *been born. Called the prophet* was done by Jesus in Matthew 11: 9. *Go before . . . to prepare his ways* pertains to the work of John in preparing a people for Christ.

Verse 77. *Knowledge of salvation* means to let the people know what would be necessary for salvation. It was to be the *remission of sins* upon repentance and baptism (Matthew 3: 11). This was preached by Jesus also (Mark 1: 15).

Verse 78. *Day spring* is a comparison of the coming of Jesus into the world with the sunrising that ushers in a new day for the inhabitants of the earth.

Verse 79. *Light* and *darkness* are figurative terms to represent truth and error. The teaching of Jesus was to show mankind the way of peace.

Verse 80. This *child* refers to the babe John, whose birth had occasioned this interesting speech of Zacharias. As the child grew he lived in *the deserts.* That was appropriate since he was to do his work there, when the time came for him to appear among the people of Israel as the forerunner of Christ.

LUKE 2

Verse 1. Caesar Augustus was the head of the Roman Empire at the time John and Jesus were born. *World* is from a Greek word that means the inhabitants of the earth. Virtually all of the civilized people of the world

were under the power of this empire (it being the fourth of the world empires predicted in Daniel 2: 36-40). *Taxed* is from APOGRAPHO which means to be enrolled. The purpose of this enrollment was to obtain a list of the citizens to be taxed, which is the reason the translators rendered the word as they did.

Verse 2. Josephus, Antiquities of the Jews, Book 18, Chapter 1, Section 1, verifies this statement of Luke. The reader may consult this historical passage for his own information, which I will not take the space to copy here.

Verse 3. *His own city.* Most countries are divided into smaller units, each with a center of jurisdiction at which the birth lists of citzens are kept on record, such as the county unit in the United States. The Jews had a similar custom of keeping their records according to the family groups to which one belonged, and such records were stored in the city that was attribuated to that family.

Verse 4. Joseph descended from David, hence he went to Bethlehem to register because that little city was known as the city of David. (See 1 Samuel 16: 1.)

Verse 5. A wife would not have to leave home to pay her taxes, but she would need to appear in person to be placed upon the enrollment of citizens according to the Roman procedure. *His espoused wife* is explained at Matthew 1: 25. Her condition of expectancy though engaged only to Joseph is explained at Matthew 1: 18-20.

Verse 6. *While they were there.* Many of the Lord's plans seem to have been done just "as occasion suggested." They may look that way to man, but God knows all about the future and can regulate it as He sees fit. It had been determined that Jesus was to be born in Bethlehem and the prophets predicted the same (Micah 5: 2; Psalms 132: 6). The Lord foresaw this edict of Caesar and planned the conditions with Joseph and Mary to coincide with it for the birth of the royal babe.

Verse 7. *Laid him in a manger.* The birth had taken place elsewhere on a birthstool, a seat so constructed that the mother could be seated while giving birth; this is what is meant by the "stools" in Exodus 1: 16. When Rachel proposed to let her maid "bear upon her knees" (Genesis 30: 3), she meant that her knees could be used instead of the birthstool. After Jesus was born, the mother found no suitable place for him as a crib, hence she put him in a manger. The lodging places in that country were combinations of bedrooms for people and stalls for their beasts of service, just as some hotels are provided with garage space for the automobiles. The word "inn" should be rendered "guestchamber" (the same word is so rendered in chapter 22: 11), where the guests would be gathered usually as they do in the lobby or waiting rooms in hotels. It was a time of large crowds on account of the decree of Caesar calling for all the people to come to the proper headquarters for registration. So the words *no room for them in the inn* have no reference to the attitude of the public towards these "humble, poor people," as a popular but erroneous statement of sentimentality represents.

Verse 8. The shepherds were guarding their flocks from robbers and wolves.

Verse 9. *Sore afraid* means they were greatly frightened by the unexpected appearance of a person out there in the darkness of the night.

Verse 10. The angel calmed their fears by telling them he was there to bring them good news. The thing he was going to tell them was a matter that concerned *all people*, not merely any certain race or nationality.

Verse 11. *Unto you* denotes that it was for their benefit the birth had occurred. The announcement of it was about the same as was predicted in Isaiah 9: 6.

Verse 12. All newborn babes look very much alike, hence some mark of recognition was necessary for the information of the shepherds. This was done by two unusual facts; the way the babe was clothed and the place used for his crib. He was bound round with a strip of cloth only, indicating that the birth had very recently taken place, and a manger was not the place where babes were generally placed as a crib.

Verse 13. The "shock" was eased by the appearance of only one angel. Then suddenly a multitude of the angel band of the heavenly army appeared shouting praises to God.

Verse 14. Moffatt renders *in the highest*, "in high heaven," and *good will toward men*, he renders, "for men whom He favors."

Verse 15. *Let us go even unto Bethlem*, shows the shepherds understood

that the "city of David," which the angel named, meant that place.

Verse 16. They found the parents near the babe that was lying in the manger.

Verse 17. That circumstance verified what the angel had told them. Doubtless they were well pleased at the combination of circumstances and reported it publicly.

Verse 18. The people wondered about the coincidence. These shepherds could not have merely guessed at what had taken place for there were too many details in the case.

Verse 19. To *ponder* means to think or meditate, wondering over the great happiness that had been poured down upon her.

Verse 20. The shepherds praised God for the combination of events with the statement of the angel, thereby constituting a verifying weight of evidence. It was such a strong evidence of divine truth they could not refrain from rejoicing.

Verse 21. See the comments at chapter 1: 59 as to naming a child at the same time with the rite of circumcision. According to Smith's Bible Dictionary, "the name *Jesus* signifies *saviour*," which made it an appropriate one to give this child.

Verse 22. See the law on this subject in Leviticus 12: 1-6.

Verse 23. To be called *holy to the Lord* means to be regarded as His, hence the reason for presenting him to the Lord at Jerusalem where the temple was located.

Verse 24. In verse 8 of the chapter in Leviticus cited, it can be seen that a woman was permitted to offer these birds only in case she was not financially able to offer a larger sacrifice, such as a four-footed animal of the clean description.

Verse 25. Various men were inspired in Biblical times when God wished to have some message spoken, and this good man Simeon was one of those persons. *The consolation* means the blessing that God had promised to Israel (and all the world) through the seed of Abraham (Genesis 12: 3; 22: 18).

Verse 26. A special promise had been made to Simeon that he would live to see the Lord's Christ, which means the Anointed One.

Verse 27. The Spirit in this verse is the same as the Holy Ghost in the preceding one. It was by this Spirit that Simeon was caused to come into the temple at the same time the parents of Jesus came in.

Verse 28. Simeon blessed God for letting him live to see Jesus.

Verse 29. Simeon was willing to die since the great wish of his last years had been realized, and if he had been called to die then he would have had "a peaceful hour to die," for his last thoughts would have been on the Saviour of the world.

Verse 30. *Have seen thy salvation* means the salvation provided of God.

Verse 31. *Hast prepared* denotes the plans and prophecies that had been formulating through the centuries, and now brought to a climax in the birth of this child.

Verse 32. *Gentiles* is from a Greek word that means "nations," and that was what God promised to Abraham as recorded in Genesis 18: 18. While all nations were to be blessed through Jesus, the people of Israel were especially honored since he was a Jew.

Verse 33. *His mother* means the mother of Jesus; she and her husband looked on and listened to the many things being done with the admiration of fond parents.

Verse 34. Simeon then directed his prophecies toward Mary concerning the child. To be *set* means "to be destined or appointed," indicating that Jesus would be the cause of the results about to be mentioned. This *fall* and *rising* is the same as Jesus taught in Matthew 23: 12. *A sign spoken against* refers to the opposition that Jesus would encounter among the people who would not like his teaching.

Verse 35. *Sword shall pierce through thy own soul* refers to the sorrow that Mary was to have at seeing her son suffering on the cross (Matthew 27: 56; Mark 15: 40; John 19: 25). Jesus was to exalt or abase men according to whether the *thoughts of their hearts* were good or evil, for he would be able to read and expose those thoughts.

Verse 36. *From her viginity* means from the time she was of marriageable age. She married at that time but her husband lived only seven years after this marriage. Women were inspired in Old Testament times as well as in the New. (See Exodus 15: 20; Judges 4: 4; 2 Kings 22: 14.)

Verse 37. This woman was a good example of the widow described in 1 Timothy 5: 5.

Verse 38. *Spake . . . looked for redemption in Jerusalem.* Only an inspired person could speak on this subject with any authentic assurance, hence this good woman used her qualification as a prophetess for that purpose.

Verse 39. Luke omits the flight into Egypt from Judea before the return to Nazareth. Matthew 2: 13-15 should be read in connection with this verse.

Verse 40. The body of Jesus was human as well as divine, and was subject to the same law of growth or development as that of any other child. His spiritual or inner man, therefore, would have to develop in accordance with his body. However, since the work to be accomplished by him was of such special importance, his Father favored him with wisdom that was "beyond his years." This will account for the beautiful story we are about to read in some following verses.

Verses 41. The law required all the males of the Jews (others might if they wished) to appear at Jerusalem at the three yearly feasts (Exodus 23: 14-17; Deuteronomy 16: 16).

Verse 42. Joseph took his wife and child Jesus with him on the occasion when the child was twelve years old. Whether they always went with him we are not told.

Verse 43. *Fulfilled the days* refers to the Passover on the fourteenth day of the first month and the seven days immediately following (Leviticus 23: 4-8). Jesus began to manifest the "special wisdom" referred to at verse 40, and he remained at Jerusalem after his parents departed. There being a large group traveling together toward Galilee, the child was not missed for a while.

Verse 44. It was the next day before the parents of Jesus observed that he was not in their family unit. They next made a search for him among acquaintances and relatives but did not find him.

Verse 45. The parents returned to Jerusalem where they had last seen their son.

Verse 46. It was three days before they found their son. The *doctors* were the teachers in the law of Moses. *Hearing* and *asking* questions shows that Jesus was conducting what is sometimes termed a "forum" in which questions and answers may be exchanged between the people in the assembly.

Verse 47. *Understanding* refers to his ability to ask proper questions, for a person needs to know something about a subject to be able to ask intelligent questions about it. His *answers* refers to the questions these doctors (teachers) were asking Jesus about the things that pertained to the *business* of God.

Verse 48. The mother of Jesus told him that she and his father had been searching for him. She meant his earthly foster father, for he it was who would need to search.

Verse 49. *About my Father's business* is rendered "in the affairs of my Father" by the Englishman's Greek New Testament. The wisdom mentioned in verse 40 taught Jesus that he was destined to perform some special work in the world that pertained to God. The temple was the official headquarters of the system of religion then in force for the Jews, hence Jesus was found in that building where his parents should have looked first.

Verse 50. This verse will help to explain why the parents were so disturbed about the disappearance of their son. *They understood not* because they did not have that special wisdom that he had, mentioned and commented upon at verse 40.

Verse 51. Whatever object God wished to accomplish in the temple at this time by this 12-year-old boy, was done, and he was then left to accompany his parents to their home. Jesus furnishes an important example of obedience to parents that all other children should imitate. Although he possessed wisdom that was given him in a special manner (which no boy or girl today can have), yet he realized his duty to his parents. All of the things that were happening were wonderful to his mother, and she *kept them in her heart* or held them as a cherished subject of meditation in her young motherly affections.

Verse 52. This verse is virtually the same in thought as verse 40.

LUKE 3

Verse 1. According to some facts of history it would seem that the fifteenth year of Tiberius Caesar is too late for the other things mentioned in this verse. The difficulty is made clear by a statement in Webster's Ancient History, page 447. "Of the successors of Augustus, the first, and by far the ablest, was his stepson, Tiberius. His merits as a soldier and administrator were well known to Augustus, who, even during his own lifetime, granted Tiberius a share in the government." The fifteen years of Tiberius mentioned by Luke includes the three years he reigned jointly with Augustus.

Verse 2. John 18: 13 calls Annas the father-in-law to Caiaphas the high priest. There was no provision made in the law of Moses for more than one high priest to be in office at the same time, but in the days of Christ the secular government was taking much part in the affairs of the Jews. In that arrangement Annas was president of the Sanhedrin and Caiaphas was high priest for religious activities. Chapter 1: 80 leaves John in the wilderness, and the present verse says the Lord called him by His word.

Verse 3. At the Lord's call, John came out of his retirement and began preaching in the region of the Jordan. *Baptism of repentance* means baptism that is preceded and prompted by repentance or a turning away from the practice of sin. *For remission of sins* denotes that repentance and baptism was in order to the remission of sins.

Verse 4. *Esaias* is the same as Isaiah, and this prophecy is in that book, chapter 40: 3, 4. *Make his paths* straight is explained at Matthew 3: 3.

Verse 5. This verse is a figurative description of preparing the path mentioned in the preceding verse, which was to be accomplished by adjusting the conditions in the lives of men to suit them for the service of Christ who was to follow soon.

Verse 6. *All flesh* signifies that the Gentiles as well as the Jews were to receive the benefits of salvation through the work of Christ.

Verse 7. This verse is explained at Matthew 3: 7.

Verse 8. *Fruits worthy of repentance* means to show by a reformation of life that they had repented. For further comments on this verse see those at Matthew 3: 9.

Verse 9. *Ax is laid* means it will be done at the proper time which will be at the judgment day. However, the way for them to avoid that "ax" was being pointed out by John, and it required the people to bring forth a life of righteousness.

Verse 10. John had been preaching in general terms, now the people wished him to specify some of the things they would be expected to do.

Verse 11. This verse pertains to the duty that one owes to another, in sharing his good things of life with those who do not have them.

Verse 12. The publicans are described by comments on Matthew 9: 10.

Verse 13. The quotation cited at the preceding verse shows that the publicans were assigned the duty of collecting the taxes from the people. Many of them had taken advantage of their appointment to demand more than the government levied, then putting the difference in their own pockets.

Verse 14. A soldier has no right to oppress the citizens just because he is a military man. To *accuse falsely* means to extort money from the people to be used on their own gratification. *Be content with your wages.* Dissatisfaction with one's wages does not make it right to use violence against the government or other employer.

Verse 15. *Mused* is properly rendered "reasoned, or debated" in the margin. The people were considering the reasons for and against the question whether John were the Christ predicted in the Scriptures.

Verse 16. *John answered.* The people had done their reasoning *in their hearts,* hence John had to be inspired to answer them. He did so by telling some of the differences between himself and "the Christ." The first one he gave was the baptism each performed. John baptized with water only but the one coming next would baptize with the Holy Ghost (Spirit) and with fire. The first one by Jesus took place on the day of Pentecost and the subjects were the apostles. The second one will take place after the judgment and the subjects will be the disobedient persons of the earth. What he says about the shoes is to illustrate his sense of inferiority to Christ.

Verse 17. *Fan* is explained by the comments on Matthew 3: 12.

Verse 18. John not only preached the truth to the people, but he exhorted them, which means to "insist on doing a known duty."

Verses 19, 20. For the information on this see Matthew 14: 3-5 and comments.

Verses 21, 22. The reader should see the comments on Matthew 3: 13-17.

Verse 23. *As was supposed* is from NOMIZO and is defined by Thayer, "to hold by custom or usage, own as a custom or usage." The people in general did not understand the whole story of Jesus and Joseph, hence Luke inserts the clause in order to make his record conform to the facts. Matthew (chapter 1) records the genealogy of Jesus from Abraham, down through David's son Solomon until he gets to the same Joseph of our chapter, who was the son-in-law of Heli, the father of Mary. Then, beginning his genealogy of Jesus on his real mother's side, Luke records it from her and her father Heli up on that side and joins the genealogy with that of Matthew when he gets to Nathan who was the full brother of Solomon. From there on Luke records the same genealogy as Matthew until he gets to Abraham, the place where Matthew begins his, but Luke goes on up until he gets to Adam who was the first man. Before going any further here, the reader should carefully consult the comments on Matthew 1: 1, 2.

Verses 24-38. I have grouped these verses into one paragraph because they have been virtually all considered in the preceding one. In ancient times certain names were used even by more than one person in the same family. If the reader observes some that he thinks he has read elsewhere he should not become confused. To clarify the subject for a final comment, let it be understood that Matthew gives the genealogy of Christ on his foster father's (Joseph) side of the house, while Luke gives it on his mother's side, both blood streams being joined in David.

LUKE 4

Verses 1-13. This paragraph is really a repetition of Matthew 4: 1-11, and to conserve space I shall request the reader to see that place in connection with this group.

Verse 14. *Power* is from DUNAMIS which means might or ability that belongs to an individual as a part of his own personality. Jesus possessed such a faculty which he exercised through the instrumentality of the Spirit. This enabled him to perform many miracles which caused him to become famous throughout all Galilee.

Verse 15. *Synagogues* is explained at Matthew 4: 23. To *glorify* is defined in the lexicon, "to praise, extol, magnify, celebrate." This honor was bestowed upon Jesus because of his wonderful teaching. (See Matthew 7: 28, 29.)

Verse 16. Nazareth was the "home town" of Jesus to which he was paying a visit. When he *stood up* in the synagogue it was a signal to the one in charge that he was ready to do some reading, that being the main purpose of the synagogues.

Verse 17. Observing the position of Jesus, the ruler of the synagogue handed him the book of Isaiah. Being divinely inspired, Jesus did not need the copy to know what it said, but it was a mark of respect for "the written word" for him to read it, and he had no trouble in locating the place he wished to read which is quoted next verse.

Verse 18. This passage is in Isaiah 61: 1-3, and is a prediction of the spiritual mission of Jesus into the world. However, some of the statements have reference also to the miraculous cures he was to perform.

Verse 19. *Acceptable year* denotes one in which the most desirable and beneficial experiences would be offered to all who would accept them.

Verse 20. Thayer defines the original for *minister* as "an attendant." It was customary, after the reading had been done, for the reader or someone else to offer some comments if it was his desire (Acts 13: 14, etc.). *All eyes were fastened on him.* They were wondering if this famous man would also become their "guest speaker."

Verse 21. He did, and this verse is the introduction to his remarks. By applying the passage to himself, Jesus raised a stir within the audience, at least in their minds, to begin with.

Verse 22. The first reaction was not so unfavorable but it caused them to begin to wonder in their minds. *Is this not Joseph's son?* The idea was whether this humble native could speak such wonderful things.

Verse 23. Jesus was aware of the reasoning the people were doing, whether he heard them with his fleshly ears or not. He knew they would wonder why he did not perform the same amount of wonderful deeds there that he was reported to have done in other countries such as that in the vicinity of Capernaum. *Physician, heal thyself* was a prediction that was fulfilled at the cross (Matthew 27: 40), but the other words of the verse were being fulfilled while Jesus was speaking.

Verse 24. This verse explains why he did not go any farther with his work while in the neighborhood of Nazareth. It was because the people would not appreciate it on the principle that *no prophet is accepted in his own country.*

Verse 25. This verse merely shows that the condition of dependency was very general in the days to which Jesus will soon refer in remarks about who was favored.

Verse 26. *Elias* is the same as Elijah in 1 Kings 17: 8-16.

Verse 27. *Eliseus* is the same as Elisha in 2 Kings 5: 1-14.

Verse 28. The people saw the point that Jesus was making. If those old prophets passed over so many people and bestowed their favors upon a few humble cases, it was because they were considered worthy of the benefits. Hence, these people in the home community of Jesus were not going to receive very much attention from him because they were not considered as being entitled to it, having given him "the cold shoulder" because he was an old home product. When they saw this lesson in the teaching of Jesus it made them to be *filled with wrath.*

Verse 29. Jesus did not resist their force until it was necessary to preserve his life. It was not time for him to die and hence he used his superior might to escape his enemies. However, he did not use force but escaped by a miraculous movement.

Verse 30. This movement enabled him to go on his way without harming them.

Verse 31. Capernaum was the other city which Jesus had previously adopted as a residence (Matthew 4: 13).

Verse 32. This verse means exactly the same as Matthew 7: 29, because the word for *power* is EXOUSIA, which is the word for "authority" in that passage.

Verse 33. *Unclean* means in regard to moral character, and this was one of the fallen angels that sinned and were cast down to hell (2 Peter 2: 4), which is explained in the notes at Matthew 8: 28, 29.

Verse 34. The note cited in the preceding paragraph explains why the devil said *I know thee who thou art*, and also why he asked to be *let alone.*

Verse 35. These devils had superhuman power and could injure human beings unless restrained. Jesus suffered this one to throw the man down but not hurt him otherwise.

Verse 36. An interesting feature of this verse is the use of both *authority* and *power* in one connection. The first comes from EXOUSIA and its first definition is the word by which it is here rendered; the second is from DUNAMIS and is properly rendered in this place. The thought is that Jesus had the right to give orders to the devils, and also had the ability to execute the orders.

Verse 37. Jesus was not performing his deeds merely to gain notoriety, but such a result was inevitable because of the natural trait of interest in the unusual things.

Verse 38. This was Simon Peter (Matthew 4: 18) whose mother-in-law was sick. We observe that Peter was married, although the Romanists forbid their clergy to marry, and yet claim that Peter was the first pope.

Verse 39. All miraculous cures were *immediate* as this one was.

Verse 40. By evening the fame of Jesus had reached so far that many afflicted persons had been gathered together, and when they were brought to him he healed them all.

Verse 41. Jesus would not suffer the devils even to confess him, because he did not want to be supported by such unworthy characters. Besides, their confession would not have been a matter of faith for *they knew that he was the Christ.*

Verse 42. Wherever Jesus went the crowds followed. *Stayed him* means they detained him; not by force to be sure, but by earnest requests.

Verse 43. Jesus was kind and did not want to disappoint the people, so he explained that other places should have the preaching of the kingdom given them also.

Verse 44. With such an explanation, Jesus left this eager crowd and preached in the same general territory, but in the synagogues where other people would be assembled.

LUKE 5

Verse 1. Gennesaret was another name for the Sea of Galilee. *The people* were the ones meant *by the common people* in Mark 12: 37. They were not prejudiced as were the priests and scribes, and manifested a hunger to hear the teaching of Jesus.

Verse 2. When a boat is said to be standing it means it is stationary in a certain spot. These two ships were thus being held while their owners were out washing their nets after a night's use in the sea.

Verse 3. Simon's full name was Simon Peter (verse 8). By moving the boat a little distance from the shore, the people could see and hear Jesus better.

Verse 4. The water was too shallow for fishing with a net where Jesus had been speaking. In bidding Simon to let the net down *for a draught* (for a "catch"), Jesus assured him that he would not be disappointed.

Verse 5. Simon's remarks indicated that his lowering of the net would be through faith in Jesus, even though the appearances were unfavorable.

Verse 6. The word *brake* is from an original that means a complete rending of the net. However, since the fish were not lost, the idea is that a full loss would have occurred had not something been done to prevent it.

Verse 7. The loss of the fish was prevented by the help of their partners in the business. *Began to sink* means the weight of the fish caused the boats to begin lowering, not that they were being submerged as yet.

Verse 8. Peter already had expressed faith in Jesus, but the success of the event was far beyond his expectation. *Depart . . . I am a sinful man.* He was so overawed by the power and wisdom of Jesus that he felt unworthy to be in his presence.

Verse 9. Doubtless the net had come into contact with a shoal or school of fish and no equipment would be able to withstand such a mass. But it required the wisdom of Jesus to know when and where to find such a group, hence the people were astonished.

Verse 10. This is the same event given notice in Matthew 4: 18-21, but that passage omits the items of the net and mass of fish.

Verse 11. *Forsook all* includes their father, who is mentioned by Matthew.

Verse 12. Lepers were under perpetual quarantine by the law of Moses (Leviticus 13: 45, 46), which accounts for the earnestness of this unfortunate man.

Verse 13. Leprosy was an incurable disease by any natural means, hence it was cured miraculously by Jesus and the recovery was *immediate.*

Verse 14. *Tell no man.* He was not to take the time for publishing the event to the people, for he had a personal duty yet to perform in connection with his recovery. The ceremony still remaining for him is described in Leviticus 14: 1-32.

Verse 15. In spite of the request, the leper spread his report to the deed until it caused the crowds to gather about Jesus to receive his favors.

Verse 16. This was the occasion when he walked on the sea towards the apostles to their terrified astonishment (Matthew 14: 23-33).

Verse 17. These Pharisees and doctors (teachers) of the law were present for the purpose of finding fault with Jesus as we shall soon learn.

Verse 18. *Sought means* refers to the crowd that was in the way about the door.

Verse 19. See the comments at Mark 2: 4 for the explanation of this verse.

Verse 20. A distinction is made between *their* and *him*. As far as the passage states, the palsied man did not have any faith to begin with.

Verse 21. This verse proves the statement made at verse 17 about the Pharisees.

Verses 22-24. For comments on this paragraph see those on Matthew 9: 5, 6.

Verse 25. *Immediately* is the important word here. Professed workers of miracles today require patients to have the faith that "holds out" long enough to effect a cure. The true miraculous healing did not call for a prolonged period of time.

Verses 26. For ordinary human beings to *glorify* God means for them to give Him the credit for the wonderful things accomplished.

Verse 27. Levi's other name was Matthew (Matthew 9: 9). The *receipt of custom* was the tax office, and Levi was there because he was a publican whose business was to receive the taxes on behalf of the government.

Verse 28. At the bidding of Jesus, Levi left his work and followed.

Verse 29. Since Levi was a publican by occupation, it was natural that many of his guests at the feast would be from that class.

Verse 30. See the notes on Matthew 9: 11 about *eating with others*.

Verse 31. If the Pharisees had been as righteous as they claimed, that would have been the very reason for Jesus to associate with the others, on the principle that the sick are the ones who need a physician.

Verse 32. This verse continues the same thought set forth in the preceding one. The sinner is the one who needs to be induced to repent.

Verse 33. John was dead and his disciples were fasting and mourning his absence. The disciples of Jesus still had him with them and hence had no occasion for mourning.

Verses 34, 35. Children of the bridechamber were the close friends of the bridegroom. After the wedding the bridegroom would leave and then it would be appropriate for them to mourn. In the illustration Jesus likens himself to the bridegroom.

Verses 36-38. This paragraph is explained by the comments on Matthew 9: 16, 17.

Verse 39. This verse has the same lesson that the preceding paragraph teaches, which is one of appropriateness. Incidentally, it also overthrows the theory referred to, that the illustration applied to the Old and New Testaments. According to that notion, Jesus teaches that every man would prefer the Old Testament as being the better.

LUKE 6

Verse 1. *Second sabbath after the first* has something to do with the relation between the religious and the civil year. It does not have much significance to us with such a translation, and most versions give it simply as "on a sabbath." For comments on taking this corn see those at Matthew 12: 1.

Verse 2. The Pharisees would not accuse the disciples of stealing, for they knew what the law said on the subject of taking the corn, but pretended to object to their doing so on the sabbath because it was a holy day.

Verses 3, 4. This paragraph is explained at Matthew 12: 4.

Verse 5. God and his Son are one in purpose and were together in giving the law. Therefore Jesus had the right to apply his own law as he saw fit.

Verse 6. Jesus was busy every day and taught the people whenever the opportunity came. His reason for entering the synagogue on sabbath days was because on that day the Jews assembled there to read and hear read the law. The man's hand was withered as a result of some obstruction in the circulation of his blood.

Verse 7. The scribes and Pharisees pretended to be zealous for the sanctity of the sabbath. That was only a screen for their envy of Jesus because of his teaching against their hypocritical life.

Verse 8. Jesus could read their thoughts and decided to head them off from their intended criticism. The man was told to stand, he being normal except the condition of his hand. This brought him into full view of the people in the building.

Verse 9. See the comments on Mark 3: 4 for the questions Jesus asked.

Verse 10. Jesus looked round to make sure of the attention to his work. The man's hand only was afflicted, hence he was able without miraculous help to stretch out his arm. With that act came the complete restoration of the afflicted hand.

Verse 11. *Madness* is from ANOIA which Thayer explains to be a condition in which they were "expressing themselves in rage." This was because they were completely baffled by the unexpected way in which Jesus handled the case. They *communed* or consulted with each other as to how they might destroy him.

Verse 12. Jesus had an important problem to solve, which was the selection of men to appoint over his kingdom that was at hand. It was fitting that he should spend the preceding hours of night in prayer to his Father.

Verse 13. Jesus had many disciples, but out of them he chose twelve only to be his apostles, to be sent into the world with the message of salvation through the Gospel.

Verses 14-16. See the notes at Matthew 10: 2-4 in connection with this paragraph.

Verses 17, 18. This paragraph corresponds with Matthew 4: 23-25, which see.

Verse 19. *Virtue* is from DUNAMIS, one of the words rendered by "power" in many places. The crowds sought to touch Jesus to obtain this power to cure their diseases.

Verse 20. Luke's account of the sermon on the mount begins with this verse. That sermon is related with more detail by Matthew, likewise my comments are more extended at that place, which are to be found in Matthew 5, 6, and 7. The reader should consult that account in connection with this chapter of Luke.

Verse 21. There is some slight variation in the way Luke words these several verses, from the way Matthew gives them, but the thoughts are the same.

Verse 22. Another word for *blessed* is "happy," and the original is so rendered in many passages. These evil treatments must have been inflicted because of their devotion to the Son of man, in order for the disciples to be given this blessing.

Verse 23. The blessing was not to be in this life but after reaching heaven.

In suffering for the sake of righteousness, the disciples were classed with the prophets.

Verse 24. This is somewhat figurative, meaning to be enjoying the pleasures of this world by neglecting the obligation of a righteous life.

Verse 25. *Full* and *hunger, laugh* and *weep*, are figures used for the purpose of contrast. The thought is the same as expressed by comments on the preceding verse.

Verse 26. A righteous man is not popular with the majority of mankind. If he does his duty he will condemn sin, and that will cause the guilty ones to speak against him.

Verse 27. *Love your enemies.* See the long note at Matthew 5: 43 on "love."

Verse 28. To *bless* means to wish for something beneficial to happen to one. It does not mean anything merely for pleasure, but that which will actually do him good.

Verse 29. See the comments at Matthew 5: 39.

Verse 30. This is explained at Matthew 5: 42 with its comments.

Verse 31. This verse is popularly spoken of as the "golden rule." It is commented upon at length at Matthew 7: 12 which the reader is urged to consult.

Verse 32. See the long note on the word "love" at Matthew 5: 43.

Verse 33. This verse refers to men who bestow favors on others with a selfish motive, thinking chiefly of their own personal gain they hope to get in return.

Verse 34. This verse deals with the same selfishness as the preceding one.

Verse 35. *Love, do good*, and the other terms of service to others, are used in the sense of unselfish ministrations for the chief purpose of doing good. If gratitude returns some reward it is right to accept it, but that should not be the motive. The Highest bestows the blessings of creation on all mankind, and His example is cited as a rule for the disciples to follow.

Verse 36. To be *merciful* means to be more lenient toward an offender than his conduct would entitle him to expect, but not to the extent of encouraging him in wrong doing.

Verse 37. *Judge not*, etc. See the comments at Matthew 7: 1.

Verse 38. Almost every rule has some exceptions, but usually if a man is kind and generous with others, they will remember him when he gets in need. That is the meaning of Proverbs 18: 24 that has been erroneously applied to Christ. That passage is explained in volume 3 of the Old Testament Commentary. The phrases in our verse are figurative, drawn from the act of crowding out unnecessary space in measuring produce.

Verse 39. A parable is a comparison. One blind man following another is like a person closing his mental eyes and letting a false teacher tell him how to go.

Verse 40. A disciple is a learner, and such a person could not know more than his teacher. *Perfect* means complete; if the disciple will absorb all of his master's teaching he will be like him which should satisfy him.

Verses 41, 42. See the comments on Matthew 7: 3-5.

Verses 43, 44. Trees and shrubs are used to illustrate the lives of men. When we see a man practicing evil we know he has an evil heart. (See Matthew 15: 19.)

Verse 45. Words as well as deeds spring from the heart, whether good or bad.

Verse 46. The word "lord" means ruler. It is inconsistent to call Jesus by a name that means one who is in the rule, but then refuse to obey what he commands.

Verses 47-49. This paragraph is explained at Matthew 7: 24-27.

LUKE 7

Verse 1. *His sayings* refers to the ones in the preceding chapter. Capernaum was the city that Jesus adopted as his residence after leaving Nazareth (Matthew 4: 13).

Verse 2. A centurion was a man having charge of a hundred soldiers.

Verse 3. The centurion was a Gentile, but was in good standing with the Jews, for they had their elders to take a message of request to Jesus from the officers.

Verse 4. Jesus had taught the principle of favoring those only who were worthy (Matthew 7: 6), hence that point was stressed in their appeal for his help.

Verse 5. Synagogues were places built for assembling to hear the law read. Strangers are not to be solicited for contributions to the Lord's cause, but their voluntary offerings may be accepted. Paul accepted help from non-Christians (Acts 28: 2, 7, 10).

Verse 6. This Gentile felt unworthy to have Jesus in his house.

Verse 7. He did not even think he was good enough to make a personal contact with the Lord, but sent others to speak for him. He expressed faith in the power of Jesus to heal his servant by just speaking the work.

Verse 8. This reasoning was to show that his remarks were not in flattery. (See the comments at Matthew 8: 9.)

Verse 9. The Jews had not produced any example of faith that was as great as this. Jesus announced this truth to the people who were following him.

Verse 10. The faith of the centurion was rewarded with the immediate healing of his servant, for the messengers found him well upon their return.

Verse 11. Nain was a village of Galilee, the same district that contained Capernaum. As usual, as Jesus journeyed toward this place the crowds followed him.

Verse 12. The death of this young man was especially saddening by the circumstance that he was the only support of his widowed mother; this explains *why much people was with her* and thus showing their sympathy for her.

Verse 13. *Compassion* means pity, and Jesus felt that way toward this sorrowing mother. (See Isaiah 53: 4.) In his sympathy for her he bade her cease weeping.

Verse 14. Jesus touched the bier (casket) to indicate he wished the pallbearers to stop. He then spoke to the dead man, showing he had power over inanimate objects.

Verse 15. In response to the command of Jesus the man came to life and sat up. It was not merely a mechanical performance upon a dead body for the young man spoke to them and then rejoined his mother.

Verse 16. This *fear* was that of deep respect, for they glorified God which means they gave Him credit for the deed performed by Jesus. It meant to the people that he was a great prophet, else God would not have enabled him to perform this deed.

Verse 17. This *rumor* means the report of what had been done for the dead.

Verse 18. John's disciples reported

this deed to him, which would be of special interest to him in view of his preparatory work for Christ.

Verses 19-22. This paragraph is so much like Matthew 11: 2-5 which is commented upon at length, that I shall ask the reader to consult that place in explanation of this.

Verse 23. This is explained with the lexicon definition at Matthew 11: 6.

Verse 24. The importance of John and his work will be the subject of some verses, all of which will show that Jesus had a high regard for him. A *reed* is a tall and slender stem that would be swayed easily by the wind. Such would illustrate a man with little stability and one who could be easily influenced. The question of Jesus implies that John was not that way.

Verse 25. A man who was accustomed to the soft and luxurious life of royal palaces would be unsuited for work out in the wilderness. But the prophets had predicted the forerunner of Jesus was to operate in the wilderness, hence no surprise should be felt over the rough outdoor raiment of the Baptist.

Verse 26. *More than a prophet.* John not only uttered prophecies, but his life and work in preparing a people for Christ constituted a fulfillment of the sayings of other prophets, which made him more than a mere prophet.

Verse 27. This prediction is recorded in Malachi 3: 1.

Verse 28. See the comments on Matthew 11: 11.

Verse 29. *Justified God* means they acknowledged God to be just in authorizing John to baptize the people. They expressed their belief on this subject by being baptized.

Verse 30. To reject an ordinance of God is interpreted as rejecting Him. The lawyers were men who were acquainted with the law of Moses and interpreted it to others.

Verses 31-35. This paragraph is explained at Matthew 11: 16-19.

Verse 36. The Pharisees were a sect of the Jews who were prominent in the time of Christ. See a description of them in the comments at Matthew 16: 12.

Verse 37. All people are *sinners* in a general sense, but there were certain outcasts who were called thus as a class. This incident must not be confused with the one in Matthew 26: 7; that woman was Mary a sister of Lazarus (John 11: 2).

Verse 38. Kissing the feet of Jesus was an act of worship (Matthew 2: 2) that was prompted by the spirit of humility. It also indicated reverence for Jesus as a holy man. Another custom of those times was the washing of the feet of a guest. This will be explained when we come to John 13.

Verse 39. Jesus knew the thoughts of men, whether they were expressed or not. This Pharisee was thinking of the woman in the light of the class she supposedly represented.

Verse 40. Jesus called for the attention of his host. The word *master* is from an original that properly means "teacher," and Simon used it in that sense.

Verse 41. A *pence* would be worth about sixteen cents in our money. The value of the individual coin is unimportant, the illustration being drawn from the difference between fifty and five hundred.

Verse 42. The question was based on the comparative favors each debtor received.

Verse 43. Simon answered the question correctly that Jesus asked.

Verse 44. Simon had other guests (verse 49), and evidently they were "rating" a little higher than Jesus, and had received the regular attention usually paid to visitors. For some reason, Jesus had been neglected and he decided to make a lesson of it.

Verse 45. The kiss was the customary form of greeting in those days. But Simon did not give Jesus the usual kiss on the mouth, while this woman kissed his feet often.

Verse 46. As a matter of refreshing, a guest was anointed on the head with olive oil. Jesus had been neglected in that by his host, while the woman anointed his feet.

Verse 47. Jesus did not deny that the woman was of the lower class and had many sins. But she was given a higher rating than the debtor who owed five hundred pence. He gave his love after receiving the favor of being forgiven the debt, but the woman loved Jesus because of her sincere faith in him even before having received any favor. In return for that attitude Jesus gave her the great reward of complete forgiveness.

Verse 48. No further condition was mentioned, for she was forgiven her sins as a reward for her loving service and her simple trust in the grace of Jesus.

Verse 49. This is the question raised by the people in Matthew 9: 1-6.

Verse 50. Her faith saved her, but it does not say faith *alone*. She had performed the works for which her sins were forgiven.

LUKE 8

Verse 1. *Shewing the glad tidings* all comes from the Greek word EUAGGE-LIZO which occurs many times in the New Testament, and the universal meaning is to tell any good news. The connection has to be noticed to learn what particular good news is meant in any given case, and in the present one it is the news that the kingdom of God is at hand. The *twelve* means the apostles (Matthew 10: 2-4; Mark 3: 14-19).

Verse 2. The closing sentence of the preceding verse is continued in this to include *certain women*, etc. One of them was Mary Magdalene who had been possessed of seven devils until Jesus relieved her of them. She was present at the cross when Jesus was crucified (Matthew 27: 56).

Verse 3. The women had been favored by Jesus miraculously, and they showed their appreciation by ministering to him *of their substance*, which means necessities of life.

Verse 4. These parables were spoken to the people, not his disciples. The reason for teaching them in this manner is explained at Matthew 13: 11.

Verses 5-15. This is the beginning of the parables, and the full explanation is given in Matthew 13 which will not be repeated in detail here. However, a few of the items of this passage will be noticed. *Thorns* means a bramble, and is the same plant of which the soldiers made a crown and placed upon the head of Jesus in mockery (Matthew 27: 29). *Devil* is from DIABOLOS which is applied to Satan as the chief of demons. *Good ground* is defined as an honest heart that causes good fruit to be produced.

Verse 16. The teaching of this verse is that a man should not hinder the influence of righteous deeds by some unwise action otherwise. (See Romans 14: 16.)

Verse 17. As a candle is not supposed to be covered, so the good things learned from Jesus should be permitted to go out for the benefit of others.

Verse 18. *That which he seemeth to have.* (See Matthew 13: 12; 25: 29.)

Verse 19. The *press* means the crowd that pressed about the door.

Verse 20. The *brethren* means the same as the word ordinarily denotes. Had Luke meant his spiritual brethren (as the Romanists teach), there would have been no reason for mentioning his *mother*, for that is a fleshly relationship.

Verse 21. See the comments at Matthew 12: 47, 48.

Verse 22. This *lake* means the Sea of Galilee which Jesus wished to cross, where he was going to do more teaching and perform his great deeds.

Verse 23. *Filled with water* is explained by the closing words, *were in jeopardy*. We know that if the boat had been literally filled they would have perished then, but instead of that they were in danger of perishing.

Verse 24. *We perish* means the same as the preceding verse about being in great danger. *Rebuked the wind* indicates control over inanimate objects by miraculous power.

Verse 25. They had heard him command intelligent creatures such as the demons, but were astonished to see him control things that have no consciousness.

Verse 26. Gadarenes (also called Gergesenes) was situated near the eastern shore of the Sea of Galilee, and that is where Jesus went ashore.

Verse 27. These tombs were cavities in the rocks, such as were sometimes used as burial places. This man was possessed with devils, which made him abnormally strong.

Verse 28. The devils knew Christ because they were fallen angels and had seen him before they were cast out of heaven. (See 2 Peter 2: 4; Jude 6.) *Torment me not.* The devils knew that if they had to leave this world they would have to go back to the place of torment into which they were cast when they first sinned.

Verse 29. The man was under the control of the devils. (See the note at Matthew 8: 28.) It explains the condition of being possessed with the devil.

Verse 30. *Legion* means an indefinite but great number of beings. But one of the devils was spokesman for the others is why the pronoun is in singular number sometimes.

Verse 31. *Deep* is from ABUSSOS which is defined by Thayer as follows: "Bottomless, unbounded; the pit; the abyss." He also explains it to mean,

"The immeasurable depth; a very deep gulf or chasm in the lowest of the earth; the common receptacle of the dead, Romans 10: 7, and especially as the abode of demons, Luke 8: 31; Revelation 9: 1; 11: 7; 17: 8; 20: 1, 3."

Verse 32. The devils did not know the swine would perish, so they requested to be let go into them rather than go back to this *deep* where they had been tormented.

Verse 33. The possession of devils made the swine mad and induced them to destroy themselves by drowning, thus forcing the spirits out of the world.

Verses 34-37. It will be well to read the comments on Matthew 8: 28-34.

Verses 38, 39. Gratitude prompted the man to wish for the privilege of accompanying Jesus, but the Lord preferred to make a messenger of him among the people of his own house. He did so and even extended his report throughout the whole city.

Verse 40. After the miracle of casting out these devils, Jesus entered the boat again and recrossed the sea, when he found people waiting for him with joy.

Verses 41-56. For detailed comments on this paragraph see the ones on Matthew 9: 18-26. For the reader's convenience, I shall make some remarks on various specific items in the present paragraph. A *ruler* was one presiding over a synagogue. The woman had a chronic hemorrhage of twelve years' standing. She was cured *immediately* which was always the case with miraculous healing. *Not dead but sleepeth* is explained in the passage cited above at Matthew 9: 24.

LUKE 9

Verse 1. *Power* means the ability to control the devils, and *authority* means the right to do so. The *twelve* were the apostles, given ability also to cure diseases.

Verse 2. The primary object of the work was to preach the news of the kingdom; the miracles were to prove the apostles were genuine.

Verse 3. A *scrip* is a provision bag, used as a modern lunch basket. No extensive provision needed to be made while Jesus was in the world to insure their care.

Verse 4. *There abide and thence depart* means for them to make only one house call in each city, except where the first one proved to be unworthy.

Verse 5. After finding one proper house for their work, they were to leave for another city. As they were leaving, they were to shake the dust from their feet. That was an ancient custom of showing disapproval of the place where they had got the dust.

Verse 6. The *gospel* they preached was the good news that the kingdom of heaven was at hand. They did the healing to prove they were not false prophets.

Verse 7. This *Herod* was a son of Herod the Great. A *tetrarch* was a ruler over a division of a general territory. *John was risen from the dead* is explained at Matthew 14: 2.

Verse 8. *Elias* is the same as Elijah in the Old Testament. Nothing is said about his rising again for he had not died (2 Kings 2: 11).

Verse 9. The beheading of John is reported in Matthew 14: 1-12 and Mark 6: 17-29. *Desired to see him* was accomplished as recorded at chapter 23: 8.

Verse 10. There were times when Jesus wished for private consultation with his apostles. Bethsaida was a city on the west shore of the Sea of Galilee.

Verse 11. It was not long until the people knew of the presence of Jesus and followed him. In his compassion he received them and gave them both spiritual teaching and physical cure for their ills.

Verse 12. The desert was on the east side of Jordan, but the country in general was unsettled and not equipped with many markets at which to buy food.

Verse 13. Jesus opened the exercises of the occasion by telling the apostles to feed the multitude. They explained how small was their supply of food at hand.

Verses 14, 15. Jesus prepared to feed the multitude by a miracle of the food. For the sake of orderliness he had them sit down in convenient groups.

Verse 16. *Looking up to heaven* was in recognition of the source of all blessings. (See James 1: 17.) The breaking was necessary because more than one person was going to partake, which was the only reason that Jesus *broke* the bread in Matthew 26: 26.

Verse 17. The twelve baskets of fragments remaining proves that being *filled* was not imaginary on the part of the multitude.

Verses 18. See Matthew 16: 13 on why Jesus asked them this question.

Verse 19. These statements of the people were made on the basis of an erroneous theory called "transmigration of souls." (See Matthew 14: 2.)

Verse 20. Peter's confession means "the Anointed one of God."

Verse 21. This is explained in the comments at Matthew 16: 20.

Verse 22. Luke's account omits the conversation about the church, but he mentions the vital fact on which it was to be built, which was to be proved by His resurrection.

Verse 23. To *deny* one's self means to disown one's earthly interests. *Take up his cross* is figurative and is based on the practice of compelling a doomed man to carry his own cross to the place of crucifixion.

Verse 24. Two kinds of life are considered here, the temporal and the spiritual. The temporal is the one meant first. If a man neglects his duty to Christ for the sake of his temporal or worldly life, he will lose his spiritual or eternal life.

Verse 25. The thought is that the things of this world altogether are not as valuable as the soul of man. If he exchanges his soul to gain the world it will be a transaction in which there will be no profit.

Verse 26. To be ashamed of one means to feel humiliated at the thought of associating with him. Christ does not expect us to become his equal in the degree of our goodness and dignity, because we are human while he is divine. But if we will obey him and do him the honor of fashioning our lives after his, he will regard it as a compliment and hence will not feel humiliated in associating with us even in the presence of his Father and the angels in the glory world.

Verse 27. If the kingdom of God has not yet been set up (as certain people teach), then the world has in it somewhere a number of persons who are many centuries old!

Verse 28. See comments at Matthew 17: 1 in connection with this verse.

Verse 29. *Fashion* is from EIDOS which Thayer defines, "Properly that which strikes the eye, which is exposed to view; the external appearance, form, figure, shape." Matthew (chapter 17: 2) says Jesus was "transfigured," and the definition is given at that place. The words used by each of the evangelists were true of Jesus then.

Verse 30. See the description of this scene at Matthew 17: 3. Elias was the Elijah of the Old Testament, and a faithful prophet of God.

Verse 31. Matthew does not tell what these men talked about, but Luke gives the subject of their conversation. *Decease* is from EXODOS which Thayer defines, "Exit, i. e., departure; departure from life, decease." This word is interesting from being the name given to the second book of the Bible. *Accomplish* is from PLEROO and the lexicon of Thayer defines it, "To make full, to fill, to fill up." The idea is that in his death Jesus completed the sacrificial service that was allotted to him by his Father. That is why he declared "it is finished" just as he was dying (John 19: 30).

Verse 32. Peter and his group were under an oppressed feeling during the conversation between Jesus and his distinguished visitors. But upon being aroused they saw the trio of glorified beings.

Verse 33. *As they departed.* That is, the conversation was ended and the guests were preparing to leave. Peter wanted to detain them and proposed that provision be made for housing them. *Not knowing what he said.* He did not realize that beings from the unseen world would not dwell in material tabernacles.

Verse 34. The word *cloud* is used a great many times in the New Testament but seldom in connection with rain. Instead, it is used to represent something that has nothing to do with moisture which would form an object that is dark. True, this verse says the cloud *overshadowed* them, but the same event is recorded in Matthew 17: 5 where it is called a "bright cloud," which would not suggest one that was leaden with condensed vapor and ready to drop rain. The idea is that something of a miraculous character was used to indicate the presence of God.

Verse 35. The words *hear him* are in addition to what was said at the time of his baptism (Matthew 3: 17; Mark 1: 11). They were said because the life's work of Jesus was nearing completion and he had proved his worthiness of the distinction.

Verse 36. *They told no man* was because of the instruction that Jesus gave them as they were coming down from the mountain (Matthew 17: 9; Mark 9: 9).

Verse 37. *Hill* and *mountain* are used in the same sense in the New Testament. The people were generally on hands whenever Jesus reappeared from his places of privacy.

Verse 38. The word *master* means "teacher," a term Jesus acquired among the people because of his many talks to them upon the subject of his kingdom. This son is the same case explained at Matthew 17: 15-18.

Verse 39. *Spirit* is from a Greek word that could apply to any disembodied being. In the present case it applies to the devil that had taken possession of the child.

Verse 40. See the comments on Matthew 17: 20, 21 for the present verse.

Verse 41. The *faithless generation* was said about the disciples, according to the statements in the verses cited at 38 and 40.

Verse 42. This *devil* is the same *spirit* mentioned in verse 39 and so termed in this. It had supernatural power and *tare* the boy. The original word for this and also in verse 39, means he was thrown into convulsions. It was an affliction, hence the Lord rebuked the unclean spirit, not the lad.

Verse 43. The words *mighty power* are from a Greek original that means "majesty," and it is so translated in 2 Peter 1: 16. This impression of *amazement* was caused by the powerful circumstance of the boy's recovery from so distressing an ailment.

Verse 44. *The sayings* include what Jesus had been expressing, also the one about his expected betrayal into the hands of men.

Verse 45. The disciples had thought from the start that Jesus was going to set up an earthly kingdom. Such a government would require the bodily presence of the king, hence they were confused over this prediction that he was to be delivered unto men.

Verse 46. Their mistaken idea of the kingdom explains why they could have these thoughts about the different ranks in it, for such distinctions exist in earthly powers.

Verse 47. Jesus could always read the thoughts of his disciples.

Verse 48. Jesus loves little children because they are pure and humble. To receive such a child *in his name* is to do so because Jesus loves him. But no one will do that as long as he is filled with the pride of his own importance. While the man who will thus humble himself is great in the true sense according to the mind of the Lord.

Verses 49, 50. See the comments on Mark 9: 38, 39.

Verse 51. *The time was come* means it was getting near the time when Jesus was to leave the earth and ascend to heaven. That made it necessary for him to be in Jerusalem, hence he turned his steps in that direction.

Verse 52. Jesus was in Galilee at this time which would make it necessary to go through Samaria. He sent some ahead to find a place for him to stop on the way.

Verse 53. The Samaritans were not on good terms with the Jews (John 4: 9), and for that reason they had a prejudice against Jerusalem. Hence they did not welcome Jesus when they learned that he was heading in that direction.

Verse 54. The brothers, James and John, were angered over the slight and suggested some physical destruction for them, citing the case of Elias (Elijah) in 2 Kings 1: 10, 12. What they suggested would have been the action that is meant by pulling up the tares in the parable of the tares. (See Matthew 13: 28.)

Verse 55. This means the brothers did not realize what kind of a spirit they were manifesting. It was just the reverse of what they should have shown.

Verse 56. The kind of spirit they should have manifested was that of Jesus, desiring to save men from spiritual destruction. And that could not be done if their lives were destroyed by physical death as these brothers wished to do.

Verses 57, 58. See the comments at Matthew 8: 19, 20.

Verses 59, 60. This paragraph is explained at Matthew 8: 21, 22.

Verse 61. Following Jesus here means the bodily traveling as explained in verse 57. This man was at that very time absent from his "loved ones," and hence had not shown any great concern for them. His sudden interest in them betrayed at least a divided state of mind between them and Jesus.

Verse 62. *Ploughs* were made with one handle according to Smith's Bible Dictionary, hence the mentioning of a single handle. To make a success of the work a farmer should keep his eye on the ground ahead of him. The work is used to illustrate what should be the attentive devotion of those professing to follow Jesus.

LUKE 10

Verse 1. The words *other seventy* are arranged as "seventy others" in the Greek text, and means seventy besides the twelve apostles. This was a special mission and intended as a hasty work of immediately preparing the people for the reception of Jesus. His work was nearing its close and he wished to accomplish as much as possible in the time. To help towards that end these disciples were sent ahead of him. He sent them in pairs, which had many advantages in that each could encourage the other.

Verse 2. There were so many people who needed help that neither Jesus or any other man could be bodily present with all of them. That is what he meant by saying *the harvest is plentious but the laborers are few,* and prayed that they might increase.

Verse 3. A lamb among wolves would be in great danger. But by great care he might not attract needless attention to himself and so would escape harm.

Verse 4. A *scrip* was a provision bag used as a lunch basket, and a *purse* was a money bag. Note they were not to carry these, which is also said about shoes. It means not to take any "spares" as will be explained at verse 7. *Salute no man* might seem unfriendly. Thayer explains the word for *salute* as follows: "As a salutation was made not merely by a slight gesture and a few words, but generally by embracing and kissing, a journey was retarded by saluting frequently."

Verse 5. Their call at a house was to begin by offering their peace to it.

Verse 6. *Son* (of peace) is from HUION which Thayer defines, "One who is worthy of a thing." The Lord was with these disciples in spirit, and if the people in a house were not worthy of the favors that were offered them, the Lord would see that none would come to them and the wishes of the disciples would return to them.

Verse 7. The work of the disciples in spreading the news of the kingdom entitled them to their living. That explains the instructions in verse 4 about not taking along their own provisions. *Go not from house to house.* They were to make only one call in each city because of the shortness of time. (See Matthew 10: 11, 23.)

Verse 8. *Eat such things as are set before you.* This is similar to Paul's instructions in 1 Corinthians 10: 27. Conscientious Jews were often afraid to eat of things unknown to them because of the restrictions of the law of Moses. Jesus did not overlook the law, yet he was about to give a new one to the world, and certain parts of the old one were to be discontinued.

Verse 9. The disciples were to preach the news of the approaching kingdom of God. By healing the sick they would prove they were true prophets.

Verse 10. A city that would not give the disciples a welcome was to be considered unworthy. The disciples were to get out of the house and into the street.

Verse 11. Shaking off the dust was an ancient custom and was used to indicate disapproval of a place. *Notwithstanding.* Even though they rejected the teaching of the disciples, that would not stop the program of the Lord, for the kingdom of God was going to come into their midst in due time.

Verse 12. *In that day* is indefinite as to date, but the same subject is handled in other passages in which the day of judgment is specified. (See Matthew 10: 15; 11: 22, 24; Mark 6: 11.) It should be noted that the tolerance is to be shown on that day, not afterward.

Verse 13. This is the same as Matthew 11: 21.

Verse 14. *At the judgment* is explained at verse 12.

Verse 15. *Exalted to heaven* is a figure of speech, based on the fact that Jesus was an inhabitant of Capernaum by choice (Matthew 4: 13), and hence it had the advantage of his presence. See the comments on Matthew 11: 23 for the meaning of *hell.*

Verse 16. Jesus ordained the apostles and the seventy and hence whatever attitude was shown to them was equivalent to showing it to Jesus. On the same principle, that attitude also pertains to God since he sent Jesus into the world. To *despise* Jesus and God means to disrespect them or belittle their authority.

Verse 17. The disciples looked upon their work of controlling the devils as an exploit of which to boast. It was much like the spirit of the Corinthians which they exhibited over the possession of spiritual gifts.

Verse 18. *I beheld Satan as light-*

ning fall from heaven. Moffatt renders this, "I watched Satan fall from heaven like a flash of lightning." John refers to this event in Revelation 12: 9. The thought is that Jesus would have more to boast of than the disciples, since he saw the chief of devils fall from heaven. But he was not making any such use of it as a personal advantage.

Verse 19. Jesus had given his disciples the ability to perform these miracles so they could prove they were not a group of false teachers.

Verse 20. This power was not intended for their personal distinction over which to rejoice. What counted the most was a spiritual favor, that of having their names written in heaven. (See Hebrews 12: 23; Revelation 21: 27.)

Verse 21. See the comments on Matthew 11: 25 for the present verse.

Verse 22. The complete mutual knowledge of the Father and Son of each other was not shared by the world. But such information as would be deemed necessary for others was to be revealed by the Son in his own manner.

Verse 23. The disciples were enjoying some bits of information that had not been granted to preceding generations, and for this Jesus called them blessed or happy.

Verse 24. It was not the time for those ancient prophets and kings to receive that information, although they had a desire for it. (See Ephesians 3: 9-11; 1 Peter 1: 10-12.)

Verse 25. A lawyer was a man informed in the law of Moses and who taught it to the people. The question he asked was a proper one as far as its form was concerned. But the inspired writer tells us the man's motive was wrong, that he wished to tempt Jesus.

Verse 26. How readest thou? This was a direct allusion to the profession of the lawyer. That being his business he should have known what he was expected to do to be saved if he had been reading the law carefully, hence the question Jesus asked him.

Verse 27. The lawyer correctly cited the requirements of the law.

Verse 28. Thou shalt live is equivalent to inheriting eternal life, the thing the lawyer inquired for. Under whatever dispensation people lived, if they did the things required by its law they were promised salvation.

Verse 29. The young man of Matthew 19: 20 affirmed he had kept all the commandments from his youth. The lawyer did not make that claim which he evidently could not do truly. To justify means to show one's self to be righteous. The lawyer thought he would clear himself of coming short of his duty by the use of a quibble over the interpretation of terms, so he asked who is my neighbor?

Verse 30. This entire story is told in answer to the lawyer's question, but there are some bits of information incidental to the main subject that will make it worth while to consider. The misfortune of this traveler could happen to any man, so that part of the story is not unusual.

Verses 31, 32. All priests were Levites, but not all Levites were priests (Exodus 29: 9; 40: 12-16; Numbers 4: 1-4), which is the reason for using the terms priest and Levite separately. But they were both Jews and considered themselves as being followers of the law which this inquirer also professed to follow.

Verses 33, 34. The Samaritans were a mixture of Jew and Gentile blood, the origin of which is recorded in 2 Kings 17: 24-33. The Jews had no dealings with them (John 4: 9), and thought that very little good ever came from them. That is what makes this part of the story significant; for the Samaritan was the one who showed a neighborly feeling toward the injured man.

Verse 35. The assistance given by the Samaritan did not consist in words of sympathy only, but he assumed the full expense of the case.

Verses 36, 37. Which . . . was neighbor? Jesus switches the direction of the subject from the neighbor to be loved to the one acting the part of a neighbor. Upon the lawyer's answering the question of Jesus correctly, he was told to go and do likewise. It all sums up the matter by answering the lawyer's question stated in verse 29 by showing that whoever needs our help is our neighbor.

Verse 38. This certain village was Bethany, the town of Lazarus and his sisters (John 11: 1). Martha seems to have been head of the house as to domestic affairs.

Verse 39. The teaching of Jesus absorbed the attention of Mary.

Verse 40. The original for cumbered is defined by Thayer as "distracted."

Martha was so interested in the entertainment of her guest that she let it crowd out her attention to spiritual things. Frequently today professed Christians will actually plan to be absent from the assembly of the saints in order to prepare a meal for expected guests. Such women are in the same class as Martha and deserve the same rebuke as she.

Verses 41, 42. Jesus does not teach that it is wrong to perform the duties of the home, but he does frown upon one's allowing them to overwhelm him with undue care. *Needful* is from a strong word meaning very necessary. The food that sustains the body will cease to exist at the same time that the fleshly body is destroyed (1 Corinthians 6: 12, 13), but the spiritual nourishment will *not be taken away*.

LUKE 11

Verse 1. *Teach us to pray.* Some people would disapprove the idea of exercises for the training in prayer, yet Jesus endorsed the request of this disciple by doing the very thing he asked for. If disciples of Christ would put in some time studying and preparing themselves for prayer, there might be fewer unscriptural efforts performed.

Verses 2-4. For comments on this prayer see those at Matthew 6: 9-13.

Verses 5-7. This parable compares an earthly *friend* with the disciple who wanted to know how to pray. The outcome of a proper prayer is the lesson of the illustration.

Verse 8. No illustration is intended to apply at all angles. God is not to be regarded as this householder is described, for that is not the point of the parable. The comparison is in the word *importunity* which means persistence. We are taught to have a faith that will not shrink because we do not receive what we need, or do not receive it as soon as desired.

Verses 9-13. This paragraph is explained in detail at Matthew 7: 7-11, which is a part of the "sermon on the mount" delivered to the disciples.

Verse 14. *It was dumb* means the devil had caused the person to be dumb, for after it was cast out the *dumb spake.* Being possessed with a devil did not affect all people alike, the reason for which is not given in the scripture.

Verse 15. See the comments at Matthew 12: 24.

Verse 16. These people were clamoring for some miracle that they imagined would be a test of the power of Jesus. Their motive was a desire to tempt the Lord.

Verses 17, 18. This is explained at Matthew 12: 25, 26.

Verse 19. See the explanation at Matthew 12: 27.

Verse 20. Explained at Matthew 12: 28.

Verses 21, 22. See the comments on Matthew 12: 29.

Verse 23. There is no "neutral" ground in matters of right and wrong. Regardless of how inactive a man may be, if he is not active for Christ he is his enemy.

Verses 24-26. This unusual passage is explained at Matthew 12: 43, 44.

Verse 27. This woman meant that the mother of Jesus was to be considered in a special sense. The Romanists make a great ado about the Virgin just as this woman did, except she did not even suggest that any worship should be offered to her.

Verse 28. Jesus did not go even to the extent of endorsing what the woman said, but stated what he would *rather* be done, which was to keep the word of God.

Verse 29. Because it was an evil generation, Jesus refused to perform any miracle at the time. However, he was willing to stake his reputation as a true prophet on an event yet to come.

Verse 30. Thayer defines the original for *sign*, "A sign, prodigy, portent," and he explains his definition to mean "an unusual occurence, transcending [going beyond] the common course of nature." Jonah lived three days and three nights in the belly of the fish, which was certainly something unusual. And Jesus predicted that he would be three days and three nights in the heart of the earth (Matthew 12: 40) and live again.

Verse 31. See the comments on Matthew 12: 42.

Verse 32. The point of the verse is one about responsibility based on opportunity. See the comments on Matthew 12: 41.

Verse 33. The common judgment shown by a man after lighting a candle, is used to compare that which disciples should show about their influence.

Verse 34. The natural eye is used for the same purpose as the candle in the preceding verse. A man has but one means of seeing and that is by his natural eye. If it is *single* (not defective) the owner will be able to see. Likewise, a man has only one life that he can live, and he should so conduct it that it will shed spiritual light upon the world about him.

Verse 35. This verse denotes that by an improper life, a man's influence will be turned into one that is for evil or spiritual darkness. (See Romans 14: 16.)

Verse 36. This verse has a thought similar to verse 23. A man is counted either for or against Christ. His influence is either one of darkness or of light.

Verse 37. Jesus accepted the invitation to dine with the Pharisee, which was not considered strange since they both were Jews. *Went in and sat down to meat*, indicates that he did this without any previous ceremony.

Verses 38, 39. The Pharisee was surprised that Jesus did not wash before coming to the table. This does not refer to ordinary cleanliness, but to a ritual the Jews had that was a mere formality. Jesus knew the mind of the Pharisee and accused him and his class of hypocrisy in the exercise of their formalities.

Verse 40. It is true that God made the outward man and wants him to be kept clean. But he also made the inner man and requires that he be kept clean, which means that he should not be defiled with pride of tradition and with acts of hypocrisy.

Verse 41. If we are helpful toward others with our good things of life, we will be edifying the inner man and will need have no fears of harm from imaginary defilement.

Verse 42. See the comments at Matthew 23: 23 for explanation of this verse.

Verse 43. These *uppermost seats* were the front pews that faced the audience. The *markets* were public gathering places, and these Pharisees craved special attention there.

Verse 44. *Appear not* means that the use being made of them is not apparent. Men walking *over* or about them do not realize that corruption is contained within. Jesus used the fact to compare the hypocrite trying to hide his wickedness.

Verse 45. *Thus saying* refers to the general denunciation Jesus has been uttering against leaders among the

Jews. The lawyer may have thought he would bring an apology from Jesus by complaining in this way, relying, perhaps, on the dignity of his profession.

Verse 46. *With one of your fingers* is a figure of speech, for a burden that could be moved with one finger would not be very heavy. It means they were not willing to exert themselves in the least toward practicing the commandments of the law.

Verse 47. The Jews were influenced much by the traditional respect for their forefathers. The devotion to their sepulchres indicated a sentimental feeling for them, and this notwithstanding their guilt of having murdered the prophets.

Verse 48. Jesus verifies the remarks on the preceding verse.

Verses 49-51. This is explained at Matthew 23: 34-36.

Verse 52. *Key* is from KLEIS, and Thayer explains it to mean, "the ability and opportunity to obtain knowledge." Robinson gives virtually the same comment. *Entered not in*, etc. They were not willing to accept the truth nor let others have it.

Verse 53. *Urge him* means to irritate him in the hope of provoking him to say many things in reply to them.

Verse 54. Their motive was to lead Jesus into saying something that would be subject to criticism. Had he done this, they would have gone to the authorities with it.

LUKE 12

Verse 1. *Trode one upon another* indicates the extent of influence that Jesus was having through his teaching. On another occasion (Matthew 16: 6-12) Jesus warned his disciples against the leaven of the Pharisees, and afterward they had to have it explained. In this instance he specifies that he means the *hypocrisy* of the Pharisees. Thayer defines the original for *leaven* by the single word "*leaven*." He then explains his application as follows: "It is applied to that which, though small in quantity, yet by its influence thoroughly pervades a thing; either in a good sense, . . . or in a bad sense."

Verse 2. The persecutors perform their evil work in an underhanded and cowardly manner. But their deeds will finally be exposed and all false accusations be disproved.

Verse 3. See the comments on Matthew 10: 27 for this verse.

Verse 4. Men can cause physical death but can do nothing against the soul of the man who serves God with a righteous life.

Verse 5. God is the one who can cast the entire being into *hell*, hence our conduct should be such that He will not regard us as deserving that awful doom. The full definition of the word hell is quoted at Matthew 5: 30.

Verse 6. The thought is that God is mindful of everything He has created, even to the comparatively unimportant case of the sparrow. He certainly will not overlook the being made in His image.

Verse 7. The thought in the preceding verse is continued in this. Each hair (a small portion of man's being) is counted by the Creator, which denotes that the whole person is of more value than the sparrows.

Verses 8, 9. See the comments on chapter 9: 26.

Verse 10. This refers to what is commonly referred to as the "unpardonable" sin. For a full discussion of this subject see the comments at Matthew 12: 24-32.

Verse 11. This does not mean they were to be unconcerned about the matter, but they were not to be planning what they were going to say.

Verse 12. The reason for the preceding verse is shown here. The Holy Ghost was to dictate the speeches as the case demanded, hence it would be *in the same hour.*

Verse 13. The subject of personal rights is an important one, but not one that should be regarded as worthy of absorbing the main interests of a man's life; certainly not worthy of claiming the attention of the busy Son of man, who was here in the interests of the kingdom of heaven and the salvation of the souls of men.

Verse 14. Jesus rebuked the man by this question which amounted to the refusal to "take the case" as a wise judge might say if asked to interfere in an outside affair.

Verse 15. A man with only a proper interest in his temporal possessions would not have thought of disrupting the work of Jesus by the subject. Therefore the Lord accused him of covetousness, and told him that the things a man possesses do not constitute the main part of his life.

Verse 16. Jesus frequently emphasized his lessons by telling a story that was adapted to the case. The man in the present instance had an unusually large crop.

Verse 17. The yield was so great that his graneries were not sufficient.

Verse 18. It was necessary to build larger facilities for the crops.

Verse 19. Up to this point there was nothing wrong in what the farmer did and said, for it is not only right but necessary to care for the product of the soil that it may not be wasted. But his mistake was in the use he was proposing to make of his crops. He thought to relax and live an indolent and luxurious manner of life, as if that were the main purpose of the good things of nature.

Verse 20. *Soul* is from PSUCHE, and Thayer's first definition is, "Breath, i. e., the breath of life; the vital force," and he adds by way of explanation, "which animates the body and shows itself in breathing." The verse does not necessarily mean that God performed a special act to take the man's life from him because of his selfishness. But the uncertainty of this life is a result of the edict of God after the sin of the first man. It was in that sense that God took the rich man's life from him that night.

Verse 21. *So is he* verifies my comments on the preceding verse, and shows that no special miracle was done to punish the farmer. The lesson of Jesus applies to all men who hoard their riches, or who trust in them for selfish enjoyment (1 Timothy 6: 17-19.)

Verses 22, 23. See the comments on Matthew 6: 25.

Verse 24. This is explained at Matthew 6: 26.

Verses 25, 26. Undue anxiety will not add the slightest amount to one's size, hence it is useless to be concerned to the extent of unreasonable worry about life.

Verse 27. See the comments on this thought at Matthew 6: 29.

Verse 28. God's care for comparatively unimportant things such as the flowers, and hence His greater care for man, is the lesson of the verse. (See Matthew 6: 30.)

Verse 29. *Seek ye not* means not to be overanxious about it.

Verse 30. The *nations of the world* have only the temporal things in mind, but the disciples of Christ should make such interests secondary.

Verse 31. This is commented upon at Matthew 6: 33.

Verse 32. *Little* is from MIKROS, which Thayer defines, "small, little," and at our verse he explains it to mean, "of quantity, i. e., number or amount." Jesus was speaking especially to his apostles who were only twelve in number, hence would constitute the *little flock*. The promise that the Father would give them the kingdom proves that it was not yet in their possession at that time, and hence was still in the future although near ("at hand").

Verses 33, 34. See the comments at Matthew 6: 19-21.

Verse 35. *Loins be girded* is an allusion to the practice of soldiers who put a belt around their body as a brace for their strength. (See Ephesians 6: 14.) *Lights burning* is a figurative admonition to be prepared. (See Matthew 25: 1-13.)

Verse 36. In the parable of the ten virgins (Matthew 25) the waiting was for the lord to come to the wedding. In this one the waiting is for him to return from it. The lesson is the same in both, which is the necessity of being prepared.

Verse 37. If a servant is watching he will not be caught with surprise, but will be ready to open the door to let him in. The happy bridegroom will regale his faithful servants by serving them with the wedding feast.

Verse 38. The second and third watches were at nine and twelve o'clock. If the servants do not go to sleep, they will be ready for their lord when he gets back home.

Verse 39. This verse is given for the same purpose as the preceding one; the necessity of watching. Incidentally, however, another lesson is taught here. Jesus speaks favorably of this householder who would resist having his house attacked. But the only way he could do so would be to oppose force with force, which shows it is right to use force if necessary in defending one's home and family.

Verse 40. This verse is the lesson of the preceding ones.

Verse 41. Much of the teaching of Jesus was to the apostles only, hence Peter asked for the application of the parable.

Verse 42. Instead of a direct answer, Jesus replied in a manner that made it apply to all who profess to be his servants. The activities described pertain to some customs in connection with weddings, but the point is in reference to the favors that Jesus will bestow on his faithful servants when he comes back to the earth.

Verses 43, 44. This is still figurative as in the preceding verse.

Verses 45, 46. This paragraph is explained at Matthew 24: 48-51.

Verses 47, 48. It would be impractical not to consider these two verses in one paragraph. A popular notion is that it teaches different degrees of punishment after the judgment. By the process of elimination we know it cannot mean that. The ones on the left of the judge (Matthew 25: 45) were guilty of only neglecting their service to needy disciples, yet they are to be cast into the same fire that is prepared for the devil and his angels. So if the mildest and strongest classes of evil will get the same punishment, it is foolish to talk about "degrees" for any of the intervening classes. The Bible speaks of but one Gehenna; one lake of fire; one hell; into which the devil and his angels and all other unsaved persons will be cast after the judgment. Being beaten with many or few stripes has nothing to do with the punishment after the judgment, but refers to the judgment itself. Jesus makes his own application of the figurative stripes and begins it with the word *for*. Then he says *unto whom much is given, of him shall much be required*. Nothing said about what will be given to the man after the judgment, but it is what was already given to him before the judgment. Upon the faithfulness or unfaithfulness of the servant in making the required use of these goods (talents) will depend the decision as to which of the TWO sides (not several) he will be assigned at the judgment. After that is done, only one sentence will be pronounced upon all in whatever group a man is placed.

Verse 49. *Fire* is from PUR. Thayer defines it in this place by, "dissension," and he explains the definition to be because "fire disorganizes and sunders things joined together and compact." Robinson says the word symbolizes "strife and disunion." These definitions and comments agree with the statements of Jesus in verses soon to follow. He does not mean that he wished people to be divided among themselves, but he did come to bring the teaching he knew would cause the dissension. *Already kindled.* Even as Jesus was speaking, there were conflicts among the people over his doctrine.

Verse 50. It might be asked why Jesus would persist in his teaching when he knew it would bring opposition: this verse answers that question. Baptism is used figuratively and refers to the sufferings he was destined to experience in order to fulfill the scripture (Matthew 26: 54). That is why he says *how am I straitened* (made completely to suffer), (according to the predictions), *until it* (the baptism of suffering) *be accomplished.*

Verse 51. Jesus continues the same line of thought but is more literal or direct in his language. Not that his motive was to cause division just for the sake of division, but he did mean to put his teaching out among people although it was bound to bring division.

Verse 52. House means household and it was destined to be divided.

Verse 53. The division was not to come between comparative strangers only, but the closest of relatives would be arrayed against each other. That would be because a father would accept the truth while his son would not, and so on through other relatives.

Verses 54, 55. Jesus referred the Jews to their own study of the conditions in nature, in which they professed to know how to figure out the future by present signs.

Verse 56. The signs of the times were as clearly portrayed in the Scriptures as were the weather signs, yet they pretended there was nothing on record to indicate the work and purposes of Jesus.

Verse 57. *Right* is from DIKAIOS and Thayer's definition at this place is, "rendering to each his due; passing just judgment on others." Robinson gives virtually the same definition. The verse reflects on the three preceding this one. If they would treat the teaching of the Scripture with the same reasoning and fairness they did the weather signs, they would be able *of themselves* to decide their duty without any miraculous signs from Jesus.

Verses 58, 59. See the comments at Matthew 5: 25, 26.

LUKE 13

Verse 1. There was more or less friction between the Jews and the Romans, although the former were suffered to carry on their religious practices. Something had occurred that angered Pilate, and he enforced his penalties upon them even while they were engaged in their sacrificial devotions. The reporters came to Jesus with the news, thinking the incident was a sort of "judgment" sent upon them by the Lord.

Verse 2. Jesus informed them that the Galilaeans were not any worse than other sinners in God's sight, even though this misfortune had come to them.

Verse 3. *Likewise* does not mean they were to meet the same fate, but that they would perish just as surely if they did not repent of their sins.

Verse 4. Jesus then added another event which they doubtless knew about, though we have no other account of it. He then asked them the same question as in verse 2.

Verse 5. He gave the same answer as he did to the question about the Galilaeans. All sinners look alike to God, when it comes to dealing with them concerning their future after their stay on earth is ended. (See comments at chapter 12: 47, 48.)

Verse 6. This *certain man* in the parable represents God, and the fig tree and vineyard is the Jewish nation (Isaiah 5: 1-6).

Verse 7. The *dresser of the vineyard* is Christ to whom God announced his determination of destroying the nation, meaning he would disown it.

Verse 8. The Jews were given many opportunities to render acceptable service to God. They were given the assistance of prophets and other teachers of truth.

Verse 9. When they proved unworthy of the favor of God, they were given over to the outside forces who laid them even with the ground. This has reference to the overthrow of the nation by the Romans.

Verse 10. The use of synagogues is explained at Matthew 4: 23.

Verse 11. *Spirit of infirmity* means the woman was bent over from weakness to such an extent that she could not straighten herself up.

Verse 12. *Her to him* is not in the original text. The passage means Jesus called to her and told her that she was released from her infirmity.

Verse 13. The woman was cured *immediately* as all miraculous cures were done. People who demand "plenty of time" for their so-called divine performances are frauds.

Verse 14. The Jews pretended to be offended at the desecration of the sabbath. But note that the ruler did not have the fairness to attack Jesus direct, although he was the one who had done the work, but condemned *the people*. This was cowardly, for there was no evidence that they had *come to be healed*.

Verse 15. Jesus had respect for the sabbath and for all other items in the law. But he knew that it was not reverence for the day that prompted the ruler to criticize him, but a desire to have a pretext for condemning him. Because of this Jesus called him a hypocrite. He further exposed the insincerity of the critic, by reminding him of his own practice of attending the care of his beast even on the sabbath.

Verse 16. *Satan hath bound.* The devil has supernatural power when God suffers him to exert it. The reader should see the comments on this subject at Exodus 8: 16-19, in volume 1 of the Old Testament Commentary. Yet there is no evidence that the present case of infirmity was a direct act of Satan. Diseases are in the world because of the sin of Adam, and it was the devil who induced him and his wife to commit it and thus bring disease and death into the world.

Verse 17. The argument of Jesus was unanswerable, which caused his critics to be ashamed. The people were truly glad to see the afflicted woman relieved.

Verse 18. To be *like* or *resemble* a thing does not mean identical in every particular. That is why the precaution was offered at Matthew 13: 3.

Verse 19. See the comments on Matthew 13: 32 for the present verse.

Verses 20, 21. *Leaven* has been misunderstood by many readers of the Bible. The same parable is discussed at Matthew 13: 33.

Verse 22. *City* and *village* are often used interchangeably in the New Testament. When named together as in this place, the former is somewhat the larger.

Verse 23. We are not told just why this question was asked Jesus by the man in the audience. It is reasonable to conclude it was because of the strict teaching he had been doing.

Verse 24. *To enter in* all comes from one Greek word, and the meaning is "to be among or of the number." That is, to be among the saved ones, since that is the question asked of Jesus. *Strive* is from AGONIZOMAI which Thayer defines, "To enter a contest; contend in the gymnastic games. To contend with adversaries, fight. To contend, struggle, with difficulties and dangers. To endeavor with strenuous zeal, strive." The word originated with the athletic performances in which opposing persons engaged against each other. It is used by Jesus with reference to the struggle for salvation, because Satan and his followers are arrayed against the man who wishes to serve the Lord. *To enter in* is the same as in the beginning of the verse, and means that many will seek to be among the saved but will not be able. There is no account of a case where sinners tried to obey the commands of the apostles or other evangelists of the Gospel, and found it impossible. Hence we must look further for the date when this disappointment will befall human beings.

Verse 25. This verse tells when the disappointment will come that was spoken of at the preceding verse. It will be when Jesus closes the door to salvation which will be at the judgment day. This is proved by the passage of Matthew 25: 31-46. *I know you not* is explained at Matthew 25: 12.

Verse 26. They thought Jesus meant he would be literally unacquainted with them, hence they made the argument about their personal association with him.

Verse 27. *I know you not* is used in the same sense as in verse 25.

Verses 28, 29. Abraham and the others named had been dead for centuries, and the kingdom on earth had not been set up when Jesus said those words, hence we know he meant the kingdom after the judgment. This paragraph is discussed at length at Matthew 8: 11, 12.

Verse 30. *First* and *last* are explained at Matthew 19: 30.

Verse 31. The Pharisees were enemies of Jesus and wanted to get him out of the community. They thought they could frighten him by a threat about Herod (Antipas).

Verse 32. Jesus disregarded the insincerity of the warning, because there was no doubt that Herod would be disposed to do the very thing the Pharisees suggested. He therefore proposed sending him a message to let him know that the good work being done would continue regardless of any supposed danger. *Fox* is used figuratively and when so used is explained by Thayer to mean, "a sly and crafty man."

Verse 33. Jesus announced that he had a three-day journey to make soon in order to arrive at Jerusalem. And that was necessary because it was determined by the Lord that he should die by violence (Acts 2: 23), yet the Jews could not lawfully condemn a man until he had been brought before the Sanhedrin which was in that city. (See Josephus, Antiquities, Book 14, Chapter 9, Section 3.)

Verses 34, 35. This is a fundamental statement and prediction. It occurs almost verbatim in Matthew 23: 37-39, which is commented upon quite fully at that place.

LUKE 14

Verse 1. The Pharisees were ever on the alert to discover something in the work of Jesus for which to condemn him. Their most convenient pretext usually came on the sabbath day. Since Jesus was always busy, it was not unusual to see him performing some act of kindness on that day.

Verse 2. Sure enough, there was a man in the group who was afflicted with *dropsy*. That word is from HYDROPS, meaning "water." It is related to the word from which we get our English word "hydrant."

Verse 3. *Jesus answering.* The text says nothing about whether the people said anything openly, but Jesus could read the thoughts of men, and he knew they were thinking of criticizing him. He anticipated them by speaking on the very subject of their wicked motives. But he did not put the question in the form they would have wished. He could have asked if it was lawful to do anything on the sabbath, but that form of question would have implied its own answer which would have been negative. So he put it on the humane basis of healing a man on the sabbath day.

Verse 4. The Pharisees were too wise to say that it would ever be wrong to heal an afflicted person, and they were too prejudiced to say yes to the question of Jesus. He then proceded to heal the man and release him cured.

Verses 5, 6. Referring to their own practice, Jesus asked them another question which they *could not* answer. It means they could not harmonize their practices with the criticism they made against Jesus in their hypocritical hearts.

Verses 7, 8. *Chief rooms* means the same as *highest rooms*, the expression used in this verse. *More honorable* means from a social standpoint, not in the sense of character.

Verse 9. The host might wish to prefer the *more honorable* in assigning a seat. It would be humiliating to be directed to step down with the other guests looking on.

Verse 10. A guest would be running no risk of embassassment to take a low place voluntarily, even should he be left there; instead, he would stand a chance of being promoted. *Worship* in this place means "honor" according to the note at Matthew 2: 2.

Verse 11. This verse states a principle that applies to human beings in general, whether in their relation to each other, or to that under the Lord and His treatment of human servants. (See Esther 7: 9, 10; Daniel 4: 37; James 4: 10.)

Verse 12. We recall that Jesus spoke the present group of parables while at the feast mentioned in verse 1. We know Jesus did not condemn showing hospitality to persons who were not actual cases for "charity," for he was at that very time enjoying a meal given for the sake of sociability and friendship. *Lest a recompense be made* denotes he should not restrict his feasts to those who would be able to repay him.

Verse 13. The classes named could not "return the call," hence if a man offered them a feast, it could be for no selfish motive as to temporal things.

Verse 14. It is right to do good to the unfortunate with a view of reward after the resurrection, for that would mean one is expecting his reward from the Lord.

Verse 15. Jesus had just spoken of the future reward for one giving a dinner to the poor. This fellow guest thought it was to be in the form of another meal in the kingdom of God, meaning a spiritual feast in heaven. With such an idea in view, he pronounced a blessing on whomsoever would have that privilege.

Verse 16. This group was evidently of the Jewish race since it was by invitation of a chief Pharisee (verse 1) that the meal was being served. Knowing the attitude the Jews as a nation were going to take toward the Gospel, Jesus saw the need for an important lesson in which a spiritual meal (the Gospel) would be served long before the one this guest had in mind, and he spoke a parable in the form of a *great supper*.

Verse 17. *Them that were bidden* means the Jews to whom the invitation was first given. (See Matthew 10: 5, 6; Acts 13: 46; Romans 1: 16.)

Verse 18. In an illustration some items need to be told to make the story intelligible, even though they are not literally applicable. *Make excuse* is rendered "excuse themselves" in the Englishman's Greek New Testament. Much speculation has been done over these "excuses," but we should see in them only a part of the parable that was intended to portray the unfavorable attitude of the Jews to the Gospel.

Verse 19. If I cared to moralize on this subject, I would say this man was more interested in his temporal products than in the good things offered by the "certain man."

Verse 20. Marriage is a divine institution, but a man should not let love for his wife be greater than the things offered him by the Lord.

Verse 21. The servant who was sent to call the invited guests was one of the preachers of Christ. He reported the cold reception he had been given by the ones originally invited. It made the master of the house angry, and he decided to extend the invitation to others who had not been previously favored. They would be Jews, but of the lower class, such as the "publicans and harlots" (Matthew 21: 31).

Verse 22. There is room enough in the plan of salvation for the whole world, hence the servant told the master that *yet there is room.*

Verse 23. *Highways and hedges* means the regions of the Gentiles. *Compel* means to use the force of truthful persuasion in bringing them into the house of the Master, which means the kingdom of heaven on earth.

Verse 24. This is explained at verse 17.

Verse 25. The crowds that walked after Jesus did not all have the same motives (John 6: 26), and that called forth the teaching of several verses following.

Verse 26. *Hate* is from MISEO which Thayer defines at this place, "to love less, to postpone in love or esteem, to slight." It is clear, therefore, that Jesus does not contradict other passages that require us to love our parents. He means for us to love the Lord above all earthly beings.

Verse 27. This is explained at Matthew 10: 38; 16: 24.

Verse 28. The lesson of the parable, beginning with this verse, is that following Christ should not be a matter of carelessness or light concern. Whoever thinks of being a disciple of Jesus should realize it will cost him many sacrifices.

Verses 29, 30. In temporal matters a man usually manifests the good judgment expressed in the preceding verse. That is not only because it is good business, but to avoid the belittling remarks that might be made by the observers. They would criticize a man for starting something before he learned whether he would be able to finish it.

Verse 31. This parable teaches the same lesson as the preceding one. A wise commander would not declare war against another until he had studied the comparative strength of the two armies and other military resources.

Verse 32. Even after hostilities have started, if he realizes that the outcome may be doubtful, he will not rashly proceed without first trying to make a settlement with the opposing forces.

Verse 33. We need not speculate on all the details of the story. Jesus gives us his own interpretation of the parable by repeating what he had previously taught, namely, that one who proposes to follow Him must sacrifice everything that would hinder.

Verses 34, 35. This is commented upon at Matthew 5: 13.

LUKE 15

Verse 1. *Publicans and sinners.* See the notes on Matthew 9: 10; 21: 28.

Verse 2. *Pharisees and scribes*, as well as the publicans and sinners, were all Jews but in different classifications according to the social castes devised by the self-righteous Jewish leaders. On the significance of *eating* with others, see the quotation from the works of reference at Matthew 9: 11.

Verse 3. *This parable* and the others in this chapter were occasioned by the complaint of the Pharisees and scribes in verse 2. The reader should bear in mind as he studies these three parables, that the lesson pertains to the two classes of Jews designated above, and not to the Jews and Gentiles. All have the same lesson, that of the Father's love for his wayward or otherwise unfortunate creatures. It is the same subject as that shown by the physician and the sick in Matthew 9: 12. However, since the stories needed to be told to make the point of application clear, I shall comment upon the verses in their order.

Verse 4. The 99 sheep, like the Pharisees and scribes (according to their pretentions), were not needing any special attention because they were within the care of the shepherd. The one that was lost (as the Pharisees considered the publicans and sinners), was the one that needed and received the attention of the shepherd.

Verse 5. *Layeth it on his shoulders* indicates a tender regard for the wandering sheep, also a willingness to help it get back to the flock.

Verse 6. It is natural for one to wish others to share with him in the event of good fortune. Paul tells Christians to "rejoice with them that do rejoice" (Romans 12: 15).

Verse 7. *Joy* does not mean love or esteem. God and the angels will always love the righteous with a divine affection. Joy denotes a spirit of active gratitude for some satisfactory event or truth, such as the recovery of an article of value that was lost.

Verses 8-10. Substitute a lost sheep for the piece of silver, and this parable is identical in thought with the preceding one.

Verse 11. The remainder of this chapter, beginning with this verse, was spoken for the same purpose as the two preceding parables, and none of the details were intended to teach any special lesson besides. Yet it will be necessary to consider the parts of the story, especially since so much speculative use has been made of it. It is commonly called "the parable of the prodigal son," but it is not so named in the text. The word "prodigal" means extravagant or wasteful, and that characteristic is given to this younger son in verse 13.

Verse 12. The younger son did not want to wait until the usual time for settling up of the estate of his father, for he did not intend to remain at home that long.

Verse 13. True to the indicated plans, the son left home with all of his part of the estate. *Riotous* is from ASOTOS and this is the only place in the New Testament where the word occurs. Thayer defines it, "dissolutely, profligately," which has the same meaning as "wastefully."

Verse 14. The famine came just after he had spent all his money.

Verse 15. Employment became scarce as it commonly does in hard times. This young man accepted a very humble job, that of a swineherd.

Verse 16. His wages evidently proved insufficient for he became hungry in spite of his job. *Husks* is described by both Thayer and Smith's Bible Dictionary as the podded fruit of a locust tree. They also say this product was used for fattening swine, and for food among the poor people. This "prodigal son" was so hungry he would gladly have supplemented his own scanty diet with this article, but due to the famine it was denied him because the owner reserved it for his swine.

Verse 17. *Came to himself* is rendered "came to his senses" in Moffatt's translation. The meaning is that he was made to realize his true condition. He recalled that even the servants at home had plenty of the good things of life.

Verse 18. He knew he could not justly request more of his father's estate for he had already received his full share. He would have to return and throw himself upon the mercy of his father. *Sinned against heaven.* When anyone does wrong, the sin is an offense against the Lord regardless of who may be affected among men.

Verse 19. This is an expression of one who realizes his unworthiness of favors.

Verse 20. The father observed his son at a great distance before he arrived at the home and ran to meet him. This detail truly represents God's attitude toward sinners. He is always casting a loving glance toward them. *Fell on his neck* is an expression that denotes affectionate feelings for another, instead of the formal kiss upon the mouth merely as a salutation that was the custom in old times.

Verse 21. This act of affection encouraged the repentant son to go on with the confession he had decided upon when he *came to himself.*

Verse 22. The father did not assign him to the low position he so humbly suggested. Penitence brings forth forgiveness instead of strict justice from the offended parent. The robe and other articles to be worn would not satisfy the hunger of the famished son, but it indicated the fullness of the father's forgiveness. The hunger will be cared for in another way.

Verse 23. It was usual for families to keep a fattened animal in readiness for any occasion of a feast that might arise, and the arrival of the "lost" son furnished one.

Verse 24. These words may have been used figuratively only, and yet this son had been dead to his father's home, since death means "separation."

Verse 25. The *elder son* represents the Pharisees and scribes in verse 2, and their envious attitude toward the younger son who represents the publicans and sinners of the same verse. As the elder son was coming in from his work he heard the *music and dancing.* Some have tried to see a significance in the mention of dancing. It has no moral application in the least since that is not the subject of the parable. It is put into the story only because it indicates the condition of joy being felt in the household.

Verse 26. When the elder son went to work, the return of the "prodigal" had not occurred, hence he did not understand the cause of the merriment.

Verses 27, 28. This *elder son* (the Pharisees and scribes) began to pout and refused to go into the house. That was not because he objected to the things being done as though they were wrong, but because of his jealousy against his brother. Ordinary human nature would have prompted the father to be "independent" and just ignore his son's action. But since this father represents the Father of mercies, the parable shows him manifesting his love for the son by making a move toward pacifying him.

Verses 29, 30. The elder son had no just ground of complaint. His brother had done wrong, but it was against his father and God only. This son was not being deprived of anything that was due him, so his attitude could be explained only on the basis of jealousy. He made two comparisons in his protest; they were between the conduct of himself and that of his brother, and between what his father had done for each son. He had always been at home and faithful, while his brother had been away living a life like that of a spendthrift. Also, his father had never as much as given him a kid (a rather inferior animal), but had given this wasteful son the choice of food animals.

Verse 31. The favors being shown the returned son did not deprive the elder one of a single possession, hence his objections were the result of his jealousy only.

Verse 32. It was meet or fitting for the father and his household to be glad. But it was not on the ground of the worthiness of the younger son for he had no just claim to the favors being accorded him. The reason assigned by the father was that a son that was lost had been found. Likewise, the Father in heaven is concerned about the spiritual safety of the lowest of human beings and is always ready to receive them as soon as they repent.

LUKE 16

Verse 1. The first seven verses of this chapter constitute another parable. Like others, it has a specific point in view, which is to show the importance of using present opportunities to prepare for the future. Keeping this in mind, let us consider the details of the story. The *rich man* in the parable represents God, and the *steward* means human beings to whom God has entrusted the use of talents and good things of life.

Verse 2. *Give an account* stands for the warning that all mankind will have to give an account of personal conduct to God (Romans 14: 12).

Verse 3. The anxiety of the steward about how he could meet the accounting, represents the concern that men should feel over the coming judgment before God and Christ.

Verse 4. The pronoun *they* in the application of the parable, refers to God and Christ as we shall see farther down in the chapter.

Verse 5. The steward still had charge of his lord's goods and the accounting of them, and he decided to manage the bookkeeping in a way to be an advantage to himself.

Verse 6. Upon payment of half the debt, this man was given full credit as if he had paid off his entire indebtedness.

Verse 7. This man's bill was marked "paid in full" upon his producing 80 per cent of the real account. The way the steward handled these accounts was wrong, but that was not the subject that Jesus had in mind when he spoke this parable as we shall see at the next verse.

Verse 8. The Lord (Jesus) did not commend the steward for his unjustness, but because he had *done wisely.* And that wisdom was shown by using his present opportunities to prepare against future needs. By favoring these debtors in this way, the steward won their good will; and when he was finally thrown out of a job and home, they would gratefully give him a place in their houses. *Children of this world are wiser* means the people of the world generally manifest more good judgment than professed Christians in many cases.

Verse 9. In this verse Jesus makes his application of the parable. The *friends* are God and Christ, and *mammon of unrighteousness* means the talents and opportunities bestowed upon men in this life. The exhortation is for us to make such use of these things that we will gain the favor of these friends by being friends to them ourselves. (See John 15: 14.) Then when we *fail*, which will be when the earth and all things therein pass away, we will be invited to enter into the mansions that are in the Father's house (John 14: 1-3).

Verse 10. We will not be judged by the *amount* of good we can do, but by whether we are faithful in doing what is within our power and opportunity.

Verse 11. *Unrighteous m a m m o n* means the temporal things of this life. If we have misused these things, we will not be regarded as worthy of those in the next life.

Verse 12. If a man is careless in handling the goods of another, he would be still more unappreciative of his own, and would feel free to do as he pleased with them.

Verse 13. See the comments on Matthew 6: 24.

Verse 14. The Pharisees had not been named in the preceding parable, yet they applied it to themselves and hence they *derided* (sneered) him. They could not make any just reply to the teaching of Christ without exposing their own covetous heart, therefore they only made fun of him.

Verse 15. To *justify* means to declare or make it appear that one is just. The Pharisees did this and deceived the public into thinking they were benevolent men by their apparent deeds of kindness. But these things that men admired (because they did not know the motive back of them), God regarded as abominable, knowing their hearts.

Verse 16. *Law and prophets until John.* After the last prophet (Malachi) laid down his pen, the world heard no more revelation from God until John broke the silence by his preaching in the wilderness. Since then the kingdom of heaven was *preached,* but that does not say it was set up by him. *Every man presseth into it.* The kingdom of God existed in preparation before it was in existence in fact. (See Matthew 11: 12.) *Presseth into it* means those who accepted the preaching of John did so under the pressure of conscience, and in spite of opposition.

Verse 17. The reference to heaven and earth is for comparison, to indicate the permanence of the law until it had accomplished its purpose under God.

Verse 18. This is discussed in detail at Matthew 19: 9.

Verse 19. I do not deny this story being a parable on the ground that it says a *certain* rich man. The word *certain* is used elsewhere where we know a parable is being spoken (chapter 20: 9). A parable requires a comparison while there is none in this case, not even any words that necessarily have to be taken figuratively. Furthermore, there are so many facts of a circumstantial nature that it shows Jesus had some particular case in mind. It was a literal fact that rich men lived in such luxuries as are described of this one.

Verse 20. *Sores* is from a Greek word that is defined "ulcers" in the lexicon. Lazarus was afflicted so badly he had to be carried to be laid at the gate of the rich man. He was placed there as an object of charity, even as beggars today seek a prominent place on the streets where they can be seen by the public.

Verse 21. In addition to what he might receive from the crowds that would be passing in and out of the gate of such an estate, he might be given the *crumbs* or scraps taken up from the table of this rich man. *The dogs licked his sores.* That was no discomfort to the afflicted man, but the fact indicates his helpless condition. There was no one to treat and bind up the sores, but they were left to run openly, else the dogs would not have cared for it.

Verse 22. *Abraham's bosom.* In old times people reclined while eating, at tables only a few inches higher than the floor. The diners would lie on their sides and rest the head on one hand while serving themselves with the other. They lay at a 45-degree angle with the table, which placed the head of one person virtually in the bosom of the one behind him, and in very intimate cases the two would be very near each other. (See John 13: 23.) Since the situation of Lazarus on earth pertained to food, it was fitting to represent him as lying in the bosom of Abraham, where he could partake with him of the good spiritual things in Paradise. Nothing is said of what disposition was made of the body of Lazarus, but the rich man was buried, which is to remind us that his body remained on the earth after his spirit was placed in Hades.

Verse 23. We have just read that the rich man was buried after his death. People are buried in the earth only, hence this man had something in his being besides his body that went elsewhere, and that could feel the sting of torments. For information about *hell*, see the note at Matthew 5: 30. *Abraham's bosom* is explained in the preceding verse, and *afar off* will be considered at verse 26.

Verse 24. *Father Abraham* was said because he was a descendant of that patriarch. The rich man's brothers had Moses and the prophets (verse 29), which were given to the Jews only, hence we know he was of that race. Objectors criticize this verse on the ground that the rich man's body was buried on the earth, therefore he had no *tongue to be tormented*. The objection shows the utter lack of considering the subject fairly. The only part of a human being that has any feeling is the inner man. While body and soul are united, the latter exercises itself through the former as a vehicle only, for the body itself has no feeling. If it did have, a dead man, or one under an anesthetic would flinch from pain caused by contact with any disagreeable object. Therefore, when the inner man is freed from the incumbrance of the flesh, it will still maintain its ability to experience feelings.

Verse 25. Abraham addressed the rich man as *son* on the same basis as the latter called Abraham his father, as was explained at the preceding verse. Abraham told the rich man to *remember* some things that he had experienced while living on the earth. This indicates that persons in Hades or the intermediate state, will be able to recall their experiences which they had on the earth. Whether the same will apply when they enter the eternal state after the judgment, is not revealed in the Scriptures.

Verse 26. *Gulf* is from CHASMA, which Thayer defines, "A gaping opening, a chasm, gulf." He then explains the definition to mean, "Equivalent to a great interval." Since this gulf is impassable, it separates the objects on each side virtually as much as if they were a great distance apart. This explains the phrase *afar off* in verse 23. Another truth that is taught here, is that no change can be made in the spiritual classification of human beings after death; this agrees with Revelation 22: 11.

Verses 27, 28. There is nothing said about what the five brothers were to do as to their manner of life. Lazarus was to be asked to testify, which means to bear witness as to the kind of place in which their dead brother was being tormented, to the end they might so live that they would avoid it. The rich man took for granted his brothers would know what changes they would have to make in their lives; also, that if they heard from one who had seen the fate of their brother, they would take warning and make the necessary reformation.

Verse 29. The brothers had the law of Moses which would lead them in the right way of life, if they would *hear* (heed) its teaching.

Verse 30. The object the rich man thought of accomplishing was the repentance of his brethren. The evidence shows that here was a family of the prosperous ranks of society, abusing their wealth and being unconcerned about the less fortunate ones.

Verse 31. *Neither will they be persuaded.* Again there is nothing said about being convinced of facts already taught in the Scriptures, but that the brothers might be induced to do what they knew was their duty. *Rose from the dead.* The rich man understood that in going back from Hades to the earth, one would need to be raised from the dead, and Abraham endorsed that idea by repeating it without any correction. This all proves that no communication ever takes place between men on earth and the spirits in the unseen world, hence the theory of spiritualism is a fraud. Even those who have been permitted to rise from the dead never said anything about information gained while dead. God expects men to be convinced by the testimony furnished them by living persons; that was verified by the miracles performed before their eyes.

LUKE 17

Verse 1. *Impossible* is from ANEN-DEKTOS which occurs in no other place in the Greek New Testament. However, the same thought is expressed in Matthew 18: 7. (See the comments at that place.) There is nothing that God cannot do as far as power or strength is concerned. But He would need to be continuously performing miracles if all *offenses* (causes of stumbling) could be avoided, and that would prevent man from developing the kind of characters fit for the kingdom of heaven. Because of this, the Greek word should be rendered "inadmissible," which is one word in Thayer's definition.

Verse 2. The foregoing paragraph does not excuse any particular man who causes another to stumble. Being drowned will not exempt a guilty man from the punishment that will otherwise be due him after the judgment. The statement is used only as a contrast, to give an idea of the severity of that punishment. Little children, in the ordinary sense of that word, are not responsible and hence cannot stumble over wrong doing. Therefore the *little ones* are those described at Matthew 18: 5, 10.

Verse 3. This verse corresponds in thought with Matthew 18: 15.

Verse 4. This verse means the same as Matthew 18: 21, 22.

Verse 5. From the strictness of the law that Jesus just gave the apostles, they realized it would require a strong faith to comply with it, and hence made this request.

Verse 6. This verse is explained at Matthew 17: 20.

Verse 7. The question Jesus asked was an introduction to an important lesson.

Verse 8. The question in the preceding verse implied a negative answer; this verse states the positive answer.

Verse 9. The servant would not even expect to be thanked for what he had done, knowing it was in line with his regular duty. *Trow* is an obsolete word for "think."

Verse 10. *Unprofitable s e r v a n t s* means they did nothing beyond their duty. To be profitable, one must contribute more to another than he receives from him. That could not be done by any human being in rendering service to an infinite God.

Verse 11. Galilee and Samaria were between where Jesus was and Jerusalem. The significance of Samaria will be brought out at verse 16.

Verse 12. *Which stood afar off* is explained at Matthew 8: 2.

Verse 13. Since they were standing off at the proper distance, the lepers had to raise their voices in order (as they thought) for Jesus to recognize their cry for mercy.

Verse 14. *Show yourselves to the priests.* This was in accordance with a law of Moses, and it is commented upon at Matthew 8: 4.

Verse 15. One of the lepers, all of whom were healed, showed his gratitude by returning to Jesus and attributing to the Lord the credit for his recovery.

Verse 16. In eastern countries, to fall at the feet of another was an expression of humility and respect. *He was a Samaritan* is a significant phrase. The Jews had a dislike for the Samaritans, and thought they were about incapable of performing anything of importance. The mere mention of this man's nationality, in connection with his exceptional conduct of gratitude, was intended as a rebuke for the Jews.

Verses 17, 18. Jesus then called this lone thankful one of the group a *stranger* because he was from an "outside" nation, that being the meaning of the word stranger.

Verse 19. *Made thee whole* included his spiritual salvation. The ten were all healed, but this blessing was not pronounced upon the nine.

Verse 20. The Pharisees thought Jesus was going to set up a kingdom like those of the world, and they were curious to see the signs of its approach. *Observation* is rendered "outward show" in the margin, which is correct.

Verse 21. It not being a kingdom with literal boundaries and material symbols, it would not be possible for any man to point to such evidences. *Is within you.* This phrase has been perverted by those who maintain that the kingdom was set up in the lifetime of Christ, because the present tense *(is)* was used by Jesus. The kingdom as a government in fact was not built then, but one phase of the word did exist as Jesus was speaking. (See the long note at Matthew 3: 2.) The heart of man is the territory of the king from heaven, and that territory was and still is *within* or on the inside of human beings. Just when that territory was fully taken over by the king is another question. That fact took place on the day of Pentecost, recorded in Acts 2.

Verse 22. From this verse through the end of the chapter the subject matter corresponds with Matthew 24, except it is much more brief. It will be well for the reader to examine that chapter with the comments, before going further in the present place. Like the chapter in Matthew, this one considers the destruction of Jerusalem and the second coming of Christ as two separate events, and he warns his disciples not to get the two mixed. During the siege of Jerusalem the distresses were to be so great that the disciples would long for the days when Jesus was with them. That is what is meant by *one of the days of the Son of man* which they would remember and long for.

Verse 23. Some would take advantage of the disturbances to declare it to be the approach of Christ in his second coming.

Verse 24. The comparison between lightning and the second coming of Christ is commented upon quite fully at Matthew 24: 27.

Verse 25. The preceding verse predicts the second coming of Christ, an event many centuries in the future when Jesus was here. Like it is in Matthew's account, Jesus alternates between the two periods. In the present verse he drops back from the second coming to predict another important fact to occur *first* (or before the second coming), which was his own personal sufferings. That experience was to end in his crucifixion and death, all of which would be a factor in the distress referred to above. (See Matthew 27: 25, with the comments.)

Verses 26, 27. These verses are identical in meaning with Matthew 24: 37, 38.

Verse 28. The remarks about what the people were doing in the days of Lot, receive the same comments that are cited from the preceding verses.

Verse 29. From this verse through 32, the Lord is speaking of the destruction of Jerusalem. He is making the point that, when the evidences of that event are apparent, the disciples should lose no time in "fleeing to the mountains" (Matthew 24: 16), because there would not be much more time for escape. As an argument on that point, he states that the raining of fire on Sodom came *the same day* that Lot escaped from the city.

Verse 30. *Son of man is revealed* means when Jesus will be represented by the fulfillment of his predictions against the wicked city of Jerusalem.

Verse 31. *In that day*, etc., means the day of the destruction of Jerusalem.

Verse 32. The preceding verse closes with the words *not return back*, and the present one recalls the fate of Lot's wife because she was too much interested in the city from which she had just escaped. Likewise, when the disciples see the destruction of Jerusalem is virtually at hand, they should flee without delay, lest a fate overtake them as serious as that of Lot's wife; not just like it, but as bad.

Verse 33. The Saviour here has in mind the spiritual preparation for the second great event, so that it may not find a man among those that will *be left*. The two kinds *of life* are explained at Matthew 10: 39.

Verses 34-36. For the meaning of this paragraph, especially on the words *taken* and *left*, see the comments at Matthew 24: 40, 41.

Verse 37. Jesus comes back to the destruction of Jerusalem. The significance of the *eagles* in connection with the event is explained at Matthew 24: 28.

LUKE 18

Verse 1. The phrase *to this end* is in italics, but the thought is justified by the Greek text. *Always* and *not to faint* means to be always a praying disciple, and not hesitate or falter just because one's prayer is not answered as soon as expected. Since the inspired writer tells us this parable was spoken for this purpose, we should not make comparisons of any other parts of it; they were spoken only to connect the story.

Verse 2. The character of this judge was revealed to show why the prayers made to him had to be persistent.

Verse 3. The justness of this widow's complaint was not questioned.

Verses 4, 5. The judge was not prompted by any regard for any being, human or divine, but because he did not want to be troubled by the widow's persistence.

Verse 6. The strength of this verse will be better realized by emphasizing *unjust*. Even that kind of a judge was finally moved to action because the widow insisted.

Verse 7. The just Judge will certainly be moved to regard the prayers of His children in the proper time, if their faith does not weaken and they continue to pray.

Verse 8. *Shall he find faith on the earth?* We must not interpret one passage in such a way that it will contradict others. It is clearly taught in the New Testament that the church with its faithful members will be here when Jesus comes. (See Matthew 24: 40, 41; 1 Corinthians 15: 24, 51; 1 Thessalonians 4: 15, 17.) Therefore the question of Jesus should be understood as a kind of warning, stirring up his hearers to beware lest their individual faith should fail them.

Verse 9. *Trusted in themselves* denotes they considered themselves *righteous* on the ground of the great display they were making of their deeds. On the same principle they would *despise* (belittle) others who could not boast of such actions.

Verse 10. It was perfectly in order for both Pharisees and publicans to pray, and to go into the temple for the purpose of prayer (Isaiah 56: 7; Matthew 21: 13).

Verses 11, 12. This paragraph contains the prayer of the Pharisee. Even if all of his claims were true, his prayer would have been objectionable because it did not include a single request; only a boastful statement of his deeds.

Verse 13. There were generally many people in the temple at "the hour of prayer" (Acts 3: 1). The publican modestly stood away from the crowd, feeling that his presence might be objectionable to them, due to the common opinion of that class. He made no claim of goodness, but instead, he classed himself with sinners and prayed for mercy.

Verse 14. *Rather* is printed in italics in the King James Version, but the American Standard Version and Moffatt's translation both use the regular type. That is evidently correct according to the reasoning of Jesus. He follows his statement about who was justified, with the declaration that *he that humbleth himself shall be exalted.* If the publican was not justified, then no one in the verse was exalted.

Verses 15-17. This paragraph is explained at Matthew 19: 13, 14.

Verses 18-27. This group of verses is almost identical with Matthew 19: 16-26. To conserve space, let the reader examine those verses and the comments.

Verse 28. This is commented upon at Matthew 19: 27.

Verses 29, 30. See the comments on Matthew 19: 28, 29.

Verse 31. The prophetic writings referred to are in Psalms 22 and Isaiah 53.

Verse 32. Spitting on one was to show the greatest of contempt.

Verse 33. It was customary to scourge all prisoners before executing them or otherwise disposing of them. The victim was stripped of all his clothing and a thong of leather was lashed across his back.

Verse 34. The apostles were baffled over these predictions about the death of Jesus. That was because they had a temporal kingdom in mind, and that would require the king to live and be present upon his throne.

Verse 35. Being blind, this man was depending upon alms for a living.

Verse 36. This wayside was a common place for people to travel, else the blind man would not have been occupying such a place to be seen by the people. *Asked what it meant* indicates that some unusual commotion was going on.

Verse 37. The fame of Jesus was frequently connected with his humble home life. It was surprising that the product of such a community could perform the deeds attributed to him. (See John 1: 46.)

Verse 38. The people told the blind man it was "Jesus of Nazareth" who was passing by, while he called him the son of *David.* This shows that at least some persons understood the Scriptures, that a descendant of David was to be called a Nazarene. (See the notes at Matthew 2: 23.)

Verse 39. As to why they rebuked him, see the notes at Matthew 20: 31.

Verse 40. It would have been a hardship for the blind man to get into the immediate presence of Jesus unaided, therefore the people were commanded to lead him to the spot.

Verse 41. A large gift of money or some regular income would have relieved the blind man of his financial worries. But instead of requesting such a favor, he asked for the restoration of his sight, which would enable him to care for himself afterwards.

Verse 42. *Saved* is from sozo, which Thayer defines at this place, "To make well, heal, restore to health." This favor was given the blind man because he believed in Jesus.

Verse 43. The recovery from blindness was immediate, which was always the case with miraculous healing.

LUKE 19

Verse 1. A traveler would come to Jericho soon after crossing the Jordan from the east side; it was not far from Jerusalem (verse 11). Jesus passed through the city on his way to the capital where he was soon to close his earthly career.

Verse 2. The publicans had access to the money of the people, and by reason of that fact they could increase their own possessions. This prominent group of citizens is described at Matthew 9: 10.

Verse 3. The *press* means the crowd, which was so great that Zacchaeus could not see Jesus, he being *little of stature*, which means he was not very tall.

Verse 4. Zacchaeus knew the usual path of travel, hence he found a tree along the route and climbed up into it. The sycamore tree was planted by waysides because it had wide-spreading branches which afforded a good shade.

Verse 5. Since Zacchaeus was a Jew (Verse 9), he was a proper subject to be commanded by Jesus, for He was sent to "the lost sheep of the house of Israel" (Matthew 15: 24).

Verse 6. *Received him joyfully.* Zacchaeus evidently was surprised (and honored) to be called upon to entertain the great Teacher, knowing the general estimate that was placed on publicans as a class.

Verse 7. The thing that happened was usual under such circumstances. The people *murmured* (among themselves after Jesus had gone with Zacchaeus) because Jesus went to be a *guest* of one whom they classed as a sinner. That was because he was a publican, most of whom were justly charged with taking unlawful amounts of taxes from the people.

Verse 8. The speech in this verse was made after reaching the home of Zacchaeus, for in his response (next verse) Jesus refers to *this house*. This helps us to understand the phrase *Zacchaeus stood*, the second word of which is defined by Thayer, "To place one's self, to stand." He evidently took a position where all that were in the house could see and hear him as he made his promises to the Lord. It is significant that he was to give half of what he had to the poor first, and then reimburse any who were wronged after the division. That adjustment would hence be made out of his half of the original stock. *False accusation* means, "To exact money wrongfully; to extort from, defraud." Such a practice was commonly done by the publicans. As this agreement was made in the hearing of the group, any man who had a complaint was given opportunity to state it.

Verse 9. *Salvation is come to this house.* Not that every member of the household was saved, for Zacchaeus was the only one who repented; it means that salvation had come to a member of that household. *A son of Abraham* entitled him to salvation on the basis of the statement of Jesus to the woman (Matthew 15: 24).

Verse 10. This verse states a truth that will apply generally.

Verse 11. People are inclined to go to extremes with their conclusions. Jesus had frequently told them that the kingdom of heaven was at hand. They concluded, therefore, that it was just upon them, especially because He was headed toward Jerusalem and was even then very near the city. *Immediately* is from PARACHREMA, and Thayer defines it, "On the spot; immediately, forthwith, instantly."

Verse 12. The inspired writer tells us why Jesus spoke this parable, that it was because the people thought the kingdom was to be set up as soon as Jesus reached Jerusalem. Were that to be done, virtually all of the preliminary details showing true devotion to the King would be over. That would be possible only under a worldly kingdom like what they expected. Jesus considered it necessary, therefore, to give this parable that would show it was to be a spiritual kingdom, and that its citizens would be placed under strict responsibility. The *nobleman* is Jesus, and the *far country* is Heaven. If he must go to that far country in order to *receive a kingdom*, it follows that he would not set it up in a few days, or as soon as he arrived at Jerusalem.

Verse 13. The specific lesson intended by this parable is the same as that of the talents in Matthew 25, namely, individual responsibility. The details of the story should not be strained into any other meaning. When

Jesus or his apostles select any particular subject for the purpose of illustration, they will give the details in order to make the main point stand out, but no other use should be made of such items. However, the items that are properly related to the principal subject under consideration will be explained accordingly. The *pounds* corresponds with the "talents" in Matthew 25, and *occupy till I come* is the same as developing one's talents.

Verse 14. This verse applies to people in the kingdom who deny the authority of King Jesus. Such persons will not make the proper use of their opportunities.

Verse 15. This verse refers to the day of judgment, when all mankind will be held to account for the way they have lived and used their talents.

Verses 16, 17. This corresponds with Matthew 25: 20, 21. In that place the faithful are told to "enter into the joy of their Lord." In our present passage it is expressed by having authority over ten cities, but the meaning is the same.

Verses 18, 19. This is equivalent to the man with two talents and the reward is to be based on the same principle, namely, faithfulness.

Verse 20. This man is in the same class as the one who buried his lord's talent, and he will be condemned for his unfaithfulness. (See Matthew 25: 24-28.)

Verses 21-26. The paragraph preceding this somewhat overlaps it, but it will be well to consider the present paragraph in connection with Matthew 25: 25-26.

Verse 27. This corresponds with Matthew 25: 30.

Verse 28. *Went before*. He took the lead in journeying toward Jerusalem.

Verses 29-35. See the notes on Matthew 21: 1-7.

Verse 36. This is explained at Matthew 21: 8.

Verses 37, 38. See Matthew 21: 9-11.

Verse 39. Evidently these Pharisees were envious of Jesus because he was receiving so much honor from the disciples. Their suggestion that He rebuke his disciples was on the pretense that it was an unnecessary disturbance, but in reality it was because of their envy. (See Matthew 21: 15, 16.)

Verse 40. The reference to the stones is figurative, to illustrate the worthiness of Jesus to be thus honored. John told the Jews that God was able to make the stones give birth to offspring for Abraham (Matthew 3: 9), and if necessary we are sure He would cause the inanimate stones to express praises for Jesus, should the devoted disciples be forced to maintain silence.

Verses 41-44. See the notes on Matthew 23: 37-39; 24: 1, 2. *Visitation* as used here means "inspection, investigation," and applies to the time when Jerusalem was to be visited with distress, as an investigation into her history would justify.

Verses 45, 46. See Matthew 21: 12, 13.

Verse 47. *He taught daily*, also the *chief* of the leaders *sought to destroy him*. The connection between these statements is not revealed here. We know, however, it was because Jesus rebuked them for their hypocrisy.

Verse 48. The people had great respect for Jesus, and these priests and scribes did not want to lose the esteem of the public lest they fail in their own popularity.

LUKE 20

Verse 1. The *priests* were a religious group, the *scribes* were those who copied the law for the people, and the *elders* were the seniors, members of the Sanhedrin.

Verses 2-8. This paragraph is explained at Matthew 21: 23-27. We should remember that Jesus never evaded answering any proper question, but He knew these people were insincere in their questioning; it was prompted by an evil motive.

Verses 9-17. The reader will find this explained at Matthew 21: 33-43.

Verse 18. The *stone* is Christ who had been rejected by the Jewish leaders. The significance of *falling on* or being *fallen upon* is explained at Matthew 21: 44.

Verse 19. The priests and scribes properly applied the preceding parable to themselves. They would have tried to do bodily harm to Jesus but for public sentiment.

Verse 20. The priests thought they could mislead Jesus into saying something that would get him into trouble with the secular government. *Spies which should feign* means men who were hired to act the hypocrite in pretending to be *just men*. That means they were supposed to be concerned about the dignity of the government.

Verse 21. These spies really did

know all the things they claimed to know, and their statements were the truth. But their motive in saying them was to flatter Jesus, which they should have known would be a failure.

Verse 22. In their ignorance of the nature of the kingdom of heaven, they thought Jesus would be opposed to all other governments. Were that the case he naturally would oppose giving them financial aid. Had he answered them to that effect, it would have been ground for accusing him of disloyalty to "the powers that be."

Verse 23. *Craftiness* means trickery which Jesus recognized to be their purpose in the question they asked him.

Verse 24. Jesus met the situation in a manner that was doubtless unexpected. Instead of answering their question with a direct yes or no, he asked for a piece of the very kind of money that was being used in paying for the government's financial support. He then asked about the image and wording on it, as to whose it was. They said it belonged to Caesar, the ruler involved in their question.

Verse 25. In their answer they committed themselves beyond recall, for they directly said the whole thing belonged to Caesar, the very thing he was asking people to give him as tribute. No one would say it is not "lawful" to give to a man what belongs to him. They had said this money belonged to Caesar, hence it would be lawful to give it back to him. And by the same token it would be right to give to God what belongs to him, namely, their religious devotion.

Verse 26. *Could not take hold* means they had no reply they could make to the reasoning of Jesus. *Marveled* is defined by Robinson, "To wonder, to be astonished, to be amazed," not that they were favorably impressed with the wisdom of the Teacher.

Verse 27. The Sadducees are described at Matthew 16: 12.

Verse 28-36. See the comments on Matthew 22: 23-30.

Verses 37, 38. This is explained at Matthew 22: 31, 32.

Verse 39. Since it was the Sadducees who had been baffled in their attempt to entrap Jesus, the scribes doubtless found much satisfaction in complimenting Him.

Verse 40. See the comments about the end of their questioning, and the reason for it, at Matthew 22: 46.

Verses 41-44. See Matthew 22: 41-45.

Verse 45. *The audience* included the masses of the people and the disciples, but in this part of his speech Jesus was speaking to his disciples.

Verse 46. *Long robes* were worn to attract attention, and obtain special salutations in public, such as in marketplaces where many people resorted. *Highest seats* were the front pews that faced the audience. *Chief rooms* means favorite places at the table.

Verse 47. *Devour widows' houses* is figurative, referring to advantages those hypocrites took of the needy and helpless among the people. (See Matthew 23: 14.) *Greater damnation* is explained at the same passage in Matthew.

LUKE 21

Verse 1. This money was a voluntary offering, made for the upkeep of the temple. The rich men were casting in much in actual count of the money.

Verse 2. The widow cast in *two* mites instead of one as is generally stated. According to Robinson's lexicon, a mite was equal to about one fifth of a cent. The widow contributed about one half of a cent to the good work. The actual amount of money was not the main point as Jesus explains.

Verses 3, 4. Jesus stated in literal language what he meant figuratively. Our contributions to worthy causes are valued in the Lord's sight on the basis of our ability to give, not in literal "dollars and cents." (See 2 Corinthians 8: 12.)

Verse 5. This adornment of the goodly stones was by way of "remodeling," which was done at various times through a period of 46 years (John 2: 20).

Verse 6. The Jews were vain in their admiration of the temple. They had the idea that it was "titanic" and hence indestructible; but Jesus rebuked their pride by predicting its utter destruction. The completeness of this destruction and the manner in which it was to be accomplished, is related in chapter 19: 43, 44.

Verse 7. According to Matthew 24: 3, it was the disciples who asked Jesus the question. But in that passage it may be seen that they really asked two questions, although they had in mind what they thought would take place as one event. It will be well for the reader to reexamine the comments on that entire chapter.

Verse 8. This corresponds with Matthew 24: 4, 5.

Verse 9. The conflict between the Jews and the Romans did not begin in Judea. Hence the people of Jerusalem would hear about wars in the farther territories, some time before it reached the capital of the nation against which Caesar was at war.

Verse 10. The Roman Empire was composed of many nations, and when the war against the Jews broke out, it threw the whole empire into commotions.

Verse 11. A state of war often produces shortages in the necessities of life, which brings famine and pestilence as a natural consequence. A literal earthquake is never caused by warfare, but God has brought them about at various times to mark His concern for the conditions. In the present case it was to be one of the signs the disciples were given by which they could see the approaching storm.

Verse 12. Many of the Christians were Jews and others were Gentiles. The disturbances of the time stirred up the Romans against them which led to persecutions.

Verse 13. This means that when the disciples undergo these persecutions, it will turn out to be a testimony for them. They will recall that Jesus foretold it and thus it will prove to them that He was a true prophet. When a prediction becomes history, it amounts to a verifying evidence. (See Exodus 3: 12.)

Verses 14, 15. See the comments on this kind of assurance at chapter 12: 11, 12.

Verse 16. Some members of various families were disciples of Christ and some were not. In the disturbed conditions, these individuals would be arrayed against each other.

Verse 17. Some would blame the war on the influence of the teaching of Christ, and in spitework would persecute the disciples.

Verse 18. *Not an hair perish* is a figurative form of speech, meaning that not the least harm would come to the disciples who heeded the instructions of Jesus. A note on Josephus, Wars, Book 2, Chapter 19, Sections 6, 7, shows how it came about that an unexpected retreat of the Roman forces from Jerusalem, for a brief period, gave the Christians an opportunity to escape from the city. "This

they did on this occasion and were preserved."

Verse 19. Christians should not let persecutions or other trials cause them to lose patience. If they will endure through to the end they will *possess* or save their souls. It means the same as Matthew 24: 13; endurance and patience are the same.

Verse 20. *Compassed with armies* will mean the siege is on.

Verse 21. Those who are outside of Jerusalem will have no difficulty as far as the hostile army is concerned, in escaping to the mountains, for the war will be directed against the cities only.

Verse 22. *Things . . . may be fulfilled.* It was predicted in Daniel 9: 27.

Verse 23. An expectant or nursing mother would find it very difficult to make a hurried escape out of the land. Jesus was not pronouncing a woe, just predicting it.

Verse 24. *Times of the Gentiles.* Jerusalem was the capital of the Jewish nation, both for its political and religious government. It continued to be such for the political government, and when the church was set up the Jews first accepted the Gospel, then they recognized it as their model (not capital) for religious government. But the Jews as a nation turned against Christ and the church, having already rejected Him and had him crucified. As a punishment, their city was doomed to be overthrown and they deprived of the possession of it. *Until* would imply that when the *times of the Gentiles* had been completed, the Jews would again come back to Jerusalem. But, they were to come back as Christians, which is predicted in Romans 11: 25.

Verses 25, 26. This paragraph is figurative and is to be explained in the same way as Matthew 24: 29; referring to the period called the "Dark Ages" in history.

Verse 27. See the notes on Matthew 24: 30.

Verse 28. *Your redemption draweth nigh* is equivalent to the gathering of the elect (the faithful) predicted in Matthew 24: 30, 31, at the second coming of Christ.

Verses 29-31. This corresponds with Matthew 24: 32, 33.

Verses 32, 33. This paragraph refers to the destruction of Jerusalem. See the notes on Matthew 24: 34, 35, giving special attention to the word "generation."

Verse 34. *Surfeiting* is from KRAI-PALE which Robinson defines, "A seizure of the head; hence intoxication, debauch, giddiness; reveling and drunkenness." The verse is a warning to disciples not to be absorbed in loose and worldly living, so as to let the day of Christ slip up on them. (See 1 Thessalonians 5: 1-8.)

Verse 35. A snare is something that takes a victim unexpectedly. The day of Christ will come upon the masses of human beings in the same way.

Verse 36. If Christians lead a prayerful and watchful life, they will be looking for Christ and will be ready to stand before him in peace.

Verses 37, 38. This was a "series" of meetings, something like some that are conducted today. An incidental difference is that ours generally are conducted in the nighttime, while that of Jesus was in the day.

LUKE 22

Verse 1. In Mark 14: 1 the passover and unleavened bread are spoken of as separate feasts. That is because there was no leaven allowed in their houses on the 14th day of the first month, nor on the seven days immediately following. Because of this, the two terms are sometimes used interchangeably. (See Leviticus 23: 4-6.)

Verse 2. *Sought how* means they wanted to plan the death of Jesus in some way that would avoid a riot among the people. (See Matthew 26: 4, 5; Mark 14: 1, 2.)

Verse 3. *Then entered Satan.* This does not mean that Satan here for the first time began to influence Judas, for he was called a devil by Jesus before this (John 6: 70, 71). But Judas had been rebuffed in his covetous attitude toward the woman with the ointment (John 12: 3-6), and began at once to plan a wicked scheme against Jesus, which was under the impulse of Satan. (See notes on Matthew 26: 14-16.)

Verse 4. Judas began his wicked plan by contacting the chief priests and captain, making a proposition to betray Jesus into their hands.

Verse 5. *They were glad* because they hated Him for his exposure of their hypocrisy.

Verse 6. *In the absence of the multitude.* This was because they did not want to get the multitude stirred up

in protest against the persecution of Jesus (Mark 14: 2).

Verse 7. *Day of unleavened bread* means the first day of the entire eight, during which no leaven was to be used. This 8-day period began with the day on which the passover was killed. (See the notes at verse 1.)

Verse 8. *Go and prepare.* Special arrangements had to be made because Jesus and his apostles were to eat their Passover two days before the regular time (Matthew 26: 2, 17).

Verses 9, 10. Jesus gave the two disciples instructions about preparing for their Passover, which they did according to Matthew 26: 18: 19.

Verses 11-13. Jesus was divine and knew just what conditions the disciples would find in the house, and also what the disposition of the men would be who were concerned in the appointment. *Guestchamber* is from the same word as "inn" in chapter 2: 7.

Verse 14. The events of this night are not all recorded in any one of the Gospel records, nor in strict chronological order. Before going any further at this place, I urgently insist that the reader see the comments at Matthew 26: 20, and keep his book open for frequent reference as he follows the comments at this verse and on through verse 23. I shall now comment on these verses as they come, making my remarks in view of the paragraph in Matthew cited above. *He sat down.* This phrase is from ANA-PIPTO, which Thayer defines, "To lie back, lie down; to recline at table." (See the comments at chapter 16: 22.)

Verse 15. This was the fourth Passover Jesus ate after his baptism, according to John 2: 13; 5: 1; 6: 4; 13: 1.

Verse 16. Jesus predicted that when he ate the Passover again, it would be of a spiritual nature, for it would be in the kingdom of God (the church).

Verse 17. *Took the cup.* According to Smith's Bible Dictionary, and Funk and Wagnalls' Standard Bible Dictionary, the Jews added the drinking of wine to the celebration of the Passover. It was this cup that Jesus took in this verse.

Verse 18. *Not drink* takes the same comments as *not eat* in verse 16.

Verse 19. Jesus is now instituting his supper that is to become the weekly "breaking of bread" in the church (Acts 20: 7). *This is my body* was not said while they were in the Passover activities (see the notes in

Matthew cited above). *This do in remembrance of me* could not apply to the Jewish feast.

Verse 20. *After supper* means after the Passover supper. "A testament is of force after men are dead" Hebrews 9: 16-18. As the animal sacrifices constituted the testament under the Mosaic system, so the blood of Christ (which will have been shed in his death), was to constitute *the new testament in my blood.*

Verse 21. The writer now goes back to the activities of the Passover. (See the notes and comments cited in Matthew 26, from verse 14 here.)

Verse 22. The betrayal and slaying of Jesus had been determined upon by the counsel of God (Acts 2: 23), to which the reference is made here.

Verse 23. *Began to enquire.* See the comments at Matthew 26: 22.

Verses 24-27. See the notes on Matthew 20: 25-28.

Verse 28. Throughout the public ministry of Jesus, he was subject to the trials of his life which he overcame completely. (See Hebrews 4: 15.)

Verse 29. See chapter 12: 32.

Verse 30. The privilege of eating at the table of another was regarded as a great favor. Jesus used the circumstance figuratively to designate the close relationship the apostles were to sustain with Christ in his kingdom. See Matthew 19: 28 for comments on *judging the twelve tribes.*

Verses 31-34. While the wording is a little different, the thoughts and subject matter of this paragraph are the same as Matthew 26: 31-35.

Verses 35, 36. See the comments on Matthew 10: 10. *Sell his garment and buy one* [a sword]. Jesus never did forbid the use of force in defence where life or home was threatened, but rather spoke favorably for it (chapter 12: 39); hence He advised his apostles to provide themselves with the necessary weapon. It might be objected that Jesus rebuked Peter when he used his sword (John 18: 10, 11). That is true, but that was not an act of defence, for no one's life was being even threatened by the use of weapons, hence Peter's act was an aggressive one. Besides, he proposed to use his sword in defence of the plan of salvation, while in our verse it was only for the purpose of defence against bodily harm. (See again the passage in chapter 12: 39.)

Verse 37. This verse was to show why the apostles would have to go on without the personal presence of Jesus; he was going to be taken from them. *Things concerning me hath an end,* means the things predicted of Him (including his death) were to be fulfilled to the end, or to be fully accomplished.

Verse 38. This is an incidental item. Jesus had instructed them to procure a sword, and they told him they already had two, which was found to be sufficient.

Verse 39. *As he was wont* denotes it was a regular practice for Jesus to go out to this mount, which was the location of Gethsemane (John 18: 1, 2).

Verse 40. On this particular occasion there was a special event about to take place, the betrayal of Jesus into the hands of the chief priests and elders.

Verses 41, 42. See the comments at Matthew 26: 41, 42.

Verse 43. After Jesus had resisted Satan in the wilderness (Matthew 4: 11), God sent an angel to minister to him. Now an angel comes to his assistance in the garden.

Verse 44. *Agony* is defined, "Severe mental struggles and emotions." It was a part of the "cup" of which Jesus prayed to be relieved in verse 42. *As it were* is from HOSEI, which Thayer defines, "As if, i. e., as it were, as though, as, like as, like." Jesus did not "sweat blood" as it is so often said. His sweat was gathered upon the surface of the body in great drops that were compared to clotted blood. The condition was caused by the intense nervous agitation over the experiences He knew were soon to be thrust upon him by the powers of darkness.

Verse 45. *Sleeping for sorrow.* It was wrong for the apostles to be sleeping even for this cause, but it was not as bad as if it was from pure indifference. A like situation exisited once with the Israelites in Egypt (Exodus 6: 9).

Verse 46. This verse gives an admonition that would be good for general guidance. In other places it is worded "watch and pray" (Matthew 26: 41).

Verse 47. Judas had left the company of Jesus and the other apostles just after eating of the Passover. See the comments at Matthew 26: 47.

Verse 48. The salutation of a kiss was a common practice in old times, hence there should not have been any surprise at the mere fact that Judas kissed Jesus, under ordinary circumstances. But it had been but a short time since he left ·the upper room where Jesus was with the other apostles, so the usual occasion for salutations was wanting. Besides, a salutation as an act of social courtesy would have been appropriate for the apostles also, for Judas had been absent from all of them the same length of time. But Jesus exposed the hypocrisy of the traitor by this statement, in question form, but really in order to show him that his Lord knew what he was doing.

Verse 49. Neither of the other records says anything about this conversation.

Verse 50. John 18: 10 tells us it was Peter who did this.

Verse 51. In this account Jesus said to Peter, "Suffer ye thus far," meaning that he should not resist the crowd that was coming to take his Master. The event is the same as recorded in Matthew 26: 52.

Verses 52, 53. This paragraph is the same in meaning as Matthew 26: 55, 56.

Verses 54, 55. See the comments at Matthew 26: 57, 58.

Verses 56-62. This paragraph has to do with Peter's threefold denial of Christ according to predictions made by Him. The sad affair is explained at Matthew 26: 69-75.

Verse 63. These actions against Jesus were to show their disrespect of Him.

Verse 64. *Prophesy* is used in the sense of a test for the superior wisdom of Jesus. If He was divine, he should be able to know who did the striking.

Verse 65. *Blasphemously spake* means they said many things in a way that would injure the good name of Jesus, were they to be heard and believed by others.

Verse 66. The *council* was the Sanhedrin, which was the highest court the Romans permitted the Jews to have in the time of Christ and the apostles.

Verses 67, 68. Jesus let the men in the council know that He regarded their question as being insincere, and not from a desire for information.

Verse 69. Jesus made a prediction they were not expecting.

Verse 70. Taking the remark of Jesus in the preceding verse as an indirect answer to their question, they repeated it in a slightly different form. *Ye say that I am* is a Biblical form of an affirmative answer.

Verse 71. This verse is explained at Matthew 26: 65, 66.

LUKE 23

Verses 1, 2. See Matthew 27: 1, 2.

Verse 3. *Thou sayest it* is the "good confession" referred to by Paul in 1 Timothy 6: 13, showing there is no set form in making the confession.

Verse 4. *I find no fault in this man.* This is virtually the same thought that is worded· in Matthew 27: 23.

Verse 5. According to Thayer, Jewry means "all Palestine."

Verses 6, 7. This was Herod Antipas, who was governor over the territory of Galilee, but was in Jerusalem at this time because of the Passover. If he could turn Jesus over to him, Pilate thought he might get rid of the problem that was worrying him, which was that of disposing of the case against Jesus. He did not believe that Jesus was guilty of any wrong, yet was hesitating about declaring him free because of political reasons (John 19: 12).

Verse 8. The desire of Herod to see Jesus was prompted largely by curiosity about His miraculous works; in chapter 9: 9 this desire is mentioned the first time.

Verse 9. Jesus knew that Herod had no just reason for his curiosity, hence He maintained the same silence before him that Pilate had received.

Verse 10. The chief priests and scribes had followed Jesus as he was escorted into the presence of Herod. But their clamor against Jesus did not have much effect on Herod, at least it did not induce him to attach any legal charge against Him.

Verse 11. The actions listed in this verse were for the purpose of belittling Jesus, not to constitute any formal accusation against Him. (See verse 15.)

Verse 12. The usual interpretation of this passage is that Pilate and Herod dropped their personal differences, in order to unite against Christ. They did not unite because of any common enmity against Christ, for neither of them had any such a feeling. But Herod wanted to see Jesus, and Pilate granted the courtesy of a personal interview with his noted prisoner. It was this judicial recognition that broke down the long-standing feud between the two political rulers.

Verse 13. This group which Pilate called together was composed of all the persons who were interested in the case. The chief priests were the ones to get Jesus into the courts (Mark 15: 10), and the people were those who had the voice about what prisoner was to be released under the custom (Matthew 27: 15), hence it was a representative audience to which Pilate was preparing to speak.

Verses 14, 15. A brief reference is made to this paragraph at verse 12. Here were two court rulers, former personal enemies, but agreeing on the innocence of Jesus.

Verse 16. It was customary to chastise all prisoners before being released, regardless of whether they were considered "guilty as charged," or not.

Verse 17. *Of necessity* denotes it was an established custom to release a prisoner at that time (Matthew 27: 15), and Pilate thought it would furnish him a way out of his problem of guarding his political interests, without directly upholding Christ.

Verse 18. *They cried out* means the people, for they alone had the legal right to speak on that subject. However, their choice was influenced by the priests and elders and scribes (Matthew 27: 20).

Verse 19. *Sedition* is from the same word as "insurrection" in Mark 15: 7. The meaning is an uprising against a legal government, of which Barabbas had been guilty.

Verse 20. *Willing to release Jesus* means his personal feelings were favorable to Jesus. He wished the people would call for His release, so that Caesar would not blame him as a disloyal officer in the Roman government.

Verse 21. This cry was the demand of a mob.

Verse 22. It is an established rule of justice that no man should be punished who is not guilty of doing wrong. Pilate realized that nothing could truly be charged against Jesus, hence his personal conclusion was that he should be discharged, after the customary *chastisement*, which means the scourging mentioned in other places.

Verse 23. The two classes in the audience (priests and people), united in the demand for the crucifixion of Jesus. The inspired writer says their *voices* prevailed. There was no additional evidence produced; just the pressure of public sentiment.

Verse 24. It is bad enough to punish a person when a court is only doubtful of his guilt; but Pilate never expressed a single doubt as to the innocence of Jesus. Not only that, but three attempts to get an expression from the audience as to His guilt had failed. So this unworthy judge condemned Jesus to the cross on the sole motive that it was *as they required.*

Verse 25. A seditious murderer was released on the same motive that Jesus was condemned, namely, he was the one *whom they desired.*

Verse 26. *After* is from OPISTHEN, and Thayer defines it, "Adverb of place, from behind, on the back, behind after." It is clear, therefore, that Simon and Jesus carried the cross together, Simon bearing one end of the instrument but walking after Jesus. See the notes at Matthew 16: 24.

Verse 27. These persons following toward the place of crucifixion were genuine sympathizers. They were not ashamed to be seen showing deep sentiments on behalf of Him, even to the extent of going with him to the place of shame. (See Hebrews 13: 13.)

Verses 28, 29. This shows a case of misplaced grief. Jesus was going to suffer the ordeal of the cross, which would be the last of all his sufferings. These people were destined to meet with distress unequaled by any case in history (Matthew 24: 21). *Blessed are the barren*, etc. When parents are forced to see the suffering imposed upon their children, they will wish that no children had been born to them.

Verse 30. *Mountains, fall on us.* This is figurative, meaning it would be a milder fate to be crushed by a mountain, than suffer the distress caused by the Romans.

Verse 31. *Green* and *dry* are used figuratively, meaning trees that are alive or dead. In the application, they represent a righteous and an unrighteous person. If such distress will be imposed upon a righteous person (Christ), what may be expected to be done to a wicked nation, and its helpless citizens were destined to share in the general calamity, brought about by the wicked leaders.

Verse 32. These malefactors (criminals) were thieves (Matthew 27: 38).

Verse 33. *Calvary* is explained at length at Matthew 27: 33.

Verse 34. This ignorance of which Jesus speaks, applies to the Jews as well as the Gentiles (Acts 3: 17). Such ignorance, therefore, does not mean they were to be excused at that time regardless of any repentance on their part. In Acts 2: 23, Peter still held the murder of Jesus against this same people. But no forgiven sin is ever "remembered against" a person who has been forgiven. The meaning of the prayer of Jesus, therefore, is that even His murderers were to be given the same access to the benefits of His death that the rest of the world would have. That prayer was answered on the day of Pentecost when hundreds of them were promised "remission of sins" upon repentance and baptism (Acts 2: 38). *Parted his raiment.* (See Matthew 27: 35.)

Verse 35. Had it been a matter of power or strength only, Jesus could have even prevented their nailing him to the cross. But the deed had to be performed in order to fulfill the scripture predictions (Matthew 26: 54).

Verses 36, 37. The soldiers were the executioners for the government; four of them (John 19: 23).

Verse 38. *Superscription* is explained at Matthew 27: 37.

Verse 39. *One of the malefactors.* This is more definite than the account in Matthew 27: 44, and it should be used as a guide in interpreting that one.

Verse 40. The fact that the one thief rebuked the other indicates he had not joined in the reproaching of Jesus. However, we can be certain that one of them took the right view of the situation at the last.

Verse 41. *This man hath done nothing amiss.* The thief who spoke the above words knew that truth when he was first placed on the cross, as well as he knew it when he made the statement. That is one of my reasons for believing he was not partaking in the reproachful language against Jesus at all.

Verse 42. This man had been leading a sinful life, yet all the circumstances indicate he had known something of the work and plans of Jesus. They both were on the cross and soon were to die, yet he believed that both would live again. The request he made of Jesus was based on his faith of a resurrection. The wish was to be granted at some date farther in the future than the one at hand.

Verse 43. Jesus granted the penitent a promise to be fulfilled sooner than the favor he requested. *Paradise* is from PARADEISOS and Thayer's general

definition is, "A garden, pleasure ground; grove, park." In our passage he defines it, "That part of Hades which was thought by the later Jews to be the abode of the souls of the pious until the resurrection." Robinson, Groves and Hickie define it virtually in the same way. We have previously learned (notes at chapter 16: 26) that persons who are assigned to this place will always be among those who are "comforted" or saved. The conclusion is, then, that the thief was saved on the cross. That does not affect the subject of baptism or any other of the specific requirements of the Gospel. The Jewish Dispensation was still in force, hence the things that are now required through the apostles were not then binding. While Jesus was living, he had the right to forgive and save people on any terms He saw fit, or without any terms at all as far as the sinner was concerned. He forgave the woman of chapter 7: 47 because of her great love, and we have no evidence that the palsied man of Matthew 9: 1, 2 even had any faith, yet the Lord forgave him. But after the church was set up in Acts 2, no case is recorded where anyone was saved except upon obedience to the Gospel.

Verses 44, 45. The sixth hour is the same as our noon, which was the hour that darkness settled over the land. The event was prophesied in Joel 2: 30, 31.

Verse 46. See the comments on Matthew 27: 50.

Verse 47. In this account the centurion describes Jesus as *a righteous man.* The account in Matthew 27: 54 describes him as the Son of God; both statements are true.

Verse 48. Smiting the breast was an ancient custom in times of mourning or humble anxiety. (See chapter 18: 13.)

Verse 49. The women were faithful to the last, but with feminine timidity they stood some distance away watching. They had come from the same district were Jesus was brought up, Galilee, and had served Him on various occasions.

Verses 50-53. The notes on Matthew 27: 57-60 are pretty full, covering the subject matter of the present paragraph. To conserve space, I request the reader to see them.

Verse 54. *The preparation* is explained at Matthew 27: 62.

Verse 55. These women saw the manner of burying for the body of

Jesus, including the rolling of a "great stone" up to the entrance (Matthew 27: 60). That explains their concern about the stone as they were going to the sepulchre (Mark 16: 3).

Verse 56. *Returned and prepared spices.* That is, they made such preparation that same day, for the next day was a sabbath or holy day, it being the regular Passover day (Leviticus 23: 4, 5), which explains the statement about resting the sabbath day *according to the commandment.*

LUKE 24

Verse 1. *They came* means the women mentioned in the last verse of the preceding chapter. For additional comments on this verse, see those at Matthew 28: 1.

Verse 2. *They found the stone rolled away* because the angel had descended from Heaven and removed it, to open the way into the sepulchre (Matthew 28: 2).

Verse 3. *They entered in.* The description of ancient sepulchres may be seen in the notes on Matthew 23: 27, 28. They entered the main cavity and looked for the spot where the body had been laid. They had seen when Joseph placed the body there (Matthew 27: 61; Mark 15: 47), and were disappointed at not seeing it as they entered.

Verse 4. These *men* were angels in human form (Matthew 28: 2).

Verse 5. *Living among the dead.* This was the angel's way of saying the One who was dead was then living, to assure the women they need not be afraid any longer.

Verses 6, 7. The conversation referred to is in Matthew 17: 22, 23.

Verse 8. *They remembered.* This is more significant than might be at first realized. One form of evidence relied upon in the Bible, is the accomplishment of predictions that were made some considerable time previously. (See Exodus 3: 12 with 24: 12, 13; Matthew 3: 11 with Acts 11: 15, 16.)

Verse 9. *The eleven* leaves out Judas who had killed himself.

Verse 10. *Mary the mother of James* was also the mother of Jesus.

Verse 11. *They believed them not.* See the comments at Mark 16: 17, 18.

Verse 12. This event will be commented upon at John twentieth chapter.

Verse 13. The most important item in this verse is the words *that same day.* Verse 1 shows it was the first

day of the week, the day of the resurrection of Christ.

Verse 14. *These things* refers to the report about the disappearance of Jesus from the tomb, that had been reported by the women returning from it.

Verses 15, 16. *Holden* is from KRATEO, which Thayer defines at this place, "To hold in check, restrain." In Mark's account of this circumstance (chapter 16: 12), he says Jesus appeared in another "form." That word is defined in the lexicon, "The form by which a person or thing strikes the vision; the external appearance." The two passages considered together makes the matter clear. The person of Jesus was not literally changed, but since the eyes of the disciples were restrained, it caused Him to look like some other human being with whom they were not acquainted.

Verse 17. The changed "form" of Jesus did not make him appear as any unusual creature, for there is no indication that his speaking to them confused them.

Verse 18. A *stranger* is one from the outside, or one lately arrived at any place. Cleopas thought a regular resident would have known about these things.

Verse 19. Jesus never had to ask men for information, for He knew all about what was in man (John 2: 24, 25). By asking this question He induced the disciples to express their belief in the One from Nazareth.

Verse 20. The disciples correctly placed the blame for the death of Jesus on the chief priests and rulers. They had caused Him to be brought into the Sanhedrin, and there the rulers pronounced a sentence of death upon Him.

Verse 21. The disciples still had a temporal kingdom in mind regarding the plans of Jesus. *Third day since these things were done;* meaning the condemnation and crucifixion of Jesus (verse 20). *Since* (or after), gives us an important key to the day on which Jesus was crucified. The disciples said *today* (the day of the resurrection, verse 1), was the third day *since* the crucifixion. Then Saturady would be the second day *since* the crucifixion; Friday would be the first day *since* the crucifixion, and hence, Thursday would be the day of the crucifixion. This disproves the Romanist doctrine of Good Friday as being the day of the crucifixion.

Verse 22. *Certain women* are the ones mentioned in verse 10.

Verse 23. These disciples were gradually unfolding their story as it was told by the women. They seemed impressed with the idea that it was a report that could not be questioned, yet was a puzzling circumstance.

Verse 24. The story of the women had been confirmed by *certain* ones who went to the sepulchre afterwards, namely, Peter (verse 12), and John (John 20: 2; 21: 20, 24).

Verses 25, 26. Jesus then chided them for being so unmindful of what had been foretold, and for speaking as if the whole event was unheard-of.

Verse 27. *Expounded unto them in all the scriptures*, means He cited them to the Scriptures which predicted those things concerning Himself. The pronoun is the word of Luke, for the disciples did not yet recognize Him.

Verse 28. Jesus did this to test their spirit of hospitality.

Verse 29. Their kindness was from a pure motive of hospitality, and not just because of the importance of the person, for they still did not know Him.

Verse 30. One part of Thayer's definition of *bless*, is "to ask God's blessing on a thing, pray Him to bless it to one's use." This act of Jesus was the same as any one of His disciples can do for the good things of life. The main point in this verse is the fact that Jesus changed from being a guest, and took the position of host. The purpose of it will be seen in the next verse.

Verse 31. *Eyes were opened*. This reversed the condition that had been over their eyes which "restrained" them. No physical miracle was performed by the act of Jesus as host. But it was such an unusual procedure for a guest, especially one who had seemed reluctant to visit with them (verses 28, 29), that it aroused their attention and stirred up their memory. They doubtless had been with Him before his death, on various occasions, and had beheld just such a performance. This, together with His conversation on the way, in which the prophecies were cited, brought them "to themselves" and they recognized Him. Having accomplished the purpose of the visit, Jesus disappeared.

Verse 32. Robinson defines the original for *burn* at this place, "to be greatly moved," and Thayer gives virtually the same explanation. These disciples turned to each other after Jesus disappeared, and recalled how they had been impressed by the remarks which he made to them *by the way;* and that was before they realized the identity of the speaker. The whole subject flowed over their minds and filled them with a restlessness that was born of genuine interest. Under such a condition they could not be still, but must go and contact others with the interesting news.

Verse 33. Yes, these happy disciples arose the *same hour*, and leaving the village of Emmaus, they returned to Jerusalem where they found the eleven (apostles) and others gathered together, engaged in earnest conversation.

Verse 34. The two disciples arriving from Emmaus found this group talking about the great subject of the hour, namely, the resurrection of Jesus. They related to the two new arrivals the same news they had themselves heard from the report of the women.

Verse 35. Then *they* (the two) joined in with their story of how Jesus had appeared to them in the way. There could be no mistake about it, for He had sat down with them to a meal, at which He was made known to them.

Verse 36. It required only a miracle for Jesus to appear in this way among them, even as a similar feat was performed when he disappeared unobserved (chapter 4: 29, 30).

Verse 37. The human mind does some strange things. This group had just been rejoicing over the report that Jesus was alive and had been seen of a number of disciples. Now when He actually appeared in their midst they were frightened. In John 20: 19 is this same event recorded, and it states the doors were closed for fear of the Jews. They evidently had the doors fastened for safety, hence when Jesus appeared in spite of the secured shutters, they considered it was a spirit that entered.

Verse 38. Jesus knew their minds and that they thought He was a spirit.

Verses 39, 40. The body of Jesus came out of the grave in the same condition it had when it entered therein. That was necessary to furnish evidence that He was the same person who was crucified. An instance of this truth is what is recorded in this paragraph. And He retained that form as long as he was on earth because the disciples were in the flesh and could profit by association with Him only in that form. But we know it was changed before He reached heaven, for Paul says (1 Corinthians 15: 50) that flesh and blood cannot inherit the kingdom of God. (See notes in the following paragraph about his having no blood.) Also, 1 John 3: 2 says, "It doth not yet appear what we shall be," and later in the verse he says that when He appears we shall be like Him. John knew what His appearance was like while on the earth, which shows that Jesus was changed between the time of the ascension from Mount Olivet and that of His arrival at the gates of heaven. From the above considerations, we know the popular theory about knowing Him "by the prints of the nails in his hand," is an erroneous notion, which should be classed with the materialistic heresies of the Sadducees.

Verses 41-43. *Believed not for joy* is an accommodative expression, used in the same sense as a familiar phrase, "too good to be true." He called for food and partook thereof, as a further proof that He was in the same form that went into the grave. This raises the question as to how He could live and make use of food when verse 39 indicates He had "flesh and bones" only, but not blood. It is true the Bible teaches that "the blood is the life," and we know also that animal creatures cannot normally live without air. But Jonah lived three days and nights in the body of the whale without normal air conditions; likewise the Father saw to it that the Son could live forty days and forty nights without blood. "Is anything too hard for the Lord?"

Verse 44. Some commentators think this verse goes over the interval of forty days, to the time of the ascension. That idea seems reasonable to me as it applies to most of the remaining verses. However, Acts 1: 3 tells us He was with his apostles throughout the forty days, during which time He spoke to them about these great subjects. Doubtless Jesus concluded His 40-day period of teaching with the verses from this through the end of the chapter, and I shall comment upon the verses in their order, with our minds centered on the last hours of the Saviour with the apostles. The *law* and *prophets* and the *Psalms* is one classification of the parts of the Old Testament, all of which contained prophecies of Christ. (See Deuteronomy 18: 18-20 for the *law;* Isaiah 53 for the *prophets,* and the *Psalms* 16: 8-10 for the *Psalms.)*

Verse 45. *Opened he their understanding.* This statement does not require any miracle upon the minds of the disciples. The *scriptures* referred to were the Old Testament, with which they were familiar as to its wording. The means Jesus used to get the disciples to understand them consisted in quoting them in connection with facts which they knew had been and were happening. Such an effort was accomplished in John 2: 22; Paul used this method in Acts 17: 2, 3, and Apollos used it in Acts 18: 28. The specific passage that Jesus used for this purpose will be considered in connection with the following verse.

Verse 46. *Thus it is written.* We know this refers to Psalms 16: 8-10, for Peter quotes it in Acts 2: 25-32, and applies it in the same way that Jesus does in our verse. Since this is the only place in the Old Testament where the prophecy of *the third day* is said to be *written,* the question would be raised about how that phrase is connected with it, when the words are not found in that text. The answer is found in the statement that Jesus was not to remain in the grave long enough for his body to begin decaying, or *see corruption.* In John 11: 39 we learn that a body would begin to decay after four days, hence Jesus must rise before that many days to prevent his body from decaying. And the other requirement of scripture was that He be in the grave three days and three nights. All of this brings the conclusion that Jesus was to rise from the dead the third day, according to the present verse. *Behoved* is from a word that means, "it was necessary and proper." In order to fulfill what was written, it was necessary for Christ to accomplish these things.

Verse 47. *Repentance and remission of sins* could not have been preached in the name of Christ, had He not met all the requirements of this important prophecy. *Among all nations* signifies that Jesus died for the whole world, not the Jews only. *Beginning* at Jerusalem. That city was the capital of the Jewish kingdom, both religiously and politically, and it was to be the model and beginning place (but not the capital) of the kingdom of Christ.

Verse 48. This work of being witnesses for Jesus is stated more fully in Acts 1: 8. The territory of their operation was to include Jerusalem as the beginning place, then reach unto "the uttermost part of the earth." According to Romans 10: 18 and Colossians 1: 23, that commission was finally carried out.

Verse 49. The *promise of the Father* pertained to the outpouring of the Spirit, and it had been made in Joel 2: 28-32. The exact date of that event was not stated to them, hence it was necessary to tarry in Jerusalem until it came. *Be endued* is from enduno, and means "to be clothed with." *Power* is from DUNAMIS, and means might or strength. This qualification was to be upon the apostles so they would be able to "preach the Gospel to every creature," as Mark 16: 15 words it. This is why it must be said that none but the apostles were able to carry out the "Great Commission."

Verse 50. Mathew says nothing about the ascension; Mark merely mentions it, and our passage precedes it with the name of the location, which was Bethany, the home town of Lazarus and his sisters (John 11: 1).

Verse 51. Before starting his journey toward heaven, Jesus lifted up his hands to bless the apostles, thereby adding dignity and solemnity to it. *He was carried up.* Jesus could have soared through space independent of any visible vehicle, but this phrase indicates He did not do so. Acts 1: 9 states "a cloud received Him out of their sight."

Verse 52. *They worshiped Him.* This was after He had disappeared, which reminds us of the various meanings of the word "worship." (See the note at Matthew 2: 2.) *The great joy* was not over the disappearance of Jesus, of course, but for the assurances of the angels that are recorded in Acts 1: 11.

Verse 53. The temple was the headquarters of the Jewish system, and the place where the national worship was conducted. It was natural for them to be spending the time at that place, waiting for the coming of the power promised by Jesus. Their activities consisted in praising and blessing God, because they believed He was the One "From whom all blessings flow."

JOHN 1

Verse 1. *In the beginning.* It should be asked, beginning of what? The almost universal answer would be, "the beginning of time." That answer would be wrong, not only from the context, but also because time never had a beginning any more than did God. The Bible makes no distinction between "time" and "eternity." The sec-

ond word occurs once in the Bible (Isaiah 57: 15), and the definition is, "duration," and that quality belongs to the word "time" as well. The popular notion is that "time" means the period before the judgment day, and "eternity" means the period afterward; the Bible makes no such distinction. The English word "time" occurs several times in the New Testament, and it comes from 12 different Greek words, but in no single place is it used as an abstract name of the space this side of the day of judgment, as distinguished from that afterwards In the Septuagint (Greek) version of the Old Testament, the first three words of Genesis are exactly the same as the original for the italicized words in this paragraph, and have exactly the same meaning. The reader should consult the first paragraph in volume 1 of the Old Testament Commentary.

The entire context shows the writer is considering the work of creation of the heavens and the earth, which is the subject of Genesis first chapter. The Being whom we call the Son of God was in existence before the creation of the universe, but He is here designated as the *Word. The Word was God* is said on the basis that God is the family name of the Deity, hence any member of that family would rightfully take that name, just as any member of the Smith family is a Smith. That is why Jesus is called God in Isaiah 9: 6; Matthew 19: 17; Acts 20: 28. And it explains why the terms "church of Christ" and "church of God" means the same, and are used interchangeably in the New Testament.

Verse 2. This verse does not change the meaning of the preceding one, but it is a significant passage, showing that while the term "God" applies to each of the Beings considered, yet they are to be understood as two separate personalities, else one of them could not be "with" the other.

Verse 3. The pronoun *him* means the Word of verse 1, and whom we know as the Son in the New Testament. *All things were made by Him.* That accounts for the plural pronoun "us" in Genesis 1: 26; 3: 22; 11: 7. In all of the domain of creation, providence and redemption, God the Father and God the Son, worked together in perfect unison although they are separate personalities.

Verse 4. A careful attention to the language of this book, will show us that John was especially impressed with the divine character of Christ, and that He has been present, either apparently or otherwise, in all of the movements and influences pertaining to the works of God. *In him was life,* then, applies from the very "beginning" which is explained above. When God breathed into man's nostrils the breath of *life,* the Word contributed to that life. Of course, the writer is not especially thinking of that fact as he writes this verse, but is viewing the subject more directly as it pertains to His influence upon the spiritual lives of men as he lived upon the earth. Thus we hear Jesus saying, "I am the light of the world" (John 8: 12).

Verse 5. *The light shineth* refers to the general favors of a spiritual character that Christ has offered to the world. What John says about the attitude of men in darkness toward the light has been and always will be true. (See chapter 3: 19, 20.) *Comprehended* is from KATALAMBANO, and Thayer defines it, "To lay hold of so as to make one's own, to obtain, to attain; to appropriate." The thought is that even though the Lord has offered the benefits of divine enlightenment to the darkened world, the men groping in darkness (as a rule) refuse to take advantage of the light.

Verse 6. The preceding 5 verses may be considered as John's preface to his account of the Gospel. The importance of the light of heaven, as it was to be shed on the world by the personal life of Christ, was of such great proportions, that God deemed it well to send a forerunner among men, to prepare a people for the reception of the Light. That man's name was John (the Baptist).

Verse 7. It is customary, when some notable person is about to appear before an audience, for another to present or introduce him. And even this temporary speaker is supposed to be a man of some importance. He will usually make a brief reference to the timeliness of the subject to be discussed before the audience, and always bears testimony of the qualifications of the speaker to handle the matter. Likewise, it is stated that the forerunner of the Light bore witness of Him, and the purpose stated is, *that all men through him might believe.*

Verse 8. *He was not that light.* John was always attentive to keep the people informed about his relation to Christ in his work, and did not want them to confuse the one with the other. (See verses 15, 20, 27.)

Verse 9. The spiritual light that Christ had to offer was for the whole mass of mankind, not just for the Jews or any other special group. The word *world* is from KOSMOS, and with the exception of chapter 9: 32, every occurrence of the word "world" in this book is from that Greek word. It has a wide range of meanings, but the one that Thayer gives for its most general application is, "The inhabitants of the earth."

Verse 10. *He was in the world,* means he was among mankind as a citizen. *Knew* is from GINOSKO, and Thayer's first and "universal" definition is, "To learn to know, get a knowledge of; passive, to become known." Robinson defines it in virtually the same words. We might recognize a certain man to be John Doe, and yet not know, or care to know much about him. In that way the people of the world did not care to know much about Christ. (See the definition of *comprehended* in verse 5.) *The world* (mankind) *was made* (caused to be) *by him.* The words in parentheses are according to lexicon definitions. Verse 3 declares that all things were made by Him; also the definition of "us" in that verse is important and should be consulted again by the reader.

Verse 11. *Came unto his own.* Luke 1: 17 says of John that he was to precede Christ, "To make ready a people prepared for the Lord." These people were Jews, and had been all of their lives, but had to be reformed before they could become a part of the "people prepared for the Lord." That is why chapter 3: 25 makes a distinction between the Jews as such, and the disciples of John. *Own received him not.* The same "own" is meant in both instances in this verse. The meaning is, that the disciples of John as a group did not receive Jesus. According to Matthew 3: 5, 6; Mark 1: 5, great multitudes from the regions named were baptized by John. However, according to Acts 1: 15, only about 120 disciples, which would include the ones made by both John and Christ, were accounted for on that day of Pentecost. This explains the words *received him not,* stated in verse 11.

Verse 12. *As many as received him.* There is a familiar saying, "All rules may have some exceptions." In the preceding verse we learned that the disciples of John, as a group, rejected Christ. That was the "rule," and the exception is indicated by the italicized words here. For instance, the apostles had all been baptized by John, and were prepared for the work of Christ as soon as He called upon them. (See the comments at Matthew 9: 9.) Hence the apostles, at least, were among "his own" who "received him." *Power* is from EXOUSIA, and its first meaning is, "right or privilege." *Sons of God* or children of God, is a term denoting family relations. While Jesus was on earth with the apostles, the spiritual family of God had not been formed. But as soon as that was done (which was on the day of Pentecost in Acts 2), all of the faithful disciples of both John and Christ became "charter members" of the new family, and in that sense they became children of God.

Verse 13. People became members of the Mosaic system by fleshly conception and birth. Being born into the spiritual family of God is accomplished according to His will, that was made known through the Gospel of Christ. However, the persons specifically referred to at first in the present passage, were those who had been baptized by John. The principles involved in their birth, though, were the same as pertain to all others who afterward were to become members of the divine family. John's disciples were baptized upon their repentance, after having believed on Him (which should come after him, Acts 19: 4), while all others were to be baptized upon believing on Him who has come.

Verse 14. The *Word* was wholly spiritual until the time for God's great "will" (Hebrews 10: 7, 9) to be carried out, the purpose of which was to have a Son begotten by His own bodily vitality, but clothed upon by the flesh, so that He could become a complete sacrifice for sin. (See the comments on Luke 1: 34, 35.) *Full of grace and truth* denotes that through Christ we are furnished completely in those blessings.

Verse 15. *Of whom I spake.* (See Matthew 3: 11; Mark 1: 7; Luke 3: 16.) The word *before* is used twice, but it is from different Greek originals. The first means before in the sense of being previous; therefore it denotes being before in the sense of rank or importance. The second means previous in time, or in any succession of things. John's reasoning is based on the priority of Christ. Since He existed before John did, he (John) felt that he ought to accord to Him the place of seniority. Christ was six months younger than John in the flesh, but

existed before the beginning of the world spiritually.

Verse 16. *Grace for grace* is the outstanding phrase in this verse. *For* is from ANTI, and Thayer explains it to mean, "grace (or favor) succeeding grace perpetually, i. e., the richest abundance of grace, John 1: 16."

Verse 17. The law of Moses was truthful, and many favors were bestowed on the Jews by it. But in contrast, the system given by Jesus Christ was far superior, because it bestowed one favor upon another in more complete measure, as the preceding verse with its comments shows.

Verse 18. No man with fleshly eyes has ever seen God, for that would have caused his death (Exodus 33: 20). Yet God wished to give man some kind of glimpse at Him that he could endure, hence the Son of God came among man in the form of flesh, who then declared, "He that hath seen me hath seen the Father" (John 14: 9).

Verse 19. For comments on *priests* and *Levites*, see at Luke 10: 31, 32.

Verse 20. The messengers the Jews sent to John asked him about his identity. He was the most unusual person who had come among them in that generation, and it had raised questions and suggestions in connection with some historic characters of the Old Testament. Many knew it was predicted that *the Christ* (the Anointed) was to come into the world, and perhaps John was that person. The inquiry was doubtless prompted by both curiosity and genuine interest. *Confessed* often implies some unfavorable charge having been made; it does not in this case. The first definition of the original shows it to mean simply, "to declare." It had been the attitude of John all along, to be humble and to show deep respect for the One who was to follow him, hence he wished to leave no uncertainty as to his position.

Verse 21. The inquirers became specific in their questioning. By *Elias*, they meant the person predicted in Malachi 4: 5. *That prophet* was their reference to a prediction of Moses in Deuteronomy 18: 15-20. To all of these questions, John gave a negative answer which left the inquirers without the desired information.

Verse 22. The negative answers did not furnish these messengers with a satisfactory report to take back with them. They insisted that John take the affirmative line and give them a specific answer as to his identity.

Everyone knew the personal and family name of John, and hence this inquiry did not pertain to that. What the messengers wanted to know pertained to his connection with the vital affairs of the Jews.

Verse 23. John's answer must have been a surprise to these men, for he had nothing to say about himself personally. *The voice of one*, etc., was to direct their attention to what he was saying to the people in the wilderness, and not to anything pertaining to him as an individual. He verified that "voice" by referring to a prediction of Esaias (Isaiah), chapter 40: 3, 4, of that prophet's book.

Verse 24. The Pharisees were a prominent sect of the Jews in the time of Christ, and they had been so for several years before. They were very formal, and made great pretensions to righteousness. For a more extended description of them, with the Sadducees, see the notes at Matthew 16: 12.

Verse 25. It is uncertain as to when the practice of baptism began among the Jews. History reveals that it became a part of the ceremonies that introduced Gentile proselytes into the religion of the Jews, and in some particulars admitted them to the privileges of the same. But since those cases were performed upon Gentiles only, and John performed his baptism on Jews only (Luke 1: 16), the Pharisees thought the work he was doing was for the purpose of introducing some new system (which was true). And such a radical movement, as they thought, should properly be initiated by some note-worthy person, such as the ones they named to John.

Verse 26. John did not say anything to lessen the importance of his work, neither did he wish them to think he regarded it as the most important. Hence he stated that his ceremony consisted of water baptism only. He further told them that an unknown (to them) person was standing among them.

Verse 27. See comments at verse 15.

Verse 28. *These things* means the conversations just reported. There is some uncertainty with the works of reference, as to the exact identity of Bethabara, but all agree that it was a town on the east shore of the Jordan, near a spot where John was baptizing at that particular period in his work.

Verse 29. *The next day* means the day after the conversations mentioned above. John saw Jesus coming towards them, and he recognized him from the events recorded in verse 33. *Behold the Lamb of God.* This should be understood as John's presentation of Jesus to his (John's) disciples, and his speech corresponds with the opening of the sheepfold in chapter 10: 3. *Taketh* is translated "beareth" in the margin, and the lexicon agrees with it. The whole sentence is worded in view of the use made of the scapegoat to "bear upon him" the iniquities of the congregation of Israel (Leviticus 16: 22). Yes, Jesus became the scapegoat for the whole world, but that does not relieve sinners of their personal obligation to appropriate the benefits of that arrangement by proper conduct of life. The ceremony with the scapegoat was for the congregation as a whole, but the individual members of the congregation had their personal duties to perform in order to benefit by the national sacrifice. Likewise, men have their individual duties to obey, in order to obtain any benefit from Crist's sacrifice.

Verse 30. This is the same as verse 15.

Verse 31. John knew some person was to come among the people of Israel, but did not know what particular man it was. He was given a cue (stated in verse 33) whereby he would have the promised one pointed out, and it was to take place while performing an act of baptism. *Therefore* signifies that because of the part water baptism was to play, John engaged in that kind of baptism, as well as to be preparing a people for that special One.

Verse 32. Luke 3: 22 says the Spirit descended in a *bodily shape* like a dove, while the other three records say the Spirit *descended like a dove.* The point is in bringing out the idea that the Spirit had to be in some visible form, in order that it could be seen by John. Not only did John see this form descend, but it alighted on Him and remained for the occasion.

Verse 33. *And I knew him not.* John means that up to that instant he did not know this person as the promised Messiah, and the One for whom he was baptizing penitent Jews. There was to be no mistake, or confusion caused by a mere incident. It might not be regarded so strange for a dove to alight momentarily, but such a timid creature would not ordinarily be seen "remaining" on the head of a man. Hence that item was added to the circumstance to give it the force of evidence. Just how long before this verse it was that the baptism had taken place, we do not know; but it was prior to the "presentation" of verse 29.

Verse 34. After John *saw* the evidence so strangely demonstrated, he became a witness in person. The subject of his testimony was the great fact that the person he baptized under such unusual circumstances, was the Son of God.

Verse 35. This was the *next day* after the presentation in verse 29.

Verse 36. *The Lamb of God.* This phrase was significant especially to the Jews, because they were familiar with the national practice of offering animal sacrifices.

Verse 37. The two *disciples* were the ones mentioned in verse 35, to whom John repeated his presentation phrase in verse 36.

Verse 38. *Saw them following.* These disciples had hitherto been disciples of John. He had told his converts they should believe on the one who was to come. Now that One was in sight, and when John bade his disciples to behold Him, it meant to them that from then on they would desire to be in His company. That is why they asked Jesus where he dwelled, which meant for the time being, for the permanent residence of Jesus had been established in Capernaum (Matthew 4: 13).

Verse 39. Jesus invited the disciples to go with him and see where he was staying. As it was about the tenth hour (our 4 o'clock), they visited the rest of the day.

Verse 40. One of the two evening guests of Jesus was Andrew, brother of Peter. He had been a disciple of John, but upon introduction to Jesus, followed Him.

Verse 41. *First* is from PROTOS according to the commonly-used Greek text, but Moffatt says it is really from PROI. Thayer's definition of that word is, "in the morning, early," and it is so translated in Matthew 16: 3, and Moffatt so renders it in our verse, making it read, "In the morning," as being the time when Andrew went in search of his brother Peter. That is a reasonable conclusion, for we have seen that it was near the end of the day when the two disciples made their call upon Jesus with whom they spent the rest of the day. Then early the next morning, Andrew went in search of his brother, and told him the good news of finding the Messiah.

Verse 42. This verse corresponds in thought (but not necessarily in chronological order) with Matthew 16: 18. In that passage Jesus is reported to have said, "Thou art Peter," while in our present verse he said, "Thou shalt be called Cephas." The two statements are identical in thought, because the Greek words for "Cephas" and "stone" have virtually the same definition.

Verses 43, 44. *Day following* means the day after the one on which Jesus had the conversation with Peter. Jesus left his place of lodging and started to go to Galilee. Upon arriving there he came to the home town of Andrew and Peter. There Jesus met Philip who was told to follow Him, and he became one of the 12 apostles.

Verse 45. I have consulted half a dozen standard works of reference, and all of them say Nathanael was another name for Bartholomew, one of the apostles. The information will be useful when we get to verse 51. Philip told Nathanael the news of finding the person whom the prophets and Moses had predicted. This announcement would have been unmingled good news for Nathanael, had it stopped there. But Philip next specified the person he meant, by saying he was *Jesus of Nazareth, the son of Joseph.*

Verse 46. The information almost dashed the interest of Nathanael, for Nazareth was not a very popular town. The question Nathanael asked was not prompted by prejudice as against some territory besides his own, for he was himself a Galilaean. The origin of the lowly repute of that district is not known with certainty. Philip made a fair and logical reply to the question; *come and see.* He believed (and rightly), that no one could come under the influence of Jesus without being convinced that He is not only a "good thing," but the best that ever lived among men.

Verse 47. *Guile* means "deceit," and Jesus described Nathanael as an Israelite who was free from that evil. He made that announcement as Nathanael approached, but after he was near enough to hear it.

Verse 48. Nathanael was surprised that Jesus knew him, even though they were in the bodily presence of each other. Then his astonishment was increased when Jesus mentioned an apparently trival circumstance such as standing under a fig tree. If Jesus knew of that circumstance while not present nor in sight of it, it would prove Him to be the very person whom Philip described in verse 45.

Verse 49. Upon the aforesaid evidence, Nathanael acknowledged Jesus to be all He had claimed to be, namely, the *Son of God* and *King of Israel.*

Verse 50. Jesus made a remark about Nathanael's belief in Him, based on the incident of relating an experience he thought no one knew. He then notified him that he was destined to see greater things than such circumstances.

Verse 51. This verse names the "greater things" referred to in the preceding one. *Upon* is from EPI, and Greenfield defines it to mean, "On account of, because of." This prediction was fulfilled at the ascension of Jesus in Acts 1: 9-11. Here the "two men" were angels, and they were seen coming down in the sight of the apostles (of whom Nathanael was one, verse 45). Their descending from heaven, then ascending thereto again, was brought about by the ascension of Jesus. They conducted this mission "upon" or "on account of" the performance of the Son of Man who had just disappeared in a cloud.

JOHN 2

Verse 1. *Third day* means after the conversation with Nathanael in the preceding chapter. Cana was a town not far from Capernaum, and it was the home of the apostle Nathanael (chapter 21: 2). The text does not state whether the mother of Jesus was there by personal invitation, or that she was a relative of the parties.

Verse 2. The disciples of Jesus would mean those he had made after entering upon his personal ministry. It was appropriate to invite the disciples along with the Master.

Verse 3. *Wanted* is from HUSTEREO, and Thayer defines it at this place, "To fail, be wanting." It indicates that they had wine provided in the beginning of the feast, but the supply had run out. The mother of Jesus very naturally appealed to her son to help them out of their embarrassment.

Verse 4. Such an appeal indicated that she expected Jesus to perform some kind of a miracle, since the occasion was too far advanced to go to a market. But Jesus had not intended launching upon his public miraculous works in full scale degree yet. Moffatt renders the question Jesus asked, "What have you to do with me?" It was a mild protest against her attempt

to press Him into his work before he was ready.

Verse 5. The statement of Jesus to his mother must not have been very severe, and there was doubtless something in the conversation (not recorded) that indicated a willingness on the part of Jesus to help the group out of their difficulty. Mary instructed them to follow whatever directions He gave to them.

Verse 6. Moffatt says these waterpots could hold about twenty gallons each.

Verse 7. It required no miraculous power to fill the pots with water, hence Jesus bade the attendants do that. The lesson of human cooperation with the Lord is taught frequently throughout the Bible, showing that He will not do for us what we can do for ourselves. Jesus raised the daughter of Jairus from death, but commanded the people to feed her (Mark 5: 43). He brought Lazarus from the grave, but told the people to remove the grave clothes (John 11: 44).

Verse 8. *Governor* in this verse, and *ruler* in the next, are from ARCHITRIKLINOS, and Thayer defines it," The superintendent of a dining-room, a tablemaster." He then explains it as follows: "It was his duty to place in order the tables and couches, arrange the courses, taste the food and wine beforehand, etc." That is why Jesus told them to bear this wine to the governor of the feast.

Verse 9. The foregoing information explains why the ruler of the feast tasted the wine. He thought it had been provided by the bridegroom for the use of his guests. He was so well pleased with it that he decided to compliment the host.

Verse 10. When a man is drunk, his mind is rendered dull so that his ability to make distinctions is weakened. Hence an entertainer would reserve his worst wine until the guests were drunk, after which they would not know the difference. Attempts have been made by some commentators to explain away the seeming objection to this circumstance, by referring to the various kinds of wine that were made in Palestine. They explain that some varieties were not as strong as others, and that when men are said to be drunk on it, it only means they are filled to the point of being stupified. But the theory does not agree with the original language. *Drunk* is from METHUSKO, which has some variety of forms in the Greek New Testament, but all have virtually the same meaning. Thayer defines the word, "To intoxicate, make drunk; to get drunk, become intoxicated." Strong defines it, "To drink to intoxication, i. e., get drunk." Greenfield defines it, "To intoxicate, inebriate, make drunk; passively, to be intoxicated, make drunk." *Good* and *worse* wine are used in the sense of superior and inferior, meaning that after wine has been fully "aged," it is more satisfactory. Of course it would be no difficult task for Jesus to put this water through all the processes that nature does in bringing it to a state of clarification.

The attempts of friends of the Bible to meet the so-called objection to this event by appealing to the meaning of the word "drunk," are not justified by the original Greek words. But the whole effort is unnecessary, for Jesus did not claim to be attempting a general reformation of the whole world all at once. (There is no evidence that the related guests were disciples either of John or Jesus.) He once told his disciples, even, that he had many things to say to them which they could not bear then (chapter 16: 12), and certainly the world in general was not yet ready for the more advanced teaching on the subject of wine as a beverage. Another thing to note in the case, is that it does not say that a single person present had actually drunk enough to make him intoxicated. In those days, people did not have any process of preserving grape juice unfermented, hence the various passages on the subject only rule against drinking enough of the wine to become drunk. (See Ephesians 5: 18; 1 Timothy 3: 3, 8; Titus 1: 7.)

Verse 11. Jesus had not planned to open his public work of performing miracles yet (verse 4), but the appeal of his mother prompted him to act. It is noteworthy that the "beginning of miracles" was enacted in the district where he was brought up. *Disciples believed on Him.* This does not denote they did not believe previously, for they could not have become disciples of Jesus without first believing; but their faith grew.

Verse 12. Jesus went on down to the city that he had adopted as a residence (Matthew 4: 13), which was not far from Cana where he had performed his first miracle. Note that his *brethren* and *disciples* are mentioned in the same sentence, which refutes the Romish theory that the "brethren" of

Christ always means his disciples. The doctrine is used to support their unscriptural notion of the perpetual virginity of His mother.

Verse 13. John's record of the Gospel is the only one of the four that refers to all the passovers Jesus attended while on earth. These events give us the Biblical basis for saying that His earthly ministry lasted between three and four years. The present verse gives the first one, and the next is in chapter 5: 1.

Verses 14-16. See notes on Matthew 21: 12, 13.

Verse 17. The saying referred to is recorded in Psalms 69: 9. See my comments on that verse in volume 3 of the Old Testament Commentary.

Verse 18. The Jews were questioning the right of Jesus to "take the law into his own hands," so to speak, and inflict this physical punishment on the dealers in necessary articles for the service of God. They challenged Him to stake his standing as an unusual person by uttering some *sign*, which means some kind of event that was to come.

Verse 19. The Jews pretended to think Jesus meant the literal temple that was the capitol of their national service. But their conversation with Pilate, recorded in Matthew 27: 62, 63, shows they fully understood what temple was meant.

Verse 20. *Forty and six years* was the length of time that Herod had used in *building* (remodeling) the temple. But even if Jesus had meant that structure, it would not have been any more difficult a task for him to have reconstructed it in three days, than to perform the other miracles recorded.

Verse 21. Jesus compared his fleshly body to a temple because it was the structure in which his spirit was dwelling. Paul makes the same comparison in 1 Corinthians 6: 19 and 12: 12-26.

Verse 22. *Believed the scripture* refers to the prediction in the Old Testament that Jesus was to rise from the dead the third day. That prediction is recorded in Psalms 16: 9, 10, and commented upon by Peter in his discourse in Acts 2: 25-27.

Verse 23. This is still the first passover, mentioned in verse 13. *Believed when they saw the miracles.* That was the primary reason why Jesus performed the miracles according to chapter 20: 30, 31.

Verse 24. *Commit* is from PISTEUO, and as used in this verse, it means to put trust in another. Jesus did not put any confidence in mankind in general, and the reason is stated in the next verse.

Verse 25. Jesus knew all about the innermost thoughts of men, and regarded them as unreliable; he knew they were not to be trusted.

JOHN 3

Verse 1. *Ruler* is from ARCHON, which Thayer defines with the simple words, "A ruler, commander, chief, leader." I have examined four other lexicons, and they give virtually the same definition. It does not necessarily mean one with official authority, although it is so used in some cases. It generally means a man of outstanding prestige among the people, in whatever position he may be found; whether religious or civil, official or unofficial; a person of much influence. Nicodemus was thus respected because of these qualities, and not merly because he was a member of the Sanhedrin. Being a Pharisee in religion, he occupied a noted position in that group. See the long note at Matthew 16: 12 for the description of the Pharisees.

Verse 2. The scripture does not even intimate why Nicodemus chose the nighttime for his visit with Jesus, hence it would be speculation for me to attempt an explanation. Had it been worth-while for us to know the reason, doubtless John would have been inspired to tell us. However, there are indications that he left the presence of Jesus with a favorable attitude toward him and his disciples. (See chapter 7: 50, 51; 19: 39.) *Rabbi* is a Greek word, and has been transferred into the text of the New Testament by the King James translators in its original form. Thayer defines it, "my great one, my honorable sir." It has been used as a proper noun 8 times, and translated by the simple term "master" 9 times. The complimentary things Nicodemus said were not mere flattery, for he gave a logical reason for his statement. In truth, the very reason he gave for saying that Jesus was from God, was the one that John states to be the purpose for performing the miracles (chapter 20: 30, 31).

Verse 3. Baptism, which is the final act in the process of the spiritual birth, is not the only important subject connected with salvation under the Gospel Dispensation, yet it is the principal one considered in this conversation with Nicodemus; there is a good reason for it. The Jews placed much of their dependence upon their fleshly birth, being in the blood line from Abraham (Matthew 3: 9), which fact entitled them to be members of the Jewish Dispensation of religion. The text does not give us any of the introductory conversation between Jesus and Nicodemus, further than the complimentary words of this verse. Perhaps that is all that was said to begin with, but Jesus knew what was in his mind (chapter 2: 25), and hence the following conversation was on the subject uppermost in the mind of this Jewish teacher. He evidently thought his birth through the blood line from Abraham, would entitle him to consideration in connection with the kingdom that Jesus was reported as being on earth to set up. Jesus took that idea away by a sweeping statement that meant his fleshly birth would not be even considered as a factor in entering the kingdom of heaven. *See* is from the Greek word EIDO, which has such a wide range of meanings that space would forbid attempting to quote all of them. The context has to be considered in each case to determine its specific meaning. The definitions of both Thayer and Robinson that apply in this verse and others like it, are condensed to the simple phrase, "To experience." A sinner may see the church as an institution of which he is not a member, but he cannot have the experience as a member without being *born again.*

Verse 4. With a fleshly birth still in mind, Nicodemus asked the question stated in this verse. He evidently was not a believer in the theory of "Transmigration of souls" (Matthew 14: 2), or he would not have thought that even that kind of a new birth would be impossible, the only difference being the said · theory did not teach that a man would enter his mother's womb, but that of another woman.

Verse 5. The necessity of a new birth in general was the form in which Jesus opened up this subject to Nicodemus; He then entered more into the details of the process. The Greek New Testament uses the same word in the process of reproduction, whether the time of begetting or that of the birth is considered. The word is GENNAO, and Thayer gives us the two definitions, "To be begotten; to be born." If the entire process is referred to in our language, it is proper to use the word "born," such as saying a child was born to Mr. and Mrs. John Doe. But if the parents are referred to separately, the correct form of speech is that a child is begotten by his father, and born of his mother. Having only the one Greek word on the subject, the King James translators often give us "born" when it should have been "begotten." A more exact wording of our passage would be, a man must be born of the water, having been begotten by the Spirit. This begetting takes place when a man believes the words of the Spirit (1 John 5: 1), because that word is the seed (of reproduction) of the kingdom (1 Peter 1: 23). After a man believes this word, he is then put under the water, and as he comes out of it he is being born of that water, because the literal meaning of "being born" is, "to come out of." The person has then been born into the kingdom of God.

Verse 6. This verse is a simple statement of the difference between things fleshly and things spiritual. The kind of birth Nicodemus thought Jesus was speaking of is fleshly only, while he was speaking of a spiritual birth. It is true the fleshly body must be acted upon even in the spiritual birth, but that is because the inner man that is being renewed or regenerated, is living within the fleshly body.

Verse 7. Jesus is still reading the mind of Nicodemus, and sees him in a state of confusion over the things that have been said. He is inclined to question the conclusions that Jesus has presented to him, because he cannot understand all about them. As an argument by way of comparison, Jesus intends to remind Nicodemus that he accepts other conclusions in the domain of his experiences, many of which are as mysterious as this one about a spiritual birth that seems to puzzle him. Yet he will accept them on the strength of the evidences, even though some phases of the cases might seem mysterious. One of those circumstances will be presented in the next verse.

Verse 8. The religious world in general is overwhelmed by erroneous ideas about the Spirit, as it is involved in the process of the new birth. Then in trying to refute those ideas, the friends of truth may go to extremes and invent other notions that are likewishe erroneous. One of such performances is the strain that is put on the present verse, which is only an illustration which Jesus draws from nature, to prove to this bewildered Jew that he is inconsistent in faltering over the new birth just because some features of it may seem mysterious to him, when he will accept the fact that the wind blows, even though he cannot tell (from any evidence of his senses) from where the wind comes nor to where it goes after it passes him. *So is every one* means that every person who is born of the Spirit is supposed to accept the proposition on the evidence of God's teaching, even though some things about it seem strange.

That the passage means just what the common translation makes it say, and that it does not call for some labored interpretation to rescue it from the hand of "sectarians," I shall give the definitions of the original words in Thayer's lexicon for this verse. *Wind* is from PNEUMA, and the definition is, "1. a movement of air, (gentle) blast; a. the wind . . . hence the wind itself, John 3: 8." *Bloweth* is from PNEO, and the definition is, "To breathe, to blow: of the wind, Matthew 7: 25, 27; Luke 12: 55; John 3: 8; 6: 18, Revelation 7: 1; Acts 27: 40."

Verse 9. Nicodemus was still confused about the subject in general. It is as if he said, "I do not see how all of this can be, or what the action of the wind has to do with the Spirit in the new birth."

Verse 10. The word *master* is from a Greek word that means "teacher." Being a teacher of Israel would not be a reason why he should understand the new birth under the Gospel system, therefore we know that *these things* refers to the subject of the temporal wind that Jesus described in verse 8.

Verse 11. Jesus gives Nicodemus a mild rebuke for stumbling over what was said to him about the things in nature, which were matters that should be accepted as facts by every person who has made any observation.

Verse 12. The only verse that has any *earthly things* in it as far as this conversation is concerned, is verse 8, the one about *the wind*. This again shows that passage refers to the literal wind, and is used to illustrate the point stated in verse 10.

Verse 13. The thought in this verse is that the Son of man had previously been in Heaven, and hence was in a position to speak on heavenly subjects, such as the new birth. This passage closed up the discussion on the subject of the new birth into the kingdom of God that Jesus was about to set up on the earth.

Verse 14. The account of the serpent is in Numbers 21: 9. There were no curative qualities in the brasen serpent, but those who looked upon it were cured by the Lord as a reward for their faith. The serpent was placed on a pole so all could see it.

Verse 15. The literal sight of Jesus on the cross is not what saves sinners, for only a few men of the world could see it. Hence the Lord makes his comparison on the principle of believing, for the death of the Son of God on the cross will benefit no one who does not have faith in that great sacrifice.

Verse 16. The word *so* is from HOUTO, and means, "in such a manner." The point is not how much God loved the world, but what kind of love He had. The answer is stated by telling how God manifested it, which was by the sacrifice He made for the sins of the world. God is the maker and owner of all that is in the universe, and no sacrifice could have been so costly that He would have been unable to produce it. But the value of the sacrifice (from the standpoint of its price or cost) is not the question. It is the fact that God gave up His *only begotten* Son. There was only one being in the universe who possessed that qualification. The subject is explained in detail at Luke 1: 35, and I urge the reader to see and carefully consider that place, then come back to the present paragraph. *Perish* and *everlasting life* are put as alternatives for the responsible members of the world. There is no middle ground; every creature that God has formed is destined to experience one or the other of these lots endlessly, after the judgment.

Verse 17. The world was all under the guilt of unbelief before Jesus came into it (Romans 11: 32), therefore his coming was not for the purpose of pronouncing condemnation upon it; that had already been done. But the condition called for something to counteract it, and the Son of God was sent among mankind for that purpose.

Verse 18. *He that believeth on him is not condemned*, since faith in Christ leads to obedience which lifts the condemnation from him. (See Romans 8:

1.) *He that believeth not is condemned already*. That is because it leaves him in the state he was in before Jesus came into the world. (See the preceding verse.)

Verse 19. The condemnation that rests upon the world is not an arbitrary decree of God, but is based on the truth that men prefer darkness to light. The reason for their unwise choice is in their wanton manner of life, which is an evil one.

Verse 20. It is a bad indication when men prefer darkness to light, for it shows they are practicing evil deeds. If they were to operate under the light, it would expose them and show them to be guilty of evil practices.

Verse 21. On the other hand, if a man is a lover of truth, he will want his life to be revealed in order to see if it is correct. A sincere man, even though he may be in error, will wish to be sure of himself, and he knows he can never be certain as to what is right, except as his conduct is regulated by the divine truth.

Verse 22. Jesus had been in Jerusalem which is in the province of Judea. *Land of Judea* means the rural or outlying territory of the district. The purpose for going out there is indicated by the statement that he tarried with his disciples and baptized, all of which could be conveniently accomplished in the country.

Verse 23. Salim was a town not far west of the Jordan, and near it was a smaller place called Aenon. John the Baptist made that his headquarters at one time, because his business was to baptize people, and there was *much water* in that locality. According to some information in Funk and Wagnalls Standard Bible Dictionary, the water supply in that vicinity was in the form of springs.

Verse 24. This is the only place where John mentions the imprisonment of John the Baptist. The manner of the injection of the subject into the story, indicates that John's work was about over, and that his imprisonment was in the near future.

Verse 25. A distinction is made between *John's disciples* and *the Jews*, although John did not baptize any but Jews (Luke 1: 16). This shows that while all of John's disciples were Jews, not all of the Jews as a nation became his disciples, and hence were not the people whom he prepared for Christ.

Verse 26. This association between John and Jesus, and John's witness that he bore for Jesus, are recorded in chapter 1: 19-29. *They* denotes John's disciples who are referred to in the preceding verse. They seemed to be concerned because their teacher was not drawing the crowds that Jesus was having.

Verse 27. John was always unselfish, and appeared pleased over any good news about Jesus. Instead of being envious, he always taught that it was expected for Jesus to increase, while he (John) would decrease. He went further and told his disciples that the success of Jesus was given him from Heaven.

Verse 28. John also reminded his disciples that he had previously predicted this very turn of affairs. Such predictions and instructions are in chapter 1: 15, 27.

Verse 29. John continued his exaltation of Jesus and the diminishing of his own work and importance. He did it under the figure of a social custom regarding weddings. The superiority of a bridegroom is manifested by the fact that he it is who possesses the bride. However, the friend of the groom finds satisfaction in hearing the voice and seeing the happiness of the bridegroom. In the illustration, John is the friend and Jesus is the bridegroom, which causes him (John) to have full rejoicing.

Verse 30. John once more makes the prediction that the difference of importance between him and Jesus was to continue and widen.

Verse 31. John was an inspired man, and his teaching was directed by the Holy Spirit. But he was a man only, and his origin was wholly through the natural laws of reproduction. Jesus was both human and divine, and hence John said he was *from above*. That is why John was to decrease while Jesus was to increase.

Verse 32. As Jesus was from above, he was able to speak from personal knowledge. Notwithstanding, *no man* (comparatively speaking) seemed willing to receive the testimony of such an infallible witness.

Verse 33. *Hath set to his seal* is all from SPHRAGIZO, which Thayer defines at this place, "To confirm, authenticate, place beyond doubt." It means that when a man receives the testimony of a personal witness like Jesus, he is thoroughly convinced that the testimony is from God and must be true.

Verse 34. *Measure* is from METRON,

and Thayer's first definition is, "An instrument for measuring." It means that God did not use any measuring instrument in bestowing the Spirit on his Son. His possession of the Spirit was total; unlimited. From this we may gather further information on the much discussed subject of receiving the Spirit. The fact of John's stating that Christ received it without measure, implies that various measures of it may be given to men. Thus the apostles received that amount required to baptize them, and empower them to bestow spiritual gifts upon Christians. Then those Christians in the days of miracles possessed that measure that enabled them to perform miracles, but not enough of it to transfer it to others. And by all these considerations, we can understand how a person could be in possession of the Holy Spirit, but in a lesser measure than would enable him to perform any miracle. Further comments will be offered on this subject as the various occasions may suggest in our study of the New Testament.

Verse 35. A part of this verse was prospective, for not until Jesus had risen from the dead did God give unto his Son this complete authority. (See Matthew 28: 18.) But the unmeasured possession of the Spirit was given to him at his baptism (chapter 1: 33), and it abided with him throughout his work while on the earth.

Verse 36. For the first part of this verse, see the comments on verses 17-19. For the word *see*, read the comments at verse 3.

JOHN 4

Verse 1. *When* is from HOS, and Thayer defines it at this place, "II. as a particle of time; a. as, when, since." The Lord always knew what men were thinking and saying (chapter 2: 25), so this word means that Jesus did a certain thing because he knew, etc. The report that He knew about was what the Pharisees had been told; namely, that Jesus was making more disciples than John. That report was true, and it harmonized with what John had been telling his audiences about how Jesus was to increase over him.

Verse 2. Things done by the disciples of Jesus and under his supervision, are said to be done by Him. The original word for *disciples* has the nominative inflection, giving it the meaning as if it said, "Jesus himself did not baptize, but his disciples did."

The validity of baptism never did depend on the one doing the baptizing (except in the case of John the Baptist), therefore it was not necessary for Jesus personally to do this work. His first disciples had been baptized by John, who had come among the Jews to baptize them and prepare a people for the Lord. When Jesus took charge of these people prepared for him, it was proper that they should do the physical work of baptizing the new converts made under the teaching of Jesus. On the same principle, it was proper for the new disciples to assist in the work of baptizing the believers.

Verse 3. Envy is a terrible condition of the mind. The Pharisees did not have any great love for John, although they pretended to be interested in his work (Matthew 3: 7), yet they could not bear to see Jesus having any special success. Rather than come out into an open conflict with them at this time, the Lord decided to leave Judea and go to Galilee, which was the home of his childhood and early manhood.

Verse 4. Samaria lay between Judea and Galilee, which is the reason this verse says *he must needs go through Samaria.*

Verse 5. The history of this transaction of Jacob may be seen in Genesis 33: 19; 42: 22; Joshua 24: 32. When the Israelites took possession of Palestine, the territory later called Samaria was allotted to the sons of Jacob.

Verse 6. Wells were important improvements in ancient times, because it required much manual labor to produce one. Jacob either dug this well, or obtained it otherwise, and left it to his posterity. These wells had a curb extending above the ground for the protection of animals. It was on this curb that Jesus sat in his journey. Being *wearied.* This word is from KOPIAO, which Thayer defines, "to grow weary, tired, exhausted." We should always think of the Saviour as possessing a body that was just like ours as far as the laws of the flesh are concerned. It is true that he was the Son of God and possessed miraculous power, but there is not a single instance recorded where he used his supernatural power to relieve his personal needs. In all the trials and necessities of life, he met the circumstances in the same way that other righteous people are expected to do. (See Hebrews 4: 15.) When Jesus became tired from walking, he sat down

to rest for the same reason that other men would do it. It was about noon, so we may expect to see some people coming to the well for water. And since it was this time of the day, the disciples had gone to the city to buy food.

Verse 7. The city of Samaria was the capital of the region of Samaria (mentioned previously in this chapter). It was near this city where the well was located where Jesus was resting. The woman of Samaria was a resident of the city with that name, and she came to the well for water. Jesus was not too tired to use the opportunity for giving this woman some spiritual instructions. He always adapted his teaching to the circumstances of the occasion. Coming to the well for water indicated the woman was needing that necessity of her temporal life, and that would find her mind prepared to appreciate some thoughts on the subject of spiritual water of life. Jesus opened the subject by asking the woman for a drink.

Verse 8. This fact is referred to at verse 6.

Verse 9. The woman was so surprised at the friendliness of Jesus that she seemed to overlook the subject of water for the moment. She expressed herself to Jesus accordingly, giving as the basis of her astonishment the attitude of the Jews toward the Samaritans, that they had no dealings with them. One of the reasons the Jews had such a dislike for the Samaritans, was their inconsistent claims about their relation to the Jewish nation. Josephus gives us a description of this subject in his *Antiquities*, Book 9, Chapter 14, Section 3, as follows: "When they [the Samaritans] see the Jews in prosperity, they pretend that they are changed, and allied to them, and call them kinsmen, as though they were derived from Joseph, and had by that means an original alliance with them. But when they see them falling into a low condition, they say they are no way related to them, and that the Jews have no right to expect any kindness or marks of kindred from them, but they declare that they are sojourners, from other countries."

Verse 10. Jesus did not make any direct reply to the woman's remarks, but continued his own line about water. He went a little farther into the subject, and suggested that she would have been the one to ask for water, had she realized who it was who was talking to her.

Verse 11. The woman is still thinking of literal drinking water. It was evidently the practice for people to bring their own cord with which to draw water from the well. Seeing that Jesus did not have such, she could not understand how he would perform the act of courtesy for her.

Verse 12. *Art thou greater.* The last word is from MEGAS, which has a wide range of meaning. As it is used in this passage it means, "stronger" or more able or better equipped." Jacob was certainly as well prepared as anyone need be to get water from this well, for he used it to supply his family and also his cattle. Yet even he had to use some means such as a cord to obtain the water. *Father* is from PATER, and Thayer's first definition is, "Generator or male ancestor," and it was in this sense the woman used the word, for the Samaritans claimed to have blood relation with the Jewish race. This was true to a limited extent, which may be learned from 2 Kings 17: 24-33, which is commented upon in volume 2 of the Old Testament Commentary.

Verse 13. We have an excellent example of the proper way to approach a subject figuratively. Jesus did not launch upon the theme with the full comparison, for the woman would not have been able to understand it; instead, he unfolded it little by little. The woman needed only to be reminded that such water as the well furnished would not give permanent relief, but must be drunk of time after time.

Verse 14. The Bible does not contradict itself, and when it may seem to, there is always a fair explanation if we will search for it. Jesus pronounced a blessing on those who hunger and thirst after righteousness (Matthew 5: 6), but here he says that if a man takes a drink of the water He provides, he *shall never thirst.* The word is from DIPSAO, and Thayer's first definition of it is, "To suffer thirst; suffer from thirst." A person can have a healthy desire for a drink of water, which will cause him to relish the water and feel satisfied afterward, and yet not have to be in actual suffering for it; such is the meaning of the statement of Jesus. The person who accepts the provision offered by Jesus need never be famished and suffer for the want of a drink, for he will have that well always with him, so that he

may keep his desire constantly satisfied. That is what Jesus meant by the beautiful statement that it will *be in him a well of water, springing up into everlasting life.*

Verse 15. The woman was still somewhat in the dark as to the kind of water Jesus was offering her. She had the idea it had such qualities that it would take the place of that in the well. It is no wonder, then, that she requested the water from Jesus.

Verse 16. Having conducted the figurative comparison to the point where the woman was ready to make some personal application, Jesus concluded to arouse her to a sense of her own moral and spiritual defects. The subject of water will not be mentioned again. Jesus opened the next phase of the lesson by telling the woman to call her husband. This was not because He thought the man should receive some teaching also, for there is no evidence that he was ever called or appeared on the scene. It was the Lord's way of stirring up her conscience.

Verse 17. The woman said she had no husband, and Jesus agreed with her.

Verse 18. In this verse Jesus gave the reason for verifying the woman's statement in the preceding verse. This has been a stumbling block for many who have been in confusion over the Biblical position on the marriage relation. The only marriage "ceremony" that God ever gave for the institution is the fleshly union of one male with one female. That law is stated in Genesis 2: 24, and verified by Jesus in Matthew 19: 5; Mark 10: 6-9, and by Paul in Ephesians 5: 31. But the objector says this woman was thus joined to the sixth man, yet Jesus said he was not her husband. That is because the laws of man came in and required certain ceremonial regulations before a union would be recognized as legal. While the Lord did not originate this ruling, yet He recognized it, and requires his creatures to obey it.

The confusion is caused largely by the term "husband," which is a legal one and not a natural one, and has been used by the translators to distinguish between a man who has complied with the legal regulations for marriage, and one who merely has relations with a woman without having done so. The terms "husband" and "man" are from the one Greek word ANER, and mean the same as far as the language is concerned. "Husband" is the wrong word to emphasize in this passage, for the word "man" would be as correct a translation as the other. So that, it would be just as correct for the verse to be translated, "Thou hast had five *men;* and he whom thou now hast is not thy *man*." All of these persons were *men*, but the one the woman was living with was not hers, because they had not complied with the laws of the land that would give her legal possession of this man. So if the reader will place the emphasis on the words "had" and "hast," which is where it belongs, showing ownership, he will be saved the confusion so prevalent over this subject. (See also my comments on Matthew 19: 5, 6.)

Verse 19. By *a prophet* the woman meant that Jesus possessed superhuman knowledge, and as such he belonged in the rank of Biblical persons who could interpret spiritual matters. She was convinced of this by what He said concerning her domestic life. To use popular language, she was secretly living with a man "to whom she was not married."

Verse 20. When the woman concluded that Jesus was a Jewish prophet, she also believed he would be informed in all the matters pertaining to the history and religious teaching of the Jews, which explains her remarks in this verse. *Our fathers* means the early ancestors of the Samaritan race and nation. The mountain referred to by the woman was Gerizim, about 25 or 30 miles north of Jerusalem. Smith's Bible Dictionary says, "Gerizim was the site of the Samaritan temple, which was built there after the captivity, in rivalry with the temple at Jerusalem." In the article "Samaritans," the same Bible Dictionary says the following: "The animosity of the Samaritans became more intense than ever. They are said to have done everything in their power to annoy the Jews. Their own temple on Gerizim they considered to be much superior to that at Jerusalem. Toward the mountain, even after the temple on it had fallen, wherever they were they directed their worship. . . . The law (i. e. the five books of Moses) was their sole code; for they rejected every other book in the Jewish canon" [accepted list of books]. This information from the authentic work of reference, explains the woman's reference to the two places of worship, and what the Samaritan "fathers," and the Jewish prophets (of whom she thought Jesus to be one) said about them.

Verse 21. Jesus did not enter into the controversy between the Samaritans and Jews as to which place was the more important. It was not worth while to do so, because He was going soon to set up a system of worship that would not depend upon any particular spot, geographically speaking, for its genuineness. That is why Jesus said, *"neither in this mountain, nor yet in Jerusalem.* Not that men would not be allowed to worship God in those places, but their services would not be accepted on the basis of where they were performed.

Verse 22. The Samaritans rejected most of the Old Testament, which ruled out all of the prophetic writings except the few passages to be found in the five books of Moses. With such a partial basis for their guide, Jesus declared they did not know what they were doing when they professed to perform their services. *Salvation is of the Jews.* Every writer of the Old Testament was a Jew except Job, and he had some of the blood of Abraham in his veins. (See notes on page 351, volume 2 of the Old Testament Commentary.) Since the entire volume of religious revelation from God was given through the Jews, they would certainly know something of the subject. (See Romans 3: 1, 2.)

Verse 23. Notwithstanding this advantage the Jews had, the time was near when all previous modes and places for religious activities were to be replaced with the final system of God, unto which and for which all those forms were instituted among men. The outstanding feature of the new system was to be its spiritual character, in contrast with the formal rituals and material requirements the old law provided.

Verse 24. *God is a Spirit.* This does not mean that He is not a personal God, but his personalities are spiritual, hence He expects the worship offered to him to be spiritual. Such worship would not depend upon literal mountains or walled cities as proper situations in which to perform it satisfactorily to the Lord.

Verse 25. Although the Jews and Samaritans had no dealings with each other, and notwithstanding the latter rejected all of the Old Testament except the five books of Moses, yet they had a belief that a great person known as the Messiah or Christ was to come. This belief would be in harmony with a passage in their own document; namely, the prediction that a prophet was to come like Moses. (See Deuteronomy 18: 18-20.) They believed this Messiah was to be a very wise person, who would be able to explain all of the points that pertained to the Scriptures. The woman must have partly suspected Jesus to be that great One, from the wisdom that he had been showing through the conversation. Doubtless she began to think along that line as far back as verse 19, when she recognized him as being a "prophet." But she finally brought Jesus to a personal acknowledgment of his identity by her remark about the Messiah to come.

Verse 26. Jesus made this "good confession" to the woman, that he virtually made later to Pilate (chapter 18: 37), and that others are asked to make of Him.

Verse 27. The disciples marveled for the same reason for which the woman was surprised at the beginning of the conversation recorded in verse 9. There is no evidence they knew anything about her personal character, but they did know she was a Samaritan. The disciples were shocked, evidently, yet their respect for their Teacher held them back from criticizing him.

Verse 28. Having been convinced that the expected Messiah had come, the woman turned into a messenger, and left her original purpose that brought her to the well, and went into the city to speak to the citizens therein.

Verse 29. *Told me all things.* This is obviously an accommodative phrase. We have the conversation on record, and the part of the woman's secret life that Jesus told her is in verse 18. But if he knew the facts about her domestic life, something that she supposed no one but the man and herself knew, then certainly He could read her entire life as if it were an open book. And such a person, in her mind, had all of the essential qualifications of the one to be anointed, which means the Christ.

Verse 30. The people of the city accepted the invitation of the woman to meet the man who had told her so much. The result of the meeting will be seen later.

Verse 31. The disciples had gone to the city to buy food, hence it was natural for them to expect Jesus to eat. Apparently he did not show much interest in the food, after they had made the trip to the city for it, hence their insisting that He should eat.

Verse 32. Doubtless, the arrival of the people from the city, presented another opportunity before Jesus to engage in something more important than partaking of temporal food. That is what He meant by the indirect or figurative remark about his having food of which they had no information.

Verse 33. The disciples thought Jesus meant temporal food, and that someone unknown to them had served it to him while they were in the city.

Verse 34. Jesus used *meat* (food) in a figurative sense. The word is from BROMA, which Thayer defines, "That which is eaten, food." He explains the way it is used in this passage to mean, "That which delights and truly satisfies the mind." The context justifies his explanation, for it would certainly satisfy the mind of Jesus to do the will of his Father. To *finish* His work meant to carry through to the end all that was in the mind of God when he sent his Son into the world.

Verse 35. Again Jesus uses some things in the temporal realm, to illustrate those in the spiritual. Temporal harvests are possible only after certain waiting periods, while the spiritual harvest is always ready to be gathered. That is because the souls of men are always subject to being gathered into the service of God.

Verse 36. *Wages* is used to represent the reward that all men will receive who do faithful work for the Lord. The production of a crop requires both a sowing and a reaping, but these are not always done by the same man. However, if they are working in harmony with each other, both will be benefited by the fruit produced.

Verse 37. Jesus only repeats the facts that are discussed in the preceding verse. It is a general principle, and the explanation will come in the next verse.

Verse 38. The *other men* means the Old Testament prophets and the work of John the Baptist. All of these servants of God had done much to prepare the way for the apostles to gather up the results. Paul teaches the same lesson in 1 Corinthians 3: 6-8.

Verse 39. The Samaritans were a mixed race, and thus were "part Jew," hence they were not regarded strictly as Gentiles. Jesus made a distinction between them in Matthew 10: 5, when he sent the apostles forth on their first mission. It also explains why the Gospel was offered to and accepted by the people of Samaria (Acts 8: 5-12), when it is generally believed (and correctly so) that it was offered to the

Gentiles for the first time when it was offered to Cornelius in Acts 10.

Verse 40. The Samaritans were so much interested in Christ, they urged him to spend some time with them. He did so, delaying his journey for two days.

Verse 41. The delay was profitable, for *many more believed* on Him.

Verse 42. There is no evidence that Jesus performed any miracle among these Samaritans. They explained their conversion on the ground of hearing His word. Jesus was able by his teaching to convince these people that he was the great One that was promised in the Scriptures and had been taught them by their leaders.

Verse 43. Galilee was an extensive territory, so that Jesus could go into that district, and yet not go into the immediate vicinity of Nazareth, which was originally considered his own country. (See Matthew 4: 13; 13: 54-57; Luke 4: 23.)

Verse 44. Because of the truth stated here, Jesus came into that part of Galilee that contained Cana (verse 46), instead of that where Nazareth was located.

Verse 45. The Galilaeans (those not in the region of Nazareth) received Jesus, because they had seen his works at the feast of the Passover in Jerusalem.

Verse 46. Smith's Bible Dictionary says Cana was not far from Capernaum, and the arrival at Cana was soon known at Capernaum. The miracle of making wine out of water had doubtless been reported generally, and the people of the neighboring towns were convinced that Jesus was able to accomplish miraculous cures. A *nobleman* was an officer serving next to a king, and therefore was an important person.

Verse 47. The nobleman went in person to Cana, and begged Jesus to come heal his son who was at the point of death from a serious fever.

Verse 48. As a test of the nobleman's faith, Jesus intimated that he would first perform some miracle, as evidence that he was able to accomplish healing the boy.

Verse 49. The nobleman was already satisfied about the ability of Jesus to work miracles. Of course Jesus knew his mind, but it is the Lord's will that people express their faith outwardly, and this was the way that Jesus brought forth the remark

of the nobleman. It was natural for him to feel anxious, because it was his son who was seriously ill, hence he pressed his request very earnestly.

Verse 50. Jesus did not accompany the father back to his home, but bade him go on his way, with the assurance that his son would live. The nobleman was satisfied to leave for home alone, because he believed the word of Jesus. Had he lingered to repeat his request for Jesus to go with him, it would have indicated that he was in doubt.

Verse 51. The nobleman did not reach home until the day after his conversation with Jesus. His servants saw him coming and went to meet him with the good news.

Verse 52. He did not question the word of his servants, but wanted to check on the saying of Jesus; he asked them when the son began to improve. The seventh hour would be the same as our 1 P. M., and it explains why the nobleman was not able to reach home until the next day.

Verse 53. The report coincided with the hour in which Jesus assured him that his son would live. We note the servants said the fever *left him* at that hour, but his full recovery was a matter of some time. This should not disturb us, for Jesus only said "thy son liveth," and to start his improvement, He caused the fever to leave him immediately. His convalescence could be taken care of by nature, without any miracle. The case caused the whole household to become believers in Jesus.

Verse 54. *Second miracle* means in Cana; the first is in chapter 2.

JOHN 5

Verse 1. This feast was the Passover, and the second one that Jesus attended after his baptism. The next one is recorded in chapter 6: 4.

Verse 2. *Sheep market* is from the Greek word PROBATIKOS, which Thayer defines, "the sheep-gate." The Greek translation of the Old Testament (the Septuagint) uses the same word, and Donnegan defines it, "Pertaining to sheep, or to cattle, especially sheep." This spot is mentioned in Nehemiah 3: 1, 32. *Porch* is from STOA, which the lexicon of Thayer defines, "a portico, a covered colonnade where people can stand or walk, protected from the weather and the heat of the sun."

Verses 3, 4. The greater part of this paragraph is omitted from some translations, on the ground that some early

Greek manuscripts do not contain it. I have consulted the information that is available to me, with the result that the subject is left in an indefinite state. Perhaps it is because there is little evidence of importance on the controversy. Various kinds of miracles were performed in ancient times, and the one described in this passage would not be entirely out of line with the Lord's manner of doing things. However, whether the miracle actually occurred as stated, or that the people had a tradition on which they relied, is immaterial as far as the work of Jesus is concerned. That some periodical disturbance of the water took place need not be disputed. Jesus did not make any controversy about the doctrine of "Transmigration of souls" (Matthew 14: 2), but healed the blind man independently of it. The writer does not show Jesus as even referring to the question of this agitation of the pool, therefore I shall comment on the remaining verses in their order.

Verse 5. This man's case was chronic, for he had been afflicted 38 years.

Verse 6. Of course Jesus knew the history of the case, but his approach to the patient was made in the spirit of a sympathetic well-wisher. The patient did not know the identity of Jesus (verse 13) until sometime afterward.

Verse 7. The impotent (weak or feeble) man had confidence in the curative properties of the water, whatever was the basis of that belief. He explained to Jesus why he was compelled to lie there from time to time, not getting any relief from his illness.

Verse 8. Jesus made no reference to the proposition in connection with the pool, but bade the man not only to arise, but to carry his bed as he walked.

Verse 9. A nervous person might be induced to bestir himself momentarily, by the influence of suggestion. But it would require something more than "mind over matter" to enable a man who had been physically helpless for 38 years, not only to walk, but to carry a bed that was large enough to support a man. His recovery was complete and immediate, because that was what Jesus willed to be accomplished in this case. In that of the nobleman's son (preceding chapter), Jesus only professed to start him on the road to recovery, which was done by causing the "temperature" to drop to normal. That feat was also immediate, for it

was done the "same hour" that Jesus spoke the word.

Verse 10. The Jews were not candid enough to object to the curing of the impotent man, but pretended to be opposed to breaking the sabbath.

Verse 11. The man did not express any conclusion, but the facts he related implied one that could not be disputed. Anyone could tell a man to get up and carry his bed, but not everyone who might say that could enable the patient to do so. This combination of facts was the strongest kind of evidence that it was no ordinary person who had befriended the impotent man.

Verse 12. We are not told whether the Jews suspected who the man's benefactor was, but it is reasonable to suppose they did, in view of their hatred for Him.

Verse 13. After Jesus cured the weak man, He took advantage of the crowd to disappear. Hence the former victim of the affliction told the truth, if he stated he did not know who it was who told him to carry his bed.

Verse 14. *Sin no more.* We are not informed what sin the man had committed, that brought on him the chronic case of physical prostration. And it did not have to be a miraculous punishment, although God did sometimes send physical judgments upon people in the days of miracles. But there are some sins of a moral nature, that can result in serious consequences to a man's health. But if this man should be so ungrateful as to sin again, the Lord would not wait for nature to inflict a penalty upon him, but would send one Himself, that would be worse than the affliction he had this time.

Verse 15. The meeting of Jesus and the man in the temple, and the conversation which they had, revealed to the former impotent man who his benefactor was. He seems to have thought the Jews had asked him the question about the identity of his friend, for the sake of information. Now that he has learned who he was, he felt that he should give them the information he could not before.

Verse 16. The Jews evidently knew that Jesus was going about doing good to the people, and that he was likely the one who had healed the impotent man. But their envy of Him was made more bitter because the man had learned about the identity of his friend, and seemed to be interested in His work. The envy of the Jews became so active they had a desire to kill Him.

Verse 17. The Jews were so bitter against Jesus that they accused him of breaking the sabbath. Jesus made his reply by asserting his relation with God as his Father, and his cooperation with Him in the good work. The Jews made great claims of respect for God, and would never admit that He would violate the very day that he had declared to be holy. Now that Jesus claimed his work (even on the sabbath) to be as a co-worker with God, it was more than they could stand.

Verse 18. A new cause for murderous hatred was furnished the Jews by the answer of Jesus. They pretended to be outraged at his claim of being the Son of God.

Verse 19. This verse expresses a situation that is generally true in principle. A dutiful son will logically imitate the actions of his father. Since God does not hesitate to bestow works of mercy on the unfortunate, even on the sabbath day, so the Son may properly do the same without being condemned as a breaker of the holy day.

Verse 20. On the principle set forth in the preceding verse, a loving and divine Father will take his Son into his confidence, and inform him of the great things that are being done through Providential benevolence. And there were to be still greater things done than the healing of an afflicted man on the sabbath day.

Verse 21. One of the works that are greater than healing a sick man, is that of raising a man from the dead. The Son was destined also to perform that great work of quickening the dead by the sound of his voice.

Verse 22. *Hath committed all judgment unto the Son.* This was said in prospect, looking to the time when the Son would complete the test. (See Matthew 28: 18.)

Verse 23. Men are required to recognize the close relationship between the Father and the Son, in order to receive the favor of either of them.

Verse 24. The subject in the preceding verse is continued in this as to the close partnership between the Father and the Son. The passage adds the results for those who recognize that union, by showing a practical belief in the same. *Death* and *life* refers to spiritual matters, because all who refuse to accept God and Christ and obey their law will be condemned to everlasting death.

Verse 25. This passage pertains to the same death and life as that in the preceding verse. To *hear* the voice of the Son of God in the sense of this statement, means to heed and obey His requirements; a dead faith will not save.

Verse 26. A father transfers his characteristics to his offspring as an established rule. This relation between God and Christ is no exception to the rule, for Jesus is able to impart spiritual life to those who will accept it, because He is the Son of the life-giving God.

Verse 27. This inheritance that Christ received from his Father, entitled him to be the executioner of the divine judgment upon the world.

Verse 28. Jesus passes from figurative and spiritual language, to literal or physical. The graves are the enclosures for the bodies of those who have died, through separation of soul and body. These dead shall be brought out of their graves literally by the call of Jesus on the day of the general resurrection.

Verse 29. There will be only one literal resurrection day, on which all of the dead will come forth. The fact of coming from the dead will not depend upon character or conduct, for the whole human family that has died will come forth. *The hour* that the voice of Christ calls is the one instant when the tremendous event will occur. But as to what will be awaiting them after coming to life again, that does depend on their conduct, as stated in this verse. This resurrection and what will follow is predicted in Daniel 12: 2.

Verse 30. This is the same teaching as that in verse 19.

Verse 31. *Bear witness of myself.* This means if His testimony is by itself, and not in harmony with that of his Father. That is why Jesus always worked in harmony with God, so that their united efforts would verify each other.

Verse 32. Not only did God verify the Sonship of Christ (Matthew 3: 17), but there was another among men who added his testimony to the divine witness, to be named soon.

Verse 33. John the Baptist was the other witness referred to above. The time the Jews sent to inquire of John is recorded in chapter 1: 19-27.

Verse 34. *I receive not testimony from man.* This denotes that Jesus did not depend on human testimony for his authority. *That ye might be saved.* The standing of Jesus did not depend upon human testimony. However, the salvation of men does depend on their faith, and Jesus was willing to cite them to any truth that would strengthen their faith. The corroborating testimony of John was a help in that direction.

Verse 35. The Jews had once shown much admiration for the work of John. If they became cool toward that testimony, that would not weaken its truthfulness.

Verse 36. The works to which Jesus refers are those mentioned in chapter 20: 30, 31. Had he been an impostor, he could not have performed these deeds.

Verse 37. No man in normal flesh ever saw the form or person of God, for to do so would mean his death (Exodus 33: 20). But God wished human beings to have the testimony of Him, hence he furnished it by aiding the Son to perform the miraculous works.

Verse 38. The gist of this verse, is that all who will nourish the word of God in their hearts, will signify it by accepting that of His Son, whom he hath sent into the world in the form of human flesh.

Verse 39. As the King James translators word this verse, it sounds like a command or directive, telling the Jews to go and search the scriptures. Several other versions have the pronoun "ye" before the word "search," and the inflection of the word in the Greek composition justifies it. The context also bears out that form of rendering. Jesus was showing the Jews another of their inconsistencies. They professed to have so much confidence in the Old Testament that they would search its pages to find the conditions on which they could obtain eternal life. And yet, that very document had told the Jews that a person like Christ was to come.

Verse 40. The one person that their Scriptures predicted should come into the world to save it, these Jews refused to accept that they might be saved.

Verse 41. This could not mean that no man honored Jesus, for even the "common people (the crowds) heard him gladly" (Mark 12: 37). It denotes that Jesus was not depending on human support for his standing.

Verse 42. This accusation that Jesus made was logical and based on the close relationship and attachment that God and his Son have for each other. If they loved God from the heart (and not merely from the lips), they would necessarily love his Son, which the Jews did not, or they would not be wanting to kill him.

Verse 43. It is hard to understand why false teachers can have more success in leading people than the true. Perhaps it is because such characters are unscrupulous about the means they will use to put over their theories.

Verse 44. Those who receive honor from men are selfish, and also feel obligated to "return the favor" to the others. Such worldly-minded persons cannot have much respect for the testimony of God, which requires them to disown themselves.

Verse 45. The thought in this verse is that Jesus is not alone in condemning these Jews. The giver of the law of which they boasted to be followers, already accused them by his predictions. In Deuteronomy 18: 18-20, Moses predicted that a prophet was to come among the Jews, and we know that was Christ. In that prophecy, a condemnation is uttered against the man who would not hearken to the words of that prophet.

Verse 46. When the Jews rejected Jesus it was the same as rejecting Moses.

Verse 47. Reasoning back the other direction, Jesus concludes they are bound to disbelieve his words, when they reject the words of their boasted lawgiver.

JOHN 6

Verse 1. John gives us two names for the same body of water, and in Luke 5: 1 it is called the "lake of Gennesaret." Jesus spent much time near this body of water.

Verse 2. Curiosity as well as genuine interest, drew great crowds after Him.

Verse 3. According to Mark 6: 31, Jesus took his disciples and went into the mountain for relief from the crowds, for they interfered even with their meals.

Verse 4. This is the third occurrence of the Passover in the course of Christ's public ministry. The fourth and last is in chapter 13.

Verse 5. The diversion from the crowds was never very long. The compassion of Jesus was always present, and at this time he realized that the people would need food, being out in the unpopulated place. Jesus aroused the interest of one of the apostles by suggesting that they provide food for the multitude.

Verse 6. *Prove* is from PEIRAZO, and Thayer's definition at this place is, "to try, make trial of, test." He then explains his definition to mean, "For the purpose of ascertaining his quality, or what he thinks, or how he will behave himself." Jesus did not have to use any such means for his own information (chapter 2: 24, 25), but wished to make it a test for the sake of an example. It was a test of faith, for the apostles had previously seen Jesus perform miracles as great as feeding a multitude.

Verse 7. Philip's remark showed that the "proof" Jesus used was testing him.

Verses 8, 9. Another apostle was being as sorely tested as Philip. He spoke as if the Lord expected them to feed the multitude with their personal supplies. John does not record any of the conversation that Jesus had on the merits of the test. But on another occasion, where this event along with another took place, He accused them of having little faith. (See Matthew 16: 8-10.)

Verse 10. *There was much grass.* This fact is mentioned to show the propriety of asking the people to sit down. It would have required another miracle to provide seats for five thousand people, hence it was perfectly reasonable to have them sit down, when there was an abundance of the green grass on which to be seated.

Verse 11. Jesus gave thanks, which was equivalent to "blessing" the bread.

Verse 12. *That nothing be lost.* This is the only instance of feeding the multitude, where the reason is given for gathering up the scraps. Jesus would never need them in his future service to the people, for even these materials had been miraculously produced. The reason for the instruction was to teach a lesson of economy.

Verse 13. People who are still hungry do not stop eating as long as there is yet something to eat at hand. The fact of having this much left after eating, proves that the multitude had a sufficiency of food.

Verse 14. The miracle served two purposes; it satisfied the hunger of the people, and also presented a proof of the personality of Jesus. This was one of the purposes of all miracles performed by Jesus. (See chapter 20: 30, 31.)

Verse 15. *Take him by force* sounds as if mere human beings could overpower the Son of God by superior strength. Of course we know that is not the idea, for He who could calm the storm and the raging sea, could certainly prevent any physical effort to take Him. But the people meant well in their intention to "draft" Jesus for the position of king. However, that was not the manner in which He was to come into his kingdom; besides, it was not the time for such a move. But rather than offend their good motives by overpowering force, Jesus quietly moved out and went into a mountain.

Verses 16-21. See the comments at Matthew 14: 22-34.

Verse 22. The people did not see when Jesus got out of the crowd to go into the mountain (verse 15), yet they realized He was not among the passengers on this boat.

Verse 23. These other boats came after the event of feeding the multitude. John mentions this to make the story clear to the reader. The people knew that Jesus did not get into the boat with the apostles. It might have been thought that Jesus was probably in one of these other boats. This is why John explains that the other boats came there *after* Jesus had given thanks, which would mean that He disappeared in some manner unknown to the crowd still remaining at that place.

Verse 24. Seeing that neither Jesus or his disciples were at that spot, they made use of these boats that had just come, and went across the sea to Capernaum, seeking for Jesus. They had no direct information that Jesus would be in Capernaum, but went to that city as the place most likely to find him, that being his residence.

Verse 25. The surprise indicated by these people in their question was doubtless sincere. However, Jesus knew their chief motive in following, and rebuked them for it.

Verse 26. The leading motive of these people was their temporal appetite. Jesus did not mean it was wrong for a person to seek to satisfy his desire for food, for such a desire is natural and needs to be gratified.

Verse 27. The Bible does not contradict itself, hence an apparent conflict in its language will be understood when all the passages involved are considered. Ephesians 4: 28 directs men to labor for the necessities of life, so we are to understand our present passage to mean that our desire for them must not be our chief purpose in the world; it should all be regarded in the light of Matthew 6: 33. *Sealed* is from SPHRAGIZO, and Thayer defines it at this place, "To confirm, authenticate, place beyond doubt." The idea is that we should seek the food that the Son of man offers which will lead to everlasting life. This is assured since the Father has placed his *seal* or stamp of approval on his Son's work.

Verse 28. The people were interested to the extent of making inquiry about carrying out the advice of Jesus that he had given for their benefit.

Verse 29. Much of John's account of the Gospel shows Jesus using temporal meat and drink to illustrate the spiritual. *Work . . . that ye believe.* Jesus meant that if a man really believes in Him, he will do the work that is required of him.

Verse 30. These Jews were still thinking of literal food, and were somewhat confused about how any improvement could be made over what God had provided for them in the wilderness. They called for some evidence that Jesus had anything better for them.

Verse 31. The Jews specified the provisions from God to which they referred in the preceding verse. They meant the manna that came down *from heaven*, a phrase quoted from Nehemiah 9: 15. The Hebrew Old Testament has but one word for the English word "heaven," whether the writer means the place of God's personal abode, or that in the material universe that surrounds the earth. It is true that the manna came literally from the latter heaven, but its true source was the Heaven of God. All of this led these Jews to think that no better food could be offered them.

Verse 32. In this verse Jesus distinguishes between the two kinds of bread. He does so by terming that from the Father as the *true bread*.

Verse 33. Jesus was presenting his comparisons in such a highly figurative form, that he drew the terms toward the application very gradually. In this verse the spiritual food is referred to as a person, without stating who that person is.

Verse 34. *Give us this bread.* This request seems to by-pass the highly figurative personal pronoun, and hold to the thought that the bread Jesus was talking about was something to be given and received, which indeed it was, except they appeared not to suspect what it was.

Verse 35. The Jews should have been prepared by this time for the direct application of the figures of which Jesus has been speaking, hence he came out with the unusual statement, *I am the bread of life.* However, this only brought the comparison far enough along to tell them for whom *he* of verse 33 stood. As to what sense in which He could be called the bread of life is still to be seen. For the meaning of *never hunger* and *never thirst*, see the comments at chapter 4: 14.

Verse 36. All through the years that Jesus was in his public ministry, the controversy between him and the Jews revolved about His divinity. They professed to have great love for God, yet were averse to the idea that Jesus was the Son of God. That is the thought in this verse, for Jesus accusses them of refusing to accept the testimony of their own eyes.

Verse 37. The manner in which the Father gives people to his Son will be brought out further on in the chapter. The point to be noted now is that being given to Jesus, and coming to him, are virtually the same. *I will in no wise cast out.* These words express the perfect cooperation between Jesus and God.

Verse 38. This verse is more along the line of cooperation between Jesus and his Father. Jesus came into the world to do that very thing (Hebrews 10: 9).

Verse 39. Whatever was included in the Father's will was included also in the purpose of the Son when he came into the world. That comprehended not only the replacing of animal sacrifices (referred to in the quotation from Paul), but the personal interest in the salvation of those who were persuaded to come to Christ. That personal interest is to continue even unto the resurrection day, when the dead in Christ shall be raised in His likeness, never to die again.

Verse 40. Man cannot see God and live, but he can see the Son, and if he will follow up that seeing with sincere belief, Jesus will bring him out of the grave to enter into life everlasting.

Verse 41. The Jews continued to stumble over their literal interpretation of the statements of Jesus. He used several terms that should have taught them that something besides material bread was meant by the subject under consideration. All of these were ignored, and they went back to the introductory sentences of the conversation.

Verse 42. The Jews could see no one in Jesus but the Galilaean, whose family relations they knew. Considering Him as a man like all others, they were in a critical mood over the claim that he came down from Heaven.

Verse 43. *Murmur* is from GOGGUZO, and Thayer defines it, "To murmur, mutter, grumble, say anything in a low tone." That explains why Jesus added the words *among yourselves*. On many occasions Jesus read even the minds of his objectors and told them about it. It is perfectly right to hold certain subjects in confidence, but when people are making complaints against what they regard as wrong doing in another, the fair thing to do is to approach that person openly.

Verse 44. Advocates of the theory of unconditional predestination m a k e much of this verse, but they do it by perverting it, and ignoring the rest of the teaching in connection with the subject. Verse 37 is virtually on the same thought, but the scriptural explanation is not given as directly as it is in the following verse.

Verse 45. *It is written.* The prophecy may be seen in Isaiah 54: 13 and Micah 4: 2. God *draws* mankind to his Son by teaching them about the ways that He would have them live. But the teaching offered to man will not avail anything unless he *hears* or heeds the things taught. This is the explanation promised the reader at verse 37.

Verse 46. See the comments on verse 40.

Verse 47. *Verily, verily*, has the idea of "most assuredly." To believe on Jesus so as to obtain life everlasting, one's faith must be proved by good works. (James 2: 26.)

Verse 48. See comments at verses 33, 35.

Verse 49. The argument of Jesus in this verse, is that the manna which their fathers ate in the wilderness was not the bread that would produce everlasting life, seeing that all of those ancestors were dead.

Verse 50. The pronoun *this* means the kind of bread Jesus was talking about. *Not die* is said in the same sense as *never hunger* in verse 35.

Verse 51. In this verse the Lord takes another step in his application of the figures that he has been using. Here the statement is made that man must eat of bread that is called the flesh of the Son of man.

Verse 52. The preceding verse makes the first move toward introducing the very important matter of eating the flesh of Jesus. Of course Jesus knew the Jews would make a literal application of the statement. That would call for the true explanation of the subject, which will include several verses because of the deep spiritual significance of the topic in hand. The reader should patiently follow the comments through this interesting group of verses.

Verse 53. When people persist in making a literal application of some declaration, it may help them to see their error to repeat the statement, but do so in a still more unusual form. The Jews should have known that it would be impossible to drink literally of the blood of Christ. That was true for two reasons; namely, that blood was to be poured out on the ground beneath the cross and never recovered. The other reason was the fact that the blood of Christ was that of a dead man when it was shed, and such blood will produce death instead of life. (See Revelation 16: 3.)

Verse 54. Literal flesh and blood will not produce endless life, hence they should have begun to understand that Jesus was not talking of that kind of material.

Verse 55. This is the same thought as the preceding verse, but in another form.

Verse 56. There is an old saying that "man is what he eats." That is true, and it applies to this verse, for if Christ dwells in the man who eats of his flesh, then the adage means that if a man eats the flesh of Christ, part of that man is Christ.

Verse 57. In this verse the general thought pertains to the merging of three beings into one; the Father, the Son and the devoted partaker of Them.

Verse 58. Jesus intersperses his speech with contrasts between the literal manna in the wilderness, and the bread that he was really considering. This is done to keep their minds alive to the main thought that it was considered necessary to impress on them.

Verse 59. The synagogues were structures erected by the Jews, and used principally for the reading of the law, and for teaching and exhortation.

Verse 60. Not only the Jews in general, but even the disciples were puzzled over this strange (to them) speech that Jesus was making. *Who can hear it.* By this the disciples meant they could not understand it.

Verse 61. The disciples did not make their complaint audibly, but Jesus always knew what was in the mind of men. He let them know about it by asking them if they were offended or caused to stumble at what they heard.

Verse 62. See the comments on verse 53. The same principle is carried out in this verse, except it is in a still more baffling form. By suggesting an event that would make it impossible to eat of the literal body of Christ, the disciples ought to see the point finally, that their Lord did not mean his fleshly body. Hence he indicated that he was going to ascend to Heaven, and that they would see it occur.

Verse 63. Many brethren use the latter part of this verse as if Jesus said, "The words that I speak unto you, they are the Holy Spirit." Such a use of this passage is not only a perversion of it, but it misses the very point that Jesus was making all through the chapter from verse 26. The Bible is nowhere spoken of as the Holy Spirit. It has been given by the work of the Holy Spirit, and it is the sword of the Spirit, but it is not the Holy Spirit itself. Jesus has been patiently laboring to show the disciples and the other Jews, that man must eat bread or die. But he wishes them to understand he does not mean temporal bread. After a number of statements along the same line, he concludes it is time to come out with the direct conclusion to his discourse on the subject of spiritual food, and he does so in this verse. It is as if he had said, "I have not been talking to you about literal flesh or literal bread, for that 'profiteth nothing.' I was meaning spiritual food; and to make you know just what I mean by that kind of food, I will inform you what it consists of. It is my words or teaching, for they are spirit (ual) and will sustain your spirit in the life for me."

Verse 64. *But . . . some . . . believe not.* This shows that eating the kind of food that Jesus had been discussing, meant to believe the words he had been saying. Jesus had specific reference to Judas, for he knew that he was going to be his betrayer. Judas had

the same opportunity of hearing the words of Christ as the other apostles, but he did not heed and believe them, therefore he was considered as an unbeliever.

Verse 65. Jesus then went back to the forepart of his speech (verses 44, 45), and made a specific application of that passage to Judas. It is not given to any man by the Father to come to Christ who will not accept the words of his Son. Judas refused to believe them in the sense of heeding them, therefore God would not permit him to be attached to his Son in the great work of human redemption.

Verse 66. The disciples who *went back* were not very much interested in spiritual matters. They were the kind described by Jesus in verse 26.

Verse 67. This pathetic question that Jesus asked the apostles doubtless was intended as an inducement to obtain an expression from them. The all-important discourse that Jesus delivered was for the benefit of all hearers, but it was especially needed by the twelve. They were the ones expected to take the same teaching to the world.

Verse 68. Peter's answer showed he had caught the point in the speech of Jesus. *Thou hast the words of eternal life.* This was the very thought with which Jesus concluded according to verse 63. The words received from the Lord constituted the spiritual food that he offered as the meat that would sustain mankind unto life everlasting.

Verse 69. In this verse Peter was speaking for the group of apostles, and as far as he knew, all of them were favorable to the teaching of Christ.

Verse 70. Jesus knew that Judas was going to betray him, but he did not point him out to the others yet. A man with the kind of heart that Judas possessed, deserved to be called by the term which Jesus used.

Verse 71. *Should betray him* is worded, "was to betray him," by Moffatt.

JOHN 7

Verse 1. *After these things* refers to the happenings unfolded in the closing verses of the preceding chapter. *Jesus walked in Galilee* means he continued to walk there, for he was already in that territory. *Jewry* is another form of "Judea," and Jesus avoided going there, at least for the time being, because of danger from the Jews.

Verse 2. This feast is described in Leviticus 23: 34-43. It brought many Jews to Jerusalem, hence the risk to his life caused Jesus to remain in Galilee for a while.

Verse 3. His *brethren* means what the word usually does, and not his disciples as the Romanists teach, for the *disciples* are mentioned also in the same verse. He was in Galilee, the home territory of his family, and thus it is clear why his own fleshly brethren would be near him.

Verse 4. His brethren made their suggestion in a critical mood. They implied that Jesus was inconsistent in avoiding publicity. If he wished to be known by mankind as the Saviour of the world, he should not be acting in such a secret manner.

Verse 5. John explains the criticism of these brethren by saying they did not believe in him. It doubtless was on the principle stated in chapter 4: 44.

Verse 6. Jesus explained his plans on the ground that it was not time yet for him to come out entirely in the open. Jesus was never afraid of man as far as his own comfort was concerned, but in his wisdom he never did anything prematurely. The brethren were not in any danger, hence their time (to appear in the gathering) would be whenever they wished to go, without waiting for the feast even to get started.

Verse 7. *Cannot hate you* does not mean it was literally impossible for the fleshly brethren of Christ to be hated. But it was wholly unlikely to occur, because all of the conditions were against it. They were regarded as ordinary citizens along with other men and were not "out on the firing line" as teachers against sin as was Jesus.

Verse 8. This verse has the same thought as verse 6, and states the reason why Jesus was not in any hurry to attend the feast.

Verse 9. Having explained his reason for not going to Jerusalem with the others, Jesus continued his stay in Galilee for a short time only.

Verse 10. After the brethren of Jesus were gone, he could go up unnoticed, being alone. This secrecy was maintained for the reason expressed in verses 6 and 8.

Verse 11. It was natural to expect Jesus at the feast, for it was a national occasion for the Jewish race. *Where is he* is explained by the statement in verse 10. Jesus did not intend to be prominently visible for a while.

Verse 12. The people were divided in their sentiments about Jesus; some for and others against him. While his presence was still generally unknown, the conflicting sentiments created an atmosphere of unrest among the crowd. The *murmuring* was as far as those sentiments exhibited themselves which is explained in the next verse.

Verse 13. The undercurrent referred to in the preceding verse was caused by fear of the Jews. Not knowing just what course they would take as to the treatment of Jesus, people did not commit themselves on the subject, for fear of finding themselves in an embarrassing situation when the issue came out entirely into the open.

Verse 14. The feast was about four days along when Jesus came out of his "hiding" and appeared first in the temple. It being the capitol of the Jewish religious system, it was proper for Jesus to show up there in order to do his teaching, which was the main purpose he had all the time he was among the people. *Taught* is from DIDASKO, which Thayer defines at this place, "To hold discourse with others in order to instruct them, deliver didactic [instructive] discourses." So Jesus did not merely utter some single sentences, but continued his speech to the extent of displaying a general knowledge of important subjects pertaining to the salvation of man in the kingdom of heaven.

Verse 15. *Letters* is from a Greek word that means something that has been written by an educated person. Jesus had never taken a course of instruction in any of their institutions of learning, hence it baffled the Jews to hear him speaking like an educated man on matters of such great concern pertaining to human conduct.

Verse 16. This verse answers the questions of the preceding one. Jesus was teaching the doctrine of his Father, and did not need the instruction coming from man.

Verse 17. The construction of this verse might seem to have things backward. We would think it to be necessary to *know of the doctrine* before one could *do his will.* That is true; however, if a person is not disposed to do the will of God, he will stumble and waver and be so unfavorably disposed toward the truth, that he will fail to grasp it when it is presented to him.

Verse 18. A man might be found who claimed to be from God, yet if he depended on the instruction given in human institutions, it would show his desire to make a display of his attainments for his own glory.

Verse 19. The particular part of the law of Moses that Jesus refers to, is the sixth commandment which is the one against murder. The sabbatarians try to make a distinction between the law of God, which they say is the Decalogue or ten commandments, and the law of Moses which is the "ceremonial law" as they call it. But here is Jesus referring to one of the ten commandments and calling it the law of Moses. All of this shows how inconsistent people will be when they wish to defend an unscriptural theory.

Verse 20. *Thou hast a devil* was their way of saying that Jesus was possessed with a devil (demon), and it had rendered him demented; they denied any desire or attempt to kill Jesus. Their memory seemed to fail them, for chapter 5: 16 says that the Jews "sought to slay him." That was after he had cured a man on the sabbath day, which they claimed was a violation of the law. But the law about the sabbath was a part of the same Decalogue that contained the commandment against murder, the very crime they sought to commit against Jesus.

Verse 21. Jesus was soon to remind them of the occasion when they sought to kill him. He first comments on the case by referring to their astonishment at the *one work* that he had done, while they also would do something even on the sabbath day that was as certainly a *work* as curing a sick man would be.

Verse 22. The Jews pretended to have great respect for Moses, whose law they accused Jesus with violating. In specifying a work they did on the sabbath, Jesus mentioned circumcision which also came from Moses. However, lest they misunderstand the real history of that ordinance, he interposed an explanation that it had been given to the fathers of old before the time of Moses. Notwithstanding this, they professed to regard the law of Moses so highly, that they insisted on performing his ordinance of circumcision, even though it should be done on the sabbath day.

Verse 23. The act of performing circumcision, which was a surgical one, was certainly as much a manual labor as was that of curing an invalid. Yet they condemned Jesus for doing that, while they persisted in doing the other.

Verse 24. There are people who resent being penalized or even criticized for their wrongs, and then will try to make a defense for their acts by quoting Matthew 7: 1. If they wanted to be fair in the matter, they would consider all that Jesus said on the same subject. In the present passage, the Lord gives more specific information on the act of judging others. *Appearance* is from OPSIS, and Thayer defines it in this passage, "The outward appearance, look." Robinson defines it, "External appearance, show." The Englishman's Greek New Testament translates it by the single word "sight." The outward or mere appearance of a situation does not always provide all the facts in the case, hence the honest thing to do is to investigate and get the whole truth. Then a judgment rendered on that basis will be a *righteous judgment*, and not the kind the first part of this verse says not to do, and the kind that Matthew 7: 1 says not to do.

Verse 25. These people *of Jerusalem* were local citizens, who knew about the plans of the rulers to kill Jesus. They thought they recognized Him as the victim who was to be slain, and were puzzled that he was still at liberty.

Verse 26. These people observed that Jesus was speaking *boldly* without being molested. They wondered if the rulers had concluded that Jesus was actually the Christ who was predicted by the Scriptures, and that they better not interfere with him.

Verse 27. There is a vein in the human mind that discounts a "home product" as being of little special value. That is why Jesus said what he did in chapter 4: 44 and similar passages. It was true these people were acquainted with the earthly surroundings of Jesus as a man, and there is no information that anything of a supernatural or even unusual nature occurred in his home life. That was because his divine personality was not to be manifested until the proper time, which would be after his baptism and he was ready to enter upon his public ministry. Another thing, these people had an idea that is not explained in any work of reference that I have, that the Messiah predicted in the Old Testament was to make his entrance into this world in some mysterious manner (which was true, but not in the way they meant), and that he would come from some unknown territory.

Verse 28. In the first part of this verse Jesus agrees with their statement, that they knew him and whence he had come. However, that applied only to his earthly family life, which is commented upon in the preceding paragraph. But as to his divine origin and personality, they did not know him because they did not know his Father.

Verse 29. The reason Jesus knew God was that he had sent his Son into the world. When Jesus came he was not in the dark as to why he had come. (See Hebrews 10: 5-9.)

Verse 30. It seems that any reference to the divinity of Christ always stirred up the anger of the Jews. Jesus asserted again that he had come from a source with which the Jews were unacquainted. That could only mean to them that the one they were hating was claiming to be of a higher origin than they. It was more than they could stand, but they were not able to do anything about it. The explanation for it is in the words *his hour was not yet come*. As long as the work of Jesus was unfinished, the Father saw to it that nothing would seriously interfere with it.

Verse 31. The people were not all as prejudiced against Jesus as were the Jewish leaders or rulers. Seeing the miracles that he was performing, they could not understand why there was any reason for looking for another to come as the Christ. On the strength of this, many of the people believed on him.

Verse 32. *Heard that the people murmured.* The last word usually means to complain in a low or undertone kind of voice, but it does not have that meaning always. One phrase in Thayer's definition of the original word is, "say anything in a low tone." The people had actually expressed themselves favorably toward Jesus, but they were doing it in a subdued voice. But the Pharisees heard about it and were envious of the kindly attention that Jesus was receiving, and decided to stop his work by arresting him. The outcome of this attempt will be learned near the close of the chapter. In the meantime Jesus delivers one of his wonderful discourses, the several verses whereof will be commented upon in their order.

Verse 33. This was a notice that the work of Jesus on earth was about to end.

Verse 34. As Jesus expected to return to his Father, he meant those unbelievers would not be able to follow him, even though curiosity might prompt them to desire to.

Verse 35. Since these Jews did not believe that Jesus came from the presence of God in the first place, they now would not grasp the thought that he was going back to Him. They wondered, therefore, if he meant he was going to disappear among some people that were beyond their visible association. *Dispersed* refers to the Jews who were scattered throughout various Gentile countries. Smith's Bible Dictionary says the following on the subject: "The Dispersion was the general title applied to those Jews who remained settled in foreign countries after the return from the Babylonian exile, and during the period of the second temple."

Verse 36. The whole subject was baffling to the Jews of Jerusalem.

Verse 37. *Last day, great day of the feast.* The day is described in Leviticus 23: 36. It is called a great day because certain religious activities were done on that day that were not done on the seven other days. Also because the closing day of any important period is regarded with special attention. The Jews had been engaged for a week, having a time of rejoicing, and enjoying the good things produced by their fields and flocks. It was hence an appropriate time for Jesus to call their attention to something else of which they might partake, that was of vastly more importance than these temporal blessings. Jesus offered to give the blessing of spiritual drink to any man who would come to him for it.

Verse 38. The original word for *belly* is defined by Thayer in this place, "The innermost part of a man, the soul, heart, as the seat of thought, feeling, choice." Robinson defines it virtually in the same way. The pronoun *his* refers both to Christ and to anyone who accepts the living water that he offers. Christ is the source of living water, and if a man opens his heart or inner being (here translated *belly*), that stream of living water will enter therein. Then such a man in turn will become a source of that precious water, supplying both himself and those he influences, with that which will contribute to his spiritual life and growth. This verse is the same in thought as the teaching of Jesus which he gave the woman of Samaria at the well. (See the comments on that instance in chapter 4: 14.)

Verse 39. The living water to which Jesus had specific reference, was the spiritual instruction to be given through the kingdom of heaven that he had been promising. That instruction would require a means of delivering it to the members of the kingdom, which was to be the Holy Ghost or Spirit. But that gift was here spoken of in prospect only, for it was not the will of God that it be sent upon the disciples until Christ was glorified, which was to be after he returned to his Father.

Verse 40. Jesus fills so large a place in the scheme of human redemption, that it takes many terms to comprehend the various parts that he was to play. Hence he is referred to as Christ which means "anointed," because he was to be a king. He is called Jesus which means "saviour," because he was to save the people from their sins. And he is termed a prophet, because he was to teach and prophecy. All of these functions and characteristics were predicted of Him, in one form or another in the Old Testament. The Jews knew about these various predictions, but did not realize they referred to the same person. For that reason we read about their mention of the different offices of Jesus as referring to separate persons. In the present verse ·they speak of him as the prophet, meaning the one predicted by Moses in Deuteronomy 18: 18.

Verse 41. Others thought of Jesus as the Christ or anointed One which means king, who had been prophesied to sit on David's throne (Acts 2: 30). But some of them rejected this idea on the ground that such an important person should have a more dignified residence than one located in Galilee.

Verse 42. They supported their idea against Galilee by citing the scripture that said Christ was to come out of Bethlehem. Their application of this scripture was correct, but they evidently did not know that while Jesus was generally known as a Galilean, yet he was born in Bethlehem according to the prophecy.

Verse 43. There was a division (in sentiment) among the people. That means with regard to their attitude toward Jesus; some for and others against him.

Verse 44. The sentiment of some who were against Jesus was so strong they would have *taken* him. The original Greek for that word is defined by Thayer at this place, "To take i. e., apprehend." He then explains his definition to mean, " a man, in order to imprison him." Among those whose sentiments were against Jesus were doubtless the officers who had been sent out by the chief priests and Pharisees. They would have acted upon authority as far as these Jewish leaders were concerned, had they arrested Jesus. They did not do so, and their excuse to their "superiors" will be stated in verse 46. However, the Lord in Heaven was watching over his Son, and was not going to permit any actual interference with his work until it was accomplished. Hence the inspired reason why these officers did not take Jesus is given in verse 30; *because his hour was not yet come.*

Verse 45. The officers who were sent to arrest Jesus returned without him. The chief priests and Pharisees doubtless were disappointed, and called for an explanation.

Verse 46. The brief but significant answer was, *never man spake like this man. Spake* is from LALEO, and it has such a wide range of meanings that the definitions will not be quoted in full. The word includes the act of speaking with authority, information, impressiveness, and on all of the subjects pertaining to human conduct. It is no wonder, then, that these officers said what they did.

Verse 47. The Pharisees concluded their officers had been captured by the teaching of Jesus, instead of capturing him as they were sent to do.

Verse 48. It was bad enough for their officers to be thus influenced by the hated Teacher, but they thought it would be a great misfortune for any of the religious leaders to be "deceived" by him.

Verse 49. *Knoweth not the law.* The statement of Nicodemus (next verse), and their reply shows the chief priests had Jesus in mind when they used the indefinite phrase, *this people.* It was not Jesus, but the chief priests who did not know the law, for it was the document that made favorable predictions of the very person whom the leaders of the Jews were condemning. (See the comments on chapter 5: 39.)

Verse 50. *Being one of them.* This means that Nicodemus was one of the

Pharisees. Chapter 3: 1 says the same thing in so many words.

Verse 51. All that Nicodemus insisted on was that the justice of the law be carried out in the case of Jesus. The question he asked would have been fair, regardless of whether Jesus was a good man or not.

Verse 52. This verse denotes that the Pharisees accused Nicodemus of siding with Jesus. The preceding verse only called for the regular procedure of the law, therefore their objection proves they did not want to do the fair thing about Jesus. The only thing they mentioned as a basis for their condemnation of Jesus, was his humble home territory of Galilee which was usually referred to unfavorably from a social standpoint.

Verse 53. The meeting "broke up" without any formal action being taken against Jesus, and the people all went to their places of stay.

JOHN 8

Verse 1. The Mount of Olives plays such a prominent part in the affairs of Palestine, especially in the time of Christ and the apostles, that I believe it will be well to quote from Smith's Bible Dictionary on the subject. "This mountain is the well-known eminence on the east of Jerusalem, intimately connected with some of the gravest events of the history of the Old Testament and the New Testament, the scene of the flight of David and the triumphal progress of the Son of David, of the idolatry of Solomon, and the agony and betrayal of Christ. It is a ridge of rather more than a mile in length, running in general direction north and south, covering the whole eastern side of the city . . . on the east the mount is close to the walls, parted only by the narrow ravine of the Kidron. It is the portion which is the real Mount of Olives of the history." The brief statement is made that *Jesus went unto the mount of Olives*, but in Luke 21: 37 it is stated that "at night he went out" and abode there.

Verse 2. The people evidently understood where Jesus spent the nights, and that he would return in the morning. In the early morning the people were on hands to greet Jesus. He did not disappoint them, but sat down and taught them.

Verse 3. The Jewish leaders had made a number of unsuccessful attempts to entrap Jesus in his teaching. They concluded to try the plan of playing upon his great compassionate nature, in the hopes of having him try to set aside one of the ordinances of Moses. They brought a woman who had been taken in the act of adultery and placed her in their midst.

Verse 4. Since the woman was taken in the act of adultery, they had the same chance of bringing the guilty man as they did the woman. The fact they did not is proof they were not concerned about the law of Moses. Leviticus 20: 10 and Deuteronomy 22: 22 is the law referred to, and it required that both the man and woman should be stoned. But they brought only the woman, because they thought the natural leniency of a man for the feminine sex would cause Jesus to set the law aside unconditionally.

Verse 5. The Pharisees made the correct interpretation of the law in the case, but their use of the word *such* condemned them, for that applied to both the man and woman. *What sayest thou?* This direct question was said in the tone of a challenge, thinking Jesus would say, "it would be harsh to stone a woman, so turn her loose." Such a statement would have furnished the Pharisees a pretext for accusations.

Verse 6. The inspired writer tells us these Jews said this to Jesus to tempt him. He knew all of that, and delayed giving them any answer at all. *As though he heard them not.* No one of these words is in the Greek text, but have been added by the King James translators as their comment on the action of Jesus in writing with his finger and saying nothing. He certainly did not pretend not to hear the accusers, for that would have been unreasonable for One who had been able even to read the minds of men before they said anything. My comment on the circumstance is that Jesus thereby showed his distaste for the whole thing. Another thing that was accomplished by ignoring them, was to force them to repeat their cowardly remarks, which would render their humiliation all the more evident when the time came. He finally stood before them and made a statement that must have surprised them. He did not advise releasing the woman (as they desired), neither did he give direct instruction to slay her. Another thing, even had Jesus directed that the woman should be stoned, they did not stop to think that they would have to be the executioners, having forgotten the stipulations in Deuteronomy 17: 7.

He that is without sin. This could not mean one who was absolutely sinless in every respect, for that requirement would have made it impossible for anyone to be punished, seeing their own Scriptures declare there is no man who "doeth good, and sinneth not" (Ecclesiastes 7: 20). The only conclusion possible is that Jesus meant the one who casts the stone must be innocent of the sin for which he wished the woman to be slain. That doubtless put them out of the right to act, for Jesus hal called that generation of Jews an "adulterous" one (Matthew 16: 4).

Verses 7, 8. Jesus placed the termination of the case at the feet of these hypocrites, then stooped down and resumed his writing to let them think upon the proposition.

Verse 9. *Conscience* is from SUNEIDESIS, and the lexicons give a various description. The outstanding definition of the word as Thayer gives it is, "The soul as distinguishing between what is morally good and bad, prompting to do the former and shun the latter, commending the one, condemning the other." These accusers were convicted by their conscience, which means it condemned their own conduct. That was because they knew they had done that which was bad, and hence were not qualified to be the executioners of the law at hand. *Went out* means they left the temple where they had been in their pretended attempt to enforce the law, leaving Jesus and the woman yet together.

Verses 10, 11. Jesus asked the woman if no man *condemned* her. This could not mean whether any man accused her, for they had already done that. The word is from KATAKRINO, and Thayer defines it, "To give judgment against one, to judge worthy of punishment, to condemn." Jesus did not excuse the woman's act, but he would not require that the ordinance be executed upon her. The accusers failed to execute it, which is what she meant when she said, *No man, Lord.* Jesus said, *neither do I condemn thee,* and immediately admonished her to *sin no more.* It was somewhat like a case where a judge hears evidence against a prisoner. He might consider all the facts in the case, and decide he would give him another chance. He would probably say, "I will let you off this time, but don't be guilty again." Another thing, the witnesses were the only ones who could lawfully execute this ordinance, and

they had left the assembly. Jesus did not care to act the part of executioners, hence bade the woman go, giving her an admonition concerning her future conduct.

Verse 12. After disposing of the incident with which the Pharisees interrupted his main work, Jesus resumed his teaching pertaining to spiritual matters. When Jesus said *I am the light of the world,* he only repeated what John the Baptist said of him in chapter 1: 6-9. Walking in this light means to conduct one's self according to the teaching that Jesus gives.

Verse 13. It is a commonly-accepted principle that one's personal testimony is lacking in force unless there is something or someone else to support it. The Pharisees knew this, and thought they could apply it to the assertion of Christ concerning himself.

Verse 14. Jesus did not call in question the rule to which they alluded, yet he maintained the truthfulness of his own testimony. He was speaking from personal experience and did not have to rely on other facts for its support. This truth gave Jesus a distinction above the situation of the Pharisees, for they did not have any "inside information" at all. But Jesus was soon to show that his own personal information was confirmed by that of another, and that therefore he was not alone.

Verse 15. *Flesh* is from SARX, which Thayer defines in this passage, "Man as he appears, such as he presents to view, man's external appearance and condition." No doubt the bodily appearance of Jesus was like that of the ordinary Jew, and the Pharisees classed him among the others on that account. Jesus did not judge any man on that basis, for he was able to see through the veil of flesh and read his mind.

Verse 16. Here Jesus states the reason for his assertion in verse 14 as to the assurance of his testimony, that it was verified by that of his Father. He testified to the divinity of his Son at the baptism (Matthew 3: 17), and also enabled him to perform miracles which no man could do on his own human strength.

Verse 17. Jesus often referred to the Old Testament for proof of his statements, because the Jews professed to have great respect for that document. (See the comments on chapter 5: 39.) In our present verse they are reminded of an established rule concerning the force of testimony that their law contained. That rule is written in various places, and one outstanding passage is Deuteronomy 19: 15.

Verse 18. Jesus and his Father would make two witnesses testifying to the same truth. According to the ordinance of their own document of law, that would establish the divinity of Jesus, the fact that was especially offensive to these Jews.

Verse 19. The Pharisees would not deny the principle that Jesus just uttered, but thought to weaken it by pretending to be unacquainted with one of his witnesses, hence they asked, *where is thy Father?* To *know* a person in the practical sense, meant to acknowledge him and give full consideration to all his claims. This the Pharisees refused to do with Jesus, consequently they did not know him nor his Father.

Verse 20. The *treasury* was one of the departments of the temple where the people came who wished to make certain financial contributions. It would be where a great many could see and hear Jesus as he was teaching. That teaching did not suit many of them, but they kept hands off because *his hour was not yet come.* (See comments on chapter 7: 30.)

Verse 21. *I go my way* refers to the return of Jesus to his Father. *Shall seek me* does not mean they will seek to find Jesus as their Saviour, for he did not intend ever to get out of reach of any man who was honestly disposed unto eternal life. It refers to the desire for the benefits that had been bestowed upon man while Jesus was in his personal ministry. (See the comments on Luke 17: 22.) With only such a selfish motive for seeking Jesus, they would fail to find him and would die unsaved, which would make it impossible for them to go into his presence.

Verse 22. *Will he kill himself?* This was not said in seriousness, for had Jesus meant that, he would not have said they could not follow him; any man can commit suicide. They took this method of "changing the subject," for they knew Jesus had predicted his own death at the hands of the Jews, but they were unwilling to recognize their connection with the sad deed.

Verse 23. The human side of the person of Christ was from beneath, but otherwise he was from above the earth. This verse is another statement of the divinity of Jesus.

Verse 24. The thought in this verse is the same as that in chapter 3: 16, for one must believe in the "Only Begotten Son of God" to have everlasting life. These Jews were persisting in their unbelief, hence Jesus warned them that they would die in their sins.

Verse 25. *Who art thou?* This question was asked in pretense of interest, for they had been told in plain terms about the personality of Jesus. He understood their motive, and only referred them to what he had said to them previously.

Verses 26, 27. Jesus could have said many things truthfully against these Jews, that he knew from personal association among them; however, he was supported in all this by his Father. But the hardness of their hearts prevented the Jews from "catching on" to what Jesus meant.

Verse 28. This lifting up refers to the crucifixion, which Jesus had predicted in chapter 3: 14. The fulfillment of that prediction, and the Gospel facts that immediately were to follow, would convince some of them that Jesus was a true prophet and teacher. Having proved that he was true, the people would have reason to believe that He was the one sent to the earth from God.

Verse 29. God was not with Jesus in person, but was in spirit, and gave evidence of it by supporting him in his great works. Jesus did not come into the world to do his own will, but to do that of his Father. (See Hebrews 10: 7.)

Verse 30. *Many believed on him.* The evident fairness of Jesus in leaving the truthfulness of his claims to rest on proposed facts to come, had its effect on some of the people, so that they professed confidence in it.

Verse 31. A mere profession of belief is not enough to satisfy the Lord. That profession must be followed up with adherence to his teaching.

Verse 32. This verse was still addressed to the believers directly, but it was in the hearing of all those present, so that its application was general.

Verse 33. *They answered him.* This means the ones who had not become believers. They interpreted the statement of Jesus to mean the bondage enforced upon people by man, in the social and political realm. But even from that standpoint, their claim was not correct if they were speaking of Abraham's descendants as a whole.

They had spent four centuries in bondage in Egypt, and 70 years in captivity in Babylon.

Verse 34. Jesus explained that he was considering another kind of bondage. *Servant* is from a Greek word that means "slave." Many people who boast of their personal liberty, are slaves under the cruelest of all masters, that of sin.

Verse 35. Passing from the moral and spiritual phase of the subject, to the social and political for the purpose of illustration, Jesus shows these self-righteous Jews that they are detsined to be thrust out unless they change.

Verse 36. A favor backed up by a servant might be of short duration, for that servant could be put out of the household at any time, and hence that favor would go out also. But a son's place in a home is permanent, and favors brought about by him would be permanent also. That is why the favor of being made free would be lasting *(free indeed)* if the son had caused it to be given.

Verse 37. Jesus did not deny the fleshly relationship of these people to Abraham, but that did not excuse their resistance to his word. Instead, it should have inclined them to think favorably upon the teaching of Jesus, for Abraham had been informed of this very great seed of his, and his belief in that promise had obtained for him the title "friend of God" (James 2: 23).

Verse 38. A rule is for a son to speak as his father speaks, and to walk in his footsteps. Jesus applied that rule to himself and to these self-important Jews.

Verse 39. *Abraham is our Father.* All that could be meant by this was their blood relationship to the patriarch. *If ye were Abraham's children.* In this phrase Jesus meant to question their true relation to Abraham in faithfulness. Had that been the case they would have shown those traits of the worthy ancestor.

Verse 40. These Jews had sought to kill Jesus for telling them the truth, which was something that Abraham would not have done. On that account, they were not worthy of being considered the children of Abraham.

Verse 41. The Jews would swing back and forth from one position to another, as they felt the need to keep up their defence. When they thought it was to their credit to be the children of Abraham, they were inclined

to boast of it. They knew that Jesus would not say anything against Abraham, yet he implied by this last statement that they were begotten of some unknown man; one among the morally promiscuous. Then they changed their base and denied any parentage but that of God.

Verse 42. Jesus made the same kind of reply to this claim that he did when they boasted of being children of Abraham (verse 39). Their conduct toward Jesus indicated they were not of God, for he was the Father of Christ whom they did not love.

Verse 43. As long as people are devoted to the devil (as these Jews were) they cannot hear (heed) the words of Christ. By the same token they would not understand his speech when he spoke to them upon the matters of correct living.

Verse 44. The Greek word for *father* is PATER, and it is used 417 times in the New Testament. The definitions are so numerous that lack of space forbids copying them all. The first definition of Thayer is, "Generator or male ancestor." As a secondary definition he gives, "The founder of a race or tribe, progenitor [ancestor in the line] of a people, forefather." In his comments or explanations of one of the secondary definitions, Thayer says, "The originator or transmitter of anything . . . one who has infused his own spirit into others, who actuates [causes to act] and governs their minds." The last sentence Thayer applies to the verse of this paragraph. That is true, for it was the spirit of the devil that caused Cain to slay his brother, then lie about it when he said he did not know where he was. It is the same spirit that has caused men to lie and commit murder all down through the centuries. Hence it was perfectly just for Jesus to call these wicked Jews the children of the devil.

Verse 45. This short verse is a logical deduction from the description of the devil as given in the preceding verse. The reason the Jews would not believe what Jesus told them was because it was the truth, for the devil does not want the truth, neither do his children who are following after his principles.

Verse 46. *Convince* is from a word that means to convict or prove one to be guilty of sin. The question of Jesus was a challenge which amounted to a denial beforehand. Since they knew they could not convict Jesus of sin, that would mean that all he said was the truth. On that basis, the only correct answer to his last question would be that their unbelief was due to their relation to the devil.

Verse 47. *Of* is from EK, and Thayer uses three whole pages in his lexicon in defining and explaining the word. The reader may thereby form some estimate of the importance of the term. But his first and general definition is, "From out of, out from, forth from, from." He also explains that it is the opposite of the terms "into" and "in." In composition such as our verse, it means one whose character and principles of life originated with God. Jesus affirmed that all whose character came from God would hear his words. These Jews were refusing to hear them, therefore it proved they were not of God, which is the conclusion which Jesus charged against them.

Verse 48. *Thou art a Samaritan.* This was said to show their contempt of Jesus, in view of the low estimate the Jews had of the Samaritans. A description of that subject is given with the comments on chapter 4: 9. *Say we not* refers to chapter 7: 20 where they first charged Jesus with having a devil. See that passage for comments on their charge as they said *thou hast a devil.*

Verse 49. A sober denial of their charge was the first reply of Jesus. He then made a logical statement, based on his relation to God. Jesus honored his Father and they dishonored Him (Jesus). That was the same as accusing them of dishonoring God also, although these Jews made great claims of respect for God.

Verse 50. The outstanding thought that John stresses in his record of Jesus, is his divinity or close relationship with God. And that seems to have been the point on which the Jews showed their bitterest feeling for Him. And that explains why Jesus so often referred to that relationship, which is the thought in the words, *I seek not mine own glory. There is one.* It is stated in many places that Jesus came into the world to do his Father's will, therefore the *one* in this phrase is God.

Verse 51. *Shall never see death.* The Bible recognizes two kinds of death, the physical and the spiritual. The man who accepts the words of Jesus and keeps them will never suffer the spiritual death. (See chapter 11: 26.)

Verses 52, 53. The Jews either did not know or they deliberately refused to recognize the two kinds of death. With that as the basis for their speech, they repeated the charge they first made at chapter 7: 20, and pretended to ascribe His statement about dying to the effects of the devil in him. Adhering to their notion of there being only the physical death, they referred to the death of Abraham and the prophets as proof against the statement of Jesus.

Verse 54. This verse has the same reasoning Jesus gives in verses 14-18.

Verse 55. The Jews made a great profession of knowing God, yet they constantly refused to recognize his Son. In rejecting Jesus they were also rejecting God, which is a principle that is taught in numerous passages throughout the New Testament. If Jesus had denied any knowledge of God, it would have been untrue, and that would have placed him in the same class as the Jews who were guilty of falsifying.

Verse 56. God told Abraham that he was to have a seed or descendant in whom the whole world would be blessed. (See Genesis 22: 18.) That promised seed was Christ, and Abraham believed the promise that was made concerning him. That is the sense in which he *rejoiced to see* the day of Christ on the earth.

Verse 57. The Jews were still thinking of Jesus as an ordinary human being only, who had been born less than fifty years before. Abraham had been dead for more than 20 centuries, hence they denied that Jesus could ever have seen him.

Verse 58. *Am* is from EIMI, a Greek verb whose fundamental meaning is, "to be." The word is used in the Greek text without inflection (suffixes), therefore it has its full original meaning. As Jesus used the word in this verse, it means that Abraham had a definite time at which he came into being, that is why he used the word *was.* Jesus existed always, hence he says *I am* with reference to himself. A noted writer has worded this much better than I can, hence I shall give the reader the benefit of it. "Divinity has no past tense, nor future tense, but always the present."

Verse 59. This assertion was completely beyond the comprehension of these Jews, and in sheer desperation they thought of stoning Jesus. But "his time had not yet come," hence he miraculously passed from their midst.

JOHN 9

Verse 1. The appearance of a man would not indicate how long he had been blind, hence they had other information concerning this case.

Verse 2. The question the disciples asked Jesus could only have been on the theory known as the "transmigration of souls." This notion is explained at Matthew 14: 2. Jesus did not endorse the theory, because it was untrue and foolish, but he did not take time to deal with every kind of error he met. However, both he and the apostles sometimes used the popular notions to illustrate a point or expose some inconsistency among the people. The present instance is one of them, which was used by Paul when he spoke of "eternal judgment" in Hebrews 6: 2. And being "baptized for [in place of] the dead in 1 Corinthians 15: 29, is another instance where the apostle used an erroneous practice without endorsing it, but to expose the inconsistency of those who did it.

Verse 3. No special act of God had been done to cause this man to be born blind. However, the misfortune will furnish the Lord an opportunity of manifesting divine power. Jesus was always able to turn unfavorable conditions into good account.

Verse 4. *Day* and *night* are used figuratively as we will see in the next verse.

Verse 5. *As long as I am in the world.* This phrase is directly connected with the words *while it is day* in the preceding verse. This would mean that *night* as used in the present instance refers to death. It was never intended that man should work day and night to make a living. Therefore, when language is used figuratively, day (the proper time for work) is likened to a life on earth, because that is the only period in which a man can work for the Lord. It is appropriate that we often sing, "Work, for the night is coming." But Jesus did not mean to teach that after he left this world all spiritual light would cease. He was considering only that light which he personally could shed upon the human beings with whom he came into contact.

Verse 6. Sometimes Jesus used certain things in connection with his miracles that could have no logical effect in the case. There was an important point in such performances. Had something been used that might have a physical relation to the result

desired and obtained, it might have been claimed that such was the cause. But since these things could have nothing to do with the actual problem, the conclusion is clear that the result was obtained through divine power.

Verse 7. Jesus never needed the help of any man in accomplishing his work, but it was well to teach the lesson of cooperation between man and God. Hence Jesus required the people to feed the daughter of Jairus (Mark 5: 43), and directed others to remove the cover from the tomb of Lazarus (John 11: 39). Had this blind man not washed the clay from his eyes he would not have been healed of his blindness.

Verse 8. In the mean time, Jesus had moved on out of the throng, and when the man was returning from the pool with his sight given to him, the people were surprised at his appearance. The absence of eyesight often makes more difference in a man's general appearance than may be thought. Yet in spite of the change wrought by the restoring of that function, some thought they recognized the former blind man.

Verse 9. Some of the people seemed to be very certain of the man's identity, while others professed only to see a resemblance. But the man settled the discussion by informing them that he was the man who had been blind.

Verse 10. This question was asked for the simple purpose of information, as they were not present at the time Jesus talked with the man.

Verse 11. *A man that is called Jesus.* All this blind man knew was what he heard, for he was blind and had to get his information by hearing only. Hence this verse is a statement of facts, without any reasoning or conclusions upon those facts.

Verse 12. While the man was going to the pool, Jesus passed on, so that up to the time of this questioning he had never seen his benefactor. The method Jesus took in this case served a purpose other than requiring the man to go wash in the pool and thus cooperate in his favor of being healed. It left him free to reason on the case without being prejudiced favorably by the appearance and personal presence of the one who had healed him. Under the circumstances, it was all the man could do to say he did not know where the person was then. We should bear in mind that all this conversation was between the man and the people who had no prejudice especially in the case, it not having been called to the attention of the Pharisees.

Verse 13. The text does not tell us why the man was brought to the Pharisees. We know, however, that they were the leading sect of the Jews, and were supposed to be interested in anything especially pertaining to miracles. The man said he was directed in his case by the one called Jesus, to go wash at the pool, with the result that he was made able to see. So it was logical that the case should be taken to these religious leaders since the very name *Jesus* brought up the subject for religious consideration.

Verse 14. There is no evidence in the life of Christ that he made any distinction between days, when he had opportunity for working a beneficial miracle. But John knew what was coming up over this case, and made the statement of this verse as an explanation beforehand, of the disturbance soon to be thrust into the work of Jesus. *Made the clay* was a manual act, and that was sufficient to give the Pharisees an excuse for their quarrel with the man for whom the work had been done.

Verse 15. The Pharisees asked this man how he received his sight, and were given the same answer that the people had received. We should note that the man said *I washed*, which was as much of a manual act as what Jesus had done. But in all of the controversy over this case, not one word will be said against the man for what he did on the sabbath day. This shows the Pharisees were not caring anything about the holy day, but were showing their hatred of Jesus and took this circumstance as a means of repeating their old hypocritically-inspired complaints.

Verse 16. This *division* was between the friends and enemies of Jesus. The former reasoned rightly, that if Jesus were a "sinner," (which means one of that particular class as listed in those days), he would be unable to work miracles, for God would not grant miraculous power to such a character. The others were merely using the question of the sabbath as an excuse for their hatred of Jesus.

Verse 17. The *blind man* did not have any more positive knowledge in the case than did the others, for he had not even seen Jesus up to this time. But the crowd wished to get him to commit himself on the subject; especially that part of the group which was Jews. Had the man expressed an unfavorable opinion of Jesus, it would have been used by the Jews as a significant circumstance. If the very man who had been benefitted by the performance was unfavorably impressed with Jesus, then surely there must have been a reason for it. But he replied with a direct and favorable verdict, *He is a prophet*. That meant not only that Jesus was a good man, but one endowed with supernatural talents to be able to do such a miracle as the one at hand.

Verse 18. The Jews failed to get any satisfaction from the man who had been blind. Their next move was to show that the whole thing was a fraud; that the man had never really been blind. Perhaps the parents can help them in their wicked design.

Verse 19. They asked the parents two questions concerning their son. One of them pertained to fact and the other to theory.

Verse 20. They answered the first question very positively, saying *we know*, etc. It would have been useless for them to deny the facts, for such as the birth of a child without eyesight, and suffering that handicap for all the years up to manhood, would be too well known to be denied.

Verse 21. The parents could literally say *we know not* on the question of how their son was healed as far as personal knowledge was concerned. But if they had been willing to show friendliness for Jesus, they would at least have referred to the case as it was reported by eyewitnesses. They therefore evaded that point for the reason mentioned in the next verse and told them to ask the son himself. *Of age* is from a Greek term defined by Thayer, "Adult age, maturity."

Verses 22, 23. *Put out of the synagogue* is all from APOSUNAGOGOS, and Thayer defines it, "Excluded from the sacred assemblies of the Israelites; excommunicated." The privilege of assembling with the Jews in their religious gatherings was indeed a valuable one. For that reason it was a strong means of punishing a man who became objectionable to the Pharisees, to cast him out of the synagogue and withdraw the fellowship from him. (See chapter 16: 2.) The parents of this man chose rather to deny to Jesus the credit due him, than lose their privilege of entering the synagogue. They took the cowardly way out of the embarrassment by referring the question to their son.

Verse 24. The Jews did not accomplish what they expected from the parents, so they thought they would make another effort with the son. But this time they did not trust the case to an unbiased question, but tried to prejudice him beforehand by framing the answer for him. It was similar to a case of our day where a judge will deliver a "directed verdict" instruction to a jury, when that jury had been sworn to decide the case themselves according to the evidence as they understood it.

Verse 25. But this blind man was not one to betray his conscience as a jury sometimes does. He did not pretend to decide for the present whether his benefactor belonged in the class known as "sinners," but he was not afraid to affirm what he did know. That statement was the simple truth that he was blind but now was able to see.

Verse 26. This question was entirely unnecessary if the Jews were honestly seeking information. The blind man had already stated all the facts in the case as he understood them, and had nothing more in that line that he could say.

Verse 27. The useless question caused the blind man to realize that his questioners were not sincere in their inquiries. Or if they were, it was just their way of pressing the investigation further in order to learn what they could of Jesus. As a means of testing whether that caused their persistence, he asked them if they were interested in becoming the disciples of Jesus.

Verse 28. The Jews realized they had committed themselves a little farther than was intended. They showed their bitterness by accusing the man of being a disciple of Jesus. That would not have been anything of which to be ashamed, but his remarks were purely logical and could have been properly uttered regardless of his personal feelings or intentions. The Jews showed their ignorance of the very document and writer they pretended to respect. Any true disciples of Moses could be disciples of Jesus also, for Moses prophesied favorably of Him. (See Deuteronomy 18: 15, 18.)

Verse 29. Jesus had shown fully as much evidence of having been inspired of God as did Moses. Therefore the statements made by these Jews were unfair and amounted to a false accusation against the doer of this good deed to the blind man.

Verse 30. The man thought it was strange they did not know from where or whom Jesus had come. He thought they ought to have known the kind of source that produced him, judging by the works he was doing. It is a law of cause and effect that is recognized by everybody, that a tree is known by its fruit. Here is a man who has given sight to a man born blind, a feat equal in principle to a creative act, and the Jews pretended not to have any evidence by which they could figure out the background of his operations and general work among mankind.

Verse 31. This verse has been misused by many well-meaning disciples. They may be discussing the question of "who has the right to pray," and they will quote this passage to show that only the children of God have that right. That sinners are outside the family of God and hence are not on "praying ground" before God. All such statements are true and are abundantly taught in the New Testament, but this passage cannot be used as a proof text. This man was uninspired and could not speak with authority, therefore his words cannot be used to prove the idea stated above. But the man could make the statement as an argument, just as one of us could do, knowing that the Word of God teaches it in various places.

Verse 32. This verse is a statement of truth that is backed up by the history of mankind, but it did not require inspiration to say it, for any person could say the same thing on the strength of history.

Verse 33. Since these were all statements of truth that could not be denied, the blind man could freely make them in his argument against the Jews. And on such a basis, he reasoned that *this man* (Jesus) must have come from God, else he could not do the wonderful things accredited to him and which were known to the public in general.

Verse 34. The truth of history agreed with the statements of this man, or the Pharisees would have confronted him with some case of healing that had been done. They knew they could not do that, so they tried to dodge the issue and call in question his right even to reason on the truth. *Born in sins* was a phrase that the Jews used to show their contempt for a truth which they could not otherwise meet. Referring to the theory of "Transmigration of souls" (see at verse 2), they wanted to weaken the force of the man's teaching by implying he was of a low origin among men. On the pretense that such a person was unworthy of their fellowship, they *cast him out*. This phrase means they excommunicated him as explained in the comments at verse 22.

Verse 35. This verse gives the first meeting of Jesus and the man after receiving the use of his eyes. The man had been insisting with the Jews that his benefactor must have been a man of God, but that was as definite as he professed to understand it. The question Jesus asked him was for the purpose of advancing him in his spiritual growth. His reasoning with the Jews before they cast him out, was evidence that he would appreciate a fuller insight pertaining to Jesus.

Verse 36. This question asked by the man is clear when we remember that he had not seen Jesus, and hence did not recognize his person. In other words, he evidently had learned that the one talking to him was a good and great man, but did not know of his Sonship with God.

Verse 37. The conversation had continued far enough for Jesus to make his claim. *Thou hast both seen him* must have been a thrilling reminder for one who had been blind all of his life until that day. How gracious it was in Jesus to seek for the man on whom he had bestowed the blessing of sight, and make it a point that among the first, if not the first, real friend he was enabled to see, was the very One who had healed him and who was his Lord in the form of man.

Verse 38. The man who had been blind made the good confession. The miracle of opening his eyes convinced him that his benefactor was a man of God, and that would mean that any claim he would make would be true. Now that they have met personally and Jesus claims to be the Son of God, the man sincerely confessed his faith. We are not told in what manner he *worshipped* Jesus, and since that word has such a wide range of meaning, it will be well to see the note in connection with Matthew 2: 2.

Verse 39. A man who has been blind physically all his life and then been given sight, would certainly be a good subject to address concerning spiritual light. In this verse Jesus speaks of both kinds. After the man had been enabled to see physically, he gladly accepted the opportunity to see spiritually, which he manifested when he professed his faith in Christ. The last sentence of the verse refers to the Jews who had normal sight physically, but their stubbornness against the spiritual light made them as blind spiritually as the man had been physically.

Verse 40. The Pharisees felt the force of the teaching of Jesus and knew it applied to them. *Are we blind also?* This is in the form of a question, but Jesus knew it was their way of denying being blind. It could have been indicated either by the tone of their voice, or it was what they were thinking in their heart. Whichever it was, Jesus was able to read their motives and so expressed it in the next verse.

Verse 41. *If ye were blind . . . no sin.* Jesus is not teaching that ignorance of one's duty will justify him in sin; the general teaching of the New Testament is against that. (See Acts 17: 30.) But if a person is actually uninformed on the matter of his duty, he would not be guilty of "sinning against light and knowledge," which is the sin Jesus meant these Jews might not have been guilty of. *Ye say, we see.* These Jews were really blind to the truths they so much needed, but their pride of self-importance kept them from giving the spiritual light a chance to shine into their heart. That caused them to be just as responsible for the obligations imposed by the spiritual enlightenment as if they actually possessed the knowledge of it.

JOHN 10

Verse 1. The first five verses constitute a certain sheepfold, the flock of which consisted of the Jews whom John baptized for Christ the "Good Shepherd," and I shall comment on the verses from that standpoint. Some people apply this verse to the church, which is incorrect for more than one reason. No one can steal into the church, for even if he does act the hypocrite in his confession, and get the local congregation to accept him into the fellowship, that will not make him actually a member of the church. Acts 2: 47 says the Lord adds to the church those that are being saved, and that can be accomplished only by sincere obedience, hence no person can get into the church as a robber. But in our case, certain ones actually get in though unlawfully. So the necessary conclusion is that it refers to men who succeeded in deceiving the people and actually gained entrance into the confidence and fellowship of the Lord's people. The cases in Acts 5: 36, 37 will serve as illustrations of this kind of deception.

Verse 2. The person entering the door into the sheepfold would thus be denoted as the true shepherd for two reasons. First, none but the true shepherd would attempt to gain entrance at that place. Second, even if anyone should try to get through it who was not entitled to enter, he would not be permitted to do so. (See next verse.)

Verse 3. When a flock was taken from the pasture in the evening, it was led through the gate into the fold. A gatekeeper was employed to guard the entrance until the shepherd was again ready to lead his sheep out for pasture. When he appeared at the gate, the keeper or *porter* as he is called here, would recognize him and open the entrance to the fold. But if a stranger should appear, claiming to be the shepherd, the porter would know he was a fraud and would not admit him, which was referred to in the preceding verse. A sheep is naturally adapted to affectionate relationship with his master, and it is stated in history, that shepherds in the east had the practice of naming each individual animal, very much as a child will name his pets.

Verse 4. The sheep recognized the voice of their master because he was the one who called them by name. It is characteristic of pets to notice when their name is mentioned. One may see an advertisement in the press for a lost animal, and probably the ad will state, "he recognizes the name," and then follows the name of the animal.

Verse 5. On the basis of the foregoing, if a stranger should come near a flock of sheep, they will flee from him instead of following. His voice will be strange to them which would make them fearful, hence they would flee in their fright.

Verse 6. *Parable* is not from the same Greek word that is generally used for the English term, but its practical purpose is the same. It means an illustration that is expressed in figurative language, where the comparison is to be discovered in the facts and truths that pertain to the subject.

Since the Jews were not informed in all those facts, it is stated that they *understood not* what Jesus spake. With the record of the case as we have it in the work of John and Jesus, we should be able to see the comparison implied in this group of verses. The fold is the ones John prepared for Jesus as explained at verse 1. John is the porter, and he *opened* the door into the confidence of his disciples when he introduced Jesus as the "Lamb of God" in chapter 1: 29. The door does not apply to that through which the sheep were to pass, but it was the shepherd who was to enter it. That door is the prophecies that had described him, and as soon as John learned the truths about Jesus he knew He was the one predicted, and then he opened the door to his disciples by the statement in chapter 1: 29.

Verse 7. Up to this point the speech of Jesus pertained exclusively to his relation with the disciples of John who constituted the "sheepfold," and to John who acted as the "porter" for that group of his disciples. From here through verse 18 Jesus enlarges the subject, and will make remarks that pertain to the church as another fold. For this reason we shall see many changes in the implied comparisons, which can be understood only by considering what the New Testament teaches about the church, and what Jesus means to those who desire salvation through the great institution. However, he will continue to use many of the same terms since they are as true in many respects in the second case as in the first. There will be one distinct reference to the first fold which will be pointed out and commented upon when we reach that verse. The word *again* is what introduces the second line of thought just mentioned a few lines above. In the second fold Jesus is the door as well as the shepherd. That is because no one can enter a saved condition now except through Christ (chapter 14: 6), and after entering thereat he must still be subject to him as his great Shepherd.

Verse 8. This verse was true from a general standpoint. It would include the cases mentioned in Acts 5: 36, 37, and also the false prophets and false Christs who rose up from time to time and claimed to be the fulfillers of the law and the prophets. To the extent of their success in misleading people, they were robbers. But others were well enough acquainted with the Old

Testament that they were not deceived, and they "turned a deaf ear" to the impostors.

Verse 9. The terms or expressions used in an illustration, are generally drawn from the characteristics of the subject, concerning which the comparison is made, and the application cannot always be made literally. One such expression is *go in and out*. Jesus had already selected a shepherd and his work for his illustration, and that made such a phrase appropriate. A shepherd will lead his flock into the fold in the evening for the night, then lead them out the next morning for pasture. In its application it simply means that if a man accepts Jesus as his Shepherd, he will be saved from the wolves of sin, and also will be abundantly supplied with spiritual pasture or food.

Verse 10. A thief attempting to get possession of a flock not belonging to him, could have no good motive for his action. He would count on slaughtering the animals, either for food or material for clothing or for both. The true shepherd would love the flock and would be interested in its growth in numbers and increase in weight.

Verse 11. *Good shepherd giveth his life.* Smith's Bible Dictionary says the following which will explain why a shepherd would run the risk of losing his life in defending the sheep: "The office of the eastern shepherd, as described in the Bible, was attended with much hardship, and even danger. He was exposed to the extremes of heat and cold, Genesis 31: 40. . . . He had to encounter the attacks of wild beasts, occasionally of the larger species, such as lions, wolves, panthers, and bears, 1 Samuel 17: 34; Isaiah 31: 4; Jeremiah 5: 6; Amos 3: 12; nor was he free from the risk of robbers or predatory [destructive] hordes."

Verse 12. A man who is hired to care for a flock of sheep would have no personal or affectionate interest in them. Such a person would not be expected to risk his life in defence of the flock, for he is acting only because of his financial interests. This would illustrate a man in the religious world who pretends to be laboring in behalf of the people of God, but who is in the business only because of personal interest in the form of money or popularity. Neither should he be expected to endure persecution or other disadvantages on account of the profession he is making. *Catcheth them and scattereth the sheep.* That is, the wolf

gets hold of some of the sheep which he mangles, while the others will flee in terror, the shepherd having already deserted them.

Verse 13. See the comments on the preceding verse about hirelings.

Verse 14. This mutual recognition is due to the affectionate relation between a shepherd and his flock, in which each sheep has its own name. See the comments on this point at verses 3 and 4.

Verse 15. The Father and Son are interested in the same flock, hence their mutual knowledge of each other is manifested in their common care for the flock. If the shepherd is called upon to give his life in defence of the sheep, the Father will give that life back to Him.

Verse 16. This is the verse that was referred to in the comments on verse 7. *This fold* means the one described in verses 1-5, consisting of the Jews whom John baptized in preparation for Christ. There was a special need for that group to be ready for Jesus, because the Jews as a nation had become so corrupt that none of them would have been good enough for the personal use of Him. But that was not because they alone were to be given a chance to save their souls. In the course of time the people of every race and nation were to be invited to come into the one fold which is the church. These are the *other sheep* of this verse. The term *I have* is in the present tense as to grammatical form, but it was spoken prospectively because Jesus knew that the Gentiles would hear his voice and come into the church. It was on the same principle that the Lord told Paul, "I have much people in this city" (Acts 18: 10). He knew that many of the Corinthians still in sin would accept the truth when they heard it, and by divine inspiration he could say, "I have." Jesus used the term *other sheep I have* in this verse in the same inspired prediction. *One fold and one shepherd* means there was to be one church, and that all of the Lord's sheep whether Jews or Gentiles would be in it.

Verse 17. Had the death of Christ been involuntary, his Father would not have raised him to life again. This willingness on his part caused God to love his Son.

Verse 18. Yes, man was the instrument through which Jesus died. But had it not been the will of the Son to die, no man would have been able to slay him. (See Matthew 26: 53.) Because of his willingness to carry out this part of his Father's will, he was given the *power* (EXOUSIA, authority) to lay his life down and then take it up again. *This commandment* refers to the will of God that his Son should come into the world and die as a sacrifice for sin. When Jesus came it was for the purpose of doing that very thing. Paul wrote about this in Hebrews 10: 5-7 in connection with the new covenant.

Verses 19-21. These verses are explained at chapter 7: 20 and 9: 16.

Verse 22. This *dedication* was not any part of the law of Moses. A wicked king of Syria named Antiochus Ephiphanes, drove the priests from the altar of sacrifices at Jerusalem and burned the flesh of swine on it. After some years of struggle, a zealous Jew by the name of Judas Maccabaeus got possession of the altar. He cleansed it and dedicated it anew to the lawful service. In honor of that event the Jews established a feast that was celebrated annually. John refers to it only as a matter of date, indicating the occasion on which the things took place of which he was writing. This sacrilege by the wicked king is predicted and commented upon at Daniel 8: 9-12, in volume 4 of the Old Testament Commentary.

Verse 23. *Solomon's porch.* Thayer explains this as follows: "A porch or portico built by Solomon in the eastern part of the temple (which in the temple's destruction by the Babylonians was left uninjured, and remained down to the times of King Agrippa, to whom the care of the temple was intrusted by the emperor Claudius, and who on account of its antiquity did not dare to demolish and build it anew)." It is elsewhere described as a covered walk where people would be protected from the weather and sun. All of this explains why we read of various gatherings of the people at this place.

Verse 24. These Jews were not really wanting information, for Jesus had already furnished an abundance of evidence that he was the Christ. They hoped that by repeated demands they would catch Jesus unawares, and that he would say something on which they could base some accusation of disloyalty to Moses or to Caesar.

Verse 25. Jesus made a very brief reply to their demand. He referred to what had previously been said and

done concerning his works in the Father's name.

Verse 26. All who accepted the teaching of John became sheep for the fold that was being prepared for Christ. If they refused to accept that work of the forerunner, they naturally would not believe the teaching of the shepherd when he came. That is why Jesus told these Jews the reason they did not believe his word was because they were *not of my sheep.*

Verse 27. Jesus made more believers through his personal teaching and that of his apostles. These became sheep also and came under the same rules that regulate a flock with its shepherd, whose voice the sheep had learned.

Verse 28. *They shall never perish* is on the condition that the sheep hear the voice of the shepherd. He will give them eternal life, whereas a temporal shepherd leads his flock into temporal pasture. This verse does not teach the false doctrine known as "once in grace always in grace." But if a man is faithful to the law of Christ, then it is true that no other person can pluck him out of the hand of the Shepherd.

Verse 29. The Father will not hold a sheep regardless of whether it is faithful and satisfied with the spiritual pasturage which He provides for him. But if the sheep is thus true to the Father, then no man can get that sheep out of His grasp.

Verse 30. The Father is greater than all other beings in existence. Since He and his Son *are one* (in spirit and purpose), the security of a sheep that is true to them is established and is based on the unfailing power and goodness of the Lord.

Verse 31. At every climax of the arguments of Jesus, the conclusion was so unanswerable that the Jews were enraged. Instead of acting in a fair manner and accepting the teaching, they would threaten him with violence.

Verse 32. In reality it was the good works of Jesus that angered the Jews. They did not like to see the favor that he was receiving from the multitude, but were not honest enough to admit it. As a screen for their envious hypocrisy, they pretended to object to some of his personal claims.

Verse 33. The specific grievance they put forward was that Jesus made himself God. He did not make such a claim directly (although he could have done so justly if taken rightly) but only had claimed to be the Son of God.

Verse 34. In reply to the charge of the Jews, Jesus made a quotation from Psalms 82: 6. Incidentally, let us note that Jesus called the book of Psalms *your law*, which tells us that the writings of Moses do not contain all of "the law" of the Jews. In this citation are the words *ye are gods;* they were addressed to the Jews of old to whom the law was sent, and in such a form of speech they were called *gods.* There is nothing strained in attributing such a title to God's people. The name God is a family one and includes every member of that family. Every member of the Jones family is a Jones, and likewise every member of the family of God is a God in the sense of relationship. It was in that sense the passage in Psalms was used.

Verse 35. The mere fact of being the ones to whom the word of God was sent, entitled them to the family relationship and the right to its name, which was God. *The scripture cannot be broken* denotes that these Jews had no right to speak of Jesus in a way that would criticize the scripture just quoted.

Verse 36. *Sanctified* is from HAGIAZO. It has such varied applications in the New Testament, sometimes pertaining to man and at others applying to the Lord, that I think it will be well to copy the definitions (the parts in italics) of Thayer. The reader should acquaint himself with these different clauses, and when using them in any given place in the scripture, always use the one that is appropriate. "1. To render or acknowledge to be venerable [worthy of high regard], to hallow. 2. To separate from things profane and dedicate to God, to consecrate. 3. To purify, to cleanse externally. To purify internally by reformation of soul." Jesus never had any impurities in his character, hence the definitions 1 and 2 should apply to him. The Father acknowledged the Son as being worthy of high regard, when he said he was his beloved Son in whom he was well pleased (Matthew 3: 17), and he dedicated him to the great work of God when he gave the command, "Hear ye him" (Matthew 17: 5). If the people who were honored only by having the law sent to them were entitled to be called gods, then certainly the One on whom God bestowed all these latter honors has the right to be called Son of God.

Verse 37. Jesus was willing to rest his reputation upon the works that he did. The Jews would not have been able to name a single thing that Jesus performed that God condemned in the Scriptures. That would indicate the works were of the Father and it should have caused them to become believers.

Verse 38. The gist of this verse is the willingness of Jesus to pass over his personality for the time. Yet he insisted that the Jews should at least accept him as a worker of good things.

Verse 39. Again the Jews were baffled by the reasoning of Jesus. Instead of acknowledging their inability to meet the issue, they were inclined to take bodily possession of him. He escaped because his time had not yet come. (See chapter 7: 6.)

Verse 40. Since it was not yet time for Jesus to be taken in hand by the Jews, he moved out of the territory of Jerusalem. It was his desire to continue his good work, and he selected a community where John had done work before he was slain. His preaching had doubtless sown the seeds of truth that prepared the soil for Jesus.

Verses 41, 42. This paragraph confirms the comments on the preceding verse. The people saw in Jesus the fulfillment of many of John's sayings, and it made believers of them. *John did no miracle.* These people used the word in its physical sense, and there is no account of any such a work done by him. However, the predictions that John made of Christ and which were fulfilled, required supernatural knowledge, and such a manifestation could rightly be called miraculous.

The word *miracle* fills such a prominent place in the New Testament that I shall explain it in detail, with the hope the reader will make a note of it for reference, as it will not again be given in full. It comes from two different Greek words, and they have also been rendered by several other English words in the King James Version. Before giving the lexicon definitions of the original words, I shall state how each has been translated and how many times. One of the Greek words is DUNAMIS, and it has been rendered ability 1 time, abundance 1, meaning 1, miracle 8, power 77, strength 7, violence 1, virtue 3, wonderful work 1. The other Greek word is SEMEION, and it has been rendered miracle 22 times, sign 51, token 1, wonder 3.

Since the last word is the one from which the significant words "miracle" and "sign" come usually, I shall give the lexicon definitions of it only. Thayer defines it, "A sign, mark, token; A sign, prodigy, portent." He also explains his definitions, "That by which a person or thing is distinguished from another and by which it is known. . . . An unusual occurence, transcending [going beyond] the common course of nature." From the foregoing information, it can be seen that the word "miracle" has a very wide range of meaning, and the specific definition to apply in any given place must be determined by the connection in which it is used. Any unusual or great or wonderful thing that is done, whether by the Lord or man, may rightly be called a miracle. But the rule is that a miracle means something that only God can do, whether he does it directly or through the agency of man.

JOHN 11

Verse 1. Bethany was a small town a short distance from Jerusalem. Though small, it was a noted place because of the frequent visits Jesus made to it, and because of the famous sisters who lived there. The importance of Lazarus was due to the relation he had with these sisters, and that importance was increased by the miracle performed upon him described in this chapter.

Verse 2. There were several Marys in those times, and John wanted his readers to know which one he was writing about, so he specified by referring to her deed of wiping the feet of Jesus with her hair. That event had not occurred at the time of Lazarus' sickness, but it had been done at the time John wrote his record. He knew it would be read, and mentioned the incident as a mark of identification. Note that John did not merely say "it was that woman which anointed the Lord," etc., for that deed was performed by another woman also (Luke 7: 36-50), and the cases were different in some respects. The other woman was classed as a "sinner" which did not apply to Mary. That woman washed the feet of Jesus with tears (of penitential sorrow), while Mary only anointed his feet before wiping them with her hair. Hence the writer says it was that *Mary* which anointed the Lord with ointment, etc.

Verse 3. *He whom thou lovest.* We are taught that Jesus was a friend of publicans and sinners, and that he loved everybody. That is true, of course, but Jesus was human as well as divine, and he could have his personal favorites as well as other human beings could have. There is nothing wrong in such affection as long as one does not allow that sentiment to influence him in the wrong direction, which we know it did not do with Jesus. But the word *love* is so much used in the New Testament, and has so many applications because of the definitions of the original Greek, that I insist the reader see the long critical note given at Matthew 5: 43.

Verse 4. *Not unto death* means the death of Lazarus was not to be permanent. Jesus knew he was going to die, but that he would be restored to life after a few days. The purpose of the event was that the Son of God might have an opportunity to be glorified by performing the miracle upon Lazarus.

Verse 5. This is commented upon at verse 3.

Verse 6. *When he had heard* has virtually the same meaning as "when the Lord knew" in chapter 4: 1; see the comments at that place. At the time the news was sent to Jesus, Lazarus was still living but nearing death. In order to have an unquestionable proof of His power, he remained two days longer where he was (verse 6), which place is named in chapter 10: 40.

Verse 7. Going into Judea did not necessarily mean going to Bethany. When Jesus proposed going into that general territory, the disciples did not know that the conditions with Lazarus had anything to do with it.

Verse 8. This intended stoning of Jesus is recorded in chapter 8: 59 and 10: 31. Having escaped the wrath of the Jews, the disciples wondered why Jesus would expose himself again and thus give them another opportunity to carry out their evil intentions.

Verse 9. Jesus used the hours of literal daylight to illustrate the idea of acting according to the light of truth and right doing. It was necessary for him to go even into Judea, in order to perform the righteous deed of raising Lazarus in the presence of witnesses. That being a proper act, it would be like a man working while he had the light of day so that he could see what he was doing. It would follow, then, that the Father would see after the safety of his Son.

Verse 10. This verse is to be understood in the light of the comments on the preceding one. That is, the *night* is just the opposite of the *day* in that passage.

Verse 11. Having given the disciples the preliminaries of the great subject, Jesus named that subject in a manner that will need further information.

Verse 12. All the disciples knew about Lazarus' condition so far was that he was sick, and they thought that since "sleep is the best medicine," it would be well not to disturb him. They did not realize the uses of figurative and literal language, which the Bible as well as other compositions uses. The reader may see a full explanation of these forms of speech in the comments at Matthew 9: 24.

Verse 13. The literal fact about Lazarus was that he was dead. The figurative appearance was that of sleep, and that is what the disciples had in mind.

Verse 14. *Plainly* is the same as saying that Jesus spoke literally.

Verse 15. This verse explains why Jesus tarried the two days in verse 6.

Verse 16. Thomas was one of the apostles, and is the one who is popularly referred to as "doubting Thomas," on account of the incident in chapter 20: 24-29. He was called Didymus as a surname, but the word in the Greek means "a twin." Why the title was applied to him as part of his name is not very clearly stated in the reference works I have seen. *Die with him* was said according to verse 8. He was so certain that Jesus would be slain as soon as he reached Judea, that he proposed to the other apostles that they share in his fate.

Verse 17. This verse with verse 39 indicates that people were buried the same day of death. When Martha suggested that the body of Lazarus was decaying, she based it on the fact that it had been dead four days. That cause for the decay would have been the same whether the body had been put into the cave or retained in the home.

Verse 18. This verse gives us about two miles for distance from Bethany to Jerusalem.

Verse 19. Jerusalem being so near to Bethany explains how *many of the Jews* could come to the home to show their sympathy for the sisters.

Verse 20. No specific reason is given why Martha only went to meet Jesus. It was not for any lack of interest or confidence in Jesus on the part of Mary, for each of them expressed the same belief in his ability to prevent death. However, from the account in Luke 10: 38-42, it seems that Martha was the head of the house and generally more forward in social and personal demonstrations.

Verse 21. Martha presumed that Jesus would have prevented the death of her brother had he been there. Whether he would have seen fit to prevent it is another matter, for he would have been able to prevent it though absent. He prevented the death of the nobleman's son though absent (chapter 4: 46-53). But the remark of Martha showed her faith in Jesus, and the feeling of friendship on which she based it.

Verse 22. Her faith was not put to any strain even by the death of her brother. Yet she recognized the cooperation that existed between Jesus and his Father, and based her expectation on their joint wills.

Verse 23. This statement was so indefinite that it did not satisfy the sorrowing sister. But Jesus took that plan of introducing the subject.

Verse 24. Martha thought Jesus had reference to the general resurrection at the last day. She spoke of that as if she had previously been informed of its truth and had fully believed it. Doubtless it was often the subject of conversation between Jesus and these dear personal friends as he was passing the time in their humble home.

Verses 25, 26. It would be difficult to do justice to these verses without including them in one paragraph. In thought or subject matter they correspond with Revelation 20: 5, 6. In the forepart of the chapter we are studying, Jesus spoke of the physical death of Lazarus in both figurative and literal language. In this paragraph the language is partially figurative, but Jesus is speaking of spiritual death and life. *I am the resurrection* means that Jesus is the giver of life. It is true of him in two senses; in him all mankind will be brought to life physically at the last day whether good or bad (chapter 5: 28, 29; 1 Corinthians 15: 22). But the spiritual death is that of men in sin, referred to by the words *though he be dead.* Such a person will be brought to spiritual life, saved from his past sins, if he will believe on Christ. After he has thus been made alive through belief in Christ (which includes primary obedience to the commands of the Gospel), he becomes one of the persons designated by the word *liveth.* But he must be faithful to the rest of the commands and so continue to show that he *believeth,* by a faithful life as a Christian. Such a person has the assurance that he *shall never die*. This death means the second one, when those who are not faithful to the end of life will be cast into the lake of fire prepared for the devil and his angels, which is the second death (Revelation 20: 14).

Verse 27. In answer to the question of Jesus, Martha made the good confession of the divinity of him as the Son of God. She coupled her confession of faith with the fact that it had been predicted of him as the one to come into the world.

Verse 28. We did not hear when Jesus made the request for Mary to come, but the statement of Martha gives us that information.

Verse 29. How sweet it was for Mary to go *quickly* to Jesus.

Verse 30. Jesus was not far from the town, but tarried until Martha could return with her sister.

Verse 31. Verse 28 says Martha called her sister "secretly," which explains why the others in the house did not know why she left the room. *Goeth to the grave to weep there.* While that was not the reason Mary left, yet the remark shows it was a practice in those times to manifest sorrow for a departed loved one in such a manner. It is natural and right for us to sorrow for our dead friends, but it is worse when we have to sorrow as those without hope. In the case of the sisters of Lazarus it was the sorrow that was lightened by their hope for the resurrection of the just.

Verse 32. Mary expressed the same faith in the power of Jesus to control disease as did Martha. See the comments on the subject at verse 21.

Verse 33. *Groaned* is from EMBBI-MAOMAI, and Thayer defines it, "To be very angry, to be moved with indignation." *Weeping* is from KLAIO, and Thayer's definition is, "To mourn, weep, lament." It has the idea of outward and audible demonstrations. We should note that Jesus not only saw Mary weeping, but also the Jews that were with her. Mary's actions were genuine and prompted by true sorrow for her dead. The Jews were merely going through it as the usual formality of mourning for the dead. Jesus knew the hearts of all of them and could see the coldness therein, notwithstanding their outward show of sympathy. It was this fact that moved him to indignation. Yet he restrained himself

from expressing his feelings, but *groaned in the spirit*.

Verse 34. Jesus never had to ask a question for information, but he wished to show a sympathetic interest in the case, and asked where they had laid him. Have you ever visited a home where death has entered? You asked to see the form of their dear dead and were told to "come this way." The look of utter dejection on the faces of the relatives as they said this, then started toward the silent chamber where lay the loved one, could not be described in words.

Verse 35. Such a look as the preceding verse describes was doubtless on the faces of these sisters as they led Jesus to the tomb of their brother. There could be no question as to the sincerity of that look or of the tone of voice when they bade the Lord to "come and see." *Jesus wept.* The second word is different from the one in verse 33. It is from DAKRUO, which Thayer defines, "To weep, shed tears." This is the only place in the Greek New Testament where this word is used. It does not indicate any audible expressions. Jesus had restrained himself from such demonstrations, even when he saw Mary convulsed in sorsow, because he wanted to ignore the hypocritical performances of the Jews. But the sight of these sorrowing sisters, and the pathos in their sweetly-sad voices, was so overyhelming that he burst into tears that were so generous that they could be seen.

Verse 36. The Jews missed the point as to why Jesus wept. It is true he loved Lazarus, and that feeling blended with his sympathy for the sisters. Yet he had as much love for him at the time of his death, although he was many miles away; but there is no indication that he wept then. This flow of tears was caused by his sympathy for the sisters. (See the comments on Verses 33-35.)

Verse 37. The Lord did not see fit to prevent the death of Lazarus, and the people implied that it was because he *could not* do so.

Verse 38. *Jesus therefore.* Because of these cruel words of the people, it caused Jesus to have a renewal of the feelings described in verse 33. Moffatt's rendering of this place is, "This made Jesus chafe afresh." By this time he had reached the grave or tomb, and found it closed by a stone.

Verse 39. Jesus told them to take the stone away. "The Lord helps those who help themselves," is an old and true saying. The people could not restore Lazarus to life, but they could remove the stone. The statement of Martha about the condition of Lazarus' body was a mild protest against opening the tomb. We are not given any explanation of this, in the light of her great faith as expressed in verse 22. She could not have doubted the ability of Jesus to raise him even out of his state of decay, when she had already affirmed belief in his ability to resurrect him out of death at the last day (verse 24), at which time the entire body will have returned to dust. Her statement was a suggestion that Jesus restore her brother to life before removing the stone, to save those present from the offensiveness due to decomposition of the body.

Verse 40. Sometimes people will propose faith in the Lord's power to do the greater things, and then manifest doubt concerning the lesser ones. For instance, they will ascribe to Him the power necessary to create the universe with its millions of items, then question his ability to cleanse a man's soul by washing his body in water. Not that one miracle really is greater than another, only it might appear to be so. Martha professed to believe that Jesus could raise the body of Lazarus out of the grave long after it had been absorbed by the elements of the earth, but manifested doubt about his ability to care for the sense of smell over a decaying body after but four days since death.

Verse 41. In obedience to the instruction of Jesus, they removed the stone from the grave or cave that was being used for burial. Before proceeding with the act of resurrecting the dead, Jesus first went to God in prayer, thereby setting a good example for others who claim to be children of God. This also was to demonstrate to the ones present that He was accomplishing his great works in cooperation with his Father. If the prayer is answered, it will show also that God is recognizing that cooperation. It was appropriate to express gratitude for the past support his Father had given him.

Verse 42. Jesus never had any doubts of his Father's assistance, but the people might have had some questioning in their minds about it. This thought is suggested by verse 37, where they intimated that Jesus had been unable to prevent the death of Lazarus. Now if these same people

hear him appeal to his Father, and then see the favorable response to that appeal, they will know they were wrong in their accusation as to his failure to intervene and prevent Lazarus from dying.

Verse 43. *Loud* is from MEGAS, and in the King James Version it has been translated by "loud" 33 times, and by "great" 145 times. It means here that the voice was not only of great volume as to degree of tone, but was one that indicated authority.

Verse 44. Even after reviving Lazarus from death, it required miraculous power to enable him to come out of the tomb, for he had been bound hand and foot. That is why Jesus instructed them to *loose him, and let him go.*

Verse 45. This miracle caused many of the Jews to believe on Jesus. That was one of the purposes for which the deed was done. (See chapter 20: 30,31.)

Verse 46. While many of the Jews believed, some of them did not. And of that class, some went to the Pharisees in the spirit of talebearers and reported the event of the resurrection of Lazarus.

Verse 47. This *council* was the Sanhedrin, the highest court the Jews were allowed to have in the time of Christ. Upon the report brought to the Pharisees from the tomb of Lazarus, they became alarmed and called a special session of the council. For detailed information about the Sanhedrin, see the note with comments on Matthew 26: 3.

Verse 48. The Jews finally lost their place (Palestine, with Jerusalem as the capital) and nation as a governmental unit. But it was because they persecuted Jesus, and not because they allowed him to teach the people. (See Matthew 23: 38, 39; 27: 25.) The first reference in the parentheses is a prediction of the desolation of Jerusalem, and the second is the rash proposition of the Jews for that very thing to happen, although they did not realize what their mad statement would mean to their people.

Verse 49. *Ye know nothing at all* means the same as if Caiaphas had said: "You have not gone far enough in your suggestion." The speakers in the Sanhedrin had suggested only that something should be done to stop the miraculous works of Jesus.

Verse 50. The proposition the high priest had to offer was the very thing that God intended should come to pass. However, the motive Caiaphas had was only that it would be a short and sure way of stopping the work of Jesus. But God used the mouth of the high priest to deliver this weighty speech to the Sanhedrin.

Verse 51. Such a use of the high priest as stated in the preceding verse was nothing new. (See Leviticus 10: 11; Deuteronomy 17: 9; Malachi 2: 7.) As time went on after the writings of Moses were completed, it was necessary occasionally to give the people further revelation of truth. That was done through the words of prophets or the lips of the priests as the passages cited show. That is why it says he spake this not *of* himself, which means it was not something that originated with him. The Holy Ghost (Spirit) was guiding him in this lofty speech, just as it had done to the prophets in Old Testament times. (See 2 Peter 1: 20, 21.)

Verse 52. No mere human being, especially a wicked man like Caiaphas, would or could make such a grand statement as this verse. *Not for that nation only* denotes that Jesus was to be the sacrifice for all nations of the world. *The children of God* is spoken prospectively, just as Jesus spoke of his "other sheep" in chapter 10: 16, referring to the Gentiles who would accept the Gospel when it was offered to them.

Verse 53. The Jews accepted the proposition made by the priest, and began at once to plot the death of Jesus. In so doing they would not only gratify their wicked personal designs upon the Lamb of God, but would unconsciously carry out the great work of Jehovah in "providing for himself a Lamb" for the atonement of the human race.

Verse 54. Jesus knew the Jews were plotting to kill him, but his time for death had not yet come, hence he maintained some privacy in his walk. He went to a city called Ephraim that was near the wilderness, and thus evaded the evil schemes of his enemies.

Verse 55. *Nigh at hand* is a comparative phrase, for the first verse of the next chapter shows that it was at least six days before. *To purify themselves.* The law of Moses required all persons to be both physically and ceremonially clean before participating in the passover. (See Leviticus 22: 1-6).

Verse 56. When these Jews gathered in the temple in the days before the feast, they became curious as to whether Jesus would come to it. He had disappeared sometime previously and gone into the region of the wilderness. This fact led some to intimate that he would be afraid to attend the passover.

Verse 57. This was like an official advertisement for the whereabouts of some wanted criminal. The Jews did not realize that whenever his "time had come," Jesus would be at hand and not make any effort to escape from them. The truth of this statement is clearly shown in chapter 18: 4-11. Jesus fully intended to let his presence be known as soon as it was the proper time. In the meantime he associated with his disciples and personal friends, making his last visit in the town of Bethany near Jerusalem, as the next chapter shows.

JOHN 12

Verse 1. Bethany was about two miles from Jerusalem, and was the scene of some of the most personal experiences of Jesus. The significance of mentioning the case of Lazarus will be seen later in this chapter.

Verse 2. According to Matthew 26: 6, this supper was in the house of "Simon the leper," who evidently had been healed by Jesus. *Made him a supper* denotes that Jesus was the honor guest, but his disciples also were present. *Martha served*, even as she did in her own house on another occasion (Luke 10: 38-40). *Lazarus was one of them.* The supper was had in honor of Jesus, but Lazarus was given special mention because of the miracle that had been performed upon him.

Verse 3. This anointing should not be confused with the one in Luke 7: 37-50. That was done by a woman from the outcast ranks and was known as a "sinner," but the present case was by the sister of Lazarus, who was one of the personal friends of Jesus.

Verse 4. *Should betray him* is translated, "was about to deliver him up," by the Englishman's Greek New Testament. The statement was made to explain the actions of Judas here and elsewhere as they pertained to money.

Verse 5. *Three hundred pence.* Weights and measures, as well as money values, changed from time to time and in different places. But in any way it is estimated, the value Judas placed on this ointment was great, which agrees with the statement of John (verse 3) that it was *very costly.*

Verse 6. No doubt Judas sincerely regretted seeing this valuable product used in this way, but it was not because of his interest in the poor. He was covetous and it hurt him to see that much value bestowed upon another. *Had the bag* means Judas was the treasurer for the group, and hence he was especially interested in anything that looked like money value. *Bare* is from BASTAZO, and Thayer defines it at this place, "To bear away, carry off." The general meaning of the word is to have charge of the money, but the more specific meaning applies to Judas according to Thayer's definition. In chapter 13: 29, 30, the bag was still in the hands of Judas just as he was ready to leave the group. He went out with the bag and was never again with Jesus and the other apostles, so that he truly "carried off" the treasury as the specific definition states, and verifies the charge of John that he was a thief.

Verse 7. *Against the day of my burying.* It was an old custom to anoint the dead and use spices at the time of burial. (See 2 Chronicles 16: 14; John 19: 40; Luke 23: 56.) Mark 14: 8 quotes Jesus as saying, "She is come aforehand to anoint my body to the burying."

Verse 8. *Poor always . . . with you.* Jesus did not criticize the idea of giving something to the poor, for he regarded that as a good work. He instructed the rich young man (Matthey 19: 21) to give his possessions to the poor. But this statement was about the idea of using present opportunities that are soon to pass. He was soon to leave the world and that would stop all chances of doing him a bodily favor, while they would never cease having opportunities for helping the poor.

Verse 9. The presence of Jesus only would have brought the people out to Bethany, but they had a sepcial interest in seeing Lazarus alive, whom Jesus had raised from the dead. This was a visible evidence of the power that Jesus possessed, for the deed had been done in that very place where Lazarus had lived, and there could be no question about his identity.

Verses 10, 11. It would be difficult to form a just description of minds as wicked as those possessed by the chief priests. We frequently hear of witnesses being slain or otherwise removed to prevent their testifying in an important case. But generally it is done on behalf of a felon who is about to be brought to trial for his crimes. Lazarus was only enjoying his natural right to live after having been restored from the dead by the Lord. And the motive for removing him was to destroy a visible but silent testimony in favor of Jesus, who had incurred the wrath of these priests by exposing their hypocrisy. No wonder such people could find it in their hearts finally to cause the death of the Teacher they hated.

Verse 12. Bethany was near Jerusalem, and the movements of Jesus were being made known in the city. The news evidently came back by the ones who had gone out to Bethany, mentioned in verse 9.

Verse 13. It was an ancient custom to honor an approaching dignitary by making a carpet of garments and the foliage of trees on which he might proceed. The season of the Passover was at hand, and great numbers of Jews from all over the world were at Jerusalem to attend it. That is why the preceding verse mentions *much people. Hosanna* is a Greek word and Robinson defines it, "Save now, succor now, be now propitious." He says further that it is from a Hebrew word that means "a joyful acclamation." Thayer's definition agrees with this but is more condensed. The passage denotes an expression of good will to Him who is able to save others because he is coming in the Lord's name.

Verse 14. *Found a young ass.* The accounts of Mark, Luke and John, leave out all mention of the mother of the colt, and the reader may be somewhat confused over it. The subject is fully discussed in the comments on Matthew's account (chapter 21: 1-7), and I urge him to see that place.

Verse 15. The passage cited is in Zechariah 9: 9. The prophet not only predicted the triumphal entrance of Jesus into Jerusalem, but said he would come "having salvation." It would be useless repetition to say this means "saving himself," as the margin renders it, for that truth is included in the fact of his riding triumphantly into the city. But Jesus was coming into the capital of the Jewish nation to bring salvation to all people in the world, whether they be Jew or Gentile.

Verse 16. The word *glorify* has several shades of meaning, and the one to apply in any given place must be determined by the context. In verse 23 it is stated that *the hour is come* (is at hand or very near), when the Son of man was to be glorified. This denotes that as yet He had not been glorified in the sense the word is used in this passage. Furthermore, chapter 7: 39 says the reason the Holy Ghost was not yet given, was because Jesus was not yet glorified, and chapter 16: 7-13 shows that the Holy Ghost was not to be given until Jesus had gone to his Father. All of these truths give us the meaning of *glorified* in this verse to be the eternal form of Jesus in Heaven; the form referred to in 1 John 3: 2. After that great circumstance of the glorification of Jesus, the disciples recalled the many things He had said to them, and the meaning of them became clear to their understanding.

Verse 17. These *people* related what they had seen and heard on the occasion of the resurrection of Lazarus. *Bare record* means they made their statements as eye and ear witnesses of the miracle that had so deeply impressed many in the community.

Verse 18. The testimony of the witnesses mentioned in the preceding verse, caused many others to believe on Him, which accounts for their actions described in verse 13.

Verse 19. *World* is from KOSMOS, which means the inhabitants of the earth. The statement of the Pharisees was one of envy and fear. Their complaint was among themselves, as if each one thought the other should "do something about it."

Verse 20. The question may arise why these Greeks (who were Gentiles) were permitted to worship at the feast, which was primarily a Jewish affair. In 1 Kings 8: 41-43 is a part of Solomon's prayer at the dedication of the temple. He predicted that "strangers" (people outside the Jewish nation) would come to the temple to pray, which is one act of worship. Solomon asked God to grant the prayer of these people. Then in chapter 9: 3 of that book, the Lord told Solomon that his prayer was heard, which means it was to be granted, and that included what was asked on behalf of the prayers of the strangers. It will help the reader to understand this matter if he will consult the note on "worship" at Matthew 2: 2. The word has such a wide range of meanings, that it would have been easy for these *Greeks* to perform some phase of it on the present occasion, without infringing upon any ceremony that was the exclusive right of the Jews.

Verse 21. Philip was of Galilee as stated here and in chapter 1: 44. It was natural, therefore, for these Greeks to contact him in their inquiry to see the greatest of Galileans. The fame of Jesus had reached so far that these visitors had heard of it.

Verse 22. I have not seen any account of the previous association of Philip with Andrew, but they seem to have been close personal friends. Philip passed on to Andrew the request of the Greeks, and together they reported it to Jesus.

Verse 23. We have no information as to what was done about the aforementioned request. However, Jesus stated to Philip and Andrew (perhaps in the hearings of these Greeks), that the hour was at hand when the Son of man was to be *glorified*. The last word is explained in the comments at verse 16. This glorification was to take place in Heaven, which had to be preceded by His death and resurrection. That brought the conversation to the point where it was necessary to say something about the death of Jesus, which will be the subject in the next verse.

Verse 24. The original word for *corn* is defined "grain" in the lexicon. Jesus used the subject to show why his death was necessary. If a grain could be kept alive, it would never be able to grow into another stock of the species. All that its owner would have would be the single grain; no reproduction. Likewise, if Christ had not died, he would never have produced others to share with him in the glorified state.

Verse 25. The meaning of this verse is set forth at some length in the comments on Matthew 10: 39, as it pertains to the two kinds of life. As the word *hate* is used here, it is defined by Thayer to mean, "To love less, to postpone in love or esteem, to slight." Robinson defines it, "Not to love, to love less, to slight."

Verse 26. *Serve* is from a different Greek word from the one that suggests a slave. It means to minister to or wait upon, such as serving one with the necessities of life. No one can render such service to Christ today directly. But that kind of service can be given to his disciples as he taught in Matthew 25: 35-40. On the principle that such service is regarded by Jesus as if it were done for him personally, so the Father will honor that servant for his loving ministry as having been done for his Son. But this material ministration should be considered only as one phase of our service to Christ. We should be even more concerned with rendering service to Him in the great Cause for which he died and "fell into the ground."

Verse 27. *Troubled* means to be agitated, which was the condition of mind that was upon the Saviour. He was beginning to feel the awful emotions that came to him in greater force later in the garden. *Save me from this hour* was equivalent to his prayer for the removal of the "cup," mentioned in Matthew 26: 39. More will be said on that subject when we come to John 18: 11. Jesus asked his Father to save him from *this hour* (not the cross). When later He prayed "if it be possible" let the cup pass, it meant virtually the same resignation of spirit that is expressed here in the words, *for this cause came I unto this hour.* The human nature of Jesus longed for relief from his mental suffering, but his divine knowledge told him that he must endure it.

Verse 28. The original word for *glorify* as used here is defined by Thayer as follows: "To make renowned, render illustrious, i. e., to cause the dignity and worth of some person or thing to become manifest and acknowledged." God answered the prayer of Jesus in an audible voice but in words the people did not understand. This made the third time God spoke with words that could be heard; at the baptism of Jesus (Matthew 3: 17), and at the transfiguration (Matthew 17: 5), being the other two. That voice was not heard in audible form again that we have any account of, but the Almighty demonstrated his majesty on behalf of his Son more than once afterward, particularly when he raised him from the dead.

Verse 29. The voice from heaven was somewhat indistinct so that the people did not understand it, yet sufficiently different from the noise of thunder that some of them knew it was some form of speech addressed to Jesus in answer to his prayer, and they interpreted it to be the voice of an angel.

Verse 30. Jesus did not need the voice of his Father to satisfy Him, but some kind of demonstration was necessary as evidence for the crowd.

Verse 31. *Now* denotes that the time was very near when the great test was to be made. Jesus was soon to be slain as a sacrifice for the sins of the world, and thus counteract the work of the *prince of this world.* Chapter 14: 30; 16: 11; Luke 4: 6; Ephesians 2: 2, shows this *prince* is Satan.

Verse 32. This verse is directly connected with the preceding one, showing that Christ was to be lifted up on the cross to accomplish the sacrifice. *Draw all men unto me.* Jesus never contradicted himself, and since he taught (Matthew 7: 13, 14) that most people will be lost, he would not here teach that all would come to him. The point is with reference to what person was to be the most important drawing power. Hitherto it had been the influence of Satan and his agents, but the lifting up on the cross of the Son of man would draw men to Him and not Satan.

Verse 33. This verse is added to indicate that the lifting up mentioned in the preceding one was to be a literal action upon his body.

Verse 34. As usual, the people failed to recognize in Jesus a person who was both human and divine. As a result, they could not understand how he could die bodily, and yet establish a kingdom that would "stand forever."

Verse 35. Jesus did not give the people a direct reply, for he had already given them many lessons about his great work in cooperation with his Father, and they seemed to be overlooked by most of them. But he intimated that his personal instructions would soon be ended, and they should make use of them while they could.

Verse 36. Jesus gave them one more parting exhortation to walk in the light that had been offered to them, then he disappeared from the crowd.

Verse 37. The hardness of men's hearts prevents them from taking a fair view of the plainest evidences. The miracles that Jesus performed were so many and under such varied circumstances, that it should have been more difficult to doubt than to believe.

Verse 38. God never did force a man to do wrong; but He knows all about the future, and can see the actions of men for centuries before they are born. With such knowledge of the future, God inspired his prophets to write about it. The common phrase "that it might be fulfilled," means the same as if it said, "and in so doing, it fulfilled," etc. The prophecy of Esaias

(Isaiah) cited is in chapter 53: 1 of his book.

Verse 39. *Could not.* The first word is from DUNAMAI, and the definitions of Thayer and Robinson agree, but the latter is clearer and I shall quote it as follows: "To be able, I can." He then adds the following explanations: "Both in a physical and moral sense, and whether depending on the disposition and faculties of the mind, on the degree of strength or skill, or on the nature and external circumstances of the case." Upon further consideration, I think it will be helpful to quote Thayer's definition also: "To be able, have power," and his comments are, "Whether by virtue of one's own ability and resources, or a state of mind, or through favorable circumstances." This information from the lexicons teaches us that these people had deliberately closed their eyes and hardened their hearts against the light of God's truth. In such a state of mind they *could not* believe in the sense of the word as explained by the lexicons. *Because that Esaias said* means that Esaias (Isaiah) said it because God knew it would happen, and caused the prophet to write it. (See comments, preceding verse.)

Verse 40. This verse is to be understood in the light of comments on verses 38, 39.

Verse 41. The account of this vision is in Isaiah 6: 1-10. *Saw his glory is* described in the first four verses of the passage cited.

Verse 42. The significance of being put out of the synagogue is set forth at chapter 9: 22, 23. But though it was a great privilege to be admitted to these assemblies, neither that nor any other personal advantage should have been counted above the honor of being a believer in Christ.

Verse 43. This verse states the motive of the conduct mentioned in the preceding one. It is hard to understand, but perhaps it is because the favor of God is connected with requirement that one shall sacrifice some of his selfish practices.

Verse 44. Jesus means that believing on him did not stop there; it includes belief in God also. The truth is that no man can truthfully say he believes on either the Father or the Son without believing on the other.

Verse 45. This verse embraces the same principle as the preceding, but the difference is due to the personalities of the two. In order for man to

see Jesus, he had to take on himself the fleshly body. But in spirit and purpose they are the same, so that seeing Jesus was virtually equivalent to seeing God.

Verse 46. By coming into the world in human form, Jesus was enabled to bring the light of Heaven within the grasp of man, thereby delivering him from spiritual darkness.

Verse 47. The original word for *judge* has several shades of meaning; one of them is, "to pronounce an opinion concerning right and wrong." The world had already been pronounced wrong or "in unbelief" (Romans 11: 32) before Jesus came into it, hence he did not come for that purpose. Instead, He came to provide a plan whereby the world might be saved from its bondage of unbelief.

Verse 48. If a man rejects the plan offered by Jesus for his salvation, then God will judge him in the last day. When that day arrives, God will bring condemnation upon the disobedient man, finding him guilty under the words that were spoken by his Son, and using him as the acting judge (Acts 17: 31).

Verse 49. It will be consistent for the Father to judge the unbeliever by the words of Jesus, because He has delivered to mankind the words that his Father gave him.

Verse 50. Jesus could speak in this positive manner about the laws of his Father, because he was with Him from the beginning, and had direct and personal knowledge of their eternal character. (See chapter 1: 1, 14.)

JOHN 13

Verse 1. This was the fourth and last passover that Jesus attended after his baptism. *Before the feast* means just before, for *the hour* of his death was in sight; he was to die the next day. *Loved them unto the end.* Regardless of the many weaknesses the apostles had shown at various times, Jesus never wavered in his love for them.

Verse 2. This chapter corresponds with Luke 22: 1-23 in most respects. There are some items of that last night given in Luke's account that John does not give, and vice versa. The most significant difference being at the point when Jesus instituted his own supper. Not that any disagreement exists, but the items are more detailed in some accounts than in the others, and I shall comment on that when we come to verse 23. Until then the comments will be made on the verses in their order. *Being ended* is translated "taking place" by the Englishman's Greek New Testament. That is correct, for the passover supper was far from being ended when Jesus did the things that are recorded now. *The devil having put.* This was done when Judas saw what he called the "waste" of the precious ointment. (See the comments at Matthew 26: 14.)

Verse 3. Jesus knew that the work his Father had given him to do was about done, and that he would soon return to Him from whom he had come into the world.

Verse 4. The *garments* Jesus laid aside were the outer ones that were worn over the closer-fitting ones next to the body. They were discarded for the time in order to give more freedom for the manual performance he intended to do.

Verse 5. A great deal of confusion has come upon the religious world over the subject of feet washing. I shall quote from Smith's Bible Dictionary concerning this: "Washing the Hands and Feet. As knives and forks were not used in the East, in Scripture times, in eating, it was necessary that the hand, which was thrust into the common dish, should be scrupulously clean; and again, as sandals were ineffectual against the dust and heat of the climate, washing the feet on entering a house was an act both of respect to the company and refreshing to the traveler. The former of these usages was transformed by the Pharisees of the New Testament age into a matter of ritual observance, Mark 7: 3, and special rules were laid down as to the time and manner of its performance. Washing the feet did not rise to the dignity of a ritual observance except in connection with the services of the sanctuary. Exodus 30: 19, 21. It held a high place, however, among the rites of hospitality. Immediately that a guest presented himself at the tent door, it was usual to offer the necessary materials for washing the feet. Genesis 18: 4; 19: 2; 24: 32; 43: 24; Judges 19: 21. It was a yet more complimentary act, betokening equally humility and affection, if the host himself performed the office for his guest. 1 Samuel 25: 41; Luke 7: 38, 44; John 13: 5-14; 1 Timothy 5: 10. Such a token of hospitality is still occasionally exhibited in the East."

Verse 6. The mere act of having his feet washed would not seem strange to Peter, but he was astonished that his Lord was going to do that for him.

Verse 7. *What I do thou knowest not now.* The customary practice of washing the feet, and the conditions that originated it, were known to Peter. (See the historical quotation at verse 5.) Hence we know that Jesus meant to teach a lesson aside from those facts, that would have a moral and spiritual significance.

Verse 8. Still seeing only the lowly service of hospitality in the act, Peter protested having Jesus wash his feet. This statement opened the way for Jesus to begin the lesson he intended by the performance. He introduced it by the assertion that such a protest was equivalent to rejecting the partnership with Him.

Verse 9. This suggested to Peter that he had missed the point of the whole performance, and that some great benefit was to be derived from his Lord that was not visible in the literal washing. With such a thought about it, he concluded he wanted even a fuller amount of the favor, and asked Jesus for a more general washing.

Verse 10. Jesus understood that Peter still had literal or material washing in his mind, although he seemed to expect some mysterious effects from it. He therefore made his first remarks from that standpoint, meaning that since they were normally clean in the main except their feet, those parts would need washing since they had just come in from a journey on foot. After saying that much on the material side of the subject, admitting them all to be clean in that respect, Jesus immediately added the exception that must be understood from the moral or spiritual standpoint, when he used the short phrase, *but not all.*

Verse 11. John explains in this verse what Jesus meant in the preceeding one. The act of Judas in betraying Jesus was planned by an unclean heart, and hence the Lord referred to him in this indefinite way as being unclean.

Verse 12. Jesus completed the feet washing while making the aforesaid speech, resumed wearing his outer garments, and again took his place at the table where the passover supper was still in progress. *Set down* is from

ANAPIPTO, which Thayer defines, "To recline at table." In old times people reclined while eating, at a table only a few inches higher than the floor. The diners would lie on their sides and rest the head on one hand while serving themselves with the other. They lay at a 45-degree angle with the table, which placed the head of one person virtually in the bosom of the one behind him, and in very intimate cases the two would be very near each other. This position explains how Jesus could wash their feet even while they were eating without disturbing them, and without getting into any inconvenient or unbecoming posture, as would have been necessary were they sitting at a modern table with their feet under it. It explains also how the woman could *stand behind* Jesus while he was eating (Luke 7: 36-38). After Jesus had taken his place again at the table, he asked them if they knew what had been done; meaning whether they knew what it signified.

Verse 13. *Master* is from a word that means teacher, and *Lord* means a ruler. The apostles had recognized Jesus as having both of these functions over them.

Verse 14. As the world would look at the matter, each of the aforesaid qualifications would entitle a man to the services of others. Instead of assuming such a superior attitude, Jesus acted the part of a servant in performing a necessary though humble favor. He specified the washing of each other's feet as an example of the kind of spirit they should manifest in their dealings with each other.

Verse 15. This verse is more general and shows Jesus intended his act to be an example of humility, a characteristic that had been wanting so many times in their conduct.

Verse 16. This verse is more teaching along the same line as the preceding ones. In the kingdom of Christ there are to be no great and small members as men count greatness.

Verse 17. This short verse contains a great principle that permeates the entire structure of man's relation to God. No one can serve Him without knowing what will please Him, but even that knowledge is useless unless it is carried out in performance.

Verse 18. *I speak not of you all.* Jesus knew his lesson of humility would not benefit all of his apostles, for a man like Judas would not be influenced by anything that did not contribute to his selfishness. Jesus did not name the traitor, but cited a prediction about him that is in Psalms 41: 9. *Lifted up his heel* is a phrase based on the ancient manner of reclining at table while eating. (See the comments at verse 12.) In that position a person could receive a morsel of bread from another, and at the same time make the personal attack against him with his heel.

Verse 19. This verse shows another instance where a prediction becomes an evidence after it is fulfilled. (See the comments at Luke 21: 13.)

Verse 20. This verse teaches the relation between God, his Son and the apostles. They all are so connected in the divine plan, that no man can either accept or reject either part of the group, without doing the same thing to the others. Jesus taught this same great truth in Matthew 10: 40, which was just after selecting his 12 apostles and was giving them their "first commission."

Verse 21. *Troubled* is from the same Greek word as that in chapter 12: 27, and the definition is the same in each place. However, the cause of His agitation in the present instance was the thought of being betrayed by one of the group at the table.

Verse 22. When Jesus announced in general terms that one of them was going to betray him, they each gave an inquiring look at the others. There was only one man among them who knew whom Jesus meant, and that was Judas the traitor.

Verse 23. The events of this last night, especially as they pertain to the Lord's supper, are not all stated in any one of the Gospel records; neither are the accounts given in chronological order. Before going any farther with this chapter, the reader should see the notes at Matthew 26: 20. I shall now comment on the verses here in their order. *Leaning on Jesus' bosom.* This act is explained by the comments on verse 12, concerning the position of the body while eating. *Whom Jesus loved.* According to chapter 21: 20, 24, this apostle was John. Jesus was human as well as divine, and had his personal friends as other men do. (See the comments at chapter 11: 3.)

Verse 24. As John was nearest to Jesus, Peter made a sign to him that he should ask Jesus to point out the traitor.

Verse 25. John then asked Jesus direct whom he meant.

Verse 26. When Jesus answered John's question Judas did not hear it. The answer was accompanied with the act of dipping a piece of bread in the dish containing the broth. He did this at the same time that Judas did, which was part of the sign to the other apostles, that answered their question of who was to be the betrayer. (See Matthew 26: 23.) There was nothing strange in their both dipping into the dish at the same time. (See the comments about hands and feet washing at verse 5.) The unusual thing was that of giving the piece to Judas when he had already served himself with one. According to Matthew 26: 25, when this act was done, Judas asked Jesus if it was he who was to betray him. Judas could not have asked the question for information, for he had already contracted with the chief priests to betray his Lord. But all of the others had asked the same question, and if he had kept silent, it would have been so conspicuous as to manifest his guilt.

Verse 27. *Satan entered into him.* Not that it was the first time (Luke 22: 3), for he had previously made his agreement with the chief priests to betray Jesus. But Satan made another and more insistent demand that he carry out his wicked promise. Jesus knew all about it, and hence he added the words of the last sentence. It means the same as if Jesus had said: "Since you have determined to betray me, do not delay to perform the act according to your agreement with the chief priests.

Verses 28, 29. *Need of against the feast.* Not the passover feast, for that was a one-day affair, and it was about over at this time. But that day was followed immediately with seven more days of unleavened bread which was also called a feast (Leviticus 23: 5, 6). The apostles thought that possibly Jesus meant for Judas to go and attend to that matter, since he was their treasurer and handled the money. They had just learned that Judas was going to betray Jesus, but they did not connect that with the suggestion of Jesus about the promptness to be exercised by Judas.

Verse 30. Judas "took Jesus at his word" and *went immediately out* after receiving the sop. He went to the chief priests and obtained a band of men for his wicked use. Thayer defines this band as "a detachment of soldiers." The *sop* was used as a part of the passover feast. Judas went out as soon as he had received the sop and never came back. The Lord's Supper was instituted after the passover supper. (See the comments at Matthew 26: 20.) From the aforesaid truths we will see that Judas was not present when the Lord's supper was instituted.

Verse 31. *Now* is accommodative and means the time was at hand when the Son of man was to be glorified, referring to the scenes that were to end with the crucifixion. *Glorified* is from DOXAZO, which Thayer defines at this place, "To exalt to a glorious rank or condition." The supreme sacrifice which Jesus was soon to make would exalt him to the highest rank of worthiness, for it would constitute Him the atoning sacrifice for the whole world. It would also glorify God since it was his Son who was to be given to the world in this great loving sacrifice. (See chapter 3: 16.)

Verse 32. This means virtually the same as the preceding verse.

Verse 33. *Little children* was an endearing term, used to indicate the nearness that Jesus felt for his apostles. *Ye shall seek me* means that after Jesus was taken from them, the apostles would long for his presence again, because they would miss his loving counsel. They would not be able to follow him *then* (verse 36), because he was going to die soon, and they must remain in the world to do the work for their Master.

Verse 34. *New commandment.* The people of God have always been commanded to love each other, hence that was not what was new. But the motive for that love was new, namely, because *I have loved you.* This was not an arbitrary reason but a logical one. If I know that Jesus loves my brother, I would conclude that the brother was entitled to that love. And if he is good enough to obtain the love of the Master, surely he is good enough for the love of me who am only a fellow-servant of the Master.

Verse 35. Since such love as the forementioned is so different, then when men see it manifested between the apostles, they will take it to mean they are disciples of Jesus.

Verse 36. Peter was referring to the statement of Jesus recorded in verse 33. Jesus repeated the statement, then added that Peter would follow him afterwards. He said this with reference to the manner in which Peter would die. (See chapter 21: 18, 19.)

Verse 37. Peter was always inclined to be rash and impulsive. In his eagerness to go with Jesus (wherever that was to be), he made this exaggerating assertion.

Verse 38. This prediction of Jesus is recorded in Matthew 26: 34; Mark 14: 30, and Luke 22: 34. In some of the passages the prediction includes a few more details than the present one. There is a special feature of the fulfillment in Luke 22: 61.

JOHN 14

Verse 1. Jesus and his apostles are still at the table where they have just concluded the passover supper. We might properly refer to this chapter as an "after-dinner" conversation between the Master and his beloved disciples. He had frequently told them that he would have to leave them, and they were naturally saddened by the announcement (chapter 16: 6). In this speech Jesus wishes to give some words of consolation for their benefit. *Troubled* means "agitated," and Jesus bids them not have such a feeling, and the basis of the opposite state of mind was to be their belief in the relationship between the Father and the Son.

Verse 2. If a dear friend is about to leave us, it would be some consolation to know that his leaving was not to be a permanent separation, and also that he was going away to arrange a special and better place than the one we now occupy. And what is especially cheering is the promise that he will find a place where we and our departing friend can again be together, never to be separated. Such a consolation Jesus offered to his apostles. The *Father's house* means Heaven, the personal dwelling place of God and the holy angels, and the place where Jesus lived before coming to the earth. *Mansions* is from MONE, and Thayer defines it, "A staying, abiding, dwelling, abode: John 14: 2." There is only one place called Heaven as the dwelling of God, and it was in existence before Jesus came to the earth. He **therefore** was not going away to build

or create such an institution. But he was going to make arrangements for the residence of his apostles in that celestial city. If a man writes ahead to a hotel for reservations, he does not expect the managers to build some more rooms, but to reserve those already there for the use of the expected guests. That is what Jesus meant he was going to do when he said, *I go to prepare a place for you.* He was going to Heaven to make "reservations" for his apostles (as well as for all others who faithfully serve Him).

Verse 3. This verse sets forth the following truths. Jesus was going away from the world to his Father's house to prepare a place for his apostles. After making that preparation he was coming to get his apostles. The purpose for coming after his apostles was that they might be with Him in the place prepared for them in his Father's house. All of this allows but one conclusion, namely, the *mansions* promised in verse 2 are in Heaven and not on the earth.

Verse 4. This short verse has two important parts, namely, the place to which Jesus was going (to his Father's house in Heaven), and the way to reach that place with reference to those who would go there after Him. The apostles should have known all this from the abundance of teaching Jesus had given them through the past three years.

Verse 5. In spite of all the teaching Jesus had given them, they seemed to be rather confused. Hence Thomas said they did not even know where he was going, much less know the way to it. His memory certainly was dull, for Jesus had just told him he was going to his Father's house. As to the way in which they (and others) could follow him, Jesus had not spoken as definitely on that point, at least not so lately.

Verse 6. In answering the last question of Thomas, Jesus made his speech more general in its application. That is, he laid down the principle on which all must act who would reach that blest abode in the Father's house. *I am the way* was the answer, and he asserted that no man would be able to reach the Father except by the Son.

Verses 7, 8. These were not new subjects, for Jesus had spoken to them many times along that same line. The human mind is sometimes very frail, especially when it is agitated. The shadow of sorrow over the near departure of their Lord, seemed to dull the thoughts of the apostles. This is directly indicated by what Jesus said in chapter 16: 6. That is why Philip requested to see the Father, although Jesus had previously taught the principle that seeing Him was equivalent to seeing the Father.

Verse 9. *Been so long time with you.* Jesus selected his apostles in the early part of his public ministry (Matthew 10: 1-4), and hence Philip had enjoyed the advantage of that association all that time. It is significant that when Philip asked to be shown the Father, Jesus asked him if he did not know Him. Not that God and Christ are one in person, but they are one in purpose and spirit, and no man can treat or mistreat either one without doing the same thing to the other.

Verse 10. Since a father and his son are of kindred flesh, so the heavenly Father and his Son are thus closely related. In this sense they are *in* each other, though they are not the same person, even as an earthly father and son are not the same person. But if an earthly father and son were as united in character, purpose and spirit, as are God and Christ, than a man would need only to become acquainted with the son to learn the character of the father.

Verse 11. The strongest evidence of the divinity of Jesus was the work he was doing. He could not have accomplished his wonderful works without the aid of his Father. That is why he told the apostles they ought to believe him *for the very works' sake.*

Verse 12. The *greater works* the apostles were to perform were not what are commonly called miracles. Jesus had raised the dead, cast out devils and cured all manner of diseases. No greater miracles of that kind could be performed by anyone. The key to this statement of Jesus is in the words, *because I go unto the Father.* The absence of Jesus did not enable the apostles to do any miracle that was greater than the ones referred to above. But Jesus could not bring men and women into the church, because that institution was not in existence until He had gone *unto the Father.* After that, the apostles could and did bring people into the kingdom of Christ by the preaching of the Gospel. Those were the *greater works* that

Jesus promised they would be able to do after he had gone to his Father.

Verses 13, 14. To ask anything in the name of Jesus means to ask it by his authority. Jesus never asked anyone to do something that would have displeased his Father (chapter 8: 29), therefore when he authorized his apostles to come for a favor or some assistance, the Father would see that it was granted.

Verse 15. This verse words the sentence in the form of a request or requirement. Verse 23 makes it more conclusive; places the keeping of the words of Jesus as proof that the apostles loved him.

Verse 16. This and the next verse contain a promise of the Holy Spirit to be sent to the apostles. This promise was made a number of times in the last hours that Jesus was with his apostles. It pertained to the same Spirit since there is but one (Ephesians 4: 4), but its work through the apostles was so extensive, that Jesus referred to it in different forms of speech. I shall give the reader the several references on the subject which he may form into a chain if he wishes, as follows: John 14: 16, 17, 26; 15: 26; 16: 7-15. I now resume my comments on the present paragraph. It was appropriate to call the Spirit a Comforter, because Jesus was about to leave his apostles and the Spirit would furnish them consolation in the absence of their Lord. *For ever* means "age-lasting," hence the Spirit was promised to abide with the apostles as long as they lived, as a personal guide. It was also to abide in connection with their work to the end of the Christian Age (Matthew 28: 20).

Verse 17. It was called the Spirit of truth because it was to guide the apostles *into all truth* (chapter 16: 13). *Whom the world cannot receive.* None but the apostles were to receive the Holy Spirit in baptismal measure (except the special case of the household of Cornelius, which was temporary), and no one else was ever promised it in any measure until after he had come out of the world into the family of God (Galatians 4: 6; Acts 5: 32). *Seeing him not.* The world does not exercise its mental or spiritual eyes, by which only anyone could see the Holy Spirit.

Verse 18. The Greek word for *comfortless* is ORPHANOS, which is so much like our English word that a lexicon definition is unnecessary. In its application here it means that Jesus would not desert his apostles whom he considered his "little children" (chapter 13: 33). *I will come to you.* This was to be fulfilled figuratively or spiritually by sending to them His representative, the Holy Spirit. It will be fulfilled personally when He comes to take them with him to the home he has gone to prepare (verse 3).

Verse 19. *See* is used in two senses, literal and figurative or spiritual. Jesus was to be slain the next day, and in a few weeks was to leave the earth. After that the world would lose sight of Him literally. But the apostles were to continue seeing him spiritually through the association made possibly by the Spirit. *Because I live.* This was to be fulfilled for Christ both bodily and spiritually. He was to come forth from the dead to die no more, and also was to live continuously in the church for which he died and in which all of his faithful disciples would live spiritually.

Verse 20. *At that day ye shall know.* The apostles had professed faith in the promises of Jesus, but when the power of the Spirit was bestowed upon them, they would have personal evidence of the divine truth of them all.

Verse 21. This is virtually explained at verse 15.

Verse 22. *Not Iscariot* is inserted to distinguish the two men of the name of Judas. This one was the same whose shorter form was Jude. Judas did not observe the difference between the material and the spiritual manner of being manifested, hence he asked Jesus the question reported in this verse.

Verse 23. *Come . . . make our abode* is explained in the first part of the verse. The spiritual association of God and Christ with the disciples, was to be based on the condition that they keep the words of Jesus.

Verse 24. As the love for Christ is proved by obedience to his sayings, so the failure to keep them requires an opposite conclusion. God and Christ are one in Spirit and purpose, hence to reject the words of Christ is the same as rejecting God.

Verse 25. As long as Jesus was with his apostles, he could keep them informed on the necessary subjects by personal conversation. But they were human and their memory would be uncertain, therefore they would need some kind of helper that could renew it after Jesus was personally gone. That called for another statement of the promise that Jesus had already made in verses 16, 17. The said statement will be seen in the next verse.

Verse 26. *Comforter* is from PARA-KLETOS, and Thayer defines it, "A helper, succorer, aider, assistant." He then explains his definition, "So of the Holy Spirit destined to take the place of Christ with the apostles (after his ascension to the Father), to lead them to the deeper knowledge of gospel truth, and to give them the divine strength needed to enable them to undergo trials and persecutions on behalf of the divine kingdom." In view of the meaning of the Greek word, we can understand why the King James translators gave us "Comforter" in these passages. The apostles had been used to leaning on the counsel of Jesus for guidance, and to have that taken from them would give them a feeling of helplessness as well as loneliness. The Spirit would thus overcome this state of mind and really give them comfort. The inaccuracy of unaided human memory would have made the historical reports of the apostles rather uncertain. But with the guidance of the Spirit, they could relate the various conversations of Jesus with infallible accuracy.

Verse 27. The Greek word for *peace* is EIRENE, and its proper or general meaning is a state of mind that is satisfied. It does not mean that no trials or hardships were to be expected, for Jesus had frequently told his apostles that such experiences were to be their lot. Notwithstanding such conditions, the assurance that Jesus would care for them was to give them a peace of mind that the world could not give. Hence Jesus again bade them not to be *troubled* or agitated.

Verse 28. They should not rejoice over the fact of His absence, but because of what it would mean for him to be again with his Father. In other words, as a feeling of unselfishness, or "rejoicing with them that do rejoice" (Romans 12: 15), they should be glad for his sake. *Father is greater than I.* Jesus and his Father were perfectly united in spirit and purpose, but there are many respects in which a parent is greater than his child, and Jesus recognized that truth.

Verse 29. *I have told you.* This is a general reference to the instances in which Jesus told his disciples of his departure from them. By telling them beforehand, they would be prepared for the shock. Also, when the sad affair came to pass, it would have the virtue of evidence based on fulfilled predictions.

Verse 30. This was the Lord's way of repeating what he had said before, namely, that his conversations with them would soon be ended. According to Luke 4: 6; John 12: 31; 16: 11; Ephesians 2: 2, the *prince of this world* is Satan. *Hath nothing in me.* 1 John 3: 5 states that "in him [the Son of God] is no sin." There was nothing in the character of Jesus that was of interest to Satan, hence he determined to have Him removed from the world, and thus from the association with his apostles.

Verse 31. The wicked motive of Satan was to drive Jesus out of this world by a shameful and violent death. But the deed was to be turned into a demonstration of the love that Jesus had for, the Father, in that he was willing to die to fulfill the will of his Father (Hebrews 10: 7-9). *Arise, let us go hence.* This meant to arise from the table since the passover supper was over. But having given his apostles the consolation speech while still at the table, recorded in the preceding chapter, the Lord concluded to spend the few remaining hours he had left to be with them, by further instructions and admonitions. But while they left the table, there is no evidence that they left the room at once. That movement did not take place till chapter 18: 1.

JOHN 15

Verse 1. One of the leading industries in Palestine was the production of grapes, which called for the cultivation of the vine. It was fitting that Jesus should use it as the subject of his parable at this time. Only a few minutes before he had partaken of the fruit of the vine while in the passover supper, at which time he said he would not drink of it again until he did so in the kingdom. That product having been before their eyes so recently, the apostles could appreciate a parable along the line of its production. *True vine* means that it is not counterfeit. The word is from ALE-THINOS which Thayer defines, "In every respect corresponding to the

idea signified by the name, real and true, genuine." The nation of Israel was compared to a vineyard (Isaiah 5: 1-6), but the vine turned out to be a false one, while Jesus asserted that He was the *true* vine. The *husbandman* was the person who planted and cared for the vine, and the Father is the one in the parable who has that part.

Verse 2. *Purge* is from KATHAIRO, and Thayer's definition is as follows: "To prune." A vinedresser will observe the branches that are inclined to be productive, and will prune off all unnecessary growths that would sap the life from the vine without producing any fruit. If he discovers a branch that has not produced any fruit, he will remove it entirely from the vine as being detrimental to the growth and productivity of the whole plant. This pruning will be given fuller attention further on in the chapter.

Verse 3. *Clean* is from the same word as "purge" in the preceding verse. Jesus teaches that the pruning is done by his word, and hence that the process is a spiritual one. Even a branch (a human being) that is alive and inclined to bear fruit, may have some useless traits developing that would finally damage the general life of the whole plant. It is the divine Husbandman's purpose to cleanse (prune) away those traits, so that it can bear more and better fruit.

Verse 4. Everyone understands the law of nature that requires continucus connection between a vine and its branches in order to bear fruit. The spiritual law is no less established concerning the relation between Jesus and his disciples. There is no salvation apart from Christ, as taught in too many passages to cite now.

Verse 5. *Ye are the branches.* Much speculation has been done over this statement. It is true that Jesus was talking *to* his apostles only at this time, but that was because no other disciples were present. It is also true that the apostles were the first branches because of their official place in the great "plant of renown" (Ezekiel 34: 29), but all vines have branches besides the first ones. Most of the things Jesus said about the branches and the necessity of their connection with the vine (Himself), are true of all disciples. *Without me ye can do nothing.* The first word is from CHORIS, which Thayer defines, "Separately, apart," and he explains his definition at this passage, "without connection and fellowship with one." It is the same truth stated in the preceding verse, of the necessity of being connected with Christ in order to bear fruit. To be connected with Christ today means to be in his body (the church), because if one is excluded from that body he is out in Satan's territory (1 Corinthians 5: 5), where he cannot bear any spiritual fruit.

Verse 6. Observe the phrase, *if a man*, which is too general to be restricted to the apostles. Everything that is said here is true of all disciples of Christ, therefore all of them are branches of one vine. *Cast forth as a branch* means he is rejected because of being separated from the vine and has become withered. As all such dead branches are burned by the men caring for the vineyard, so all disciples who are severed from Christ will be cast into the fire at the judgment day. (See Matthew 25: 41.)

Verse 7. *Ask what ye will* seems unlimited if considered alone. The proviso is in the words about abiding in Jesus, and letting them abide in the apostles. As long as a person's requests are according to the words of Jesus, they will be lawful and will have the assurance of being granted. The line of comparison is still drawn from the vine and its branches. A branch obtains the sap and germinating principles from the vine. Everything that the branch is expected to produce, will be fully supplied for it by the vine. Should the branch call upon the vine to furnish it with the materials necessary to produce apples, the vine would ignore such a request because the branch is not supposed to produce such fruit. Likewise, if a branch of this spiritual vine should *ask* the vine (Christ) for ability to start a wild plant, that request would be denied because the branches (disciples) are not supposed to produce any such fruit.

Verse 8. *Disciples* is a more general term than apostles, although Jesus was talking to the latter. The idea is that what Jesus was teaching was true of all disciples of Jesus. If a person should see grapes growing on a branch, he might not be able to see anything but the branch due to its being uncovered only, while the vine was hidden from view. But later he might be permitted to see a vine only of a tame variety. From this combined circumstance he would be able to conclude that the branch on which he saw the tame grapes was connected with that tame vine, because no other kind of plant could produce such fruit. Also, when people see certain kinds of spiritual fruit being produced by men and women, they will know them to be disciples of Jesus, seeing that no other relationship can produce that kind of life. That is why Jesus said, *so shall ye be my disciples* in the eyes of the world.

Verse 9. A husbandman supplies his vine with soil and other necessary material for producing fruit so that it can pass on the material to the branches that are still connected. Likewise, the Father has bestowed infinite love on his vine (the Son), so that he can pass that love on to the branches (the disciples), that are still connected with the vine. Hence Jesus here exhorts them to *continue ye in my love.*

Verse 10. The figurative form of speech is discarded now, and Jesus expresses the same thoughts in direct language, and exhorts his disciples to keep the commandments in order to abide in His love. (See chapter 14: 23).

Verse 11. Jesus was about to be crucified, yet he speaks of his joy; Paul refers to this joy in Hebrews 12: 2. Jesus would never pretend having a joy that he could not or did not have, and the joy attributed to him was not the literal experience of the scenes at the cross, for the very anticipation of that ordeal caused his sweat to coagulate while in the garden (Luke 22: 44). The joy was over what He knew would result from the great sacrifice. He wished this joy to be shared by his apostles, and that was why he had taken so much care about giving them an abundance of information.

Verse 12. This is virtually the same as verse 11.

Verse 13. True friendship and love are best manifested by what a man is willing to do on behalf of the ones whom he professes to love. He will be willing even to give up his life for their sake if the necessity arises. Jesus was soon to do that very thing, and hence he wished his disciples to be prepared in mind for the separation.

Verse 14. Jesus did not ask his disciples to give up their lives in the physical sense as he was required to do. Of course, if the enemy should bring bodily persecution upon them, they should be willing to die rather than betray their devotion to Him. But that would be a result of their services, and not a deliberate part of it according to their own arrangement. What Jesus meant was that the true followers of Him would devote their lives to his service. That is why he said what he did in this verse about showing their friendship for Him. They were to be regarded as his friends *IF* they did whatever he commanded of them. Hence if a man specializes on being a "Friend" of Jesus religiously, yet at the same time refuse to obey the commands of the Lord (one of which is to be baptized), such a man is making a false claim and is not a true friend of Jesus.

Verse 15. There were different kinds of *servants* in Bible times, and the distinction should be considered to avoid confusion. In the present passage the word is from DOULOS, and Thayer's definition is, "A slave, bondman, man of servile condition." Robinson comments on the word as follows: "In a family the DOULOS was one bound to serve, a slave, and was the property of his master, 'a living possession' as Aristotle calls him. . . . According to the same writer a complete household consisted of slaves and freemen. . . . The DOULOS therefore was never a hired servant." It was in that view of the word that Jesus said he would not call his disciples his *servants*. The distinction is set forth by the confidential relation between Jesus and his religious household which was composed of his faithful disciples. A hired servant was not informed about the intimate affairs of his master, while Jesus wishes his disciples to know all about the things that pertain thereto. Of course this was especially true of the apostles, since the Master depended upon them to pass the information on to the unofficial household members.

Verse 16. See the comments on the preceding verse as to the special need for information to be given the apostles. The English word *ordain* occurs a number of times in the New Testament, and does not always have the same meaning. Much confusion has existed in the religious world over this word, and most of it is due to the erroneous principles taught by Rome, and brought over into the so-called Protestant groups by their teachers. It will be helpful to give the reader a complete view of this word as it comes from the various Greek originals. It will not be quoted in full again, hence he should make note of its location for ready reference. The following table gives all the words in the Greek New Testament that are rendered "ordain" in Authorized Version, together with the references where they are found, followed by the definitions according to Thayer.

DIATASSO. 1 Corinthians 7: 17; 9: 14; Galatians 3: 19. "To arrange, appoint, ordain, prescribe, give order." KATHISTEMI. Titus 1: 5; Hebrews 5: 1; 8: 3. "To set, place, put; to appoint one to administer an office; to set down as, constitute, to declare, show to be." KATASKEUAZO. Hebrews 9: 6. "To furnish, equip, prepare, make ready; to construct, erect; adorning and equipping with all things necessary." KRINO. Acts 16: 4. "To determine, resolve, decree." HORIZO. Acts 10: 42; 17: 31. "To ordain, determine, appoint." POIEO. Mark 3: 14. "To (make i. e.) constitute or appoint one anything." PROORIZO. 1 Corinthians 2: 7. "To predetermine, decide beforehand." TASSO. Acts 13: 48; Romans 13: 1. "To place in a certain order, to arrange, to assign a place, to appoint." TITHEMI. John 15: 16; 1 Timothy 2: 7. "To set, put, place." CHEIROTONEO. Acts 14: 23. "To vote by stretching out the hand; to elect, appoint, create." PROGRAPHO. Jude 4. "To write before." PROETOIMAZO. Ephesians 2: 10. "To prepare before, to make ready beforehand." GINOMAI. Acts 1: 22. "To become, i. e., to come into existence." The reader should note that most of these Greek words have been translated also by other words in the New Testament, but I have given only the places where they have been rendered "ordain." The latter part of the verse is explained at verse 7.

Verse 17. This verse is a repetition of verse 12.

Verse 18. It should have been regarded as an honor for a disciple of Christ to be hated by the world. Such hatred began when He attacked the wickedness of the world, and it would be logical for the followers of such a teacher to be accorded the same sentiments. The truth is that one of the evidences of a man's relation to Christ morally is the persecution that is heaped upon him (2 Timothy 3: 12).

Verse 19. The clannish characteristics of the people of the world will lead them to love their own. See Matthew 5: 43-47.) By the same token, when they see that a man's manner of life is the opposite of theirs they will naturally hate him. Such a sentiment is a form of envy or a feeling of (moral) inferiority complex. It is similar to the motive of a spoiled boy who tries to puncture the balloon of his playmate, because he does not have one himself.

Verse 20. The thoughts of this verse are the same that have been mentioned in preceding ones under different terms of relationship. In this passage the relation of ruler and servant is considered.

Verse 21. *Know not him* is said in two senses. The people of the world did not have an understanding of the goodness and greatness of God. Also, they were unwilling to recognize Him for his greatness and hence would not respect his Son's disciples.

Verse 22. The subject of responsibility is what Jesus is teaching in this verse, especially that which is dependent upon instruction. The Lord will not hold men responsible for not accepting any truth that was never offered to them. Jesus had come personally among mankind and been teaching by word of mouth. It is true that most of them stopped their ears so they would not hear, yet the opportunity for receiving the gracious truths made them fully responsible for all the teaching offered to them.

Verse 23. This is taught in chapter 14: 23, 24 and other places.

Verse 24. This verse teaches the same principle of responsibility as verse 22, but from a different standpoint. No intelligent man should fail to grasp the evidence of his own eyes. The people had seen the miraculous works of Jesus through a period of more than three years, and they should have known that no one like them could perform such deeds. The conclusion which they could not avoid was that Jesus was doing the things by the help of God. That is why Jesus accused them of both seeing and hating him and his Father.

Verse 25. *Their law.* The pronoun refers to the Jews who had rejected the teachings of John and Christ. The Sabbattarians teach that the law of Moses was intended to be perpetual and hence to be in force over all mankind. Had that been true, then the

Old Testament would not have been "their" law any more than it was that of Christ and his apostles. The writing cited is in Psalms 35: 19, and according to chapter 10: 34, the Psalms were a part of the law.

Verse 26. This verse is a link in the chain of passages about the Holy Spirit, that was suggested at chapter 14: 16. Jesus was to send this Spirit as a Comforter, and it was to be obtained of the Father. Everything that the Spirit would say would be according to what Jesus had said, and in that sense he was to *testify of Him.*

Verse 27. The apostles had been personally with Jesus from the beginning of his personal work (Mark 3: 14; Acts 1: 21, 22). That would qualify them to speak as eye and ear witnesses, and the *Spirit of truth* would see that their memory was accurate.

JOHN 16

Verse 1. *To stumble* is from SKANDALIZO, and Thayer defines it at this place, "To cause a person to begin to distrust and desert one whom he ought to trust and obey; to cause to fall away." Jesus warned his apostles of what they would have to encounter in their service for Him. The information was to forearm them so that they would not be surprised into error when it came.

Verse 2. *They* refers to the people, especially the leaders of the Jews, of whom Jesus had been saying much in the preceding chapter. Being put out of the synagogue is explained at chapter 9: 22, 23. Paul was a prominent case of this form of persecution as is revealed in Acts 26: 9-11.

Verse 3. Jesus always emphasized the close relationship between his Father and Himself. He maintained that all treatment that was accorded either of the two, was to be considered as being done to the other. Not *knowing* the Father meant not to acknowlelge him and not to accept his truth. The Jews had rejected the teaching of Jesus, and he used that fact as evidence that they did not know his Father.

Verse 4. *That . . . ye may remember.* A prediction becomes evidence after it has been fulfilled. (See Exodus 3: 12 and Luke 21: 13.) *Said not . . . was with you.* Being with the disciples in person, Jesus did not consider it necessary to go into as much detail with his teaching as he did when he was about to leave them.

Verse 5. Jesus knew about the question asked in chapter 13: 36 and 14: 5, but he meant they were not repeating it; the explanation is in the next verse.

Verse 6. Their great sorrow so overwhelmed the apostles that they did not "have the heart" to inquire into the subject of their Lord's departure.

Verse 7. This verse through 15 forms the final link in the chain that was suggested at chapter 14: 16, 17. This passage gives a more itemized statement of what was to be accomplished by the Spirit through the apostles. I shall comment on the present verse, also the others in their order. *Expedient* means "to help or be profitable," according to Thayer. As long as Jesus was with the apostles in person, the Comforter or Holy Spirit would not come to them, for it was not the Father's will that two persons of the Deity should be working personally on the earth at the same time. That being true, it was necessary for Jesus to "retire" from the scene and give way to the other. The Spirit would come to stay with the apostles throughout their work, which would give Him the opportunity to accomplish certain ends that it was not intended for Christ to do.

Verse 8. This verse is a general statement of the work of the Spirit after it has come upon the apostles. *Reprove* is from ELEGCHO and has various shades of meaning, including the conviction of those who are guilty of wrongdoing, and bringing to light what constitutes a life of righteousness. The work of the Spirit (through the mouths and pens of the apostles) that is stated in general terms in this verse, will be considered in its several parts in some verses to follow.

Verse 9. *Of sin.* The Holy Spirit was to convict the world of the sin of unbelief. John 3: 18 teaches that unbelief in Christ constitutes sin, and the apostles were to bring that truth before the attention of the world, inspired by the Comforter which is the Holy Spirit.

Verse 10. We have seen at verse 8 that a part of the definition of *reprove* is to bring to light what constitutes a life of righteousness. While Jesus was in the world personally, he taught such principles orally. But after going back

to his Father, that teaching would have to be done otherwise, and He purposed to do it through the guidance of the Holy Spirit working through the apostles.

Verse 11. The *prince of this world* is Satan (chapter 12: 31; 14: 30; Luke 4: 6; Ephesians 2: 2) who is to be judged. But Matthew 25: 41 states that unsaved men and women will be cast into the same place as the devil and his angels. That denotes the unsaved will be judged likewise, hence the Comforter was to teach and warn mankind of the judgment day and the only way to prepare for it.

Verse 12. *Bear* is from BASTAZO, which Thayer defines at this place, "To take up in order to carry or bear; to put upon one's self something to be carried." Things which would be spoken are not literal or material such as would be taken by one upon his body. The meaning of the statement, then, is that their understanding and memory would not be able to embrace all of the things that Jesus wished his apostles to hear. This thought will be verified by the following verse.

Verse 13. With the Spirit to *guide* them *into all truth*, the apostles would not need to be overburdened with the load, but could always have the assurance that no truth would be omitted that was necessary for their work. The Holy Spirit is the third being in the Godhead, and is wholly subject to the authority of God and Christ who are the two other members thereof. That is why Jesus said that he would *not speak of himself. Will show you things to come.* Romans 8: 27 and 1 Corinthians 2: 10, 11 teaches us that the Holy Spirit is fully aware of the purposes and desires of God. That is why he was able to tell the apostles *things* to come; he would learn it from God.

Verse 14. The Holy Spirit would glorify Jesus by receiving the truth, then passing it on to the apostles. Jesus called this truth his *(mine)*, and by giving it over to the ones whom He had chosen, it would redound to the glory of the Son.

Verse 15. This verse is Christ's explanation of the statement he made in the preceding verse. The Father and Son were so united in the great scheme of human redemption, that what pertained to one was a concern of the other.

Verse 16. *A little while* is uttered twice; the first means the time until Jesus was to be crucified and buried; the second is the time of three days he would be in the grave. After Jesus went to his Father the disciples could not see him, it is true, but in order for him to go to the Father, it was necessary for him to come forth from the grave, and then would come the period that would make the second absence a *little while* also to which Jesus referred in this important conversation.

Verses 17, 18. These remarks were made among the apostles, unknown to Jesus (as they thought), but he always knew what men were thinking about.

Verse 19. Knowing the tension in the minds of the apostles over his remarks, Jesus relieved it by taking up the subject without waiting for them to ask him.

Verse 20. This verse was said in view of the same periods of time that were meant in verse 16. When Jesus was dead, his disciples wept and lamented (Mark 16: 10). At that time the enemies of the Lord were in rejoicing because they thought they had conquered the man who exposed their wickedness. But after the resurrection, and the disciples came to realize that their Lord had risen again, their sorrow was *turned into joy*. (See Matthew 28: 8; Luke 24: 41; John 20: 20.)

Verse 21. The original word for *sorrow* also means "pain," so that it applies to the bodily feeling in this case, as well as the state of nervous anxiety of a woman at such a time. That condition would make the contrast all the more apparent when the joy of the happy termination was experienced. Likewise, the sorrow of the disciples at the death of their Master was more than overbalanced by the rejoicing that came upon his ⊕resurrection and reappearance among them.

Verse 22. *Joy no man taketh from you.* The enemies could plunge the disciples into sadness by slaying their Lord, but the joy that would follow could not be taken from them. That was because He would be the final victor over the grave, and ascend to the Father after having filled them with joy over the resurrection.

Verse 23. The ascension of Jesus was soon followed by the outpouring of the Holy Spirit upon the apostles. That was to guide them in *all truth*, so that they would not need to ask Jesus personally for information, as they did when he was with them. That was the time meant by *that day*. When that time arrived, instead of asking Jesus for favors and information directly, they were to ask the Father, but were to do it in the name of Jesus or by his authority.

Verse 24. *Hitherto* they had not asked anything *in His name* which would mean by his authority. The time finally was to come when he would have "all power" (Matthew 28: 18), to which he refers here by words *ask, and ye shall receive*.

Verse 25. *Proverbs* means a figure of speech, and Jesus evidently refers to his comparison of the expectant mother. *The time cometh* meant the occasion when the apostles were to receive the Holy Spirit in baptismal measure. As that would guide them "into all truth," they would not require any explanatory passages.

Verse 26. *At that day* still has reference to the complete inspiration of the apostles, at which time they would make their requests *in the name* or by the authority of Jesus. *Say not . . . will pray the father*, yet chapter 14: 16 expressly says that he would pray the Father. We are sure that Jesus never contradicted himself, but the next verse will show he meant that the favor of God upon the apostles did not depend solely on the prayer of his Son.

Verse 27. The love of the Father for the apostles of his Son, would be a sufficient motive for sending the Spirit upon them for their guidance.

Verse 28. The former intimate association of Jesus with his Father, agrees with the idea that God would be inclined to honor his Son's apostles by sending them the Spirit. It also would make it appropriate for the Son to return to his Father, after his work on earth was finished.

Verse 29. The apostles grasped the meaning of the words of Jesus, and they admitted that he had already fulfilled the prediction made in verse 25, to speak to them in direct language, and not depend upon figures of speech.

Verse 30. The apostles did not mean to express any previous doubt. The passage denotes that the conversation of Jesus had strengthened their faith and understanding.

Verse 31. Jesus knew the weakness of the human being. He did not question the sincerity of their faith when he asked them *do ye now believe?* But he was using that as an introduction for the sad prediction about to be made when their human weakness would prevail over their faith for a time.

Verse 32. *Every man to his own.* The margin adds the word "home" to the pronoun, and Moffatt's translation does the same. Jesus predicted that the apostles would desert him in his hour of trial, and Mark 14: 50 states the fulfillment of the prediction. *Leave me alone* meant as far as the apostles were concerned Jesus would be alone, but he would still have the comfort of his Father.

Verse 33. All of the foregoing conversation of Jesus was for the purpose of preparing the minds of his apostles for the great crisis that was near. He knew it would be a severe trial of their courage, and he wished to leave them all the consoling assurances they were able to comprehend.

JOHN 17

Verse 1. The passage in Matthew 6: 9-13 is popularly referred to as "The Lord's Prayer." That is not accurate, but in refuting it we may hear another statement that is likewise not accurate. After criticizing the aforesaid phrase, a speaker may ask, "where do we find the Lord's Prayer," and with an air of finality another person will say, "John 17 is the Lord's Prayer." One would get the impression from the above conversation that Jesus uttered just one prayer while on earth. It is true that this chapter is the longest prayer of Jesus that is recorded, but prayers of Jesus are recorded in Matthew 11: 25, 26; 26: 39, 42; 27: 46; John 11: 41, 42 and Luke 23: 34. Besides these recorded prayers, Luke 6: 12 tells of one instance when he prayed all night. *Hour* is from HORA, and Thayer defines it at this place, "The fatal hour, the hour of death." Jesus knew that ere the setting of another sun, he would lie in death at the hands of his enemies. But that very tragedy was to bring glory on both the Father and the Son. *Lifted up his eyes to heaven* means he looked up toward the sky, that being one of the definitions of the Greek word translated "heaven." Heaven as the place where God dwells, is neither up or down, since those words are relative only, and would not mean anything as to direction were it not for the existence of the earth.

Verse 2. *Power* is from EXOUSIA, and its first definition is "authority," and it is the same word that is rendered "power" in Matthew 28: 18. *Over all flesh* means Jesus was to have dominion over the Gentile as well as the Jew, and that he would exercise that dominion for their salvation.

Verse 3. *This is life eternal* denotes that the fruit of knowing (recognizing and obeying) God and Christ is eternal life. There is no way of obtaining such a reward except through a life on earth that is patterned faithfully according to divine law.

Verse 4. The verb *glorify* is from DOXAZO, and Thayer's definitions of it include, "1. To think, suppose, be of opinion. 2. To praise, extol, magnify, celebrate. 3. To honor, do honor to, hold in honor. 4. To make glorious, adorn with lustre, clothe with splendor. To cause the dignity and worth of some person or thing to become manifest and acknowledged. To exalt to a glorious rank or condition." The word has such a wide range of meanings, that we need to consider who is being glorified and who is doing it, before we can know which part of the definition should be applied. By *finishing* the work on earth that God gave him to do, Jesus did honor to the name of God.

Verse 5. *Glory* is the noun form of the same word for *glorify*. Before Jesus came to the earth he was wholly divine. In order to fulfill the work his Father had for him to do, it was necessary for him to take upon him the nature of man in the flesh. That required him to "lay aside his robes of glory" and humble himself to the rank of a servant (Philippians 2: 7). Now that his mission was performed, and he was about ready to leave the earth, he prayed his Father to restore him to his former place in the glory world. The passage in 1 John 3: 2 indicates that his prayer was answered, since "flesh and blood cannot inherit the kingdom of God" (1 Corinthians 15: 50).

Verse 6. This refers to the apostles who had been chosen from among the men whom John baptized. *Thine they were.* John did not baptize any of the Jews into the name of Christ; he only baptized them for the remission of sins, and they belonged to God in a special sense as those who had been reformed according to Malachi 4: 5, 6. The pronoun "I" in that passage refers to God personally, who was to send John into the world. After that great era came, the Jews who came under the influence of John's work were prepared for the service of Christ when he came upon the scene. When he did so and received the men to be his apostles, baptized and prepared for his service, Jesus regarded them as having been given him of God. *Manifested thy name unto the men.* Throughout his association with the apostles, Jesus kept his Father's name and honor before their attention, impressing them with his dependence upon God in all that he did upon the earth.

Verse 7. The apostles were made to know this by the fact that Jesus constantly kept his Father's name before them. By such a procedure, they accounted for the forcefulness of the work of their Master by considering the might of God.

Verse 8. This verse has virtually the same thoughts as the preceding one, but with the application being made specifically to the teaching of Jesus. The perfect agreement between the words of Jesus and those of his Father (as far as they had heard them), was evidence that God sent Jesus into the world. He would not have corroborated the sayings of Jesus had his coming been without the authority of his Father.

Verse 9. *I pray not for the world.* That is, he was not praying for the world in that part of his prayer; that will come later in his petition. *They are thine* is explained by the comments on verse 6.

Verse 10. This beautiful verse shows the complete and affectionate unity that existed between Jesus and God, in all of the affairs concerning the plan of salvation.

Verse 11. *Am no more in the world* is accommodative language. It means that the life work of Jesus was so near the end that his departure from the world was virtually at hand. *These* (apostles) *are in the world.* They were to live on in the work for which Jesus had chosen them. *I come to thee.* This was true spiritually at that very instant, in that Jesus was coming to God in prayer on behalf of his apostles. It was true personally in that the time was near when He would leave his

chosen ones on earth and go to his Father. Hence Jesus saw the need for the grace of his Father to keep the apostles in the bonds of love that their work required. *One* is from HEIS, and Thayer's definition consists solely of the one word in the passage as we have it, which is "one." But he uses one whole page in his lexicon in discussing and commenting on the many phases of the word as it is used in the Greek Testament, and then indicates that he has not exhausted the subject. That is because the word may be used with regard to its numerical value, or in cases where various persons or things are being distinguished, or in compositions where unity of principle is the subject. Under the numerical phase of the word, it would be considering whether the things being spoken of were one in principle only, or one thing literally and bodily. We know that God and Christ were not one in person, hence the oneness of the apostles which was to be *as we are* could not mean they could be one personally. The only conclusion possible is that Christ wished his apostles to be one in purpose and activities in the Master's service.

Verse 12. *While I was with them* refers to the personal association of Jesus with his apostles. Such direct contact would be a strong preventive against being corrupted by the evils of the world. Jesus offered his good influence to all of his apostles alike, and it was not his fault that one man among them failed to profit by it. But such an event was to be expected because it had been predicted that one of the chosen apostles would betray his Lord. *Son of perdition* means that Judas went to perdition because of his deed of suicide. The first word is from HUIOS and is used figuratively. Thayer's explanation of this Greek word for *son* when used figuratively is, "One who is worthy of a thing." By destroying himself, Judas put it out of his reach to be saved, for there is no provision made for salvation that can be embraced after one has passed from this life. *That the scripture might be fulfilled* means as if it said, "and in so doing, the scripture was fulfilled."

Verse 13. *These things I speak in the world.* While Jesus was still with his apostles in person, he spoke the gracious words of instruction and consolation, so that He could thus leave with them the benediction of his hallowed memory.

Verse 14. *I have given them thy word.* This is the oft-repeated truth that is so important that it cannot be spoken too often. Everything Jesus said to his apostles he received from his Father, because he was always in communion with Him. Such instructions could be delivered to them orally while he was with them, but he was soon to depart from them, hence they would need more direct instruction from God.

Verse 15. The work of God and Christ for the salvation of the world, required the personal presence and services of the apostles. That is why Jesus did not ask his Father to take them out of the world, but to protect them from the evils of the world, while they were fulfilling their task for the kingdom that was so great.

Verse 16. While the apostles were human beings and hence were creatures of earthly birth, yet their conversion to the cause of Christ had lifted them to a "higher plane" of living, even as He had shown them the better way of life.

Verse 17. *Sanctify* is explained in a full quotation from the lexicon, in the comments at chapter 10: 36. If the reader will consult that place, he will see why Jesus asked his Father to sanctify the apostles by *His truth* which is the word of God.

Verse 18. God sent his Son from Heaven into the world in the form of a human being. He accomplished his mission within that part of the world that was in Palestine. The apostles were to accomplish theirs by going into "all the world" (Mark 16: 15). The part Jesus was to perform in the scheme of human redemption, did not require his bodily presence anywhere except the country that had been the headquarters of God's nation of Israel. That which the apostles were expected to accomplish required them to contact all peoples and languages in every land.

Verse 19. *Sanctify myself.* Jesus never had any impurities from which to be cleansed, hence the definitions 1 and 2 (at chapter 10: 36) should apply to him. *For their sakes* denotes that Jesus consecrated himself to the great work for the sake of the apostles. One result of the consecration of Jesus was the bestowal of divine truth, and

that was to be the means by which the apostles were to be sanctified. (See verse 17.)

Verse 20. Up to this point the prayer of Jesus has been on behalf of his apostles. Of course he was desirous that they should be saved, and also he wished their work for him to be effective. They were to take the words of truth concerning Christ to the people of the earth, and hence he now includes them in his prayer along with the apostles.

Verse 21. See the comments at verse 11 on the meaning of "one." The believers were to be *one* as God and Christ were, which would rule out the idea of their being only one person. It has to mean oneness of purpose and work. Not only must the believers be united in their work, but Christ prayed that they should be one *in us.* If the whole religious world should become a perfect unit in its practices, it would not avail anything unless its people were in Christ and God. The great object of that unity for which Christ prayed was *that the world may believe that thou has sent me.* No doubt many thousands of infidels are made by the divided condition of those who profess to be followers of Christ. It is not enough for the professed disciples of the Lord to insist that "at heart we are united and believe the same things." The *world* cannot see that, but the outward or bodily activities of the religious groups can be seen, and that is what Jesus was counting on as evidence of the truthfulness of the claims of the Gospel.

Verse 22. One of the commonest words in the definition of *glory* is "*honor.*" It certainly is among the highest of honors to be in the service of Christ. That honor is emphasized by the fact that Jesus bestowed it upon his servants, having received it himself from the Father. Best of all considerations, is the object of the bestowing such honor, namely, that the whole group of interested persons, God, Christ and his disciples, should form a unit in the great cause of human salvation.

Verse 23. This is an emphatic repetition of verse 21.

Verse 24. This part of the prayer was looking forward to the time after the judgment. It is the same thing that Jesus promised them in chapter 14: 3. Again he refers to the glory he had with the Father when he was wholly divine. In order for that to be possible with the disciples, so that they could also have at least some measure of the same personal glory, they would have to be faithful servants of their Master to the end of life. After the resurrection they will be in the glorified state and fit for the association with Jesus in glory. *World* is from KOSMOS which means the inhabitants of the earth. Jesus existed before all other beings except his Father, and enjoyed His love such as a fond parent bestows on his child.

Verse 25. The world in general did not know God in the sense of recognizing and obeying the divine law. *These* means the apostles, who had learned of the Father through their association with the Son and the teaching that he gave unto them.

Verse 26. The general unity of purpose and spirit between God and Christ, including the faithful apostles, makes up this closing verse of Christ's memorable prayer.

JOHN 18

Verse 1. After Jesus finished his prayer, he left the room where they had eaten the passover supper, in company with his apostles. He took them out of the city and crossed *the brook Cedron*, which is otherwise called Kidron. Funk and Wagnalls New Standard Bible Dictionary describes this place as follows: "Kidron: The name of the valley east of Jerusalem, the stream of which is dry during the greater part of the year. Originally the spring Gihon emptied its waters into this part of the valley." Thayer defines the original word for *brook*, "Flowing in winter, a torrent," which agrees with the note from the dictionary just quoted. It shows why it was no barrier against their walking on out to the desired destination. *Where was a garden* means the garden was *over* or beyond this Cedron. This garden is named Gethsemane in Matthew 26: 36 and Mark 14: 32, and a description is given of it at the first-named passage.

Verse 2. This garden had often been the resting place of Jesus with his disciples. A quiet retreat, he would retire to its shade amid the olive and other fruit trees, and there talk to his beloved disciples about the great work of the future. Had Jesus wanted to evade the mob that he knew would be hunting for him, he would never have come into this place on the present occasion. He knew that Judas *knew the place*, and would bring his officers to it. But after *his time* had come, he made no effort to escape or to resist his capture, but submitted like a lamb being led to the slaughter.

Verse 3. John omits the events between the arrival of Jesus at the garden, and the coming of Judas with the mob. Those events are recorded in Matthew 26: 36-46; Mark 14: 26-42, and Luke 22: 39-46. *Band* is from SPEIRA, and Thayer defines it at this place, "Any band, company, or detachment of soldiers." This force had been delivered to Judas by authority of the chief priests and Pharisees. It was altogether unnecessary to form this posse, for Jesus had frequently predicted his own fate, and there never was any intimation on his part that he would give them any trouble. They were equipped with *torches and weapons*, which means clubs, as if Jesus would be hiding among the trees, and would have to be found with the aid of a torch, and then perhaps have to be taken by force.

Verse 4. The crowd was due a surprise, for instead of having to search for Jesus, he anticipated them and came forward saying, *whom seek ye?* The crowd as a whole was unaware of the person who asked them the question. It was night and they had not been around him enough even to recognize his voice.

Verse 5. When the band announced the name of the person they were wanting, Jesus identified himself as the man they were after. All that John records about Judas' part is that he *stood with them*. But the accounts of the other writers show us that sometime in the course of this conversation, he approached Jesus and gave him the betrayal kiss. It might seem that the kiss was unnecessary since Jesus was making himself known and showing no inclination to evade the crowd. But he had made his contract at a time when he did not know what the circumstances would be, and it was "according to form" for him to go through with his agreement for which he was to receive the money.

Verse 6. Had Jesus said nothing, and let them pursue their man hunt unopposed, they doubtless would have been surprised. But when he took a leading part in the search, even to the extent of boldly announcing himself as their wanted victim, they were amazed and stunned, and fell prostrate to the ground.

Verse 7. We do not know what they would have done or said next, if Jesus had not aroused them from their daze by repeating his question. They had recovered sufficiently to answer the question as they did the first time.

Verse 8. *Let these go their way* refers to the apostles. Since Jesus plainly identified himself as the man they wanted, it was not necessary to hold the apostles as if the investigation had to be continued.

Verse 9. *Have I lost none* refers to the saying of Jesus in chapter 17: 12. It is true that the Saviour was to be deprived of the company of his apostles for the time being, but they would be free from the clutches of the officers, so they could take up His work when the proper time came, and hence would not be *lost* to Him.

Verse 10. Peter was always impulsive and rash, and seemed ready to defend his Lord as long as he could do so with material force. But he was a coward later when called upon to show moral courage in behalf of Christ.

Verse 11. This is not the same *cup* that is mentioned in Matthew 26: 39. In that instance Jesus meant the mental suffering he was just beginning to feel, which is more fully described in Luke 22: 42-44. Jesus asked to be spared that present suffering if God willed it so. The *cup* in the present verse means the ordeal of the crucifixion, against which Peter thought to defend his Lord. *Put up thy sword* is commented upon at length in the notes at Matthew 26: 52.

Verse 12. It was at this point that the apostles fled from Jesus, which is shown in Mark 14: 50. Binding Jesus was another unnecessary performance as far as actual security of the prisoner was concerned, for the conversation that had taken place immediately preceding it, showed that Jesus was not even protesting his arrest. But that was another routine act in connection with the services of an armed force of officers.

Verse 13. *Led him away to Annas first.* There was no provision made in the law of Moses for more than one high priest to be in office at the same time, but in the days of Christ the secular government was taking much part in the affairs of the Jews. In that arrangement Annas was president of the Sanhedrin and Caiaphas was high priest. Verse 24 shows that Annas sent Jesus to Caiaphas in the bonds put there by the mob.

Verse 14. This speech of Caiaphas with comments is given at chapter 11: 50, 51. John regarded him as an official of some note, hence made the second mention of him.

Verse 15. The *other disciple* evidently was John, judging from the indirect way he is mentioned in other connections. (See chapter 13: 23; 21: 20, 24.) *Was known* denotes that he had some personal acquaintance with the high priest that gave him more freedom in approaching his presence. By reason of this special intimacy, when they led Jesus into the palace of the high priest, John went in also.

Verse 16. Peter lingered at the door while John went on into the palace, doubtless for the purpose of obtaining permission to bring in also his brother apostle Peter. With such authority, he went to the damsel who was guarding the door, and from her he obtained the privilege of bringing Peter on in.

Verse 17. The foregoing conversation evidently called the attention of the damsel to Peter, and she asked him about his relationship with *this man*, meaning Jesus. Peter denied being his disciple, fearing that it might involve him in some trouble.

Verse 18. The reader should refer to the comments on Matthew 26: 69 for information concerning the palace. That will throw some light on how there could be a fire at the place. Being within hearing distance of the immediate presence of the high priest, it gave Peter an opportunity to "see the end" (Matthew 26: 58).

Verse 19. Jesus was never ashamed of his doctrine (teaching), and really wished it to be known. But the question of the high priest included the disciples as well as the doctrine, which opened the way for the next statement of Jesus.

Verse 20. *In secret have I said nothing.* All statements should be considered in the light of all circumstances and the context generally. We know the facts would not admit the conclusion that Jesus never said anything to his disciples away from the public, hence we should look for the explanation in the meaning of the language. *Secret* is from KRUPTOS, which

Thayer defines, "hidden, concealed, secret." The idea is that Jesus never tried to keep his doctrine from the public. We know that is what he meant here, for in Matthew 10: 27 he told his disciples to preach upon the housetops what they heard in the ear, which means what they heard from Jesus in their private hours.

Verse 21. An officer does not take a man into court and then ask him to make out a case against himself. If one has spoken things against the government, then certainly someone knows about it, and he would be the proper person from whom to obtain testimony. That is why Jesus told the high priest to *ask them which heard me.* Jesus had stated in the preceding verse that he had done his teaching in the synagogue and temple, which were public buildings in which great crowds generally assembled. It surely should not be difficult to obtain legal witnesses if Jesus had been guilty of criminal activities in his teaching.

Verse 22. *Palm* is from RHAPISMA, which seems to have a rather indefinite meaning. It is rendered "a rod" in the margin, but the lexicons do not require that translation, though they admit that the word sometimes may have that meaning. Both Thayer and Robinson prefer the definition, "A blow with the flat of the hand, a slap in the face." It was intended as an insult and indignity. *Answerest thou the high priest so?* They pretended that Jesus had shown disrespect to the dignity of the court.

Verse 23. Jesus had only exercised his "constitutional right" in demanding that if any charge was to be lodged against him, it should be upon the statements of eye or ear witnesses. In the absence of even any attempt to secure such testimony, he protested that they had no right to smite him.

Verse 24. This is commented upon at verse 13.

Verse 25. This was Peter's second denial of Jesus.

Verse 26. It had not been long since Peter had attacked this servant and cut off his ear, and he surely would recognize him. However, he leaves out mentioning the matter of being a disciple, directly, and treats the same subject by asking if he had not seen him *with him.* This conversation is significant, for it means that in the estimation of this servant, being *with*

Jesus was evidence of his being a disciple. His idea was correct as the scripture elsewhere teaches. (See Obadiah 11; 1 Corinthins 15: 33.) Many professed disciples of Christ today will deny any sympathy with the enemies of the church just because they have not taken any formal stand with them. At the same time, they may be seen often associating with them and thus giving them encouragement.

Verse 27. This was the third time Peter denied his Lord. According to Luke 22: 60, 61, Jesus looked upon Peter at this time which reminded him of their conversation, and in remorse the apostle went out of the crowd and wept bitterly.

Verse 28. *Hall of judgment* is from PRAITORION, which Thayer defines as follows: "The palace in which the governor or procurator [administrator] of a province resided." Smith's Bible Dictionary says of this place, "It is the residence which Pilate occupied when he visited Jerusalem." (See notes on Matthew 27: 2 as to the position of Pilate.) Pilate represented the secular government, and it was necessary to bring Jesus before him to obtain a legal sentence of death (verse 31). The pronoun *they* occurs four times in this verse; the first means the Roman soldiers, the others are the "chief priests and elders of the people" (Matthew 27: 1). The soldiers had the charge of personally handling Jesus when he was turned over into the jurisdiction of the secular court; that is why *they* led him into this *judgment hall.* But *they,* the Jews, would not enter into that place, *lest they should be defiled.* It being a Gentile spot, they imagined it would defile them (ceremonially) to come in contact with such a place, and that would render them unfit to partake of the passover feast that was about due. The law of Moses required the Jews to be ceremonially (as well as physically) clean before they could participate in this feast. (See chapter 11: 55).

Verse 29. The Jewish leaders were waiting outside for the reason stated in the preceding verse. *What accusation bring ye?* Pilate was an officer in the secular government, representing that part of the Roman Empire known as Palestine. It was supposed that when a man was brought bound into a hearing of the penal courts, there was some specific and serious charge to be tried against him.

Verse 30. This verse states a cowardly reply to the question asked by the governor. The word *malefactor* is indefinite, meaning an evildoer of any rank or degree. The statement of these Jewish leaders implied that Pilate should take for granted that Jesus was guilty of lawlessness from the mere fact of their bringing him into court. This was contrary to the usages of all courts in any civilized land.

Verse 31. Their failure to name any specific charge, left Pilate to conclude that Jesus had not violated any ordinance of the Roman government, hence he should have no jurisdiction in the case. That is why he told them to *judge him according to your law.* The Jews stated the truth when they said it was not lawful for them to put any man to death, but that was not the true reason they did not want to act in the case. They did not let that truth keep them from killing Stephen, although they did not have even a judicial sentence of death against him.

Verse 32. The whole transaction was being directed by the Lord, who decreed that Jesus was to die on the cross, and the secular government only would put a man to death in that manner. That is why John says that it would be according to the kind of death Jesus had signified would be imposed upon him. (See Matthew 20: 19).

Verse 33. Luke gives us a fuller statement, which includes some false accusations against Jesus (Luke 23: 2). Pilate concluded that the complaint the Jews had was based on some claims of the prisoner that were opposed to the government of Rome. He therefore thought he could bring the issue to the foreground by asking him directly, *art thou the king of the Jews?* The whole situation was based on the idea that no two governments of whatever kinds, could lawfully exist in the same territory at the same time. That idea would be correct if the two were necessarily opposed to each other. But Pilate did not know anything about the character of the kingdom Jesus was heading, hence he asked the question quoted here.

Verse 34. Jesus never asked questions for his own information, for he knew all about men (chapter 2: 24, 25). He took this method of introducing the important conversation to follow concerning the nature of his kingdom.

Verse 35. Pilate represented the matter correctly by referring to his nationality. He stated the truth when he told Jesus that it was his own people who had brought him into this court to be tried before him as a representative of the government of Caesar.

Verse 36. The reply of Jesus was not evasive, but it was not direct, as yet. He wished to set forth the principle on which he could claim to be a king, and still not be any rival of the government represented by Pilate. That was what Jesus had in mind when he said *my kingdom is not of this world.* Jesus never intended to establish a kingdom of a secular nature, while the government of Rome was that kind. That was the reason why Jesus was making the claim of being a king, yet not admitting any charge of rebellion that was being made by the Jews. This verse has been perverted by extremists among professed disciples of Christ. They make Jesus teach that his disciples have no right to take part in the activities of secular governments, particularly those of doing military services, even in defense of their country. They not only err in their position, but make this statement of Jesus teach the very opposite of what he intended. Jesus plainly shows that citizens of secular governments have the right to *fight* in a defensive war for their country. But that does not make it right for Christians to resort to carnal warfare in defense of the kingdom of Christ. And that also does not touch the question of whether they may be citizens of an earthly government (which we know they may since Paul the apostle was one, Acts 22: 25-28), but that subject was not under consideration at all in the present case of Jesus and Pilate.

Verse 37. The speech of Jesus in the preceding verse was taken by Pilate as an affirmative answer to his question, yet he wished a more direct one. He therefore repeated his inquiry, except he said nothing about what people Jesus was to rule. And the answer of Jesus was also without any reference to the people who were to compose the citizenship of his kingdom. *To this end was I born* is in direct agreement with the question of the wise men, when they asked for him who was "born king of the Jews" (Matthew 2: 2). Very logically, if Jesus was to be born as a king, it would be necessary that he *come into the world*. Also, the principles that were to rule in his kingdom would be so different from any the world had even known, that the king himself would have to bring the truth about them into the world. The citizens of the new kingdom would be those who showed a disposition to accept this truth. This is why Jesus exhorted men to take his "yoke" (government) upon them and "learn of me" (Matthew 11: 29).

Verse 38. *What is truth!* I do not believe that Pilate asked this question with any evil motive. The entire situation was new and somewhat bewildering to him. Here was a man brought bound into his court with a clamor for the death sentence from his complainants, yet against whom no specific charge was made. The nearest he could get to their grievance was the fact that the prisoner claimed to be a king. Furthermore, he seemed to claim kingship only over those who accepted the *truth* that he delivered to them. No wonder, then, that he asked *what is truth*. But he did not have time for further details into the mysterious subject, for the plaintiffs were outside waiting for some kind of answer from him. Going out to them, he said *I find in him no fault at all*. In a court where justice is carried out, such a verdict would have been followed by the dismissal of the prisoner.

Verse 39. Although Jesus was found "not guilty" by the court into which he was brought, yet he was not released from custody. Pilate was afraid of public sentiment and wanted to shift the responsibility of terminating the case from his own shoulders to others. He thought of a custom that had been followed, whereby the time of the passover was celebrated by releasing a prisoner. The guilt or innocence of a prisoner did not seem to have any bearing on the selection of the man, except as it might affect the sentiments of the people whose right it was to name the fortunate person. If Pilate could persuade the people to select Jesus for the occasion, it would effect a compromise whereby an innocent man (as Pilate believed Jesus to be) would be let go, without directly denying the clamorous demand of the crowd.

Verse 40. The plan of Pilate did not work. The people did not wish to abandon their custom either, so they gave their unanimous voice that the release was to be given to Barabbas who was a robber and murderer (Luke 23: 18, 19).

JOHN 19

Verse 1. Pilate failed in his effort to get Jesus released under the custom of the times in connection with the passover. He then tried to hope that he could work on the sympathy of the Jews, after they saw the appearance of Jesus as the regular procedure was followed. That began by scourging him, which was usually done to victims about to be executed. It was a cruel ordeal which is described by Smith's Bible Dictionary as follows: "Under the Roman method the culprit was stripped, stretched with cords or thongs on a frame and beaten with rods. (Another form of scourge consisted of a handle with three lashes or thongs of leather or cord, sometimes with pieces of metal fastened to them. Romans citizens were exempt by their law from scourging.)"

Verse 2. Matthew 27: 27 should be read in connection with this verse. The scourging had been done in the court, then Jesus was led into the common hall, where the whole band of soldiers was gathered to see the indignities to be imposed on him. He had said he was a king, and in mockery they put a crown of thorns upon his head. The thorns were those of a brier or bramble bush. Purple was one of the royal colors, so they put such a robe on Jesus which was also in mockery of his claim to being a king.

Verse 3. These derisive words were said in mockery with the same motive that prompted their actions in the preceding verse. *Smote him.* See the comments on chapter 18: 22 for the description and significance of this shameful act.

Verse 4. Having put Jesus through these cruel indignities, Pilate announced to the Jews in waiting that he was bringing their prisoner out to them. *That ye may know* was said with the meaning, "Although your prisoner has been treated with such indignities as you can see, yet no final sentence has been pronounced upon him. I am therefore offering him *to you* because I still *find no fault in him*."

Verse 5. With this "introduction," Jesus appeared on the scene, wearing the crown of thorns with its thousands of prickles having been pressed down upon his head, and robed in the colors that only belonged to Roman kings. His appearance was plainly visible to all the mob, yet Pilate thought to arouse their pity by a pointed phrase, *behold the man.* The first word is from IDE, and Thayer defines it, "see! behold! lo!" He then explains it, "as the utterance of one who wishes that something should not be negelected by another." Robinson gives the same definition as Thayer, thén follows with the comment, "As calling attention to something present."

Verse 6. When the chief priests had their attention especially directed to Jesus, it had the opposite effect upon them to what Pilate expected. They were enraged and caused to repeat their demand that Jesus be crucified. *Take ye him and crucify him.* This was not a judicial sentence; that came later. But it was another effort of Pilate to evade responsibility for punishing a man in whom he still found *no fault.*

Verse 7. *Made himself the Son of God.* This was a new charge as far as Pilate had heard. Up to the present he could get only the idea of a rival against the government, but which was not in any of the evidence so far produced. Pilate was a heathen in religion, and could not realize fully what it would mean to be called by such a title as the Jews named. Yet he was not entirely unacquainted with Jewish history as was indicated by washing his hands (Matthew 27: 24), an act based on Deuteronomy 21: 1-6.

Verse 8. From his knowledge of Jewish history, referred to in the preceding verse, Pilate had some idea of the importance attached to their God. Now here was a man in his court who claimed to be the Son of that God. If such claim was true, then it might be dangerous to mistreat him. All of this in connection with his wife's dream (Matthew 27: 19), filled him with uneasiness so that the record says *he was the more afraid.*

Verse 9. Pilate was still unwilling to let the matter drop, but made another effort to get Jesus to commit himself. The question *whence art thou* was related to the claim just made that he was the *Son of God.* Jesus made no answer to the question, but that was not because he could not do so, neither was it from pure contempt of the court, for he did speak presently. In the appearances of Jesus be-

fore the rulers, he was silent when his personal comfort or safety was all that was involved, and that fulfilled the predictions in Isaiah 53: 7. But when an important issue was called up, he would speak out and give the teaching upon it, as we shall see very soon.

Verse 10. Pilate thought Jesus was maintaining silence in contempt. He thought he would goad him into speaking by a sort of "threat of the law." The self-importance which he felt he possessed was expressed in the words, *I have power.*

Verse 11. Jesus considered it was the proper time for him to speak. He did not deny the power (or authority) that Pilate claimed to have, but informed him that this power was not his directly, but that it had been given him *from above.* It meant that Pilate was acting as the instrument of a Higher Power, and hence that his part in the solemn drama was not purely upon his own motive; he personally did not wish it to be so. But the Jewish leaders, though also acting in fulfillment of the prophecies, were yet carrying out their personal desires. That is why Jesus told Pilate that *he that delivered me unto thee hath the greater sin.*

Verse 12. It seems that every turn of the conversation and events only confirmed Pilate in his belief that Jesus was an innocent man. But his political interests outweighed his conscience, so that he made only such attempts at releasing the prisoner as would not endanger his standing with the government of Caesar. The Jews realized this situation, and used it with telling effect in this verse.

Verse 13. Pilate yielded to the political pressure which the Jews brought to bear upon him in the preceding verse, and concluded he would pass the sentence of death against Jesus. *Judgment seat* is from BEMA, which Thayer defines, "A raised place mounted by steps; a platform, tribune." He further says it was used as the official seat of a judge. This was the spot where Pilate brought Jesus for the final act in the tragedy.

Verse 14. The meaning of *preparation* will be fully explained at verse 31. The present verse puts the time of the crucifixion *about the sixth hour,* which seems to disagree with the account in Mark 15: 25 which puts it at the *third hour.* There is no contradiction in thought when the various kinds of calendars that were used are considered. One method of dividing the day was by the single hours, starting in the morning at what corresponds with our six o'clock, which was the first hour in New Testament times. The hours were then numbered from one to twelve, and a reference to any certain hour (such as 3rd or 6th) meant a period of one hour only. Another form of calendar divided the twelve hours into four periods of three hours each and each period was named by the last hour of that period. By that method, the *sixth hour* would mean the period that really began with the hour that was called the *third* in the single hour method. John's statement is based on this calendar. As the source of my information, I will quote from Owen C. Whitehouse, Professor of Hebrew, Chesnut College, near London, on the Hebrew Calendar: "The later division of the day was: *Third hour*, 6 to 9 A. M.; *Sixth hour*, 9 to 12 A. M.; *Ninth hour*, 12 to 3 P. M.; *Twelfth hour*, 3 to 6 P. M." This same information is given by The Oxford Cyclopedic Concordance, under article "Day."

Verse 15. When Pilate asked the Jews to behold their king (in preceding verse), it enraged them still more and made them want the execution performed at once. Pilate gave them one last chance just before giving Jesus over to the executioners, to change their minds and snatch him as it were from the cross. He made the appeal as pointed as possible by asking, "Shall I crucify your King?" This desperate move of his reminds us of the language of Peter in Acts 3: 13, where he says of Pilate's attitude toward Jesus, "he was determined to let him go." The chief priests rejected all of Pilate's suggestions. Their statement, *We have no king but Caesar*, was not made except as a retort to Pilate's question, and not in the spirit of patriotic loyalty.

Verse 16. Pilate regarded the remark in the close of the preceding verse as final, and at once delivered Jesus unto the soldiers, who led him away to be crucified.

Verse 17. *Bearing his cross.* According to Luke 23: 26, Simon was compelled to help Jesus bear the cross. There was a rule that if a victim condemned to the cross was unable physically to carry it alone, someone would be made to take up the rear part and help

carry it, walking after the other to the place of execution. *Place of a skull.* There is a long note on this phrase at Matthew 27: 33, containing information gleaned from the lexicons and other authentic works of reference.

Verse 18. The *two other* were thieves according to Matthew 27: 38.

Verse 19. The *title* also means an inscription, in the form of a placard or poster, placed on the cross in full view of the passers-by. The wording on this poster was, *Jesus of Nazareth the king of the Jews.* The inscription was to inform the public of the charge on which the victim had been crucified. This one showed that Jesus was nailed to the cross for the "crime" of being king of the Jews.

Verse 20. The inscription was written in the three languages named, because people of those tongues were present at Jerusalem at that time and thus they could read it.

Verse 21. The title on the cross was such a flimsy reason for having Jesus slain, that the chief priests were ashamed as they saw the crowds reading it. They thought it could be made to seem more fitting if the charge would read so as to represent Jesus as an arch impostor; they requested Pilate to change the wording to that effect.

Verse 22. *What I have written I have written*, was a brief way of saying, "I have written the inscription as I wanted it, and I will not let it be changed."

Verse 23. We may learn from Smith's Bible Dictionary (article—"crucifixion"), that the victim to be crucified was stripped of his clothing before crucifixion. It was a custom that the soldiers performing the execution should have the victim's raiment as an extra pay in addition to their wages as soldiers. According to the present verse there were four of the soldiers, corresponding to the four parts of the body to be nailed; the two hands and two feet. This would call for four divisions to be made of the garments so each soldier could have a share. But the coat was woven in one piece in such a way that it could not be divided without ruining it.

Verse 24. In the case of the one-piece garment, the soldiers agreed to decide the question by casting lots for it. *That the scripture might be ful-*

filled means, "and in so doing the scripture was fulfilled," etc.; the prediction is in Psalm 22: 18.

Verse 25. This verse corresponds with Matthew 27: 56, with some variation in the names of some of the women. Mary the mother of Jesus was the same as the mother of James and Joses (Mark 6: 3).

Verse 26. The disciple *whom he loved* was John, the writer of this book (chapter 21: 20, 24). *Behold thy son.* The term *son* comes from HUIOS, which has a great many shades of meaning besides the one commonly used. Thayer says it is sometimes used "of one who depends on another." Jesus used it in that sense as may be seen in the following verse. When he told his mother to *behold* John as her son, he meant for her to depend on him for support.

Verse 27. By the same token as set forth in the preceding verse, when Jesus told John to behold his mother, he meant for him to let Mary depend on him for support. John also understood it that way, for he began at once to take her as a member of his own household. And the arrangement was exactly on the same principle that was taught by Paul in 1 Timothy 5: 4, 16. In that place the apostle was writing about dependent widows, and the obligation of nephews to care for them. The same idea would hold good in the case of others who are able to care for worthy disciples who are dependent.

Verse 28. Not until after *all things were accomplished* did Jesus give expression to his dying desires. In the throes of his feverish last hours, he complained of being thirsty. *That the scripture might be fulfilled* denotes that in his thirst and its quenching he would fulfill the scripture.

Verse 29. The scripture prediction that was fulfilled by this is in Psalm 69: 21. When Jesus expressed his wants by stating the condition of thirst, someone dipped a sponge in vinegar (sour wine) and placed it upon hyssop so as to reach it up to the parched lips of the dying Saviour. This was the most convenient way either of serving or receiving it under the circumstances. It was done merely to quench his thirst and not as an opiate, since it did not have the gall mixed with it which he had refused (Matthew 27: 34). Some confusion might occur over this word *hyssop,*

since both Matthew and Mark say it was put on a reed. I shall quote from Smith's Bible Dictionary on the article in question. "Besides being thus fit for sprinkling, having cleansing properties, and growing on walls, the true hyssop should be a plant common to Egypt, Sinai and Palestine, and capable of producing a stick three or four feet long."

Verse 30. *It is finished.* In chapter 17: 4 as Jesus was praying he said, "I have finished the work which thou gavest me to do." That was said prospectively, because his work on earth was virtually completed then. In the present instance it was said literally, because it was among the last words Jesus uttered before death. *Gave up the ghost* (spirit), indicates that when a man dies, something in his body leaves it, which proves that the human being is not wholly material.

Verse 31. *Preparation.* Funk and Wagnalls New Standard Bible Dictionary says of this day, "This term signifies in general any day which preceded a great feast. The usage is somewhat analogous [similar] to that of the English 'eve' (Christmas eve, New-year's eve, etc.)." The call for such a day lay in the restrictions of the law of Moses regarding holy days. On them it was unlawful to perform any manual labor, even to the gathering of sticks for fuel (Numbers 15: 32-36). It was therefore directed that all their baking and boiling be done the day before by way of *preparation* for the sabbath or holy day to come (Exodus 16: 23).

The law of Moses forbade letting a body on a tree (or cross) over night (Deuteronomy 21: 22, 23). The Jews were attentive to such items as this, and especially as it would have caused a dead body to be thus exposed on a *sabbath day.* What was still more important in this case was that it would have been on a *high* day. The word is from MEGAS, which Thayer defines at this place, "Of great moment, of great weight, important; solemn, sacred." Even without the definition from the lexicon, the way it is used indicates that the sabbath day referred to was not the ordinary or weekly one.

The explanation is in the fact that the day following the crucifixion was the Jewish Passover. Leviticus 23: 1-7 clearly shows that day was a holy one which made it a sabbath day. The regular sabbath came each week, while this other came only once a year, and was commemorative of the deliverance of Israel from Egyptian bondage. No wonder, then, that John called it a 'high day. Crucifixion caused a slow death 'as a rule, so that the victims might linger on into the night and even up till the following day before dying. It was not lawful to permit them thus to remain there, neither could they take them down from the cross while alive. Hence it was a rule to hasten death before night by breaking the legs with clubs, the shock on top of what they had already endured being the final cause of death. That is why the Jews requested Pilate to have the legs of the three broken.

Verse 32. We are not told why the soldiers came to the thieves before Jesus. It was not because of their order on the crosses, for verse 18 says they were on the sides of Jesus. We might speculate and suggest that a humane feeling prompted them to put off the brutal performance as long as possible, but that would be a guess only, and I merely offer it for what it is worth. But the custom of the occasion was carried out under the authority of Pilate.

Verse 33. Jesus had suffered so much physical shock in addition to his intense nervous strain (Luke 22: 44), that he anticipated the soldiers and died before they arrived at the cross. The fact was unusual, and hence Pilate was surprised when he heard that Jesus was dead (Mark 15: 44). The only reason the soldiers had for not breaking the legs of Jesus was that the purpose for the act (to hasten death) was not present. But their refraining from doing it fulfilled another prediction, that his bones were not to be broken (Psalm 34: 20). The same fact was also typified by the restrictions on observing the first passover in Egypt, "neither shall ye break a bone thereof" (Exodus 12: 46).

Verse 34. The scripture does not tell us the motive of the soldier in piercing the body of Jesus with his spear. Doubtless the hand of God was in the act, using the heathen servant as the instrument in producing the greatest event in all history. *Blood and water.* In the very nature of the case, the source of the *water* had to be the circulatory system. The word is from HUDOR, and Robinson defines it, "A watery fluid, serum," and explains it at this place, "which flowed

from the wound in Jesus' side." This critical authority will justify another note, in the form of a medical comment, by Henry H. Halley, as follows: "Some medical authorities have said that in the case of heart rupture, and in that case only, the blood collects in the pericardium (the lining around the wall of the heart), and divides into a sort of bloody clot and a watery serum. If this is a fact, then the actual physical cause of Jesus' death was heart rupture. Under intense pain, and the pressure of his wildly raging blood, his heart burst open." Thus the spear of the Roman soldier started the flowing of the most precious stream that ever existed in the universe. In it was fulfilled the prophetic words, "In that day there shall be a fountain opened in the house of David and to the inhabitants of Jerusalem for sin and for uncleanness" (Zechariah 13: 1). And with that amazing circumstance in our minds, we sing the beautifully solemn words, "There is a fountain filled with blood, Drawn from Emmanuel's veins; And sinners plunged beneath that flood, Lose all their guilty stains."

Verse 35. This verse is virtually the same as chapter 21: 24, which lets us know that it means John. He *knew* that his record was true, not only because he was an eye witness (verse 26), but was one of the inspired apostles and wrote by the Holy Spirit.

Verse 36. This is commented upon at verse 33.

Verse 37. This prediction is in Zechariah 12: 10. The mere act of looking on Jesus might seem as an unimportant item. But Matthew 27: 36 says, "And sitting down they watched him there." This was not from mere morbid curiosity, but it was a part of their duty. Smith's Bible Dictionary says, "The crucified was watched, according to custom, by a party of four soldiers, John 19: 23, with their centurion, Matthew 27: 66, whose express office was to prevent the stealing of the body. This was necessary from the lingering character of the death, which sometimes did not supervene even for three days, and was at last the result of gradual benumbing and starvation. But for this guard, the persons might have been taken down and recovered as was actually done in the case of a friend of Josephus."

Verse 38. *Secretly for fear of the Jews* means that his being a disciple had been kept secret up to this time. But he maintained that secrecy no longer, which he could not do if he performed the act he planned on doing in taking charge of the body of Jesus. The soldiers would not have permitted him to take the body, had he not been authorized to do so by Pilate, hence the record says that he "commanded the body to be delivered" (Matthew 27: 58)." And the open manner of Joseph's actions is expressed in Mark 15: 43, that he "went in boldly unto Pilate, and craved the body of Jesus."

Verse 39. The visit of Nicodemus with Jesus is recorded in chapter 3 of this book. Nothing is said at that place as to the impression made on the ruler, nor of what his attitude was afterward; but the present verse indicates that it left him with a favorable feeling. Also the protest he made against the unfair treatment accorded to Jesus by the Jews (chapter 7: 50, 51) agrees with that attitude. Hence he joined with Joseph in giving the body of Jesus this honorable burial. Thayer says that *myrrh* is, "a bitter gum and costly perfume which exudes from a certain tree or shrub in Arabia and Ethiopia, or is obtained by incisions made in the bark; as an antiseptic it was used in embalming." Of *aloes* he says it is "the name of an aromatic tree which grows in eastern India and Cochin China, and whose soft bitter wood the Orientals used in fumigation and in embalming the dead." The immense weight of these materials that Nicodemus brought would indicate his respect for Jesus.

Verse 40. The products mentioned in the preceding verse were bound to the body of Jesus with the linen cloth, after which it was prepared for burial according to the Jewish custom in practice at that time and in that country.

Verse 41. *A new sepulchre.* This place had become the property of Joseph according to Matthew 27: 60. We are not informed when nor why Joseph had acquired this tomb, but having done so evidently for his own use whenever the occasion came that it would be needed, it was at this time unoccupied. That gave the occasion for the body of Jesus to be placed "wherein was never man yet laid" (stated here and in Luke 23: 53).

Verse 42. *Because of the Jews' preparation day.* Luke 23: 54 says it was the day of the preparation, "and the sabbath drew on." The preparation day was a busy time for the Jews (see notes at verse 31), hence it was convenient from that standpoint to bury Jesus at this place, *for the sepulchre was nigh at hand.*

JOHN 20

Verse 1. It is unnecessary to quibble over the particular hour in which Jesus arose from the grave. Neither should any of the indefinite statements about "darkness" be an occasion for confusion. Mark 16: 9 plainly says "Jesus was risen early the first day of the week." No one of the other accounts disagrees with this, hence the conclusion is that the first day of the week was the day on which Jesus arose from the dead. Matthew 28: 1 and Mark 16: 1 shows that Mary Magdalene was not alone in coming to the sepulchre. These women were coming with the intention of anointing the body of Jesus (Mark 16: 1; Luke 24: 1). But when they got to the tomb they saw that the stone was taken away. Matthew 28: 1-6 and Mark 16: 5, 6 adds the information that they found the grave empty, and that Jesus was alive although they did not realize it at first.

Verse 2. Luke 24: 3 tells why the woman ran to meet Peter. She had looked in and seen the empty tomb and thought the body had been removed and laid elsewhere.

Verse 3. The *other disciple* was the one *whom Jesus loved* (chapter 21: 20, 24), who was John. The two disciples started running toward the sepulchre.

Verse 4. John outran Peter and arrived first at the sepulchre.

Verse 5. John went near enough only to see the empty clothes.

Verse 6. Peter reached the sepulchre, and when he did, he did not pause on the outside as did John. *Went into the sepulchre.* This phrase will be better understood by reading the notes at Matthew 27: 60 on the description of tombs.

Verse 7. The order in which the clothes and napkin were neatly folded and laid back, indicates that no confusion or violence was present when Jesus was ready to depart from the tomb. The *linen clothes* was all the clothing the body of Jesus wore as he was laid away in this tomb, as all of his own raiment was taken from him before he was crucified. (See the notes at Matthew 27: 35.) We are not told how he obtained clothing suitable for public appearances, but we know he was wearing some ordinary kind, for Mary thought he was the gardner when she saw him (verse 15).

Verse 8. By this time John was ready to enter the cave or tomb. The statement is that *he saw and believed.* This may be the origin of an old saying, "seeing is believing." The phrase is not strictly true, for what one sees, he knows, which is not the same as belief. However, the present passage is true, for the thing that John *saw* was not what he *believed.* He *saw* the empty tomb and the unoccupied grave clothes. This caused him to *believe* that Jesus was alive, though at that moment he could not see him.

Verse 9. *Knew not* means they did not realize the meaning of the scripture that predicted the rising from the dead. The writer makes this statement as an explanation of why it took these plain evidences to convince them that Jesus was really alive. The scripture prediction referred to is in Psalms 16: 8-10.

Verse 10. *The disciples* means Peter and John who had run to the sepulchre.

Verse 11. In the meantime, Mary had returned to the tomb, and was weeping in grief for her Lord. Her interest would not let her be inactive, so she stooped down and looked into the tomb.

Verse 12. This gave her a view of the place where the body of Jesus had lain, which was in the same condition it was when she was first at the sepulchre (Luke 24: 3). But this time she saw something she did not see the first•time. That was *two angels in white* sitting at the head and foot of the place where Jesus had lain.

Verse 13. Mary still thought that someone had removed the body of her Lord; she told the angels this in answer to their question why she was weeping.

Verse 14. While this conversation was going on, Jesus had returned to the tomb and was standing near Mary. She *knew not that it was Jesus.* One meaning of the Greek word for *knew* is "to perceive." The circumstance here was perfectly natural because of the unexpectedness of the appearance of Jesus. Mary was so positive that

the body of her Lord had been stolen, that it caused her eyes to be restrained from their usual functioning. (See the notes on Luke 24: 15, 16.)

Verse 15. The salutation of *woman* was so formal and distant, that it helped to keep her in the dark as to his identity. She could think of no one who would be addressing her in this unfamiliar way but the man who had care of the garden. In that case he would likely be the one who had removed the body to some spot more convenient to his work. That is why she offered to take charge of it if he would tell her of it.

Verse 16. Jesus pronounced the one word *Mary,* which was so personal and direct that it roused her from her far-away state of mind. *She turned herself* does not mean that her back had been toward him before, for she had looked at him closely enough that she took him to be the gardener. The idea is that she assumed a more direct and deliberate attitude toward Jesus, for she then recognized him. In her surprised joy she saluted him with one of the most reverent title she knew, which was the Greek word RHABBOUNI, which John interprets to mean *Master.*

Verse 17. *Touch* is from the Greek word HAPTO, and Thayer's definition is, "To fasten to, make adhere to; to fasten one's self to, adhere to, cling to." As the word is used in this verse, Thayer explains it, "Do not handle me to see whether I am still clothed with a body; there is no need of such an examination." I believe this explanation is correct, and that Jesus did not mean merely that no personal contact with him would be right. We may be sure of such a conclusion, for a little later (verse 27), Jesus told Thomas to make a very decided contact with him, and his body was then in the same condition it was when he was talking to Mary. A similar use of words is in the instruction of Jesus to the apostles not to "salute" anyone in the way (Luke 10: 4). The explanation given in that place is as follows: "As a salutation was made not merely by a slight gesture and a few words, but generally by embracing and kissing, a journey was retarded by saluting frequently." *For I am not yet ascended to my Father.* This remark is plainly a logical one under the circumstances. Whenever Jesus went back to Heaven, he would no longer have the fleshly body and other evidences of the eyes as to his identity. But since he had not yet made that change, her own eyes should tell her that it was the same Lord who was crucified. Therefore, instead of spending time with unnecessary handling of his body, she should *go to his brethren* and tell the good news to them. She was to tell them also that their Lord would soon ascend back to their God.

Verse 18. Mary obeyed the instructions of the Master.

Verse 19. *Same day . . . being the first day of the week.* This statement is another proof that the first day of the week was the one on which Jesus arose from the dead. The persecuting spirit of the Jews still hovered in the community, causing the disciples to meet "behind closed doors." Luke 24: 33-35 tells us the subject they were discussing was the report that Jesus had risen from the dead. *Jesus stood in the midst.* This is taken by some to mean that Jesus had already undergone a change in his body, since he was able to appear in their midst in spite of the closed doors. However, that act would not require any greater miracle than did his disappearance from them unnoticed before his death (Luke 4: 29, 30).

Verse 20. Jesus knew the disciples were puzzled by his sudden appearance, and Luke 24: 37 says they thought he was a spirit. But he clarified their confusion by showing them his hands and his side, which still had the wounds inflicted on him at the cross. This satisfied the disciples and made them glad to recognize their risen Lord.

Verse 21. Whenever Jesus promised peace for his disciples, it was always the kind that was backed up by his Father. The same is true of the *sending* mentioned in this place. The wording shows that Jesus was sending his apostles out with the same authority by which He had been sent by his Father. The verse is the same in thought as Matthew 28: 18, where Jesus declared that all power (or authority) in heaven and in earth had been given to him.

Verse 22. *Receive ye the Holy Ghost* was a promise, and not a gift bestowed at that moment. It was the same "promise" that is stated in Luke 24: 49, and the same that Luke meant in Acts 1: 4 when he was preparing to appoint another apostle.

Verse 23. This verse is equivalent in thought and application to Matthew 16: 19. In order for the apostles to be correct in their remitting and retaining of sins, it was necessary for them to be inspired by the Holy Ghost or Spirit, hence the command for them to tarry in Jerusalem until they received the Spirit.

Verse 24. See the notes at chapter 11: 16 on the fact of Thomas' being a twin, also with regard to the popular phrase, "doubting Thomas," applied to him because of the present circumstance. He was not in the group when Jesus showed his hands and side.

Verse 25. The disciples told the story to Thomas, but he demanded to have even more positive evidence of the identity of Jesus than merely seeing the wounds. No severe criticism should be made of Thomas, for he seemed only to be more exacting or cautious than the others, and might not have realized how convincing the very sight of the wounds would be in establishing the identity of Jesus.

Verse 26. In a little more than a week, Thomas had the opportunity he said he would require before he would believe. The disciples were again assembled behind closed doors, and Thomas was present. Jesus came again as he did in verse 19, but his presence did not excite them this time for they understood the situation.

Verse 27. We are not told whether the disciples had reported the statement of Thomas to Jesus, or that it was a part of his general knowledge of all men (2: 24, 25). But he quoted the words of Thomas verbatim as to thrusting his hand in the side wound.

Verse 28. After all the demand that Thomas had made to the other disciples, there is no indication that he took the advantage that Jesus offered him. Instead, the response he made to the invitation was only to *answer* Jesus, and make the full confession of faith, *My Lord and my God.*

Verse 29. Here is the plain statement of Jesus that Thomas believed because he had seen the wounds, which proves the comment above that he did not thrust his hand in the side of his Lord. This passage has the two words *seen* and *believed* in about the same connection they are used in verse 8. That is, Thomas *saw* the wounds which

Jesus only could have exhibited at that time. This identified Him as the one who had been dead but now was alive, and that caused Thomas to *believe* that he was his Lord and God. Jesus did not condemn Thomas for arriving at his faith from the things he had seen. The point is that he had enjoyed an advantage that few others could have, for the world in general was to be left to believe on the strength of sound testimony. All such were to be *blessed* or be considered happy, because mankind could not all have the bodily presence of Christ for an evidence.

Verse 30. This verse corresponds with the thought in chapter 21: 25, as to the immensity of the things that went to make up the life of Christ.

Verse 31. John wrote these last two verses for the information of the readers, the pronoun *ye* referring to them. The immediate purpose of recording the *signs* or miracles was to make believers by them, as Jesus stated in verse 29. The ultimate purpose was to give the believers spiritual life and salvation through His name.

JOHN 21

Verse 1. *After these things* means the events of the preceding chapter. *Tiberias* was another name for the Sea of Galilee. It was according to previous appointment that Jesus met his disciples at this place. (See Matthew 28: 7).

Verse 2. Among the men named as *disciples* was *Nathanael*, the same man who figured in the interesting conversation of chapter 1: 45-51. (See the notes at that place.) The other name for him was Bartholomew, which may be learned from the lists given by the Gospel records. Matthew 10, Mark 3 and Luke 6, name twelve apostles including Bartholomew, but never mention Nathanael, while John mentions Nathanael six times, but never refers to Bartholomew by name one time. The verse merely states that these disciples *were together*, but does not tell the exact spot where they were nor what they were doing; the next verse will give us that information.

Verse 3. The disciples named were together somewhere in the vicinity of the Sea of Galilee, when Peter proposed going fishing, his original occupation. The others of the group said they would join him, and thus they returned to the secular business they were in when Jesus first called them into his service (Matthew 4: 18-22). They did their fishing in a boat by using a net, but although they spent the whole night in their efforts, *they caught nothing*.

Verse 4. In the meantime Jesus had come to the sea and was standing on the shore when morning came, or at least as it was getting on towards daylight. But it was still somewhat dark, so that the disciples could not recognize Jesus.

Verse 5. *Children* is from PAIDION, and its literal meaning is "little ones." It is not used literally in this verse, but is spoken "in affectionate address" according to Thayer. The margin renders it "sirs," and Moffatt translates it "lads." *Have ye any meat* meant to ask if they had been successful in their fishing, which they had not.

Verse 6. The word *right* is used in the sense of right-hand, and has no reference to the distinction between right and wrong, or "right" as contrasted with "incorrect." A school of fish was coming along that side of the boat at that moment. Jesus had divine power as well as divine knowledge. He could have caused the school of fish to come to that spot at the appropriate time, or he could have known that it was occurring by ordinary causes. In either case it would have been a miraculous demonstration on the part of Jesus. *Not able to draw it* without help. (See verse 8.)

Verse 7. By this time it was light enough to recognize an acquaintance, especially by the help of hearing his voice. The disciple *whom Jesus loved* (John according to verses 20, 24), was the first to recognize Jesus, and he announced the fact to Peter. *Naked* is from GUMNOS, which Thayer defines at this place, "clad only in the undergarment." The cloak or outer garment had been laid aside for convenience in the activities of fishing. Peter did not feel "presentable" to come into the presence of Jesus, and threw his fisher's coat over the undergarment. He did not wait to come to land by boat, but plunged into the water and either swam or waded out as it was only 300 feet (verse 8).

Verse 8. The short distance from land is mentioned to explain why they came in a *little ship*. At that distance the water would be shallow, so that a larger boat would not navigate so well, especially when it had to serve as a sort of a "tug" to draw the filled net toward shore.

Verse 9. By having fish on the fire, with bread to eat with them, Jesus taught the disciples that he did not need to depend upon them for the necessities of life.

Verse 10. But the Lord has always taught that man must contribute to his own needs as he is able, hence the disciples were commanded to bring some of the fish they had caught.

Verse 11. The disciples had reached the edge of the water when Jesus told Peter to bring some of his fish. The writer mentions the fact of the net being unbroken notwithstanding the number and size of the fishes, and such reference to it indicates that another miracle was worked to preserve the net.

Verse 12. *Dine* is from ARISTAO. Both Thayer and Robinson define it, "To breakfast," and the latter adds, "to lunch, i. e., to take an early meal before the chief meal." *Durst* is a form of "dare." The thought is that none of the disciples would dare or venture to ask Jesus to identify himself, for they all knew it was the Lord. Curiosity, as well as a desire to be doubly certain, would have prompted them to ask Jesus the question, but the evidences of his identity were so great they did not have the courage to ask him.

Verse 13. The fish having been cooked by the fire that Jesus had kindled before the arrival of the disciples, he served them with bread to them.

Verse 14. *Third time . . . to his disciples*, or apostles. The two other times are in chapter 20: 19 and 26. His first appearance was to Mary Magdalene (Mark 16: 9), but she was not an apostle.

Verses 15-17. I believe these verses should be studied as one paragraph for the best results. Some unnecessary labor has been done by some in the way of technical distinctions between certain words, which might cause us to overlook the main point Jesus had in mind. It is true that the Greek originals for *love, feed, sheep* and *lambs* has each some meanings different from the others. And yet, those distinctions are not great enough to affect the lesson Jesus was giving the apostles. Peter was engaged in the fishing business when Jesus called him (Matthew 4: 18-20). He left his net and followed the call, and later insisted that nothing could separate him from his service to the Master (Mark 14: 31). Notwithstanding such a profession of loyalty, Peter denied his Lord three times (Matthew 26: 75), and in verse 3 of the present chapter he led the others in returning to their former occupation. Now it was the time and place to make him "take his stand" with reference to his service to the Lord. The masculine and neuter genders for the original of *these* are the same in form, hence the Greek grammar will not help us in determining to what the pronoun refers. Strong defines the word, "Of (from or concerning) these (persons or things)." From all the foregoing considerations, the question of Jesus means, "lovest thou me more than you do this fishing business?" Upon his three-fold assertion that he did, Jesus very logically directed him to prove it by devoting his efforts towards the spiritual business of teaching His people.

Verse 18. The Greek word for *young* has the comparative form, which makes it mean "younger." Jesus is speaking of the days when Peter was in his prime physically and able to care for himself, even to the extent of self-defense if necessary. But the time was coming when he would be subject to the will and strength of others. This prediction is so general that we only could have guessed at its meaning, had the writer not given us the key to it in the next verse.

Verse 19. *By what death* indicates not only that the death of Peter would be to glorify (do honor) God, but that the manner of that death was to be a significant item in the affair. I do not believe it requires me to pay any special attention to the tradition that Peter was crucified with his head downward, nor even that he was crucified at all, though that is probable. The point is that he was to die by violence because of his devotion to God. In that kind of experience he would be imitating the example of his Lord, which is what he was exhorted to do in the words, follow me.

Verse 20. This entire verse is given to identify the disciple of whom Peter was about to ask his question. That disciple was John according to verse 24.

Verse 21. In this verse Peter manifests a very natural curiosity, but which will be interpreted by Christ as an intrusion by Peter into matters that should not have concerned him. Jesus had exhorted Peter to follow Him by faithfulness even to the extent of a violent death. The question of the apostle means as if he had said, "And what do you expect John to do; will he have to die a violent death also?"

Verse 22. Jesus did not answer Peter's question directly. *Tarry till I come* means not only that he would not die a violent death, but would not die at all before Jesus returned to earth. But Jesus did not say that such a thing would happen, only that if it did, it would be no concern of Peter's; his duty was to follow Jesus.

Verse 23. This verse gives a clear example of the disposition of men to formulate rumors with no truth as a basis. Jesus only asked Peter a hypothetical question by way of rebuking him for his meddlesome attitude. Then the gossiping spirit of the disciples made an affirmation out of it, and made Jesus say that John was promised that he would live to see the second coming of Christ.

Verse 24. This verse, together with other passages, shows us that the disciple "whom Jesus loved" was John. (See chapter 13: 23.)

Verse 25. Jesus lived and worked with his disciples and among men for more than three years. It would have made a volume or volumes of immense size had all of His deeds been recorded. *World* means the people of the earth. *Contain* is from CHOREO, and as Thayer defines it, the meaning is, "To receive with the mind or understanding, to understand; to be ready to receive, keep in mind." The entire Bible is very brief, and the Lord has placed before mankind enough only to make the necessary preparation for usefulness in this life, and happiness in the next.

ACTS 1

Verse 1. The Greek word for *treatise* is LOGOS. The definitions in the lexicon are very numerous, likewise the word is translated by a great variety of terms in the King James Version. I believe it will be well to state the different terms, and the number of times it is so rendered by each, so the reader may form a general idea of the scope of the original. It has been translated by account, 8 times; cause, 1; communication, 3; doctrine, 1; game, 1; intent, 1; matter, 4; mouth, 1; rumor, 1; saying, 50; shew, 1; speech, 8; talk, 1; thing, 4; things to say, 1; tidings, 1; treatise, 1; utterance, 4; word, 208; Word, 7; words, 4; work, 2. In our present passage it means volume or document, since it refers to the Gospel of Luke. The salutation to *Theophilus* is the same as in Luke 1: 3, which proves that one man is the author of both books. All of the writers in the Nicene Library, a work composed by scholars in the church in the first four centuries of the Christian Era, agree that Luke is the author of the book we are now studying, as well as the Gospel bearing his name. Referring to his former work (his Gospel record), the author says it was a *treatise of all that Jesus began both to do and teach.*

Verse 2. The preceding verse states something of the subject matter of Luke's former book, and the present tells of the event at which it concluded its narrative. *Was taken up* refers to the ascension of Jesus, recorded in Luke 24: 51. These *commandments* pertain to the "Great Commission" given to the apostles, to go and preach the Gospel in all the world. (See Matthew 28: 19, 20; Mark 16: 15, 16; Luke 24: 47, 48.)

Verse 3. *Whom* means the apostles referred to in the preceding verse, who were to be the witnesses for Jesus in the nations of the world. In order for them to be qualified as witnesses to the fact that Jesus had risen from the dead, it was necessary for him to show himself to them. *Passion* is from PASCHO, and Thayer's general definition is, "to feel, have a sensible experience, to undergo; to suffer sadly, be in bad plight." As Luke uses it, it refers to the sufferings and death of Jesus on the cross. *Showed himself alive* indicates how long after his death it was that he showed himself, namely, after his resurrection, since he was *alive. Infallible proofs* comes from one Greek word TEKMERION, and Thayer's definition is, "That from which something is surely and plainly known; an indubitable [unquestionable] evidence, a proof." A proof that was merely reasonably sure was not enough, but it must be so evident that it would be impossible to misunderstand it, and there were to be *many* of them. That would enable the apostles to say, "we know that Jesus lived after his death on the cross, for we saw him, heard him speak, and had this experience so often that it could not have been any delusion or imagination. And this kind of experience extended over a period of forty days, which would make it impossible to have been mistaken about it. Another thing that confirmed their recognition of the identity of Jesus, was the fact that he talked with them of the things pertaining to the kingdom of God, a subject that no stranger would have known anything about, especially if he had been an impostor.

Verse 4. This book reaches back over the last part of the Gospel record, which connects the line of thought regarding Christ. The assembling mentioned in this verse took place before Jesus made his ascension, at which event this book is supposed to begin. The *promise of the Father* was the bestowal of the Holy Spirit to guide the apostles into all truth. That promise may be found in Joel 2: 28-29; John 14: 16, 17; 15: 26; Matthew 3: 11. The apostles were *not to depart from Jerusalem* until they had received this Spirit, since it was necessary for their guidance in the work assigned to them.

Verse 5. When John predicted the baptism of the Holy Spirit (Matthew 3: 11), he also included that of fire. But he was talking to a mixed multitude, in which were some whom John knew would live and die in sin and finally be cast into the lake of fire. And there also were some in his audience who were destined to become apostles, and hence would receive the baptism of the Holy Spirit. John's speech was addressed to the multitude as a whole. But when Jesus uttered the promise of this verse, he was talking to his apostles only, so it was unnecessary to say anything about the baptism of fire.

Verse 6. The apostles held to their notion that Christ was going to erect a temporal kingdom like the one the Jews had before, and deliver it to them as a restoration of their power as a nation. They had given up that hope for a time on account of the death of Jesus (Luke 24: 21). But after his resurrection, they seemed to think they had been a little hasty in their despondency, and that now perhaps he would give them the kingdom, hence the question of this verse.

Verse 7. The specific *time* or date of the plans of the Father were not to be announced beforehand to the apostles. That is why they were told to tarry in Jerusalem until they received the Holy Spirit, and then they would know all they needed to know to carry on the work for which they had been called.

Verse 8. *Power* is from DUNAMIS, which means might or ability. The Holy Ghost or Spirit was to impart this qualification to the apostles, so that they could take the testimony to the uttermost parts of the earth. The need for such power was the reason they were told to wait in Jerusalem for the descent of the Spirit as promised through the prophets.

Verse 9. This verse corresponds with the closing ones of the book of Luke. Both places record the ascension of Jesus, but the present one only mentions the cloud; the other merely says he disappeared. The cloud feature in the ascension is significant, because Revelation 1: 7 says that He will come in the clouds. That agrees also with what will be stated in verse 11 of the present chapter.

Verse 10. *Looked steadfastly toward heaven.* The last word is from OURANOS, which is the only word in the Greek New Testament for the English word "heaven." Yet the inspired writers speak of the third heaven (2 Corinthians 12: 2) which means there are a first and second. Hence we have three definitions of the word in Thayer's lexicon, which I will quote in their order: "1. The vaulted expanse of the sky with all things visible in it. 2. The sideral or starry heavens. 3. The region above the sideral [starry] heavens, the seat of an order of things eternal and consummately [entirely] perfect, where God dwells and the other heavenly beings." Jesus finally entered the third heaven, but the one the disciples saw Him enter was the first. It was logical that Jesus went "up" to heaven, since that is the only direction that can be realized by human eyes. But the term is accommodative only, for literal directions as to altitude are based on the earth; "up" meaning away from the earth, and down meaning toward it. Were the earth and other material bodies destroyed, there would be no "up" or "down" as we use those terms. Whether Jesus left the earth at noon or midnight, he would still have gone "up" as we use the word. The *two men* in *white apparel* were the "angels" of John 1: 51.

Verse 11. Jesus will come in *like manner*, which is why Revelation 1: 7 says he will come in clouds, and also adds that "every eye shall see him." That prediction explodes the heresy that Jesus has come to the earth in such a manner that only the self-styled "witnesses" can see him.

Verse 12. In Luke's Gospel record, he merely states (chapter 24: 52) that the disciples returned to Jerusalem with great joy. In our present verse he states from where they made the journey, namely, from the mount called *Olivet*, which is the same as the Mount of Olives, a distance from Jerusalem of *a sabbath day's journey*, or about three-quarters of a mile. The law of Moses has nothing to say about "a sabbath day's journey," but that was a tradition of the Jews, based on a strained interpretation of Exodus 16: 29 and Joshua 3: 4. Neither Jesus nor the inspired writers endorsed the tradition, but on account of its common use, the term came to have a secular meaning as to distance.

Verse 13. *Where abode* does not mean they resided there, as the word generally denotes, but that they were remaining or passing the time there. That was in obedience to the command of Jesus that they "tarry" and wait for the coming of the "power from on high" (Luke 24: 49). The word *both* commonly denotes that two things only are being considered, but Thayer explains the Greek as meaning, "things are thus connected which are akin, or which are united to each other by some inner bond, whether logical or real." The men named were related to each other as apostles of Christ.

Verse 14. While waiting for the coming of the Holy Spirit, the disciples were improving the time by religious devotions. These exercises included the *women*, for it says they continued thus *with* the women. This is the last time the mother of Jesus is mentioned by name in the New Testament; others are named of that term, but not His mother. *His brethren* means the children of Joseph and Mary; not his disciples, for they were already named in verse 13.

Verse 15. As usual, Peter was the spokesman on this occasion. The *hundred and twenty* disciples means the ones who were present in this assembly. In 1 Corinthians 15: 6 Paul says that Jesus was seen (after his resurrection) by "above five hundred brethren," most of whom were living when the apostle wrote the epistle. Just where they were when the assembly was going on mentioned in the present verse we do not know, for only the apostles had been commanded to tarry at Jerusalem; the others were there by their own voluntary desire only.

Verse 16. The Holy Spirit had not yet come down, but the divine record afterwards indicates full approval of all the proceedings, hence we must conclude that what Peter and the others said and did was by the guidance of the Lord. Peter began his speech with a reference to Psalms 69: 22-25, pertaining to the conduct and fate of Judas.

Verse 17. This means that Judas had been included among the apostles. The verse also indicates that the purpose of the present session was to secure a man to become an apostle in the place of Judas.

Verse 18. *Purchased a field* refers to the "potter's field," mentioned in Matthew 27: 7. *With the reward of iniquity.* Judas did not personally have any part in purchasing this field, for it was done after his death (Matthew 27: 5-8). The phrase means the field was bought with the money that Judas had received as a reward for betraying Jesus. *Falling headlong.* If two statements seem to disagree, they should not be taken as a contradiction if it is possible for both to be true. The other record of the death of Judas says he "hanged himself." There were no "up-to-date" scaffolds available in those days, so Judas would naturally select a place, such as a tree near a precipice, for clearance of his body when he plunged from the footing under him. Then when his weight pulled suddenly on the limb (as the tradition reports it), his body broke it off and he was ruptured as he fell down upon the rocks below.

Verse 19. There is nothing strange in the general knowledge of the affair of Judas. The suicide of a man prominently associated with Jesus could not escape the attention of the people. And the setting aside of a piece of land that ordinarily was discarded, would naturally bring forth many inquiries, and that in turn would suggest the title given to the place. *Field of blood.* Judas did not actually shed the blood of Jesus, neither did the crucifixion directly shed it. The law of capital punishment in Genesis 9: 6 says, "He that sheddeth man's blood, by man shall his blood be shed." Nobody would think this is restricted to cases where the veins of another were literally opened and the blood poured out, either in the act of murder or the punishment for it. Were that the case, a murderer could escape the penalty by merely using some other method of slaying his victim besides bloodletting. The origin of the term is in the declaration of God that the blood is the life (Genesis 9: 4). From this truth the term "bloodshed" came to mean any act of violence that would cause one to lose his life. Judas caused Jesus to lose his life by violence, and hence he was properly charged with bloodshed.

Verse 20. The quotation being cited is in Psalm 69: 25. *Habitation* means a house or place of dwelling, and to be *desolate* means that it was to be deserted. There is no information that the home of Judas was ever occupied by others, or that he left any family to take charge of it. *Bishoprick* is from EPISKOPE, and is the word for "office of a bishop" in 1 Timothy 3: 1. Thayer defines the word as, "oversight, office, charge," which explains why it was applied to the apostle Judas. *Let another take* denotes clearly that the man who is about to be appointed as apostle was to take the place of Judas, and should therefore be regarded as an apostle after the Lord has indicated his choice.

Verse 21. One of the qualifications required in the man to be placed in office as an apostle, is that of constant association with the others and with the Lord Jesus. This idea of being "with him" is set forth in Mark 3: 14.

Verse 22. The extent of time when this association was to have been had was from the baptism of John to the ascension of Jesus. Such an experience would qualify him to be a witness of the resurrection of Jesus, because the death and return to life of the Lord took place between those two events. The proper man would be *ordained* to the office of apostle. (See the notes on ordain at John 15: 16.)

Verse 23. *Appointed* is from HISTEMI, which Thayer defines in this place,

"To bid to stand by." It has the same meaning as our modern word "nominate," but not placed in any office as yet. They named Barsabas called Justus, and Matthias, who were to "stand by" and be ready for whatever might be determined upon.

Verse 24. As far as the apostles knew, each of these men named for the office left vacant by Judas' death was qualified. But the Lord could see defects that man could not, or could observe superior qualities of one over the other that could not be known by human beings. That is why they prayed to the Lord who *knoweth the hearts of all men,* to make the final choice between their candidates.

Verse 25. *Ministry* is from DIAKONIA, and its general meaning is "service." The word will apply to anyone and to any activity that is of service to the Cause of Christ. The *apostleship* was a specific service to be administered only by those qualified and authorized to do it. Judas fell from his position as apostle *by transgression,* hence was responsible for his actions. *His own place* meant perdition according to John 17: 12.

Verse 26. The appointment of an apostle was such an important event, that I believe a full explanation should be made of the *lot* as a means of determining the selection. The word is from KLEROS, which Thayer defines, "An object used in casting or drawing lots." He than explains the performance, "which was either a pebble, or a potsherd, or a bit of wood . . . the lots of the several persons concerned, inscribed with their names, were thrown together into a vase, which was then shaken, and he whose lot first fell out upon the ground was the one chosen." *Fell* is used figuratively, as it is used in Romans 14: 4, where Paul uses the statement, "*to* his own master he standeth or *falleth.*" This also is according to Robinson's definition for the Greek word for "fall" which is, "To fall *to* or upon any one, Acts 1: 26." A natural question would be why such a thing as a "game of chance" would be used in determining the selection of an apostle. That was still in the period when the Lord used "sundry times and diverse manners" (Hebrews 1: 1) to communicate his will to mankind. When He was pleased to use the lot on any matter, he would see that the proper piece would come out. That is the meaning of Proverbs 16: 33, and it is the reason the apostles prayed that the Lord would "show whether [which] of these two thou hast chosen." The inspired writer is the one who says Matthias was numbered with the eleven *apostles*, which he would not have done, had the proceeding not been in harmony with the divine will. Hence we must understand that Matthias was the man divinely selected to take the place of Judas, and to fill out the original quota of the "twelve apostles."

ACTS 2

Verse 1. *Pentecost* is from PENTE-KOSTE, which Thayer describes as follows: "Properly the fiftieth day after the Passover, the second of the three great Jewish festivals; celebrated at Jerusalem yearly, the seventh week after the Passover, in grateful recognition of the completed harvest." Being a Greek word, it is not found in the Old Testament, but the feast is referred to in other terms. It is called "feast of harvests" in Exodus 23: 16; "new meat offering" in Leviticus 23: 16; "feast of weeks" in Deuteronomy 16: 10. *Fully* does not have any original as a separate word, but *fully come* is from the one Greek word SUMPLEROO, and one phrase in Thayer's definition is, "be fulfilled." After the Passover observance, with the 7-day period of unleavened bread immediately following, the next great event with the Jews was Pentecost. During that space of fifty days, the devoted people of Israel were waiting and looking forward to this feast that was observed for one day only. The phrase *fully come*, then, merely means that the waiting days were over and the important day at last had come. *They* is a pronoun that stands for the "apostles," the last word of the preceding chapter. These men had two reasons for being in Jerusalem at this time. They were Jews who were loyal toward the institutions of the law, and more important, they had been commanded to tarry in that city while waiting for the Holy Spirit or "power from on high" (Luke 24: 49). *All with one accord* includes Matthias, the apostle newly ordained, which gives us the significant information that the entire group of apostles was of one mind.

Verse 2. The *sound* was what filled all the house; not the wind nor the Spirit. The sound came *from heaven* or the region of the atmosphere, since that is the place where winds originate, being the movements of the air.

Verse 3. There appeared unto *them*, the apostles, these tongues, for none but they had been promised the "power from on high" on this occasion. *Cloven* is from a Greek word that has been translated by such terms as "parted, disparted, distributed, separated," etc. The significance was that the apostles were to speak in various tongues or languages. That was not only for use on this occasion, but they were expected to "go into all the world and preach the Gospel to every creature," and to do that it would be necessary for them to be able to speak several hundred languages. These c l o v e n tongues were *like fire*, but it does not say they were fire. They sat upon *each* of the apostles, indicating that each apostle would be able to speak in as many kinds of tongues as occasion required when he got out into the world.

Verse 4. It was the house that was filled with the sound, but it was *they*, the apostles, who were filled with the Holy Ghost. This enabled them, *each of them*, to speak with other tongues. This refutes the theory that the Lord assigned to each apostle the ability to speak with some specific foreign tongue, giving him the task of speaking to some of the foreigners present. That will not do anyway, for there were fifteen or more tongues represented at Jerusalem, but there were only twelve apostles, and hence there would not have been enough speakers to go round on that plan.

Verse 5. These Jews were *dwelling* at Jerusalem temporarily only. They had come there to attend the feast of Pentecost as required by the law of Moses.

Verse 6. *When this was noised abroad.* I believe the pronoun "this" refers to the circumstance as a whole, not merely to the "sound," for the text states only that it "filled the house," not the whole vicinity. But such a performance as happened on that occasion could not but be reported by those nearest the scene, and that would bring the multitude to the place to see "what it was all about." When they got to the place they were *confounded*, which means they were confused or amazed, to discover that these men could all so speak that each of them in the multitude could understand the speakers, although no two of them spoke the same tongue, whenever they used that of the country where they were born.

Verse 7. *Are not all these which speak Galileans?* It is true that Galilee and its people did not have a very exalted place in the estimation of many in the time of Christ and the apostles. However, that was not the reason the multitude made the remark here. It was in reference to the fact that all of these spokesmen were of that group and generally spoke in a tongue peculiar to themselves. (See Mark 14: 70; Luke 22: 59.) But here they were departing from their own native speech, and using those of the Jews from other countries all over the world "under heaven."

Verse 8. *Wherein we were born* denotes the language peculiar to the country where they were born and where they had acquired the individual speech.

Verses 9, 10. This paragraph with a part of the next, names the various countries from where these Jews had come to be present at the feast of Pentecost. The number of the different places has been given a variety of counts, ranging from 15 to 17, depending on how technically the distinctions are made. The information as to their location is a matter of simple history or geography, and I do not think that space needs to be used here for that purpose.

Verse 11. The pronouns *we* and *our* refer to the people from the several countries named; *them* means the apostles. *Tongues* being plural is significant, and denotes that the apostles were speaking in more than one tongue. All of this was done for the purpose of demonstrating the miraculous power and divine authority being vested in the apostles, and not with the intention of imparting any doctrinal information to the multitude. That was to come later, after the attention or interest had been sufficiently fixed for them to listen thoughtfully. *Wonderful works* as a phrase comes from the Greek word MEGALEIOS, and Thayer's definition is, "magnificent, excellent, splendid, wonderful." It does not mean "works" as some physical or material deeds, but that God's ability to enable these apostles to speak in this extraordinary manner was wonderful.

Verse 12. *Doubt* is from DIAPOREO which Thayer defines, "To be entirely at a loss, to be in perplexity." Some of the multitude had a respectful attitude toward the situation, but were perplexed over it and honestly wondered what it all meant.

Verse 13. *Mocking* means to sneer or make fun, which was done by a different part of the people than the ones who were honestly and respectfully perplexed. *New wine* is from the one Greek word GLEUKOS, and Thayer defines it, "sweet wine," and he explains the definition to mean, "The sweet juice pressed from the grape." I have consulted seven other lexicons, and they all agree with Thayer on the meaning of the word. If that be true, then the question would arise, how could the apostles be drunk on such an article? They could not, but it was an indirect and cowardly way these scoffers took of accusing the apostles of being drunk. And Peter took it to mean that, for in his reply he did not deny the accusation on the ground that new wine would not make anyone drunk; he knew they were insincere in the foolish charge.

Verse 14. *Peter, standing up with the eleven.* The apostles all stood up as a token that what Peter was about to say would be the word of all the apostles. They did not all speak at this time, for that would have been disorderly. Besides, the miraculous demonstrations had all been done as far as was necessary for the purpose of evidence. There will not be any further miracle performed except that of inspiration, to enable Peter to preach the Gospel with unerring accuracy and authority. We are not told just what language he used, but we know it was one that the entire multitude could understand. Verse 7 tells us the multitude (assembled from 15 or 17 countries), *said one to another*, etc. This shows they knew some kind of tongue that was common to all of them, else they could not have conversed with each other. Whatever that tongue was, it doubtless was the one the apostle used. Having stood up for a more effective way of addressing that vast throng, Peter urged them to give serious attention to his words.

Verse 15. *These are not drunken.* The unkind critics had only accused the apostles of being *full of new wine*, but Peter knew they were wanting to besmirch them with the charge of drunkenness, and hence he treated their remark from that viewpoint only. The *third hour* is the same as our 9 A. M. Isaiah 5: 11 indicates that it was not the common practice to begin drinking in the early part of the day. Those people who arose early in the morning for that purpose were of a class that the prophet was condemning. Peter meant that it was too early in the day for these apostles to have become drunken, even if they had been using fermented wine, as that is a slow intoxicant anyway. And that would be especially true of these men who had been in the assembled condition all day, due to the sacredness of the occasion.

Verse 16. The passage to which Peter refers and quotes is in Joel 2: 28-32. The pronoun *this* refers to the entire line of events that was predicted by the prophet, and that had just started with the descent of the Holy Spirit upon the apostles. Having made the reference to Joel's prediction, Peter goes ahead and quotes the entire passage, although some of the things will not take place on the day of Pentecost. The things predicted were to begin their fulfillment at that time, and others were to come at the proper time later, which will be explained as the commenting on the verses proceeds.

Verses 17, 18. *Last days* means the closing days of the Jewish Dispensation. That era was still in force until the Holy Spirit came upon the apostles, and Peter then introduced the Gospel of Christ and the church was set up. *Upon all flesh* indicated that the Gospel was to be given to the Gentiles as well as the Jews. That was one of the things that Joel saw in the over-all vision that was to start on this day of Pentecost. But that item did not come until the conversion of Cornelius in chapter 10. *Sons and daughters shall prophesy* was another item that came later, but it was actually fulfilled according to chapter 21: 9.

Verses 19, 20. This paragraph refers to the events recorded in Matthew 27: 45; Mark 15: 33; Luke 23: 44, 45. Of course no literal changing into blood and smoke took place, but the conditions were such that the terms were a fitting illustration. *Before* is used as if it said, "just before," or "only a short while before." The darkness that came as Jesus was on the cross came only 50 days before the day of Pentecost. In a period of time spread out over as large a scale as several centuries, a space of 50 days would be virtually the same date for each of the events predicted. The circumstance is mentioned by way of identifying the noted prediction. Such an event as the failing of sunshine in the middle of a day, that happened as Jesus was on the cross, had never occurred before. And when it did come so short a time before the *day* on which the Holy Spirit came down, the people would easily associate the two events as parts of the same prediction. Another thing to consider, the time of the Passover (which was also that of the crucifixion) was so near the feast of Pentecost that many pious Jews just "remained over," hence among those on this great day now at hand, were many who had personally seen that darkening of the sun, which would help to verify the prediction.

Verse 21. *Call* is from EPIKALEO, and Thayer defines it at this place, "To call upon (on one's behalf) the name of the Lord, i. e., to invoke, adore, worship, the Lord, i. e., Christ." It is the same Greek word for "calling" in chapter 22: 16, where the context shows that calling on the name of the Lord for salvation means to obey His commands.

Verse 22. Having quoted in full the prophecy of Joel, Peter proceeded to recite the story of Jesus, describing briefly the outstanding deeds of his life, which he will do through several verses, bringing the narrative down to His death and resurrection, and even to the very hour then at hand. He asserted that men were not asked to receive Christ merely on the claims of God, but that He had testified to his Son's divinity by enabling him to perform *wonders and signs.* The apostle further reminded them that they knew about these things, and they never disputed it as we shall find. And the fact that Peter accused this very crowd of guilt in the crucifying of Jesus, verifies my remarks on verses 19, 20, that many of these people had been in Jerusalem at the time when Jesus was on the cross and the sun was darkened for three hours.

Verse 23. *Determinate counsel.* It was determined by the Lord God that his Son should die by violence, and it was also foretold through the foreknowledge of God. (See Luke 22: 22; Revelation 13: 8.) Had it not been the will of God that Jesus should be delivered into the hands of wicked men, they never could have taken and killed him. (See Matthew 26: 53, 54.) But this determination of God did not excuse the wicked Jews, for their motive was an unrighteous one. *Ye have taken* was what the Jews did by their perverted Sanhedrin, and *by wicked hands* means those of the Roman soldiers, because the Jews could not legally put a man to death.

Verse 24. *Loosed the pains of death.* Death does not bring any pain afterward to a righteous man. The statement means that God released his Son who had been bound in a death that had been accompanied by pain. *Not possible.* The impossibility was on the part of the bondage of death, not God, for he determined his Son should rise again.

Verse 25. *David speaketh concerning him* means that David made a prophecy concerning Christ. (See Psalms 16: 8-11.) In this passage David represents Christ as saying the things that are set down in this verse through 28. In these verses all of the pronouns of the first person refer to Christ, while the second and third person pronouns mean God. The present verse expresses the confidence of Christ that God would always be at hand to support and comfort him.

Verse 26. Christ rejoiced because of a hope he had concerning his fleshly body. He knew that he must die, and that his fleshly body would be without its soul for a time. The usual result of such a separation of soul and body is for the latter to decay. Jesus not only had hope that involved his soul (inner man), but also one that was favorable for his fleshly body. That twofold hope will be revealed in the next verse.

Verse 27. When a man dies, his soul (inner man) goes to the unseen or intermediate realm, called Hades in the Greek New Testament, which is rendered "hell" by the King James translators. His body remains on the earth, and after three days it will begin to decompose or *see corruption.* This fact explains the words of Martha in John 11: 39. But this noted passage means that the soul of Jesus was not to remain in hell (Hades) long enough for his body that had been placed in the tomb of Joseph to start decaying. That was why it was neces-

sary for Jesus to be raised from the dead after three days.

Verse 28. *Hast made known* is past tense as to grammatical form, but it is a prediction that God would fully reveal to his Son the *ways of life,* or plan of salvation through his own blood. This assurance filled Jesus with joy because of the agreeable *countenance* or face of his Father.

Verse 29. The listeners might not understand the form of language where one writer would speak as if meaning himself, but was really talking for another. To show them that David was not writing about himself personally, Peter reminded them that he had been dead all these years, because his tomb (still occupied) was yet with them, whereas his prediction concerned a person who was to leave his grave after three days.

Verse 30. Having explained that David was not writing about himself, Peter thought it well to account for his statements. They showed that he was personally interested in Christ because he was to be his (David's) own famous descendant. The most significant item was that this descendant was some day to sit upon the throne (of course in a spiritual sense) left vacant by the change in dispensations.

Verse 31. To do as just predicted, it would be necessary for him to come forth from the grave so that he could establish that throne. "Being a prophet," it was possible for David to make the prediction of the resurrection.

Verse 32. *We* means the apostles who had seen Jesus after his resurrection.

Verse 33. After all these verses from 16, Peter comes directly again to the purpose of his speech; to explain the meaning of what the multitude had seen and heard. That it was according to a promise that the Holy Ghost was to be *shed forth* upon the apostles.

Verses 34, 35. Coming back to David, Peter reminds them again that the prophet had not ascended to heaven and was therefore not at God's right hand. That would explain that another noted prophecy could not have meant him (David), for it says that the Lord (who was Christ) was to sit on the right hand of God, until he (Christ) had become a universal conquerer. This prediction is in Psalms 110: 1.

Verse 36. Peter laid the foundation consisting of prophecy and its fulfillment, citing facts that could not be doubted nor disputed. Upon that foundation he declared that Jesus, the very one they had crucified, had been made by the God of Heaven, both *Lord* and *Christ*. The first word means a ruler, and the second denotes one who is anointed. The sentence means that God had anointed his Son to be the ruler of His people.

Verse 37. *Pricked* is from KATA-NUSSO which Thayer defines, "To pain the mind sharply, agitate it vehemently." They were pained because they were convinced they had killed the very One whom God ordained to be the Saviour of the world. That fact also meant to them that some great condemnation was in store for them unless something could be done about it. In their grief and feeling of guilt, the only thing they could say was to ask the apostles what they should do.

Verse 38. This verse has two distinct parts; command and promise. The command would have to be obeyed at once in order to obtain the desired result, while the promise would be carried out according to the Lord's own plan, to be observed as we consider the conditions connected therewith. *Repent* means to turn from a sinful course and choose a righteous one. *Be baptized* means to be buried in water, the details of which will be discussed at chapter 8: 38. *For* is from EIS, which means in order to, or into, the remission of sins. The gift of the Holy Ghost (or Spirit) was the promise, and it meant that the Holy Ghost was to be given, not that it was to give something to anyone, for it is in no place spoken of as a giver. Besides, in chapter 10: 44, 45, the terms "Holy Ghost" and "the gift of the Holy Ghost" are used in the same sense, proving that the promise that Peter meant in this verse was the Holy Ghost was to be given. The inevitable question that comes up, is what was this gift or when was it to be given? This verse does not answer that question, hence we must look elsewhere for the answer. Chapter 19: 2 shows that men did not receive this Holy Ghost simultaneously with repentance and baptism, else Paul would not have asked the question he did, for he thought he was talking to people who had been baptized with "Christian baptism." The information we are seeking may be

found in chapter 8: 14-17. The people of Samaria had been baptized just as Peter commanded, yet they had not received the Holy Ghost until the apostles came and laid hands on them. Hence the conclusion is unavoidable, that when Peter made the promise in chapter 2: 38, he meant that if they would repent and be baptized, they would be entitled to the gift of the Holy Ghost whenever an apostle laid hands on them.

Verse 39. *The promise* that is meant may be learned from the companion passage in chapter 3: 25, where Peter is speaking on the same subject, but where he calls it "the covenant." It was first made to Abraham (Genesis 12: 3), and concerned both Jews and Gentiles. That is why our present verse says it is to all that are *afar off*. That same phrase is used in Ephesians 2: 17, where the context plainly indicates that it means the Gentiles. The promise was that both Jew and Gentile were to be offered the blessing of salvation through Christ, who was the promised descendant of Abraham.

Verse 40. To *exhort* means to insist on doing one's known duty. Peter had clearly shown the Jews their duty, then it was fitting that he should exhort them to do it. *Save yourselves* means for them to do their part in their salvation by performing the duty mentioned in verse 38. *Untoward* is from SKOLIOS which is defined, "perverse, wicked." To save themselves from that wicked generation, means to escape the fate awaiting it, by obeying the commands the apostle had just given.

Verse 41. *They that gladly received his word were baptized.* This is a very significant statement. Baptism, like all other commandments from the Lord, must be acts of faith in order to benefit one. And when a man has been convinced of the truth, and has been shown his duty as set forth in that truth, he will obey it without hesitation or question. As we proceed in the study of this book, it will frequently be observed that the act of baptism followed the belief of a sinner, and it will be stated in a manner that implies it to be a matter-of-course that if he believes the word he will obey. *Unto them* is not in the original but is supplied by the translators. However, the last verse of the chapter furnishes information that people who were saved (by obedience to the Gospel) were added to the church. We do not know how many of the *three thousand* were baptized on that day, since the text does not deal with that question. But we may properly conclude that ere the day was gone, the "membership" of the newly-founded church had come to be that numerous. And then, as the days passed by, whenever a person obeyed the Gospel, the Lord added him to the church.

Verse 42. *They* means the *three thousand* (and all others daily being saved). *Continued steadfastly.* Both words come from the Greek word PROS-KARTEREO, which Thayer defines, "to give constant attention to a thing." That explains how some of the items of the verse could be observed as the Lord expected, even though the nature of them required only that they be done periodically. One such item is the *breaking of bread*, which we know was to be done only on the first day of the week (chapter 20: 7). This verse is a historical statement of the general practice of the early disciples, and not a set form or order of worship for the public assembly. Besides, some of the items are too individual in their character to be restricted to the public assembly. *Apostles' doctrine* means the teaching of the apostles. In all of their religious activities, whether private or public, they were guided by the teaching that the inspired apostles had given and were giving them. *Fellowship* is from KOINONIA, which is defined in Thayer's lexicon, "The share which one has in anything, participation." That would include financial contribution, but does not apply to that item exclusively. And of course all true disciples would make their entire life a matter of prayer, in recognition of the need for divine guidance, and as expressions of their love for and devotion to the Lord.

Verse 43. This *fear* was not one of terror, but rather a feeling of profound awe settled upon the vast throng who had seen and heard such great things. They had witnessed the demonstrations that followed the descent of the Holy Spirit. They had also been brought to see the light of divine truth, and made to rejoice in the pardon of their sins. The *wonders and signs* were done by the apostles, not by the ones who had been baptized that day. This is another proof that they did not receive the gift of the Holy Ghost at the time of their bap-

tism, for if they had they would have been able to perform signs and wonders (chapter 10: 45, 46; 19: 6).

Verse 44. *Common* is from KOINOS, and Thayer defines it at this place with the one word that is used in the text. He then explains it to mean, "belonging to several." Robinson defines it, "common, shared alike by all." This will be more specifically brought out in the next verse.

Verse 45. *Possessions* is from KTEMA, and Robinson defines it, "a possession, property, estate," which agrees with the definition of Thayer. *Goods* is from a Greek word that has a more general meaning. But since the first word in the passage is shown to apply specifically to real estate, we know the second refers to their personal belongings. Many of these disciples had come from far countries to attend the feast of Pentecost. They had not intended remaining at Jerusalem so long, consequently had not made preparation for such a prolonged stay. In their new-found joy they were loath to leave the community. This induced the resident disciples to create this common fund by turning all their property into money and placing it in one pool, to be drawn from according to the needs of the various members. It should be remembered that no apostle instructed the disciples to start this movement, but it was purely a voluntary action upon the part of the disciples. The Bible in no place teaches or encourages the practice of communism or socialism. On the contrary, it teaches the principle of individual holding of property, granted and guaranteed by the law of the land, with the result that as long as the world stands there will be men who have titles to property, and those who have not; there will be rich and will also be poor people. (See Genesis 23: 17-20; Matthew 26: 11; 1 Corinthians 16: 2; Galations 2: 10; James 2: 1-5; 4: 13, 14.) This arrangement of the community of goods was not instituted in any city outside of Jerusalem that we know of. It was not a divine system, and finally got some people into serious trouble as we shall see in a later chapter.

Verse 46. *Continuing* is from the same word as *continued steadfastly* in verse 42, and has the same definition in each passage. The *continuing* was done *daily*, hence we know the *breaking bread* was not the Lord's Supper, for that was done only on the first day of the week (chapter 20: 7); it referred to partaking of food for material purposes in this passage. It was a season of general visiting and social happy times together as brothers and sisters in Christ. *Did eat their meat* means they partook of their food. *Singleness of heart* means with humbleness and sincerity.

Verse 47. *Favor* means good will and admiration. It was *the people* who had this feeling for the disciples, when they beheld how they loved each other. The opposition of the rulers had not yet been aroused, hence the general good attitude of the multitude had not been corrupted by the spirit of persecution. *Added* is from PROSTIHEMI, which Thayer defines, "To add, i. e., join to, gather with." *Should* does not occur in the original as a separate word, but *should be saved* all comes from SOZO. That word is defined by Robert Young, "To make or keep sound or safe." Robinson defines it, "To save, to deliver, to preserve safe." Thayer defines it, "To save, to keep safe and sound, to rescue from danger or destruction." The Englishman's Greek New Testament translates it, "were being saved." The Lord *added* these *saved* ones to the church, which agrees with Ephesians 5: 23, which says that Christ is the Saviour of the body, which is the church (Ephesians 1: 22, 23). Outward forms of church membership are necessary for the sake of order in the divine government, but unless the law pertaining to salvation (which is completed in baptism) is obeyed, all such forms of becoming members of a congregation will be ignored by the Lord.

ACTS 3

Verse 1. The *ninth* hour was 3 o'clock in the afternoon. There is no ordinance in either Old or New Testament that designates any certain time as *the hour of prayer.* Some pious Jews formed a practice of praying daily at regular hours (Psalms 55: 17; Daniel 6: 10), but it was a voluntary service. The "daily sacrifice" was required by the law of Moses (Numbers 28: 3-6), and this called for two lambs each day. The second one was offered "at even," and the margin words it, "between the two evenings," which was the same as our 3 o'clock, called *the ninth hour* in the present verse. The Jews formed the practice of going into the temple and engaging in a

prayer service at that time, while the priests were out at the altar performing the sacrifice. The apostles were going up to the temple at that time because they knew they would have opportunity of meeting the people, to whom they could preach the Gospel.

Verse 2. As the apostles approached the temple the following events took place. An "object of charity" was lying just outside of the temple, where the people coming and going would see him and perhaps bestow upon him a gift of money. This man was forty years old and had been a cripple from birth. The Old Testament does not give the special name of *beautiful* to any gate of the temple. The passage says it was *called* that, which indicates that the people had come to speak of it in that way, which probably was because of its appearance after Herod had remodeled and adorned the building (Luke 21: 5). Robinson has the following to say of this gate: "Supposed by some to have been the large gate leading from the court of the Gentiles to the court of the Israelites, over against the eastern side of the building, called by the Rabbins the gate of Nicanor, and described by Josephus as covered with plates of gold and silver, and very splendid and massive."

Verse 3. The original word for *alms* means generally any favor or mercy or pity bestowed upon an unfortunate person, but its most specific definition is, "a donation for the poor," and this is what the lame man asked of Peter and John.

Verse 4. When Peter told the lame man *to look on us,* he should have concluded that some kind of favor was in store for him other than a gift of money, for such an action would not have required that he look at them.

Verse 5. But the lame man had never been treated to anything but the kindness of those who carried him to the place daily, and the alms that people bestowed on him. Hence he did not form the conclusion here suggested, but instead he gave the apostles an earnest look, expecting to receive some money.

Verse 6. *Silver and gold have I none.* We are not to suppose that the apostles were paupers, but they had no occasion for carrying supplies of money around with them, for Jesus had assured them that the necessities of life would be given them. In the present case however, if Peter had possessed an abundance of money, it would not have benefited the lame man physically as to his infirmity. He told the man to *rise up and walk*, but preceded the order with a statement as to the source of the power. We should understand that not only did Peter derive his ability to heal the man from the Lord, but he wished him also to know upon whom he was to trust for his recovery.

Verse 7. Miraculous cures may be performed with or without any outward cooperation on the part of the patient. Jesus required the blind man to go wash the clay off his eyes, but He previously had put the anointment on the eyes of the patient. Peter commanded the lame man to rise up and walk, but he encouraged him by taking the initiative and grasping his hand and helping him to arise. This verse tells us in what way the man was lame; it was a weakness in his feet. The mere act of taking him by the hand did not heal him, for any other person could have done that; there had to be some miraculous power exerted by the apostle. It is stated that the healing was *immediate*, which was always the case with genuine miraculous cures. Professed divine healers of today always require "time and patience" for their cases, which proves they are frauds.

Verse 8. A lame man might use enough will power to come to his feet, but he would not be able to show much energy in the enforced action. This man leaped up, and he did not stop with that; he walked and leaped alternately, and continued his movements along with the apostles, so that he entered with them into the temple. While doing all this he was *praising God.* Why did he do that, when it was Peter who had lifted him up? The answer is in the statement of the apostle that he was to arise in the name of Jesus of Nazareth. The man had been carried each day and laid by the gate. He knew that in that act those men had used more physical force upon him than Peter did, as far as the outward performance was concerned, and yet no improvement in his condition had ever been experienced. The only conclusion he could reach was that it was God working through Peter, and that caused him to give his praise to the right one.

Verse 9. The whole event was so evident and public that all the people saw it, and that means there were a great many who witnessed it, for it was in a prominent spot, and there were thousands of Jews in the city at that time.

Verse 10. *They knew* it was the man who had been seen at the gate of the temple, for he had appeared there daily for a long time, and it was easy to recognize him. The natural effect upon the people was that they were filled with wonder and amazement. They knew it was not their own imagination that was affecting them, nor could it have been a forced action on the part of the lame man, for they were too well acquainted with the nature of his case to allow such a conclusion.

Verse 11. *Held* is from KRATEO, and Robinson defines it in this place, "So to hold one fast, i. e., to hold fast to him, to cleave to him." Thayer defines it in the same way then gives the explanation, "To hold one fast in order not to be sent away." This action was perfectly natural. The man had been a cripple since his birth, and had to depend upon alms for a living. Now he was healed and had become an able-bodied man so that he could be on his own. However, since the condition was another one that might be described by the familiar phrase "too good to be true," he had a feeling of dependency that made him afraid to leave the apostles. Another thing that should be considered about his action, it emphasized the part the apostles had in the recovery. When the people saw this man clinging so firmly to the apostles, it announced publicly that they were the actors in the deed, and that the former lame man knew it. Another result that was natural was the gathering of *all the people* near the scene, for it was an extraordinary thing that had happened. *Solomon's porch* was a convenient and comfortable place for the crowd to gather; a description of this porch is given at John 10: 23.

Verse 12. Peter was able to speak with inspiration, but ordinary reasoning would have brought the conclusion indicated here. The people could see the lame man holding fast to the apostles, and as they were *greatly wondering*, it was because they thought these men had caused the patient to be cured through some mysterious virtue of their own. It would have been easy for them to obtain a following from this multitude because of the frame of mind that possessed them. But Peter was the faithful apostle of Christ, and humbly told the crowd that it was not in them' (the apostles) that the lame man had found his recovery.

Verse 13. The circumstance gave Peter another opportunity for preaching Christ to the people. The crowd was composed of Jews, and they were the people who were responsible for the condemnation of Jesus. They were acquainted with the Old Testament (John 5: 39), and knew about the promise that was made to the fathers that a descendant of theirs was to come into the world to bless the nations of the earth. Now Peter connected that promise with the very man they of this audience had caused to die. Peter showed them as being worse even than Pilate, who would have been willing to let Jesus go. The apostle told them that God had glorified that very man in spite of their intended destruction of his great plans. *Glorified* is from DOXAZO, which Thayer defines in this passage, "To exalt to a glorious rank or condition." It was a stinging rebuke to these people, not only to accuse them of condemning Jesus, but to be told that God had over-ruled their malicious attempt and had exalted their victim to a rank in glory.

Verse 14. This verse names two distinct crimes the Jews committed, either of which would have entitled them to the serverest condemnation. It refers to the time when they were to name the prisoner to be released under a custom of that season (Luke 23: 16-21). They denied freedom to a holy and just person against whom no charge had been sustained. In their choice of prisoners they did not name one who was even an ordinary evildoer, but called for a man who was a murderer and a member of a seditious gang.

Verse 15. The Jews could not lawfully put any man to death, and did not personally put Jesus on the cross. But Peter told them that they had killed Him, and it was because they were the ones who caused it to be done. *Prince* is from a word that means the author or leader in an important movement. That is true of Christ as announced by John, "In him was life, and the life was the light of men" (John 1: 4). The apostles almost invariably mentioned the resurrection of Jesus when-

ever they told of his death. Many persons have been killed by the people who were objectionable to them for some reason, but none of them ever lived again until the event of Christ. He not only came back to life, but God did the raising of him, thereby defeating the plans of the Jews who pretended to believe in Him, while disbelieving in his Son. Peter was not relating this to the multitude on some mere hearsay, but declared *we are witnesses.*

Verse 16. *Through faith in his name.* The name and power of Jesus would not have caused this man to be healed, had he not manifested faith in that name by making what attempt he could to arise. *The faith which is by him.* Not only was the lame man required to have faith in the name of Jesus, but Peter could perform the miracle only because he also had faith in the name of Jesus.

Verse 17. *Ignorance* does not excuse anyone in wrongdoing, but it may explain how it came about. The word is from AGNOIA, which Thayer defines, "Want of knowledge." The idea is different from being lacking in common intelligence, for then they might not have been held so strictly to account. But the information was available had they made use of it; they did not, and were like Israel of old who did not know, simply because they did not consider (Isaiah 1: 3). *Wot* is an obsolete word for "know" as the apostle was considering his own frame of mind. As to the *rulers*, they were the ones in power and who were chiefly responsible for the death of Jesus.

Verse 18. The Jews were condemned for having Jesus slain, because they had an evil motive in the act. But Peter informed them that in doing so, they fulfilled the words of the prophets concerning the fate that was to come upon the Son of God.

Verse 19. The first Gospel discourse is in chapter 2, which consists mainly of the story of Jesus, and closes with an exhortation for the hearers to recognize Him as the Lord. The present passage is the second discourse that is recorded, and consists of the same matter as the first, although the wording is somewhat different. The present verse corresponds with chapter 2: 38 in thought. "Repent and be baptized" is equivalent to *repent and be converted.* "For the remission of sins" is the same as *that your sins may be blotted out.* "Gift of the Holy Ghost" corresponds with *times of refreshing,* and of course it all comes *from the presence of the Lord.*

Verse 20. Peter then deviates slightly in his subject matter, and speaks of the *sending of Jesus Christ* which refers to His second coming to earth; the same Jesus who was *preached* (prophesied about) before in the Scriptures.

Verse 21. The next phase of this discourse explains some things that must take place before Jesus comes again. *Receive* is used in the sense of giving a guest continued hospitality or reception, until it is the desired and proper time for him to leave. In the case of Jesus, that time will not come until certain things that were predicted of him have been fulfilled. Robinson defines the word in the Greek for *restitution,* "full establishment," and Peter tells us that he refers to the predictions that had been made by the holy prophets, that were to be accomplished by Christ. We understand these things were to be brought to pass through the services of the apostles, while Jesus is still on his Father's right hand in Heaven.

Verse 22. Peter next specifies one of the predictions that Moses made concerning the prophet who was to come up from among the Jewish people (Deuteronomy 18: 18-20). That prediction called upon the people to hear the prophet in whatever he said to them.

Verse 23. The fate of all who refused to hear (heed) that prophet was that he *be destroyed from among the people.* The form of that threat is based on the usages of the times of Moses, when the "law of sin and death" was in force (Romans 8: 2). Its meaning under Christ is that all who refuse to hear him, will be condemned as disobedient in this world, and will be "punished with everlasting destruction from the presence of the Lord" when he comes again (2 Thessalonians 1: 9).

Verse 24. *Prophets, from Samuel.* There were other men before the days of Samuel who made prophetical statements, so there must have been a special sense in which he was regarded as one. The Schaff-Herzog Encyclopedia says: "Samuel was not only a prophet like others, but he was also the first of the regular succession of

prophets." 1 Kings 19: 16 says God spoke to Elijah as follows: "Elisha the son of Shaphat shalt thou anoint to be prophet in thy room," which verifies the quotation from the Encyclopedia, and shows there was a succession of national prophets. The mention of Samuel by Peter indicates that he was the first of the prophets in that succession. Other prophets after Samuel spoke of the time when the promise made to the fathers would be fulfilled.

Verse 25. *Covenant* in this verse is the same as *the promise* in chapter 2: 39. *Children of the prophets and of the covenant.* How could men be children of a covenant? The word *children* is from HUIOS, and Thayer explains that one meaning of the word is, "One to whom anything belongs; those to whom the prophetic and covenant promises belong; for whom a thing is destined." Peter meant that the people to whom he was speaking were intended by the Lord as among those who were to be benefited by the covenant. It is the same as the statement in chapter 2: 39 that" the promise is unto you and your children."

Verse 26. *Unto you first.* Peter was speaking to Jews, and he meant to tell them that they were to receive the blessings of the promised seed of Abraham before the Gentiles. (See chapter 13: 46; Romans 1: 16.) *Turning away every one of you from his iniquities* in this discourse, corresponds with "save yourselves from this untoward generation," in chapter 2: 40.

ACTS 4

Verse 1. The first Gospel discourse was delivered in some building suitable for an auditorium, not especially connected with the Jewish institutions. The present one was in the temple, which was the capitol of the religious system that had been established by Moses. That is why the *priests* and other public men became stirred up over the preaching. *Captain* is from STRATEGOS, which originally means "the commander of an army." Thayer explains it (citing a passage in Josephus) to mean, "The commander of the Levites, who kept guard in and around the temple." The Sadducees were a sect of the Jews who did not believe in the resurrection. A full description of this sect is given with the comments on Matthew 16: 12. All of the classes named came upon the apostles as they were preaching to the people in the temple.

Verse 2. *Grieved* is from DIAPONEO, which the Thayer lexicon defines at this place," "To be troubled, displeased, offended, pained, worked up." The Sadducees did not believe in the resurrection and would naturally resent any teaching in favor of the subject. The main cause of this displeasure, however, was that the apostles were telling that it was *through Jesus* that the dead would be resurrected. They had already come to hate Him because of His exposure of their sins and inconsistencies (Matthew 16: 1-4; 22: 23, 34), and now to have Him held up to the people as the hope of the resurrection, a doctrine they rejected with all the bitterness possible, was more than they could stand.

Verse 3. *Laid hands on them* means they arrested the apostles. *Hold* is another word for "prison," but they were put there and held "without charge" for the time, because it was too late in the day to have any hearing on the case.

Verse 4. *Howbeit* is not in the original text, and does not serve any important purpose, although it is not out of line with the thought of the passage. The original does justify the statement that *many believed.* That is a frequent expression used by the inspired writers to mean that the people obeyed the commands given them. If the word is used in a restricted sense it will say so, as in the case of the rulers in John 12: 42. *Number of the men was*, etc. The Englishmen's Greek New Testament renders this passage, "the number of men became about five thousand." Moffatt translates it, "bringing up their number to about five thousand." It means that the new believers made on this occasion, added to what they already had, made the total number of disciples in fellowship with the apostles about five thousand.

Verses 5, 6. This paragraph shows a meeting of the *council* or Sanhedrin (verse 15), to see what could be done about the stir that was being caused over the work and preaching of the apostles. According to Thayer, the *rulers* were leading men of the Jews who were members of the Sanhedrin. The *elders* in this case is defined by Thayer, "Members of the great council or Sanhedrin," then explains "because in early times the rulers of the people, judges, etc., were selected from the elderly men." *Scribes* came to have a very influential position in the time of Christ and the apostles. A full description of the word is given with the comments at Matthew 13: 52. *Annas* and *Caiaphas* are both mentioned in connection with the high priesthood. That was due to some interference by the secular government in the affairs of the Jews. (See the comments at Luke 3: 2.) All we know of *John and Alexander* is that they were leading men in Jerusalem at this time, and related in some way to the high priest. Others of the high priesthood who were not so outstanding are merely referred to as such.

Verse 7. After this meeting of the Sanhedrin was called, they brought Peter and John out of the prison where they had been held overnight, and placed them in the midst of the assembly. The last word of the verse is a pronoun that refers to the healing of the lame man. No attempt was made to deny the fact for it was too well known for them to try that plan in their persecution of the apostles (verse 16). Hence they were foolish enough to think they could oppose the work by showing that it was done illegally. As though any law could be made that would forbid curing a man of a physical infirmity! *Power* is from DUNAMIS and means strength or ability. This was another question that showed how desperate the council was in its desire to punish the apostles. Whatever might have been the power that was used, if it actually healed a man of a life-long infirmity, and without doing anyone else any harm, there could not possibly be any wrong about it. But these persecutors would not depend solely on the one point of attack; they also demanded to know by what *name* they had done the deed, which means by what authority they did it. One of Thayer's definitions of the original word is, "To do a thing by one's command and authority, acting on his behalf, promoting his cause." This was also a foolish question, and could not in any way touch the matter of right and wrong in the deed performed. If a man was pretending to offer remedial services to the public independent of the laws of the land, and was suspected of defrauding people, it would be entirely proper to require him to "show his license." But nothing of that kind was being done, for the actual healing of the patient had been done without any infringement of authority, either human or divine. However, the apostles did actually perform their deed under authority to act, as we shall soon see.

Verse 8. *Filled with the Holy Ghost.* This does not mean that Peter just then was filled with the Spirit, for he received that in the second chapter in fulfillment of the promise made the apostles by Jesus (John 14: 16), and it was to *abide with them forever.* The writer means that Peter was qualified to speak with authority to this audience, because he was in possession of the Holy Ghost or Spirit. All persons present were expected to hear what Peter said, but the rulers and elders were the ones who had taken the lead in this action against the apostles, hence it was appropriate to make his address especially to them.

Verse 9. To *be examined* means to be questioned and investigated. Peter did not object to being questioned, but he did not consider that they had even accused him of anything wrong, much less been shown any testimony that was claimed to hint at such a thing. Instead, he virtually held his investigators up to shame by the statement that the investigation was over a *good deed done to the impotent* (weak) *man.*

Verse 10. In all of the circumstances that ever came upon the apostles that concerned their work, they never failed to use the opportunity for preaching Christ to the hearers. Peter not only told them that it was in the name of Jesus that the deed was done, but he reminded them that it was the same person whom they had crucified. This was not said in the spirit of petty resentment, for an inspired apostle would not need to resort to that sort of speech. It was in order to show them that even death on the cross did not prevent Him from accomplishing his intended work for mankind. As definite proof that death could not overthrow the plans of Jesus, Peter reminded them that God had raised his Son from the grave.

Verse 11. While the vital facts concerning the experiences of Christ were under consideration in this "investigation," Peter cited these leading Jews to a prophecy in Psalms 118: 22, which they had fulfilled by slaying Jesus. And when God overruled their wicked deed and brought his Son out from the grave, and seated him on the throne in Hea *ven,* he caused that Son to be the *head of the corner.*

Verse 12. All of the discourses of the apostles contained the same thoughts, even though they were not always worded alike. This verse corresponds to chapter 2: 36, 38 and 3: 16, 19, and is similar in thought to the "closing exhortations" of evangelistic sermons today. Peter made a strong and exclusive claim for Christ. He not only declared that salvation could be had in Him, but that no salvation could be found in any other. *Under heaven given among men.* There is much truth involved in this phrase, for it designates the only part of the universe where any means of salvation is being offered. *Under heaven* would denote that no salvation is planned (or needed) for beings living in Heaven. *Among men* restricts the realm outside of heaven to the place where men live as human beings, and that would exclude those in the unseen world or Hades, even though they are "under heaven." *Must* is from DEI which Thayer defines, "It is necessary, there is need of, it behooves, is right and proper." Robinson gives the general definition, "It is binding on anyone, it behooves one to do, i. e., one must, one ought." He then says that in the New Testament it means, "It behooves, it must needs, one must or ought." The passage does not teach that anyone *must* be saved at all, for the matter of accepting salvation is one to be decided by man; "Whosoever *will* may come." The verse means that if a man is saved, it *must* be through the name (or authority) of Christ.

Verse 13. The lexicon defines the original for *boldness* to mean, "Freedom in speaking, unreservedness in speech; openly, frankly; free and fearless confidence, cheerful courage." *Perceived* is from KATALAMBANO, which Thayer defines at this place, "To lay hold of with the mind; to understand, learn, comprehend." *Unlearned* and *ignorant* does not refer to their natural intelligence, for even their enemies did not think the apostles were lacking along that line; had they thought so, they would not have been so uneasy about their influence with the people. The phrase means the apostles were not cultured in the art of learning as taught in the public institutions, but were private citizens without what the world would call "education." The leaders in the Sanhedrin *perceived* (realized) that the apostles were without these advantages of learning, yet beheld their boldness and ability of speech, and that caused them to marvel. They had to account for it in some way, which they did by concluding that the men *had been with Jesus*. These Jewish leaders did not know what Jesus had taught his apostles, but many of them had heard Him speak and had known how bold and outspoken he was. Now they conclude that the apostles had been with Jesus so much that they had imbibed the same spirit of courage and force of speech, which made them (the leaders in the Sanhedrin) fearful of the influence they might have over the common people.

Verse 14. *It* refers to the *boldness of Peter and John.* The reason the Jews could not say anything against their outspoken claims for the power of Jesus by which they were working, was that the man whom they had healed was right there with them, and was *standing*, something no one had ever seen him do before.

Verse 15. *Commanded them* means they ordered the apostles to leave the Sanhedrin while a consultation was being held. It was much like the circumstance where a jury is taken out of the court room, while the lawyers argue over some question of the testimony, as if they feared the men might catch some truth they did not want them to hear.

Verse 16. These Jews knew they could not deny the fact of the lame man's recovery. And it would not have been so bad if only they knew about it; but it was *manifest to all them that dwell in Jerusalem.*

Verse 17. *Threaten* means an indefinite warning that something very bad will be done, without stating what that will be. It is an intimation that does not have any specific charge, as the word is being used in this case. It is very much like the warning of some irresponsible parent or guardian, "If you do not behave yourself, you will wish that you had." These rulers knew they could not cite any law that was being violated by the preaching of the apostles, hence they thought they could daunt them by their cowardly threats.

Verse 18. The leaders in the Sanhedrin concluded that they did not have any recourse to the law, hence all they could do was to threaten the apostles.

They brought their victims back into the assembly and ordered them to cease speaking in Christ's name.

Verse 19. The apostles made a respectful but firm reply to the order against speaking in the name of Christ. They made no reference to the *threat*, doubtless regarding such a subject such a petty thing that it was beneath their dignity. But they put the issue in its true light by showing that the leaders of the Sanhedrin were demanding more consideration for themselves than they allowed the apostles to show for God.

Verse 20. *Cannot but speak* has a double force as to obligation. The apostles had seen Jesus after his resurrection, and had heard him command them to tell the story to others. Therefore when they preached the Gospel of Christ they were dealing with matters of evidence on which they could speak without any guesswork. They also were under the duty to speak these things to the world, or else they would be guilty of failing in their obligation to Him who had commissioned them for the work.

Verse 21. *Because of the people.* Public sentiment is a powerful influence, and when it is aroused in favor of a good cause, not many leaders are willing to defy it, especially if they are desirous of maintaining a popular standing. The Sanhedrin officials knew there was nothing in the deed of healing a lame man that could call for any punishment, and if they attempted such a thing the public would unite against it, because they had already expressed an attitude of glory to God for the good deed.

Verse 22. It would have been useless to claim the whole circumstance was a delusion, for the man was more than forty years old who had been healed. A mere child or very young man might have been said to be ready for improvement through the course of nature. Such a theory would not be accepted concerning a man forty years old.

Verse 23. *Their own company* means the believers who were assembled (verse 31), no doubt waiting to see the outcome of the action against the apostles. When Peter and John were released they went and joined the gathering of disciples and made a report.

Verse 24. The report did not discourage the believers but strengthened their faith. It did not even cause any dissension among them, for they spoke *with one accord.* They offered a prayer to God whom they recognized to be the Maker of all things.

Verse 25. One reason the disciples were not discouraged, was the fact that what had occurred to the apostles was a fulfillment of one of the prophecies. They were acquainted with the predictions that David made in Psalms 2: 1, 2, but acknowledged that it was God speaking through the mouth of the Psalmist. The prediction is in the form of a question, because the prophetic style is not always in the regular form of literal language. *Heathen* is from ETHNOS, which means the nations in general who are not Jews. The leaders of the Sanhedrin were Jews, but they could accomplish their purposes against Christ and the apostles only by resorting to the Roman courts which were Gentile. *Rage* is from PHRUSSO, and its general definition is, "To neigh, stamp the ground, prance, snort; to be high-spirited." *Imagine* is from MELETAO, which Thayer defines, "To meditate or devise, contrive." *Vain* is from KENOS and is defined, "Vain, fruitless, without effect." The idea is that the enemies of the Lord planned and schemed to destroy the work He was doing on the earth, even to the extent of persecuting his Son first, then the servants who were doing His work. But the prediction was that their schemes would prove to be in vain, for God would finally overrule all to the good of the world.

Verse 26. This verse is somewhat indefinite, meaning that the powers of government in various domains among men would be arrayed against the Lord (the Divine Ruler) and his Christ (or Anointed One).

Verse 27. *Of a truth.* It was a true prediction that David made, for such opposition actually took place within the knowledge of these disciples. Herod was in the line set up by the Maccabees, and was supposed to represent the interests of the Jews. Pilate was a governor in the Roman Empire, and represented the heathen or Gentile nations. *Gentiles* and *people of Israel* are named as a general summing up of the forces that worked against the Lord. The Herod who is named in this verse is Antipas, son of Herod the

Great; he is the one mentioned in Luke 23: 7-12.

Verse 28. They did not do this planning for the purpose of carrying out the work of God, for they were enemies of Him. The statement means that their schemes were what God had aforetime determined should be done. But although their work was according to the plans of God, they were not justified, for their motive was wicked throughout.

Verse 29. The disciples called the attention of the Lord to the threatenings of the Sanhedrin, but not to ask for any personal relief from persecutions. Instead, they prayed for divine help for the speakers of truth, that they might be able to speak the word *with all boldness.* The last word is from the same original as in 13, meaning to be outspoken and fearless in proclaiming the truth. They were not worrying about what sufferings it might bring on them; they were concerned only in the effectiveness of the truth that was going to be offered to the people.

Verse 30. Knowing that human might alone would not avail, they asked the Lord to confirm the preaching by demonstrations of miraculous power. It should be observed that they wished all of this to be done in the name of Jesus, the very One whose name they had been forbidden by the Sanhedrin to proclaim.

Verse 31. In the days of miracles, God sometimes answered prayers with a physical demonstration, or by something that could be discerned by the natural sense (John 12: 27-30), and the present case is another of such an evidence. *Were all filled with the Holy Ghost.* In the book of Acts there are no less than ten places where the expression to be "full" or "filled" with the Holy Ghost is used. It is said of both official and unofficial disciples; sometimes applying to the apostles and at others referring to the ordinary disciples. Since we know that the qualifications of the apostles were greater than those of any other Christians, we should understand that the expression under consideration is one with various shades of meaning, and the connection must always be considered in each instance for determining the force of the term. It would be natural to ask how two people could be "full" of anything, and yet one of them have more of it than the other. The passage in John 3: 34 should always be remembered when the subject of the Holy Ghost or Spirit is being studied. That statement shows that the Spirit can be measured or limited according to the will of God. But the mistake that is commonly made is to limit the word "full" or "measure" to the one quality of volume. But that is not a correct or necessary conclusion. A room could be "full" of smoke and still be capable of admitting more of it by making it more dense. A disciple could be full of the Holy Ghost, yet the density of it not be such as to enable the possessor to perform the same works as could the apostles. And so in the present verse, they were filled with the Holy Ghost in such measure or density or strength, that it encouraged them to speak the word *with boldness*. In the case of the apostles, the measure was such that they could testify *with great power*, which was what the other disciples prayed for in verse 30.

Verse 32. *Was his own* (personally), but that it was to be deposited in the common stock of money. For a complete discussion of this subject, see chapter 2: 44, 45.

Verse 33. The *great power* came in answer to the prayer of the other disciples in verse 30, and it consisted in the miraculous deeds that they performed upon the people. The question might be asked, what would the miraculous performances of the apostles have to do with the resurrection of Jesus. It confirmed the testimony they were giving that they had seen Jesus alive after his death on the cross. Had they been false witnesses of that claim, they never could have performed the miracles, for God would not work with them in their activities. All of this proved that when they affirmed that Jesus had appeared to them after his resurrection, they were telling the truth.

Verse 34. As to the merits of this community of resources, see the comments at chapter 2: 44, 45. For the present verse and onward, we shall study the outworkings of the system with various kinds of disciples.

Verse 35. The money received for their property was deposited with the apostles. That was logical since no other officials had been designated for any special work.

Verse 36, 37: We might wonder at the purpose of this paragraph, as it seems to be mentioned casually without any connection with the line of narrative being run. But it really does have a related purpose in what Luke knew he was about to report on the subject. There was to be given the sad story of some people who met with disaster because of their dishonesty. The present instance was given first to show that some disciples fulfilled their promise and came up to the agreement without a fault. The details of identity for this man are important because of the prominent place Barnabas occupies later in the work of the Lord. We shall hear much of him while studying this book, and even in one of the epistles of Paul he will be named (1 Corinthians 9: 6).

ACTS 5

Verse 1. This verse gives the brief but important information that both Ananias and his wife acted in the transaction. I do not know what arrangements could be had in those times as to joint titles to property. However, the fact remains that the husband and wife acted jointly in the disposal of their property.

Verse 2. *Kept back part of the price.* There was no wrong in this for the whole system was voluntary to begin with. This item will be noticed again in a later verse. *Being privy to it.* This phrase is from SUNEIDON which Thayer defines, "To see (have seen) together with others." The Englishman's Greek New Testament renders it, "being aware of it." The husband doubtless took the lead in the transaction, but the wife's knowledge of what was being done made her a full partaker in the deed. The whole family of Achan was stoned because the goods was stored in the tent, so that they had knowledge of it (Joshua 7: 21). If a person has knowledge of an evil deed and does not object to it, he is thereby made as guilty as the actual perpetrator. However, the wife of Ananias went further than guilty knowledge as we shall soon learn.

Verse 3. Jesus said that the devil is the father of lies (John 8: 44), hence Peter told Ananias that Satan had caused him to lie. Keeping back part of the money is mentioned again in connection with the sin of Ananias, but that is still not what constituted his sin. The mere fact of retaining part of the money would not be a lie, but the cause of his guilt will be shown before the case is finished.

Verse 4. This verse clearly shows that Ananias could have kept possession of his land and not been blamed. And even after he sold it, he could have kept all of the money and still been guiltless, since no divine command had been given for any of this arrangement. Not only so, but Ananias could have brought a part of the money only and have been accepted. The sin is mentioned in the close of this verse, which was the committing of a lie as will be explained soon. And what made it all the more condemnable was their attempt to deceive man, thinking thereby to escape the judgment of God. But Peter informed Ananias that he had not lied to men (only) but unto God.

Verse 5. *Hearing these words.* Even a human court of justice does not sentence and execute a prisoner without first informing him of the crime laid against him. Hence it was just for Ananias first to hear the accusation he was under, after which he was stricken with immediate death. *Great fear* means that a profound feeling of awe came over all the people by the mighty demonstration of the Lord's wrath against sin. Peter never as much as touched Ananias, yet at his words of denunciation of the shameful attempt to deceive the Lord, he fell down dead as if by a stroke of lightning. The crowd was thus made to know that the Lord had sent the punishment.

Verse 6. *Wound him up* means the young men drew his garments up close around him, which was the only burial shroud that was given this unworthy character. He was taken out for immediate burial, as it was sometimes the custom anyway to bury on the day of death.

Verse 7. Had Ananias and his wife come together in the first place, she might have tried to change her story when she saw the fate of her husband. But that would have been a change outwardly only, and one born of terror and not from a godly sorrow. The text says only that she *came in;* nothing said about her having any of the money. Of course it would have been foolish for her to bring it, for her husband had already brought all of the amount they had received for the

land according to the story in their conspiracy. So her presence at this time was only to confirm the statement of her husband.

Verse 8. *For so much.* This phrase is all from TOSOUTOS which Thayer defines at this place, "For so much," just as it is in the text. Robinson combines his definition and explanation in one sentence and gives us, "Of a specific amount, so much and no more." The necessary conclusion is that when Sapphira came into Peter's presence, he named the amount that her husband had brought, then asked her if that was exactly the price they had received for their property. She confirmed it by repeating the very word the apostle had used. This was the first time that the lie of which they were accused of doing was directly stated as far as the record informs us. But Peter did not have to hear the falsehood verbally for his own information; he was being informed by the Holy Spirit. The statement was drawn from her so that all could know about the wicked attempt of this couple to practice deception.

Verse 9. It is always bad for men to commit wrong when they act individually, but worse when they conspire with others in the act. The daughters of Zelophehad made this point in their plea for their fathers' estate (Numbers 27: 1-7), and the Lord accepted their reasoning. Peter charged Ananias and his wife with *agreeing together* in their covetous lie. He accused them of trying to *tempt the Spirit of the Lord,* and such a sin was condemned even in the Old Testament (Deuteronomy 6: 16). The text does not inform us directly as to any instructions previously given to these burial servants. However, the necessary inference is that they were told to "stand by" and complete their task when it was ready for them. In compliance with such an understanding, they were at that very moment *at the door,* waiting to perform their duty in the sad affair.

Verse 10. *Yielded up the ghost* means her spirit left her body as was done in the case of her husband. This gives us another instance that proves there is something in a human being besides his body and that they separate when death occurs. This woman's body was buried in the same tomb as that of her husband.

Verse 11. This was the same kind of *fear* that is mentioned in verse 5, except that with *the church* it would include a feeling of reverence for the majesty of the Lord.

Verse 12. There was a continual need for the evidence of signs and wonders at that time, because the New Testament had not been composed and the people did not have any written instructions. But when the apostles performed the miracles it proved them to be the true servants of God. When they spoke to the multitudes, therefore, they were heard as the authentic representatives of the Lord. At the time of these events the assembly of all the people in general was in Solomon's porch, the same place where they saw the lame man who had been healed (chapter 3: 11).

Verse 13. *The rest* refers to unconverted persons, but not to all such, for it immediately says *the people* magnified them. Hence the *rest* must refer especially to those not favorably disposed toward the apostles and other faithful disciples. They would not *join themselves* to them means they stayed away from the assembly. But some others were sufficiently interested to remain in the gathering, and even *magnified* (lauded or admired) the apostles.

Verse 14. The aforesaid conclusion is justified by this verse which says that *believers were added to the Lord*.

Verse 15. *Insomuch* should be connected with the statement in verse 12, about the "signs and wonders" that were performed by the apostles. Those wonders had produced so much interest among the people that they began to bring their sick folks into the vicinity. They had so much faith in the work of the apostles that even the presence of Peter was thought by them to be sufficient to heal them. Such an act was like those performed by the woman in Mark 5: 27, and the men in Matthew 14: 36.

Verse 16. This verse tells us that the people were not disappointed in their efforts recorded in the preceding one, for they were *healed every one*. The healing was done by the Lord as a reward for the faith that had been shown by their actions. *Vexed with unclean spirits* is the same as being possessed of devils. (See the note on the subject of being possessed of devils at Matthew 8: 28.)

Verse 17. The Sadducees are mentioned especially as being in sympathy with the high priest in opposition to the apostles. That is understandable because they were disbelievers in the resurrection, which was the outstanding fact that the apostles had been stressing in their work in connection with the story of Christ.

Verse 18. It has been a prominent weakness of man from the beginning that if he does not like the teaching someone is giving, the way to stop it is by persecuting the teacher. Jeremiah was put into a dungeon because the king did not like his teaching (Jeremiah 38: 6), and John the Baptist was imprisoned and slain because of his teaching that was objectionable to some wicked people (Matthew 14: 1-11). The Sadducees thought they could stop the preaching of a resurrection by imprisoning the apostles. *Common prison* means one "belonging to the people or state, public." It was the kind of detention place where captives in time of war were locked up.

Verse 19. The tomb of Joseph that had been sealed with a Roman stamp was no hindrance to the act of an angel in opening the place (Matthew 28: 2). Likewise, the Lord's angel was able to open the door of this public prison and free the apostles.

Verse 20. The angel did not tell them to "make good their escape" and flee while they had a chance. That is what he would have done, had his purpose been only to help them to avoid further persecution. Instead, he told them to go into the temple, the most public place in the city, and resume their preaching of the same facts that had got them into trouble in the first place. Life is from ZOE, which Thayer defines at this place, "Real life after the resurrection." Robinson defines it, "Eternal life, salvation." Since the Greek word generally means life of any kind, we can understand why the angel specified *this* life in his instruction to the apostles. The great issue at that time was the question of the resurrection which the Sadducees denied. That would make it especially appropriate for them to emphasize the truth of the resurrection, even in the face of possible further and more bitter persecution.

Verse 21. This "jail delivery" by the angel was made in the night, and the apostles made no delay in carrying out the instructions of the angel, but entered the temple *early in the morning* and taught. All of this was unknown to the Jews, who called a meeting of the Sanhedrin in the morning to handle the case of the apostles, and sent officers to the prison to bring the captives into court.

Verses 22, 23. In another case where Peter was miraculously released from prison (chapter 12: 19), the keepers were put to death; we are not told why it was not done in this instance. An angel may be invisible if he wishes to be, but that was not indicated here, for no uncertainty was manifested by the apostles about whether they had actually seen or heard anyone speaking to them. The only explanation that can be offered is that some kind of miracle was performed that prevented the keepers from seeing what was done. The men were not taken out through some "hole in the wall" at the rear of the building, for the account states that the angel opened the prison doors, the very spot where the keepers were found standing faithfully attending to their duty. It was a demonstration that God is able to care for his own, even in circumstances where "no earthly help is nigh."

Verse 24. *Doubted* is from a word that means to wonder or be perplexed. Grow is from GINOMAI, which has such a wide range of meanings that it would be hard to settle on a definite one in any one place. Some idea of the word may be gathered from the fact that in the King James Version, the word is translated by 39 different terms; one of them is "be," used 249 times. The verse simply means the captain and chief priests did not know what to make of the situation revealed by the report.

Verse 25. It would be difficult to imagine the surprise these Jewish leaders must have felt upon the news of this verse. They were already perplexed over the mere absence of the apostles from the prison, with the parts of the building intact and the keepers at their post of duty. They might finally have recomposed themselves and made further investigation with a view of discovering some unfaithfulness in the keepers. But before they had time for anything of the kind, here came the officers with this strange report. That would shut out any surmise of crookedness on the part of the keepers, for had the apostles been able and disposed to bribe the keepers, it would have been from a motive of cowardice, and in that case they would have fled from the city.

Verse 26. In view of the foregoing considerations, they could but conclude that some unseen power stronger than theirs was working on behalf of the apostles, and that it would be dangerous for them to mistreat their prisoners. *Without violence* means they did not use or even threaten to use physical force upon the apostles. Had they done so, public sentiment that was on the side of the apostles was so strong, that the officers would have suffered violence from the people.

Verse 27. The *council* was the Sanhedrin, the highest court the Jews were allowed to have in the time of Christ and the apostles. It had the power to arrest a man and examine him, and pass its own judgment upon the case. But if it passed a verdict of capital punishment, the case had to be taken before the secular court that operated under the Romans before it could be executed.

Verse 28. The faithfulness of the apostles in preaching the Gospel of Christ was proved by the statement of these enemies, that they had *filled Jerusalem* with it. *Bring this man's blood upon us.* These rulers knew that if the people were fully informed of the story of Jesus as he was dealt with in Jerusalem, they would hold them (the Jewish rulers) responsible for His death. In a threatening attitude, they reminded the apostles of their order not to teach in the name of Christ.

Verse 29. *We ought to obey God rather than men.* This is one of the most important sentences in the New Testament concerning the conduct of man. It states a rule or principle that should be observed whenever two or more requirements are made on one that conflict with each other, and yet where they come from sources that are supposed to have authority to command. For instance, children are commanded to obey their parents in all things (Colossians 3: 20); wives are commanded to submit themselves unto their husbands (Ephesians 5: 22), and Christians are commanded to be subject unto the *higher powers* or laws of the land (Romans 13: 1). If any one of these sources of authority should give a command that would interfere with one's duty to God, then that child or wife or disciple should refuse to obey it, regardless of the possible consequences.

Verse 30. Having made the reply shown in the preceding verse, the apostles began to preach to these wicked Jews the very doctrine they had forbidden them to preach anywhere. As was always the case, they began their story with the resurrection of Jesus. But they also connected that subject with the guilt of their hearers in the death of the One in whose name they were preaching.

Verse 31. *Exalted with his right hand.* Other translations word it "at" or "to" his right hand, and likewise the lexicon so defines it. The word *right* in this place comes from DEXIOS, which never means "right" in contrast with "wrong," but always means the right hand instead of the left, and hence has no moral significance. It is the rule for men to use their right hand in their one-handed manual activities, while it is an exception to use the left. When such an exception exists the writer will generally call attention to it (Judges 3: 15; 20: 16). There is no information in the Bible why God created man thus, we only know it is so. And the fact has been a source of some figurative uses of the word, meaning the more exalted or honorable place with reference to the person of God or Christ or any other being of dignity. God overruled the wicked purposes of the Jews and exalted his Son to be a Prince (leader) and a Saviour for all who would accept him. *Give repentance* means to give Israel the chance to repent (reform) their lives, with the promise that their sins would be forgiven.

Verse 32. *We are his witnesses.* This denotes that the apostles were witnesses to the fact that Jesus had risen from the dead. *So is also the Holy Ghost.* Jesus had said (John 16: 7) that if he did not go away (back to Heaven) the Comforter (Holy Ghost) would not come. Therefore, the fact that He did come and was possessed by disciples, was a proof (witness or testimony) that Jesus had arisen from the dead and had ascended to his Father. As to how or when the gift of the Holy Ghost was received, see the comments on chapter 2: 38.

Verse 33. *Cut* is from DIAPRIO, which Thayer defines at this place, "to be sawn through mentally," and explains it to mean, "to be rent with vexation." This was different from the case in chapter 2: 37, which says they were "pricked in their heart," which means they were overwhelmed with a conviction of guilt. In the present instance the Jewish leaders were overcome with anger, because they realized that everything the apostles said was true, yet they were not in a penitent frame of mind. Instead of wanting to do the right thing as did the ones on Pentecost, they plotted to bring violence upon the apostles. *Took counsel* denotes that they held a consultation to decide on some means by which they could have the apostles slain. They knew they would have to do some kind of scheming to get it done, for they could not lawfully slay anybody (John 18: 31).

Verse 34. Gamaliel was a member of the Sanhedrin, the man referred to by Paul in Chapter 22: 3. He was a *doctor* or teacher of the law of Moses. We know nothing about his qualifications of education in the branches of secular learning. The frequent expressions that represent him as a "professor" in the sense that term is used in connection with schools of literary training are only guesswork. But he did have a good reputation among the people, and his advice was regarded with respect.

Verse 35. Gamaliel advised the council to be careful how they proceeded against the apostles. But he did not ask them to act solely on his general suggestion; he proposed to support it with some facts with which they were evidently acquainted, or at least which they accepted as true due to their respect for Gamaliel.

Verse 36. Funk and Wagnalls New Standard Bible Dictionary says the following about this Theudas: "A Jewish revolutionist in the reign of Augustus [Caesar] who instigated a political uprising in Palestine that came to an inglorious end." We may also read the account of Josephus in his Antiquities, Book 20, Chapter 5, Section 1, as follows: "Now it came to pass, while Fadus was procurator pass, while Fadus was procurator [agent] of Judea, that a certain magician, whose name was Theudas, persuaded a great part of the people to take their effects with them, and follow him to the river Jordan; for he told them he was a prophet, and that he would, by his own command, divide the river, and afford them an easy passage over it; and many were deluded by his words. However, Fadus did not permit them to make any advantage of his wild attempt, but sent a troop of horsemen out against them; who, falling upon them unexpectedly, slew many of them and took many of them alive. They also took Theudas alive, and cut off his head, and carried it to Jerusalem." Some historians question whether this is the same Theudas as the one Luke writes about, while others say he is the same. All agree, however, that the account in Josephus is true, and we know it corresponds with the description as Gamaliel gave it.

Verse 37. I shall quote from Josephus, Wars. Book 2, Chapter 8, Section 1: "Under his [Coponius, an agent] administration it was that a certain Galilean, whose name was Judas, prevailed with his countrymen to revolt; and said they were cowards if they would endure to pay a tax to the Romans, and would, after God, submit to mortal men as their lords. This man was a teacher of a peculiar sect of his own, and was not at all like the rest of those their leaders." As a further support of the account of Gamaliel touching the downfall of the claims of Judas, I shall quote Josephus, Antiquities, Book 20, Chapter 5, Section 2: "And besides this, the sons of Judas of Galilee were now slain; I mean of that Judas who caused the people to revolt, when Cyrenius came to take account of the estates of the Jews" [for the purpose of taxing them].

Verses 38. 39. Gamaliel based his reasoning on the outcome of the historic cases to which he referred. He was considering the subject very much along the line of some familiar sayings that "history repeats itself," or that "time will tell." On that principle, he thought these Jewish leaders need not be so concerned about the activities of the apostles. He was correct in saying that if their work was of God, they would not be able to overthrow it. This passage has been used by professed disciples today, to show that we should not oppose any new doctrine or institution that might appear among us, but should let time decide whether it is right or wrong. There are at least two phases of this reasoning that shows it to be a perversion. Gamaliel was only a member of the Jewish Sanhedrin, and had no special authority that we know of.

The most that could be said about his speech was that it was his personal judgment as to the better procedure to follow toward the apostles, and hence it was no authentic principle on which to handle the question of conduct in the affairs of the church.

Again, even if it had been a statement produced by approval of the Lord, that would not make it a proper rule today. The New Testament was not in existence at that time, and hence there was no written document by which to test new teachers or new propositions. Today we have the completed book given to the church by the inspired apostles. If something appears among us that is new (to us), and that could easily occur, we do not have to wait until experience has tested it, but can learn at once whether it is "of God," by examining it in the light of the New Testament. (See 1 Peter 4: 11.)

Verse 40. The leaders of the Sanhedrin accepted the advice of Gamaliel, not to do anything too rash against the apostles. It was not because of any just feeling of righteousness or fair consideration for the prisoners, for they just could not stand to let them go until they had given them a parting threat accompanied with a beating.

Verse 41. It was and still is an honor to suffer persecution for the name of Jesus (1 Peter 4: 16): it indicates that one is living a godly life (2 Timothy 3: 12).

Verse 42. Their persecutions did not intimidate the apostles, even to the extent of decreasing the amount or frequency of their preaching, but they preached *daily*. Neither did they seek for private spots or places of safety to do their work. They preached in the temple, the most public building, and in every private house, where they ran a risk constantly of coming in contact with some telltale member of the Sanhedrin.

ACTS 6

Verse 1. *Number of the disciples was multiplied.* This was said as an explanation of how there came to be some difficulty over caring for the needs of the dependent ones. The *Grecians* were Jews who spoke the Greek language; I shall quote from history: "The church, though consisting wholly of Hebrews, comprised two classes of persons; one party understood only the Hebrew and Chaldee languages, which was used in their synagogues at Jerusalem and its vicinity, while the other had been accustomed chiefly to use the Greek language, into which the Old Testament scriptures had been translated (the version which we now call the Septuagint), and which had been for some time in common use, previous to the coming of Christ, in all the Jewish synagogues dispersed throughout the cities of Greece, as well as Egypt. These last were called Hellenists or Grecians." Jones' Church History, Chapter 1, Section 2. The Hebrew-speaking Jews had a feeling of superiority over the others, and the Grecians thought that feeling had crept into the church, so that partiality was being shown in the distribution of food. *Daily ministration* refers to the disbursements that were made out of the funds of the "community of goods" that was introduced in chapter 2: 44, 45 and 4: 34, 35. It should be observed that this distribution was made on the basis of need or dependency. The statement in connection with the work is worded, "according as he had need." This idea is further set forth by the fact that it was the *widows* for whose sake the disturbance of our present verse was caused. And this point should not be overlooked when we come to considering the work of the men who will be chosen later in this chapter.

Verse 2. This is the only place in the New Testament where the work of the deacons is shown. Their qualifications are stated in another passage (1 Timothy 3: 8-12), but the work belonging to men as official deacons is not to be found in any passage but this verse. *The twelve* means the apostles who were busy delivering instructions to the people on spiritual matters. *Not reason* denotes it would not be acting with good judgment. *Leave the word of God* would mean a ceasing of their preaching the word of God. *Serve* is from DIAKONEO, and Thayer's definition at this place is, "To minister, i. e., supply food and the necessaries of life." He then comments, "To provide, take care of, distribute, the things necessary to sustain life, Acts 6: 2. Absolutely, those are said to take care of the poor and the sick, who administer the office of deacon in the Christian churches, to serve as deacons." It is interesting to know that the six words "use the office of a dea-

con" in 1 Timothy 3: 10 all come from this one Greek word translated *serve* in our present verse. Incidentally, this shows that we should regard the men whom the apostles appointed as being deacons. In truth, were we to reject them as deacons, then we would be left with the baffling situation of having been given important qualifications of deacons, but no instructions as to what they were to do, for no information on that subject is in any other place.

It is true that the Greek word DIAKONEO in general, without any consideration of the context, could mean unofficial as well as official deacons, and also their work might consist of any manner of service. In that general sense, all members of the church are deacons, both men and women. But we cannot put that meaning unto the word in the present instance, for the apostles stated the kind of service for which they proposed to *appoint* (making them officials) the men; that was shown in the word *tables*. This is from TRAPEZA, which Thayer defines, "a table," then gives his explanation, "a table on which food is placed, an eating table." He gives a specific definition of the word in our verse which is, "To set a table, i. e., food before one." This settles the question of the work belonging to men as deacons, that it is to see that food is provided for those who are needy.

The amount of loose thinking and acting on this subject that has been done is deplorable. Many people think that the work of the deacons is to "pass the emblems." Others even today will insist that it is the place of the deacons to "attend to any of the temporal affairs of the congregation." They will then expose the weakness and inconsistency of their position by allowing those things to be done by almost any member of the congregation, even though they may not possess half of the qualifications required of deacons. If the elders see fit to ask the deacons to perform some of the temporal affairs of the church, that is their right, and these men may comply with the request of the rulers. But they should not do so as deacons, for such things are no part of the office of deacons.

Verse 3. *Look ye out* is from EPISKEPTOMAI, which Thayer defines, "To look (about) for, look out." Robinson combines his definition and explanation in one sentence as follows: "To look at in order to select, to look out, to seek out, e. g., persons for office." The *brethren* were to find the men, but the qualifications were stipulated by the apostles. Some of the qualifications that are required of deacons in 1 Timothy 3: 8-12 are not mentioned in the present instance. This was in the beginning of the church, and also was while the apostles were present in person. As time went on and the organization of the institution of Christ was being made more complete, He added other qualifications, but nothing was added to their work as deacons. For the phrase *full of the Holy Ghost*, see the comments at chapter 4: 31. That information will explain why these men could have some measure of the Holy Ghost at the time of their selection, and yet require the laying on of the apostles' hands (verses 6, 8) for them to work miracles. *Wisdom* is from SOPHIA, and Thayer defines it in general as follows: "Wisdom, broad and full intelligence." He explains that any particular shade of meaning must be determined by the context in which it is used. Hence in the passage of this paragraph he says it means, "skill in the management of affairs." That is appropriate since these men were to handle the distribution of goods. And being full of the *Holy Ghost* corresponds with the requirement in 1 Timothy 3: 8 that they be "not greedy of filthy lucre." The wording is different in the two places, but both refer to the qualification that would be needed in the work of handling the funds that were contributed by the disciples. A man who is *full of the Holy Ghost* would not be so interested in his own temporal affairs that he would come short of his duty on such a matter.

Verse 4. After completing the arrangements for taking care of the temporal needs, the apostles said they would devote their time to spiritual matters.

Verse 5. A spirit of cooperation prevailed between the apostles and the multitude of disciples. Stephen is mentioned especially in connection with being full of the Holy Ghost. It was fitting to give him special mention in view of the glorious work he did in defending the faith, and sealing his courage in a violent death. But we know the others also had the qualifications, for they were required of them all and the apostles would not have appointed them had they not been qualified as stipulated. Philip is the same one who became known as "the evangelist," who preached to the people of Samaria. Nothing is said of any of the others that we know about, except what is said of them as a group working in conjunction with the apostles.

Verse 6. Having selected these men according to instructions, the multitude presented them to the apostles who laid hands on them, accompanying the act with prayer.

Verse 7. *Word of God increased.* After the deacons were appointed to handle the temporal needs of the disciples, the disturbances were evidently calmed. That gave the apostles fuller opportunity for preaching the word of God, and this is why the word *increased* is used, meaning increased occasions for offering it to the people. The aforesaid furtherance of the preaching resulted in the increase of disciples in Jerusalem. Another thing that helped the spread of the Gospel, was the work of the deacons who engaged in the preaching as well as attending to their official work. For while the specific function of the deacons is to care for the temporal needs of the congregation, that does not need to prevent them from spiritual activities as their talents and opportunities permitted. The mention of priests becoming obedient to the faith is for the purpose of showing the growing influence that the word of God was having among those who were usually opposed to the work of Christ.

Verse 8. Stephen could do these miracles because the hands of an apostle were laid on him (verse 6). The New Testament was not in existence yet and it was necessary to have men equipped to support their preaching with such special evidence. This is taught in Ephesians 4: 8-14, where Paul is considering both the temporary and the permanent form of the plan of salvation under Christ. But while these deacons could preach the word, and even confirm it with miracles, they could not bestow such power upon others, not having that "measure" of the Spirit. Hence after they would make converts to the Gospel, it required the hands of an apostle to confer miraculous power on them. (See chapter 8: 14-17.)

Verse 9. *Certain of the synagogue.* The first definition in the lexicon for synagogue is, "In the New Testament, an assembly of men." It is used in the same sense as "a congregation." For a full description of the subject, see the notes at Matthew 4: 23. *Libertines.* In his historical comments of this word Thayer gives the following: "Jews who had been made captives by the Romans under Pompey but were afterward set free; and who, although they had fixed their abode at Rome, had built at their own expense a synagogue at Jerusalem which they frequented when in that city. The name Libertines adhered to them to distinguish them from the free-born Jews who had subsequently [afterward] taken up their residence in Rome." *Cyrenians* were Jewish dwellers in Cyrenaica who were in Jerusalem at Pentecost (Acts 2: 10), and gave their name to one of the synagogues of that city. *Alexandrians* were Jewish colonists of Alexandria in Egypt, who were admitted to the privileges of citizenship and had a synagogue in Jerusalem. *Cilicia* was a province lying on the northeast shore of the Mediterranean Sea, and was the native country of Paul. The *Asia* that is meant here is a part of the province of Asia Minor (today known as Turkey). Jews from these various places were in Jerusalem on account of the feast of Pentecost, and were displeased with the teaching of Stephen.

Verse 10. One part of the definition for *resist* in the lexicon is "to withstand," and means that although the Jews from all the places named combined in disputing with Stephen, they were not able to meet his claims for the doctrine of Christ. *Wisdom* is from SOPHIA which Thayer defines, "Wisdom, broad and full intelligence." *Spirit* is from PNEUMA which the same lexicon defines in this passage, "The disposition or influence which fills and governs the soul of any one; the efficient source of any power, affection, emotion, desire." The personal intelligence of Stephen was backed up by the Spirit that was given him through the laying on of the hands of an apostle. This explains why those envious Jews could not "meet the arguments" that he put before them.

Verse 11. *Suborned* is from HUPO-BALLO which Thayer defines, "To instruct privately; instigate, suborn." It means they influenced these false witnesses in an underhanded sort of way that was in the nature of a bribe. The inspired writer says that Stephen spoke with *wisdom* and *spirit*, so we know these witnesses made false statements, even though we do not have any record of what they said up to this point. But his speech that is recorded in the next chapter will show us that they were the ones who had blasphemed, for that speech is made up of a respectful recital of the history of many centuries, and that account was written by Moses whose inspiration Stephen recognized.

Verse 12. Stephen was out before the public where he had a perfect right to be; he was preaching the Gospel, which every Christian has a right to do. *They* means the people from the different countries named in verse 9, who had disputed with Stephen but could not show anything wrong with his teaching. On the strength of the false witnesses of verse 11, they worked up a riotous spirit among the people under their leaders. These men ignored all rules of justice and forced him into the *council* (Sanhedrin).

Verse 13. Once within the grasp of that prejudiced assembly it was not hard to produce false witnesses, for they had already been prepared in mind for such a work by the crookedness mentioned in verse 11. The accusations of this verse are general, and if looked at without any explanation would certainly make an unfavorable impression on any court, and more so on one that was already ill-disposed toward a prisoner. It would be a very wicked thing to *blaspheme* the *holy place* (Jerusalem with its temple) and *the law* (of Moses). To blaspheme means to speak reproachfully, rail at, revile, calumniate" [falsely accuse.]

Verse 14. These false witnesses pretended to specify concerning the general accusations of verse 13. The falsity of the charges will be realized by all who will follow the teaching of Jesus while he was on the earth. He always spoke respectfully concerning Moses, and censured the hypocritical Jews for not being true to the law. *Change the customs.* Jesus never taught that in the sense those enemies placed in the term. It is true He often announced that a change of rules was to take place among God's people, but he showed that even Moses predicted such a change. (Deuteronomy 18: 18-20.)

Verse 15. *Angel* is from AGGELOS, and its primary meaning is, "A messenger, one who is sent," according to both Thayer and Robinson. There could be nothing in the face of a man from the physical standpoint that would show any indication of his being a messenger, except when considered on the negative basis. Had Stephen been guilty of the evil things charged against him, his face or countenance would have reflected it, for he certainly would have had "a guilty look." Instead of such an expression, the countenance of this righteous man had the appearance of one who was faithfully delivering the message (the business of an angel) of Him whose truth was offered for man's benefit. Stephen was not cowed or in the least intimidated by the brazen stare fixed toward him by the crowd in the council.

ACTS 7

Verse 1. We are still in the Sanhedrin where the false witnesses have just made the serious charge of blasphemy against Stephen. *Are these things so?* This was said by the high priest, because under a practice started by the Jews, he was the presiding judge of the Sanhedrin. The act of proposing this question was about the only just thing that was done for Stephen. It was the order in any fair court, religious or otherwise, to permit a prisoner to speak for himself concerning accusations being brought against him. (See John 7: 51; Acts 22: 25.)

Verse 2. From this verse through verse 50 is Stephen's answer to the question put to him by the high priest. A simple denial of the accusations would have been the whole truth, but Stephen's purpose was to give the entire historical background of the issue at stake; not only to show their charges to be false, but also to present a basis of truths and facts for the conclusion he intended to draw in their hearing. We shall see that when all this was done, it showed up these false accusers to be really the ones who could justly be charged with the things they maliciously said against him. The speech will consist of the history that began with Abraham and ended with Solomon. In addition to Stephen's principal reason for reciting these historical matters, I shall comment on the verses in their order because of their general interest. *Fathers* is used in the sense of respect for them as being among the older members of the Jewish nation, and hence those who should be respectfully interested in the history of their race. *Before he dwelt in Charran* (Haran). Genesis 12: 1 says that God *had said* for Abraham to make this move, even before the command stated in that verse, and that is the reason for Stephen's phrase underlined in this place.

Verse 3. *Which I shall show thee* is significant, and denotes that the patriarch was not told even what country it was when the Lord first appeared to him. He was to obey the command purely upon his faith in the wisdom and goodness of God. That is why Paul says, "and he went out, not knowing whither he went" (Hebrews 11: 8).

Verse 4. Abraham moved immediately out of his home territory which was the *land of the Chaldeans* (called "Ur of the Chaldees" in Genesis 11: 31). This place was in the general territory of that later containing the city of Babylon. To reach the land of Canaan (where God intended him to go), it was necessary for Abraham to journey up and around the northern extremity of the country, due to the geographical character of the land. (See the historical note given with Isaiah 14: 31, in volume 3 of the Old Testament Commentary.) *When his father was dead.* The necessary inference is that Abraham's father became more infirm on account of old age, so that the Lord suffered Abraham to pause in this land of Haran until his father was dead. We know this pause was not displeasing to God, for Stephen says that after the death of his father, *he* (meaning God) *removed him into this land*, which indicates that Abraham was acting in God's favor.

Verse 5. *Gave him none inheritance.* Let us not become confused over this phrase and the account in Genesis 23: 9-20. Abraham became a possessor of that real estate in the land of Canaan, but he bought it with money, and thus obtained it by his own business transaction; he even refused to accept it as a gift from the owners. But *inheritance* is from KLERONOMAI, and Thayer defines it, "an inheritance, property received by inheritance." Abraham did not receive a foot of that land in that way, but it was promised that he would indirectly receive it some day through his descendants. *When he had no child* is mentioned to show Abraham's faith in the promises of God.

Verse 6. This prediction is recorded in Genesis 15: 13, and refers to the hardships of the Israelites in Egypt. *Strange land* means one outside their own promised land.

Verse 7. *Will I judge* refers to the plagues that God brought upon the Egyptians (Exodus 7 to 12). *Serve me in this place* means their service at Mount Sinai.

Verse 8. This verse includes the years from Abraham's 99th to the birth of Jacob's sons in Mesopotamia and Canaan.

Verse 9. *The patriarchs* means the brethren of Joseph who sold him to travelers going to Egypt. *God was with him* denotes that assistance was given Joseph from the Lord because he was righteous and was being persecuted.

Verse 10. This verse includes the events of Genesis 41.

Verse 11. This verse includes the events of Genesis 41: 30, 31.

Verse 12. See Genesis 42: 1-3.

Verse 13. This is recorded in Genesis 43, 44, and 45.

Verse 14. *Threescore and fifteen souls.* For an explanation of this phrase, see the comments on Genesis 46: 26, 27, in volume 1 of the Old Testament Commentary.

Verse 15. *Our fathers* means the sons of Jacob and other early ancestors.

Verse 16. The last word in the preceding verse is "fathers," and they are the ones who were buried in Sychem. No explanation is offered by the historians or critical works of reference of the name of Abraham in the place of Jacob, concerning the purchase of this burying place. But all of them are agreed as to the particulars of the transaction, and hence we may be assured that some incidental fact or custom in use at the time of Stephen's speech would explain it if we had access to the literature of those days.

Verse 17. God promised to Abraham that his posterity would become a great nation, and would be delivered from their bondage in a strange land. It was getting along near the time for the fulfillment of that promise, hence the people were becoming numerous.

Verse 18. *Knew not Joseph.* (See the comments on Exodus 1: 8.)

Verse 19. *Dealt subtilly* means to use schemes or tricks to get advantage of them. One of such was to take the supply of straw from them, when they knew that the crop had been gathered and that nothing but stubble could be found. (See Exodus 5: 10-14.) *Cast out their young children* refers to the decree that all male infants should be drowned.

Verse 20. *Exceeding fair* is explained by Thayer to mean he was fair "unto God," and the Greek text does have those words. The significance of this subject will be realized when we consider the history that will be cited at verse 25.

Verse 21. Read this history in Exodus 2: 3-10.

Verse 22. This information is not given in any other place in the Bible, but Stephen was speaking by the Spirit and his report is authentic.

Verse 23. *Full forty years* is more definite than the account in Exodus 2: 11, which says he "was grown." *Came into his heart.* Moses acted on his own authority only, for there is no information that God told him to take on the work at that time.

Verse 24. There is no question about the injustice of the Egyptian's attack upon the Hebrew. The point is that Moses acted before he was told to by the Lord. The details of this episode are given in Exodus 2: 11-14.

Verse 25. *He supposed his brethren would have understood, etc.* This proves the point made in the two preceding paragraphs; Moses acted on his own supposition. The question will be raised as to why Moses formed this notion. The information is given in Josephus, Antiquities, Book 2, Chapter 9, Section 3. That paragraph is too long to be quoted in full, but I shall give the gist of it, and the reader may verify it by consulting the history of Josephus. The father of Moses had gone to God in prayer concerning the danger his people were in and had received assurances that deliverance would be provided. That, as Abraham had been blessed with a son who meant so much to him, so, through the child soon to be born to him and his wife, great deliverance would be experienced by their people. It is reasonable to conclude that Moses' father had told him about that prayer and the promise, and hence Moses "supposed" all of his brethren had heard about it also.

Verse 26. *Them* means his brethren mentioned in the preceding verse. Exodus 2: 13 states that it was two Hebrews who were striving. Moses thought he would interfere with the wrangle, and no doubt he was acting on the *supposition* just explained above.

Verse 27. The one who objected to the attempt of Moses was the one who was in the wrong. That is frequently the case today, for when a man is doing what is wrong he will resent any interference with what he says is "his business." However, Moses could not have given a satisfactory answer to the question asked by this Hebrew.

Verse 28. When Moses "looked this way and that way" (Exodus 2: 12), he either did not see everybody who was near, or the avenged Hebrew reported the event.

Verse 29. Exodus 2: 15 tells us that Pharoah heard about the deed of Moses and tried to have him slain. That caused him to flee the country in fear, and go into the land of Midian, a country lying between the two arms of the Red Sea. *Where he begat two sons* condenses the history in Exodus 2: 15-22.

Verse 30. *Forty years were expired* from the time Moses came into the land of Midian. In the course of this period Moses cared for the flocks of his father-in-law. He was with them when he came into the region of Sinai, where the angel appeared to him.

Verse 31. *He wondered* because the bush was burning but was not being consumed, and decided to investigate the situation. (See Exodus 3: 1-3.)

Verse 32. *Fathers* is often used as a general reference to the early ancestors of the race, but here it applied to Abraham, Isaac and Jacob. Moses was overawed by the voice and the scene before him.

Verse 33. *Put off thy shoes*. It was customary in that country to remove one's shoes in the presence of a dignitary as an act of courtesy, very much as a man will lift his hat under like circumstances. *Holy ground* did not refer to the essential quality of the earth, for it was the same place where Moses had been taking the sheep for

pasture. But in the present instance it was holy because of the person who was present, and the purpose for the appearance of the angel. A place is holy where and when holy proceeding takes place.

Verse 34. *I have seen, I have seen.* Both phrases are in the original, and the inflection of the terms is somewhat different in each case, showing the purpose of the statement is for emphasis. God was speaking to Moses by the angel in the bush. Having seen the afflictions of his people in Egypt, God proposed sending Moses to deliver them.

Verse 35. Stephen does not include the conversations between God and Moses about his (Moses') fitness for the commission: that record is in Exodus 3 and 4. But he reminds his hearers that the very man whom the Hebrew resented was the one God sent to rule over them. He is getting his speech shaped up for application to his hearers.

Verse 36. This brief verse covers the history from Exodus 7 to Joshua 5.

Verse 37. This prophecy is in Deuteronomy 18: 18-20.

Verse 38. *Church* is from EKKLESIA, and Thayer gives its primary meaning to be, "A gathering of citizens called out from their homes into some public place; an assembly." In the present passage he defines it, "The assembly of the Israelites." *With the angel which spake to him in the mount Sina.* God gave the law at Sinai through the services of angels (Galatians 3: 19).

Verse 39. *In their hearts turned back.* The Israelites could not return to Egypt literally, but their desire to do so made them as guilty as if they had done so.

Verse 40. Moses had gone up into the mountain to receive the law, and the people became restless because of his absence; they demanded of Aaron that he make the idol.

Verse 41. In response to the cry of the people, Aaron made the calf out of the gold they had brought from Egypt.

Verse 42. *Gave them up* denotes that if a man is determined to do wrong God will not use force to prevent it. *Host of heaven* means the sun and other heavenly bodies. *As it is written* refers to Amos 5: 25. The statement is in question form, but the thought is an admission from God that his people went through that form for forty years.

Verse 43. The preceding verse seems to speak well of ancient Israel but the present one shows the other side of the story. It begins with the word *yea*, while the corresponding verse in Amos 5: 26 starts with "but." The point is that Israel was not satisfied to sacrifice to the true God but also took up idolatrous worship. *Moloch* and *Remphan* were heathen gods that the Israelites worshipped by making *figures* (images) of them for that purpose. The last sentence is a prediction of the Babylonian captivity.

Verse 44. *Tabernacle of witness.* The tabernacle was a visible and constant symbol of the wisdom and goodness of God, so that Israel could always have His presence.

Verse 45. *Fathers that came after.* Most of the older men died in the wilderness for the sin at Kadesh-barnea (Exodus 32: 8-11), and it was their descendants who *brought* in the tabernacle to Canaan. *Jesus* is from IESOUS, and Smith's Bible Dictionary says it is "the Greek form of the name Joshua," and Thayer's lexicon agrees with it. Joshua was the leader of the Israelites when they crossed the Jordan. *Possession of the Gentiles.* These were heathen nations living in Canaan when the Israelites came, and they were attacked by Joshua and driven out (Joshua 12). *Unto the days of David.* Joshua did his duty in fighting the heathen, but on account of the unfaithfulness of Israel, God suffered some of the nations to remain in the land to harass them for many years.

Verse 46. The preceding verse does not mean that no heathen existed in the land after David's time. The pause in the narrative at him is because of his outstanding importance in the affairs of Israel, the ancestors of these rebellious Jews to whom Stephen was speaking. David was in the favor of God and desired to *find a tabernacle*, referring to his desire to build the temple (2 Samuel 7: 1-3).

Verse 47. The reason that Solomon and not David was permitted to build the temple is shown in 1 Chronicles 22: 6-10.

Verse 48. God permitted Solomon to build the temple to replace the tabernacle. That was not because He wanted a better building in which to dwell for he does not *dwell* ("settle down") in man-made temples. *Saith the prophet* is reference to Isaiah 66: 1. He uses earthly structures only as a place for people to meet with him spiritually.

Verse 49. God is a personal (though spiritual) Being, and his dwelling place is in Heaven. *What house will ye build me* was quoted by Stephen because these Jews had boasted so often of their temple, and pretended to be offended at anyone who even intimated that it would ever be destroyed. (See chapter 6: 14.)

Verse 50. God was already the Maker of all things in the universe, hence it was foolish for the Jews to think they could build a temple as a permanent dwelling for Him.

Verse 51. Stephen made his long speech to portray the history of the Jews, showing a record of continual rebellion against the law of God and persecution of His true servants. His application was by showing these Jews before him that their conduct was running "true to form." *Stiffnecked* means stubborn, and *uncircumcised in heart and ears* denotes their unconsecrated minds as manifested by resistance against the Holy Ghost.

Verse 52. A man is not to be blamed for the sins of his forefathers, unless he imitates those sins and boasts of his relation to the ancestors. These rebellious Jews had done that very thing, and were following in the steps of their immediate fathers who had slain Jesus as predicted by the holy prophets of God.

Verse 53. The law which the disobedient Jews were resisting had been given through the agency of angels (Galatians 3: 19).

Verse 54. To be *cut to the heart* means to be rent asunder in mind, and caused to *gnash* or grind their teeth in an insane fit of anger.

Verse 55. *Full of the Holy Ghost* is explained at chapter 4: 31. *Saw the glory of God.* No man in normal condition can see God and live (Exodus 33: 20). When He wanted Saul to see Jesus in the glorified state, he performed a miracle for the purpose; he did the same thing for Stephen.

Verse 56. In defiance of their threatening gesture, Stephen declared his vision of the very One whom they had murdered, standing in glory at the right hand of God.

Verse 57. *Stopped their ears* was an admission that the truth being spoken by Stephen was unwelcome to them, but they had no honorable means of meeting it.

Verse 58. The Jews told Pilate it was not lawful for them to put any man to death. That was true, but it was not the real motive for their plea that Pilate have Jesus slain. It did not prevent them from carrying out their murderous rage upon Stephen, who had not even been sentenced by any court, religious or secular. *Witnesses.* The law (Deuteronomy 17: 7) required that the witnesses to a crime must be first in an execution. That is why Jesus said what he did to the men who had witnessed the sin of the woman (John 8: 7). *Laid down their clothes.* When any manual action was to be done, it was the usual practice for the men to lay aside their loose outer garments. As a guard to protect them, they were placed in charge of someone standing by, and this was done by placing the garments at the feet of Saul, of whom we will hear much in later chapters.

Verse 59. Stephen was calling upon God while the Jews were hurling stones at him. *Receive my spirit* shows Stephen had an inner being that was not within reach of these murderers. (See Matthew 10: 28.)

Verse 60. Before his body collapsed, Stephen kneeled in prayer to God. *Cried with a loud voice.* The first word is from KRAZO which Thayer defines at this place, "to call out aloud, speak with a loud voice." It was not the involuntary outburst of a body because of pain, but an intelligent utterance so expressed that all in the crowd could hear. *Charge* is from HISTEMI and Thayer defines it, "to cause to stand." It does not mean that these men were to be declared innocent, for that would be endorsing sin. The prayer meant for God not to hold it against them. Jesus prayed for his Father to forgive his murderers, but that did not mean it should be done before they repented, which they did on Pentecost. Likewise, the prayer of Stephen means for God to forgive these murderers whenever they repented. *Fell asleep* is a figurative way of saying that Stephen died. (See notes on literal and figurative language at Matthew 9: 24.) Stephen's death is the first one on record that was imposed in persecution for faith in Jesus. There will be others committed to which reference will be made later.

ACTS 8

Verse 1. *Consenting* is from SUNEU-DOKEO, which Thayer defines at this place, "To approve together," and Robinson gives virtually the same definition. Paul verifies the definition in his statement in chapter 22: 20. *At this time* is rendered "on that day" by the Englishman's Greek New Testament. Like a ravenous beast that gets a taste of blood, these murderers became infuriated by the case of Stephen and started a general persecution of the church in Jerusalem. The disciples were scattered on account of the danger to their lives. A Christian has the right to save his life when he can do so without compromising any truth. I do not know why the apostles did not have to flee.

Verse 2. The original for *lamentation* is defined by Thayer, "lamentation with beating of the breast," and Robinson defines it in the same way. It was a formal demonstration of grief that such a righteous man should die as he did.

Verse 3. The church as an established organization cannot be overthrown, for it was destined to "stand for ever" (Daniel 2: 44). But it can be hindered in its work, and its individual members can be persecuted and even put to death in certain instances. That is what Saul did, for *havoc* means to "treat shamefully or with injury." It states he was *entering into every house,* which shows he was not attacking the church as an assembled unit. *Haling* is defined "to draw, drag," and denotes that disciples were used roughly while being taken to prison.

Verse 4. *Therefore* indicates a conclusion is to be drawn from facts stated or understood. Saul was persecuting the disciples so cruelly that they fled from the community and went into various territories. *Preaching the word* was not a part of the conclusion from *therefore,* but was added for our information to show that the disciples were not weakening in their love for the word. Their being scattered is the only part that is offered as a conclusion after the word *therefore.* The motive in preserving their lives was that they might be able still to defend the faith in other places. Chapter 11: 19 names some of the places where they went preaching.

Verse 5. Cornelius is commonly referred to as the first Gentile convert to the Gospel, which is correct. This verse says that *Philip* (one of the seven deacons) preached to the people of Samaria. All people who were not full blooded Jews were regarded as Gentiles, hence some confusion might arise here. But the explanation is in the fact that the Samaritans were distinguished from the Gentiles proper because they were a mixed race, part Jew and part Gentile, both in their blood and in their religion. The history of their origin is in 2 Kings 17, volume 2 of the Old Testament Commentary.

Verse 6. *With one accord* denotes that no dissension arose among the people over the preaching of Philip. He was able to perform these miracles by the laying on of the apostles' hands in chapter 6, verse 6.

Verse 7. *Unclean spirits* is another name for devils or demons with which people were possessed. *Palsies* and *lame* were afflictions of the body that were healed by Philip.

Verse 8. This joy was natural, for doubtless the afflictions had been suffered for many years. Both the afflicted and their friends would rejoice over the miraculous relief.

Verse 9. *Used sorcery* is from MAGEUO which Thayer defines, "To be a magician; to practice magical arts." In past ages, God suffered Satan to exert supernatural power through the agency of men (Exodus 7: 11, 12, 22; 8: 18, 19). Because of the real existence of such works, it was possible for men to impose on the credulity of the people and thus pass for such supernaturally-endowed performers even though they were frauds. Whether Simon was the former or the latter kind of actor we are not informed.

Verse 10. Any such demonstrations that would seem to be divine would have a profound effect on the people, and cause them to think the performer was a man of God.

Verse 11. *Bewitched* is from EXISTEMI which means, "to amaze, astonish, throw into wonderment," hence it refers to some effect Simon had on the mind and not the body.

Verse 12. *When they believed . . . they were baptized.* It will be seen that the inspired writer takes it for granted when a man believes the Gospel he will also obey it. (See the com-ments at chapter 2: 41.) *Men and women.* We never read in the scriptures that infants or young children were baptized; it is always men or women.

Verse 13. *Simon himself believed.* This is the statement of Luke and therefore must be taken as the truth, and not merely that Simon pretended to believe. *And when he was baptized.* (See the comments on the preceding verse about this form of expression.) *Continued* is from PROSKARTEREO, and Thayer defines it at this place, "To adhere to one, to be his adherent; to be devoted or constant to one." We have no reason to think that Simon was not genuinely interested in the work of Philip. The record says that Simon continued with Philip because he saw the miracles that were performed, and John 20: 30, 31 expressly says that the signs and wonders were performed to produce belief.

Verse 14, 15. Philip preached the word of God and even performed miracles in proof of his authority. But he could not confer the Holy Ghost on his converts in the measure necessary to enable them to work miracles; none by apostles could do that. And since converts in those days were promised such a gift (chapter 2: 38), the apostles went down to Samaria to confer it.

Verse 16. These people had obeyed the Gospel but had not received the Holy Ghost, which shows that the gift was not bestowed simultaneously with baptism.

Verse 17. This gift was not to make them Christians or bring them forgiveness of sins; their obedience to the Gospel did that for them.

Verse 18. The inspired Luke says that Simon *saw* a certain fact, not that he only thought he saw it. Hence this verse is insipred authority for saying it was *through laying on of the apostles' hands the Holy Ghost was given. He offered them money.* This was what constituted the sin of Simon (see next verse). It does not indicate that Simon's primary obedience was not sincere. (See the comments on verse 13.) Disciples who have been in the church for years are known to commit sin, so it is not to be doubted that a babe scarcely out of his spiritual swaddling clothes might backslide also.

Verse 19. Simon was not asking merely for the power to perform miracles; he might have received that sooner or later as the others did. But he wanted the power that was possessed by the apostles, so he could lay hands on others and give them ability to perform miracles. The sight of the performance of the apostles seemed to arouse his former interest in that which was marvelous, so that he yielded to the temptation and offered to buy that which cannot be valued in "dollars and cents."

Verse 20. *Money perish with thee* is a declaration of solemn truth, not in the sense of a special denunciation. We know that money is destined to pass away some day, and so also will evil men if they do not repent. *Money perish . . . because*, etc. This was an evil thought and constituted the sin of Simon.

Verse 21. *Part* means a share of something that is "assigned" to one, and *lot* denotes something won or "obtained by lot." There is not a great deal of difference between the two words in question, but the use of them together makes a statement that is more emphatic, and rules out both measures of the Holy Ghost. That which the apostles only could possess would not have been given Simon even if he had not been corrupt in heart. But that condition prevented him from receiving even the measure that other disciples were promised to receive.

Verse 22. The original word for *wickedness* often means some very bad bodily conduct, but Simon had not done anything of that kind. One word in Thayer's definition is "depravity," and that would apply in this case. Nothing but a depraved mind would think the Holy Ghost could be bought with money. Hence Peter told him to repent of the *thought of his heart*. Perhaps ordinarily denotes a doubt, which would not be a proper sense to attach to the word when thinking of the mercy of God. The original carries the idea of an earnest frame of mind on the part of Simon as if he should say, "Lord, I beseech thee," etc. *Repent and pray* is the law of pardon for a disciple when he has sinned. Chapter 2: 38 gives the law for one who has never been a child of God, and that is to "repent and be baptized." An alien sinner would not avail himself anything to repent and pray, neither would it avail anything for an erring disciple to repent and be

baptized, because baptism is to be performed only once.

Verse 23. *Gall* and *bitterness* are virtually the same in thought, and are used together for the sake of emphasis. It denotes a state of mind that is poisoned with depravity. *Iniquity* is defined in the lexicon, "unrighteousness of heart." The heart of Simon was bound up in a state of depravity, indicated by the sordid estimate that he placed on the value of the Holy Ghost.

Verse 24. Simon wished Peter to pray that he be released from the guilt of *these things*, meaning the state of corruption in his mind and the judgment of God that such a condition of mind would deserve. The scripture does not tell us anything about the conduct of Simon after this, and secular history is uncertain about the subject.

Verse 25. *They* means Peter and John who returned to Jerusalem, but preached in many of the Samaritan villages on their way.

Verse 26. The New Testament was not completed and the apostolic period was still with the world. In that situation God used various means to get his will to men. It should be carefully noted that he never did tell a sinner directly what to do to be saved. But until the plan of salvation was put on record where everyone could read it, the Lord used miraculous means to contact the sinner. In the present instance an angel (in what form he appeared we are not told) appeared to Philip who had just done his wonderful work in Samaria. The only thing the angel did was to tell Philip where to go. God knew where the preacher would meet the man to whom the Gospel message was to be delivered. *Desert* is from EREMOS which means an "uninhabited wilderness," and has reference to the physical condition of the land.

Verse 27. There is no history available that tells us whether this eunuch was a Jew or Gentile. If he was a Jew born in Ethiopia, he would be an Ethiopian by nation. The question that is sometimes raised is how it can be said that Cornelius was the first Gentile convert, if this eunuch was an Ethiopian by race. That need cause no confusion, for there were proselytes to the Jewish religion all through the years, and such persons were regarded as Jews. That is why this man had gone to Jerusalem to worship, for that was the headquarters of the Jewish system. It also explains why he was reading the book of Isaiah. (For notes on the proselytes, see Matthew 23: 15.)

Verse 28. Chariots were made for two purposes: war, and transportation in times of peace. The eunuch was riding in one of the latter.

Verse 29. The angel was used to direct Philip into the general location of the eunuch, and after arriving there, the Spirit gave him specific instructions about joining the chariot. But it should be noted in each case that the eunuch never learned anything about his duty until he got it from the preacher. (See Romans 10: 14.)

Verse 30. Philip was evidently traveling on foot, for after reaching the chariot (and entering it) he journeyed on with the eunuch. The speed of the chariot also was slow enough that Philip was able to overhear what the eunuch was reading, and also to enter into conversation with him.

Verse 31. In answer to Philip's question, the eunuch said he could not understand what he was reading without a guide. This should not surprise us, for he was reading in one of the prophetic books, and we are told that even the prophets themselves did not know "what it was all about" when they were inspired to do their writing. (See Matthew 13: 17; 1 Peter 1: 10-12). The attitude of Philip indicated his willingness to explain the scripture, and the eunuch asked him to sit with him in the chariot.

Verses 32, 33. This scripture is in Isaiah 53: 7, 8; it is in the past tense as to grammatical form, but that is a common thing in the prophetic writings. It pictures the unresisting attitude of Jesus when he was sentenced and executed upon the cross. *Judgment was taken away* means Jesus was treated with injustice. *Declare* is defined, "to set forth, recount, relate in full," and *generation* means one's family descent. The question is asked in the sense of asserting that no one can declare the family descent of Jesus. The reason is given in the words, his *life is taken from the earth*. Jesus died without having produced any fleshly offspring, because his only purpose in this world was to leave behind him a spiritual family. (See Ephesians 3: 15.)

Verse 34. See the comments on verse 31 for the eunuch's question.

Verse 35. *Opened his mouth.* No sinner was ever induced to accept salvation by miraculous means, but it was always by the use of words. (See chapter 11: 14.) *Began at the same scripture* denotes he explained the passage to be referring to Jesus. But after that start of his speech, the context indicates that he taught the eunuch the acts of faith that Jesus requires of sinners in order to receive forgiveness of sins.

Verse 36. The Old Testament says nothing about baptism, hence the eunuch could have learned about it only from Philip. This proves beyond any question that to *preach Jesus* means to tell of His requirements, including baptism in water. *Certain* is from TIS which Thayer defines, "a certain, a certain one." *Water* is from HUDOR, and the definitions of Thayer and Robinson agree, but the latter is fuller at this passage which is, "A stream, river." Hence *a certain water* means a permanent body of water, and one large enough for two men to enter. (See verses 38, 39.) The only material element necessary for baptism being present, the eunuch wished to know if he might be baptized.

Verse 37. There was just one item in his duty still undone that had to precede baptism, which was the good confession. (See Romans 10: 9, 10.) Philip told the eunuch that if he believed with all his heart *thou mayest.* The last two words are from EXESTI, which Thayer defines, "it is lawful." Robinson defines it, "It is lawful, it is right, it is permitted, one may." Philip meant it would be scriptural for him to baptize the eunuch if he was a believer in Jesus. The contrary would necessarily be true, that it would be unscriptural to baptize a person who is not a believer. That would make it unscriptural to baptize infants since they cannot believe. The confession of the eunuch was his own as far as the wording was concerned, for no one told him just how it was to be made. In 1 Timothy 6: 13 Paul says that Jesus made a good confession before Pilate, yet his words were merely "thou sayest" in answer to the governor's question (Matthew 27: 11.) This shows that no formal kind of confession should be considered necessary. The form the eunuch used is all right, and so is any other that means that one believes Jesus to be the Son of God.

Verse 38. A chariot is an inanimate object and cannot receive an intelligent order. Hence Philip addressed his command to the driver, for had he been doing his own driving he would not have commanded the chariot either. All of this proves that at least three persons were present at this baptism. The remark and question of the eunuch, also the answer of Philip and the eunuch's confession all took place after they came in sight of the "certain water," and they were still in sight of it when the command was given for the chariot to stop. This is another proof that the water was of some considerable size. *Into* is from EIS and is properly translated in the King James version. They both had to go down *into* the water for the act of baptism. The word *baptize* is from BAPTIZO, and Thayer defines it, "To dip repeatedly, to immerge, submerge." Robinson defines it, "To dip in, to sink, to immerse." Groves defines it, "To dip, immerse, plunge." Greenfield's definition is, "To immerse, immerge, submerge, sink." In its noun form, Donnegan defines it, "An object immersed, submerged, soaked."

Verse 39. *Come up out of the water* gives emphasis to the comments in the preceding verse on the necessity of going down *into* the water. *Into* and *out of* are opposite terms, and agree with the necessary movements in performing baptism. However, the purpose for the statement is to inform the reader that no supernatural act was done until the baptismal service was concluded. Philip had to make his way into this territory in whatever manner was available, but now that the object of his journey was accomplished, the Spirit of the Lord used some means of snatching him away suddenly out of the eunuch's sight; but he went on his way rejoicing in his new relation to the Lord.

Verse 40. Azotus was a town north of Gaza, the place to which Philip was told by the angel to go. Going on in his northward journey, he preached in all the cities to which he came until he reached his destination which was Caesarea on the coast.

ACTS 9

Verse 1. *Breathing out* is from EMPNEO and is defined, "to breathe in or on." When a person has a "bad breath" it is supposed to come from some undesirable condition within his body. It is used to illustrate the attitude and conduct of Saul towards the disciples. His mental breath was coming from a mind filled with desire to persecute them. He went unto the high priest because he was the president of the Sanhedrin, which was the highest court allowed the Jews.

Verse 2. *Desired of him letters.* Paul says he was "mad" against the saints (chapter 26: 11), but there was "method in his madness." He never acted independently of the authorities whom he regarded as having the right to punish offenders. These letters showed his authority to arrest the disciples, and they designated even the city and circumstances in which he was empowered to act. The original word for *way* means a way of life, and in our passage it refers to the way being professed by the disciples. Saul had the authority to bind disciples as an officer would put irons on a criminal.

Verse 3. The Lord let Saul proceed until he was near his destination (Damascus), then caused the light to envelop him. Saul afterward described this light as being "above the brightness of the sun" (chapter 26: 13).

Verse 4. Chapter 26: 14 says they all fell to the ground, but in Luke's original account of the event we have only *he* falling to the ground. That evidently was because Saul was the only one in the group who was to receive the full effect of the shock. The other men did not even know the source or meaning of the voice. (See comments verse 7).

Verse 5. *Who art thou?* Saul did not know it was the Lord speaking or he would not have asked the question. The word translated *Lord* is rendered "sir" 12 times in the King James version, which means merely a title of respect and was all that Saul meant. It is Luke that tells us it was the Lord speaking, who told Saul that He was the person whom he was persecuting. This charge was made on the principle of Matthew 25: 45. *Pricks* is from KENTRON which Thayer defines, "an iron goad," and explains it to mean, "for urging on oxen, horses and other beasts of burden." If an animal kicks back when his master prods him with the goad, it only makes it pierce him the more. Likewise, if Saul continues to rebel against the authority of the Lord, it will make his experience that much more disagreeable at last.

Verse 6. Saul then addressed Jesus as *Lord* in the true sense. He was convinced of his terrible error and began to tremble. Unlike Felix (chapter 24: 25) who trembled only, Saul asked what he should do. Of course, that meant with reference to his personal duty to get right with the Lord. But Jesus would not give him that information, and told him where to go for it. (See comments at chapter 8: 26.) However, Jesus did give him some other information, which is written in chapter 26: 16-18.

Verse 7. *Hear* is from ΑΚΟΥΟ, and the lexicon gives several distinct meanings, but they may be classified under three heads; I shall quote Thayer's definitions for the three: "1. To be endowed with the faculty of hearing. 2. To attend to, consider. 3. To understand, perceive the sense of what is said." The particular sense of the word in any given place must be determined by the context. Hence we know the word is used with the first meaning here; they merely knew by their ears that a voice was speaking, while in chapter 22: 9 the third meaning is used. *Seeing no man* was because the voice came from Heaven, and no one but Saul was to see Jesus then.

Verse 8. When the remarks of the Lord were concluded, Saul arose from the earth. The dazzling light that struck him to the ground also closed his eyes, and upon arising he naturally opened them. However, he was unable to see on account of what the light had done to his sight. (See chapter 22: 11.) He had to be led by the men who had come with him, who took him into the city of Damascus.

Verse 9. Smith's Bible Dictionary says, "The instance given of individual fasting under the influence of grief, vexation or anxiety are numerous." It was natural, therefore, for Saul to fast in view of the change in his plans, including the strange blindness.

Verse 10. Any disciple has the right to tell the story of Jesus and baptize the believers. We have seen that the Lord never told any man directly what he must do to be saved (chapter 8: 26), hence this disciple was to do that for Saul.

Verse 11. The Lord mentioned the fact of Saul's praying to assist Ananias in identifying him. Saul was a Jew and would have the right to pray under the Mosaic religion. We are not told specifically the subject of Saul's prayer, but it is not strange that he would be praying under the circumstances. It would also be reasonable to think he was praying for help in his undone condition, and that it was in reply to his prayer that the Lord permitted him to have the vision of Ananias coming to heal his blindness.

Verse 12. All inspired visions are one form of predictions. God had caused Saul to see this vision, now He was sending Ananias to fulfill it for him.

Verses 13, 14. The report of Saul's activities against the disciples was so widespread it had reached the city of Damascus before he arrived. The remarks of Ananias were not made with the idea of giving the Lord any information; so worthy a disciple would know better than that. They were the natural expression of his sincere emotions, and the Lord regarded them as such since he did not give him any rebuke.

Verse 15. The Lord's reassurance consisted in telling Ananias that Saul had been chosen by Him to bear his name before others, both Gentiles and Israelites. Of course, the Lord would not suffer such a chosen servant to harm any disciple sent to him.

Verse 16. The fulfillment of this prediction is described at chapter 20: 23; 21: 11; 2 Corinthians 6: 4-10; 11: 23-28. After such a devoted life filled with persecutions, Paul closed it by shedding his blood upon the block (2 Timothy 4: 6).

Verse 17. It will be well to take another look at the matter of being *filled with the Holy Ghost*. (See the comments at chapter 4: 31.) Also the subject of the "measure" of the Spirit should receive further consideration. The measure that would cause one to be baptized with the Holy Ghost, even, has some variation. The Gentiles in the house of Cornelius were baptized with the Holy Ghost (chapter 11: 15-17), yet all they could do was to speak in tongues (chapter 10: 46). Ananias did not lay hands on Saul for the same purpose that the apostles laid hands on others, for they did that to baptized believers only, while this was done to Saul before he was baptized (as it was done in the case of Cornelius' groups, it being an emergency): that shows it was another emergency or special case. God needed another apostle, and instead of sending the Holy Ghost as it was done on Pentecost, He gave Ananias the special commission and power to install the man Saul into office. Ananias called him *brother Saul* because they were members of the same Jewish race.

Verse 18. *As it had been* means that what fell from his eyes was like scales. The reason Saul was baptized is given at chapter 22: 16. In both passages it should be noted that Saul *arose* to be baptized, because that ordinance is done by immersion.

Verse 19. *Received meat* means he took food after his period of fasting. *Certain days* is really indefinite, and denotes merely that Saul remained with the disciples in the city where he had become one himself.

Verse 20. Saul began at once to discharge his assignment of preaching Christ. He did this in the synagogue where the Jews assembled to read the law.

Verse 21. It should be expected that the people would be amazed at the preaching of Saul. He did not merely subside from his persecution of the disciples, but became an active proclaimer of the faith he had been opposing.

Verse 22. *Increased in strength* denotes that he became more powerful in proclaiming the Gospel. He *confounded* (confused and bewildered) the Jews by showing from their own scriptures that Jesus was the Christ predicted therein.

Verse 23. The preaching of Saul finally roused the Jews to anger, and they plotted to kill him whenever he came outside the city walls.

Verse 24. They lay secretly near the gates, where they expected to attack him as he came through. Saul learned about their plot, which really proved to be to his advantage. Knowing that his enemies were lying near the gates, he was left to feel safe in escaping if he could by-pass those places.

Verse 25. According to 2 Corinthians 11: 32, 33, the secular officers joined with the Jews in their plot by maintaining a military guard near the gates of Damascus. But the disciples helped Saul to escape by lowering him down the outside of the wall in a *basket*, a vessel made by plaiting reeds or ropes.

Verse 26. *When Saul was come to Jerusalem*. This was after he had been in Arabia and returned to Damascus, a period of three years after his conversion (Galatians 1: 16-18). When he *assayed* (tried) to join the disciples they were afraid of him, thinking he was only posing as a disciple in order to get an advantage of them.

Verses 27, 28. Barnabas was a native of Cyprus (chapter 4: 36) which was not far from Damascus. It was natural that he would be more or less familiar with the events that took place in that city, especially as they concerned the religion he professed. His introduction of Saul to the apostles was satisfactory, so that he was with them in their movements in and out of Jerusalem.

Verse 29. Wherever Saul went, he was persecuted for preaching in the name of Jesus. *Grecians* were Greek-speaking Jews as explained at chapter 6: 1.

Verse 30. Caesarea was a seaport from which Saul sailed for his old home Tarsus. He was not idle while there, but preached "the faith he once destroyed" (Galatians 1: 21).

Verse 31. *Rest* is from EIRENE which Thayer defines, "a state of national tranquility; exemption from the rage and havoc of war." Then in its application to our passage he explains it to mean, "of the church free from persecutions." This indicates the extent and success of Saul's persecutions of the church as it pertained to the uneasiness caused among the disciples. *Fear* is used in the sense of reverence for the Lord. It shows us that while persecutions will not take from true disciples their love for Christ (Romans 8: 35-39), yet they may hinder them from advancing in numbers and strength. This will be the last we will hear of Saul until we get to chapter 11: 25, 26.

Verse 32. The condition of "rest" which the churches were enjoying opened up opportunities for the further spread of the Gospel. Peter used this situation to travel among the churches of Palestine and made Lydda one of his stopping places.

Verses 33, 34. *Palsy* was a form of paralysis that rendered the victim helpless from weakness. This man's case was of eight years' standing and hence was not imaginary. To make his bed was especially appropriate since his ailment was one of weakness. The cure was *immediate* as were all of the cases of miraculous healing.

Verse 35. *Saw him and turned to the Lord.* While the New Testament was in the making, the Lord empowered his apostles and other workers to perform miracles as evidence of their connection with Him. (See John 20: 30, 31; Ephesians 4: 8-14.)

Verse 36. Joppa was a seaport about ten miles from Lydda. The original word for *good works* means the general conduct is good and practical, and *almsdeeds* refers especially to things done for those in need, which is indicated in verse 39.

Verse 37. Thayer defines the original for *upper chamber*, "The highest part of the house, the upper rooms or story where the women resided." Here is where they laid Dorcas after preparing her body for burial.

Verse 38. The miraculous work of Peter had become known to the people of Joppa. Desiring him to come could have been only in the hope of restoring Dorcas to life.

Verse 39. *Widows stood by.* These were the ones for whom the "almsdeeds" of verse 36 were done. Their weeping was a sincere expression of appreciation for what Dorcas had done for them. *While she was with them.* Her body lay in their presence as they did this, which is another proof that there is something in a human being that leaves the body and the world when death occurs.

Verse 40. We are not told why Peter wished to be alone while performing this miracle, but it was not the first time such a thing was done. (See 1 Kings 17: 19-23; 2 Kings 4: 32-36; Matthew 9: 25.) Life was restored to the woman at the voice of Peter, and she opened her eyes only upon hearing it. She had enough physical strength to sit up, but was evidently somewhat weak from her recent illness.

Verse 41. *Gave her his hand.* Peter restored the woman to life independent of any cooperation on her part, as a matter of course, but he encouraged her to "arise" by giving her his hand. The miracle having been performed, he called her friends back into the room and presented her alive to them.

Verse 42. *Many believed.* See notes on verse 35 for the use of miracles in making believers. The case of Dorcas was reported throughout the city of Joppa.

Verse 43. The decision to spend more time in the city is mentioned as a mere incident, but it connects up with the events of the next chapter.

ACTS 10

Verse 1. This Caesarea was on the coast of Palestine. It was the official headquarters for the Roman government in that province. That is why Cornelius was stationed there, he being a military officer of the government, a centurion or commander of a hundred soldiers. *Italian band* means soldiers recruited from captives out of Italy.

Verse 2. Cornelius was a Gentile and lived under the Patriarchial Dispensation, which made it appropriate for him to worship God in the manner described. That dispensation, like the two others, had its better as well as less devoted members, and Cornelius was one of the best. He was a busy man in practical matters, so his praying to God *always* means he was continually a praying man.

Verse 3. He saw *evidently* denoted it was so plain that it could not leave any doubt as to what he saw. God was about to put an end to the Patriarchial Dispensation, and selected one of the best men in that system for the occasion. That was significant and showed that the change was not made just because the system was an absolute failure. The angel was not to tell Cornelius what to do to be saved, but to direct him to a man who would tell him. (See the comments at chapter 8: 26.)

Verse 4. Was *afraid* means he was overcome with awe at the appearance of this being. It was at the *ninth hour* which is three o'clock P. M., in broad daylight, so that no mysterious condition surrounded the place. He used the word *lord* in the sense of "sir," a title of great respect, and inquired what he wanted of him. Before telling him of his duty, the angel first quieted his fears with some words of commendation for his past life. *Memorial* is from MNEMOSUNON which Thayer defines, "a memorial (that by which the memory of any person or thing is preserved), a remembrance." It denotes that God had not overlooked his righteous life, and was going to use him as the first Gentile to be offered membership in the Christian Dispensation.

Verse 5. Up until *now* Cornelius had lived in accordance with the obligations of the Patriarchal Dispensation. That system was for the Gentiles and had been in force since the days of Adam. In the meantime the Jewish Dispensation had been "added" (Galatians 3: 19) as the system for the Jews, and that was lifted from them by the cross (Colossians 2: 14), leaving the Gentiles still under the Patriarchal Dispensation for a few years. *Now* that, too, was to be discontinued, and Cornelius was to do something else. That placed him under a new obligation, cancelling the authority of the former system. From *now* he was expected to do something else in order to be saved, and he was told to send for Peter at Joppa that he might tell him what it was.

Verse 6. Specific directions were given so that the right Simon would be called for. *Oughtest* is from DEI which Thayer defines, "It is necessary, there is need of, it behooves, is right and proper," and he explains it at this place to mean, "Necessity in reference to what is required to attain some end." It has been rendered "must" 58 times in the King James translation. *He shall tell thee.* This is in keeping with the Lord's plan not to tell sinners directly what to do to be saved. (See chapter 8: 26.)

Verses 7, 8. Most public officers have their servants to wait on them in the affairs of the home, and military men who compose a bodyguard. Cornelius sent a group of three from these two classes to go to Joppa.

Verses 9, 10. The story now leaves the three men in their journey but nearing the city of Joppa the following day. Meanwhile Peter went upon the roof of the house to pray. Homes had flat roofs and they were occupied in much the same way as verandas are used today. It was at noon and Peter was hungry, but the meal was not ready, hence it furnished an opportunity for the Lord to add another portion to the story. A *trance* differs from a dream in that it occurs while the person is physically awake, but is lost to the immediate surroundings; a sort of "daydream." When the Lord

uses that plan for making a special revelation, he will cause the person to "draw in his mind from the things around him," and see with his mind's eye the things He wishes him to see.

Verse 11. *Saw heaven opened* refers to the region above him that could be seen with the natural eye under ordinary circumstances. A square piece of cloth could be gathered up by the four corners and thus form a vessel in which objects could be held. The four corners represented the "four corners of the earth," and denoted that God was about to offer an additional opportunity to mankind for salvation, that would include the Gentiles or nations of the whole earth.

Verses 12, 13. The Jews were restricted against eating certain kinds of animals that were considered unclean (ceremonially). They likewise held themselves above the Gentiles and regarded them as "dogs" (Matthew 15: 26, 27). The time had come when the Lord was going to consider any of the nations of the world good enough to be offered the Gospel, and he was introducing the subject by this object lesson. It was to be literally true that under the new dispensation no religious objections would be made against any kind of meat (1 Timothy 4: 3, 4). Likewise, no discriminations were to be made against any race of mankind, whether Jew or Gentile.

Verse 14. Peter took the language of the Lord to be used literally of these living creatures, and that perhaps He was putting him to the test. *Common* means food that the common classes of mankind used.

Verse 15. *What God hath cleansed* is explained at verses 12, 13.

Verse 16. This (conversation) was done thrice, the second being mentioned in the preceding verse. After the three times, the vessel was taken back out of Peter's sight.

Verse 17. Peter pondered over the vision as to what it signified, and by that time the men sent by Cornelius had arrived at Simon's gate.

Verse 18. The men specified whom they wanted according to the instructions they received from Cornelius.

Verse 19. The Lord was supervising this whole drama and bringing the various parts of it together at just the right time. Peter was still wondering about the vision at the time these men were making their inquiry. The "voice" of verses 13 and 15 is here seen to have been the Spirit, speaking on behalf of the Lord.

Verse 20. The purpose of the Spirit in speaking was to reassure Peter that the call was legitimate. That would prepare him to receive whatever message they gave him.

Verse 21. Peter identified himself to the three men, which was the only response we have recorded as to their inquiry when they arrived at the gate. The Spirit had not told him what the men wanted, but simply assured him they were there because of Him.

Verse 22. In answer to Peter's question the men told their story. The original for *warned* at this place is defined by Thayer, "To be divinely commanded, admonished, instructed." Admonition always implies that some danger is possible for the one being admonished. Cornelius had been asked to learn his duty from Peter, and should he neglect it his soul would be in danger. This verse adds the information that Cornelius (though a Gentile) had a good reputation among the Jews.

Verse 23. It being evening of the day after the men started from home, Peter procured lodging for them over night; the next chapter will explain about *certain brethren.*

Verse 24. *Morrow after* means the next day after the group left the house of Simon the tanner. By way of tabulating the days, if the men left the house of Cornelius on Monday, they got back on Thursday. Cornelius was not selfish about the good words he expected to hear, but had assembled his relatives and friends who were waiting for Peter.

Verse 25. It was very natural for Cornelius to offer worship to the man who was to show him the way of salvation. We do not know what actions he attempted further than his falling down at the feet of Peter. For information on the various meanings of the word "worship," see the notes on Matthew 2: 2.

Verse 26. Peter's remark that he was himself *also a man* indicates that what Cornelius was attempting to offer was a kind due only to the Lord.

Verse 27. The above conversation took place near the entrance of the house of Cornelius. Peter then went on in and observed that quite an audience had assembled.

Verse 28. The first part of this verse states the long-standing attitude of the Jews toward the Gentiles. Peter makes his application of this vision of the sheet and the conversation in connection with it. In that instance nothing was said about common or unclean men; only articles of food. But the apostle understood the lesson and stated it to this assembled audience.

Verse 29. Acting upon the lesson as he understood it, he came *without gainsaying,* which means without calling it in question. Being convinced that whatever was the purpose in calling him, it was proper, he asked them what that purpose was.

Verses 30-32. This paragraph corresponds with verses 3-6 in its main thoughts. It adds the information that he was fasting at the time the *man* (angel) appeared.

Verse 33. Cornelius was the spokesman in this reply to Peter's question. He was appreciative of the fact that Peter had come at his request. In the original conversation there was nothing said directly about the commandments coming from the Lord, but Cornelius recognized that He was back of all this, because the angel told him it was God who had remembered his good deeds. *We are all here . . . to hear.* This denotes an audience that was open to the words of the Lord.

Verse 34. *Opened his mouth.* (See the comments at Matthew 5: 2.) God is no *respector of persons* is from PROSOPOLEPTER which Thayer defines, "an accepter." It has the idea of one who can be bribed or induced to show partiality in bestowing mercy.

Verse 35. Through the combination of several circumstances, Peter was convinced that all races were equally acceptable to God if they feared him and lived righteously.

Verse 36. Peter then began his sermon about Jesus, whose life's story was begun among the children of Israel, and which declared that Jesus was Lord (or ruler) of all.

Verse 37. The work for Jesus began with the introductory labors of John in the wilderness, and consisted of his baptism of the people, connected with belief of the story that Jesus was to come.

Verse 38. Literal anointing was

done by rubbing oil over a person being introduced into an office. Figurative anointing was done by bestowing the Holy Spirit upon someone who was expected to have a prominent work under God. When the word is extended to apply to unofficial persons, it means to be endowed with the words which the Holy Spirit gave the disciples through the apostles. (See 1 John 2: 27.) Jesus was anointed with the Holy Ghost and power at his baptism (Matthew 3: 16, 17). *Devil* is from DIABOLOS which means the being called Satan, who is considered responsible for the entrance of sin and disease into the world.

Verse 39. *We are witnesses* was made possible by the arrangement recorded in Mark 3: 14, which also is in line with Peter's statement in chapter 1: 21, 22.

Verses 40, 41. *Openly* does not mean generally, but evidently, "by many infallible proofs" (chapter 1: 3). The *witnesses* were the apostles, who were chosen beforehand for that purpose. Having seen Jesus alive, and eaten with him and handled him, they could testify from personal knowledge that Jesus lived again after his three days and three nights in the tomb.

Verse 42. Unlike his previous speeches, Peter did not accuse his hearers of guilt when he mentioned the death of Jesus, but the event needed to be told in connection with the resurrection. For the meaning of *ordained*, see the notes at John 15: 16. The *quick* are the people who will be living when Jesus comes. The dead will be raised, and all will be judged by this One who was ordained for that work. (See chapter 17: 31.)

Verse 43. *All the prophets witness.* The Gentiles were not expected to be acquainted with the Old Testament prophecies. The purpose Peter had in mentioning this was to show Cornelius and his group that it had long been God's will to offer salvation to all the world who would believe, whether they were Jews or Gentiles.

Verses 44, 45. It is better to consider these two verses together because of their relation to each other. Notice that the terms *Holy Ghost* and *gifts of the Holy Ghost* are used for the same event, showing that the Holy Ghost was the thing given. The gift was not bestowed to make them disciples, for they were told next to be

baptized. The reference to the astonishment of the disciples of the Jewish nation, and the argument Peter makes in verse 47, shows that God bestowed the gift as an evidence that from then on the Gentiles would be acceptable to become converts to Christ. (See Romans 15: 16.)

Verses 46-48. These verses may be bracketed and entitled, "end of the Patriarchal Dispensation." *Speaking with tongues* was necessary as evidence that these Gentiles had received the Holy Ghost. Upon all the accumulated evidence before Peter, which began with his trance on the roof of the house, he proposed baptism in water for these believers. *In His name.* The first word is from EN, and means upon the authority of the Lord. It shows Peter's right to command the baptism, and not as a "formula" to be uttered by the baptizer. It was natural for them to wish Peter to spend some time with them.

ACTS 11

Verse 1. Much of this chapter is a rehearsal of the preceding one, and I shall try to avoid unnecessary repetition of the comments. The brethren around Jerusalem heard the news of the conversion of the Gentiles before Peter returned.

Verse 2. When Peter got back to Jerusalem, they of the *circumcism*, meaning the Jews, had a contention with him.

Verse 3. It was objectionable to them for Peter to have associated with the Gentiles, but it was made worse for him to *eat* with them. In those days it was regarded as one of the strongest signs of social intimacy, to sit down together with others at a meal. (See 1 Corinthians 5: 11.) See the notes at Matthew 9: 11 about eating with others.

Verses 4-11. See the notes on chapter 10: 9-18.

Verse 12. These *six brethren* are the "certain brethren" of chapter 10: 23. They were taken along to be witnesses of the events in the household of Cornelius. Peter referred to them as a verification of what he was reporting.

Verses 13, 14. See the comments on chapter 10: 30-33.

Verse 15. See notes on chapter 10: 44, 45. Also note that Peter says the Holy Ghost fell on them *as it did* on the apostles at the beginning. As to what "measure" it was that was given them, see the comments at chapter 4: 31.

Verse 16. *Then* is an adverb of time and refers to the moment when the Holy Ghost fell. That event reminded Peter of what John said in Matthew 3: 11. See the comments on that verse as to why Peter does not mention the baptism of fire.

Verse 17. Peter again calls the gift received by them and the Gentiles a *like gift.* Had he even hesitated about baptizing these Gentiles he would have been resisting God, for the bestowal of the Holy Ghost on them was to show that they were acceptable to God upon obedience to the Gospel ordinance.

Verse 18. The brethren showed the right spirit when Peter presented the facts to them. They did not merely give a reluctant agreement, but gave God the glory for what he had bestowed on the Gentiles. *Granted repentance unto life* means God gave the Gentiles the chance to repent (reform their lives), with the promise of forgiveness of sins.

Verse 19. This subject is mentioned in chapter 8: 1, 4, but the places are not named in that passage. *To the Jews only.* That was because they had left Jerusalem before the Gentiles had been accepted into the Gospel work.

Verse 20. The Grecians were Jews who spoke the Greek language.

Verse 21. The Lord blessed the labors of these men by causing their work to be received. The result was that a great number became disciples.

Verse 22. The church in Jerusalem sent Barnabas to Antioch (in Syria), because the scattered disciples had carried the Gospel message as far as to that city.

Verse 23. The mission of Barnabas was to encourage the new converts, also to exhort them regarding their responsibility. *Purpose of heart* denotes a service into which one puts his whole heart.

Verse 24. *Full of the Holy Ghost.* (See the notes at chapter 4: 31.) The work and influence of Barnabas resulted in many more conversions.

Verse 25. The last account we had of Saul was when the brethren helped him get started towards this town of Tarsus (chapter 9: 30). The work at Antioch was growing in numbers and influence, and Barnabas believed that the help of Saul would be beneficial, hence he went to Tarsus to find him.

Verse 26. These two men spent a year with the church, teaching them their duties that follow induction into the Lord's service. *Called Christians.* The second word is defined in the lexicon, "a follower of Christ," hence it is not likely that enemies would attach that title to them as in disrespect, for the disciples themselves claimed to be that, and rejoiced in the thought of being known by that name. The first word is from CHREMATIZO, and Thayer defines it at this place, "to assume or take to one's self a name from one's public business." That is exactly what was done in this case, for the (religious) business of the disciples was to work for Christ which made the name Christian an approprite one for them.

Verse 27. Among the miraculous gifts bestowed upon the disciples in the early period of the church was that of prophesying. Peter cited the prediction of it in his reference to Joel's writings, in chapter 2: 17.

Verse 28. This famine is verified by Josephus; Antiquities, Book 20, Chapter 2, Section 5. I shall quote only one sentence from his lengthy paragraph: "Whereas a famine did oppress them at that time, and many people died for want of what was necessary to procure food withal." The context shows Josephus was writing of the days of Claudius Caesar. *All the world* was a common phrase to refer to the Roman Empire.

Verse 29. The disciples at Antioch were in better circumstances than those in Judea, and concluded to send them some relief. This was done on the basis of voluntary contributions, and the giving was according to each man's ability. That is the principle on which all giving is to be done by Christians (1 Corinthians 16: 2).

Verse 30. *Sent it to the elders.* We learned at chapter 6: 2 that the deacons are the ones whose *work* is to distribute the funds for the necessities of life. That was always true, but the work of those officials, like everything else pertaining to the affairs of the church, is under the supervision of the elders.

ACTS 12

Verse 1. This was Herod Agrippa, I, the grandson of Herod the Great. After a career of "ups and downs" with various powers, he was finally placed in a ruling position over Palestine by authority of the Roman Emperor. His idea in vexing persons of the church was to win the favor of the Pharisaic Jews. (See verse 3.)

Verse 2. This James was one of the sons of Zebedee (Matthew 4: 21).

Verse 3. Peter was not slain but was put into prison. *Days of unleavened bread* denotes it was the time of the feast of the Passover (Leviticus 23: 4-8).

Verse 4. A quaternion consisted of four soldiers, and four of them would make 16 soldiers charged with the guarding of the prison, changing their shifts every three hours. Two of the ones on duty were with the prisoner and two watched the gate. *Easter* is from PASCHA. Thayer defines it, "The paschal festival, the feast of Passover." It has no connection with Easter as that term is used today.

Verse 5. *Without ceasing* is from the Greek word EKTENES, and Thayer defines it, "Intent, earnest, assiduous [persistent]." The prayers were continuous and earnest.

Verse 6. *Sleeping between two soldiers.* (See the notes at verse 4.)

Verse 7. An angel of the Lord would be given supernatural power, by which he could perform this service to Peter unknown to the soldiers. (See Hebrews 1: 13, 14.)

Verse 8. Peter had taken off his sandals and outer garment when he was preparing for sleep. The angel meant for him to resume them, tightening his belt about him.

Verse 9. *Wist* [knew] *not that it was true.* The last word is from ALETHES, which Thayer defines with the same word used in the text, and adds by way of explanation, "an actual occurrence." Peter thought he was in a trance and was seeing a vision only.

Verse 10. *First and second ward* were the two soldiers stationed some distance apart to guard the prison. (See notes at verse 4.) The same supernatural power that loosened the chains unknown to the soldiers in the prison (verse 7), enabled them to pass these other soldiers unseen. The *iron gate* was what closed the outer wall of the entire prison structure. *Opened of his own accord.* The Lord was still working in the case and miraculously

removing all the barriers to Peter's freedom. *Passed through one street.* The angel remained with Peter until they were safely out of reach of the prison officers and guardsmen, then disappeared.

Verse 11. *Come to himself.* After the angel disappeared, Peter observed that he was on one of the streets of the city, out of the vicinity of the prison. He knew that to be there it was necessary to escape the two soldiers lying by him, and the two near the gate, likewise get through the iron gate in the prison outer wall. This is what caused him to come to himself and to conclude that his experience was not "only a dream."

Verse 12. *Considered the thing.* The last two words are not in the original. The phrase means that after Peter had come to himself he considered the whole situation and decided to call at the home of one of the disciples. It was at the home of Mark's mother, where a prayer service was being conducted on his behalf.

Verse 13. *Door of the gate.* The last word refers to the porch in front of a house, and the first is the smaller opening through which to pass into the porch. *Came to hearken* means to inquire or to ask, "who is it?"

Verse 14. When Peter answered her question she recognized his voice. She was so joyously surprised she seemed to forget to open the door. She left Peter standing and knocking and went to tell the group that Peter was at the gate.

Verse 15. We are not told just what the church said in its prayer for Peter. If it was a scriptural prayer, the disciples placed their request on condition "if the Lord will." The favorable answer to the prayer was so gladdening that they thought it was "too good to be true." The girl was so positive about her report they thought some explanation should be resorted to that would harmonize all the phases of the situation. Their solution was that it was *his angel.* After his definition of the Greek word for *angel,* Thayer explains that "guardian angels of individuals are mentioned in Matthew 18: 10; Acts 12: 15." Funk and Wagnalls Standard Bible Dictionary says the following: "There was a popular idea that each person had assigned to him a special guardian angel, and it is to this that Jesus refers in Matthew 18:

10. Peter's escape from prison (Acts 12: 15) is an illustration of the thought that when such guardian angel appeared on earth he took the form of the person guarded." Luke does not say anything for or against such a theory, since in the present instance the experssion was that of the astonished group, and their statement had no authority in the nature of inspiration.

Verse 16. The continual knocking made it necessary to open the door. Their amazement caused them to make some kind of clamor. (See next verse.)

Verse 17. Peter indicated with his hand that he wished them to be quiet and listen. He then rehearsed the manner in which he was released from prison. He asked them to tell the good news, first to James and then to the other brethren. This was James the Lord's brother, and the writer of the epistle that bears his name. Special mention is made of him because of his prominence in the work at Jerusalem. (See chapter 15: 13; 21: 18; 1 Cortinthians 15: 7; Galatians 1: 19; 2: 9, 12.) After giving the group his request, Peter went into another *place*. That meant some spot in Jerusalem, for in chapter 15: 7 we find him in the city and speaking to the assembly on the issue before it.

Verse 18. By the aid of the angel, Peter had escaped prison unseen by the soldiers, hence the confusion over his absence, but we know that the soldiers were innocent.

Verse 19. *Examined* is from ANA-KRINO, and Thayer defines it, "To hold an investigation; to interrogate, examine, the accused or witnesses." The keepers would not be able to give Herod any information as to the escape of their prisoner, hence they were condemned to a death they did not deserve. Caesarea "was the official residency of the Herodian kings," according to Smith's Bible Dictionary, hence we have the statement that Herod went there and abode.

Verse 20. *Highly displeased* is from THUMOMACHEO, which is defined in Thayer's lexicon, "to carry on war with great animosity; to be very angry, be exasperated." Adjoining countries frequently have trouble with each other; we do not know what was the cause of Herod's displeasure. But the country of Tyre and Sidon became anxious for peace because it depended

on Palestine for necessary products. (See 1 Kings 5: 11; Ezekiel 27; 17.) A chamberlain is an intimate servant to a king, and the people of Tyre and Sidon induced this one to use his influence with his master. As a result, Herod agreed to drop hostilities and fixed a date when he would grant a hearing to the interested partisans.

Verse 21. When the set day arrived, Herod put on his royal garments and made a speech (of conciliation) to the people, which aroused them to making foolish compliments.

Verse 22. In their wild joy the people said that Herod was a god.

Verse 23. Josephus, Antiquities, Book 19, Chapter 8, Section 2, says that Herod did not rebuke the people for their flattery. Our passage merely states that Herod was eaten of worms and died. But the passage in Josephus cited above says, "A severe pain arose in his abdomen, and began in a most violent manner. . . . When he had said this, his pain was become violent. . . . And when he had been quite worn out by the pain in his abdomen for five days, he departed this life."

Verse 24. The significance of this verse is that in spite of all the disturbances going on between rival countries, the word of God gained many adherents.

Verse 25. *Fulfilled their ministry.* Chapter 11: 29, 30 shows this mission was to take the contribution collected at Antioch for the famine-stricken disciples in Judea. When they came back to Antioch they brought with them Mark, who is the writer of the book that bears his name.

ACTS 13

Verse 1. I shall quote from the Schaff-Herzog Encyclopedia: "Antioch in Syria, the second capital of Christianity, and the third city of the Roman Empire in population (500,000), wealth, and commercial activity, was situated about 300 miles north of Jerusalem, upon the left bank of the Orontes, and 16 miles from the Mediterranean." The importance of this city is indicated by the fact that Paul had it for his starting place for the "missionary journeys" that he made, returning each time to report his work to the church there. It was the place where the disciples first called themselves Christians (chapter 11: 26). The church there was strong in numbers and talented men, including the ones whose names are mentioned in this verse.

Verse 2. See the notes on Matthew 6: 16 on the subject of fasting. The Holy Ghost speaks only through men, so this instruction was made through one of the prophets in the church. *Separate* is from APHORIZO which Thayer defines, "To appoint, set apart, one for some purpose." Barnabas and Saul were to be thus appointed for a special work to which the Lord had called them.

Verse 3. We know from chapter 8: 18 that it required the laying on of an apostle's hands to confer any miraculous gift. Besides, Saul was already an apostle of Christ with the power to confer such gifts, hence no hands were laid on him for that purpose. But since such a manual act was used in those days for that important office, it came to be also a gesture of approval, similar to giving the "right hand of fellowship" (Galatians 2: 9). The church at Antioch *sent them* on this mission, which is one of the meanings of being an apostle.

Verse 4. The Holy Ghost sent them forth by speaking through the church. This was the start of the first "missionary journey." Seleucia was a seaport town, from where they sailed to Cyprus, an island in the Mediterranean Sea.

Verse 5. Salamis was one of the two chief cities of Cyprus, situated on its eastern coast. Here the missionaries preached in the synagogue of the Jews because they could meet people there. It was John Mark who was going with them as a *minister.* The original for that word is defined in the lexicon, "Any one who serves with his hands, a servant." John Mark went with them as an attendant to do whatever service that was needed.

Verse 6. Paphos was the other chief city of the island and it was situated on the western shore. *Sorcerer* is from MAGOS which is the word for "wise men" in Matthew 2: 1. See the notes at that place for a fuller explanation of the word. This sorcerer was using whatever talent of wisdom he had to make false predictions and to oppose the truth. Bar-jesus was the proper name given to this man as his personal name. Elymas (verse 8) was a common noun applied to him because

of some special meaning derived from the name.

Verse 7. Sergius Paulus was the *deputy* (acting governor) of the island, which was a part of the Roman Empire. This man was *prudent* (very intelligent) and wished to hear what Barnabas and Saul were preaching.

Verse 8. *Elymas the sorcerer* (See verse 6) was associated with the deputy in some way, and tried to prevent him from believing the Gospel. He was a Jew by race, and feared that if the deputy became a believer it would affect his standing with him.

Verse 9. *Also is called Paul.* A common but erroneous saying is that Saul's name was changed to Paul. The text only says that he was *also* called Paul. Thayer says that Saul was his Jewish name, while Paul (from PAULUS) was a Latin proper name. From here on the name Saul will not be applied to him except historically when referring to his conversion. *Filled with the Holy Ghost.* (See notes at chapter 4: 31.)

Verse 10. *Subtilty* means deceitfulness, which the sorcerer used with a *mischievous* motive. *Child of the devil.* The first word is explained at John 17: 12.

Verse 11. *Hand of the Lord* was said to let the deputy know that he (Paul) was working under Him. A man who is so blind that he cannot see even the sun is certainly very much so, although this was to be on this man only *for a season.* This miracle was *immediate,* as all of them were that the Lord brought to pass. The fact the man sought for someone to lead him proved the genuineness of the deed.

Verse 12. The deputy *believed* when he saw the miracle. That was according to the Lord's purpose for miracles, stated in John 20: 30, 31.

Verse 13. Pamphylia was in Asia Minor, and was a province of the Roman Empire. We are not told why John (Mark) deserted them, but the act was so distasteful to Paul that it later caused a serious dispute between him and Barnabas (chapter 15: 37-40).

Verse 14. Pisidia was another province in Asia Minor adjoining Pamphylia, in which the present Antioch was situated. The Jews assembled in the synagogues on the sabbath day to hear the reading of the law, since copies of it were scarce and only a few people could possess it. The preachers went into it because it gave them an opportunity to speak to the people about the Gospel. It was the custom to invite persons in the audience to speak, after the reading service was completed.

Verse 15. *Sent unto them, saying.* The first word is from APOSTELLO, which Thayer defines at this place, "to say through a messenger." In a large room and in a numerous gathering of people, it would be more courteous and orderly for the rulers at the front of the auditorium to have a messenger go to the visitor and personally invite him to speak.

Verse 16. Paul *stood up* according to the custom in that community for public speakers. *Beckoning with his hand* was a gesture as an invitation or request for the people to give their attention to him. *Ye that fear God* was not said in flattery, but was an honest comment based on the fact that they were at that place for the purpose of hearing the reading of the law of God.

Verse 17. As a preparation for his main subject, the story of Christ, Paul rehearsed the history of the Jews, beginning with their sojourn in Egypt. *High arm* means one of great might and authority.

Verse 18. *Suffered he their manners* means that God tolerated them, not that He endorsed them. Instead, He frequently punished them for their sins.

Verse 19. The *seven nations* are named in Deuteronomy 7: 1. Joshua conquered 31 kings (chapter 12: 24), but many of them ruled only over single cities. The *seven nations* were important groups in Canaan. The division of the land is in Joshua, chapters 15, 16 and 17, and the division was decided by means of the lot.

Verse 20. This is the only passage that states the entire period of the judges. *Until Samuel* is said because he was the last one of the judges (1 Samuel 7: 15).

Verse 21. This is the only passage that states the length of Saul's reign.

Verse 22. The throne was not only removed from Saul's house but also from his tribe (Benjamin), and given to David of the tribe of Judah. It remained in that tribe as long as the kingdom existed.

Verse 23. The importance of David was due to the fact that he was to become the ancestor, both fleshly and spiritually, of the Saviour of Israel and all the world.

Verse 24. *John had first preached* refers to the work of John as the forerunner of Jesus, baptizing people in preparation for His service. *Baptism of repentance* means that John baptized those only who repented. (See Matthew 3: 7, 8.)

Verse 25. This verse is explained at John 1: 19-27.

Verse 26. Paul was showing these Jews that they were the ones who were first to be concerned in the promise made to Abraham. (See verse 46.)

Verse 27. The leaders among the Jews did not know (recognize) Jesus nor the prophecies that went before concerning h i m. Notwithstanding, when they condemned *him* (Jesus), they fulfilled *them* (the prophecies that foretold that condemnation).

Verse 28. In spite of there being no charge sustained against Jesus, the Jews called for his death. In so doing they fulfilled the prophecies about him. (See verse 27.)

Verse 29. The pronoun *they* refers to both the enemies and the friends of Jesus, for it was the friends who placed him in the tomb. But the next verse shows that the enemies were still interested in His death, for they placed a guard about the tomb in the hope that he would not be able to come out alive. In this sense *they laid him in the tomb.*

Verse 30. This brief verse means that God overruled the acts and expectations of the Jews, by raising his Son to life.

Verse 31. As a rebuke to the murderers of Jesus, God saw to it that many "disinterested" people would have full opportunity to see Jesus after his resurrection.

Verses 32, 33. *Glad tidings* is another term for "Gospel," and Paul was announcing it to this synagogue audience. *Second Psalm.* The quotation stated by Paul can be found in no other place than the Psalm that is so numbered today. This proves that the Book of Psalms was arranged as to chapter numbers then the same as today.

Verse 34. *No more to return to corruption* means that Jesus arose from the dead to die no more. *Sure mercies of David.* The second word is from HOSIOS which Thayer defines at this place, "The holy things (of God) promised to David." These things included the resurrection of his illustrious descendant, Jesus, to die no more.

Verses 35, 36. Jesus was to be raised from the dead, but God also promised David that his "son" was not to remain in the grave long enough to decay. (Psalms 16: 9, 10.)

Verse 37. *Served his own generation* denotes that David did his duty in serving God in that age or generation. After doing that, however, he died and his body went back to the dust, while the One concerning whom the promise was made to David was raised before His body had time to decay, thus fulfilling the promise made to the patriarch.

Verse 38. *This man* was said to emphasize that Christ and not David—the new law and not the old—is the only means by which one must obtain forgiveness of sins.

Verse 39. *By him* has the same force as the italicized words in the preceding verse. The law of Moses could not bring the justification that is possible by belief in Christ.

Verse 40. Paul referred to a statement in Habakkuk 1: 5.

Verse 41. The prophet was writing about ancient Israel and the judgments that were brought upon them through the Chaldeans. Paul warned the Jews in his audience that a like judgment might come upon them. It was similar to his statements in Romans 15: 4 and 1 Corinthians 10: 11.

Verse 42. The synagogues were public places and came to be attended by Gentiles as visitors. They were less prejudiced than the Jews and wished to hear more of the subject that Paul was preaching. *Next sabbath* would be the next gathering in the synagogue.

Verse 43. *Congregation* is from the same Greek word as *synagogue.* (See the notes at Matthew 4: 23.) The more favorable among the Jews, also the Gentiles who had become proselytes to the Jewish faith, were so well impressed that they accompanied Paul and Barnabas as they went on their way out into the city. Seeing their attitude, Paul encouraged them to continue in the good life they were following. He was not ready to make a direct appeal for them to take their stand for the Gospel; that will come soon.

Verse 44. In the week following the events just mentioned, the news of them was spread so that a large crowd came the next sabbath to hear the word.

Verse 45. No outspoken opposition was manifested against the preaching of Paul until the Jews saw the great throng of people. Their envy was so bitter that they even blasphemed the work of the preachers, denying the truths they were uttering.

Verse 46. The Gospel was intended for the whole world, but the Jews were to be given the "first chance" for it. Indeed, it was not even offered to the Gentiles until the case of Cornelius. And on that principle Paul made his first appeals to the Jews in his preaching. But when they rejected the favor, Paul considered it as rendering themselves *unworthy of everlasting life.* In turning to the Gentiles he was acting in keeping with the events of chapter 10.

Verse 47. Paul verified his work by quoting Isaiah 49: 6.

Verse 48. *Gentiles heard this* means the announcement of Paul that he was turning to them with the word of God. The Bible does not contradict itself, and the whole of God's dealings with man shows that no person will be either saved or lost by any predestined decree, but that all who will may be saved. The passages on the subject are too numerous to be cited here, but the reader should see 2 Peter 3: 9. All of the words in our verse are correctly translated, but the construction of the sentence is inaccurate. The proper form is, "As many as believed were ordained to eternal life," and the reader should see the notes at John 15: 16 on the word "ordain."

Verse 49. This publishing of the word was due to the conversion of the Gentiles throughout that territory, who repeated the good news to others.

Verse 50. These *devout and honorable women* were of the better class of citizens, who generally had much respect for established law. The Jews worked on their emotions and got them so excited that they became uneasy about the work of Paul and Barnabas. The result of the excitement was a movement of persecution against the preachers. This expelling was not a formal or legal act, but a persecuting one that forced them to leave.

Verse 51. *Shook off the dust.* (See the notes on Matthew 10: 14.) Iconium was a large city in the next province, a place of many wealthy people.

Verse 52. Notwithstanding the opposition of the envious Jews the disciples were happy. (See the notes on chapter 4: 31 on being filled with the Holy Ghost.)

ACTS 14

Verse 1. As his manner was, Paul went into the synagogue to have opportunity to preach the word. Both Jews and Greeks believed the word, due to the convincing way in which Paul (and Barnabas) spoke the truth.

Verse 2. The Jews ordinarily had little or no interest in the Gentiles, but it grieved them to see these people becoming interested in the work of the brethren. They agitated them so much that it turned their minds against Paul and Barnabas.

Verse 3. *Gave testimony* was done as it was in Mark 16: 20. This was necessary because the New Testament had not been produced, and something was required to prove that the preachers were not frauds.

Verse 4. The multitude was divided in sentiment between the Jews and the *apostles.* The last word will be explained at verse 14.

Verses 5, 6. This *assault* did not reach the stage of actual attack, for the men heard about it and escaped. The word means "a hostile movement" according to Thayer, and would have ended in violence had Paul and Barnabas remained in the city. Lystra and Derbe were in another province nearby, and the preachers stopped at Lystra first.

Verse 7. Persecution did not dampen the devotion of the missionaries, for at every opportunity they preached the Gospel to all who would hear it.

Verse 8. *Impotent* means to be weak, and this man had been too lame in his feet to walk, having been that way since his birth.

Verse 9. *Faith to be healed.* Paul knew the man showed the proper attitude toward the preaching, and that frame of mind would prompt him to cooperate with the apostle.

Verse 10. Paul put that faith to a test by telling the man to stand. Sure enough, he proved his faith by his works by leaping and walking.

Verse 11. Lycaonia was the province where Lystra was situated. This miracle was so unusual that the heathen people of the country thought Paul and Barnabas were gods; that is, the planets (which these people worshiped) in the form of men.

Verse 12. The planets *Mercurius* and *Jupiter* had these characteristics as indicated in the work of Paul and Barnabas, according to the heathen mythology.

Verse 13. True to their opinion of the preachers, the heathen priest of that city was preparing to do homage to them as gods. The oxen were for the purpose of sacrifice, and the garlands were to be used as crowns.

Verse 14. *Apostles Barnabas and Paul.* The first word is from APOSTOLOS which Thayer defines, "A delegate, messenger, one sent forth with orders." The outstanding idea in the word is, "one sent." Both these men had been "sent" out by the church at Antioch (chapter 13: 3, 4), and hence were apostles of that church. It is true that Paul was an apostle of Christ independent of the church at Antioch, but when the two are mentioned together as apostles, it means their commission from that church. They manifested much displeasure at the attempt to treat them as gods.

Verse 15. Some men would be vain enough to enjoy being worshiped, but Paul and Barnabas were true worshipers of the God of creation. A part of their mission among the heathen was to lead them out of such vain worship. Instead of worshiping the planets, men should honor Him who created those planets. (See James 1: 16, 17.)

Verse 16. God *suffered* nations to walk in their own ways. That is different from permitting it, for that would be equivalent to endorsing it.

Verse 17. The *witness* consisted of the blessings of nature. These heathen should know that none of the planets could bestow such things on the world.

Verse 18. It took all of this teaching to prevent the people from performing religious services to Paul and Barnabas.

Verses 19, 20. Persecution is a persistent evil, even following the victims from place to place. Note the inspired writer says only that they *supposed* that Paul was dead. There is no evidence of any miracle having been performed upon Paul to revive him. Neither is there any proof that he was unconscious. A man can be so stunned that he would be unable either to move or speak for a while, and yet retain full consciousness. But this condition did not continue very long, for the disciples were standing about him, and they certainly would not have neglected doing something for his body before long. But without any help, while they were looking on, Paul got up and went into the city, with no sign of bodily injury indicated. Therefore, to connect this incident with 2 Corinthians 12: 1-4 is pure speculation.

Verse 21. Derbe was the farthest city to which they went in this part of their journey, which was given advance notice in verse 6. After preaching here, they retraced their steps and entered the very city where Paul was *supposed* to have been killed, then going on as far as Antioch where they did some work with the disciples they made at the previous visit.

Verse 22. Paul's persecution did not discourage him, but he did not want the disciples to be so either. The work in this city consisted in *confirming* or strengthening these brethren. And lest they might think that the things just happening showed that "something was wrong," he told them that entrance into the kingdom of God must be accompanied with much tribulation.

Verse 23. The original word for *ordain* in this place is defined by Thayer "To elect, appoint, create." Notice that they ordained *elders in every church*, which clearly shows that a plurality of elders in each congregation is the Lord's arrangement. Prayer and fasting was a voluntary devotional service performed in keeping with the solemnity of the occasion.

Verse 24. They passed through these places before (chapter 13: 13? 14).

Verse 25. Perga was in Pamphylia, the city where Mark deserted the work. They again preached in that city before going on to the seaport town of Attalia in Lycia.

Verse 26. From Attalia they sailed to Antioch in Syria, the place from which they started out on the work for which the church had recommended them.

Verse 27. The first thing Paul and Barnabas did was to report their work to the church. That gives us a good example of how evangelists should act toward the congregation that is sponsoring their work. The church has the right to know where their evangelists have been and what they have been doing. The most important item of news was the opening of the door of faith to the Gentiles.

Verse 28. This *long time* of their stay with the disciples will include an important visit to Jerusalem, which is reported in the next chapter.

ACTS 15

Verse 1. This chapter introduces what is commonly called Judaism. The term is not to be found in the New Testament, but the doctrine is reported at various places. It was the principal error that afflicted the church in the first century, and whole chapters and books had to be written to expose it, which will be commented upon as we come to them in the COMMENTARY. The doctrine is that people under the Christian Dispensation must keep the Jewish law also in order to please God. The men who taught that doctrine are called Judaizers. These *certain men* who came to Antioch with this agitation did not truly represent the church at Jerusalem. (See verse 24.)

Verse 2. Paul and Barnabas understood the subject but could not satisfy the brethren. It was decided that they should go to Jerusalem about the matter, that being the first church, and the place where the other apostles were making their headquarters. Certain brethren from Antioch were to go with Paul and Barnabas.

Verse 3. *Being brought on their way* was done by an escort of honor, similar to the circumstance in chapter 21: 5. Phenice and Samaria lay between Antioch and Jerusalem, and in passing through those regions Paul and Barnabas informed the brethren of the Gentile conversions, which was good news and caused much rejoicing.

Verse 4. The church and its elders with the apostles, gave Paul and Barnabas a favorable reception, and listened to their report of good work done for God.

Verse 5. *Which believed* is said to denote that these Pharisees had accepted the Gospel. These were the kind of *brethren* who had caused the disturbance at Antioch, and they were agitating the same heresy before the group from that city.

Verse 6. The authority of the twelve apostles was universal (Matthew 19: 28; 28: 19, 20), but they were then working especially with the Jerusalem church; at the same time they respected the elders of the congregation and worked with them. It should be noted that this whole matter was in the hands of the church at Jerusalem, and it was thus not a "church council" as Rome uses that term.

Verse 7. After the discussion had gone on for some time, Peter "took the floor" to make a fundamental report touching the issue involved, referring to his own personal experience. The *choice* that God made is recorded in chapter 10: 5, 6, which made it fitting that Peter should "speak up" at the turn of the discussion.

Verse 8. *Knoweth the hearts.* God would not have chosen the household of Cornelius for this initial work of offering the Gospel to the Gentiles, had He not seen in them a heart that was worthy of the great epoch.

Verse 9. He *put no difference* in that both Jew and Gentile could become pure in heart by accepting the faith of the Gospel and not by the law of Moses.

Verse 10. *Nor we were able to bear.* The last word is defined in the lexicon by "endure," and the term *able* does not refer to physical strength, but that it was more than they felt prepared to endure. God never intended the ritualistic yoke of the law to be perpetual, but these Judaizers would have made it permanent.

Verse 11. Instead of that formal, severe yoke of the law, Peter declared that he and the Gentiles could be saved by the grace of God through Christ.

Verse 12. The disturbers of verse 5 were quieted by the speech of Peter, which gave Paul and Barnabas an uninterrupted opportunity to report their work among the Gentiles. They proved the righteousness of their work by detailing the miracles God enabled them to perform among the people.

Verse 13. This James was not one of the twelve apostles, but he was a very outstanding man in the church at Jerusalem. (See the notes and references on the subject at chapter 12: 17.) He was the next spokesman and his advice will be respected.

Verse 14. *Simeon* means Simon Peter, and James is referring to what he declared in verse 7. *A people for his name* means that the Gentiles were to become a part of God's people and wear His name.

Verses 15-17. James not only endorsed the statement of Peter, but quoted the prophecy that foretold it. (See the prediction in Amos 9: 11, 12).

Verse 18. All of this was according to what God always knew he was going to do. With Him all dates are the same as "now" (Isaiah 46: 10).

Verse 19. *Sentence* is from KRINO, and Thayer's definition at this place is, "To be of opinion, deem, think." But we must bear in mind that this opinion was inspired by the Holy Ghost. (See verse 28.) That opinion was that the Gentiles converted to Christ were not to be troubled with the Jewish ordinances.

Verse 20. The law against eating blood is older than the law of Moses, having been given in Genesis 9: 4. And that against fornication is still older, being implied by the statement in Genesis 2: 24. For if this union makes them one flesh, then no other person can have relations with one of this pair without committing fornication. Hence these two laws are permanent regardless of what Dispensation is in force. But the subject of eating meat that had been offered to idols is a later one, and the law against it is based on special conditions that are more or less local. The Gentiles had practiced it so much that the Jews had an abhorrence for it. For that reason these Gentile Christians were told to abstain from it because of the Jews who were already somewhat prejudiced against the Gentiles; otherwise there would not have been any wrong in itself for them to eat it. That is the reason Paul taught as he did in 1 Corinthians 8 and 10 on this subject. *Things strangled* were forbidden because the blood would not have been all removed from the beast.

Verse 21. Because this law of Moses was known wherever there was a synagogue of the Jews, it was not expedient to offend them unnecessarily by eating this meat.

Verse 22. The judgment of James was accepted by the entire group, the apostles, elders and the whole church. Paul and Barnabas were not left to return to Antioch and expect the church there to rely solely on their word for the decision of the Jerusalem church. They selected two *chief men among the brethren* to go with them, carrying a written document backed up by the apostles and elders.

Verse 23. This document began as a greeting to the Gentile brethren, not only those in Antioch, but also those in the whole provinces of Syria and Cilicia.

Verse 24. *We have heard . . . went out from us.* This shows that the disturbers were acting without the knowledge and consent of the church in Jerusalem. The original word for *subverting* is defined by Thayer, "to unsettle." The agitation of these Judaizers confused the minds of the Gentile Christians.

Verse 25. The *chosen men* were Judas and Silas (verse 22).

Verse 26. *Hazarded their lives* means they had risked their lives for the sake of the Gospel. One notable case was that of Paul at Lystra, chapter 14: 19.

Verse 27. The main purpose of sending Judas and Silas was to confirm the letter by their oral testimony. That would prove the document was genuine as from the church.

Verse 28. This denotes that the letter was inspired by the Holy Ghost.

Verse 29. This is the same as verse 20, with a friendly closing additional.

Verse 30. When Paul and his group reached Antioch, they assembled the multitude to which the epistle was delivered, since all were interested.

Verse 31. *Consolation* is properly translated, for a part of Thayer's definition of the original word is "encouragement." It was reassuring to these Gentile brethren to know they did not have to take up the burdensome ordinances of the Jewish system. They also looked favorably upon the exhortation to abstain from the evils named in the letter.

Verse 32. *Judas and Silas being prophets.* Those were the days of spiritual gifts and these brethren possessed that of prophecy. That was doubtless the reason they were named as *chief men* and sent along with Paul and Barnabas to confirm the letter.

Verses 33, 34. *They were let go.* Silas and Judas were given friendly release so that they could return to Jerusalem, but Silas preferred to remain at Antioch longer.

Verse 35. Paul and Barnabas remained at Antioch for the time, since that was their regular headquarters. They employed their time *teaching* and *preaching* the word. The italicized words are used interchangeably all through the New Testament because the distinction is slight. The second has special reference to the first announcement of the Gospel, and the first meaning to give further instruction concerning the things preached.

Verse 36. The term "missionary" is commonly used to mean a worker in new fields, but the present verse says they were to revisit the places where they had been. Hence the "second missionary journey" of Paul does not start until chapter 16, verse 10.

Verse 37. Mark was a cousin to Barnabas (Colossians 4: 10). I do not know whether that influenced him in this contention or not.

Verse 38. Paul mistrusted Mark's stability on account of his desertion of the work at Pamphylia. (See chapter 13: 13 for the account of this circumstance.)

Verse 39. The original for *contention* is defined in Thayer's lexicon by the one word "irritation." Robinson defines it, "A paroxysm, sharp contention." It should be noted that no "doctrinal" difference came up between these brethren; it was only a matter of judgment. And after they each went his own way, they preached the same Gospel; neither was there ever any personal ill feeling between them. Instead, Paul made favorable mention of Barnabas afterward (1 Corinthians 9: 6; Galations 2: 9).

Verse 40. Silas had come with Judas from Jerusalem (verses 22, 34) and had remained. That made him available for the work with Paul on the next journey. *Being recommended* means they started on this journey with the good wishes of the brethren. Nothing is said on that subject about Barnabas, either for or against him. That is because the writer is continuing only with his report of Paul's work.

Verse 41. *Confirming the churches* means to strengthen and establish them.

ACTS 16

Verse 1. Paul had been in this city before and taught many people (chapter 14: 20, 21). Timothy is the other form of this *disciple's* name, of whom we will hear later.

Verse 2. This disciple had a good reputation at Lystra and Iconium.

Verse 3. Circumcism was a Jewish rite, and the national blood was in the veins of Timothy which made it right for him to be circumcized. *Because of the Jews.* The rite was not necessary to salvation (Galatians 5: 6), but Paul performed it on Timothy on the principle of 1 Corinthians 9: 20.

Verse 4. The *decrees* refers to the requirements stated in chapter 15: 29. Note that they were ordained by the apostles and the elders of the Jerusalem church, hence not a decision of a "council of churches" as Rome teaches.

Verse 5. *Churches established.* The starting of a church is not the same as establishing one. That has to be done by additional instruction concerning Christian duties.

Verse 6. This *Asia* was one of the smaller provinces of Asia Minor. We are not told why the Lord did not want them to do any preaching in that territory.

Verse 7. Mysia and Bithynia were in another part of Asia Minor than the *Asia* of the preceding verse. Paul *assayed* or made plans to do some work in those parts but was not permitted to do so because the Lord had other work for them to do.

Verses 8, 9. In obedience to the divine orders, Paul journeyed on until he came to *Troas*, the Troy of history. This is the time and place where the familiar Macedonian call was made upon Paul in a vision. The Gospel had never been preached in Macedonia, hence this will be new territory and the real start of his "second missionary journey."

Verse 10. *Vision* is from HOROMA which Thayer defines, "That which is seen, a sight, spectacle; a sight divinely granted in an ecstacy, a vision." *We endeavored* means they made preparations for the voyage. The first personal pronoun *we* denotes that Luke was in the group with Paul. *Assuredly gathering* means that they concluded with certainty.

Verses 11, 12. *Samothracia* was an island where Paul made his first stop over night. Next day he sailed on and landed at Neapolis on the coast of Macedonia. He went on to Philippi for the first stop of some days. This place was important because of its being a Roman colony. That means a commu-nity of Roman citizens located there in Macedonia, but remaining subject to the mother country. (See verse 21.)

Verse 13. The *sabbath* did not mean anything special to Paul except as an opportunity to preach to some people. Out by a river side some women were *wont* (accustomed) to conduct a prayer meeting on the sabbath day. Paul entered into the group and began talking to them about the Gospel.

Verse 14. Smith's Bible Dictionary says Lydia was a Jewish proselyte, which accounts for her being present at the prayer meeting on the sabbath day, and also explains why she *worshipped God.* One meaning of *opened* is to have things explained so that the heart (mind) could understand what is said. The Lord did this for Lydia through the preaching of Paul, and the result was that she *attended* or accepted it.

Verse 15. *When she was baptized.* The wording of this phrase takes it for granted that a penitent believer in the Gospel will obey it. *Her household.* One part of the lexicon definition of this word is, "the inmates of a house"; it does not necessarily mean that they are related to each other. The inmates of Lydia's house were able to *attend* to the things spoken by Paul. *Judged me to be faithful* means that they regarded her as a true convert, and would be pleased to be her guests for some time.

Verse 16. This damsel did not possess anything supernatural as a bestowal from God. She had some kind of factulty by which she bewitched her patrons and made them think she could foretell events. She was somewhat like the modern "fortunetellers," and brought a good income for her sponsors.

Verse 17. All that the girl said was the truth concerning Paul and his group, but the Lord will not accept testimony from such characters as she.

Verse 18. Paul became tired of being hounded by this troublesome person. *Said to the spirit.* Whatever faculty she had of an extraordinary kind was what Paul commanded to leave the damsel, so that she would not have ability to mislead the people.

Verse 19. The love of money is a strong sentiment (1 Timothy 6: 10), and it caused these wicked masters of the girl to plan the persecution of Paul and Silas. They drew them by force into the *marketplace*, "a place where assemblies are held."—Thayer.

Verses 20, 21. They were not fair enough to state their true grievance, that they had been shorn of their means of unrighteous gain. Instead, they dealt only in generalities, and made false charges against Paul and Silas about their teaching. *Being Romans* is explained at verse 12.

Verse 22. *Rent off their clothes* in order to administer a scourging. That was done by requiring the victim to lie down with his naked back exposed to the scourger, and a heavy thong of leather or ropes was lashed across the body.

Verse 23. *Stripes* means wounds made by blows inflicted with a heavy whip. The original for *safely* is defined "assuredly" in Thayer's lexicon, which denotes to take every precaution possible to prevent the prisoners from escaping.

Verse 24. *Such a charge* indicated that the jailor felt a special responsibility for keeping of the prisoners. *Stocks* is from XULON and the primary definition is, "that which is made of wood." Thayer describes the instrument as follows: "A log or timber with holes in which the feet, hands, neck of prisoners were inserted and fastened with thongs." *Inner prison* means a cell with its own door locked, on the inside of the general prison which is also enclosed with locked doors.

Verse 25. Persecution can torture and hamper the body, but it cannot affect the spirit of a devoted servant of God, except to stir it to greater praises to Him who always hears the prayers of the righteous. Those of Paul and Silas were expressed at an hour of the night when men are usually asleep. The righteous men here were, tortured into sleeplessness, but their songs of praise to God rang out into the midnight darkness and awakened the other prisoners.

Verse 26. The power that loosened the doors and bands was the same that released Peter in chapter 12: 7-10. With God one miracle is as easy as another.

Verse 27. The Lord would not interfere with the just operation of secular government. Doubtless the other prisoners were being held lawfully, and God would not perform a "jail delivery" in opposition to the law. Hence he unfastened all the fetters but saw to it that no one escaped. It was sure death to a jailor to let his prisoners escape, especially after receiving *such a charge* (verse 24). He thought he would prefer suicide to the shame of being executed for failure in his duties.

Verse 28. All was darkness, yet Paul knew the jailor was about to kill himself. *Loud noise* was necessary to overcome the frenzy of the officer. *We are all here* was spoken by divine knowledge, for Paul could not have seen all the conditions naturally.

Verse 29. *Called for a light* was necessary because it was utter darkness in the cell where Paul and Silas were held. *Sprang in* means he rushed in excitedly and with trembling. He fell down before Paul and Silas because the miracle convinced him these men had been imprisoned unjustly.

Verse 30. *Brought them out* indicates the preachers were taken outside the jail. *What must I do to be saved?* The jailor knew that Paul and Silas were religious men, and that their imprisonment was in connection with their religious belief. But being a heathen, he knew nothing of the merits of their teachings. Now the miraculous demonstration on behalf of them convinced him that they represented some great and righteous Being, whose law it would be dangerous to ignore. That also made him realize that he was due to suffer some kind of punishment unless something was done to prevent it, hence the question he asked of Paul and Silas.

Verses 31, 32. The jailor was a heathen and knew only the worship of idol gods. Paul's answer to his question meant only to cite him to the proper source of salvation. It was like telling an inquiring patient to put his trust in Doctor Blank, with the understanding, of course, that he would show confidence by doing what the doctor told him to do. We know that was all the statement of Paul meant, for he immediately *spake unto him the word of the Lord*, which would have been unnecessary had the answer in verse 31 been all the jailor needed to do to be saved.

Verses 33, 34. Here was a situation similar to that in chapter 8: 35, 36. In one verse Philip preached Jesus and in the next the eunuch asked to be baptized. In our present case the preachers spoke the word of the Lord, then the hearer arranged to be baptized. All of this shows that "the word of the Lord" means the commandments of the Lord including baptism. Verse 30 says the jailor *brought them out,* and then verse 34 says he brought them into his house. The baptizing took place between the two movements, which is explained by the act of immersion which requires their going to some place where there was plenty of water. *Washed their stripes* means the jailor bathed the wounds that the magistrates had inflicted on Paul and Silas, as a means of giving them some relief from their injuries. After the baptism the jailor served food to the preachers, while he and his household rejoiced in their newly-found religion.

Verses 35, 36. The officers evidently had learned something of the situation, and knew they had violated the law by their brutal treatment of the missionaries. They wished to get rid of them in as quiet a manner as possible. The jailor passed the word on to Paul and Silas and told them they might go.

Verse 37. Paul felt that such an unjust treatment as had been publicly inflicted on them should be reversed in as public a manner also. He refused to go in such a humiliating manner and demanded the responsible officers come in person and release them.

Verse 38. Being a Roman citizen entitled one to special consideration, and Paul and Silas had been denied such favors.

Verse 39. In their anxiety over the unlawful treatment of the prisoners, the officers came in person and very respectfully requested them to leave.

Verse 40. Paul and Silas did not leave the city until they had first visited the church in the house of Lydia, the first convert they had made in the place. It is remarkable that the very ones who had been the victims of cruel persecution were the ones to offer comforting words to others.

ACTS 17

Verse 1. Amphipolis and Apollonia were cities in Macedonia, but Paul did not pause for any work until he reached Thessalonica, another Macedonian city. The existence of a synagogue made it desirable to stop in this place.

Verse 2. *Three sabbath days.* The Jews would be engaged in their regular occupations through the week, and on the sabbath days they would assemble to hear the reading of the Scriptures. Paul based his reasoning on things written in that very book.

Verse 3. Thayer defines *opening* as follows: "To explain, expound," and *alleging* is virtually the same, except that it is a somewhat closer application of the statements in the Old Testament. Paul showed these Jews that their own Scriptures set forth the doctrine that he was giving them, namely, the death and resurrection of Jesus (Psalms 16: 8-10). Having proved by their own sacred writings that Jesus was to fulfill such predictions, he declared Him to be the Christ.

Verse 4. *Consorted* means they associated with Paul and Silas because they believed their teaching. The *devout Greeks* were the ones religiously inclined, and *chief women* were the leading persons among the female sex.

Verse 5. The original for *lewd* is defined "bad" and *baser sort* means the loafers around the markets. Such characters would be inclined toward the kind of service these envious Jews needed in their wicked plots. Paul and Silas were staying in the house of Jason (verse 7), but at the present time were not "at home."

Verse 6. Being disappointed at not finding the preachers, they took their spite out on Jason and other brethren by forcing them before the rulers of the city. *Turned the world upside down* was a reference to the success accomplished by Paul's preaching.

Verse 7. *Whom Jason hath received* was said as explanation for having him now in the presence of the rulers. *Do contrary to the decree of Caesar* was a false charge. Paul always taught obedience to the laws of the land, but he did not agree with the contentions of the Jews about the law of Moses.

Verse 8. The *rulers* owed their official position to Caesar, and did not want any condition to arise that might endanger their place in the public affairs. That is why the report of the envious Jews *troubled* them and the people.

Verse 9. *Taken security* denotes that they either required a deposit of money, or found some responsible person to stand good for their conduct toward the laws of the land. Such an arrangement would satisfy Caesar should he hear about the commotion in one of his provinces in Macedonia.

Verse 10. When Paul was chased from one city to another he continued his work for Christ. Berea was another city of Macedonia and contained a synagogue.

Verse 11. *Noble* is from *eugenes* and it means of better breeding; more highly cultured. Such a character caused them to be more reasonable in their attitude toward the preaching of Paul and Silas. Instead of attacking them enviously, they investigated their claims by reading up on the subject. If the preachers made an argument based on the statements of the Old Testament, the Bereans looked into the book to see if they were telling the truth: that was fair for both speaker and hearer.

Verse 12. Finding that Paul was giving them the truth, many were made believers. *Honorable* is from EUSCHEMON which Thayer defines, "of good standing, honorable, influential, wealthy, respectable." All classes need and are offered the benefits of the Gospel, but it is well to know that it found those who accepted it among the high ranks of society as well as the lower classes.

Verse 13. The envy of the Jews knew no bounds, so when they heard of the work of the Gospel at Berea they pursued the preachers there. *Stirred up the people* means they worked up a sentiment against Paul which cut off further opportunity for his work there.

Verse 14. The feeling seemed to be more sharp against Paul than against Silas and Timotheus, so that he was induced to leave for other parts leaving them for the present.

Verse 15. An escort of brethren went with Paul on his sea voyage until they came to Athens, which was the chief city of Greece, the province joining Macedonia on the south. From there they returned to Berea, taking back with them an order for Silas and Timotheus to come to Paul as soon as possible.

Verse 16. Paul could not wait until Silas and Timotheus came to him when he saw the conditions. *Given to idolatry* is rendered "full of idols" in the margin, which is correct as may be seen by other verses in this chapter.

Verse 17. *Therefore* is not a conclusion from the preceding verse because the synagogue was a meeting place of the Jews who were not idolaters. But the people in the *market* were a mixed group and contained idolaters. The verse means that Paul followed his usual practice of preaching the Gospel, first in the synagogue where he could meet the Jews, then in any other place where he could find some hearers.

Verse 18. Athens was the chief city of Greece and the seat of learning and civilization for that province. Hence Paul would encounter various classes of citizens whose ears were alert for any literary or philosophical subject that might be introduced. The Epicureans were a class founded by Epicurus, who taught that fleshly pleasure should be the chief purpose of man on earth. The theory of the Stoicks was almost opposite of the Epicureans, but it was based chiefly on the supposed importance of philosophy. It is easy to see why both these groups would criticize the Gospel which seeks to find true pleasure in humble devotion to the risen Lord.

Verse 19. Areopagus and Mars' hill (verse 22) were names for the same place, which was the highest court in Athens in the days of the apostles. Not only were criminal cases tried in this court, but also any subject thought to affect the public welfare.

Verse 20. Thus far there was nothing particularly objectionable to the Athenians in the teaching of Paul, but he had raised their curiosity by introducing a new subject, or one that was *strange* which means an outside or unknown (to them) matter. They told him they wished to know what it all meant.

Verse 21. The inspired writer throws in this verse by way of explanation of the curious inquiry of the people. Nothing was as exciting to them as the prospect of hearing something that had not been told them before. It will develop that what Paul had to offer the Athenians was *new* to them, but yet did not meet their demands that it must be something new along the lines of philosophy.

Verse 22. Paul was invited to speak before this highest court in Athens. His audience was composed of idolaters and various classes of philosophers and Greek statesmen. His introduction was not intended as a criticism but rather a friendly comment. The adverb *too* is not justified by the Greek original, for it does not have any separate word in the Greek at this place. It is a part of the original for superstitious, so the phrase *too superstitious* should be rendered "very religious." This extensive religious attitude was indicated by the presence of so many idols or altars. (See verse 16.)

Verse 23. Paul had not seen them engaging in their idolatrous services. *Devotions* is from SEBASMA which Thayer defines, "whatever is religiously honored, an object of worship." An *altar* was an elevated place on which to offer sacrifices. Among the places Paul saw was one that had an inscription written upon it which read *to the unknown god.* The occasion for such an altar is explained by Horne, Introduction, Volume 1, Page 90, as follows: "The Athenians, being afflicted with a pestilence, invited Epimenides to lustrate [purify with sacrifice] their city. The method adopted by him was, to carry several sheep to the Areopagus, whence they were left to wander as they pleased, under the observation of persons to attend them. As each sheep lay down, it was sacrificed on the spot to the propitious [gracious] God. By this ceremony, it is said, the deity was satisfied; but as it was still unknown what deity was gracious, an altar was erected to the unknown God on every spot where a sheep had been sacrificed." It is not known just what actually took place, but since all blessings come from the true God, if any miraculous cure was bestowed upon the community, it was through the goodness of Him; hence the Athenians ignorantly gave the credit for their great blessing to the right One, whose existence and power Paul *declared unto them.* These idolaters actually did *worship* the true God though ignorantly. (See the note at Matthew 2: 2 on *worship.*)

Verse 24. The God who made everything in the universe could not be expected to *dwell* (be confined) in manmade temples, and certainly not in as small and lifeless a thing as an altar of earth or stone, such as the Athenians had erected for the purpose.

Verse 25. The Athenians offered their worship to God in connection with a supposed case of healing, hence Paul selected a word from their vocabulary that pertains to the art of medicine and healing. *Worship* in this passage is from THERAPEUO which Thayer defines, "to heal, cure, restore to health." The word also means "to serve," but Paul used it in the first sense because the Athenians were worshiping God (unknowingly) in connection with their experience in the healing of the epidemic. Since God

is the source of all the creatures of life and health, it would be foolish for such to think they could grant healing to Him through the works of their hands.

Verse 26. *One blood.* The Lord said that the blood is the life of all flesh (Leviticus 17: 14), and God is the creator of all flesh. The conclusion is that all life originated with Him, therefore it is foolish to think that he can be represented by objects made of metal or stone. *Determined the times before appointed.* Not that the moral conduct of man has been predetermined by the Lord regardless of his own will, for that would rule out any human responsibility. But the statement just means that the universe did not come "by chance," but was the intelligent work of God, who did set a boundary to the habitation of man which is *the face of the earth.*

Verse 27. This restricted location for man's habitation away from the visible presence of God made it necessary *that they seek the Lord. If haply,* etc., is said in the sense as if it said, "with the intent that man would seek or feel after the invisible God and succeed in finding Him through the evidence shown in chapter 14: 17."

Verse 28. If we live in Him with all our activities of life, it follows that He is greater than any of us or anything that we can make, which is another argument against man-made images of God. Making reference to their own heathen poets was good psychology. They would be bound to accept their own authors, and finding that they taught the same things as Paul, it would incline them to think favorably of the statements of the apostle. Chief of the quotations was the one that spoke of man as the offspring of God.

Verse 29. It would be inconsistent to think that living, intelligent beings like men could be the offspring of a God who was represented by objects made of stone or metal.

Verse 30. *Winked at* is from HUPER-EIDON which Thayer defines, "to overlook, take no notice of, not attend to." The heathen in times past did not have the complete information that was to be given the whole world through the Gospel, hence God did not hold them to strict account. That leniency was to end with the period of the law of Christ, and all men were then required to come to repentance. (See 2 Peter 3: 9.)

Verse 31. *Appointed a day* but not a "date." If God has predetermined just when the judgment day is come, it must be learned from some passage other than this one. It means only that God has made an appointment with the risen One to be the judge of the people of the world whenever the proper day arrives. By raising Jesus from the dead, God not only proved that He is able to manage "all things after the counsel of his own will" (Ephesians 1: 11), but gave notice that all must meet the risen Jesus as the Judge.

Verse 32. The Athenians were interested in philosophical subjects only, as they regarded them, and the resurrection from the dead did not come under that classification in their estimation. Some of them made fun of the matter, but others were a little more polite and promised to give it their attention at some other time.

Verse 33. Paul did not take their promise seriously, but departed from the court and went elsewhere in the city.

Verse 34. The preaching of Paul was not an entire failure as to results, for one member of the Aeropagite court became a believer, also some private persons.

ACTS 18

Verse 1. Paul is traveling without his companions, Silas and Timotheus, who have not reached him yet (verse 5). Corinth was another important city of Greece, in which was planted what became one of the most noted churches of the apostolic period.

Verse 2. Aquila was not a native of Italy but had resided for some time in Rome. Claudius (Caesar) was the Roman emperor, and for some reason (not very clearly explained by the historians and commentators) had formed a dislike for the Jews and had banished them from the city; Paul met this man and his wife Priscilla.

Verse 3. *Same craft* means the same trade or occupation, which was tentmaking. That was Paul's trade also, which naturally caused them to have a common interest in each other, so that Paul made his stay with them. This association gave him an opportunity to instruct them thoroughly in the Gospel, so that they became earnest disciples who were able to teach others. (See verse 26).

Verse 4. *Reasoned* is from the same word as "disputed" in chapter 17: 17.

Paul did this on the sabbath days because the Jews met then to read the law, and the Greeks often attended as spectators.

Verse 5. The original for *pressed* is defined by Thayer, "to urge, impel." Silas and Timotheus finally reached Paul (chapter 17: 15), and their arrival encouraged him to put all the more pressure in his preaching of the Gospel, affirming in the ears of the Jews that Jesus was Christ (the Anointed).

Verse 6. *Opposed themselves* means they set themselves in opposition to the teaching of Paul. *Shook his raiment* was an old custom of expressing one's attitude toward something very evil. *Blood be upon your own heads.* Whatever punishment they suffered would be their own fault because they had refused to hear the warnings of the Gospel. Paul usually gave the Jews first chance in his teaching, but if they rejected it he would turn to the Gentiles. (See chapter 13: 46.)

Verse 7. Paul left the synagogue and went into a nearby house, whose owner was a worshiper of God. (See the note at Matthew 2: 2 on *worship.)*

Verse 8. The audience in the synagogue had rejected Paul's teaching, but the chief ruler was an exception and became a believer, together with the members of his household. *Hearing, believed, and were baptized.* That was the scriptural procedure then and it is so today. A sinner must hear in order to believe (Romans 10: 14), and if he truly believes, he will be baptized in obedience to the One in whom he believes.

Verse 9. *Be not afraid* of the opposition mentioned in verse 6 or any other that might be threatened against him, but preach the Gospel to all he can meet.

Verse 10. *No man . . . to hurt thee.* Paul was to be opposed, but he would not be overcome by the enemy because the Lord assured him that He would be with him. This is the same assurance that he wrote to the brethren in Rome (Romans 8: 31). *I have much people in this city.* This was said in prospect because the Lord knew there were many who would accept the Gospel when Paul reached them with it. It was said on the same principle that Jesus meant when he said "I *have* other sheep" in John 10: 16.

Verse 11. Verse 8 says that many of the Corinthians became obedient believers, so it was *among them* that

Paul taught the word. And in a period of 18 months many more would hear and obey, so that the church in that city became one of the largest in numbers.

Verse 12. A *deputy* was an inferior officer in the government of Rome in one of the provinces. Achaia was a name given to Greece by the Romans. The ever-envious Jews brought Paul before the secular ruler in a disorderly manner.

Verse 13. *Contrary to the law.* They charged that Paul's teaching was contrary to the law of Moses. That was a false charge, because Paul had shown on more than one occasion that the Gospel system had even been predicted by the Old Testament.

Verse 14. Paul could and would have answered the false charge, but the "judge on the bench" interrupted him. He told the Jews that he would hear their complaints on any matter that pertained to lawlessness against the laws of the land.

Verse 15. The thought in this verse is that the Jews were wanting this man who was a secular judge, to hear a case of theirs that was strictly a religious dispute. He told them that he would not be a judge of such matters.

Verse 16. This verse means that Gallio dismissed the case and cleared the court room of the complainants. This judge set a precedent that should be observed today. No secular court has any business meddling in religious controversies, and professed disciples of Christ ought to know better than to bring religious disputes into such courts.

Verse 17. The Greeks were the Gentile spectators in the court of Gallio and had heard the remarks to the Jews that he made in answer to their complaint. Sosthenes was a Jew and doubtless was a leader in the uprising against Paul. Their sympathy would naturally be for the apostles and against the Jews who had not always shown a favorable attitude toward the Gentiles. Hearing the declaration of Gallio, that he would not interfere with any dispute of the Jews concerning their religion, they decided to take the opportunity of showing their feeling against this would-be persecutor of Paul by this personal attack. While this action was one pertaining to "law and order," yet Gallio knew it was caused by religious agitation, and, being disgusted by the attempt of the

Jews to invade his court with an improper issue, took some satisfaction out of seeing them thus punished, hence he *cared for none of those things*.

Verse 18. Cenchrea was a port of Corinth, from which Paul sailed for the shores of Asia Minor. *Shorn his head.* The Jews had a custom of making personal vows, and at the termination of the period a man was to cut his hair that had been let grow while the vow was in force. This part of the formality was similar to the Nazarite vow in Numbers 6: 5-18, but it was not otherwise bound by the other requirements. For the custom of voluntary vows, see Leviticus 27: 2; 1 Samuel 1: 11; 2 Samuel 15: 7.

Verse 19. When Paul and his companions, Aquila and Priscilla, arrived at Ephesus, he separated from them and went into a synagogue as he was accustomed to do to preach.

Verse 20. Paul's teaching seemed to meet with favor among his hearers, for they asked him to remain longer, which his plans would not permit.

Verse 21. *Keep this feast.* It was the feast of Pentecost, one of the national feasts of the Jews. Paul was a Jew and had a right to observe the national customs of his race. (See chapter 16: 3.) After a brief stay at Ephesus he again sailed.

Verse 22. Paul landed at Caesarea on the coast of Palestine. As a brief "side trip" he went to Jerusalem to salute the church. We are not given any account of this visit further than the present statement. After this incident the great apostle to the Gentiles went to Antioch (in Syria), thus ending his second missionary journey.

Verse 23. This is the beginning of what is commonly called Paul's third "missionary journey." (See the comments at chapter 15: 36.) But he really revisited some churches that had been started previously, to *strengthen* or establish them. A church can be started in a little while, but it takes time and further teaching to establish it.

Verse 24. *Eloquent* is defined "skilled in speech" in Thayer's lexicon. *Mighty in the scriptures* means he was well acquainted with the Old Testament, and had learned something of the early teaching pertaining to the New. He was regarded as a good man and one devoted to the Lord.

Verse 25. Apollos was not a careless

man, and always taught others accurately as far as he had learned, but at this time he knew no baptism except what John preached and practiced. That subject will be explained at chapter 19: 4.

Verse 26. Aquila and Priscilla had been instructed by Paul (verses 2, 3), and were able to supply the points that Apollos lacked. It should be noted that *they* expounded the way of God, showing an instance where a woman helped to get a preacher better acquainted with the teaching of the Gospel.

Verse 27. Achaia was a name that the Romans gave to Greece. After Apollos was through with his work at Ephesus he wished to go over into Greece, and we will find that he stopped at Corinth. He left Ephesus with the recommendation of the brethren. After arriving in Greece he helped the believers who had experienced the *grace* of God.

Verse 28. Apollos approached the Jews with the same kind of arguments that Paul had used, namely, showing them that their own scriptures (the Old Testament) predicted the coming of Jesus as the Christ or the Anointed One.

ACTS 19

Verse 1. Paul came to Ephesus after Apollos had left that city and gone to Corinth in Greece. (See chapter 18: 27, 28.) The *disciples* he found at Ephesus were evidently the persons whom Apollos had baptized (chapter 18: 25).

Verse 2. Paul knew that in those days a baptized believer was entitled to the gift of the Holy Ghost (see the comments at chapter 2: 38), but he also knew that even their baptism did not automatically bestow that gift until an apostle had laid hands on them (chapter 8: 18). He did not know whether that special favor had yet been given to them, hence the question stated in this place. When they told him they had not heard anything about such a subject as the Holy Ghost, it showed that something was wrong.

Verse 3. In answer to his question about their baptism, they told Paul that they had been baptized unto John's baptism. (See chapter 18: 25.)

Verse 4. The difference between "John's baptism" and "Christian baptism" is indicated in this verse. When John baptized a man he was required to believe on Christ who *was to come.* He had not yet come and hence no person could be baptized into His name or by his authority. But John was dead and Christ had come when Apollos was preaching, hence it was unscriptural to use John's baptism. Both baptisms were "for the remission of sins," and both had to be preceded by repentance (Mark 1: 4; Acts 2: 38). But the latter was by the authority of Christ which put the believer into His name.

Verse 5. These were rebaptized and it was into the name of Christ. No person but John could use his baptism, but the ones whom he baptized never had to be baptized again, for they were then *prepared for the service of Christ.*

Verses 6, 7. What happened when Paul laid hands on them, was what he was inquiring about in verse 2. Only those who were baptized with "Christian baptism" were entitled to that gift, and even then it required the hands of an apostle.

Verse 8. *Disputing* is from the same word as "reasoned" in chapter 17: 2. By reasoning on the subject, Paul was able to *persuade* some in favor of the kingdom of God.

Verse 9. After three months of effort before the general multitudes assembling in the synagogue, the opposition to the truth became such that Paul concluded he could accomplish more by working elsewhere. *Separated the disciples* means he withdrew with the ones who were truly interested and who were eager to hear more of the truth. *School* is from the Greek word SCHOLE. Robinson defines it, "leisure, rest, vacation, attention, devotion, study." He then explains it to mean, "A place of learned leisure, where a teacher and his disciples came together and held discussions and disputations." Thayer defines it, "Freedom from labor, leisure; a place where there is leisure for anything, a school." Moffatt renders it, "lecture-room." This "school," then, was a place maintained by Tyrannus, a kind of public auditorium that was open to the public for the free use of any persons who wished to engage in cultural and recreational activities.

Verse 10. This *school* was frequented by many people of all races and from all over Asia, for in the two years that Paul spent in his teaching there, the word of the Lord was heard throughout that area.

Verses 11, 12. *Special miracles* denotes those that were not commonly performed even in the days of miracles. God is able to accomplish any kind of wonders and by whatever means He wills. As an encouraging support for the work of the apostle in this center of various thought and activity, the Lord saw fit to use the pieces miraculously that had been in contact with the preacher.

Verse 13. *Vagabond* Jews were some who were wandering around from house to house. An *exorcist* was a person who expelled demons from men by pronouncing some mysterious sentence, or by commanding the evil spirit by some important name. But even evil characters can be imitated and their work be pretended to be done by mere impostors. The present ones were frauds and pretended to be working through the name of Jesus; and to add weight to their pretense, they used the name of Paul.

Verse 14. *Sceva* was a high priest, and he had seven sons who were practicing this fraud, attempting to cast out a devil from an unfortunate man.

Verse 15. *Jesus I know.* This evil spirit was telling the truth, for the devils were originally in heaven and had been cast out because of sin (2 Peter 2: 4), and it was there that they had their acquaintance with Jesus. That accounts for the statements in Mark 1: 24, 34. Since these men were frauds the spirit did not recognize them.

Verse 16. Being possessed with a devil did not have the same effect on every person. In the present instance it produced unusual physical strength and activity. Acting through the man in whom the devil was dwelling, it pounced upon these pretenders and they fled from the house in fright and stripped of their clothing.

Verse 17. The word *fear* is used in the sense of respect in this verse, since it caused the name of the Lord Jesus to be magnified by both Jews and Greeks.

Verse 18. This respectful fear was proved by their confession of evil deeds.

Verse 19. These penitent Jews and Greeks did not stop with mere confessions, for the event about the exorcists convinced them that the business of dealing in trifles was wrong. *Curious arts* is from PERIERGOS, which is defined by Thayer as things "impertinent and superflous," and he explains it to mean "arts of magic." These were chiefly a system of superstitious performances, and they had their recipes written in books by which they would mislead their victims. When they became penitent over their sinful practices, they proved their sincerity by burning the collection of their evil formulas. Moffatt renders the value of the books to be 2,000 pounds of silver.

Verse 20. The word of God grew, because every genuine demonstration of repentance was attributed to the power of that word over the minds of men. The increase of the word means that the number of believers in the word was increased.

Verse 21. *Purposed in the spirit* means that it was Paul's personal plans to accomplish the things stated. While he always intended doing and saying the things that were in harmony with the Holy Spirit, this was not an inspired purpose, for part of it was not carried out as he had *purposed.* He did actually *see Rome,* but not until he was taken there as a prisoner (chapter 28: 16).

Verse 22. Paul's purpose was to leave Ephesus and go through Macedonia and Achaia (Greece), but he did not intend starting at once, for he wished to spend some more time in the city. Timotheus and Erastus usually traveled with Paul as coworkers, but he released them to go ahead and work in the region of Macedonia while he was still in Asia.

Verse 23. *That way* is a phrase applying to the Gospel plan, so used because of its preeminence. (See verse 9; chapter 9: 2.) The original word for *stir* is defined, "commotion, stir, tumult" in Thayer's lexicon. It was because of the interference it was making with the many of the evils in the community.

Verse 24. Diana was a heathen goddess and a temple was built for her at Ephesus. Demetrius and his fellow workers made a great deal of money by forming *shrines*, which were small models of the temple, selling them to travelers who wished them for souvenirs.

Verse 25. Demetrius became concerned over the prospect of losing this business and he called a meeting of his partners in the trade.

Verse 26. Demetrius called attention of his fellows to the preaching of Paul, stating that it had extended throughout Asia. The part of Paul's preaching that worried him was that against idolatry, especially the kind that was the work of human hands.

Verse 27. These men were not concerned about the merits of the religious issue, but feared that financial loss would come to them if people were made to believe in the one living God. That is the meaning of the statement, *our craft* [business or occupation] *is in danger*. It was the old story of men being more interested in their financial than in their spiritual welfare. Yet they pretended to be concerned about the dignity of the idolatrous goddess, that was worshiped by the world.

Verse 28. The inflamatory speech of Demetrius aroused the mob spirit of these tradesmen, causing them to make a boistrous shout in behalf of the goddess.

Verse 29. The cry spread until it affected the whole city, throwing it into confusion. The excited people let their wrath be exhibited against the associates of Paul. They took them by force into a place where public performances were put on.

Verse 30. Paul wished to appear in this public place to reply to the complaints of the mob. Fearing that he might be harmed by the angry populace, the disciples prevented him from entering the theatre.

Verse 31. *Sent unto him* denotes that a general state of confusion existed, so that special means had to be used to communicate with Paul.

Verse 32. This state of disorder made it impossible to discern just what the concourse was about or what the issue was.

Verse 33. A riot is regarded by all civilized nations as something worthy of being condemned. The Jews feared that their people would be blamed by the Greeks for the present uprising. They selected this prominent member of their race to speak in their behalf, and he prepared to make an address for that purpose.

Verse 34. This outcry was the opposite of an ovation. It was a disorderly explosion of anger and disrespect against the attempt of a Jew to make a speech in the public theatre of the Greek people. This raving mob was so worked up and tumultuous that it took two hours to get it quieted.

Verse 35. A *townclerk* was a secretary or public scribe; a man supposed to be informed in matters of law and order. After two hours he was able to get the uproar subdued so that he could speak to the people. His purpose was to state the legal and fair aspects of the situation. He proposed to show that there was no call for such a demonstration in defense of the temple of Diana. That it was common knowledge that the people were devoted worshipers of their goddess, which it was believed had come down from Jupiter, another god of the Greeks.

Verse 36. The reputation of the goddess in the eyes of the Greek people was not even questioned by them, hence there was no reason for being reckless or unnecessarily hasty in acting against Paul and his companions.

Verse 37. The townclerk was not siding with Paul in his teaching, but wished to show his fellow citizens that they were mistreating him and his friends contrary to the principles of human rights. *Robbers of churches* is from HIEROSULOS which means those who commit sacrilege or who rob temples. Paul had not made any vicious attack on the goddess of the Greeks, but had emphasized the authority of the God of Heaven. But these heathen had correctly concluded that if the God whom Paul preached was the only true one, then all manmade objects of worship were false.

Verse 38. The reasoning of the townclerk was that provision had been made by the law of the land, whereby all just complaints could be handled. *Deputies* were men authorized to represent the government in the disputes arising between man and man.

Verse 39. By *other matters* he meant subjects that were differences of opinion only and not involving any personal misconduct. *Lawful assembly* means one called by the proper authorities and in accordance with the law.

Verse 40. The townclerk feared that the higher authorities might bring a complaint against the community because of the riot.

Verse 41. The mob was dispersed without further disorder, because the people had been shown the lawlessness of their actions.

ACTS 20

Verse 1. *The uproar* refers to the disturbances recorded in the preceding chapter. After some parting words, Paul left for Macedonia which was his previous purpose according to chapter 19: 21.

Verse 2. Paul spent some time with the churches in Macedonia, such as Philippi, Thessalonica and Berea. Greece was the province immediately south of Macedonia.

Verse 3. Syria was a part of Asia, and it contained such important places as Troas and Ephesus. After spending some time in Greece, Paul intended crossing by water over to Asia. Hearing of a plot of some kind being formed by the Jews, he changed his plans and retraced his journey through Macedonia.

Verses 4, 5. These persons were associated with Paul in the good work, but were evidently not involved in the plot of the Jews. They went on ahead across the sea and stopped at Troas where they awaited the coming of Paul and Luke, he being with Paul as the first personal pronoun *us* denotes, and as he is the author of this book (chapter 1: 1).

Verse 6. Having been in Philippi some time (verse 3) on this return journey, he and Luke went aboard a ship bound for Troas, where the group of the preceding paragraph was waiting for them. *Days of unleavened bread* is mentioned only by way of indicating the date or time of year that had arrived.

Verse 7. *Break* is from the same Greek word as it is in other places, regardless of whether a common meal is meant or that of the Lord's Supper. The connection must determine in each case as to what sense is used. In the present passage it could not mean a common meal, for the disciples would not come together for that purpose; they went "from house to house" (chapter 2: 46). Likewise, they would not have done so especially on the Lord's day any more than on some other day. The conclusion, then, is that it means the Lord's Supper. Another unavoidable conclusion is that the Lord's Supper is to be observed by disciples who come together, and not done as a private performance in some convenient place suitable to the personal program of temporal entertainment. The preaching of Paul was incidental because he chanced to be present, not that they came together for that purpose. However, the incident gives us an apostolic precedent for having preaching at the time of the regular Lord's day assembly if a preacher is present. The long sermon was occasioned by the plans of Paul who intended continuing his journey the next day, and the interest in such a rare opportunity of hearing this great apostle held the services to the late hour.

Verse 8. *Lights* is from the Greek word LAMPAS, which was a device used as a torch and was fed with olive oil. The writer had just stated that Paul continued his speech until midnight, and his mention of the *many lights* was to explain how an assembly could conveniently extend its services that far into the night.

Verse 9. This verse is a simple statement of an event not especially important in itself, but furnishing an opportunity for Paul to work a miracle. The inspired writer is the one who says that the young man *was taken up dead*, so that it was not just the imgination of an excited crowd.

Verse 10. It should be observed that Paul said *his life is in him* after he had embraced him. The act of embracing the young man was when the miracle was performed that brought the life back into his dead body. (See similar acts in 1 Kings 17: 21; 2 Kings 4: 34.)

Verse 11. *Broken bread.* This was not the act for which the disciples had come together, for they did not know that such a lengthy service would be had when they assembled. But having been awake most of the night, and as Paul was soon to leave on a journey, it was courteous for them to set refreshments before him for his support.

Verse 12. This verse is an afterthought upon the event of the miracle of verse 10, showing the joyful effect of the apostle's performance for the young man and friends.

Verse 13. The entire group was making its way in the return from this third missionary journey, but Paul went on foot as far as Assos where the party was to join him.

Verse 14. At Assos the boat landed and took in Paul, then proceeded and came to Mitylene, a town on the island of Lesbos.

Verse 15. Three days after leaving Mitylene the group reached Miletus.

Verse 16. Miletus was 36 miles south of Ephesus, and in the time of Paul it was on the coast. He did not wish to spend much time in Asia (a small district in Asia Minor), because the feast of Pentecost was near at hand, and he was eager to be in Jerusalem at that time. For information about observing Jewish customs and days, see the comments at chapter 16: 3 and 18: 21.

Verse 17. Paul knew he would lose less time by calling these elders to him while waiting for the ship to resume its journey, than for him to make this "detour" to Ephesus to see them. Chapter 14: 23 states that Paul ordained elders in every church, and evidently that included those at Ephesus.

Verse 18. The Ephesian elders complied with the request of Paul by coming to Miletus to meet him. This was to be a very important occasion, for Paul was to have a heart-to-heart talk with these rulers of the church, in which there will be some outstanding information that will be useful for all of us.

Verse 19. These elders knew about the severe trials the apostles had suffered, for many of them had taken place in their city (chapter 19).

Verse 20. *That was profitable.* The apostle never imposed any obligations or information upon the elders of the churches that would not be of assistance to them in their great work for the Lord. There are no "nonessentials" in the things the inspired writers have left to the world. Paul's teaching was done in the synagogue *(publicly)* and in the homes *(from house to house)*.

Verse 21. Repentance here seems to be required before faith, which is really not the order of the items pertaining to the Gospel. (See the comments at Mark 1: 15.)

Verse 22. The original word for *bound* is defined "To put under obligation" by Thayer. Paul was always guided in his teaching and conduct of his office as an apostle, by the Holy Spirit that was sent to "guide him into all truth" (John 16: 13).

Verse 23. The Spirit did not give Paul the details of what was to come upon him, but he was told that he was to have a hard time. This "blanket" information really made a severer test of his faith than a minute statement might have been.

Verse 24. *None of these things move me* means that Paul was not disturbed by the prospect of persecutions, nor did he let it change his purpose to serve Christ faithfully to the end. *Finish my course with joy.* The true servant of God expects to receive his reward at the end of the race, not while the conflict of this life is going on. *The ministry* refers to the charge delivered to Paul to "fight the good fight" (2 Timothy 4: 7) by testifying for the Gospel.

Verse 25. Paul did not make this sad prediction by inspiration. He did not know what particular experiences were awaiting him, but he knew that he would not be permitted to labor among the churches as extensively as before.

Verse 26. *Take you to record* means he was testifying to these elders with regard to his work among them. *Pure from the blood* denotes that he would not be held responsible for any unfavorable lot that might come upon them in the future.

Verse 27. This verse explains the statement in the preceding one. A preacher of the Gospel may not have the ability or opportunity to declare everything that pertains to the plan of salvation, and if so he will not be held accountable for such lack. But if he shuns or evades to proclaim a single requirement of the *counsel of God* that he could have made known, he will be charged with the full results of such evasion of duty.

Verse 28. *Overseers* is from EPIS-KOPOS and is the same word that is translated "bishop" in other passages. The word is defined by Thayer, "An overseer, any curator, guardian or superintendent." There is but one class of ruling officers in the church of the New Testament, and they are called by the three words, elders, overseers and bishops. The exception is the case of evangelists who have charge of churches not having elders (Titus 1: 5). *God* is the family name of the Deity, of which Christ is a member, making that word his own name as well as that of his Father. Hence the name *church of God* is equivalent to "church of Christ." It is his church because he purchased it with his own blood. The elders are commanded to *feed* this church which is likened to a flock, and the word in the original is POIMAINO, which is also defined, "To rule, govern." The Holy Ghost makes men overseers by revealing the qualifications and manner of appointment of such officers (1 Timothy 3: 1-7; Titus 1: 6-9).

Verse 29. The warning of this verse refers to false teachers from the outside, who would creep into the congregation and corrupt the members.

Verse 30. *Of your own selves* means that false teachers would arise among the elders. It is a fact borne out by history, that the great apostasy known as the "Dark Ages," was started within the eldership of the church, but this is not the most appropriate place to go into the details of that subject.

Verse 31. The three main duties of the elders are to feed, rule and watch. The first two are commanded in verse 28, and the third is stated here. Hebrews 13: 17 states for what or why the rulers are to watch, namely, for the souls of the flock, because the elders will have to give an account of their work with the members of the flock. The warning of three years included that recorded in chapter 19: 8, 10.

Verse 32. *Commend you to God* denotes that he advised them to look to God and to his word. That word is able to build them up or edify them in their work for Him. Such a life would make them heirs of the reward that is prepared for all who are sanctified or set apart for the service of the Lord.

Verse 33. Paul was not preaching the Gospel with the motive of obtaining the personal possessions of the brethren.

Verse 34. As proof of the preceding statement, Paul reminded them of his manual labor for the temporal support of himself and his traveling companions. (See chapter 18: 3.) Not that it would not have been right for him to receive financial support in his work, for he taught elsewhere that such support would have been right (1 Corinthians 9: 4, 14). But he refers to his own secular work as proof that temporal support was not his purpose in preaching the Gospel.

Verse 35. Another purpose Paul had in his manual labor was to set an example of working to supply the needs of those who cannot work. The words of Jesus quoted are not recorded elsewhere in the New Testament, but Paul could repeat them by inspiration.

Verses 36-38. This paragraph does not require any particular explanation. It is a word picture of a very pathetic leave-taking between Paul and the elders. His conviction that they would never meet again was the saddest item in the circumstance. The labors in the midst of many trials and persecutions for the cause of Christ, had a tendency to bind the followers of the Lord close together. The manner of embracing upon the neck was a custom of those times. The elders went with Paul as far as they could, then parted from him as he entered the ship.

ACTS 21

Verses 1, 2. The ship they took at Miletus went as far as Patara only, where the group had to change over to another vessel bound for Phenicia. That was a small tract of country on the east coast of the Mediterranean Sea.

Verse 3. *Discovered Cyprus* means they came in sight of that island, but passing it on their left they sailed on into Syria, the larger territory of which Phenicia was a small part. The ship landed at Tyre, an important seaport of the last named country. Here the ship was to unload its cargo which made a delay in the journey of seven days.

Verse 4. *Through the Spirit* applies to the general condition of persecution that would beset Paul, not that it was an inspired directive for him not to go.

Verse 5. *Brought us on our way* means that they all went with them to "see them off." Leave-taking was often done in connection with a prayer service. It was done when Paul and the elders separated (chapter 20: 36).

Verse 6. After saying good-bye they separated. The disciples went to their homes and Paul and his company went into the ship which was ready to sail again.

Verse 7. Paul and his group ended their sea travel at this town. There were some brethren here with whom they visited for one day.

Verse 8. This traveling was done by land, bringing them to Caesarea which was the headquarters of the Roman government in Palestine. Philip was one of the deacons appointed in chapter 6. He is called the evangelist because of such work as he did as recorded in chapter 8.

Verse 9. These *virgins* were the maidens mentioned elsewhere and their prophesying fulfilled the prediction made in Joel 2: 28, 29 and quoted by Peter in Acts 2: 17, 18.

Verse 10. This is the same *Agabus* who made a prediction in chapter 11: 28. The primary meaning of a prophet is a foreteller, although it is not restricted to that definition, but sometimes is used of those who edify or exhort (1 Corinthians 14: 3). Agabus was a prophet of the former kind, those being the days of spiritual gifts.

Verse 11. See the note on "prophets acting" at 1 Kings 20: 35 in volume 2 of the Old Testament Commentary. Agabus took this dramatic manner of making his prediction to impress its importance upon the group.

Verse 12. The whole group believed the prediction of Agabus, and in their anxiety and love for Paul, tried to persuade him not to go up to Jerusalem.

Verse 13. Paul did not worry over the prediction, but he was vexed because of the attitude of the group. He declared his willingness to go even further in his endurance for the sake of Jesus. He was willing to die for him if need be, although Agabus had not included that in his prediction.

Verse 14. *The will of the Lord be done* indicates their resignation to whatever lot might befall the beloved apostle. His fortitude had the effect of reconciling them to the program that Christ might have mapped out for him.

Verse 15. *Took up our carriages* is all from APOSKEUAZO, which Thayer defines, "To pack up and carry off." *We* means Luke, Paul and the others of their company.

Verse 16. *Mnason* was formerly of the island of Cyprus but was now living in Jerusalem. He was returning home with this group and arrangements were made for them to stay with him.

Verse 17. *Brethren received us gladly* indicated a friendly attitude toward the brethren of Paul's group. This was not only because of the common interest they had in the cause of Christ, but there were certain questions that had arisen among the Jewish Christians that they wished Paul to clarify.

Verse 18. The prominence of this James has been mentioned before. He is the one called "the Lord's brother" in Galatians 1: 19, and is the one in Acts 12: 17; 21: 18; 1 Corinthians 15: 7 and Galatians 2: 12. It is understandable, then, why Paul sought his company in the presence of the elders.

Verse 19. One of the main subjects of interest in those days was the admittance of the Gentiles to the benefits of the Gospel.

Verse 20. While many of the brethren rejoiced in the conversion of the Gentiles, they were confused as to their proper relation to the national customs of the Jews under the law of Moses. *Zealous* of the law means they had a desire to continue the aforesaid customs of the law even though they had embraced the Gospel. They had the right to do so (chapter 16: 3; 18: 21), but did not understand why the Gentiles did not also.

Verse 21. Paul taught that no one was to be justified by the law of Moses. This teaching of the apostle was misunderstood and some thought that he also opposed the Jews who observed the old practices even though they did it merely as national customs. These elders understood Paul's position on the subject, but many of the Jewish brethren did not, and they were informing him of the situation.

Verse 22. Paul was told that there would be an assembling of these zealous Jewish disciples in order to inquire into the subject.

Verses 23, 24. As a proof that Paul had not turned against the law as far as the national customs were concerned, they told him of an opportunity just at hand where he could engage in one of those customs, which was in regard to vows and the formalities required. The directions for observing this vow are in Numbers 6th chapter.

Verse 25. This refers to chapter 15: 23-29.

Verse 26. Paul complied with the advice of the elders. When he did so he carried out a principle he set forth in 1 Corinthians 9: 20.

Verse 27. Paul had to be in the temple to perform the custom mentioned in the preceding verse. That attracted the attention of the *Jews of Asia*, a small Roman province in which was the city of Ephesus. They had known of Paul's work in their home city and still had a prejudice against him. They raised a commotion among the people and caused them to threaten Paul with violence.

Verse 28. Like most riotous demonstrations, the motive was a false accusation. The mob accused Paul of opposing the law. (See comments at verses 20, 21.) They even accused him of bringing some Greeks (Gentiles) into the temple for the purpose of corrupting it

Verse 29. When people have the motive of persecuting a man whose teaching they do not like but cannot meet, they will take things for granted and form wrongful conclusions. Paul was seen with one Trophimus somewhere in the city, then the people presumed that he had taken him into the temple to corrupt it.

Verse 30. A general uproar was caused and Paul was forcibly taken out of the temple. The doors were closed to prevent him from returning should he get loose.

Verse 31. *Went about to kill him* means they were actually beginning their acts of violence, and intended to continue until they had him killed (verse 32). Word of the riot reached the ears of the captain of the military.

Verse 32. The captain took a crew of soldiers with him to the scene of the riot. The appearance of this company caused the mob to cease beating Paul.

Verse 33. The captain partook of the mob spirit and mistreated Paul, although the apostle had not even been accused by any officer.

Verse 34. The riotous clamor of the mob confused the captain so that he concluded to remove Paul from them for further investigation, all the while treating him very roughly. The *castle* was the place that contained the barracks of the soldiers.

Verse 35. The mob spirit was so violent that Paul had to be carried by the soldiers to get him through the crowd to a place of personal safety.

Verse 36. *Away with him* was an outburst of rage prompted by the spirit of murder, for Paul had not even been accused by any legal witness.

Verse 37. While this military police was pushing Paul along, he asked permission to make a speech to the people in his own behalf. This request was made in the Greek language, which surprised the captain who thought Paul was an Egyptian.

Verse 38. The only fact that was present in both the case of the Egyptian and that of Paul, was that there was an uproar among the people. But the apostle was not to blame for the present riot, a truth seemingly unknown to the chief captain.

Verse 39. Paul did not answer the captain with a direct "no," but stated in brief his identity. Instead of being an Egyptian he was a Jew. Tarsus was *no mean city* which means it was no insignificant place. Paul's nativity, then, was an honorable and noted one.

On that basis he again asked permission to speak to the people.

Verse 40. After being given *license* or permission to speak, Paul stood on the stairway to be in sight and hearing of the people, making a signal with his hand requesting their attention. When talking to the captain (verse 37) who was a Gentile, Paul used the Greek tongue. Now that the crowd was mostly Jewish, he used their own language which he knew they could understand and would respect.

ACTS 22

Verse 1. Paul's *defence* was to meet the charge, that he was trying to influence the Jews to disrespect the customs of the Mosaic system.

Verse 2. *The more silence.* An audience will be more willing to listen to a speaker if it knows that the language to be used is one that can be understood. As soon as Paul began to speak the people realized that he was using the dialect that was being spoken in that territory.

Verse 3. A part of Paul's *defence* consisted in answering the question of the chief captain in chapter 21: 33 as to "who he was." He was a Jew of Tarsus, which was recognized even by the Romans as an important city, to the extent that Augustus had made it a "free city," which means that all of its population would be classed as Roman citizens with all the privileges and honors accorded to such residents. As to Paul's cultural training, he had been instructed in Jerusalem by Gamaliel, a great teacher of the law. As to his religious attitude, he was as zealous toward God as were these Jews before him.

Verse 4. *This way* means the Gospel system of living. Paul's mention of persecuting its followers was to show that he had once shared the same opinion of them that was now being held by his hearers. That should at least suggest that he must have good reasons for his present position.

Verse 5. Paul referred to the facts mentioned in this verse to show that his former opposition to the *way* was done under the recognized authorities of the Jews, and that he was not merely a fanatic acting for the purpose of acquiring personal notoriety.

Verse 6. The original account of Paul's conversion is in chapter 9, and it is repeated here to show the background of his activities that had brought him into conflict with the Jews. He had almost reached Damascus, the destination in the commission authorized by the Sanhedrin, when his progress was halted by a light from heaven over which neither Jews nor Gentiles had any control.

Verse 7. The account here and that in chapter 9: 4 mentions simply that Paul fell to the ground, while chapter 26: 14 says they *all* fell down. Both accounts are true, but Paul was the only one who heard the question from the *voice*.

Verse 8. Paul (or Saul) knew that the person to whom he was talking was not on the earth. When he was told that it was the person whom he was persecuting, he did not express any surprise or question as to how he could be persecuting anyone who was not among men. He understood the subject of responsibility and association to mean that "he that despiseth you [the disciples] despiseth me" [Jesus].

Verse 9. For comments on *heard*, see chapter 9: 7.

Verse 10. See the comments at chapter 9: 6.

Verse 11. The glorious power of the light was due to the personality of Jesus, who was then at his Father's right hand in the glory world.

Verse 12. Ananias was a disciple of Christ as well as having been devout under the regulations of the law. (See chapter 9: 12.)

Verse 13. Ananias called him *Brother Saul* because they were both Jews, and had been servants of God under the Mosaic system.

Verse 14. Saul had to *see the Just One* in order to be a witness of his resurrection. It was the wisdom of God that Saul should also hear the voice of Jesus, which would add weight to his testimony for the divinity of the risen Christ.

Verse 15. The testimony of Saul was to be based on seeing and hearing.

Verse 16. Both in this instance and in chapter 9: 18, Saul is said to have risen to be baptized. That was because the rite had to be performed by immersion. *Wash away thy sins.* The first word is used literally because the act of baptism really washes the body, and that act is necessary for the remission of sins. (See Titus 3: 5; Hebrews 10: 22). *Calling on the name of the Lord* is associated with the act of

obedience to the command of the Lord, which shows how such *calling* is to be done.

Verse 17. *Come again to Jerusalem* was three years later (Galatians 1: 17, 18).

Verse 18. The Lord knew the stubborness of the people of Jerusalem, that they would not receive Paul's preaching, and hence he should not waste it on them.

Verses 19, 20. Paul refers to his former persecution of the disciples as an argument that the people of the city would certainly believe him to be sincere now. A man who had taken as active a part as he in opposition to the cause of Christ, would certainly leave no doubts of the genuineness of his conversion.

Verse 21. The Lord still knew best and was not willing for Paul's labors to be given to these inappreciative people. The apostle was to be sent away to preach the Gospel among the Gentiles.

Verse 22. *Gave him audience unto this word.* The Jews had an envious feeling against the Gentiles, and when Paul made his remark of being sent to this hated race by the Lord, they could not stand it any longer.

Verse 23. This verse manifests a state of mind that is disordered, and it explains why they cried out in the preceding verse that Paul should be destroyed. They did not even intimate any specific reason for their demand against the apostle, but instead they acted like madmen.

Verse 24. The chief captain was a Roman and a Gentile, and did not understand what that commotion was all about. He ordered Paul to be brought into the *castle* (the place that contained the soldiers' barracks) for bodily protection from the rage of the crowd. He also intended to torture (scourge) him in order to force him to tell the truth, which was an ancient practice that served as a form of "lie detector." As if the great apostle Paul had to be forced into telling the truth!

Verse 25. The centurion was the military officer assigned the duty of taking Paul into custody. Being *a Roman* will be explained at verse 28.

Verse 26. It was a serious offence to claim falsely to be a Roman. The mere statement of Paul, therefore, made a deep impression on the centurion.

Verse 27. Again Paul's word was all that was required, yet the captain wished to have the word personally from the lips of the apostle.

Verse 28. *Freedom* is from POLITEIA, which Thayer defines, "Citizenship, the rights of a citizen," and Robinson defines it in the same way. Being born within the territory of the Roman Empire did not always confer upon one the full rights of citizenship. Some special favors might be conferred upon a region that made all of its population full citizens of the Empire. That had been done for Tarsus, the city where Paul was born, which made him a full citizen of the nation. Sometimes a man could bribe the officers in charge and buy his citizenship, which was the way the captain obtained his.

Verse 29. *Examine him* means to make a judicial investigation, and it was to have been done in connection with a scourging. (See verse 24). The persons who had been called to carry out the scourging were dismissed. The captain was afraid because he had acted rashly in his rough handling of a Roman citizen. He felt that he might be called to account for improper conduct of his office.

Verse 30. On the morrow the captain concluded to take a more orderly course and "sift the case to the bottom" by calling in the accusers of his prisoner. He loosed him from his bonds and summoned the Sanhedrin to take charge of the situation.

ACTS 23

Verse 1. No specific charge had been made against Paul, hence he had none to deny. It was appropriate, therefore, for him to make a statement to the effect that he was not conscious of any wrong ever having been committed. Paul had caused Christians to be slain and had committed general persecution against the church, yet his *good conscience included* that time. This proves that a man can be conscientious in doing wrong, which also gives us the conclusion that a good conscience alone will not justify one before God.

Verse 2. Ananias had the common but erroneous idea that if a man is conscientious he is right. To him the statement of Paul meant that he had never done anything wrong. He thought that such an assertion from one who had been opposing Judaism so persistently was one of arrogance. Smiting one on the mouth was an act of contempt and humiliation, and not one especially considered as a physical punishment.

Verse 3. *Whited wall* was a figure of speech that meant Ananias was a hypocrite. It was similar to the words of Jesus in Matthew 23: 27. The hypocrisy of Ananias consisted in his posing as an administrator of justice under the law, and then directing an unlawful action against a prisoner who had not so much as been legally accused. It was like a judge in the courts of our land who will swear a jury to decide a case according to the law and evidence, then require it to bring in a "directed verdict." *God shall smite thee* was doubtless an inspired prediction. Smith's Bible Dictionary says Ananias was assassinated at the beginning of the last Jewish war.

Verses 4, 5. Paul agreed that the rulers of God's people should not be spoken against, and even cited the law that forbids such a speech (Exodus 22: 28). But the history of those times shows that Ananias was an evil character, who had been in difficulties with the civil authorities and had once been deposed from his office. Afterward, however, he assumed the place as president of the Sanhedrin, which is the meaning of Paul's words "sittest thou to judge" (verse 3). Knowing him to have been a usurper, the remark of the apostle, *I wist* [knew] not, etc., was the apostle's way of ignoring his assumption, thus showing him not to be entitled to the usual judicial courtesy.

Verse 6. Having disposed of their quibble over the highpriesthood of Ananias, Paul used the divided condition of sentiment in the Sanhedrin to bring to the fore the fundamental principle of the Gospel, the truth of which was the basis of his difficulties with the Jews. (See the note at Matthew 16: 12 on the differences between the Pharisees and Sadducees.) With regard to the most important difference between these sects, the belief in the resurrection, Paul declared he was a Pharisee.

Verse 7. Paul's declaration of faith in the doctrine of the resurrection, divided the multitude and set them at variance among themselves.

Verse 8. See the comments at verse 6.

Verse 9. Paul's declaration of faith had the effect he expected. The Pharisees believed in the existence of angels and spirits (verse 8), hence they were prepared to listen to Paul as an inspired man. Moreover, they have given us a point on the subject of authoritative teaching, namely, to oppose the word of an inspired man is the same as fighting against God.

Verse 10. In the riot among the two sects of the Jews, their attention was turned upon Paul who was regarded as the cause of the disturbance. There was even so much indication of violence against him that the chief captain feared for his bodily safety. The reader should note that this act of soldiers under lawful direction was solely for the purpose of protecting Paul from mob violence. This should be remembered when considering the falsehoods of Tertullus in chapter 24: 6, 7. Paul was removed from the Sanhedrin by the soldiers and taken into the *castle* for his bodily safety.

Verse 11. The imprisonment of Paul in the soldiers' barracks was a friendly act as it pertained to his personal safety, but the whole situation was one of apparent danger, and one that had many discouraging phases. It was an appropriate time for the Lord to speak words of cheer to him. *Bear witness also at Rome.* See the comments at chapter 19: 21 as to when he would bear this testimony at Rome.

Verses 12, 13. A *curse* means some kind of harm to be wished upon one. This harm was to come upon these Jews if they ate or drank until they had killed Paul. It was a rash proposal, but there is no evidence that they stuck to it though Paul was not killed.

Verse 14. They notified the chief priests of their curse, thinking it would impress them with the genuineness of their determination.

Verse 15. Paul was in the castle or barracks, and these Jews suggested that the priests ask the captain to bring the prisoner before the Sanhedrin again on the pretext of a fuller hearing. That would have given them an opportunity of killing him.

Verse 16. Paul's nephew heard of the plot and told him of it.

Verses 17, 18. Paul arranged a meeting of his nephew with the captain.

Verses 19, 20. The young man first told the captain of the request that was soon to be made of him by this wicked band of 40 Jews.

Verse 21. The young man then told him of the plot to kill Paul if he should be allowed to appear outside the castle, and he urged him to deny their request.

Verse 22. The captain bound the young man to secrecy and then dismissed him, but he intended to act on behalf of Paul's safety.

Verse 23. This was a military escort to conduct Paul to Caesarea, the headquarters of the Roman government in Palestine. Altogether there were 470 military men in the escort, some of whom had special services to perform. The horsemen were included to continue the guarded journey after the others returned to Jerusalem (verse 32). This journey was begun at 9 P. M. according to our time.

Verse 24. *Felix the governor* was a ruler at Caesarea on behalf of the Roman Empire.

Verses 25, 26. Claudius Lysias was the chief captain at Jerusalem. As a judicial courtesy, he wrote a letter to Felix explaining why he was sending Paul to him.

Verse 27. This part of the letter is a truthful report of the rescue of Paul by the soldiers of the captain, recorded in chapter 21: 32-34.

Verse 28. The captain understood that the *council* (Sanhedrin) was a place where the Jews held their examinations of accused persons.

Verse 29. The captain regarded the dispute between Paul and the Jews to be mostly a religious one and not such as he should try.

Verse 30. The court of Felix also was a secular one, but the captain felt that Paul's personal safety required that he appear there. Besides, the Jews had intimated that Paul was a general disturber of the peace (chapter 21: 28), and hence it seemed proper for the court at Caesarea to hear what the accusers had against him, they having been commanded also to appear at Caesarea for that purpose.

Verses 31, 32. Antipatris was about halfway between Jerusalem and Caesarea. The entire military escort went that far, at which place it was thought that most of the danger was over. The day after leaving Jerusalem they reached that place, from which all of the escort except the horsemen started back to Jerusalem, and the horsemen conducted Paul the rest of the jorney to Caesarea.

Verse 33. Upon arrival, the horsemen presented Paul to the governor, and also delivered the epistle that was sent by the chief captain.

Verse 34. This inquiry was to learn whether he should have jurisdiction in the case. Cilicia (the province containing the birthplace of Paul) was in such jurisdiction.

Verse 35. While waiting for the accusers to appear, Paul was to be kept in a place built by Herod, but now being occupied by Felix. Some one of the buildings attached thereto was Paul's prison, pending the arrival of his accusers.

ACTS 24

Verse 1. The word *descended* is used with reference to direction, as to or from Jerusalem, in view of its importance. Thayer defines the original word, "To come down," then explains it to mean, "as from the temple at Jerusalem, from the city of Jerusalem." Tertullus was a professional speaker whom the Jews employed to argue their case against Paul before Felix. What his nationality was is not clearly shown in the history, but he was acquainted with the procedure of courts.

Verses 2-4. Tertullus, like many court lawyers of our day, was not scrupulous in handling the truth, or in his manner of treating a serious case that pertained to the personal rights of a citizen. This paragraph is devoted to pure flattery of the governor, for the purpose of prejudicing him against Paul. I do not think this part of his speech needs any further comments.

Verse 5. An orator is supposed to make his speech before a court after the accusers and witnesses have said their part. But Tertullus acted both as accuser and witness, before the legal accusers were even present, like the unprincipled lawyer that he was. The most of this verse is false, but the part pertaining to Paul's leadership among the *Nazarenes* is true. And that was the chief grievance the Jews had against Paul, because they had previously had that feeling against Jesus, the founder of the *sect of the Nazarenes*. The last word was applied to Christians by the Jews, in reference to Jesus who had lived at Nazareth.

Verses 6, 7. This was a falsehood. (See chapter 21: 30-34.)

Verse 8. *By examining of whom* was an admission that the court had not heard any testimony furnished by Paul's accusers, thereby convicting himself (and the court) of gross injustice.

Verse 9. *Assented* means the Jews agreed with what Tertullus had said; yet they did not even pretend to have any witnesses to present to Felix.

Verse 10. Paul began his speech with remarks that were respectful and complimentary, but not in the nature of flattery. Having been in a public position over Judea for many years, Felix could appreciate the truths Paul intended stating before him.

Verse 11. *But twelve days.* The events to which Paul refers had occurred so recently, that it would be easy to find testimony to the contrary if any doubt was felt by Felix.

Verses 12, 13. This paragraph is a general denial of all the charges of disorder made against Paul, and he challenged his accusers to present their testimony.

Verse 14. To *confess* does not mean to admit any wrongdoing; it is only an admission of certain facts of which he was not ashamed, but which were objectionable to his critics. Paul does not admit that he is worshiping God through heresy, but that he is serving Him with the system that his accusers called by such a name. He further states that the law (of Moses) and the prophets had taught that same system to be coming sometime.

Verse 15. In this verse the apostle expressed the real subject that was the motive for their objection to him, namely, a belief in the resurrection. *Which they themselves also allow.* The Pharisees professed to believe in the resurrection, but denied that it was through Jesus whom they had crucified (chapter 4: 2).

Verse 16. *Conscience* is from SUNEIDESIS and Thayer's main definition is, "The soul as distinguishing between what is morally good and bad, prompting to do the former and shun the latter, commending the one, condemning the other." This definition states the action of the conscience, but it can act on improper information as well as proper. When Paul was persecuting Christians his conscience commended him for it, because his information (which was erroneous) was to the effect that the disciples of Christ were evildoers. In our present verse he means he had always exercised himself in a way that he thought would be right regarding both God and man. His good conscience while persecuting

Christians was due to the improper information that he had received. The popular idea is not true that the conscience is "A creature of education," for it is a part of every human being. However, it is true that the conscience may be educated, and it depends on the character of that education whether it will commend or condemn what it should.

Verse 17. The *alms* refers to the collections that were made by the various churches (Romans 15: 25-31; 1 Corinthians 16: 1-4). The *offerings* were according to some Jewish customs that Paul still had the right to perform as a Jew, since they were both secular and religious, and Paul did them as the former.

Verses 18-20. This paragraph is explained at chapter 21: 27-29.

Verse 21. See the comments on verses 14 and 15.

Verse 22. Felix now had a somewhat clearer view of the situation, to the extent that he wanted to see the case through after the other parties to it appeared. He promised Paul to hear the whole matter when the captain arrived. It might be stated, however, that so far as the record shows, neither Lysias nor witnesses ever appeared.

Verse 23. Paul was detained as a prisoner, but the soldier who was made responsible for his keeping was commanded to let him have many liberties usually not given.

Verse 24. *Felix came.* He was not residing outside the community; the second word means, "to make a public appearance," according to the lexicons. His interest had been aroused by Paul's speech to the extent he wished to hear more about the faith he was preaching. We will hear more about his wife in the next verse.

Verse 25. The subjects of this verse are in response to the request in the preceding one, to discuss *the faith in Christ,* which shows that the Gospel contains more than just the "first principles." These subjects were especially appropriate at this time, for both Felix and his wife were very unrighteous people. He had induced her to desert her former husband to marry him, for no other motive than lust on the part of each. Thayer defines the original word for *temperance,* "Self-control," then explains it to mean "the virtue of one who masters his desires and passions, especially his sensual

[fleshly or carnal] appetites." *Judgment to come* is defined by Thayer, "The last or final judgment." Being a judge himself and acquainted with the dignity of judicial sentences, Felix could feel the weight of Paul's prediction and was made to *tremble,* which is defined in the lexicon "to be terrified." *A convenient season.* The second word does not appear in the original Greek as a separate term. The phrase is from KAIROS which Thayer defines "opportune or seasonable time." The word has been translated in the King James Version by the single word "time" in 63 places.

Verse 26. The "convenient season" never appeared as far as the record informs us, for the same purpose that Paul had been called the first time. However, Felix was so depraved as to think the apostle would try to bribe the court into releasing him, and for that purpose he did call for him frequently.

Verse 27. After two years Felix was replaced by Festus because he had incurred the displeasure of the Romans. During those two years Paul was kept as a prisoner, his accusers never having appeared. In spite of this situation, to gratify the hatred of the Jews toward him, Felix kept Paul bound when he relinquished his office to Festus.

ACTS 25

Verse 1. Caesarea was the political headquarters of the Roman Empire in Palestine, but Jerusalem was the chief city of the province from many standpoints. Hence when Festus had been in his own official city three days, he went to Jerusalem to acquaint himself with conditions in that metropolis.

Verse 2. The leading Jews lost no time in approaching Festus with their complaints against Paul.

Verse 3. *Desired favor* means they asked Festus to grant them the favor of having Paul brought from Caesarea to Jerusalem. The inspired writer is the one who is telling the purpose of the Jews to lie in wait and kill Paul in the journey.

Verse 4. Festus evidently knew nothing of the murderous intent of the Jews, but supposed they preferred having Paul tried in their own court; it was in keeping with court form to refuse their request under the circumstances.

Verse 5. Festus invited the proper persons to accompany him to Caesarea and press their complaint aginst Paul. *If there be any wickedness* indicates he thought the Jews had some serious charge against the defendant.

Verse 6. After spending ten days in Jerusalem, Festus returned to his own jurisdiction at Caesarea. He did not delay the matter at hand, but summoned Paul to be brought before him the next day after arriving from Jerusalem.

Verse 7. The Jews had never appeared at Caesarea while Felix was in office, though they had two years to do so. For some reason they seemed to think they would succeed better with their case before Festus. *Many and grievous complaints* were doubtless general, and it was not definitely shown whether Paul was accused as an offender against the secular or the religious laws, or both.

Verse 8. Whichever they meant, Paul denied having transgressed against either.

Verse 9. For reasons of political policy, Festus changed his attitude toward the request of the Jews. He proposed to try Paul at Jerusalem as they had requested.

Verse 10. In view of the twofold phase of the complaints made against him, Paul insisted that he should stand trial before Caesar, the secular ruler.

Verse 11. *If I . . . committed anything worthy of death, I refuse not to die.* This sentence is against the sentimentalists who oppose capital punishment, and who claim the New Testament does not endorse it. If that penalty is wrong in God's sight, then it would be impossible for a man to commit anything worthy of death, and Paul would not have admitted such a possibility, which he did by the words "if I have." Also, if capital punishment is wrong, then Paul would not have given his consent to it, which he did by *not refusing to die.* But since he denied any guilt whatsoever, and was a Roman citizen entitled to the rights of such a standing, he appealed his case to the highest secular court in the world, whose headquarters were at Rome.

Verse 12. This *council* was not the Sanhedrin, but a consultation with the advisers of Festus. After the consultation, Festus, as the "lower court," granted the appeal.

Verse 13. The full name of this man was Herod Agrippa II, who was a ruler in another part of the Roman

Empire, and who came to make a friendly judicial call upon Festus. He was accompanied by his sister Bernice, with whom he was suspected to be living in the intimacy of husband and wife.

Verses 14, 15. Festus told his royal guest of Paul, and of the circumstances that brought him as a defendant before him.

Verse 16. In this verse Festus states the just procedure of the Roman government in the case of one facing trial for life. The present "recess" in the case was caused by the absence of Paul's accusers who were supposed to appear soon.

Verses 17, 18. The preliminary hearing showed to Festus that the charges against the defendant were nothing like what was expected to be offered.

Verse 19. In the opinion of Festus, the issue between Paul and the Jews was only a matter of superstition with Paul; that he was affirming the resurrection of a man by the name of Jesus who had died. As far as Festus could see, such a question was not worth all the bother the Jews were making, and hence there certainly must be something more serious that had not been brought out.

Verse 20. The above opinions are all that Festus stated to Agrippa as his reason for proposing moving the case to the Jewish courts in Jerusalem, there to be tried by him. However, verse 9 gives us another motive he had for the proposal.

Verse 21. When Festus granted the appeal of Paul, that took the case out of his hands, and he was waiting to get the "appeal papers" ready to send up to the higher court. *Augustus* is from a Greek word that was one of the titles of the Roman emperors, not a personal name as in other cases.

Verse 22. Doubtless it was curiosity mainly that prompted the request of Agrippa, but verses 26, 27 show the real motive of Festus in granting it.

Verse 23. This verse describes the important audience that gathered in the official auditorium to see and hear the speech of Paul.

Verse 24. Festus gave Paul a respectful introduction to his audience.

Verse 25. Agrippa had not been asked to listen as a trial judge, for Paul had already taken his case to another court. The statement of Festus, therefore, in declaring Paul innocent of any capital crime, was not an effort to prejudice Agrippa.

Verses 26, 27. *My lord* means the Roman emperor, whose personal name was Nero. Here was a strange situation; Festus had agreed to send a prisoner up to the highest secular court in the world, and yet had no charge of any importance on which to send him. He thought that if Paul were allowed to speak, something might be said as a basis for a charge.

ACTS 26

Verse 1. Agrippa was courteously invited to share the judicial "bench" with Festus. Under such a privilege, he bade the defendant to make a speech in his own behalf. *Stretched forth his hand* was a gesture of respect for the court, and a call to attention.

Verse 2. Paul made a complimentary speech to Agrippa, but it was not flattery as we shall see. He had good reasons for his happy feelings over the situation.

Verse 3. Paul here states the reasons for his happiness expressed in the preceding verse. Agrippa was not of pure Jewish blood, yet he was brought up under the influence of Jewish teaching, and was acquainted with the law of Moses. This would qualify him to appreciate the things that Paul would say.

Verse 4. Paul was brought up in Jerusalem (chapter 22: 3), so that the leaders of his own nation had full opportunity for knowing about his manner of life.

Verse 5. *Most straitest* is a double superlative and hence is an improper translation. The two words are derived from AKRIBES (by superlative inflection), and Thayer defines it "most exact." Paul means that he was a member of the Pharisees who were the most exacting of the Jews in their adherence to the law of Moses. They should have known, therefore, that he would not violate that law as the Jewish leaders charged him.

Verses 6, 7. The *promise* has a general reference to the benefits expected to come to the world through the seed of Abraham (Christ), but the special item of those benefits was the resurrection from the dead (verse 8). The Pharisees professed to believe in the resurrection as well as did Paul, but they resented his teaching that it was to be accomplished through Jesus (chapter 4: 2).

Verse 8. *Why should it be thought,* etc. The resurrection from the dead would not be any more impossible with God than any of the other works of His providence, therefore it was unreasonable to call that particular miracle in question.

Verse 9. The apostle then took up the history of his personal case to show that his present conduct and teaching was a complete change from what it had once been. (See the comments on this subject at chapter 22: 4.)

Verse 10. A *saint* is one who is "set apart for God, to be, as it were, exclusively his," according to Thayer. It is one of the names applied to the followers of Christ who are elsewhere called Christians and disciples. Paul's mention of the authority of the chief priests was to show he acted according to the recognized law of the Jews.

Verse 11. *Compelled them to blaspheme.* The American Standard Version translates this clause, "strove to make them blaspheme," which is evidently the meaning of the apostle. The first word is from the same original as "compellest" in Galatians 2: 14, where we know that Peter did not actually induce the Gentiles to do the things mentioned, for Paul's rebuke put a stop to his perversion. But he was using pressure for the purpose of forcing them to do as he contended. Likewise, Paul tried to terrorize the disciples into blaspheming the name of Christ, but they suffered death or imprisonment before denying their Lord. *Unto strange cities* means those on the outside. His last campaign was to reach to Damascus which was a city "outside" Palestine.

Verses 12, 13. At *midday* the sun would be straight over them, hence a light that would be *above the brightness of the sun* would indeed be a strong one.

Verse 14. All of the group fell to the ground but only Paul (or Saul) heard the voice. (See the comments at chapter 9: 5 for the meaning of *pricks.)*

Verse 15. This is also explained at chapter 9: 5.

Verse 16. Jesus did not appear to Paul to make him a Christian; men were appointed for that work. But an apostle must have seen the Lord after his resurrection, and that is why he *appeared* to Paul. Having been a *witness* of the fact that Jesus was alive, he was also to *minister* or serve Him by telling it to others.

Verse 17. Paul's delivery from his enemies was to be continued until the work for which he had been appointed had been accomplished.

Verse 18. *Open their eyes spiritually* to the truths of the Gospel. *Darkness* is ignorance of those truths, and *light* is the knowledge of them. Satan is the minister of darkness, and God is the source of divine light. *Forgiveness of sins* was to be the personal benefit conferred on those who accepted these truths. *Inheritance* means a share of the spiritual possessions enjoyed by the *sanctified*, which denotes the same as the "saints" in verse 10, and this state was to be obtained by faith in the risen Lord.

Verse 19. *Not disobedient* refers to the assignment to preach as the next verse shows. Chapter 9: 20 says he "straightway" preached Christ in the synagogues.

Verse 20. *First unto them of Damascus, and at Jerusalem.* According to Galatians 1: 18 it was three years before Paul preached at Jerusalem and other places in Judea.

Verse 21. Paul had done nothing that called for any punishment whatsoever, much less that of being slain. He therefore wished this court to know the truth of the motive for being persecuted by the Jews.

Verse 22. Paul again declared that his preaching was according to the predictions of the very writings that the Jews professed to believe. It is good to hear him give God the glory for his endurance, as he stood in the hearing of this mixed judicial court.

Verse 23. In this verse Paul specifies the most important one of the "things" of which he made mention in the preceding one. That was the fact that Christ was the first that rose from the dead (to die no more, Romans 6: 9). And that this great fact was bringing light to the Gentiles (as well as to the Jews).

Verse 24. *Learning* is from GRAMMA which Thayer defines, "Any writing, a document or record." Paul had made such wide reference to the writings of ancient scribes that Festus thought such knowledge had thrown him into a state of frenzy, to the extent that he had lost control of himself.

Verse 25. Paul made a direct denial of the charge concerning his mental condition, *soberness* being from a Greek word that means "self-control." But his reply to Festus was respectful

and one that recognized his standing. Thayer says the word for *noble* is "used in addressing men of conspicuous rank or office."

Verse 26. *The king* means Agrippa for whose special hearing Paul was making this speech, and who was acquainted with the ancient writings to which the apostle had referred. *Corner* is from GONIA which Thayer defines, "A secret place." *This thing* means the story of Jesus including his public life, crucifixion and evidences of his resurrection, all of which was known to thousands of people.

Verse 27. Agrippa was acquainted with the Old Testament writings, and this question of Paul was a challenge to the king to make a consistent application of them.

Verse 28. Agrippa was logical enough to see the conclusion required from the premises that Paul had cited. He really believed the truth of the prophetic statements, and the facts and truths connected with the story of Christ clearly connected Him with the prophecies. His unwillingness to go all the way that his conclusions would lead, was not from any doubts as to the rightful claims of the Gospel upon his life. But many personal interests of a worldly nature intervened against his better judgment. He was willing only to make the concession to Paul that is expressed by the famous sentence that has become the subject of song and poetry in various literature.

Verse 29. This verse expresses the sincere interest of the apostle in the spiritual welfare of his distinguished listeners. There is no sign of personal triumph in his remarks, for he realizes that nothing short of wholehearted obedience to Christ will avail anything for the unsaved, hence his wish was for the completeness of the conviction that was acknowledged by Agrippa. *Except these bonds.* How gracious was this remark, which shows the complete absence of bitterness, or any feeling that others too should be humiliated who were no better than he.

Verses 30, 31. At the conclusion of Paul's speech the meeting "broke up" and the royal hearers went aside to confer with each other. That was not in order to decide on a verdict, for such action had been taken from them by the appeal of the prisoner. But to see if either of them had discovered "somewhat to write" to Caesar (chapter 25: 26). It was admitted that no such discovery had been made, but rather that the prisoner was not worthy even of bonds.

Verse 32. Agrippa was the visiting jurist who was invited to give a critical ear to the speech of the prisoner. It was proper, therefore, for him to express the opinion that we have recorded. Had it not been for the appeal that Paul had made, he could have been released from all custody at this time.

ACTS 27

Verse 1. This chapter and half of the next has to do with the voyage to Rome in Italy, the capital city of the Roman Empire. The voyage was made necessary by Paul's appeal from the lower courts (chapter 25: 11; 26: 32). *Augustus' band.* Josephus writes of a "Troop of Sebaste [the Greek word for Augustus], of Caesarea," and it was an officer of this band of soldiers who was given charge of Paul and the other prisoners.

Verse 2. The first ship sailing in the desired direction was from the city of Adramyttium. This Aristarchus was the same who was with Paul in chapter 19: 29.

Verse 3. The ship landed next day at Sidon, a seaport on the *coasts of Asia.* While the ship was anchored here, Paul was permitted to visit his friends among the disciples.

Verse 4. To *sail under* means "to sail close by," according to Thayer. They sailed near the shore of this island to shield them from the winds that were blowing against them.

Verse 5. Sea of Cilicia and Pamphylia means the waters bordering on those provinces. Passing on they landed at Myra in Lycia, another province of the Roman Empire.

Verse 6. At Myra all on board had to change to another ship.

Verse 7. *Scarce were come* means they just barely made it to reach Cnidus on account of the opposing wind. Going on in a southwestern direction, they sailed between the islands of Salmone and Crete, passing nearer the former.

Verse 8. *Hardly* (with difficulty) they sailed round along the southern shore of Crete and came to a harbor called *fair havens,* near the city of Lasea.

Verse 9. *The fast was now already past.* The *fast* was the period of the Atonement which came on the 10th day of the 7th month (Leviticus 23: 27). This ceremonial day had nothing to do with the sailing, but it so happened that it came about the beginning of a stormy season on the Mediterranean. The reference to it was merely as a date, indicating the season of the year when it was generally dangerous to sail.

Verse 10. *I perceive* is from THEOREO, and the several definitions in the lexicon present the idea of a conclusion based on what one has seen or can see, in connection with his better judgment. From such a basis, Paul advised that it would be a risk to both their lives and to the ship for them to sail.

Verse 11. It was natural to prefer the judgment of these men to that of Paul since they were experienced seamen, and should have been in position to judge.

Verse 12. Just because the place was not *commodious* (convenient) where they were in which to winter, the majority of the crew advised leaving. They thought they could reach the haven of *Phenice* which faced the northwest and southeast. Due to some "weather conditions" with which I am not acquainted, this was thought to offer a safe place in which to remain until spring.

Verse 13. *South wind blew softly.* Such a wind seemed favorable, both as to direction and intensity. It would gently press them north and west along Crete.

Verse 14. The chief characteristic of *Euroclydon* was that of churning up the water into huge waves, which accounts for the difficulties they had with the body of the ship. Thayer defines the word, "A S. E. wind raising mighty waves."

Verse 15. *Let her drive* means they did not try to control the direction of the ship, but let it float in whatever direction the wind and waves drove it.

Verse 16. *Running under* denotes going south of the island and passing near the shore. At this place the conditions had become so severe that they had difficulty to *come by the boat,* which means they could hardly manage the boat.

Verse 17. The *boat* referred to was a lifeboat, which had been towed up to now because the waters were calm when they started. The word for *boat* is from SKAPHE which Robinson defines, "A skiff, boat." They hoisted this boat (with "much work," verse 16) up on deck, then gave their attention to the ship. To strengthen the hull, they passed ropes or chains around it and drew them up tight. *Strake sail* means they lowered the sails for fear the wind in them would force the ship *into the quicksands.* From now on they let the ship drift as it would with the wind and waves.

Verse 18. *Lightened the ship* means they threw overboard some of the goods, thereby easing the weight the ship was compelled to carry in the storm.

Verse 19. *Tackling* means the furniture, apparatuses and all other equipment of the ship. The situation was so grave the disciples assisted in throwing these things out.

Verse 20. The obscurity of *sun* and *stars* indicates the storm continued throughout day and night. Not having any compass in those days, mariners had to depend on the heavenly bodies for their direction. This condition continued for so many days that all on board (except Paul) despaired of ever reaching land.

Verse 21. The *long abstinence* was natural under the terrible strain of the conditions. Paul was very kind and respectful, yet properly chided the group for having rejected the advice he offered them while at Crete.

Verse 22. Paul bade them to be of good cheer since the only loss that was to come to them would be regarding the ship; he then explained why he was thus assured.

Verses 23, 24. *Stood by me . . . angel.* (See Hebrews 1: 13, 14.) It was God's will for Paul to appear before Caesar; many results were to come from that great event.

Verses 25, 26. Paul predicted the wreck of the ship, which was to intervene before the personal rescue of the crowd or his appearance before Caesar.

Verse 27. Two weeks after leaving Crete the mariners thought they saw indications of being near land. They were being driven back and forth in *Adria,* the Adriatic Sea, which is that part of the Mediterranean between Greece and Italy.

Verse 28. They *sounded* (measured the depth with a line and weight) and found it *twenty fathoms,* or about 120 feet. After going only a *little further*

they found it *fifteen fathoms,* or about 90 feet.

Verse 29. At that rate they feared the water would soon be too shallow for the ship to float. They cast four anchors out of the rear of the boat to hold it from moving, while waiting for daylight to come when they could see better about conditions.

Verse 30. The sailors lowered the lifeboat *under color* (pretending) that they intended placing some anchors at the forepart of the ship, but in reality for the purpose of abandoning the ship and taking to the lifeboat.

Verse 31. The Lord promised to bring all the persons on board alive through the storm. However, He expected the cooperation of all concerned, especially the ones who were trained in affairs of water travel, hence Paul made this statement to the soldiers.

Verse 32. To prevent the escape of the shipmen, the soldiers cut the ropes and let the lifeboat go. As it was an emergency, the military men acted in this commandeering manner to save the lives of the whole group.

Verses 33, 34. While waiting for daylight, Paul advised them to break their fast *for their health.* Too long abstinence from food would be injurious, and besides, as their ultimate escape was assured, there was no reason for them to punish themselves more.

Verses 35-37. Paul led the way and began to eat, after giving thanks for the bread. The group of 276 persons then took courage and also partook of the food.

Verse 38. After satisfying their hunger, they decided to ease the strain on the boat further by casting the wheat into the sea.

Verse 39. *Knew not the land* denotes that they did not recognize it. All *creeks* of necessity have *shores,* so we learn that a clearer translation would be that they thought they saw a bay with a beach that would be a desirable place for a "forced landing."

Verse 40. *Had taken up* all comes from one Greek word which Thayer defines, "to cast loose." The italicized word *themselves* refers to the anchors which they abandoned in order to relieve the ship of the weight. The rudders were large oars used to steer the ship. While at anchor they would be hoisted out of the water and held by *bands* or ropes; these were now cut loose. They next raised the mainsail and started toward the "bay" mentioned in the preceding verse.

Verse 41. *Where two seas met* all comes from DITHALASSOS, which Thayer defines, "an isthmus or tongue of land," and he explains it, "the extremity of which is covered by the waves." Both sides of this projection of land were washed by the sea which formed a sort of whirlpool, into which the forepart of the ship was thrust and stranded. The rear part of the boat was then lashed with the violence of this "whirlpool" and crushed.

Verse 42. When the jailer in chapter 16: 27 thought his prisoners had escaped, he intended killing himself rather than be executed (as he thought) by the officers. The soldiers in our verse wanted to kill the prisoners, rather than face their superior officers under the charge of allowing the prisoners to escape. This indicates the harsh rules the Roman government established regarding the responsibility of those having charge of prisoners. It also explains why the Jews felt the necessity of assuring protection for the watchers at the tomb of Jesus. (Matthew 28: 12-14.)

Verse 43. Paul was one of the prisoners and would have shared the fate of the others, had the soldiers been suffered to carry out their purpose. Whether the centurion cared much for the other prisoners we are not told. But his respect for the apostle Paul moved him to dissuade the soldiers from their evil design. Instead, he gave orders for all to get to land in whatever way they could.

Verse 44. Some of the crowd were able to swim to shore. Others made it to safety by the aid of boards and pieces of the ship that helped them to float.

ACTS 28

Verse 1. Smith's Bible Dictionary says the following: "Melita, the modern Malta. . . . It is 17 miles long by 9 or 10 broad. It is naturally a barren rock, with no high mountains, but has been rendered fertile by industry and toil."

Verse 2. *Barbarous* sometimes means to be rude in speech; rough, harsh. It also means to speak in a foreign tongue. At our place Thayer says it is not used reproachfully, and that the inhabitants were of Phoenician origin, who had some refinement of manners.

These facts explain the kind treatment they gave the shipwrecked group.

Verse 3. A cold rain was falling and Paul was building a fire for warmth. A *viper* is a poisonous snake that came out of the sticks and clung to his hand. It had evidently been sheltering itself among the sticks and was numb from the cold. The heat brought it to its feeling and caused it to attack him as might be expected to be done by such a creature.

Verse 4. The islanders were rather superstitious and thought this incident was the work of some supreme being. They thought Paul was trying to escape just punishment.

Verses 5, 6. They fully expected to see Paul drop dead. Seeing his mastery over it, they reversed their opinion and said he was a god. While that was not the object of the miracle, it did serve to prove Paul and his companions to be good men.

Verse 7. *Same quarters* means that same part of the island. Publius was probably the governor of the island, because he had possessions sufficient to give hospitality to Paul and his group for a period of three days.

Verse 8. Paul had a chance to "return the favor" by healing the father of Publius of a serious disease, which he did by laying his hands miraculously on him.

Verse 9. The good deed done for Publius' father was reported over the island. As a result, others came to Paul and were healed of diseases.

Verse 10. We are not told just how these *honors* were manifested while Paul and his companions remained on the island. But when they were ready to leave, the natives gave them a supply of the necessities of life.

Verse 11. *Castor and Pollux* was the label inscribed on the side of the ship. The words were derived from some legend about heathen gods.

Verses 12, 13. The stop of three days at Syracuse was either because of the conditions of the weather, or to perform the regular business of a vessel. *Fetched a compass* means they took a circuitous route by the place, and coming to Puteoli they landed for a few days.

Verse 14. Smith's Bible Dictionary says Puteoli was "the great landing-place of travelers to Italy," so it is not surprising that some brethren would be there.

Verse 15. The brethren at Rome heard of Paul's voyage toward their city and came to meet him. According to Smith's Bible Dictionary, *Appi forum* was 43 miles from Rome and *Three taverns* was 33. The same information is given in Thayer's lexicon under the word TABERNAI. Paul was heartened by seeing this brotherly welcome from those who were willing to brave the uncertainties of the sea to meet this "prisoner of Jesus Christ."

Verse 16. Thayer says the *captain of the guard* was the "captain of the Roman emperor's body-guard." To this officer the centurion delivered his prisoners, thus discharging the duty that was imposed upon him at Caesarea. But Paul was not placed in the soldiers' camp; instead, he was permitted to dwell separately with a single soldier as his guard. This would give him opportunity for seeing persons in whom he was interested.

Verse 17. Paul called these Jews *men and brethren* because of their common blood, not that they were brethren in Christ. He related how he was made a prisoner of the Romans by the Jews, though he was not guilty of wrong-doing against any laws.

Verse 18. *Who* means the Romans into whose hands Paul had been delivered. Finding nothing wrong in him, they were disposed to discharge him from all accusations.

Verse 19. Paul appealed unto Caesar as a defendant, and not as a complainant against his nation. That is, he merely wished to clear his own good name, not that he wanted to cause his Jewish brethren any trouble.

Verse 20. Lest he might be misjudged by his Jewish brethren, however, he thought it well to explain the presence of the chain that was attached to him. *Hope of Israel* refers to the hope of a resurrection through Christ. That was the reason why he called them to him three days after arriving in their city.

Verse 21. These Jews had heard the report about the disciples in general, but had not received any news of accusations against Paul personally.

Verse 22. Because of the unfavorable report these Jews had heard about the disciples, they wished to have Paul's personal story. *Sect* is from HAIRESIS, and Thayer defines it at this place, "a sect or party."

Verse 23. These Jews professed to believe the Old Testament, hence Paul used it as a basis for his speeches. He showed them that their own religious literature had foretold the coming of the kingdom of God, the institution referred to as a "sect."

Verse 24. As usual, the hearers disagreed among themselves over what they heard.

Verse 25. Because of the disagreement between themselves the Jews departed. Before they left Paul spoke *one word*, meaning one quotation from Esaias (Isaiah).

Verse 26. *Go unto this people* denotes that Isaiah was to carry a message to *this* people, the Jews. Hear . . . *not understand* . . . *see* . . . *not perceive*. This all means the Jews would refuse to make the proper use of their mental faculties.

Verse 27. *Waxed gross* denotes they had become stupid through their own prejudice. Their motive for such an attitude was to reject the reformation of life that the teaching of the Gospel might work in them.

Verse 28. This announcement to the Jews was on the same basis as set forth in such passages as chapter 13: 46. The Jews were given the first opportunity of hearing the Gospel. When the Gentiles had the divine truth offered to them, they showed a greater readiness to receive it.

Verse 29. *Had great reasoning*. The Jews did not agree among themselves upon the teaching of Paul, hence they got into dispute over it. They were familiar with the law as Paul quoted it, but their prejudice prevented them from accepting his teaching.

Verse 30. *Hired house* means a rented building which Paul used at his own expense. He was still in custody, hence could preach only to those who *came in unto him*.

Verse 31. *No man forbidding him* all comes from AKOLUTOS which Thayer defines, "without hindrance." We know that men objected to the preaching of Paul, but God sustained him so that the preaching of the cause of Jesus Christ continued with great zeal.

ROMANS 1

Verse 1. Paul first mentions his relation as a servant of Christ, which means "one who gives himself up wholly to another's will." He next refers to his position as apostle, and says he was *called* to that office. The word is from KLETOS which Thayer defines at this place, "called to some office," which he explains to mean "divinely selected and appointed." *Separated unto the Gospel* means he was appointed to the work.

Verse 2. *Which* has reference to the Gospel which had been predicted in old time. This fact is referred to in Galatians 3: 8 and 1 Peter 1: 10. When God told Abraham (Genesis 12: 3) that all the families of the earth would be blessed through him, He was meaning the Gospel that was to be given to the world through Christ.

Verse 3. The promise was first given to Abraham, but it was to be fulfilled through the lineage of one of his great descendants, David. *Made* is from GINOMAI which means "caused to be." This part of the great promise pertained to the fleshly nature of Christ.

Verse 4. It became generally known that Jesus was a descendant of David as to his fleshly or human relationship, but some special event was necessary to *declare* or prove him to be also the Son of God. That was accomplished by his resurrection from the dead, for God would not have raised him had he been an impostor.

Verse 5. By *we* Paul includes himself with the other apostles, and he regards the appointment as *grace* or divine favor. *For* is from EIS, and it means the apostleship was in order to call men of all nations to believe on the name of Jesus.

Verse 6. *Ye* means the brethren to whom the apostle was writing this epistle.

Verse 7. *To all that be in Rome* applies to all the disciples of Christ, whether they be Jews or Gentiles. The church in that city was composed of both, and that must be remembered throughout the study of this epistle, in order to grasp the purpose of much of the apostle's reasoning. The Jewish brethren admitted that the Gentiles were their equals as far as the chances of salvation were concerned, yet they still had a feeling of superiority because of having been God's special people for so long. On the other hand, the Gentile brethren had the attitude of persons who had been underestimated, but whose real merits had finally been recognized by the Lord so that He had admitted them to the benefits of the Gospel because of those merits. Paul will show in various passages that God had never favored either Jews or Gentiles by reason of

their inherent virtues (since all have sinned and come short of the glory of God), but that it was through the abundant mercy of the Lord that any man in the world could be saved at all. This is a fundamental key to many passages of this book, and the reader should note the passage for reference, as the notes will not be repeated in full.

Saints is from HAGIOS, and means a person "set apart for God, to be, as it were, exclusively his." — Thayer. This setting apart is accomplished by obedience to the Gospel. In the New Testament the terms Christians, disciples, saints, brethren and children of God, are used interchangeably, and are applied thus to the same people because they possess the qualifications that are denoted by the terms. They are called saints for the reason just stated; disciples means learners or followers; brethren means they have a common relation to the Father; children because they have been begotten of Him, and Christians because they wear the name of Christ.

Verse 8. *World* is from KOSMOS and means the people of the earth. Rome was a center of population, being the capital of the Roman Empire. People coming and going to and from this capital would learn of the church and would carry the information back home.

Verse 9. *God is my witness.* Since God knows the hearts of all, He knew that Paul's service was from the heart, and for that reason the prayers of the apostle would be heard.

Verse 10. Having been faithful to the service of Christ elsewhere, Paul prayed trustingly for the opportunity of preaching the Gospel in Rome.

Verse 11. No one but an apostle could impart spiritual gifts (Acts 8: 18), hence Paul's wish to do that for the brethren at Rome denotes that no apostle had ever been in that city. We have no direct information as to how the church was started in Rome, but we know (from the above) that no apostle did it. This refutes the claim of the Romanists that Peter established it and that he was its first bishop.

Verse 12. The motive for this wish of Paul was not far the sake of glory, but he longed for the comfort that comes from association with those of like faith.

Verse 13. *Let* is an old word that

means to hinder. For some reason which he does not state, he had been hindered from coming to Rome. *Other Gentiles* shows that the church in Rome had Gentiles in it as well as Jews.

Verse 14. *Debtor* means one who is under obligation to another, and Paul means he has the obligation to preach the Gospel to these classes mentioned. A barbarian is one who speaks a foreign language, and the word is used in contrast with the Greeks because they were the native people of Greece and also recognized the people of Italy as their equals socially. The *wise* refers to those skilled in the philosophy of the time in contrast with those who were not.

Verse 15. The foregoing considerations made Paul feel obligated to preach the Gospel to the people of Rome to the extent of his ability.

Verse 16. Paul had been persecuted for the sake of the Gospel, yet he was not ashamed of it. The reason for his attitude was the great truth that *it* is the power of God unto salvation. *Power* is from DUNAMIS, which is one of the strongest words in the Greek New Testament for the thought of what may bring about a desired result. But it has such an effect only on those who believe it. *Jew first . . . Greek.* That denotes the Gospel was offered to the Jews before it was to the Greeks (or Gentiles).

Verse 17. *Righteousness of God* means the system of life that will produce a state of righteousness acceptable to God. That system is revealed in the Gospel (not in the law of works in the Mosaic system). The original for *from* is EK which denotes the source of something or the means by which it is accomplished. Hence the thought is that the system of God's righteousness is revealed by means of the faith (in Jesus), and not by the works of the law. *To faith.* The first word is from EIS and is defined "in order to," and as applied here it means that this system of God's righteousness is revealed "in order to" produce faith in the hearer. *The just shall live by* (the) *faith* in Christ, and not by the works of the law. The Judaizers were trying to force the Christians into observing the works of the law as the proper system of righteousness.

Verse 18. The Gospel not only reveals God's system of righteousness, but it also tells of the divine wrath against all ungodliness. *Hold* means to hold back or restrain. The unrighteousness of men is a hindrance to the spread and reception of the truth.

Verse 19. From here to the close of the chapter the apostle deals with the corruptions of the heathen or Gentile world. Those people did not have the law of Moses, but they did have the principles of righteousness that nature offered them, and they refused to abide by them. *In them* means the evidences of God's goodness were visible to them.

Verse 20. This verse corresponds in thought with Psalms 19: 1, meaning the evidences in nature of the existence of a Supreme Being. The *invisible things of him* are *His eternal power and Godhead*. Though invisible to man, yet the evidences of them are *clearly seen* in the world that was created and whose objects "declare the glory of God" (Psalms 19: 1). This leaves the heathen *without excuse* for their unbelief.

Verse 21. The heathen did not live up to the information offered them by the things in creation. They did not respect God as he deserved, but estimated Him on the basis of their foolish imaginations, which are described in verse 23.

Verse 22. When a man professes to be wiser than a Being who can create the universe, he becomes the most deplorable of fools.

Verse 23. This verse outlines the idolatry of the heathen, and shows why Paul applied the term "fools" to them. They were bound to know that the brute creatures of the earth could not originate anything, yet they pretended to represent the Creator by making images of these dumb animals and calling them gods.

Verse 24. The original Greek for *gave them up* is defined by Thayer, "To give over into (one's) power or use." Robinson's definition is virtually the same. When men persist in going contrary to the light and information in their reach, He will abandon them and suffer them to go full length into their preferred practices. They dishonored their own bodies by the unnatural immoral practices to be considered at verses 26, 27.

Verse 25. The truth of God cannot actually be changed into a lie, for divine truth is eternal. The definitions of Robinson and Thayer of the word for *changed* are the same in thought, but the former is more direct which is, "To exchange one thing for another." The heathen gave up the truth of God and accepted the lie of idolatry in exchange. *Served the creature more* [marginal "rather"] *than the Creator.* See verse 23.

Verse 26. *Gave them up* is explained at verse 24. *Vile affections* is defined "depraved passion" by Thayer. *Change* means the same as in verse 25. The iniquity of which these women were guilty is called "homosexuality" in Webster's Dictionary. Liddell and Scott's Greek lexicon defines such a woman as one "who practices lewdness with herself or with other women."

Verse 27. The common name for the iniquity referred to in this verse is sodomy. It is the sin meant in 1 Corinthians 6: 9, last sentence. A case of it is that predicted in Daniel 11: 37, and the man was a Syrian king by the name of Antiochus Epiphanes. The historical fulfillment of that prediction is recorded in Prideaux's Connexion, year 175. *Recompence of their error.* This is not described in any work that I have seen, but the circumstances indicate it refers to some physical derangement of the organs involved in the shameless act. We know that the promiscuous intimacies between the sexes has produced the well-known "social disease," and in a similar manner some terrible disorder was the result of the horrible practice of sodomy, which is the unnatural immorality between men and men.

Verse 28. This is the same as verse 24.

Verse 29. The "reprobate mind" in the preceding verse would crave and secure the evils named here, many of which are general in their meaning and do not require extended comments. *Fornication* is unlawful intimacy between the sexes. *Covetousness* is the unlawful desire for the belongings of another. *Maliciousness* is a desire and determination to do injury to another. *Envy* is a feeling that regrets seeing someone enjoying a favor. *Debate* as used here means wrangling or quarreling. *Deceit* is an effort to mislead another to his injury. *Malignity* is virtually the same as maliciousness. *Whisperers* are "secret slanderers" according to Thayer.

Verse 30. *Backbiters* means about the same as "whisperers" in the preceding verse; those who would slander you "behind your back." *Haters of God* is proved by their worship of false gods. *Despiteful* is similar to malicious, and such characters also will show their pride. *Boasters* are those who love to practice those evils and want others to know about it. *Inventors of evil things.* They not only follow in the steps of wicked persons, but also devise evil ways of their own. *Disobedient to parents* means they have repudiated the rightful authority of their father and mother.

Verse 31. *Without understanding* denotes they are too stupid to recognize their folly. *Covenantbreakers* are those who disregard their promises. *Without natural affection* explains why they are "disobedient to parents" in the preceding verse. *Implacable* is defined by Thayer, "That cannot be persuaded to enter into a covenant"; not willing even to talk of "terms" of agreement. It is no wonder that such persons would be *unmerciful* in their dealings with others.

Verse 32. *The judgment of God* is that all who do such things are worthy of death. But that is not all; that same judgment will be meted out to them who have pleasure in those who practice them. It is as bad to rejoice in iniquity as it is to practice it.

ROMANS 2

Verse 1. Before reading further into this chapter, I shall insist that the reader see the comments on chapter 1: 7, then come back to this place. The closing verses of that chapter pertain to the evil practices of the Gentiles. The Jews were free in their condemnation of the Gentiles, yet they were just as guilty, in principle, as were the Gentiles; therefore this chapter will be directed against them. In condemning the Gentiles for their iniquities, they condemned themselves for things as bad in principle.

Verse 2. *We* means Paul and all others who were acquainted with the ways of God. His judgments are always in harmony with the truth, whether against Jews or Gentiles.

Verse 3. *O man* means the Jew who was condemning the Gentile. He thought that his being a Jew would exempt him from the judgment of God.

Verse 4. *Despisest* means to belittle or disregard, and the Jew did that with reference to the goodness of God. It was the quality of goodness and longsuffering of God that caused him to put up with the unrighteousness of both Gentile and Jew. The goodness of God would lead the self-righteous Jew to repentance if he did not "despise" or overlook it.

Verse 5. A hard and impenitent heart is one that stubbornly persists in a course of wrongdoing. *Treasurest up* means that such a life is sure to make a record that will bring the wrath of God upon it in the *day of wrath;* that will be the day of judgment spoken of by Paul in Acts 17: 31.

Verse 6. *According to his deeds* does not teach "degrees of reward or punishment," but only whether they are good or evil. (See 2 Corinthians 5: 10.)

Verse 7. *Eternal life* will be rendered to one class of persons. They are the ones who *seek for glory, honor and immortality.* They are to do this seeking by *patient continuance in well doing.*

Verses 8, 9. These verses designate the other class as those who are *contentious* (resort to trickery), resist the truth and obey unrighteous instructions. To this class God will render *indignation and wrath, tribulation and anguish.* The apostle gives additional reasons why they will receive such from God; it is because they are souls that do evil. *Jew first and also of the Gentile* again suggests comments at chapter 1: 7.

Verse 10. This verse is for emphasis on verse 7.

Verse 11. *Respect of persons* all comes from one Greek word, and it is defined "partiality" by Thayer. It means God will not favor the Jew any more than the Gentile.

Verse 12. All sinners, whether Jews or Gentiles, will be punished for their sins. The word *law* in this verse means the law of Moses; the Jews will be judged for their sins under that law. The Gentiles will be judged for their sins, but it will be *without law;* that is, not by the law of Moses, for they did not live under that. The law by which they will be judged is stated in verses 14, 15.

Verses 13. The principle set forth in this verse applies to whatever law the people lived under, whether they were Jews or Gentiles.

Verse 14. The Gentiles *have not the law* (of Moses), yet they do have the law and evidences of nature (creation, chapter 1: 20). If they make use of such law it will serve as a rule of action for themselves. Many of the requirements stipulated in the law of Moses were in line with natural principles (such as love of parents and children, and respect for a neighbor's wife, etc.) The Gentile was expected to respect these natural laws, and he will be condemned if he does not. It must be remembered that all of the aforesaid comments about the two laws apply to the years before the giving of the Gospel of Christ. After that, all persons everywhere were commanded to be subject to that universal law. (See Acts 10:35 and 17: 31.)

Verse 15. Another part of the law in nature for the Gentile was his conscience. That is a part of every human being and he was born with it. For an extended definition of the word see the comments at Acts 24: 16. The conscience may be erroneously informed, hence a man might follow it and still be wrong. But no man can go contrary to his conscience without being guilty of wrong. The Gentile was required never to do anything for which his conscience would condemn him.

Verse 16. This verse states the day on which the judging will be done; it is the one Paul mentions in Acts 17: 31. *My Gospel* does not denote origin or ownership, but the one that Paul was preaching; the Gospel that was the subject of *his* preaching.

Verse 17. This and the following three verses set forth the claims (which were true) of the Jew. He could boast (glory) because God had given the law to his nation.

Verse 18. God's will was made known in the law, hence the Jew could have knowledge of it. *Approvest* means to decide between right and wrong, and the Jew could do that by the instruction the law provided him.

Verse 19. The knowledge furnished by the law, enabled the Jew to feel that he could extend guidance and enlightenment to others less fortunate.

Verse 20. Even persons without ordinary discernment could be instructed by one who had the law for his own support. Teacher of babes is figurative, meaning the Jew could give information to the most unlearned, because he had the background of the inspired law. The Jew was not restricted to the mere principles of right doing, but he had the *form* or ritual in which they were to be carried out.

Verse 21. With all of the forementioned advantages, the Jew had no reason for coming short of the proper conduct in his own life. However, many of them were satisfied to rest on their knowledge of what was right, without setting an example of the things they told others to do. They would steal to enrich their own purse, yet condemn the Gentiles for the sin of theft.

Verse 22. An adulterer would be condemning himself when he told another not to commit that wrong. Commit sacrilege means to rob a temple. The Jews would profess a horror for idols, yet would not hesitate to enter the idols' temple to steal the metals.

Verse 23. It is wrong to commit any lawlessness; it is worse to break the very law that one has praised as being the law of God.

Verse 24. The Gentiles could see the disorderly conduct of the Jews, and it led them to speak against the God whom they professed to serve. *As it is written.* "My name continually every day is blasphemed" Isaiah 52: 5.

Verse 25. Circumcision was one of the rites required by the law. These Jews were insisting that it be attended to, yet were indifferent about the many practical duties that the same law required. (See Matthew 23: 23.)

Verse 26. *The uncircumcision* is used figuratively, meaning the Gentiles to whom the rite was never given. *Keep the righteousness of the law* means the same as doing them by nature as set forth in verse 14.

Verse 27. *Uncircumcision* and *circumsion* are used to mean the Gentiles and Jews. *By nature* (see verse 14) means the Gentile did by nature what the Jew did not do, though he had the written law that showed him plainly what his duty was. By this better example of the Gentile, he *judged* (condemned) the Jew in his transgression of the law that had been given to him by *letter* (had been written in words).

Verse 28. The word *Jew* is used to designate a real servant of God, not one who merely professes to be one just because he wears the national name. On the same principle, fleshly circumcision has ceased to count favorably for anyone whose general life does not harmonize with the spiritual significance of the rite, namely, the cutting off of the sins of his life.

Verse 29. The real Jew in God's sight is one whose circumcision has been of a spiritual character, cutting off from the heart that which is evil. Such circumcision is not *in the letter* (is not literal), but is spiritual. And such a rite will obtain the *praise* (approval) of God, although the Jew with his love of rituals will not approve. This circumcision is stated in Colossians 2: 11.

ROMANS 3

Verse 1. *Advantage* means "preeminence or superiority," and not some special favor that would give him any more assurance of salvation. After all that Paul had just written about the equality of the Jews and Gentiles as far as it concerned their spiritual worth, they might feel grieved and think that no other kind of superiority was acknowledged for them, hence the question the apostle asks.

Verse 2. Paul answers the question of the preceding verse, stating that unto the Jews were committed the *oracles* (words) of God. With the exception of one writer (Job), every writer of the Old Testament was a Jew. That shows the great affection of God for the descendants of Abraham, Isaac and Jacob, the founders of the Jewish race.

Verse 3. The Jews were not to be blamed if some refused to believe the oracles. They would be shown to be true and a basis of faith in God in spite of the unbelief of many.

Verse 4. *God forbid* is the same as saying "by no means." Even if every man in the world should reject the oracles of God, it would not prove them to be untrue, for man cannot be compared with God, who "cannot lie" (Titus 1: 2). Instead, the rejection by man of the oracles of God will prove man to be a liar. Unless this principle is recognized, we would have to conclude that God could not justly condemn those who reject His word. *As it is written* is a citation to Psalms 51: 4.

Verse 5. Paul does not agree with the complaints of men, but uses some of them to show the greatness of God. For instance, the unrighteousness of man emphasizes the righteousness of God by contrast. *I speak as a man* means he was using the arguments of men to show that they were wrong.

Verse 6. Men argued that since the unrighteousness of mankind *commended* or emphasized the righteousness of God, then He should not punish man for his wrongdoing. The apostle is here showing that on that principle God could not rightfully judge the world, although it was admitted (even by these objectors) that a general judgment was necessary.

Verse 7. Paul makes the same point with *lie* and *truth* that he makes with unrighteousness and righteousness in the preceding verse.

Verse 8. *And not* is a contrast with the closing words of the preceding verse. Taken together it means that instead of the liar being judged as a sinner, he should be encouraged to do evil that good might come. Paul had even been accused (slanderously) of teaching such a theory. Then in his own direct language, the apostle says that all such slanderers will be justly condemned.

Verse 9. *We* means the Jews and *they the Gentiles*. After the exposure that Paul just made against unrighteous men, the Jews were disposed to apply it all to the Gentiles. He is denying that and declaring that both Jews and Gentiles are alike under sin.

Verse 10-12. This paragraph describes the character of both Jews and Gentiles as nations and not as individuals. We know that the word *one* does not mean an individual, for that would contradict some facts of sacred history. The scripture plainly teaches that Abel and Job were righteous individuals (Hebrews 11: 4; Job 1: 8), and they were Gentiles. And the righteousness of Daniel and many other individuals of the Jewish nation is too well known to need references. So the paragraph means that there was *not one* nation as a whole that was righteous. That is, neither one of the nations was so righteous that God chose it in preference to the other as the Jews pretended.

Verse 13. Through several verses Paul is describing the evil conduct of many persons in both Jewish and Gentile nations. When a sepulchre is opened, the corruptions in it are manifest. These characters were so bold in their sinful utterances that Paul compares their throats to the sepulchre. Deceitful language is as dangerous as the poison of asps, a very venomous kind of snake.

Verse 14. *Cursing and bitterness* shows their hateful attitude toward others.

Verse 15. *Swift to shed blood* means they are ever ready and anxious to do so.

Verse 16. *In their ways* denotes that the ways of these characters leave such results behind them. They destroy the lives of others, or otherwise make them miserable.

Verse 17. *Not known* in the sense of having a practical knowledge of it. They seek not the peace of others, but prefer to heap trouble upon them.

Verse 18. They have *no fear*, which would mean that they have no respect for God, nor do they act as if they were afraid of His righteous judgments.

Verse 19. The law has jurisdiction over those only who are under it, and that is the Jews. *Every mouth may be stopped.* The mouth of the Jew was stopped in the sense that he had no excuse to make for his sins. All the world (the people of the Jewish nation) was *become guilty* (made subject) to the judgment of God.

Verse 20. *Be justified* is used in the sense of being declared personally meritorious. The very law that requires certain deeds implies the unworthiness of the subject to whom the command is given. Therefore the doing of the deeds of the law only brings the sinner to a state of having done what he was obligated to do, so that he does not deserve any special praise (or justification) for it. The Jew would not have had even any *knowledge of sin* had it not been for the law, therefore the complying with its requirements only gave him credit for having "done that which was his duty to do."

Verse 21. *Righteousness of God without the law* means that system of *God's righteousness* explained at chapter 1: 17. That system was predicted by the Old Testament writers, the very men whose writings the Jews in Rome professed to respect. Yet these Judaizers were speaking as if the righteousness taught in the Gospel was not sufficient, but that both Jew and Gentile should go to the old law for justification.

Verse 22. *Righteousness . . . of Jesus Christ* means the Gospel, the same as set forth in chapter 1: 17. *There is no difference* between Jew and Gentile before the Gospel.

Verse 23. See the comments covering verses 9-12.

Verse 24. *His grace* means the grace of God that was offered the world through Christ. The deeds of man could not save upon their virtue, but the favor made possible by the sacrifice of God's Son brought free justification to all who accepted the terms.

Verse 25. *Propitiation* means something that satisfies a demand made by one person of another, or that was justly due another whether it had been demanded or not. A man might be in debt to another to the amount of one million dollars, which it would be impossible for him to pay. The creditor, having a son who wished to receive the services of a faithful attendant, would agree to consider the debt "settled" if the debtor would become such an attendant. That is what God proposes to man, if he will become a faithful servant of his Son. *Sins that are past* is represented in the illustration by the million dollars for which the debtor had become indebted but could not pay.

Verse 26. *Might be just, and the justifier.* The word *and* is the key to this profound proposition. The justice of God demanded payment of the million dollars, which man was unable to meet. But God cannot be anything but just, for that is a part of His eternal personality. The blood of Christ was offered in payment of that great debt on condition that the debtor believe on this divine blood Donor. By that arrangement it was possible for God to show mercy to the debtor (the sinner), and at the same time retain the eternal attribute of justice.

Verse 27. The works of the law could not pay that huge debt, neither could the regretful poverty of the debtor satisfy his creditor. But the service to the creditor's son satisfied the creditors just as the blood of Christ atones for those who will do or have done what the great Creditor requires. In view of such a plan, neither the doer of the works of the law nor the servant of Christ has anything of which to boast.

Verse 28. Paul now draws his conclusion from the foregoing premises. A man is justified by *faith* (the Gospel of Christ), and not by virtue of the deeds of the law of Moses.

Verse 29. Another conclusion logically following upon the aforesaid truths, is that God is the God of the Gentiles as well as of the Jews. It also explains how He can accept the services of the Gentiles who did not have any benefit of the law.

Verse 30. *Circumcision* and *uncircumcision* means the Jews and the Gentile. The first *faith* does not have the definite article before it, and it denotes the simple act of faith shown by the Jew individually when he performed the rites of the law of Moses. Even those services had to be accompanied with faith or the Jew would not receive the favor of God in that age. (Read the entire 11th chapter of Hebrews, especially verse 6.) The second *faith* is preceded by *the*, which makes it mean the Gospel which is often termed "the faith." And the benefits thus received by both the Jew under the law, and the Gentile under the Gospel, are bestowed by the *one God.*

Verse 31. In this verse the word *faith* is also preceded by the article "the" in the original. Paul is saying that the law was not made void nor disrespected by the *faith* or the Gospel, but rather it is given a high recommendation for being true (is established), because it had predicted the coming in of the Gospel and the new prophet. (See Deuteronomy 18: 18-20.)

ROMANS 4

Verse 1. Paul's question is to introduce his remarks about the works of Abraham and what they meant to him. The Jews not only claimed that God chose them over the Gentiles because of their better qualities, but that they and their law were good enough to be continued in authority for the sake of righteousness before God. That was the reason the Judaizers in Rome (and elsewhere) were so persistent in disturbing the Gentile Christians with their notions. And in defence of their position, they referred to Abraham who was said to be righteous on the ground that he was justified by works (James 2: 21), jumping from the works of the law to those practiced by Abraham centuries before the law.

Verse 2. Abraham did not have to rely on his works to have something of which to glory in God's sight. The Jews were boasting of Abraham's works, for his sake, but there was no need for the patriarch to boast on that ground.

Verse 3. God had already given Abraham the favor of justification for being righteous, on the ground that he believed on Him (Genesis 15: 6). Why, then, should Abraham look to works for justification when God had already counted him righteous without them?

Verse 4. *To him that worketh* means the man who depends on the merits of his works for justification. In that case, if he receives that reward, it will be *reckoned* (considered) on the basis of debt, something actually delivered to him because he had earned it. But that would exclude any credit to the idea of *grace* or favor.

Verse 5. This is just the opposite to the preceding verse.

Verse 6. The principle of receiving favor from the Lord as a gift, and not on the basis of meritorious work, was even taught by David in old time. (Psalms 32: 1, 2.)

Verse 7. If a man's debts are forgiven, that is not the same as actually paying them. (See Matthew 18: 27, 32, 34.) When God forgives a man of his sins, it is not because he has actually paid the debt with meritorious works, for that cannot be done. Instead, it is because the debt has been *covered* by the blood of Christ (chapter 3: 26, 27).

Verse 8. *Not impute sin* means to forgive them. (See the preceding verse.)

Verse 9. *This blessedness* refers to the grace of God bestowed because of *faith* and not on the virtue of works. Paul asks if it was bestowed on the *circumcision* (Jews) only, or on the *uncircumcision* (Gentiles) also. He then cites the fact that such *blessedness* was given to Abraham. The Jew would reply that he had a point in that very case, for Abraham was the first man to be circumcised. The apostle expected that reply, and he met it in the next verse.

Verse 10. Abraham was reckoned righteous while he was uncircumcised, hence the favor could not have been by virtue of circumcision as the Jews claimed.

Verse 11. Circumcision was given to Abraham as a *sign* or *seal* of the righteousness which he already had displayed. An inspector does not put his stamp of approval on an article of food to make it pure, but to indicate that it was already pure. Circumcision did not make Abraham righteous, but it was given to him because he was that kind of man previously. He had been declared righteous 24 years before the rite of circumcision was given him. (See Genesis 12: 4; 15: 6; 17: 24.) This fact has an important bearing on the world in general. By attributing the quality of righteousness to Abraham because of his faith before he even knew anything about circumcision, it would be made possible for others to become the spiritual descendants of the patriarch, even though they were the ones who did not have circumcision, namely, the Gentiles. This great argument of Paul was especially directed against the Jews in Rome, who made more ado over circumcision than over the other requirements of the law.

Verse 12. That would make Abraham the spiritual father (ancestor) of *circumcision* (spiritual, chapter 2: 28, 29), to those who are not of the fleshly circumcision. That refers to the Gentiles who, though not circumcised fleshly, yet imitate the faith that Abraham had before he was circumcised.

Verse 13. To be an *heir* of anything means to receive that possession by allotment or gracious gift. Abraham and *his seed* which means his spiritual descendants by faith, became heirs or possessors of the grace of God's favor. That favor was connected with the promise of Christ who was to bless *the world.* But that favor was not bestowed on the merits of law (of works), but *through the righteousness of faith.*

Verse 14. If the promise made to Abraham and his seed was to be fulfilled by the works of the law, then the *faith* (the Gospel) would be made of no avail.

Verse 15. Transgression means going beyond a law, therefore where there is no law there could be no transgression, though there could be other forms of sin.

Verse 16. The words *it is* are not in the original as separate words. The thought of the verse is that the favor of God is the most important subject and the thing that should be the most desired. That is why the divine plan was to bestow such a favor on the basis of grace to the faithful of all nations, not only to the adherents of the law.

Verse 17. Such a grand scheme opened up the way for all to become the spiritual descendants of Abraham, who was set forth as a model of righteousness by faith long before there was any law of Moses. That also made it possible for him to have the promise of being the *father of many nations,* which would include both Gentiles and Jews. *Things which be not as though they were* refers to the apparent impossibility for Abraham to be a father at all when the promise was made.

Verse 18. *Against hope believed in hope* means the same as the last clause in the preceding verse, concerning the improbability of Abraham's parenthood.

Verse 19. This verse comes down to the time when the son of promise was soon to be born. Such a son had been promised a number of times, but the exact time of it had not been set. When Abraham was 99 years old God set the time for the birth of this son (Genesis 17: 1, 21). *Own body now dead* is figurative as Abraham was of such advanced age. *Deadness of Sarah's womb* is literal as far as reproduction function is concerned. She was barren to begin with (Genesis 11: 30), and she also had passed the childbearing period (Genesis 18: 11). In spite of all these natural impediments, Abraham believed that God was able to give him and his wife a son who would be the joint offspring of their bodies, by overcoming the defects that nature had placed in the way.

Verse 20. *Staggered not* denotes that he did not waver in the least in his faith concerning the promise of God, but he was firm and absolute in that faith.

Verse 21. Such a faith not only means that God is able to perform what he had promised, but that He would not have promised it had he not known he could do it.

Verse 22. *Imputed to him* denotes that he was considered as a righteous man.

Verse 23. Abraham would have rejoiced at the simple assurance that he was considered righteous, but the fact was written also for the sake of others besides himself.

Verse 24. It was written as an encouragement for *us* (all people of our day, whether Jew or Gentile), to the intent that we believe on God who raised up his Son, the great Seed that was promised to Abraham.

Verse 25. *Was delivered* refers to Jesus being turned over into the hands of his enemies, to be slain because of the offences of the world, that by his sacrifice they might be atoned for. Had Jesus not been raised from the dead, he could not have perfected that system of faith by which man could be justified before God.

ROMANS 5

Verse 1. The principle of individual faith has been required from the days of Abel on down (Hebrews 11: 4, 6), therefore the word in this verse means "the faith" or the Gospel of Christ. That brings to us justification through Jesus Christ and not the law of Moses. The reader should constantly keep in mind that the predominating thought

of the book of Romans, is the virtue of faith in Christ as against the works of the law, which the Judaizers were urging upon Christians, and which was causing much confusion especially among those of the Gentile nation.

Verse 2. *By whom* means by Christ, and *this grace* means the favor of justification before God. Such justification could not have been obtained by virtue of the works of the law, therefore *we* (Christians) stand and rejoice in the hope of partaking of the glory of God. Of course that glory is to come at the end of the world (Colossians 3: 4).

Verse 3. Since the glory is to be received in the future, we welcome the experience of tribulations. It is not the pleasure of tribulations in which we glory, but it is the good fruit of patience produced thereby.

Verse 4. Patience results in experience, because it can come only by persistent practice, and we would not do that if we were not patient. All of this results in hope, because, having adhered to a course of righteousness in spite of tribulations, we have reason to look for final victory.

Verse 5. The hope we have of a life with Christ when this present period of tribulation is over, keeps us from being ashamed of that which we have endured for His sake (Acts 5: 41). The Holy Ghost (or Spirit) was given to the early Christians in miraculous measure (Acts 2: 38; 8: 14-18). After the complete New Testament was produced, the Spirit dwelled in the church which is the "temple of God" (1 Corinthians 3: 16, 17). However, this indwelling is not in miraculous measure, because that form of it was to cease after the complete rule of faith in Christ was given (Ephesians 4: 8-16).

Verse 6. *Without strength* means we were powerless to save ourselves, or to devise any system by which mankind could be saved. Of necessity, then, we were ungodly as to our spiritual standing, and hence when Christ died his death was *for the ungodly.*

Verse 7. For all practical purposes the words *righteous* and *good* mean the same, and they are generally so used in the New Testament. But when used in distinction from each other, the first means a man who does what is right because the law under which he is living requires it. The second means a man who is naturally of an agreeable disposition so that "everybody likes him," although he may not be living in obedience to any laws. There are people who would die for such a person if the circumstances called for it.

Verse 8. God and Christ went beyond all these conditions and showed their love for us while we were sinners—neither righteous nor good—by having Christ to die for our sins.

Verse 9. *Justified by his blood* is explained at chapter 3: 25, 26. Through such a complete satisfaction offered by the blood of Christ, the wrath of God against sin will be turned away from us.

Verse 10. Jesus found us in sin and reconciled us to his Father through his blood, which denotes that He put us into the position of praying terms with God. In that relation with God, we could "work out our salvation" by following the example that Jesus set by his own life.

Verse 11. There is a considerable amount of repetition of thought in several verses. Reconciliation is the same as *atonement*, and Paul adds it for the sake of emphasis.

Verse 12. *The one man* by whom sin entered into the world was Adam. He is the only one who is regarded as a personal sinner in this verse. However, it was his sin that caused the separation from the tree of life with its consequent death of the body for all his descendants, we must regard the phrase *all have sinned* as meaning only that all human beings regardless of age or mental or moral qualification, are physical partakers of the results of Adam's sin. We know it cannot mean that infants were thereby forced to become sinners as to their character, for they are represented by Jesus as already possessing the character that adults are required to develop before they can enter the kingdom of heaven (Matthew 18: 3).

Verse 13. *Sin* in this verse is in the ordinary sense, pertaining to the personal conduct of human beings. Adam introduced the knowledge of it, but a person must be old enough to possess knowledge before he can actually perform it responsibly. *Not imputed* means it is not taken into account, and the particular form of sin meant in this verse is that which is the transgression of law. (See the comments on this at chapter 4: 15.) In view of this, before there was any law given, men could not be counted as sinners by transgression since there was no law to transgress.

Verse 14. It might be (erroneously) concluded from the foregoing, that since men were not adjudged as sinners before the law was given, therefore nobody died before that. Yet the apostle affirms that death did reign through all that period, even over those who had not sinned after the *simili-tude*—after the manner—of Adam's transgression. This shows that sin in this verse as applied to all mankind is used in the same sense as it is in verse 12. That is, they had to suffer the physical death that resulted from Adam's sin, because it caused them to be born outside the garden of Eden and away from the tree of life. The last clause, *who is the figure of him that was to come*, is introduced to prepare the reader for the comparison a little later on, that deals with the principle of sharing in the *results* of one man's righteousness in the same sense as sharing in the *results* of one man's sin.

Verse 15. An illustration may be used either by comparison or contrast, or by both, and the present one is used in the last sense. The comparison is in the fact that all mankind will have to partake of the physical results of Adam's sin which means death of the body. Likewise, all will partake of the physical resurrection from death as a result of the resurrection of Christ. The contrast is in the fact that the *grace of God*, which means justification from personal sin, is offered to all mankind through Christ, in addition to the resurrection of the body.

Verse 16. This verse means virtually the same as the preceding one, but expressed in slightly different language.

Verse 17. The comparison and contrast are again repeated. The phrase *much more* denotes that the opportunity to receive *abundance of grace* is of more value than the mere resurrection of the body which also will be effected through that of Christ.

Verse 18. This is virtually the same in thought as the preceding verses, but the subject is so vital to the happiness of mankind, that the apostle regarded the repetition of it as necessary. *Offence of one* refers to the sin of Adam, and the *condemnation* means the physical death that resulted upon all mankind. *Even so* again includes both the resurrection of the body, and also the *justification of life*, which means the offer of forgiveness of personal sins to all who will accept it on the Lord's terms.

Verse 19. *Many were made sinners* is explained at verse 12. *Obedience of one* refers to the great deed of Christ in providing a sacrifice that could cleanse all from sin who would avail themselves of it by their own individual obedience.

Verse 20. The word *law* does not have the definite article before it in the original, so it is used with reference to law in general. That is, man has always had some form of law by which he could live and then be judged. With the Gentile it was the law of conscience and nature (chapter 1: 19, 20; 2: 14, 15), and with the Jew it was the law of Moses. *Offence might abound* denotes that no man was with "excuse" for his sins, since he had a law that taught him to do better. This condition of responsibility made it all the more necessary for the grace or favor of God to be used so that sin could be atoned for.

Verse 21. This verse is the grand conclusion of Paul's argument. The sin of Adam brought physical death upon all mankind, and bringing in a law of conduct brought spiritual death upon all who failed to obey that law. Then the great work of Christ brought physical life to all mankind unconditionally, and spiritual life to all who avail themselves of the "unspeakable gift" of this human-divine sacrifice of the Son of God.

ROMANS 6

Verse 1. Paul was a master in logic, and he refuted beforehand an erroneous conclusion that some would draw from what he had said. They would argue that if there was more grace where more sin abounded, then it would be well to sin so as to bring that grace.

Verse 2. Even without the statement of the apostle, we can see that such was false reasoning. It would be like arguing that, since doctors have more opportunity for doing the good deed of curing the sick wherever there is more sickness, therefore let us do something to cause more sickness. *God forbid* is Paul's ways of saying "by no means," and he then shows the logical objection to the reasoning. Christians claim to have died to sin by repentance, which would preclude the living in or practicing sin.

Verse 3. Death means separation regardless of when or how the word is used. The body and spirit of Christ were separated at his death, and it was done for the sins of man. He died *for* sin, but in order for it to benefit a man, he likewise must die—must die *to* sin, which means that he is to be separated from the practice of sin by repentance. In order for this figurative death of a man to be benefited by the literal death of Christ, it is necessary for him to get into that death. Divine wisdom has decreed that such an experience is to be accomplished by baptism.

Verse 4. This verse incidentally shows how baptism is performed—by a burial and rising—but it was not written for that purpose. In truth, no passage was written to show the form or "mode" of baptism, for the word itself shows that. Whenever a person goes to quibbling about the "mode" of baptism, he is not ready for the ordinance anyway. What he needs but lacks is a sincere belief in Jesus Christ. It is not an arbitrary declaration that baptism is necessary for the new life with Christ. The principle has already been shown in the preceding verse that it is in baptism that we get into the death of Christ. Well, all people should know that Jesus was dead when he shed his blood (John 19: 33, 34), and it is his blood that saves, therefore a man has to be baptized in order to come in contact with the blood. The comparison of death and burial is continued. When Christ came from the grave alive, he was never to die again (verse 9); likewise, when a man has died to sin and has been buried with Christ in baptism, he is thereby made alive spiritually, and when he comes out of that watery grave, he too is expected to live a new life in Christ, and not again become dead in sins.

Verse 5. The word *planted* means to be united with, and likeness denotes only a comparison. Sinners who die to sin and are baptized, will be in spiritual likeness to Him.

Verse 6. *Old man* is a figurative name for our life of sin. To *crucify* figuratively means to have the life of sin put to death as regards general practice.

Verses 7, 8. *He that is dead* to sin by repentance is freed from the bondage of sin, and becomes alive through Christ with whom he has been buried by baptism.

Verses 9, 10. Christ arose never to die again, and likewise it is expected that sinners who die to sin and are buried with Christ, will follow a life of righteousness.

Verse 11. The *death* and *life* of this verse both have a spiritual sense.

Verse 12. All Christians will make mistakes and sin incidentally (1 John 1: 8), but that is not the same as to permit sin to *reign* in the body.

Verse 13. *Yield ye your members* denotes to consent or give one's body over to a life of unrighteousness, and not sinning incidentally according to 1 John 1: 8.

Verse 14. For sin to have dominion over us is equivalent to making a practice of sinning. *Under grace* means that the New Testament system is one made possible by merciful favor of God, so that one's mistakes are atoned for constantly by the blood stream of Christ. (See 1 John 1: 7; 2: 1.)

Verse 15. This is the same in thought as that set forth in verse 1.

Verse 16. Again the key to the passage is *yield yourselves*, which means a deliberate surrender to some ruler, and not the incidental event of sin due to weakness.

Verse 17. *God be thanked* cannot be understood until the entire verse is considered. That will show that the rescue from a sinful service is the fact for which Paul thanked God. *Form* is from TUPOS and one of Thayer's definitions is, "A pattern in conformity to which a thing must be made." The "pattern" is the example that Jesus set when he died for sin, then was raised from the grave to die no more. The sinner must die to sin, be buried with Christ by baptism, then arise to walk in a new life.

Verse 18. This is the same in thought as verse 11.

Verse 19. *After the manner of men* is all from one Greek word, and means that Paul uses human language because he is speaking to human beings. *Infirmity* is explained by Thayer to mean inability to understand another language due to the frailty of the flesh. Had Paul used the "tongue of angels" man could not have grasped its meaning. Therefore, their natural reasoning would show them that when they formerly yielded themselves servants of uncleanness, the result of it was *iniquity*. So now, by yielding themselves to righteousness, the result will be holiness.

Verse 20. This means that a man cannot be a servant of sin and still be a servant of righteousness; that would be like serving two masters. (See Matthew 6: 24.)

Verse 21. What *fruit* does not imply they had no fruit, but it asks, "what kind of fruit was it," and then Paul answers it by saying, *the end* [fruit] . . . *is death.*

Verse 22. Verses 17, 18 tell when one is made free from sin and hence when he begins to bear holy fruit. The final reward for such sowing and reaping is *everlasting life.*

Verse 23. *Wages* is from OPSONION which Thayer defines, "a soldier's pay, allowance." It denotes, therefore, that a life devoted to the service of sin will earn or merit the wages of *death.* Not physical death, for all have to go through that, but the second death, designated in Revelation 21: 8. *Eternal life* is a gift, because it is impossible for any man to earn such a treasure by his own service.

ROMANS 7

Verse 1. The fact that his brethren understood the working principles of law as it pertained to marriage, prompted Paul to draw comparison between Christ and Moses.

Verse 2. A woman cannot be lawfully bound to more than one man at a time, neither can a person be subject to more than one religious law at the same time.

Verse 3. Jesus taught in Matthew 19: 9 that fornication of a married person is the only lawful ground for the remarriage of the innocent one. Such a sin virtually causes the guilty one to be *dead* to the other. *Adulteress* is used by some to support the notion of "living in adultery," something the Bible does not teach, since the single act of adultery unites the two permanently. (See the comments at Matthew 19: 9.) The word italicized is defined by Thayer as a person with "eyes from which adulterous desire beams forth." It means a frame of mind rather than any physical performance.

Verse 4. As physical death breaks the union of persons in marriage, so when Jewish penitent believers died with Christ, that broke the bond between them and the law of Moses. Being free from the law they could become married to Christ, and the offspring of such a union would be *fruit unto God.*

Verses 5, 6. The outstanding difference between the law of Moses and that of Christ, is that the former was ritualistic and its penalty was physical death in extreme cases. The latter is spiritual in its character, and makes provision for the weakness of the human fleshly nature through the grace of God.

Verse 7. The foregoing does not blame the law for the existence of sin; it only revealed it and thus made man responsible. But it could not clear man of guilt by its virtue, hence it was necessary for the law of Christ to come in, to accomplish that which "the law could not do" (chapter 8: 3).

Verse 8. The purpose of this verse is to defend the law against unjust criticism. The revelation of sin by the law seemed to increase it, whereas it was the carnal disposition of man to crave that which he was forbidden to have, that brought about the apparent increase of sin.

Verse 9. *I was alive.* Paul is speaking of humanity in general. While man was ignorant of his sin he was not responsible for it—it was not imputed (chapter 5: 13). As sin was dead at that time, it follows that the conscience was alive—was free from the sting of guilt. The law brought sin to life and then man became "dead in sin."

Verse 10. The commandment that would bring spiritual life to the man if he obeyed it, would result in death "in trespass and sins," until he repented.

Verse 11. This is virtually the same as verse 9.

Verse 12. See the comments on verse 10.

Verse 13. The law (which would mean good to man if he obeyed it), was not responsible for the spiritual death of the human being. No, the law only revealed the existence of sin and decreed a penalty. It was the sin itself, springing into life or action, that brought on the condition of spiritual death. The law served to show how *exceeding sinful* such a life is.

Verse 14. This is explained at verse 10.

Verses 15-21. In the foregoing verses of this chapter, Paul has said much of the carnal or fleshly part of man's personality. He has shown that its tendencies were responsible for the difficulties with the law of Moses, which was not adapted to the needs of man on its own merits, therefore leaving it necessary to bring in the spiritual law of Christ. The remainder of the chapter is devoted to a description of these two parts of man's being, which I shall refer to by the terms, "inner man" and "outer man." I shall quote the verses of this paragraph, substituting these terms for the pronouns, and making such other changes as the grammatical rules require.

"For that which the outer man does, the inner man allows [endorses] not. For what the inner man would, the outer man does not. What the inner man hates, that does the outer man. If then the outer man does that which the inner man would not, the inner man consents unto the law [against sin] that it is good. Now then it is no more the inner man that does it, but sin that dwells in the outer man. For the inner man knows that in the flesh dwells no good thing. For to will is present with the inner man, but how to perform that which is good the outer man will not do; but the evil which the inner man would not do, the outer man does. Now if the outer man does what the inner man would not, it is no more the inner man that does it, but sin that dwells in the outer man. The inner man finds a law, that, when he would do good, evil is present with the outer man." The reader should understand that both parts of a man are not operating at the same time. The paragraph shows only the tendencies of each, and whichever is in the lead at any given time, will determine whether the person is a servant of Christ or Satan.

Verse 22. This is direct proof of the foregoing description of the "inner man."

Verse 23. This verse should be understood in the light of the paragraph of verses 15-21. *Members* means all the parts that go to make up a human being. The conflict between the fleshly law (rule) of sin and that of the mind or spirit or better part of said being, is the subject of this verse.

Verse 24. Roman convicts were sometimes chained to a dead body as a means of punishment. Paul likens the carnal man whose tendencies lead to spiritual death, to the dead body thus chained to the inner man. Only the proper officer can release a convict from the chain, and Paul asks who can release one from the control of the fleshly man.

Verse 25. Paul answers his question by saying it is Christ who can give the sinner such release, for which he thanks God. The chapter closes with the proposition running through several verses, namely, the conflict between the mind and the flesh.

ROMANS 8

Verse 1. *No condemnation* refers to the deliverance from the dead body in chapter 7: 24. However, to continue in the freedom, one must continue to walk according to the inclinations of the "inner man," instructed and guided by the law of the Spirit.

Verse 2. *Law of the Spirit* is the Gospel, and it is called *of life* because it will guide one into a spiritual life in this world, and prepare him for eternal life in the next. *Sin and death* is explained at chapter 7: 5, 6.

Verse 3. The law was not adapted to meet (through its own merits) the needs of fleshly weakness. Jesus came in the flesh, the same kind of body that sinful men have. While in that body He condemned sin by living free from it, then offering that body as a sacrifice for sin.

Verse 4. *Righteousness of the law* means that required by it, but unattained on account of the weakness of the flesh as explained in the preceding verse.

Verse 5. See the paragraph of verses 15-21, of chapter 7.

Verse 6. *Carnally minded* denotes a yearning for fleshly pleasure.

Verses 7, 8. See paragraph of chapter 7: 5, 6.

Verse 9. *Not in the flesh* is explained at verse 1. *Spirit of Christ* is equivalent to "Christ be in you" in the following verse.

Verse 10. *The body* means the "old man" of chapter 6: 6. It died to sin by repentance, and the *spirit* (inner man) came to life through the righteousness of Christ.

Verse 11. The good and bad will all be raised through Christ, but the good only will be raised to life everlasting. (See John 11: 26; 1 Corinthians 15: 49-53.)

Verse 12. *Are debtors.* Are obligated, but not to the flesh to live after it.

Verse 13. This is the same as verse 6.

Verse 14. The Spirit of God operates through the Gospel (John 14: 16, 17). Being willing to be led by that instruction shows one to have been begotten of God.

Verse 15. This verse makes a comparison of the difference between a servant and an heir. (See Galatians 4: 1-7.) These Jewish Christians had been made free from the law through Christ, which entitled them to recognize God as their Father.

Verse 16. *Beareth witness with* all comes from one Greek word, SUMMARTUREO, which Thayer defines, "To bear witness with, bear joint witness." Hence the phrase does not indicate any communication between these two witnesses, but that each one gives the same testimony on the subject, namely, that the persons are children of God. That is, the Spirit states through the Gospel what it takes to make one a child of God, and the spirit (mind) of a man knows whether he has done that. If he has, the conclusion is that he is a child of God.

Verse 17. This relationship makes one an heir of God, since only his children can inherit the divine riches. Such a man is a joint-heir with Christ in that He too is the Son of God. *If so be* is virtually the same proviso mentioned in verse 1.

Verse 18. Following Christ includes suffering persecutions with him if need be. Such sufferings are nothing in comparison with the glorious reward to be received.

Verse 19. *The creature* signifies human beings in general. Every man (though some unconsciously) wants something better than he is enjoying in his frail, decaying body. Paul calls the state that is thus yearned for the *manifestation of the sons of God,* and that is the same as *the redemption of our body* in verse 23.

Verse 20. *Vanity* is from MATAIOTES which Thayer defines in this place, "Frailty, want of vigor." It means the human creature was made subject to decay of the body, and that took place when he was driven from the tree of life. *Not willingly.* No, he had to be driven out (Genesis 3: 24). *Him* means God, who subjected man to an existence that would end in death of the body, but at the same time gave him hope of a deathless body in another world. (See verse 23.)

Verse 21. The promise in this verse is for those only who are faithful *children of* God. The corruption and incorruption are explained by 1 Corinthians 15: 52-54.

Verse 22. This is the same as verse 19.

Verse 23. *Not only they* means not only the human family in general. *Firstfruits* of the Spirit means the indwelling of the Holy Spirit that is the possession of all who come into the body of Christ. (See the comments on Acts 5: 32.) To *groan* means to sigh or earnestly to long for the *redemption of the body*, which means the resurrection.

Verses 24, 25. *Saved by hope* denotes that our hope for everlasting life prompts us to persevere in the kind of conduct that is necessary to receive everlasting life.

Verse 26. A safe rule is to let one passage help us understand another, when both are on the same subject, and one seems more difficult than the other. A companion passage for our present one is Ephesians 3: 20, which the reader should see at once. We know that no communication is given to man today on spiritual matters except what can be read in the Bible. Therefore, that which the Spirit does for Christians is a part of the plan of God and Christ for taking care of the Christians' prayers. The Spirit (which can read our minds) forms our prayers as to the wording, so that they are in presentable form to offer before the throne, doing it with *groanings* (sighing) which *cannot be uttered* (by us).

Verse 27. This verse verifies the comments on the preceding one. *He* means the Lord, who not only can read the mind of the saints (Christians), but also knows the mind of the Spirit, since he is the third member of the Godhead, and is subject to the Father and the Son. Therefore, when the Spirit presents the intercessions of the saints to the throne, in groanings that man cannot utter, that form of the prayer virtually becomes the petition of the Christian, addressed to God through Christ who is the official or authoritative Advocate.

Verse 28. This verse does not teach "special providence" as some believe. It means that if a man loves the Lord, he will make "stepping-stones" out of his "stumbling-stones." He will so work on the conditions of life (even his sufferings, verse 18), that they will assure him the *good* reward that God has promised to the faithful. *The called* refers to the men and women who have heard and accepted the call through the Gospel to serve the Lord. The final reward for such service will be to receive a body that can never die, fashioned after that of Christ (Philippians 3: 21); and as an evidence that God can do such a marvelous work, He decreed to bestow that very favor on some of the saints before the general resurrection, which is the subject of verses 29, 30.

Verses 29, 30. Of course the Lord will not grant the glorious resurrection to any but faithful saints, hence Paul begins his account of this particular group with the event of their entrance into His service. That was when they were *called* by the law in force in their day. Those who accepted the call were justified or made free from their past sins. It was required, also, that these persons be faithful till death, which would constitute them "saints that slept." God never predestinates any certain person as to his character, but He did predetermine what kind of conduct would receive certain favors. The Lord foresaw some who were going to develop such a character, and among them He predestinated a group to come out of their graves to die no more, giving them the same form or bodily image that the Son received, so that he (the Son) could be the *firstborn* (from the grave to die no more) *among* many brethren. To be *among* them would mean to be associated with them in the same event. Hence we read (Matthew 27: 52, 53) about these saints that arose after the resurrection of Jesus. They are the *glorified* ones of verse 30 here, who were given bodies to die no more. As such, they would not remain on earth, hence when Jesus ascended to Heaven he took them with him. This is what Paul means in Ephesians 4: 8 where he says Christ "led captivity captive." (Marginal, "led a multitude of captives.") These had been captives in the unseen state, but were now made free forever and taken along with their Lord in a *glorified* state. When Jesus comes again he will bring them back with him to witness the execution of judgment upon the ungodly (Jude 14, 15).

Verse 31. If God can thus give glorified life to thousands of his saints so long before the general resurrection, He certainly can do the same for all others who will be faithful until death. No wonder the apostle said as to these things that since God is for us, *no one can be against us.*

Verse 32. Paul reasons that God will freely give us all these things, since He did not spare his Son to make the provision on our behalf, who also led the way by being faithful to God, and then going triumphant through the unseen world.

Verse 33. *God's elect* means those who are chosen of God, and such are the ones who obey God's law. It also means those whom God *justifieth* or declares freed from sin. What reason, then, would anyone have to charge anything to such persons?

Verse 34. This question is similar to the one in the preceding verse. Since Christ died for these chosen ones, and took his place by the Father's right hand after his resurrection, He will intercede for them when enemies condemn them.

Verse 35. This question implies a similar answer to the foregoing. When Christ loves us, these hardships cannot separate us from Him.

Verse 36. *Killed all the day long* denotes that the Lord's disciples were threatened with death constantly, as if they were fit only for slaughter.

Verse 37. *More than conquerors* is defined in the lexicon as, "a surpassing victory." A man might win in a physical combat with another athlete, which would be a simple victory only. But if it was a struggle to repossess a treasure that the other contestant had taken from him, the success would be more than a simple victory. Our combat with Satan is to redeem our soul which he had caused to be endangered.

Verses 38, 39. Note that none of these things can rob us of the love of God. But that does not say that we ourselves could not forfeit it by becoming unfaithful to Him.

ROMANS 9

Verses 1, 2. See the comments at Acts 24: 16 for the meaning of *conscience*. *Witness in the Holy Ghost* means his conscience had the testimony of the Holy Ghost (or Spirit), recorded in the scripture. The *great heaviness* refers to his great concern.

Verse 3. Paul had said so much in criticism of his Jewish brethren that some might think it was prompted by a personal grudge against them. To offset such an impression, he refers to evidences of the past that showed his personal love for them. *I could wish* is all from EUCHOMAI. The Englishman's Greek New Testament translates

it, "I was wishing," thus putting it in the past tense as it should be. It is just another expression in Paul's effort to show his Jewish kinsmen how devoted he had been to their interests. (See the comments on the preceding paragraph, also the passage in Acts 26: 9, 10.) *Accursed* means to be separated from Christ—having nothing to do with him except to oppose him as shown in the passage cited in Acts.

Verse 4. This is virtually the same as chapter 3: 1, 2.

Verse 5. *Whose are the fathers* means the Israelites descended from the fathers, Abraham, Isaac and Jacob. Christ came from them as regards his fleshly ancestry.

Verse 6. *Word . . . taken none effect* is explained at chapter 3: 3. *Not all Israel . . . of Israel.* There are two Israels being considered, the fleshly and the spiritual.

Verse 7. Not all of Abraham's descendants were *children* or in the line coming down to Christ; only those who descended from Abraham through Isaac.

Verse 8. *Flesh* and *promise* refers to Ishmael and Isaac. The regular law of fleshly reproduction was all that was necessary to produce Ishmael (Genesis 16: 1-3). But Sarah was barren and a miracle was needed to produce Isaac, which God *promised* to do for her.

Verse 9. *At this time.* God worked a miracle to enable Sarah to conceive, then let nature go through the usual *time* of expectancy for the forming of the child.

Verse 10. We learned at chapter 3: 9-18 that God did not choose any particular nation because of its personal goodness, for all were corrupt as nations. His choice, then, was solely because He so willed it, as he certainly had the right to do. Paul is making the same argument in several verses, beginning with our present one.

Verse 11. As an illustration of God's practice of making official selections regardless of personal merit, Paul cites the case of the twin brothers where God made the choice before they were born and before they could have done anything, good or evil.

Verse 12. *Elder* and *younger* are changed to "greater" and "lesser" in the margin. That is proper, for while Esau was elder in the order of their births and thus of *greater* age, yet God decreed that he and his descendants should give place to Jacob in His plans.

Verse 13. The original word for *hated* is defined by Thayer in this place, "to love less," hence it does not mean a feeling against Esau as if He detested him.

Verse 14. Since no personal injury was done to Esau by this choice, there was no unrighteousness on the part of God in making this official selection.

Verse 15. The *mercy* and *compassion* of this verse does not refer to the personal treatment of the individuals, but to selecting them for national or official purposes.

Verse 16. The selection is not left to the person to do his own choosing, since it was not for personal advantage, but to God whose will is supreme.

Verse 17. In some cases the selection did result in the personal welfare or fate of the one selected, and then God selected one who was already fitted by character for the place. Pharaoh was brought to the throne of Egypt by the Lord at the right time to go through the humiliating experiences related in Exodus, but he was a wicked character to begin with (Exodus 1: 8), so the experience did him no injustice.

Verse 18. Verses 15 and 17 should be considered with this one.

Verses 19, 20. To criticize God for using his divine right of choice would be like a vessel complaining against the one who formed it. It would be similar to the foolish argument about deliberately sinning in chapter 6: 1, 15.

Verse 21. A potter is the one to decide what kind of vessel is to be made out of a lump of clay. The facts that determine it are such as the case of Pharaoh.

Verses 22, 23. A potter might delay his decision about a vessel, when an onlooker would think it very clear as to which vessel deserved to be retained and which discarded. Yet he would not know the mind of the potter, neither would it be his affair.

Verse 24. The apparent unwise action of the potter in the preceding paragraph refers to the Jews and Gentiles. Each of these nations thought the other should have been discarded as an undesirable vessel. (See the comments at chapter 3: 9-12.)

Verses 25, 26. *Osee* means Hosea, and it is a prediction that the Gentiles

were to become God's people, even though the Jews thought them unworthy of it.

Verse 27. *Esaias* is Isaiah, whose prophecy was concerning the Jews also. But this prediction was not so complimentary for this nation, although it was the vessel at first selected by the Potter. Notwithstanding its number was as the sand of the sea, a remnant only was to be salvaged because of unbelief of the majority.

Verse 28. The first application of this verse as well as the preceding one, is that only a remnant of the Jewish nation was to return from the Babylonian captivity. The context of the passage cited in Isaiah 10: 22, 23 shows clearly that such is the meaning. Then later the nation was reduced still more by the wars with the Romans.

Verse 29. *Lord of Sabaoth* means Lord of hosts. *Left us a seed* applies to the *remnant* of verse 27, and to the "elect" for whose sake the days of the siege of Jerusalem were to be shortened according to Matthew 24: 22. The reference to Sodoma and Gomorrha is to show how complete the destruction of Israel would have been had it not been for the mercy of God.

Verse 30, 31. *Followed not after righteousness.* The Gentiles were not under the law of Moses and did not profess to follow the life of righteousness. The Gentiles were not under the law of Moses and did not profess to follow the life of righteousness that it prescribed. Yet when the righteousness set forth by *faith* (the Gospel) was offered to them, they were more ready to accept it than was Israel. (Chapter 8: 4 and Acts 13: 42, 46.)

Verse 32. Paul explains that the failure of the Jews came because they did not seek to attain to righteousness by *faith* (the Gospel). Instead, while professing to accept the preaching of the apostles, they insisted on clinging to the merits of the works of the law. The apostle gives an additional explanation of their failure which is in the fact that they *stumbled at that stumbling-stone.*

Verse 33. The stumbling of the people of Israel had been predicted, and Paul cites it which is in Isaiah 8: 14; 28: 16. It is also in Psalms 118: 22 and 1 Peter 2: 6-8. The Jews' prejudice against Christ caused them to reject His system of righteousness.

ROMANS 10

Verse 1. Paul's personal interest in his Jewish kinsmen is still one of his main concerns. (See the comments at chapter 9: 3.) His wish *that they might be saved* proves they were in an unsaved state at that time.

Verse 2. The apostle freely gave them credit for what was commendable, but also disapproved of all that was wrong about them. A prominent phrase in Thayer's definition of the original word for *zeal* is, "ardor in embracing." Israel was not sluggish in religious activities on behalf of God. *Knowledge* is from EPIGNOSIS, and Thayer defines it at this place, "Precise and correct knowledge." The Jews displayed a heated interest in their form of righteousness, without bothering to learn if it was the correct one.

Verse 3. *God's righteousness* is that performed "through the faith of Christ," and *own righteousness* is that "which is of the law" (Philippians 3: 9). Their lack of knowledge mentioned in the preceding verse, is here specified to consist of their being *ignorant of God's righteousness*.

Verse 4. *Righteousness* is from DIKAIOSUNE, and the part of Thayer's definition that is needed here is, "The state acceptable to God which becomes a sinner's possession." This definition shows the word to have a religious sense, meaning the kind of life necessary to salvation. Christ put an end to the law for that purpose, but He did not intend to interfere with the observance of its institutions as national customs. That is why Paul, though a Christian, did the things recorded in Acts 16: 3; 18: 21. See also the comments at Acts 21: 20-26. But none except Jews have the right to any of these things, even as customs (Galatians 2: 21; 5: 1-4).

Verse 5. All who served God acceptably, from Abel onward, were required to do their performances with faith. But the New Testament system is the only one that is designated as one of faith. In contrast with this, the Mosaic system was one of works, the predominating idea being that the "doing" of the works was what was acceptable to God.

Verse 6. *Righteousness which is of faith* still means the Gospel system. Paul quotes from Deuteronomy 30: 11-13, but adds some words to make it apply to the law of Christ, whose active principle is faith; "take God at his word," without demanding why or how the divine truths and facts were accomplished. On this basis, one should not be concerned about "who" or "how" it was that Christ came down from above.

Verse 7. And by the same rule as the preceding verse, we need not be concerned about the "hows" of the death, burial and resurrection of Christ. *Deep* is from ABUSSOS, and Thayer's definition of it is, "Bottomless, unbounded, the abyss." He then explains it to mean, "the common receptacle of the dead."

Verse 8. Our concern is not so far away as the foregoing inquiries would indicate, for all necessary information is nigh at hand in the divine Word.

Verse 9. The simple belief that the resurrection took place, and the confession on our part of such a belief, is sufficient to bring salvation within reach as far as what we must believe is concerned.

Verse 10. The *heart* is the mind and it must accept the divine testimony that Christ arose from the dead, then the believer must make a confession of this belief. Paul does not say that this belief and confession *alone* will bring one into a saved state. But they are a part of the terms that pertain to the "righteousness" discussed above, which leads one *unto* or in the direction of salvation. Other items will logically follow if this belief is "from the heart" (chapter 6: 17).

Verse 11. *Not be ashamed* means "not be disappointed." The emphasis should be on the word *whosoever*, in view of the self-importance felt by the Jews.

Verse 12. This verse shows why "whosoever" in the preceding one is emphasized. The Jews thought they occupied a place of superiority in the Lord's sight.

Verse 13. See Acts 22: 16 for the practical meaning of "calling on the name of the Lord." It denotes more than merely pronouncing the holy name.

Verse 14. If believing in the Lord is necessary to calling on him, it explains the comments in the preceding verse. Even unbelievers can say "Lord, Lord," but to no avail. Faith is not an emotion miraculously produced, but is the effect of something heard. Also, before the New Testament was written, someone had to preach the word so that the sinner could hear it. (See 1 Corinthians 1: 21 and Titus 1: 3.)

Verse 15. *Except they be sent* also pertains especially to the time before the New Testament was written. The original for the last italicized word is APOSTELLO, and Thayer's first definition is, "To order one to go to a place appointed." That is why Christ "ordered" his apostles to "go" as recorded in Matthew 28: 19, 20, but told them to tarry in Jerusalem until they were "endued with power from on high" (Luke 24: 49). That was because they would not know what to preach without this "power," since the New Testament had not been written. This great work of the apostles was predicted in Isaiah 52: 7. *Beautiful are the feet* means their footsteps are beautiful because they bring the promise of peace and other good things.

Verse 16. This is similar in thought to chapter 3: 3.

Verse 17. This verse clearly shows that faith does not come to a sinner as a direct gift from God. It can be produced only by hearing the word of God. That accounts for the items set forth in verse 14, 15.

Verse 18. The pronoun *their* refers to the *preachers* of verses 14, 15, who were the inspired apostles. Paul affirms that their word had at that time gone *unto the ends of the world*. This same fact is declared in Colossians 1: 23. Therefore, when a man applies the "Great Commission" to preachers of today he is perverting the scripture.

Verse 19. *Did not Israel know* that the Gospel was to be preached throughout the world, to both Gentile and Jew? They did not, but they should have known had they "considered" (Isaiah 1: 3), for their own lawgiver Moses prophesied it in Deuteronomy 32: 21. Had the Jews "considered" it, they would have realized that *no people* and *foolish nation* meant the Gentiles.

Verse 20. *Very bold* means his language is very strong, sounding almost like a disagreement, such as a man finding something that he was not looking for. This, of course, has the same meaning as chapter 9: 30.

Verse 21. Here is a contrast to the foregoing. The Gentiles were not seeking God through any system of religion, yet they were offered one which they gladly accepted. Israel was constantly exhorted to hear and obey, yet they stubbornly disobeyed and were a *gainsaying* (calling in question) people.

ROMANS 11

Verse 1. The last verses in the preceding chapter indicates a dismal prospect for God's ancient people. Realizing such a possible conclusion being formed by his readers, Paul clarifies the subject in this chapter. The Jews were stubborn, and as a nation had alienated themselves from God; there were some exceptions such as the apostle Paul.

Verses 2, 3. While the nation had departed from God, he had not cast it off nor regarded its departure as final. *Which he foreknew* refers to the promise to Abraham to make of him "a great nation" (Genesis 12: 2). The apostle then cites a former time when *Elias* (Elijah) thought the whole nation was gone (1 Kings 19: 10).

Verse 4. God told the prophet that seven thousand men were still faithful to Him, although the majority had gone into idolatry.

Verse 5. The Jewish nation was chosen as the people to bring the Saviour into the world, and that is what Paul means by *the election of grace*. There has always been a sufficient portion of the nation (though small in number), to carry out the divine plan for the salvation of the world. The individuals of this "remnant" were good enough that God preserved them for the predestined purposes.

Verse 6. The leading thought in this verse is that *grace* and *works* cannot both be given the credit for the salvation of this "election" or "remnant." If the merits of the works of the law are to be given the credit, then grace (the Gospel) is excluded from consideration, and vice versa.

Verse 7. Paul concludes that *Israel* (as a whole) had not obtained what he sought for, namely, justification (because he thought to obtain it through the works of the law). But the *election* (verse 5) had obtained it through the faith of the Gospel. *Rest were blinded.* Israel as a whole was hardened by the national prejudice against Christ.

Verse 8. *God hath given them.* He abandoned them to their unbelief for the time, but expects them finally to change and recognize Christ (verse 26).

Verses 9, 10. The original for *table* is defined by Thayer at this place, "a banquet, feast." The passage is a prediction that even the feasts of the Jews would be used by their foes to *snare* or entrap them to their detriment. The rest of the paragraph is a further prediction of the fate to come to the Jews for their stubborn unbelief. *Bow down their back* predicts the subject condition of Israel at the heathen's hands.

Verse 11. There is a vast difference between causing an event to happen for a certain purpose, and using the event for that purpose if it does happen. A man might not place his foot in the path of another in order to cause him to stumble and fall, yet he might have his foot where he had a perfect right to have it, and then another man, not "looking where he was going," might stumble and fall. God did not place his Son in the path of the Jews for the purpose of making them stumble and fall, yet He did put his Son in the world where He had every right to have him, then the Jews stumbled over him and fell through their blind unbelief. God then used the situation as an advantage for the Gentiles. *Provoke them to jealousy* means that the favored state of the Gentiles would cause the Jews to realize what they had lost, and finally come back to their former favor with God by recognizing his Son. (See verse 26.)

Verse 12. If such benefit came to mankind through the fall of the Jews, certainly more will come when they as a nation (the meaning of *their fulness*) come back.

Verse 13. *Magnify* means "to honor" according to Thayer. Since Paul was especially the apostle of the Gentiles (chapter 15: 16; Galatians 2: 9), he honored that office (work) by showing to them their favored standing with God.

Verse 14. *Emulation* means a stimulation into action by the good example of another. It is virtually the same in thought as that expressed at verse 11.

Verse 15. This is the same in thought as verse 12.

Verse 16. A great part of this chapter is for the information of the Gentile Christians who were disposed to make too much of their acceptance with God, over the Jews who had been the "chosen people" for so long. Paul wants them to know that the present alienated state of the nation of Israel was not to be permanent, but that when it gave up its stubborn unbelief and acknowledged Christ to be the promised Messiah, the nation would be as *holy* (acceptable) to God as it

always was. The subject is illustrated by a reference to the practice under the Mosaic system. (See Leviticus 23: 10; Numbers 15: 19, 20.) In the application it means that if the Jewish Christians who were first converted to Christ (Acts 13: 46) were *holy* (acceptable), then the whole nation would be when it also turned away from its unbelief (verse 26).

Verses 17, 18. The olive tree is used as an illustration of the subject. The branches being *broken off* is the same as the "stumbling and fall" of verses 11, 12. (See comments on those verses.) The Gentiles are compared to a wild olive tree.

Verses 19, 20. This is the same argument as in most of the preceding verses. The Gentiles were warned not to feel boastful of their favorable standing with God.

Verse 21. If God cast off the Jews because of their unbelief, He surely will not continue his favor to the Gentiles if they become unfaithful.

Verses 22, 23. The *goodness* and *severity* of God are applied to those only who deserve it, depending on whether men are believers or unbelievers. And this is true regardless of whether they are Jews or Gentiles. (See Acts 10: 34, 35.)

Verse 24. *Graffed contrary to nature.* In the grafting process when a graft from one tree is put into the limb of another, the fruit will be like the graft and not that of the tree into which it is inserted. Paul uses the illustration contrary to nature and represents the Gentiles (the wild olive) as being graffed into the tame olive (the Jewish stock). Yet, instead of being required to bear its own natural fruit (wild olive), God counteracts the rule of nature to enable this wild graft to bear tame fruit. That being the case, these Gentile Christians should realize that God would graft the natural branches (the Jews) back into their own stock. The point is the same as was made before, namely, the Gentiles should not be too boastful of their standing.

Verse 25. *Blindness* (or unbelief) *in part* proves that the condition of unbelief with Israel was not total, and the latter part of the verse shows that even that state of partial unbelief was not to be permanent. *Fulness of the Gentiles* means until they have had a *full* time with the Gospel all to themselves while the Jews are out. Just when that fact will be accomplished the apostle does not say.

Verse 26. *All Israel shall be saved.* This cannot mean that every individual Jew will be saved, for that is not true of the Gentiles, and it was never true of any nation as such. It means that the Jews as a nation will give up its stand against Christ and acknowledge him to be the Messiah of the Scriptures. That will open the way for individual Jews to have *ungodliness turned away* from them, by themselves "turning from transgression" (Isaiah 59: 20). This is the only unfulfilled prophecy between now and the second coming of Christ.

Verse 27. When the Jews turn unto Christ and from their transgressions, God will fulfill his covenant unto them, namely, to *take away their sins.*

Verse 28. The nation as a whole had rejected the Gospel, and God regarded it as a group of enemies, then turned the situation in favor of the Gentiles *(for your sakes);* this is according to verse 11. *Touching the election* (verse 5). For the sake of the fathers, Abraham, Isaac and Jacob, God still loves the nation in spite of its temporary state of unbelief, and is ready to receive it again when it gives up its unbelief.

Verse 29. *Gifts* means the favors of God, and the *calling* is the invitation of the Lord for all men, Jew and Gentile alike, to accept those favors on His terms. *Without repentance* denotes that God does not regret making those offers, and He will fulfill them whenever men comply with the terms.

Verses 30, 31. This is virtually the same as verses 11, 12. *Not believed that.* Note especially the comments on "stumbled that" in the verses cited.

Verse 32. *Concluded them all in unbelief* does not say God caused them to become unbelievers. The truths and facts disclosed to God that all nations were unbelievers, and for that reason He put them all in that class, which would make them all the subjects of divine mercy.

Verse 33. No wonder the apostle exclaims on the *depth of the riches* of God, in providing a way for the exercise of His mercy. *Unsearchable* means the judgments of God are beyond the full comprehension of man.

Verses 34, 35. Not knowing the infinite mind of the Lord, it would be foolish for man to think of advising Him. Nor can man give any favors to God that would obligate Him to recompence them back to man.

Verse 36. The thought of this verse is that the Lord is infinite in wisdom and every other greatness, and man is entirely dependent upon Him.

ROMANS 12

Verse 1. *Beseech* or earnestly exhort, *by the mercies of God,* in view of the mercy shown in chapter 11: 32. *Present* means to offer willingly something to another, not to have it taken from us by force. *Living sacrifice* in contrast with the dead creatures that were offered on the brazen altar. *Holy, acceptable to God.* The Jews could offer only such animals as were not defective. Christians must have their bodies "washed with pure water" (Hebrews 10: 22), and also have the carnal thoughts and practices "mortified" (put to death, Colossians 3: 5). *Reasonable* is explained by Thayer to mean, "the worship which is rendered by the reason or soul." It is a contrast to the literal or fleshly sacrifices offered under the Mosaic system.

Verse 2. *Be not conformed* or be not like the things of this world. *Be transformed* means to be changed to a different form of living. *Renewing of your mind* denotes a "complete change for the better" in the desires and motives of the mind. *Prove* or demonstrate by living it out that the *will of God* is a good and acceptable way of living.

Verse 3. The *grace given unto* Paul was the favor of inspiration. That authorized him to make the following statements. To *think more highly* means esteeming oneself overmuch; being "vain and arrogant." *Think soberly* or moderately concerning one's talents or natural gifts. We know the apostle means such gifts for chapter 1: 11 shows this church did not then possess any miraculous or spiritual gifts. *Measure of faith* means that God-given natural capacity to absorb the instruction in the word of God (the source of faith, chapter 10: 17), thus becoming able to try out in practice the particular talent or talents that one has.

Verses 4, 5. The human body is used as an illustration of the body of Christ, because the members of the fleshly body each have a separate *office* or use. The various members of the body of

Christ have individual parts to perform in the spiritual life.

Verse 6. *Gifts* is from the same Greek word as "gift" in 1 Corinthians 7: 7, where the context shows it means a gift of nature and not a miraculous one. *According to the grace* is explained at verse 3. According to Thayer's lexicon, *to prophesy* means, "To break forth under sudden impulse in lofty discourse or in praise of the divine counsels." In 1 Corinthians 14: 3, 4, Paul shows that one form of prophesying is to speak "to edification, and exhortation, and comfort." Prophesying, then, does not necessarily mean to speak with a spiritual gift.

Verse 7. *Ministry* means that service to others that their condition requires. If a man has the ability to teach, let him attend to that as his personal work.

Verse 8. To *exhort* means to insist on the performance of known duties. *Giveth* is from METADIDOMI, and Thayer's first definition is, "To share a thing with any one." *Simplicity* is from HAPLOTES, and it has been rendered in the King James Version by, bountifulness, liberality, singleness. *He that ruleth* applies to the elders since they are the only rulers in the church. They are to be diligent and "watch" the conduct of the members to see that it is not such as to endanger their souls. (See Hebrews 13: 17.) When administering to the distress of another let it be done cheerfully, and not in the spirit of one who does it merely because it is a duty he has to perform.

Verse 9. *Dissimulation* means hypocrisy; do not merely pretend to love another. *Abhor* is from APOSTUGEO which Strong defines, "to detest utterly," and *cleave* is from KALLAO, which the same author defines, "to glue, i.e., to stick." The thought is that Christians should not be half-hearted in their opposition to evil or support of the good.

Verse 10. *Kindly affectioned* is defined in the lexicon, "loving affection, prone to love, loving tenderly." *Brotherly love* is from PHILADELPHIA, and Thayer's definition is, "in the New Testament the love which Christians cherish for each other as 'brethren.'" *Honor* means respect or esteem, and *preferring* is defined, "To go before and show the way." The thought is to be a leader and set an example in showing respect for others.

Verse 11. *Business* is from SPOUDE, which Thayer defines, "Haste, with haste; earnestness, diligence," and the original for *slothful* is defined, "sluggish, slothful, backward." The thought is that Christians should not be indifferent about the activities of the service for Christ. The remainder of the verse means virtually the same thing.

Verse 12. *Rejoicing in hope.* A Christian does not have to be in possession of the crown of life to rejoice, but he can rejoice over the hope of receiving it; that will cause him to be patient in tribulation, and continue to be a prayerful disciple.

Verse 13. *Necessity* is from a word that means a state of destitution that the Christian is here told to relieve. Thayer defines the original for *given*, "to seek after eagerly," and that for *hospitality*, "love to strangers" (Hebrews 13: 2).

Verse 14. *Bless* is from EULOGEO and means "to invoke [wish for] blessings," while *curse* means to wish that some ill fortune will come upon our persecutors.

Verse 15. This verse means to share in the feelings of others over their condition, whether it be favorable or otherwise. This is taught also in 1 Corinthians 12: 26.

Verse 16. *Be of the same mind.* Be interested in the same things that concern our brother. (See preceding verse.) *Men* is not in the original; the sentence denotes an interest in common or lowly things rather than craving that which is lofty. *Own conceits* is from the original terms that mean "yourselves." The sentence means not to be conceited over one's individual wisdom, being like Job's friends to whom he said in irony, "Wisdom shall die with you" (Job 12: 2).

Verse 17. The first sentence means not to retaliate or do an enemy a wrong because he has done to us that way. *Provide things honest.* Live so that no one can reproach you.

Verse 18. James 3: 17 teaches that divine wisdom requires peace that is in harmony with the truth "from above." Our present verse requires peace on the same terms.

Verse 19. An evildoer deserves to be treated with revenge, but Christians are not the ones to inflict it. The Lord says *vengeance is mine*, therefore the passage means to give place unto [divine] wrath.

Verse 20. The first part of this verse is the same in thought as that in verse 14. *Coals of fire* is figurative, meaning that an act of kindness will bring a tortured conscience upon an enemy that will be like fire on top of his head.

Verse 21. In the conflict between *evil* and *good*, let the disciple of Christ so conduct himself that he will be the conqueror and win the battle for the good. This is virtually the same thought as that in the preceding verse.

ROMANS 13

Verses 1, 2. *Higher* is from HUPER-ECHO, which Thayer defines at this place, "to be above, be superior in rank, authority, power." *Power* is from EXOUSIA which the same author defines at this place, "one who possesses authority; a ruler, human magistrate." *Be subject* is from HUPOTASSO, and both Thayer and Strong define it in this passage, "to obey." The sentence, then, means that every person must obey the rulers of human governments. The same command is given in direct terms in Titus 3: 1 and 1 Peter 2: 13, 14. *Ordained* is from TASSO, which Thayer defines here, "to place in a certain order, to arrange, to assign a place, to appoint," and Paul says this is done of God. The Mosaic system was both religious and civil, or secular as a government. But when the New Testament age came in, the Lord dropped the civil use and ordered man to form his own government, with the understanding, of course, that he was not to pass any laws that would violate the religious principles of His law. That is why it is the same as resisting the ordinance of God for a man to disobey the laws of the land.

Verse 3. In most of the verses Paul is considering the penal parts of the law. To *be afraid* of these rulers means to respect their laws against wrongdoing. *Have praise of the same.* If a man does right he will be regarded as a good citizen.

Verse 4. *Minister of God* is explained in the first paragraph. *Beareth not the sword in vain.* There is only one use for a sword and that is to take life; in the hands of an officer it would mean capital punishment. Here we have the teaching that when an officer executes capital punishment, he is acting as a "minister of God."

Verse 5. A Christian will obey the laws with a twofold motive. He wishes to avoid punishment, and he also desires to have a good conscience.

Verse 6. This *tribute* means tax on property. The rulers protect our property, which makes it necessary to support them while they are *attending upon this very thing.*

Verse 7. *Custom* is defined by Thayer, "toll, custom," and explains it to mean, "an indirect tax on goods." The two words, *tribute* and *custom* means "all taxes, personal and real." We should *fear* the penal officer (verse 3) and respect or honor the rulers.

Verse 8. A part of Thayer's explanation of *owe* is, "that which is due." It does not forbid honorable debts such as accounts, for Paul and Philemon conducted such transactions (Philemon 18), but a man should regard his debts and deal honestly. The debt of *love* can never be "paid in full," hence one may always *owe* that without criticism.

Verse 9. The Jews regretted giving up the law that contained what they thought were such important principles. Paul is showing that those principles are not lost by receiving the Gospel. It requires Christians to love their neighbors as themselves, and if they do, they will necessarily do all the things that are named in this verse.

Verse 10. Love (one of the requirements of the Gospel) fulfills the law by prompting one to do these neighborly acts specified by the law.

Verse 11. *Wake out of sleep* denotes arousing from indifference and becoming more active in the service of the Lord. *Salvation nearer.* If we are faithful until death or until Jesus comes — whichever occurs first — our salvation will be assured. Of necessity, then, the passing of the days brings us nearer to that reward.

Verse 12. *The night* is a figurative term for the period of waiting, and the *day* (of *our salvation*, verse 11) is *at hand* or *nearer* as stated in the preceding verse. Moralizing on these truths, the apostle exhorts us to cast off the works of darkness and put on the *armor* ("implements") of light, which means divine truth.

Verse 13. *Honestly* means "decently," and the *day* here means the condition of spiritual light. *Chambering* is from KOITE which Thayer defines "cohabitation," then explains it to mean, "whether lawful or unlawful." *Wantonness* is from ASELGEIA and Thayer's definition is more specific than on the preceding word: "Unbridled lust, excess, licentiousness," etc. He then explains it at our passage to mean, "filthy words, indecent bodily movements, unchaste handling of males and females." Such a life as the foregoing describes will not prepare one for salvation when the "day arrives.

Verse 14. Galatians 3: 27 tells us how we can "put on Christ." *Make no provision* means not to look forward to the lusts of the flesh, in order to have the opportunity for gratification.

ROMANS 14

Verse 1. This chapter deals with two subjects on which the Lord has made no legislation as to their being right or wrong. *Him that is weak in the faith* does not pertain to matters that are necessary to salvation, for on that subject all Christians are commanded to be "strong in the Lord" (Ephesians 6: 10). But it means one who is weak as to whether he should participate in the things others were doing. *Receive ye* denotes that we should accept him as a brother in Christ, but not with the idea of judging or condemning him on these unlegislated things on which he has some doubts.

Verse 2. *Who is weak* explains the *weak* person in verse 1. He is weak in that he thinks he should not eat any kind of food but herbs.

Verse 3. *Him that eateth* is the one who will *eat all things* in the preced-ceding verse. To *despise* means to belittle or look down upon one, and Paul forbids the one man thus to treat a brother who restricts himself to vegetables. Likewise, this latter man has no right to condemn the one who *eats all things,* for *God hath received him* or recognized him as an acceptable servant.

Verse 4. The relation of master and slave, a common one in the Roman Empire, is used for the purpose of illustration. If a slave deserves correction, his own master is the one to administer it. Likewise the servant of God has to answer to Him only in regard to these unlegislated matters. In the present case He will hold up for his servant because he has not disobeyed any divine law.

Verse 5. Having dealt with one subject pertaining to the individual conscience, on which the Lord has not legislated, Paul introduces another which is the observance of days.

Thayer defines the original word for *esteemeth,* "to prefer." One man has some preference for a certain day while another has not. The Lord does not care which view a man takes, just so he is fully persuaded in his own mind, and does not try to force his views on another.

Verse 6. *Regardeth* is from PHRONEO which Thayer defines, "to direct one's mind to a thing," and he explains it at this place to mean, "to regard a day, observe it as sacred." Robinson's definition of the word is, "to regard, to keep." Both the lexicon definitions and the language of Paul show he is writing of men who prefer to "keep" some certain day in a religious way since he regards such a day as sacred. But that is his individual privilege, even as it is the privilege of another not to keep any day as sacred. The same privilege applies to eating or not eating certain foods.

Verses 7, 8. I have combined these verses to prevent a wrong conclusion. We are not under obligation to any *man* with regard to this liberty described in verse 6, but we are subject to the Lord, who forbids us to press our views on another in this matter.

Verses 9, 10. Even if there should be anything objectionable to Christ in the exercise of this liberty, it is between the individual and Him, and he will answer at the judgment.

Verse 11. Every tongue will confess, but those who wait till the judgment to do so will bestow glory on the Father only but will receive no reward (Philippians 2: 10, 11).

Verse 12. The word *himself* is the one to be emphasized in this verse.

Verse 13. The word *judge* is from KRINO which has several meanings, and two of them are "condemn" and "conclude." The verse means for one brother not to *condemn* another regarding these unlegislated matters. Rather he should *conclude* not to put a stumbling-block in his way by trying to force him to eat what he believes it is wrong to eat.

Verse 14. *I know* denotes that Paul is speaking by inspiration. No kind of food is unclean in fact (1 Timothy 4: 4), but it is unclean to the man who believes it is.

Verse 15. This is the first time in this chapter that the word *meat* is used. Had the word "herbs" not been used in contrast to it in verse 2, we would have no reason for saying it means the flesh of animals, for the lexicon only defines it, "that which is eaten, food." Hence the principle Paul is discussing is that God does not care what kind of food one eats, as long as he has no conscientious objections to it. If a brother has such objections, another should not induce him to eat it, defiling his conscience.

Verse 16. *Your good* means the right for the "strong" to eat meat. If he tries to force that privilege on the weak brother, he will speak evil of this strong brother.

Verse 17. If salvation depended on eating or not eating certain foods, then it would be necessary to insist on one or the other. Since it does not, we should not disturb anyone on it, but give our attention to righteousness and peace.

Verses 18, 19. By observing this rule of respect for a weak brother's conscscience, we not only serve God acceptably, but all good men will approve of it.

Verse 20. For the sake of meat, do not destroy the work of the Lord. *All things are pure,* etc., is explained by the comments on verse 14.

Verse 21. This verse is a generalization of the arguments of the chapter. We should not press our "rights" on a brother who is weak concerning these practices.

Verse 22. *Faith* here is upon the testimony of the conscience that it is right to *eat all things;* he should exercise that to himself. It is wrong to press it upon a weak brother, and if he does so the Lord will condemn him, for imposing upon another that thing that is *allowed* for a strong brother.

Verse 23. *Whatsoever is not of faith is sin.* This is the same *faith* that is described in verse 22, namely, that which is produced by the testimony of one's conscience. Since the Lord has not legislated for or against the observance of days or the eating of foods, a man's conscience must be his sole guide and basis of his faith.

ROMANS 15

Verse 1. This is virtually the same as chapter 14: 21.

Verse 2. *Please his neighbor* is to be accomplished by respecting his views on the matters discussed in the preceding chapter. This will have the effect of edifying him, or building him up in his service to the Lord. Such a

result would be the opposite to that set forth by the comments at verse 16 of that chapter.

Verse 3. None of the things Christ did for man brought Him any selfish pleasure. The quotation is from Psalms 69: 9. Many of the passages of David are worded as if they pertained to his own experiences. To some extent they do so apply, but the main thought is that they are prophecies to be fulfilled in his illustrious descendant, Jesus the Christ. *Thee* and *me* in our verse means God and Christ. The reproaches that were aimed at the Father were like arrows that missed their mark and struck the Son.

Verse 4. Paul had just quoted from the Psalms, therefore we know his word *aforetime* means the things written in the Old Testament. *Learning* is from DIDASKALIA, and Thayer defines it, "teaching, instruction." They were not written, then, as our law, for this whole book is in opposition to that. But by learning of God's dealing with his servants in old time, and observing how they came through their trials by the help of God, the disciples of Christ may be encouraged to press on in their own duties, even though unpleasant sometimes, in the hope of a life of joy and freedom from trial in the world to come. If God caused these Old Testament things to be recorded *for our learning,* it is our duty to study and learn them.

Verse 5. *Likeminded* is similar to the thought in chapter 12: 16. The brethren should be united in their care for each other, and to have that unity *according to Christ Jesus.* Such a mutual consideration for each other will cause them to suppress their personal preference and give their attention to the instructions of the Lord.

Verse 6. Being united in *mind* concerning the things of God and Christ, they will also be united in speech *(one mouth)* in their praise of the Lord.

Verse 7. This is the same as verse 5.

Verse 8. *The circumcision* is a term meaning the Mosaic system, Jesus was a Jew and his entire life on earth was under that dispensation. *To confirm the promises.* God promised Abraham that the person who was to bless all the families of the earth should be of his seed (Genesis 22: 18). Had Jesus come through the Gentile nation, it would not have fulfilled the promise to Abraham.

Verses 9-11. The Jewish birth of Jesus fulfilled the promise as to His being of Abraham's seed, and also the offering of the Gospel to the Gentiles fulfilled that part of the promise that "all nations" would be blessed through this seed.

Verse 12. This verse pertains to the same promise made to Abraham, but extends it on down to one of his great descendants; for David (the son of Jesse) was a lineal descendant of Abraham to whom the promise was first made. The quotation showing this promise is in *Esaias* (Isaiah) 11: 10.

Verse 13. No apostle had been in Rome when this epistle was written, and hence no spiritual gifts were possessed by that church. The power of the Holy Ghost (or Spirit) was exerted through the word of God which is the "sword of the Spirit" (Ephesians 6: 17). By *believing* this word, the brethren could be filled with *joy* and *peace*, all of which would give them their *hope*.

Verse 14. Paul had much confidence in the brethren at Rome, and wrote this complimentary passage for their encouragement.

Verse 15. Notwithstanding his confidence in them, Paul thought it well to stir up their minds on the important matter. Being favored with the apostolic work under God, Paul was acting properly in thus writing to the brethren.

Verse 16. Paul's special mission was to the Gentiles (chapter 11: 13; Acts 9: 15), and most of the brethren in Rome were of that nation. *Being sanctified by the Holy Ghost.* Acts 11: 15-18 records the giving of the Holy Ghost to the Gentiles, which was a public announcement from God that the Gentiles would be acceptable Gospel subjects.

Verse 17. Paul gloried (took great pleasure) in the work among the Gentiles, especially since that constituted the things pertaining to God.

Verse 18. *Not dare to speak . . . not wrought by me.* He would not take credit for work that had been done by others.

Verse 19. His own field of labor had furnished him much cause for rejoicing. That work had been performed under God through the aid of the Spirit of God, inspiring him. The territory Paul mentions had not been "covered" by other preachers, hence it was virtually new territory where the apostle felt free to labor.

Verse 20. By working in new fields he would not be building on another man's foundation. This idea is also set forth in 2 Corinthians 10: 15, 16.

Verse 21. These new fields were predicted in Isaiah 52: 15.

Verse 22. *For which cause* refers to his plan to confine his labors to new fields, so that he did not have time to make the journey to Rome until the present.

Verse 23. *Having no more place in these parts* denotes the field had been "worked out," so he was free to go elsewhere in his labors.

Verse 24. This purpose of Paul was never accomplished that we have any substantial account of, nor any record of labors performed in that territory.

Verse 25. This ministering was to consist in taking some contributions from various brethren, and delivering them to the *saints* (disciples) at Jerusalem.

Verse 26. This verse tells who were making the contributions, namely, the disciples in Macedonia, and those in another Greek country called Achaia.

Verse 27. *Their debtors they are* means the brethren in the countries named are indebted (under obligation) to the *poor saints* at Jerusalem. The latter had supplied the former with spiritual things (the Gospel), now in turn they should help them with *carnal* (temporal) necessities of life. This is exactly the same as Galatians 6: 6.

Verse 28. See the comments at verse 24.

Verse 29. No fuller blessing could be brought to a community, than that provided by the Gospel of Christ that Paul was preaching.

Verse 30. Paul here teaches that the prayers of disciples in behalf of each other are one means of having a part in their labors for the Lord.

Verse 31. Paul expected to encounter some foes in Judea. He accounts for this opposition by the fact that they were unbelievers. He also desired to be understood and received by the saints in that region.

Verse 32. *By the will of God* denotes that he would be able to carry out the desire as to visiting the brethren in Rome "if the Lord will."

Verse 33. This is an expression of good will. There is only one God, so the expression *God of peace* means that he is such a God.

ROMANS 16

Verse 1. *Servant* is from DIAKONOS which is usually translated "deacon." Having the feminine inflection in the composition at this place, it could be rendered "deaconess," and it is so defined by Thayer. He then explains it to mean "a woman to whom the care of either poor or sick women was entrusted." Robinson gives the same information; but neither the New Testament nor any secular authors that I have seen, say anything about official deaconesses. Phebe was a member of the church at Cenchrea, a harbor of Corinth, and she served there in the capacity described above.

Verse 2. *Business* is from PRAGMA, which Thayer defines at this place, "a matter of law, case, suit." Phebe needed to go to Rome on some legal affair, and in that big city she would naturally need some assistance. Paul tells the brethren to receive her as a saint (disciple of Christ), and to help her for her good example of assisting others, including himself.

Verses 3, 4. These worthy disciples had once been banished from Rome (Acts 18: 2), but had returned home after some time. While at Ephesus they did some important work just preceding that of the apostle (Acts 18: 24-26), and they otherwise rendered faithful service to him. *Laid down their own necks* is figurative, referring to the risks to their own lives they had run for him.

Verse 5. *The church that is in their house.* In the early years of the church, the disciples did not have church buildings in every place, hence they conducted their services in the homes of the brethren; the home of Priscilla and Aquila was one of such places. *Achaia* is another name for "Asia" at this place according to both Moffatt and the American Standard Version. 1 Corinthians 16: 15 says that the house of Stephanas was the first fruits of Achaia.

Verse 6. All we can know of this woman is what is said here. She had rendered some kind of service for Paul for which he wished her to be remembered.

Verse 7. In the King James Version, the terms "greet" and "salute" are used interchangeably as they well may be, since they both come from the word ASPAZOMAI, which means a gesture of good will in whatever form it may be performed. *Who also were in Christ before me.* This statement is against the theory of unconditional predestination, which claims that God determined "from all eternity" just who was to be saved. If that were true, it would be impossible for any person to be in Christ before another, since all would have been placed in Him by divine decree at the same time.

Verses 8, 9. The persons named had helped the apostle in some way. I have no information as to the nature of their services.

Verse 10. There is no separate word in the Greek for *household.* The marginal reading is "friends," which is correct as the name Aristobulus is in the possessive form. Smith's Bible Dictionary says he is reputed by legend to have been a preacher.

Verses 11, 12. Kinsman is used in the sense of a fellow-countryman. All of the persons here are given "honorable mention" because they had *labored much in the Lord.*

Verse 13. *His mother and mine* is a term of tender appreciation for the favors Rufus' mother had shown to Paul; she had been like a mother to him.

Verses 14, 15. The works of reference that I have seen do not know much about these persons, other than to ascribe to them an active interest in the Lord's work.

Verse 16. *Holy kiss.* I have examined a number of dictionaries and histories, as well as four lexicons, and they all represent the kiss to have been a form of salute between persons of both sexes, the custom dating back to ancient times. The instruction of the apostle, then, was not to start any new form of salutation for the kiss was in use centuries before he was born. The point is in the word *holy,* and it means for the salutation to be sincere and not one of hypocrisy as was that of Judas. The word "church" in the King James Version of the New Testament is always from EKKLESIA, and its primary meaning according to Thayer is, "A gathering of citizens called out from their homes into some public place; an assembly." Robinson gives the simple definition, "A convocation, assembly, congregation." The word has no religious significance unless it is associated with some other word. Hence our phrase means those who have been "called out" by Christ to "assemble in His name." Any group of men and women thus called out would be one of the assemblies or congregations or churches of Christ.

Verse 17. To *mark* means to observe very carefully in order to discover the nature of the person's conduct. There is not much difference between *divisions* and *offences*, considering their results. The first means that which causes disunion in a body of people, and the second means that which causes someone to stumble along the pathway of life. These things are always wrong, hence the proviso *contrary to the doctrine which you have learned* is stated to signify that such theories have not been taught by any true teacher of the Gospel. To *avoid* is more than merely a refusal to accept, but Thayer defines it to "keep aloof from, one's society; to shun one." Christians should keep no company with such characters, but should shun them as they would Satan.

Verse 18. *Belly* is from KOILIA, and Thayer defines it at this place, "the gullet [throat, or what goes down it], and he explains it to mean, "to be given up to the pleasures of the palate, to gluttony." The motive of these divisive characters is to gain the confidence of their victims, in the hope of obtaining something from them to consume upon their appetite. *The simple* refers to those who do not suspect anything wrong in the workings of these teachers, and hence are easily deceived thereby.

Verse 19. *Obedience is come* denotes that the report of their obedience had become generally known, and for this the apostle was rejoicing. *Wise* and *simple* are used as contrasts, with the idea that no one can know too much about that which is good, but the less we have to do with things that are evil, the better will be our condition.

Verse 20. *Shortly* is a comparative term, for the final victory over Satan is not to be until the end. "Be thou faithful unto death, and I will give thee a crown of life" (Revelation 2: 10). The endless life of happiness awaiting the faithful after death is so great that the span of life is "but for a moment" (2 Corinthians 4: 17).

Verse 21. *Timotheus* is the same as Timothy, and he is called the workfellow of Paul because he was associated with him in his travels (Acts 16: 1-3), and also was a close friend in Christ in many of the trials of the apostle. He had good reason to join

in the salutations to the brethren at Rome, because he had been in contact with many of them in other places. Paul refers to *Lucius* among his *kinsmen*, and the Funk and Wagnalls New Standard Bible Dictionary places him with the one mentioned in Acts 13: 1. Smith's Bible Dictionary says he was a fellow tribesman of Paul, and that tradition recognized him as a bishop of the church of Chenchrea. Jason was the man who entertained Paul and Silas in Acts 17: 5-9, for which he was persecuted by the mob. It is significant that he would join his salutation with others being sent by Paul. There is not much said about Sosipater, but he was of sufficient importance to have Paul include him with the group that was sending salutations to the brethren at Rome.

Verse 22. The Funk and Wagnalls New Standard Bible Dictionary says the following of Tertius: "The amannuensis [secretary] who penned Paul's Epistle to the Romans and who sent his salutation, along with others' to the church at Rome." Paul usually had someone else to do the writing of the epistles as he dictated them, then he signed them which made them his epistles officially.

Verse 23. *Gaius mine host* means he was the one who provided headquarters for Paul when he was in Corinth. He was also the one whom the apostle baptized in that city (1 Corinthians 1: 14). He was said to be very hospitable, and that accounts for the fact that he entertained a whole congregation. *Erastus the chamberlain.* The third word is from OIKONOMOS which Thayer defines as follows: "The superintendent of the city's finances, the treasurer of the city." It is important to know that a disciple of Christ would be entrusted with such an important position. This circumstance is also against the theory of some professed disciples today, who say that it is wrong for Christians to have anything to do with civil government, and who even go so far as to object to casting a vote. Yet we here have an instance of one of the brethren of Paul who did "take part in politics" to the extent that he held an important position as a servant of the government. What is commonly called "politics" is usually very corrupt, but that is because a good thing is being abused. Since civil governments exist by divine ordinance (chapter 13: 1-6), it is a serious error to assert that Christians do wrong to have any part in their administration.

Verse 24. *Grace* is from CHARIS and it has been so rendered 129 times in the King James Version. It is rendered also by benefit 1 time, favor 6, liberality 1, thank 3, thanks 4. Thayer gives as its primary definition, "sweetness, charm, loveliness," and explains it to signify "that which affords joy, pleasure, delight." Other definitions are, "good-will, loving kindness, favor; kindness which bestows upon one what he has not deserved." *Amen* is from the Greek word AMEN; it occurs in the Greek New Testament 150 times, and has been rendered "amen" 50 times, and "verily" 100 times in the King James Version. Thayer says that at the beginning of a discourse it means "surely, of a truth, truly." He says a repetition of the word as John alone uses it, has the force of a superlative, "most assuredly," and at the close of a sentence it means, "so it is, so be it, may it be fulfilled." Thayer further says historically, "it was a custom, which passed over from the synagogues into the Christian assemblies, that when he who had read or discoursed had offered up a solemn pray to God, the others in attendance responded *Amen*, and thus made the substance of what was uttered their own." With this short but impressive sentence, Paul begins the closing words of apostolic and brotherly interest in his brethren at Rome.

Verse 25. *My Gospel* means the Gospel that Paul was preaching, and that it was the power by which they were to be *stablished (*made firm*)*, communicated to them by preaching. A *mystery* is anything not known, and such was the case regarding the great system of salvation through Christ.

Verse 26. It was then (in Paul's day) made manifest *by the scriptures of the prophets*, referring to the predictions in the Old Testament. *It was made known to all nations.* (See chapter 10: 18; Colossians 1: 23.) *For the obelience of faith* means it was revealed to all nations to the end that all might obey it from the motive of faith.

Verse 27. This is similar in sentiment to verse 24. *God only wise* means to give Him credit for the origin of all true wisdom. Such a Being is worthy of all glory, and it should be offered through the name of His only begotten Son, Jesus the Christ, and it should be attributed to him for all the coming ages. AMEN.

CPSIA information can be obtained at www.ICGtesting.com
Printed in the USA
LVOW07s2032270715

447816LV00002B/411/P